Wissenschaftliche Untersuchungen
zum Neuen Testament · 2. Reihe

Herausgeber / Editor
Jörg Frey (Zürich)

Mitherausgeber/Associate Editors
Markus Bockmuehl (Oxford) · James A. Kelhoffer (Uppsala)
Tobias Nicklas (Regensburg) · Janet Spittler (Charlottesville, VA)
J. Ross Wagner (Durham, NC)

545

D1555030

Llewellyn Howes

The Formative Stratum of the Sayings Gospel Q

Reconsidering Its Extent, Message, and Unity

Mohr Siebeck

Llewellyn Howes, born 1980; 1999–2002 studied Theology at the University of Pretoria; 2012 PhD in New Testament Studies; since 2019 Associate Professor of Mythology, University of Johannesburg.
orcid.org/0000-0001-7759-8088

ISBN 978-3-16-160094-4 / eISBN 978-3-16-160095-1
DOI 10.1628/978-3-16-160095-1

ISSN 0340-9570 / eISSN 2568-7484
(Wissenschaftliche Untersuchungen zum Neuen Testament, 2. Reihe)

The Deutsche Nationalbibliothek lists this publication in the Deutsche Nationalbibliographie; detailed bibliographic data are available at *http://dnb.dnb.de*.

The book was printed on non-aging paper by Laupp & Göbel in Gomaringen, and bound by Buchbinderei Nädele in Nehren.

Printed in Germany.

For Lurinda Maree,
who gives light to everyone in the house (cf. Q 11:33)

Table of Contents

List of Abbreviations

[Oec.]	Aristotle's *Oeconomica*
Clem.	Clement
11Q13	Qumran Scroll *Melchizedek* from Cave 11 (a.k.a. 11QMelch)
1Q22	Qumran Scroll *Words of Moses* from Cave 1 (a.k.a. 1QDM)
1QS	Qumran Scroll *Community Rule* from Cave 1
Bar.	Baruch
4Q264	Qumran fragment of *Community Rule* from Cave 4
4Q416-418	Qumran fragments of *Sapiential Work A* from Cave 4 (a.k.a. 4Qinstruction)
4Q421	Fragmentary Qumran Scroll *Ways of Righteousness* from Cave 4 (a.k.a. 4QWays of Righteousness)
'Abot R. Nat.	'Abot de Rabbi Nathan
Agr.	Cato's *De agricultura (De re rustica)*
A.J.	Josephus's *Antiquitates judaicae*
Alleg. Interp.	Philo's *Allegorical Interpretation*
Ant.	Josephus's *Jewish Antiquities*
Apoc. Adam	Apocalypse of Adam
Asin.	Plautus's *Asinaria*
ASV	American Standard Version
b. B. Meṣ.	Tractate Baba Meṣi'a from the Babylonian Talmud
b. Ber.	Tractate Berakot from the Babylonian Talmud
b. Ḥul.	Tractate Ḥallah from the Babylonian Talmud
b. Ketub.	Tractate Ketubbot from the Babylonian Talmud
b. Qidd.	Tractate Qiddušin from the Babylonian Talmud
b. Šabb.	Tractate Šabbat from the Babylonian Talmud
b. Ta'an.	Tractate Ta'anit from the Babylonian Talmud
B.J.	Josephus's *Bellum judaicum*
Bacch.	Plautus's *Bacchae*
BETL	Bibliotheca Ephemeridum Theologicarum Lovaniensium
BibInt	Biblical Interpretation Series
BibInt	*Biblical Interpretation*
BZNW	Beihefte zur Zeitschrift fur die neutestamentliche Wissenschaft
Cant. Rab.	Canticle of Canticles Rabbah (a.k.a. Song of Songs Rabbah)
Cat. Maj.	Plutarch's *Cato Major* (a.k.a. *Cato the Elder*)
Cherubim	Philo's *On the Cherubim*
Der. Er. Zuṭ	Derek Ereṣ Zuṭa
Dial.	Justin's *Dialogus cum Tryphone*
Dig.	Justinian's *Digesta seu Pandectae*
Dreams	Philo's *On Dreams*

Ep.	Seneca the Younger's *Epistulae morales* or Pliny the Younger's *Epistulae*, as indicated by the context
ESV	English Standard Version
ET	English translation
Good Person	Philo's *That Every Good Person Is Free*
Gos. Thom.	Gospel of Thomas
Hom.	Pseudo-Clement's *Homilies*
HTR	*Harvard Theological Review*
HTS	*Hervormde Teologiese Studies*
ICC	International Critical Commentary
J.W.	Josephus's *Jewish War*
JBL	*Journal of Biblical Literature*
Jos. Asen.	Joseph and Aseneth
Joseph	Philo's *On the Life of Joseph*
JSNTSup	Journal for the Study of the New Testament Supplement Series
Jub.	Jubilees
KJV	King James Version
Leg.	Plato's *Leges*
LNTS	The Library of New Testament Studies
LXX	Septuagint
m. 'Abot	Tractate 'Abot from the Mishnah
m. B. Bat.	Tractate Baba Batra from the Mishnah
m. B. Meṣ.	Tractate Baba Meṣi'a from the Mishnah
m. Naz.	Tractate Nazir from the Mishnah
m. Nid.	Tractate Niddah from the Mishnah
m. Ṭehar.	Tractate Ṭeharot from the Mishnah
Macc	Maccabees
Magn.	Ignatius's *To the Magnesians*
Mek.	Mekilta
Merc.	Plautus's *The Merchant*
Metam.	Apuleius's *Metamorphoses* (a.k.a. *The Golden Ass*)
Migration	Philo's *On the Migration of Abraham*
Most.	Plautus's *Mostellaria*
MT	Masoretic Text
Names	Philo's *On the Change of Names*
NASB	New American Standard Bible
Nat.	Pliny the Elder's *Natural History*
NIGTC	New International Greek Testament Commentary
NIV	The New International Version
NKJV	The New King James Version
NovT	*Novum Testamentum*
NovTSup	Supplements to Novum Testamentum
NRSV	The New Revised Standard Version
O.Mich.	*Greek Ostraca in the University of Michigan Collection* (see bibliography: Amundsen 1935).
Oec.	Xenophon's *Oeconomicus*
P.Cair.Zen.	*Zenon Papyri, Catalogue général des antiquités égyptiennes du Musée du Caire* (see bibliography: Edgar 1925–1940)

P.Col.	*Columbia Papyri* (see bibliography: Westermann and Hasenoehrl 1934; Bagnall and Obbink 1996)
P.Col.inv.	*Columbia Papyri* (unpublished; referenced according to inventory number)
P.Corn.	*Greek Papyri in the Library of Cornell University* (see bibliography: Westermann and Kraemer 1926)
P.Duk.inv.	*Duke Papyrus Archive* (unpublished; see https://library.duke.edu/rubenstein/scriptorium/papyrus/texts/homepage.html)
P.Enteux.	*ΕΝΤΕΥΞΕΙΣ: Requêtes et plaintes adressées au Roi d'Égypte au IIIe siècle avant J.-C.* (see bibliography: Guéraud 1931–1932).
P.Fay.	*Fayûm Towns and their Papyri* (see bibliography: Grenfell, Hunt, and Hogarth 1900)
P.Haun.	*Papyri Graecae Haunienses* (see bibliography: Bülow-Jacobsen 1981)
P.Kar.Goodsp.	*Papyri from Karanis* (see bibliography: Goodspeed 1902)
P.Köln	*Kölner Papyri* (see bibliography: Gronewald and Maresch 1991)
P.Lond.	*Greek Papyri in the British Museum* (see bibliography: Skeat 1974)
P.Mich.	*Michigan Papyri* (see bibliography: Edgar 1931; Winter *et al.* 1936; Husselman 1971; Shelton 1971; Browne 1975; Sijpesteijn 1982)
P.Mich.inv.	*Michigan Papyri* (unpublished; referenced according to inventory number)
P.NYU	*Greek Papyri in the Collection of New York University* (see bibliography: Nielson and Worp 2010)
P.Oslo	*Papyri Osloenses* (see bibliography: Eitrem and Amundsen 1931)
P.Oxy.	*The Oxyrhynchus Papyri* (see bibliography: Hunt 1912; Gonis and Colomo 2008; Leith *et al.* 2009; Maehler, Römer, and Hatzilambrou 2010)
P.Petaus.	*Das Archiv des Petaus* (see bibliography: Hagedorn *et al.* 1969)
P.Petr.	*The Flinders Petrie Papyri* (see bibliography: Mahaffy 1891)
P.Princ.	*Papyri in the Princeton University Collections* (see bibliography: Kase 1936)
P.Ryl.	*Catalogue of the Greek and Latin Papyri in the John Rylands Library, Manchester* (see bibliography: Johnson, Martin, and Hunt 1915)
P.Stras.	*Griechische Papyrus der Kaiserlichen Universitäts- und Landesbibliothek zu Straßburg* (see bibliography: Schwartz 1963)
P.Tebt.	*The Tebtunis Papyri* (see bibliography: Grenfell, Hunt, and Smyly 1902; Grenfell, Hunt, and Goodspeed 1907; Hunt and Smyly 1933)
P.Theon.	*The Family of the Tiberii Iulii Theones* (see bibliography: Sijpesteijn 1976)
P.Wisc.	*The Wisconsin Papyri* (see bibliography: Sijpesteijn 1967)
P.Zen.Pestm.	*Greek and Demotic Texts from the Zenon Archive* (see bibliography: Pestman 1980)
Pesiq. Rab Kah.	Pesiqta de Rab Kahana
Pol.	Aristotle's *Politica*
Prob.	Philo's *Quod omnis probus liber sit*
Pss. Sol.	Psalms of Solomon
m. B. Qam.	Tractate Baba Qamma from the Mishnah
QE	Philo's *Quaestiones et solutiones in Exodum*
Quaest. rom.	Plutarch's *Quaestiones romanae et graecae* (*Aetia romana et graeca*)
Rust.	Columella's *De re rustica*

Sat.	Macrobius's *Saturnalia*
SB	*Sammelbuch griechischer Urkunden aus Ägypten* (see bibliography: Preisigke, Bilabel, and Kießling 1931; Bilabel, Preisigke, and Rupprecht 1981–1983; Rupprecht and Kießling 1985–1988; Preisigke 1997)
SBL	Society of Biblical Literature
Sem.	Semaḥot
Sent. Sextus	Sentences of Sextus
Sir	Sirach
SNTSMS	Society for New Testament Studies Monograph Series
Sobriety	Philo's *On Sobriety*
Spec.	Philo's *De specialibus legibus*
T. Ab.	Testament of Abraham
T. Jos.	Testament of Joseph
T. Levi	Testament of Levi
t. Maʿaś.	Tractate Maʿaśerot from the Tosefta
Rust.	Varro's *De re rustica*
Vid.	Plautus's *Vidularia*
Wis	Wisdom of Solomon
Worse	Philo's *That the Worse Attacks the Better*
WUNT	Wissenschaftliche Untersuchungen zum Neuen Testament
y. Ber.	Tractate Berakot from the Jerusalem Talmud
Yal.	Yalquṭ
ZNW	*Zeitschrift für die neutestamentliche Wissenschaft und die Kunde der älteren Kirche*

Introduction

As the book's title indicates, this is a study about the formative stratum (or earliest redactional layer) of the Sayings Gospel Q. And as the subtitle indicates, the book reconsiders three aspects of Q's formative stratum, namely its extent, message, and unity. Regarding its extent, the book argues that certain texts in Q that have traditionally been excluded from its earliest layer should rather be included. In the process of arguing for the inclusion of these individual texts, the book also reconsiders the message of Q's earliest redactional layer, the second item listed above. It would seem that Q's formative stratum was much more concerned with actual daily survival than earlier scholars might have thought. Besides the extent and message of Q's formative layer, the book also considers its unity. It is possible, the book argues, to regard the first layer of Q as a unified document or tradition even though it is made up of individual traditions. If I am correct about the addition of certain individual traditions to Q's formative stratum, what impact does this have on its overarching unity and flow?

More than 30 years ago, John S. Kloppenborg published *The Formation of Q*, identifying three redactional layers in the Sayings Gospel Q, namely the "formative stratum" (or Q[1]), the "main redaction" (or Q[2]), and the "final recension" (or Q[3]).[1] The formative stratum came first, to which the main redaction was added at a later stage. The final recension was last to be added and consisted only of the temptation passage (Q 4:1–13) and two interpolations (Q 11:42c; Q 16:17). I have argued elsewhere that the latter two interpolations belong to the main redaction rather than the final recension, so that the final recension would include only the temptation passage.[2] The current study focuses on the formative stratum, with occasional reference to the main redaction. Kloppenborg used the following criteria to distinguish between these two redactional layers: (1) characteristic forms; (2) characteristic motifs; and (3) implied audience. Regarding characteristic forms, the formative stratum features sapiential small forms like maxims and aphorisms, while the main redaction features *chreia* with prophetic and/or apocalyptic logia. Regarding characteristic motifs, the formative stratum discusses the radical wisdom of God's

---

[1] Kloppenborg 1987.
[2] Howes 2015a, 85–86.

kingdom, while the main redaction discusses apocalyptic judgment. When it comes to the criterion of implied audience, the formative stratum is unilaterally addressed to the Q people as insiders, while the main redaction is simultaneously addressed to insiders as the actual, stated audience and outsiders who reject the Q people and their message as the "projected" or "implied" audience. Kloppenborg's stratigraphy confirmed earlier proposals by scholars that deuteronomistic traditions about the condemnation of "this generation" represent redactional elaboration of the Q material during a later stage when boundary demarcation became important for the in-group.[3] Although there had been other attempts to determine the redactional layering of Q, Kloppenborg's proposal was the first to gain wide acceptance in scholarship.[4] Subsequent proposals of Q's stratigraphy have also failed to replace Kloppenborg's proposal by convincing any number of scholars.[5] As one would expect, not all scholars accept Kloppenborg's proposed stratigraphy or even believe that the redactional make-up of Q can be determined in the first place.[6] The impact of Kloppenborg's monograph was to divide scholars clearly into two camps: those for and those against his proposed stratigraphy. The former group of scholars accepted his proposed stratigraphy, sometimes uncritically, and used it as a basis for further study.[7] The latter group rejected it out of hand without engaging the detail of his exegetical analysis.[8] Lacking on both sides has been a critical engagement with the details of Kloppenborg's exegesis and argumentation. I intend to do just that here. Accepting Kloppenborg's proposed stratigraphy for the most part, this monograph focuses on those individual texts that have in my opinion been wrongly ascribed to the main redaction instead of the formative stratum.

Thirty-plus years after the publication of Kloppenborg's ground-breaking monograph, the time has come to re-evaluate his proposed stratigraphy in the exegetical detail it deserves. Developments over the last thirty years in both Q research and historical Jesus studies have contributed to the proposals and interpretations offered here. In my analysis, I will use the same three criteria as Kloppenborg to determine the redactional placement of individual traditions, namely characteristic forms, characteristic motifs, and implied audience. Although the focus is on Q's redaction and stratigraphy, the current analysis includes interesting and novel interpretations of certain Q texts, aided in no small way by advances in our knowledge of not only the logia and parables of Jesus,

---

[3] E.g. Steck 1967; Lührmann 1969.

[4] Tuckett 1996, 69, 70; Horsley 1999, 62; Freyne 2000, 227.

[5] E.g. Jacobson 1992; Ra 2016.

[6] For a discussion of criticism against Kloppenborg's proposal and arguments against such criticism, see Howes 2015a, 68–88.

[7] E.g. Cotter 1995, 117; Arnal 2001, 5; Rollens 2014a, 94–95, 105, 109–113; Oakman 2015, 100.

[8] Arnal 2001, 4; Kloppenborg 2001, 164.

but also the ancient Jewish world. A good example is my reinterpretation of the parable of the loyal and wise slave in Matthew 24:45–51 and Luke (Q) 12:42–46, which draws on a thorough understanding of servile farm management in antiquity.[9] Another example is my proposed interpretation of the logion in Matthew 5:25–26 and Luke (Q) 12:58–59 about making peace with one's opponent on the way to court, which takes full account of recent Q studies that appeal to Egyptian papyri.[10] A final example is my reinterpretation of the parables of the mustard seed and leaven, which fully engages recent parable scholarship.[11] As such, the current study contributes not only to our understanding of Q's redactional stratification, but also to our interpretation of the Jesus tradition, including especially his sayings and parables recorded in the earliest layer of Q. The content of this monograph should therefore be useful not only to Q scholarship, but also to scholarship on the parables of Jesus, the historical Jesus, the Synoptic Gospels, and the New Testament in general.

The novelty of my interpretations are not only a result of advances in scholarship, but also a consequence of my positionality on the African continent. Although my goal with this publication was not to read Q texts from a liberationist or African perspective, my situatedness on the African continent contributed in no small way to my reading of these texts.[12] My experience both of and with poverty, for example, affects how I look at the world and how I read texts, allowing me to see elements and nuances that others might miss. My reading of Q texts is therefore typically "from below." Scholars often use the terms "from below" and "from above" to reference the opposing perspectives of the underclass and the elite, respectively. Reading a text "from below" therefore means to read it from the perspective of those who find themselves at the bottom of society's socio-economic (as well as politico-religious) hierarchy, whether ancient or modern. The economic situation of many Africans today bears a striking resemblance to the economic situation of many Jews in the first century.[13] I have been convinced by the content of Q's formative stratum that this text was in the first place directed at poor people and struggling peasants in ancient Judaism.[14] This is not to deny that Q was most likely written by "village scribes" (κωμογραμματεύς).[15] In general terms, I tend to agree with the "village scribe" hypothesis. Yet, unlike some proponents of this hypothesis,

---

[9] See chapter 4 below.

[10] See chapter 5 below.

[11] See chapter 6 below.

[12] For an overview of how Q has been interpreted in South Africa, see Howes 2019a.

[13] See Van Aarde 2009, esp. 535–536; cf. Van Eck, Renkin, and Ntakirutimana 2016. For an overview of poverty in first-century Galilee, see Häkkinen 2016.

[14] Cf. esp. Horsley 1995a, 44–45; 1999; Uro 1996, 89, 90; Park 2019, 52. Both the oral prehistory and the agricultural imagery of Q support the idea that it emerged in a non-elite agrarian context (Park 2019, 41–42, 44).

[15] See Kloppenborg 1991; Arnal 2001; cf. Rollens 2014b; Bazzana 2015.

I do not perceive any contradiction between the idea that the *authors* of Q were socio-economic "middling" figures, to use the vocabulary of Rollens,[16] on the one hand, and the idea that the primary *audiences* of Q were made up of the peasantry and poor, on the other.[17] In antiquity, "the poor" (οἱ πτωχοί) was a specific class of people, who were on a lower socio-economic scale than peasants.[18] Although the peasantry constituted a socio-economic group above "the poor," most peasants were likewise very poor. It is true that the peasantry was made up of various socio-economic strata,[19] but there should be little doubt that an overwhelming majority of them lived in poverty, especially in Palestine during the first century.[20] In fact, "the poor" also included dispossessed peasants, who lost their land due to economic pressures, making the line between these two classes of people blurry and easy to cross.[21] It is therefore not impossible to imagine that "the poor" would in certain ancient references have included peasants struggling economically. According to Häkkinen, the Jesus movement

seems to have attracted especially, like some other anti-Roman movements, the landless: peasant children without inheritance, expropriated smallholders and all kinds of people who were deprived of access to the land. The changed situation from a landowner, a peasant farmer, into a tenant farmer or day labourer was dramatic for many Galileans. The peasant farmers were permanently poor and in continuous danger to fall under the subsistence level.[22]

To distinguish between the different socio-economic strata in the ancient peasant class, Boer and Petterson, for example, speak of "small," "middle," and "big" peasants.[23] In this book, I will use the terms "small peasants" and "small peasantry" to reference peasants who were struggling to survive due to economic pressures, which included most peasants. Although the term "peasant" is often used in scholarship to reference a socio-economic *class* of people, including, for example, ancillary workers like fishermen and artisans,[24] I will mainly use the term here to reference peasant *farmers*. The term "the poor" will reference the landless class, including dispossessed peasants, although some peasants would have been so desperately close to losing their smallholdings that it would not be unreasonable to include at least some of them in this group as well. According to Ukpong, "[t]he poor comprised the urban non-elite and

---

[16] Rollens 2014b.

[17] Cf. Park 2019, 44.

[18] Cf. Van Aarde 2009, 536; Häkkinen 2016, 2, 4.

[19] See Freyne 1988, 211–212; Mattila 2010, 291–313; Boer and Petterson 2017, 68–72; cf. Rollens 2014b, 12, 21, 36; Häkkinen 2016, 3.

[20] See Häkkinen 2016, 1–9, esp. 3, 5–8; cf. Ukpong 2012, 200; Jacobs 2018, 121–126.

[21] Häkkinen 2016, 4, 8.

[22] Häkkinen 2016, 7.

[23] Boer and Petterson 2017, esp. 68, 70.

[24] See Boer and Petterson 2017, 71–72.

the rural small landowners, landless day labourers, slaves, the handicapped, tenant farmers, beggars (the blind, lame, lepers, destitute), widows and orphans."[25] This study will therefore regard "the poor" and the "small peasantry" as separate but overlapping categories.

Although this book represents a critical reassessment of Kloppenborg's redactional model, it is at the same time also an attempt to reinforce and buttress his proposed stratigraphy. The current author has defended his acceptance and approval of Kloppenborg's stratigraphy of Q at length elsewhere.[26] This does not mean that every aspect and argument of Kloppenborg's stratigraphy is simply taken over without question. In fact, this publication functions as an example of how one may accept Kloppenborg's stratigraphy in principle, but still question and critically re-examine some of the more specific arguments and conclusions that pertain to particular texts. Although the book calls into question Kloppenborg's attribution of individual texts to the main redaction, it defends his overarching proposal that an earlier layer of instructional material was subsequently expanded by the addition of prophetic and/or apocalyptic traditions. This is done in two distinct ways. Firstly, the current analysis will argue that individual traditions were expanded in exactly the same direction. For example, it will be argued that the traditions in Q 12:39–40, Q 12:42–46, Q 13:24–27, and Q 19:12–13, 15–24, 26 all show signs of development from non-eschatological traditions about the present kingdom of God to parables about the final judgment. This happened through the addition of material that changed the meaning of these parables to support the message of the main redaction, so that these individual traditions represent a microcosm for the procedure by which the Q document as a whole was edited. In other cases, the same goal was achieved without elaborating the tradition, but simply by placing it within a literary context that treats eschatological/apocalyptic themes. This is true for at least Q 11:33, 34–35, Q 12:58–59, and Q 14:16–21, 23. Secondly, the current study will attempt to show that Q's formative stratum was a literary unity before the main redaction was added to it. This is in response to critics of Kloppenborg's stratigraphy who point out that Q's formative stratum might not have been a unified document before the addition of redactional material.[27] According to them, Kloppenborg's proposal would be dealt a serious blow if the formative stratum was not a unified document or tradition in its own right before its redactional expansion. Instead of adding material to an existing document, editorial activity would then consist merely of assembling a host of disparate sayings (and/or clusters of sayings) into one document.[28] Against

---

[25] Ukpong 2012, 200.

[26] See Howes 2015a, 61–89, 151.

[27] E.g. Hoffman 1995, 187; Tuckett 1996, 71–74; Horsley 1999, 67; Dunn 2003, 156–157.

[28] Cf. Kloppenborg 1996a, 27.

this, the current study will argue that a strong case can indeed be made for the original unity of Q's formative stratum.

One of the criteria used here for distinguishing between the formative stratum and main redaction is whether individual traditions are sapiential, prophetic, eschatological, and/or apocalyptic in form and content. Kloppenborg claims that his stratigraphical analysis of Q was *not* based on determining whether the thematic content of particular logia or traditions were "sapiential," "prophetic," "eschatological," or "apocalyptic."[29] He explains further: "Thus when one speaks of a formative 'sapiential' stratum, this is a *secondary* characterization of the *result* of literary-critical analysis, and not the description of the *primary criteria* for strata separation."[30] True as this may be, the ultimate result that the formative stratum is a sapiential stratum and that the main redaction harbours apocalyptic eschatology and prophecy justifies the subsequent use of these findings as criteria when considering the placement of individual traditions in Q. Since the present study accepts Kloppenborg's stratigraphical analysis and uses it as a starting point for further analysis, it is entirely legitimate to use his *result* that the content of Q[1] is sapiential and that the content of Q[2] is apocalyptic, eschatological, and prophetic as *criteria* for distinguishing between the two layers. Formal literary criteria will not be ignored in the process. It is true that Kloppenborg allows for the presence of eschatological and apocalyptic themes in the formative stratum, but I have argued elsewhere that the formative stratum does not develop *futurist* eschatology or apocalypticism at all.[31] This explains my high level of confidence in using categories like "sapiential" and "eschatological," in relation to both literary form and thematic content, when separating between the two main layers of Q.

The focus of this study on Q's first redactional layer introduces the question of Q's relation to the historical Jesus. A number of historical Jesus scholars have appealed to Kloppenborg's model as part of their larger arguments that the historical Jesus was not an eschatological or apocalyptic prophet, but rather a teacher of wisdom.[32] Yet Kloppenborg's division is not as clear-cut as many of these scholars assume. For example, Kloppenborg does regard some of the traditions in Q's formative stratum as eschatological and/or apocalyptic. As noted above, I have argued elsewhere that none of the traditions in Q's formative stratum promote a futurist eschatology, apocalyptic or otherwise.[33] At any rate, Kloppenborg warns against equating the redactional development of Q

---

[29] See e.g. Kloppenborg 1996a, 51–52.

[30] Kloppenborg 1996a, 52, emphasis original; cf. Vaage 1995a, 75.

[31] See Howes 2015a, 111–125, 151, 221–283, 286.

[32] E.g. Mack 1993, 36–37; Borg 1994, 15 n. 13; Patterson 1998, 171–172; cf. Kloppenborg 1996a, 52.

[33] See Howes 2015a, 111–125, 151, 221–283, 286.

with the historical development of the Jesus tradition or Q materials.[34] In other words, Kloppenborg cautions against the automatic assumption that Q's earliest redactional layer represents an earlier layer of the Jesus tradition.[35] It is not unimaginable that certain individual traditions in the main redaction might be authentic, while certain traditions in the formative stratum might likewise be inauthentic. What is more, Q's Jesus and the historical Jesus might be two completely different entities and should not automatically be equated.[36] Despite these words of caution, I am personally convinced not only that the Sayings Gospel Q brings us closer to the historical Jesus than most, if not all, of the canonical material, but also that Q's formative stratum brings us closer to the historical Jesus than any other material in the Sayings Gospel Q. Q's chronological and geographical proximity to the historical Jesus in all likelihood indicates conceptual and essential proximity between Q's Jesus and the historical Jesus.[37] There is likely to be a great degree of overlap between the two figures.[38] Q does not only predate the canonical Gospels in the source-critical sense, but also in the tradition-historical sense, containing a more primitive theology and Christology than the rest of the New Testament. Despite Kloppenborg's justified insistence that tradition history and redaction history should not be equated, it seems that there might very well be a great degree of overlap between the two. As Dunn observes, Kloppenborg's archaeological imagery of "excavation" and "stratigraphy" more than suggests that the "earliest layer" from a redactional point of view is also earliest from a historical point of view.[39] Robinson addresses this topic directly, stating that older and later traditions about Jesus "do not necessarily conform to the layering of Q, although by and large this would seem to be the case."[40] If Robinson is correct, it would follow that although individual traditions in the formative stratum are not automatically authentic and individual traditions in the main redaction are not automatically inauthentic, the presence of a saying in the formative stratum is suggestive of authenticity, while the presence of a saying in the main redaction is similarly suggestive of inauthenticity. Stated differently, although the redaction history of Q should not be *equated* with the tradition history of Jesus material, the former can indeed be *related* to the latter to some degree. This is supported by the likely sociological and polemical reasons for adding the main

---

[34] Kloppenborg 1987, 99, 244–245; 1996a, 52; 2000a, 150–151.

[35] See Freyne 2000, 227–228; Allison 2010, 120–125; cf. Vaage 1995, 75; Tuckett 1996, 68; 2001a, 383, 388; Crossan 2001, 119; Dunn 2013, 81.

[36] Kloppenborg 2001, 163; cf. Holmén 2001, 513; Robinson 2011, 471.

[37] Robinson 1991, 192; 1993, 9; 2001a, 14; 2007, vii, viii; 2011, 470; Vaage 2001, 479; cf. Theissen and Merz 1998, 27, 29; Kloppenborg 2001, 152, 171; Horsley 2012, 103, 117, 154; Park 2019, 41.

[38] Kloppenborg 2001, 158.

[39] Dunn 2013, 81; cf. Perkins 2007, 90.

[40] Robinson 1995a, 260; cf. 2011, 471; cf. Järvinen 2001, 516–517.

redaction. The main redaction seems to have been added to strengthen internal group solidarity in the midst of hostility from outsiders. Although it is possible that they drew on existing Jesus material for this purpose, it is more likely that they created much of this material *ex nihilo* to address this new situation. This is in stark contrast to the probable reasons for creating Q's formative stratum. From the content of Q's formative stratum one can easily deduce that the early followers of Jesus compiled it for the express purpose of implementing the teachings of Jesus in their daily lives. Committing the Jesus material to writing was a way to ensure that the teachings of Jesus would not be forgotten and would find practical expression in the lives of his post-mortem followers. In other words, the respective reasons for creating each of Q's two principle layers support the notion that the formative stratum would generally be more authentic and historically trustworthy than the main redaction. All of this is to say that the message of Q's formative stratum brings us very close indeed to the message of the historical Jesus. This book therefore adds to our understanding of the historical Jesus by considering the extent and message of Q's formative stratum.

More specifically, the main purpose of the current book is to argue that the following texts belong in Q's formative stratum, even though Kloppenborg originally attributed them to Q's main redaction: Q 10:21, 23–24 (chapter 1); Q 11:33–35 (chapter 2); Q 12:39 (chapter 3); Q 12:42–44 (chapter 4); Q 12:58–59 (chapter 5); Q 13:25 (chapter 7); Q 14:16–21, 23 (chapter 8); and Q 19:12–13, 15–24 (chapter 9). An exceptional case regards Q 13:18–21 (chapter 6), which was originally attributed to the formative stratum by Kloppenborg, but for which I propose a non-traditional reading that is important to the book's overarching argumentation. Each of the first nine chapters represents a reworked and elaborated version – sometimes extensively so – of one or more scholarly articles formerly published by me. These articles are referenced in the first footnote of each chapter. The last two chapters bring everything together: chapter 10 considers the unity and flow of the formative stratum as a whole, and chapter 11 concludes the study by summarising the main themes of the formative stratum, discussing the level of creativity showcased during the redactional process, and considering what we can take away from this study about both the parables of Jesus and the historical Jesus. Finally, Annexure A reproduces the extent or scope of the formative stratum given the alterations suggested in this book.

All reconstructions and translations of Q in this book are from the International Q Project's *Critical Edition of Q*.[41] I explain my reasons in the relevant contexts whenever my reconstruction or translation differs from the *Critical Edition of Q*. I use the same sigla as the *Critical Edition of Q* when reconstructing the Q text. Double square brackets (i.e. [[...]]) indicate a probability of {C},

---

[41] Robinson, Hoffmann, and Kloppenborg 2000; 2002.

which is lower than {A} or {B}, but higher than {D} or {U}. Pointed brackets (i.e. <...>) indicate some measure of conjecture, but with reference to the Matthean and Lukan texts. Guillemets (i.e. «...») indicate phrases that seem to have originated in Q, but for which it is impossible to produce a verbatim or close-to verbatim reading with any degree of certainty. For a more detailed description of the application of these sigla, see the *Critical Edition of Q*.[42] Chapter and verse references of the Sayings Gospel Q are according to Luke's Gospel.

Throughout this book, the term "main redactor" is used, even though more than one person were probably responsible for adding the main redaction. The title "main redactor" seems appropriate for the following reasons: (1) the material added by this redactor was dubbed the "main redaction" by Kloppenborg; (2) quantitively, this redactor added more material at one stage than the redactor(s) responsible for the final recension; and (3) qualitively, the material added by this redactor had more of an impact on the content and meaning of the document than the material added by the redactor(s) responsible for the final recension.

---

[42] Robinson, Hoffmann, and Kloppenborg 2000, 563–564; 2002, 153–155.

Chapter 1

Q 10:21–24, "Blessed Are Those Who See"[1]

²¹ἐν ... εἶπεν· ἐξομολογοῦμαί σοι, πάτερ, κύριε τοῦ οὐρανοῦ καὶ τῆς γῆς, ὅτι ἔκρυψας ταῦτα ἀπὸ σοφῶν καὶ συνετῶν καὶ ἀπεκάλυψας αὐτὰ νηπίοις· ναὶ ὁ πατήρ, ὅτι οὕτως εὐδοκία ἐγένετο ἔμπροσθέν σου. ²²πάντα μοι παρεδόθη ὑπὸ τοῦ πατρός μου, καὶ οὐδεὶς γινώσκει τὸν υἱὸν εἰ μὴ ὁ πατήρ, οὐδὲ τὸν πατέρα ⟦τις γινώσκει⟧ εἰ μὴ ὁ υἱὸς καὶ ᾧ ἐὰν βούληται ὁ υἱὸς ἀποκαλύψαι. ²³μακάριοι οἱ ὀφθαλμοὶ οἱ βλέποντες ἃ βλέπετε ... ²⁴λέγω γὰρ ὑμῖν ὅτι πολλοὶ προφῆται καὶ βασιλεῖς ... ησαν ἰδεῖν ἃ βλέπετε καὶ οὐκ εἶδαν, καὶ ἀκοῦσαι ἃ ἀκούετε καὶ οὐκ ἤκουσαν.

²¹At «that time» he said: I thank you, Father, Lord of heaven and earth, for you hid these things from sages and the learned, and disclosed them to children. Yes, Father, for that is what it has pleased you to do. ²²Everything has been entrusted to me by my Father, and no one knows the Son except the Father, nor ⟦does anyone know⟧ the Father except the Son, and to whomever the Son chooses to reveal him. ²³Blessed are the eyes that see what you see ... ²⁴For I tell you: Many prophets and kings wanted to see what you see, but never saw it, and to hear what you hear, but never heard it.

The composite nature of Q 10:21–24 is accepted by most.[2] Even a superficial reading of this cluster of sayings reveals that verse 22 interrupts the progression of thought from verse 21 to verses 23–24. A number of interpreters have noticed and commented on the intruding nature of verse 22.[3] These scholars tend to see verse 22 as a late addition not only to this pericope, but also to Q as a whole.[4] Unlike verse 21, the authenticity of verse 22 is also generally denied.[5] Yet, in the scholarly analyses of Q 10:21–24, these logia are persistently treated together, especially verses 21 and 22.[6] During these analyses, there seems to

---

[1] An earlier version of this chapter was published as an article in *Ekklesiastikos Pharos* 95 (see Howes 2013a).

[2] See Marshall 1978, 431–432; cf. Kloppenborg 1987, 198; Lee 2005, 137.

[3] Cf. e.g. Percy 1953, 260; Bultmann 1963, 159–160; Hahn 1969, 309; Lührmann 1969, 65; Schulz 1972, 215; Hoffmann 1975, 109; Marshall 1978, 431; Wanke 1980, 218; Zeller 1982, 405; 1984, 55; Kloppenborg 1987, 198; Sato 1988, 38; Denaux 1992, 170; Jacobson 1992, 150.

[4] Cf. Kloppenborg 1996a, 11–12; Tuckett 2001b, 287; Lee 2005, 137.

[5] Cf. Lee 2005, 137. It is worth noting, however, that an increasing number of scholars view this logion as typical of the way in which the historical Jesus spoke of himself (cf. Harvey 1982, 160).

[6] See e.g. Robinson 1964, 226–228; Jacobson 1978, 140–143; Piper 1989, 170–173; Allison 1997, 13–14; 2000, 43–51, 232–233; Kirk 1998, 340–364; Broadhead 2001, 294–295; Fleddermann 2005a, 447–454.

be a disregard for the formal, thematic, and other differences between these logia. Whenever these differences are indeed noted, scholars nonetheless continue discussing these logia together, as if these discrepancies were trivial.[7] This matter seems particularly pertinent if one considers that the *Critical Edition of Q* subdivides Q 10:21–24 into three distinct sayings, each with its own heading.[8] Whenever scholarly treatments of these sayings follow the *Critical Edition of Q* by formally subdividing the logia of Q 10:21–24, they nonetheless continue to discuss these sayings as if the disparities between them did not exist.[9]

Kloppenborg places Q 10:21–24 as a whole with the main redaction. Although Kloppenborg agrees that verse 22 was at some stage added to the pericope in Q 10:21–24, he claims that this addition was made during the prehistory of Q 10:21–24.[10] In a subsequent publication, Kloppenborg does concede the possibility that verses 23–24 might rather belong with Q's formative layer.[11] Yet Kloppenborg continues to treat verses 21 and 22 together and to regard verse 21 as part of the main redaction.[12] Kloppenborg's attribution of Q 10:21–24 to the main redaction depends on arguments drawn largely, if not exclusively, from the content and nature of verse 22. Against this, the present chapter will consider each of the three logia individually and on their own terms.

1.1 Characteristic Forms

Kirk classifies Q 10:21–22 as a "hymnic thanksgiving and revelation unit."[13] On a thematic level, both verses surely deal with "revelation," but on a genre level, only verse 21 can properly be labelled a "hymnic thanksgiving." Kirk continues to explain both verses solely in terms of a hymnic thanksgiving.[14] Fleddermann distinguishes between verses 21 and 22 by calling the former a "prayer" and the latter a "comment by Jesus."[15] Jacobson similarly distinguishes between the "thanksgiving" of verse 21 and Jesus's "claim" in verse

---

[7] See e.g. Kloppenborg 1987, 197–199, 201–203; Jacobson 1992, 149–151; Lee 2005, 137–143.

[8] Cf. Robinson, Hoffmann, and Kloppenborg 2002, 103. Verse 21 is dubbed "Thanksgiving that God Reveals Only to Children"; verse 22 is called "Knowing the Father through the Son"; and verses 23–24 are classified as "The Beatitude for the Eyes that See."

[9] See e.g. Denaux 1992, 163–199; Valantasis 2005, 110–116, esp. 113.

[10] Kloppenborg 1987, 198.

[11] Kloppenborg 2000a, 145, 147 n. 63; cf. Sato 1988, 32.

[12] Kloppenborg 2000a, 128, 147, 160, 187, 202, 330, 348, 375, 376, 387.

[13] Kirk 1998, 362; cf. also Piper 1989, 173.

[14] See also Robinson 1964, 226–228.

[15] Fleddermann 2005a, 448.

22.[16] Fleddermann is certainly correct in labelling verse 21 a "prayer."[17] Kirk is also correct in his more precise classification of verse 21 as a (hymnic) "thanksgiving."[18] The tell-tale signs of this small form are all present: (1) Jesus, the subject delivering the prayer, emphatically refers to himself in the first person singular (ἐξομολογοῦμαί σοι);[19] (2) Jesus addresses God directly, using not only the second person personal pronoun on two separate occasions (σοι and σου), but also the vocative case on two separate occasions (πάτερ and κύριε);[20] (3) Jesus affectionately refers to God as "Father" (πάτερ);[21] (4) Jesus directly and unmistakably expresses "praise and thanks" (ἐξομολογέω) to God;[22] (5) Jesus purposely mentions God's honoured vocation as the undisputed ruler over heaven and earth (κύριε τοῦ οὐρανοῦ καὶ τῆς γῆς);[23] (6) in typical sapiential fashion, Jesus then continues to explain with a causal clause (cf. ὅτι) the reason for his thanksgiving and praise;[24] and (7) Jesus ends the prayer with a statement about God doing what pleases him, thereby giving expression not only to God's might and autonomy, but also to Jesus's humility and dependence.[25]

As a *Mikrogattung*, hymnic thanksgivings like the one in Q 10:21 occur frequently in sapiential instructions.[26] Considering form only, verse 21 belongs properly with the traditional sapiential genre of instruction and thus with Q's formative layer. Conversely, Q 10:21 exhibits none of the formal characteristics of apocalyptic or prophetic sayings, including the prophetic or apocalyptic correlative.[27] Neither can the saying be classified as a *chreia*. The introductory words "at that time he said" certainly do not introduce the logion in a manner typical of either *chreiai* in general or other *chreiai* in Q.[28] Rather, this short introduction reminds one of similar introductions used by Q's Jesus to introduce the sapiential clusters of the formative stratum.[29]

---

[16] Jacobson 1992, 150.

[17] Cf. also Dibelius 1971, 281; Marshall 1978, 430, 431; Horsley 1992, 189; Valantasis 2005, 110.

[18] Cf. also Dibelius 1971, 281; Marshall 1978, 433; Denaux 1992, 169, 170.

[19] Cf. Robinson 1964, 197.

[20] Cf. Robinson 1964, 197, 208, 227, 230; Jacobson 1992, 149.

[21] Cf. Robinson 1964, 211, 227, 230; Marshall 1978, 433; Allison 1997, 14; Lee 2005, 142.

[22] See Robinson 1964, 198–201; cf. Fleddermann 2005a, 449; cf. e.g. 2 Sam 22:50; Ps 6:5; 9:1; 35:18; 45:17; 86:12; 118:28.

[23] Cf. Gammie 1990, 62; Fleddermann 2005a, 450.

[24] See Robinson 1964, 197, 208, 211–213, 227.

[25] Cf. Harvey 1982, 159; Gammie 1990, 62.

[26] See Gammie 1990, 49–50, 61–63; cf. Marshall 1978, 432; Kirk 1998, 362; cf. e.g. Golden Verses 61–62.

[27] See Edwards 1969, 9–20; 1976, 41, 142; Schmidt 1977, 517–522.

[28] Cf. Kloppenborg 1987, 168; cf. e.g. Q 3:7; 7:1, 3, 18–19; 11:14–15, 16; 17:20.

[29] Cf. e.g. Q 6:20; 9:58, 60; 10:2; 11:2, 9; 12:22; 13:18, 20.

There should be no doubt that Q 10:22 introduces a new small form.[30] To my knowledge, Robinson was the first to recognise that Q 10:21 constitutes a "thanksgiving."[31] Unfortunately, he treated verses 21 and 22 together and baptised both of them "thanksgiving." This formal linkage between the two verses has been very influential. Yet not in one of the numerous other examples of the "thanksgiving" small form held up by Robinson is there a change from addressing God directly in the second person to addressing him indirectly in the third person.[32] Logically, if this micro-genre constitutes a prayer of some kind, the end of the prayer would be signalled the moment when God is no longer addressed directly. This is exactly what happens in Q 10:22. As indicated earlier, the thanksgiving in verse 21 ends properly with the closing statement that God does whatever pleases him – a claim that is addressed directly to God in the second person. That verse 22 no longer addresses God directly is indicated by two features: (1) although God is still called "Father," he is now repeatedly referred to in the third person; and (2) the *second* person personal pronouns that referred to God in verse 21 now give way to *first* person personal pronouns (μοι and μου) that instead refer to Jesus. That verse 22 comprises a new *Mikrogattung* is both undeniable and straightforward.[33] Classifying the *Mikrogattung* of verse 22 is, however, much more challenging. The middle part of the logion[34] certainly has the gnomic feel of a sapiential maxim, but the particularising force of the introductory[35] and closing[36] statements cancel this out.[37] In essence, there are no definitive markers of genre in the logion itself.

As such, redactional observations are more determinative at this point. As already mentioned, a great number of scholars have noted that verse 22 was secondarily added to the complex of logia in Q 10:21, 23–24. These scholars can be divided into two categories:[38] (1) those who regard verse 22 as a redactional creation *ex nihilo*, added to this cluster of sayings as an interpretive

---

[30] Cf. Marshall 1978, 431–432; Kloppenborg 1987, 198; Denaux 1992, 170; Lee 2005, 137, 138; Rodriquez 2008, 250 n. 132.

[31] Robinson 1964, 226.

[32] Robinson 1964, 194–235. Paul sometimes *indirectly* refers to the thanksgiving prayer itself. In these cases, God is referenced in the third person, not in the second person (cf. e.g. 1 Cor 1:4–5; 1 Thes 2:13; 2 Thes 1:3; 2:13). Even so, the indirect manner of address remains stable in these cases.

[33] Cf. Rodriquez 2008, 250 n. 132.

[34] "…no one knows the Son except the Father, nor does anyone know the Father except the Son" (οὐδεὶς γινώσκει τὸν υἱὸν εἰ μὴ ὁ πατήρ, οὐδὲ τὸν πατέρα τις γινώσκει εἰ μὴ ὁ υἱός).

[35] "Everything has been entrusted to me by my Father" (πάντα μοι παρεδόθη ὑπὸ τοῦ πατρός μου).

[36] "…and to whomever the Son chooses to reveal him" (καὶ ᾧ ἐὰν βούληται ὁ υἱὸς ἀποκαλύψαι).

[37] Cf. Marshall 1978, 437; Harvey 1982, 160; Denaux 1992, 167, 174–175; Lee 2005, 140.

[38] Cf. Denaux 1992, 170; Lee 2005, 137–138.

gloss;[39] and (2) those who regard verse 22 as a pre-existing, free-floating logion, added to this cluster of sayings as a *Kommentarwort*.[40] Kloppenborg opts
for the latter because "the two sayings [in verses 21 and 22 respectively] differ
markedly in form, structure and motif." Yet two other textual features seem
more decisive at this point, suggesting the former option instead. Firstly, the
lack of any determinative genre markers in verse 22, referred to above, supports
the notion that this saying was created *ex nihilo*. Secondly, the reintroduction
in verse 22 of the catchwords "father" (πατήρ) and "reveal" (ἀποκαλύπτω)
seems deliberate, suggesting that an author purposely reproduced them.[41] Be
that as it may, the specific small form of the saying in Q 10:22 cannot be determined with any measure of certainty, which means that any decision regarding its proper placement in either the formative stratum or the main redaction
remains premature at this stage.

    Few would dispute that Q 10:23–24 constitutes a beatitude or makarism with
an extended causal clause.[42] The former determination is made clear by the
word "blessed" (μακάριος) in verse 23, while the latter is made clear by the
conjunction "for" or "because" (γάρ) in verse 24. The beatitude of verse 23 is
itself a well-established form of traditional wisdom literature.[43] The manner in
which verse 24 buttresses the beatitude with deductive reasoning also signals
the proper place of the logion in traditional wisdom literature. These formal
features indicate that Q 10:23–24 belongs to the formative stratum. Although
Kloppenborg mentions the introductory formula "I tell you" (λέγω ὑμῖν) as a
typical feature of the formative stratum, this aspect of verse 24 should not be
pressed too hard, since the same formula also occurs on occasion in the prophetic sayings of the main redaction.[44] At any rate, none of the representative
formal features of prophetic or apocalyptic small forms occur in this logion.
What is more, neither the saying itself nor the cluster it features in can be classified as a *chreia*.

    In the end, the status of verse 22 as an interpretive addition contrasts mark-
edly with the proverbial small forms that appear in the rest of the pericope.
Irrespective of whether verse 22 appropriately belongs to the first or second
layer of Q, it is clear, based on its formal features alone, that this saying seems

---

[39] Cf. e.g. Schulz 1972, 215; Hoffmann 1975, 109; Marshall 1978, 431; Sabbe 1982, 363;
Zeller 1982, 405; Sato 1988, 38; Luz 2001, 158, 164.

[40] Cf. e.g. Percy 1953, 260; Bultmann 1963, 159–160; Hahn 1969, 309; Lührmann 1969,
65; Wanke 1980, 218; Kloppenborg 1987, 198.

[41] Cf. Marshall 1978, 431; Zeller 1982, 405; Kloppenborg 1987, 198; Denaux 1992, 170;
Allison 1997, 14; Lee 2005, 137; Fleddermann 2005a, 448.

[42] Cf. Marshall 1978, 438; Sato 1988, 37; Denaux 1992, 169; Kirk 1998, 312, 315, 334;
Fleddermann 2005a, 448.

[43] Cf. Kirk 1998, 334.

[44] Kloppenborg 1987, 239.

ill at home in Q 10:21–24.[45] The saying seems alien and intrusive in its syntagmatic literary context in Q. On the other hand, the formal features of Q 10:21, 23–24 seem to indicate that these logia belong to the formative stratum.

1.2 Characteristic Motifs

The most apparent and persistent theme in Q 10:21–24 is that of "divine revelation."[46] Incontestably, all four verses deal in one way or another with divine revelation. Verse 21 claims that "these things" (ταῦτα) were "revealed" (ἀποκρύπτω) by God to infants, as opposed to sages and educated men. Verse 22 claims that "revelation" (ἀποκρύπτω)[47] occurs from God the Father to Jesus, his son, and then from Jesus to a selected group of people.[48] Verses 23–24 use the words "seeing" (βλέπω) and "hearing" (ἀκούω) as metaphors of divine revelation, claiming that the recipients of such revelation are more "blessed" (μακάριοι) than prophets and kings.[49] Thus, the thematic thread that holds the three logia of Q 10:21–24 together is the concept of divine revelation.

Kloppenborg claims that Q 10:21–24 "is unified by the theme of the reception and acceptance of the revelation of the kingdom by the 'simple.'"[50] However, a number of considerations speak against this claim. Firstly, as will be argued in more detail below, verse 22 fails to make any mention of social, economic, or intellectual hierarchy, indicating that it does not have the "simple" in view. Secondly, it will also be argued in more detail below that the focus is not in any of these sayings on human "reception" or "acceptance." Instead, the spotlight falls on God's generous acts of revelation. Kloppenborg's proposal

---

[45] Cf. Kloppenborg 1987, 198.

[46] Cf. Jacobson 1978, 142; Lee 2005, 138.

[47] The verb "entrust" (παραδίδωμι) actually describes the first level of revelation, while the verb "reveal" (ἀποκρύπτω) describes the second. Conceptually, however, both should be understood in terms of "revelation" (cf. Allison 2000, 47 n. 103). By describing the first level of revelation with the verb "entrust" (παραδίδωμι), the author might have implied a form of (divine) authority that was afforded Jesus as a result of the knowledge revealed to him (see Denaux 1992, 173–174; Lee 2005, 142–143; cf. Marshall 1978, 436; Sabbe 1982, 363).

[48] That is, of course, if "son" (υἱός) here does indeed refer exclusively to Jesus (cf. Marshall 1978, 437; Tuckett 2001b, 287). The latter seems highly likely for the following reasons: (1) the dual appearance of a first person personal pronoun (μοι and μου) in the former part of the saying; (2) the consistent use of a definite article before "son" (ὁ υἱός); (3) the appearance of the noun υἱός in the singular; (4) the exclusivity of the phrase "no one knows the son" (οὐδεὶς γινώσκει ὁ υἱός); and (5) the son's role as exclusive mediator (cf. Marshall 1978, 437, 438; Piper 1989, 172; Denaux 1992, 174–175; Lee 2005, 140).

[49] Cf. Bultmann 1963, 109; Marshall 1978, 438; Kloppenborg 1987, 198; Kirk 1998, 334, 344–345.

[50] Kloppenborg 1987, 201.

of a unified theme applies solely to Q 10:21, 23–24, which supports the observation that verse 22 fits awkwardly with its immediate literary surroundings. Fleddermann argues persuasively that "desire" is an integral motif to all three logia in Q 10:21–24.[51] If anything, the cluster in Q 10:21–24 is unified by both the principal theme of "divine revelation" and the subordinate theme of "desire," but that is where it ends.

Although each saying deals with the broad idea of "revelation," they differ about the narrower content of what is in fact being claimed *about* the phenomenon of revelation. In the first instance, they differ about the method of *how* this revelation actually takes place. In verse 21, Jesus thanks God for revealing "these things" to infants, which indicates that God reveals "these things" *directly* to the infants.[52] In verse 22, on the other hand, Jesus claims that God the Father *mediates* his revelation through his son.[53] In this way, verse 22 seems to contradict verse 21.[54] It is not expressly stated by the beatitude in Q 10:23–24 whether the revelation in view is mediated or not. Theoretically, the recipients could be pronounced fortunate either because they "saw" and "heard" God's revelation directly or because they "saw" and "heard" God's revelation as it was mediated through Jesus. Nevertheless, preference should be given to the former option.[55] Failure to mention a mediator in the closing logion is certainly noteworthy after the central position afforded Jesus as mediator in the preceding verse.

The second thematic discrepancy between the three logia concerns the content of *what* is essentially being revealed.[56] As others have noted,[57] the opening phrase "at that time" (ἐν ἐκείνῳ τῷ καιρῷ // ἐν αὐτῇ τῇ ὥρᾳ) intentionally connects verse 21 to the foregoing material. That it reaches back *solely* to the mission discourse seems unlikely.[58] Rather, the phrase probably has all the preceding (Q¹) material in mind, including the inaugural sermon. Resultantly, the words "these things" (ταῦτα) and "it" (αὐτά) refer comprehensively to Jesus's

---

[51] Fleddermann 2005a, 448, 451, 452, 453.

[52] See Howes 2016a, 20–21.

[53] Cf. Jacobson 1978, 141–142; 1992, 149; Marshall 1978, 438; Denaux 1992, 170; Kirk 1998, 315, 347; Fleddermann 2005a, 451.

[54] See Piper 1989, 170–173; cf. Zeller 1982, 405; Kloppenborg 1987, 198; *pace* Lee 2005, 142.

[55] Cf. Zeller 1982, 405.

[56] Cf. Zeller 1982, 405; Jacobson 1992, 150; *pace* Dibelius 1971, 280.

[57] E.g. Marshall 1978, 430, 432; Zeller 1982, 405; Kloppenborg 1987, 197; 2000a, 128; Sato 1988, 37; Denaux 1992, 169; Allison 1997, 14; Fleddermann 2005a, 449.

[58] Cf. Horsley 1992, 190.

message *in toto*.[59] The thanksgiving therefore understands the content of revelation to be the sapiential message of Jesus, which the "infants" are receiving
as they listen.[60]

There are two levels of revelation in verse 22.[61] The content of what is revealed by God to Jesus is vaguely, but comprehensively, described as "everything" (πάντα).[62] The second level of revelation occurs between Jesus and others.[63] The content of this second level of revelation seems to be privileged
knowledge of the innate nature and identity of God the Father.[64] This is primarily indicated by the phrase "know the Father" (τὸν πατέρα γινώσκει).
Fleddermann claims that the neuter plural words "these things" (ταῦτα), "it"
(αὐτά), "all things" (πάντα), and "which" (ἅ) tie the three logia of this cluster
together.[65] This grammatical similarity between the three logia is by far out-
weighed by the fact that the neuter plural words of the thanksgiving and beatitude refer to the restricted revelation of something specific, while the neuter
plural word of verse 22 claims unrestricted revelation of everything.[66] This
disparity represents more than a mere change in focus or rhetorical strategy; it
represents a direct contradiction.[67]

Although the beatitude is not entirely lucid in its description of what is being
revealed, the verbs "see" (βλέπω) and "hear" (ἀκούω) both render highly unlikely the possibility that it also has the nature and identity of God in mind.[68]
The use of the present tense in verses 23–24 for the verbs "see" (βλέπετε) and
"hear" (ἀκούετε) indicate that the recipients are in the process of receiving the
imagined revelation as they are listening to Jesus.[69] This strongly suggests that

---

[59] Cf. Marshall 1978, 434; Denaux 1992, 169, 172; Fleddermann 2005a, 451, 453.

[60] Cf. Zeller 1982, 405.

[61] See Valantasis 2005, 113–114; cf. Sato 1988, 38; Hartin 2000, 275; Lee 2005, 137.

[62] Kloppenborg 1987, 201; 2000a, 375; Sato 1988, 38; Denaux 1992, 173; Jacobson 1992,
150; Allison 2000, 45, 47; Broadhead 2001, 295; Fleddermann 2005a, 451; Lee 2005, 137;
Valantasis 2005, 114.

[63] Marshall 1978, 437; Sato 1988, 38; Jacobson 1992, 150; Fleddermann 2005a, 451; Lee
2005, 137; see Valantasis 2005, 113–114.

[64] Davies 1953, 138; Marshall 1978, 431, 437; Kloppenborg 1987, 201; 2000a, 375;
Jacobson 1992, 150; Allison 2000, 45; Fleddermann 2005a, 451, 452.

[65] Fleddermann 2005a, 448, 450, 451, 452–453. Fleddermann (2005a, 451, 454) even
uses this grammatical overlap as evidence against the obvious composite nature of Q 10:21–
24.

[66] Cf. Marshall 1978, 431; Zeller 1982, 405; Jacobson 1992, 150; Allison 2000, 47;
Valantasis 2005, 114.

[67] *Pace* Dibelius 1971, 280; Lee 2005, 142.

[68] Cf. Marshall 1978, 431.

[69] Cf. Horsley 1992, 190. The use of the present tense in verse 23 is not to be compared
with the use of the present tense in verse 22. The latter is a gnomic present, whereas the
former is a true indication of time (cf. Denaux 1992, 167).

the content of the revelation is the sapiential message itself.[70] In particular, the verb "hear" (ἀκούω) seems to suggest a message of some kind. The verb "see," however, indicates that this message was not only spoken by Jesus, but also demonstrated by him.[71] In Q 7:22, Jesus likewise refers to his ministry as something that is both "seen" (βλέπω) and "heard" (ἀκούω).[72] In Q 7:22, the "seeing" part of Jesus's ministry refers specifically to his humanitarian miracles, while the "hearing" part refers specifically to his humanitarian act of "bringing good news" (εὐαγγελίζω) to the poor.[73]

The most direct, effective, and memorable way in which Jesus demonstrated his sapiential message was through his humanitarian miracles.[74] There were, however, other ways as well. In Q 10:21, Jesus demonstrates one of the central themes of his sapiential message, namely that God the Father is accessible to everyone at any time and place, by praying directly and audibly to God in front of a live audience.[75] Among other types of exhibition, the beatitude probably had the demonstration of verse 21 specifically in mind when it mentioned "seeing" (βλέπω) the wisdom of Jesus.[76] Just as important in this regard is the repetitive use in the beatitude of a *neuter* relative pronoun (ἅ) as the object of both "hear" and "see."[77] The latter is almost determinative as an indication that the sapiential message of Jesus, and not the person of Jesus, is here intended as the content of revelation. This supports our former result that, in all likelihood, the beatitude in verses 23–24 did not have a mediated form of revelation in mind.[78] Both the sapiential content and the immediacy of the revelation tie this logion to the one in verse 21.

That Q 10:21, 23–24 has the sapiential message *of Jesus* in view opens up the possibility that these verses also understood the revelation as something that was mediated.[79] After all, without the person of Jesus to relay this specific brand of divine wisdom, how could the "infants" ever have received it? This is certainly a legitimate argument. Yet there is a fundamental difference in this regard between verse 22 and the other sayings. In verse 22, Jesus remains essential to the process of revelation.[80] In the remainder of the passage, however,

---

[70] Cf. Valantasis 2005, 115.

[71] Cf. Dibelius 1971, 281; Marshall 1978, 431, 438; Kloppenborg 1987, 197.

[72] Cf. Fleddermann 2005a, 453.

[73] Cf. Marshall 1978, 431, 434, 438; Horsley 1992, 190; Fleddermann 2005a, 453. For teaching and healing as two ways of proclaiming God's kingdom, see Du Toit 2016, 67.

[74] See Kirk 1998, 334–335; cf. Dube 2015.

[75] See Allison 1997, 13–14; Valantasis 2005, 110–112; cf. Dibelius 1971, 281; Kirk 1998, 326, 334.

[76] Cf. Dibelius 1971, 281; Kloppenborg 1987, 197.

[77] Fleddermann 2005a, 448.

[78] *Pace* Kirk 1998, 313–314.

[79] Cf. Kloppenborg 1986, 460; Kirk 1998, 313–314.

[80] Cf. Valantasis 2005, 113.

the process of revelation may continue if Jesus is removed from the equation.[81] Once the message has been delivered, the messenger becomes irrelevant. In verses 21, 23–24, it is the message that remains essential to the process of revelation, not the messenger.[82] This is comparable to the intent of wisdom material in general.[83] Whether contemporaneous with the ministry of Q's Jesus or posthumously, parts of the Sayings Gospel Q clearly betray a belief that both the seeing and the hearing parts of Jesus's sapiential message could be delivered without the help of Jesus himself.[84] Q 10:21, 23–24 should be read in the same light. In many ways, unmediated access to God is precisely what the formative stratum is about.[85] In verse 22, on the other hand, it is the messenger who remains essential as the mediator of revelation.[86] In verse 22, Jesus is the exclusive avenue through which access and knowledge of God are possible. This motif corresponds to the content of the main redaction.[87] At a number of turns in the main redaction, the messenger seems to have become the message.

Beside the "how" and the "what" of the perceived revelation, there is also discontinuity as far as the "who" is concerned. According to all three logia, the ultimate subject of revelation is God the Father. However, the recipients of revelation do not remain the same throughout the pericope. In the thanksgiving, the objects of revelation are the "infants" (νηπίοι). Similarly, in the beatitude, the recipients of revelation are spoken of in the plural.[88] In verse 22, the unidentified and undefined "infants" are replaced by the singular and specific "son" (ὁ υἱός) of God.[89] The mentioning of additional recipients, namely "whomever the son chooses" (ᾧ ἐὰν βούληται ὁ υἱὸς), may be equated with the "infants" of verse 21, but the generic nature of this description differs markedly from the identification of a specific socio-economic group in verse 21.[90] One also gets the distinct impression that the phrase "whomever the son chooses" is added as an afterthought or side-note to the central issue of revelation from God to Jesus. The focus is surely on the "son," meaning Jesus, as the prime recipient.[91] This observation obviously ties into the aforementioned distinction

---

[81] Cf. Zeller 1982, 405.

[82] Cf. Zeller 1982, 405.

[83] Cf. Kloppenborg 1986, 460.

[84] Cf. Jacobson 1992, 149; see Kirk 1998, 334–335. For the "hearing" part, cf. esp. Q 10:2–11, 16; 12:2–3, 8–9, 11–12; for the "seeing" part, cf. esp. Q 11:2–4, 19; 17:6. In possible reference to both, see also Q 6:40, 46; 7:35; 11:29–32.

[85] Cf. e.g. Q 11:2–4, 9–13; 12:12, 22–31.

[86] Cf. Marshall 1978, 438; Jacobson 1992, 149; Valantasis 2005, 113.

[87] Cf. Fleddermann 2005a, 451; cf. e.g. Q 3:16–17; 7:6–8, 18–19, 22–23; 11:23, 29–32; 12:8–9, 40, [49], 51, 53; 13:35; 17:23–24, 26–27, 30; 22:28, 30.

[88] Cf. esp. μακάριοι, οἱ ὀφθαλμοί, οἱ βλέποντες, βλέπετε (x2), ὑμῖν, ἀκούετε.

[89] Cf. Zeller 1982, 405; Fleddermann 2005a, 449.

[90] See below.

[91] Cf. Jacobson 1992, 149; Valantasis 2005, 113.

between direct and mediated revelation.[92] Nevertheless, the difference between many unnamed "children" (νήπιοι) and one privileged "child" (ὁ υἱός) is striking enough to be held up as a separate thematic dissimilarity between verse 22 and the remainder of the sayings-cluster.[93]

Turning to eschatology, there is no *direct* indication of its presence in Q 10:21–24. There are neither any future-tense verbs, nor any apocalyptic images or references to the end. The appearance of the word "revealed" (ἀποκρύπτω) in verses 21 and 22 does not automatically turn these verses into "apocalyptic" small forms. Neither does the word "hidden" (ἔκρυψας // ἀπέκρυψας).[94] There are many examples from contemporaneous literature of "hidden" but typical this-worldly wisdom being "revealed" to specified recipients, without intending apocalypticism or eschatology.[95] Whether or not these sayings have some type of eschatological revelation in mind depends almost exclusively on the content of what is being revealed according to each individual logion. Concerning verse 21, this entails primarily what is understood to be the referent of "these things" (ταῦτα).[96] As we saw, the content of what is "revealed" (ἀπεκάλυψας) in verse 21 has very little to do with the end times, but has everything to do with the common and corporeal wisdom that is being delivered by Jesus as he speaks.[97] The same is true of verses 23–24. One could argue for a *realised* eschatology in Q 10:21, 23–24,[98] but that would not be an argument in favour of a Q² position for either logion, seeing as the formative stratum also develops the theme of "realised eschatology."[99]

Like the two logia just examined, the question of whether or not verse 22 contains any hint of eschatology depends not on the presence of future-tense verbs or the word "reveal" (ἀποκρύπτω). Both wisdom and apocalyptic literature contain traditions where divine secrets are revealed to selected persons, but hidden from others.[100] Instead, settling this issue depends largely on the content of what is being revealed. As we saw, according to verse 22 revelation occurs in two distinct stages. Firstly, "everything" is revealed to Jesus, including the innate nature and identity of God the Father. Secondly, this

---

[92] Cf. Jacobson 1992, 149.

[93] Cf. Robinson 1964, 228; Sato 1988, 38; Denaux 1992, 170; Jacobson 1992, 149, 150; Kirk 1998, 357.

[94] *Pace* Piper 1989, 171.

[95] Cf. Jacobson 1978, 142–143; Denaux 1992, 172; Kirk 1998, 334; cf. e.g. Wis 7–9; Sir 24.

[96] Cf. Sato 1988, 37; Horsley 1992, 190.

[97] Cf. Denaux 1992, 172; Kirk 1998, 334; *pace* Sato 1988, 37; Allison 2000, 233; Fleddermann 2005a, 450.

[98] As many others have done: e.g. Bultmann 1963, 126, 128; Marshall 1978, 438; Sato 1988, 32, 37; Denaux 1992, 169, 172; Horsley 1992, 190.

[99] See Howes 2015a, 122–124; cf. e.g. Q 6:21–23b; 10:5–9; 13:18–21; 16:16.

[100] Cf. Kloppenborg 1986, 460; Denaux 1992, 172, 175–176.

"knowledge" (γινώσκω) of the divine is then revealed to whomever Jesus chooses. The specified content of each level of revelation strongly suggest apocalyptic revelation.[101] The confident claim that "everything," including all the secrets of earth, heaven, and God, has been revealed to a certain individual is characteristic of the apocalyptic and prophetic genres.[102] Also, the specific combination of the verbs "know" (γινώσκω) and "reveal" (ἀποκρύπτω) with the notion of mediation strongly suggests an interpretation of Q 10:22 that takes apocalyptic eschatology seriously.[103]

Conversely, the humble idea that there is much about the world, about heaven, and especially about God, that sages do not yet have any knowledge of is more commensurate with sapiential literature.[104] Ancient wisdom is generally less concerned with the unknowable aspects of God's nature and person. Whenever the nature of God becomes a sapiential motif, it is mostly to emphasise how little can be known of him.[105] The fact that verse 22 claims exclusive knowledge of the ever-elusive nature and identity of God strongly suggests that it should be read as an apocalyptic saying.[106] This distinction between wisdom and apocalypticism should not be pressed too far. Others[107] have indeed identified certain sapiential themes in Q 10:22, including perhaps the Sophia motif. Conversely, the presence in this logion of apocalyptic eschatology should likewise not be denied. If the presence of apocalyptic eschatology is combined with other indicators, it functions as fairly strong supportive evidence that Q 10:22 belongs with the main redaction. Equally, the absence of apocalyptic motifs in the rest of this passage strongly suggests that it suitably belongs with the formative stratum.

If I understand him correctly, Kloppenborg basically has two reasons for placing Q 10:21–24 in the main redaction.[108] The first is that the heightened

---

[101] Cf. Sabbe 1982, 363; Zeller 1982, 405; *pace* Jacobson 1992, 150.

[102] See Allison 2000, 47–48, esp. n. 104; cf. Horsley 1992, 190; cf. e.g. Dan 2:22; 1 Enoch 46:3.

[103] See Davies 1953, 113–139.

[104] Cf. Jacobson 1978, 143; cf. e.g. Job 8:8–9; 9:1–19; 26:5–14; 28:1–28; 36:27–33; 37:1–24; 38:1–38; 39:1–38; 40:1–28; 41:1–25; Prov 3:7, 19–20; 8:22–31; 13:11; 15:33; 16:18; 25:3; 30:2–4, 18–19; Eccl 5:1; 7:23–24, 29; 8:1, 6–8, 16–17; 11:5.

[105] Cf. e.g. Job 5:9; 9:1–19; 11:7–9; 21:22; 22:12–14; 25:1–6; 26:5–14; 33:13; 34:10–28; 36:22–33; 37:1–24; 38:1–38; 39:1–38; 40:1–28; 41:1–25; Prov 3:19–20; 15:3, 11; 20:24, 27; 21:30; Eccl 3:11; 9:1; 11:5.

[106] Although this logion might at some stage in its prehistory have consisted only of a sapiential maxim: οὐδεὶς γινώσκει τὸν υἱὸν εἰ μὴ ὁ πατήρ, οὐδὲ τὸν πατέρα τις γινώσκει εἰ μὴ ὁ υἱός.

[107] Cf. e.g. Robinson 1964, 228; Marshall 1978, 432; Sabbe 1982, 364; Kloppenborg 2000a, 348, 375; Tuckett 2001b, 288–289; see Jacobson 1978, 141–143; Piper 1989, 171–173; Denaux 1992, 175–176.

[108] Kloppenborg 1987, 201–203.

Christology (and soteriology) of Q 10:21–22 is comparable to the high Christology (and soteriology) of the main redaction.[109] This is certainly true, but it
is only true of verse 22.[110] The rest of the pericope has no Christology to speak
of.[111] In verses 21, 23, and 24, God the Father is the subject who either "hid"
(ἔκρυψας // ἀπέκρυψας) or "disclosed" (ἀπεκάλυψας) "these things," not Jesus.[112] It is only in verse 22 that the role of Jesus as mediator is referenced.[113]
As such, the oft-noted[114] affinities of this Q pericope with Johannine Christology apply *solely* to verse 22.[115] The same is true of the potential allusion to
Jesus's role as an envoy of Sophia. It is only verse 22, and not the pericope as
a whole, that potentially alludes to the Christological role of Jesus as prophetic
envoy of Sophia.[116] In this regard, it is certainly telling that the reference to
"Sophia" appears elsewhere in the main redaction,[117] but not at all in the formative stratum. Kloppenborg acknowledges that "[t]he effect of the association
of vv. 21 and 22 is to introduce a new focus: the unique authority of Jesus and
the exclusivity of his mediation of revelation."[118] It can certainly be judged
typical of the main redactor to introduce a saying with a high Christology into
other material.[119]

The same remarks are applicable to the "soteriology" of Q 10:21–24. Out of
the three sayings, only verse 22 opens itself up to soteriological interpretation.
As will be argued in the subsequent section, the intent of the other two sayings
was plainly to underscore the fortuitousness and privilege of the "infants" to
be receiving the sapiential message of Jesus. No claim is made that this message has the ability or power to "save" anyone in a soteriological sense.[120] More
crucially, it does not seem as though the content of these logia imply or enable

---

[109] Cf. also Robinson 1964, 228; Jacobson 1978, 141; Denaux 1992, 163, 176; Jacobson
1992, 149; Kirk 1998, 340, 357; Fleddermann 2005a, 454.

[110] See Tuckett 2001b, 286–287; cf. Zeller 1982, 405; Sato 1988, 38, 45; Piper 1989, 172;
Denaux 1992, 163, 170, 176; Valantasis 2005, 113;.

[111] Cf. Marshall 1978, 431; Zeller 1982, 405; Jacobson 1992, 158; *pace* Kirk 1998, 313–
314.

[112] Cf. Valantasis 2005, 111.

[113] Cf. Zeller 1982, 405; Piper 1989, 172; Fleddermann 2005a, 451.

[114] See e.g. Denaux 1992, 163–199; Allison 2000, 46–47; Broadhead 2001, 294–295; Lee
2005, 139–140; cf. e.g. Robinson 1964, 228; Jacobson 1978, 144; Kloppenborg 2000a, 330;
Tuckett 2001b, 283.

[115] See Sabbe 1982, 363–371; Denaux 1992, 176–187; Tuckett 2001b, 286–288; cf. Rodriquez 2008, 250 n. 133.

[116] Cf. Kloppenborg 1986, 461; 1987, 199; Jacobson 1992, 149.

[117] Cf. Q 7:35; 11:49.

[118] Kloppenborg 1987, 198; see Piper 1989, 170–173; Denaux 1992, 173–175, 184–187;
cf. also Jacobson 1978, 142; 1992, 150; Marshall 1978, 431, 438; Broadhead 2001, 295;
Fleddermann 2005a, 448, 451.

[119] Cf. Zeller 1982, 405; Sato 1988, 38, 45.

[120] *Pace* Jacobson 1978, 142; Kirk 1998, 315.

a soteriological interpretation. Although verse 22 likewise fails to make any overt claim about soteriology, it does imply and open itself up to such interpretations. Not only the exclusivity of the knowledge about God, but also the privileged position of Jesus hint towards a soteriological application.[121] Furthermore, it was argued above that verse 22 was probably intended to be read as an apocalyptic saying. Like most apocalyptic literature, it must have looked ahead at the salvation of the in-group and the destruction of the out-group.[122] The dividing salvific factor seems to have had everything to do with the choice and person of Jesus.

1.3 Stated and Implied Audiences

Kloppenborg's second reason for attributing Q 10:21–24 to the main redaction is that the polemical intent of the cluster is to accuse greater Israel of failing to accept the eschatological message of Jesus and/or the kingdom of God.[123] Kloppenborg argues that the polemical intent of Q 10:21–24 is comparable to the theme of "failed response" in the main redaction. Kloppenborg has argued persuasively that one of the chief foci of the main redaction is Israel's failed response to God's revelation.[124] The broad strokes of this observation are well-argued and should be accepted without much hesitation. The current question, however, is whether or not the same is true of Q 10:21–24. In the thanksgiving, God the Father acts as the subject of both "revelation" (ἀποκαλύπτω) and "non-disclosure" (κρύπτω).[125] Regardless of who the (non-)recipients are, they have no choice in the matter.[126] Some receive revelation, while others do not. God is the subject who makes this determination.[127] The concluding exclamation confirms this in no uncertain terms: "Yes, Father, for that is what it has pleased you to do" (ναὶ ὁ πατήρ, ὅτι οὕτως εὐδοκία ἐγένετο ἔμπροσθέν σου).[128] The second person personal pronoun (σου) emphasises the fact that God is the acting subject. It follows that this logion did not have the (positive, negative, or neutral) *response* of anyone in mind.

In verse 22, the first level of revelation takes place between God and Jesus. The verb used to express this act of "entrustment" appears in the passive voice (παρεδόθη), functioning here as a divine passive. God "the Father" (ὁ πατήρ)

---

[121] Cf. Broadhead 2001, 295.
[122] Cf. Jacobson 1992, 149; cf. e.g. 1 Enoch 48:7.
[123] Kloppenborg 1987, 201–202.
[124] Kloppenborg 1987.
[125] Cf. Valantasis 2005, 111.
[126] Cf. Kloppenborg 1987, 201.
[127] Cf. Jacobson 1992, 149.
[128] Cf. Fleddermann 2005a, 451.

is specifically mentioned in this sentence as the semantic subject of the verb "entrust" (παραδίδωμι). In two distinct ways, then, God is highlighted as the acting subject of the revelatory act.[129] The second level of revelation happens between Jesus the son and "whomever he chooses" (ᾧ ἐὰν βούληται). Not unlike the previous logion, this saying focuses on the choice of Jesus. Jesus is the one who chooses and distinguishes, not the (non-)recipients. In this regard, the main difference between verses 21 and 22 is that, in the former, God chooses who will and will not receive revelation, whereas, in the latter, Jesus is "entrusted" to make this choice on God's behalf.[130] Regardless of whether Jesus or God separates between those who will and those who will not receive revelation, in neither logion does the response of anyone come into focus.

In verses 23–24, those who receive revelation are uncharacteristically described as the *subjects* of the actions "see" (βλέπω) and "hear" (ἀκούω). Yet there is no mention or suggestion of them having a choice in the matter. Nothing is said of their (positive, negative, or neutral) *response* to the revelation. In truth, there are two factors indicating that the recipients are no more than passive receivers of God's revelation. Firstly, the recipients are pronounced "fortunate" (μακάριος) as receivers of revelation.[131] Secondly, noteworthy people from Israel's past were not fortunate enough to receive this revelation. Both of these factors imply that the (non-)recipients have no choice in the matter, irrespective of their precise identity. All in all, it seems that the focus of Q 10:21–24 is on *God's act of revelation*, not on anyone's response to it.

In all three logia that make up Q 10:21–24, a distinction is made between those who receive revelation and those who do not.[132] Upon closer examination, however, one finds that the specific representatives of these groups differ from one saying to the next. According to verse 21, God revealed "these things" to "infants" (νήπιοι), but obscured them from "sages" (σοφοί) and "intelligent men" (συνετοί).[133] This is not primarily an individualistic distinction between intelligent and unintelligent people. Such a reading would be anachronistic. Rather, the thanksgiving intends a socio-economic distinction between those selected few who were privileged enough to have received some form of education, like sages and scribes, on the one hand, and the illiterate masses, on the other.[134]

Since both the verb "revealed" (ἀπεκάλυψας) and the verb "concealed" (ἔκρυψας) appear in the aorist tense, it is difficult to determine whether or not

---

[129] Cf. Kloppenborg 1987, 201.

[130] Cf. Marshall 1978, 437; Denaux 1992, 170.

[131] Cf. Marshall 1978, 438; Kirk 1998, 334; Valantasis 2005, 115.

[132] Cf. Valantasis 2005, 111.

[133] Cf. Robinson 1964, 228; Fleddermann 2005a, 450.

[134] Cf. Marshall 1978, 434; Zeller 1982, 405; Kloppenborg 1987, 198; 2000a, 387; Denaux 1992, 172; Horsley 1992, 190.

a temporal distinction between past and present is also implied here.[135] Some scholars do not think so. Marshall, for example, distinguishes between Q 10:21 and Q 10:23–24 on the basis that "the former contrasts [the disciples] with their contemporaries, the latter with their predecessors."[136] If the vague term "these things" (ταῦτα) does indeed refer to the sapiential message of Jesus, the verb "revealed" (ἀπεκάλυψας) most probably refers back to that recent past during which Jesus proclaimed his message.[137] It seems unlikely, however, that the other aorist verb, "concealed" (ἔκρυψας), similarly refers exclusively to the recent past during which Jesus proclaimed his message. Logically, it is difficult to see how God could have been "concealing" something while that very same thing was simultaneously being revealed. Put differently, it is difficult to imagine that God was using the delivery of Jesus's message to a certain audience as a tool to conceal that very same message from a different audience. Much more reasonable is the possibility that God concealed the sapiential message of Jesus from sages and educated men throughout Israel's history, including the concurrent age, but that he finally revealed it through Jesus.[138] The sequence of events in the structure of the logion confirms this notion of "revelatory progression." God is first mentioned as "concealing these things from sages and the learned" (ὅτι ἔκρυψας ταῦτα ἀπὸ σοφῶν καὶ συνετῶν) and only thereafter is he described as "revealing them to infants" (ἀπεκάλυψας αὐτὰ νηπίοις). It does therefore seem as though this logion implies a temporal division as well.[139] This confirms our earlier contention that verse 21 might have intended some form of realised eschatology.

There are no indications whatsoever that verse 22 makes either a socio-economic or a temporal distinction. What is rather at stake in this saying, as we have mentioned before, is exclusive and unrestricted knowledge of the innate nature and identity of God.[140] Jesus is entrusted with clandestine knowledge over "everything" (πᾶς), but reveals knowledge about the divine in particular to "whomever he chooses" (ᾧ ἐὰν βούληται).[141] Unlike verse 21, this logion distinguishes between those who were and those who were not chosen by Jesus to receive exclusive knowledge of God. Such a distinction is typical of ancient breakaway groups and sectarian movements, especially Gnostic groups (like those responsible for the *Gospel of Thomas*) and apocalyptic groups (like the

---

[135] Cf. also Rom 16:25–26; Col 1:26; Eph 3:3–5, 9–10.
[136] Marshall 1987, 431; cf. also Denaux 1992, 170.
[137] Cf. Marshall 1978, 434.
[138] Cf. Fleddermann 2005a, 448.
[139] Cf. Kloppenborg 1987, 198.
[140] Cf. Marshall 1978, 431; Jacobson 1992, 150; Allison 2000, 45.
[141] Cf. Marshall 1978, 431, 437; Jacobson 1992, 150; Allison 2000, 47.

Qumran community).[142] The distinction is clearly polemical, being as it is between the in-group, who are in possession of restricted knowledge, and the out-group, who are not.[143]

It was pointed out earlier that the verbs of verse 21 are both in the aorist tense. In verse 22, the verb "entrust" (παραδίδωμι), which describes the first level of revelation between God and Jesus, similarly appears in the aorist tense. This indicates that the first level of revelation had happened sometime in the past. The gnomic nature of the rest of the saying indicates that both the special relationship between God and Jesus and the role of Jesus in revealing the nature of God to "whomever he chooses" remain applicable after the historical person had passed away. In other words, in the daily life of the Q movement, Jesus continued to determine who were worthy of revelation and who not. The division of verse 22 differs markedly from the division of verse 21.[144] In verse 21, the division is between the few educated elite, who did not receive the message of Jesus, and the uneducated masses, who did.[145] In verse 22, on the other hand, the division is between the few who received exclusive knowledge of God from Jesus and the many who did not.[146] In short, the former division is indicative of socio-economic concerns, while the latter is indicative of polemical concerns.[147]

As we saw, the criteria of characteristic forms and motifs seem to indicate that Q 10:21 and Q 10:22–23 belong together. The criterion of implied audience corroborates this finding. It is likely that both the word "infants" in verse 21 and the repeated appearance of the plural "you"[148] in verses 23–24 refer to the same group of people.[149] Like the thanksgiving in verse 21, the beatitude in verses 23–24 makes a socio-economic distinction.[150] Those who are in the process of receiving the message of Jesus (i.e. the "infants" of verse 21) are distinguished from more important Jewish figures, like "prophets" (προφῆται) and "kings" (βασιλεῖς).[151] That the reference to "prophets" and "kings" is utilised to designate a socio-economic distinction is confirmed by a similar application of these epithets in Q 7:25–26.[152]

---

[142] Cf. Jacobson 1992, 149, 150; cf. e.g. Gos. Thom. 61–62; 1 Enoch 48:7.

[143] Cf. Fleddermann 2005a, 450.

[144] *Pace* Fleddermann 2005a, 450.

[145] Cf. Robinson 1964, 228; Horsley 1992, 190.

[146] Cf. Jacobson 1992, 149.

[147] *Pace* Fleddermann 2005a, 450.

[148] Cf. esp. βλέπετε (x2), ὑμῖν, ἀκούετε.

[149] Cf. Denaux 1992, 170; *pace* Jacobson 1992, 158.

[150] Cf. Kloppenborg 1987, 198; 2000a, 387.

[151] Cf. Marshall 1978, 438; Horsley 1992, 190; cf. also 1 Cor 2:6–10.

[152] See Howes 2019b, 2–4; cf. Marshall 1978, 438; Jacobson 1992, 157.

The distinction is not only socio-economic, but temporal as well.[153] The be-atitude is much clearer than the thanksgiving in this regard.[154] In fact, the grammar of the beatitude puts this temporal demarcation beyond serious doubt and also affords additional support to the likelihood that the thanksgiving does indeed harbour a temporal distinction. The beatitude consistently uses aorist verbs[155] in reference to those who did not receive revelation, and no less consistently uses present verbs[156] in reference to those who were lucky enough to in fact receive revelation. If the socio-economic and temporal distinctions are combined, the differentiation is particularly between the socio-economically privileged of a bygone era and the socio-economically underprivileged of the concurrent age.[157] More specifically, the demarcation seems to be between the traditional receivers of sapiential revelation in Israel's past and the concurrent receivers of sapiential revelation through the ministry of Jesus.[158] Whereas the former constitutes important persons, like kings, sages, and prophets, the latter constitutes seemingly insignificant people.[159] The message is clear: through the wisdom revealed by Jesus, the underprivileged now become just as privileged as the leaders of old, if not more so.[160]

The most apparent audiences of each logion have now been identified. The subsequent and more important question is whether or not these stated audiences are in any way representative of other implied audiences; and if so, who do they represent? It is perhaps easier to answer these questions in relation to verse 22. As we saw, this saying is most naturally understood as a polemical attempt to differentiate between the in-group and the out-group. If this is accepted, then those who are chosen by Jesus to receive privileged knowledge of God should be equated with the Q people.[161] Those on the other side of this divide should, as a consequence, be equated with those opposing the Q movement, including (perhaps exclusively) "this generation."[162] This polemical division situates verse 22 within the main redaction. The purpose of the saying was not only to legitimise the exclusivity of the Q people, but also to justify

---

[153] Cf. Fleddermann 2005a, 448.

[154] Cf. Kloppenborg 1987, 198; Horsley 1992, 190.

[155] I.e. ἐπεθύμησαν // ἠθέλησαν ("wanted"), εἶδαν ("saw"), and ἤκουσαν ("heard").

[156] I.e. βλέποντες // βλέπουσιν and βλέπετε ("see") and ἀκούετε ("hear").

[157] Cf. Kloppenborg 2000a, 387.

[158] Cf. Bultmann 1963, 109; Marshall 1978, 434, 439; Denaux 1992, 170; Horsley 1992, 190; Fleddermann 2005a, 453.

[159] See Valantasis 2005, 111–112; cf. Kloppenborg 1987, 198; Horsley 1992, 190; Allison 2000, 230.

[160] Cf. Denaux 1992, 172; Kirk 1998, 344; Fleddermann 2005a, 453.

[161] Cf. Kloppenborg 1987, 202; Denaux 1992, 170; Jacobson 1992, 151; Kirk 1998, 343.

[162] Cf. Zeller 1982, 405; Kloppenborg 1987, 202; Jacobson 1992, 149, 151; Kirk 1998, 343.

their continued association with and stubborn proclamation of Jesus.[163] Both
the need to legitimate their defence and the outward-directed view towards an
implied outsider-audience concretise the place of verse 22 in the main redaction.[164]

Those listening to the message of Jesus, previously in the Sayings Gospel
specifically identified as "the disciples" (οἱ μαθηταῖ),[165] would most likely
themselves have identified with the "infants" of Q 10:21, 23–24.[166] That such
an identification is intended by Q's Jesus is suggested by both the phrase "at
that time" (ἐν ἐκείνῳ τῷ καιρῷ // ἐν αὐτῇ τῇ ὥρᾳ) and the placement of Q
10:21, 23–24 in the overall structure of Q('). In the midst of delivering his
sapiential message, Jesus rudely interrupts himself to direct a prayer of thanksgiving to God. The intent of the prayer is not merely to communicate with God,
but also to deliver a message and to underscore the privilege of the "infants"
to be receiving this message.[167] Jesus then continues in verses 23–24 to expli-
cate the prayer.[168] By means of a beatitude, Jesus brings home his intention
with the foregoing prayer, which is to underscore the significance of seeing
and hearing his wisdom. In his commentary on his own prayer, Jesus repeatedly
refers to those who receive his revelatory wisdom in the second person plural.[169] These features all point to the intention of Q's Jesus to invite an equation
between the "infants" of his prayer and his concurrent audience.[170] Whereas
the thanksgiving addresses Jesus's concurrent audience (or "the disciples") indirectly, the beatitude does so directly.[171]

The word "infant" (νήπιος) is obviously ambiguous in this context. On the
one hand, it points to the socio-economic status of Jesus's audience, which has
already been discussed. On the other, it points to the family metaphor that is so
prevalent in the rest of the Sayings Gospel, focusing on the special and unique
relationship between God the Father and his children.[172] Both levels of meaning would have invited the audience of Q's Jesus to identify with the "infants"
of Jesus's prayer. Regarding the second meaning, this is true mainly because

---

[163] See Kirk 1998, 342–343; Kloppenborg 2000a, 375–376; cf. Zeller 1982, 405.

[164] Cf. Zeller 1982, 405; Kloppenborg 1987, 202, 203.

[165] Cf. Q 6:20; 10:2.

[166] Cf. Marshall 1978, 430; Kloppenborg 1987, 197; Sato 1988, 38; Denaux 1992, 170;
Lee 2005, 137; Fleddermann 2005a, 452; Valantasis 2005, 111–112.

[167] See Valantasis 2005, 110–111; cf. Dibelius 1971, 281.

[168] Cf. Robinson 2005a, 117. This function of Q 10:23–24 is not evidence that it should
be taken as a secondary addition to Q 10:21–22 (*pace* Robinson 2005a, 117–118; cf. Kloppenborg 2000a, 147 n. 63).

[169] Cf. esp. βλέπετε (x2), ὑμῖν, ἀκούετε.

[170] See Kloppenborg 1987, 197; Denaux 1992, 170; Valantasis 2005, 111–112.

[171] Cf. Sato 1988, 38; Fleddermann 2005a, 452.

[172] See Moxnes 2003, 115–121, 152; Howes 2015a, 149–150; cf. Kirk 1998, 343, 357;
Tuckett 2001b, 287.

Q's Jesus has himself, in what has gone before, more than once identified the children in God's family and kingdom with his underprivileged and deprived audience(s).[173] In the very next passage (Q 11:2–4, 9–13), Q's Jesus in fact takes up this theme and teaches his audience how to speak directly to their Father.[174]

On the level of the Sayings Gospel Q, these "infants" obviously represent the Q people themselves.[175] The Q document was in all likelihood collected and composed to direct the behaviour and belief-system of the in-group.[176] The Q people applied the message of Jesus to their own lives and circumstances, as if they were continually hearing his message anew. It follows that if Q's Jesus intended his immediate audience to identify themselves with the "infants" of his prayer, then the Q people who subsequently read and listened to Q would also have identified themselves with these "infants."[177] This conclusion is almost inescapable given the propensity of the Q people to see and describe themselves, through the mouth of Q's Jesus, as the children of God.[178]

Unlike verse 22, the rest of the cluster is not in any way polemical.[179] As we know, the main redaction is polemically opposed to "this generation" and, more specifically, to the Pharisees, scribes, and Jerusalem elite.[180] Elsewhere in Q (11:49–51), these same outsiders are accused of killing the "sages" (σοφοί) and "prophets" (προφῆται) of old. Here, the "sages" (σοφοί) and "prophets" (προφῆται) from Israel's history not only receive a positive valuation from the main redactor, but are also clearly distinguished from the intended out-group. That prominent figures from Israel's history could form part of the in-group even though they had never heard the message of Jesus is indicated by Q 13:28–29.[181] It logically and incontrovertibly follows that the "sages," "prophets," and "kings" of Q 10:21, 23–24 cannot possibly be identified with the out-group of

---

[173] See Fleddermann 2005a, 449–450; cf. Kirk 1998, 343, 357; cf. e.g. Q 6:20–23, 35, 36; 7:28, 35; 9:59–60; 10:8–9.

[174] See Allison 1997, 13–14; cf. Horsley 1992, 189, 190; Jacobson 1992, 149–150; Kirk 1998, 326, 334, 344–345; Robinson 2005a, 117; Valantasis 2005, 110.

[175] Cf. Zeller 1982, 405; Kloppenborg 1987, 198, 202; Denaux 1992, 170; Jacobson 1992, 151; Kirk 1998, 344; Valantasis 2005, 112.

[176] Valantasis 2005, 116.

[177] Cf. Zeller 1982, 405; Valantasis 2005, 112, 116.

[178] See Moxnes 2003, 115–121, 152; Howes 2015a, 149–150; cf. e.g. Q 6:35–36; Q 11:2–3, 13; Q 10:21–22; Q 12:22–31.

[179] *Pace* Denaux 1992, 172–173; Fleddermann 2005a, 450; Valantasis 2005, 111–112.

[180] Cf. esp. Q 11:29–32, 39, 41–44, 46–52.

[181] Likewise, the purpose of Q 11:29–32 could surely not have been to place Solomon, one of the most important kings in Jewish history, and Jonah, one of the most important prophets of Jewish history, on the outside.

the main redaction.[182] Neither the thanksgiving nor the beatitude can legitimately be interpreted as some form of "attack against the [Jewish] leadership."[183] Far from being an "attack," these logia represent a mere *comparison* between "infants" and prominent historic figures from Israel's past.[184] This is supported by the fact that none of the traditional Q terms for the out-group appear in these two logia, including "this generation," Pharisees, scribes, or Jerusalem elite. If these sayings were intended for Q's opponents, one would have expected them to explicitly name these traditional opponents. Although this is an argument *ad silencium*, it is especially valid in *this* literary context, since the actual objects of comparison with the "infants" are indeed expressly named. Particularly striking is the fact that the term "this generation," which is Q's standard designation for (a segment of) greater Israel,[185] is entirely missing in these sayings. The sting of this argument *ad silencium* is highlighted by the fact that Denaux feels the need to surmise that "the wise" might have been one of Q's technical terms for (a segment of) greater Israel.[186] Moreover, if Q 10:21, 23–24 had greater Israel in mind, it would summarily contradict the deuteronomistic theme, which is undoubtedly one of the most important redactional motifs in Q.[187]

The phrase "blessed are the eyes that see what you see" (μακάριοι οἱ ὀφθαλμοὶ οἱ βλέποντες ἃ βλέπετε) implies that outsiders could, hypothetically, also be blessed, provided that they are lucky enough to receive God's revelation (in the form of Jesus's message).[188] If anything, the phrase in question betrays an openness to outsiders that is uncharacteristic of the main redaction, including Q 10:22. There is no hint of a judgmental, polemical, or accusatory tone in Q 10:21, 23–24. That some received revelation while others did not is matter-of-factly stated, without any attempt to use this status quo against outsiders. Unlike the main redaction, Q 10:21, 23–24 is not directed at outsiders at all, either directly or indirectly.[189] These features of Q 10:21, 23–24 are in stark contrast to the content of verse 22, which seems to accuse outsiders of knowing neither God nor Jesus.[190]

---

[182] *Pace* Jacobson 1978, 140–142, 144; 1992, 152, 182; Denaux 1992, 172; Kirk 1998, 343; Valantasis 2005, 111–112.

[183] Piper 1989, 171. In addition to calling verse 21 an "attack" against the Jewish elite, Piper (1989, 171) also calls it an "implicit rebuke."

[184] Cf. Allison 2000, 230.

[185] See Horsley 1992, 191; 1995a, 38–40; 1999, 64–65; Tuckett 1996, 196–201; cf. Uro 1996, 93.

[186] Denaux 1992, 172.

[187] Cf. Jacobson 1978, 141, 144.

[188] Cf. Marshall 1978, 438; Jacobson 1992, 158.

[189] Cf. Piper 1989, 171.

[190] Cf. Jacobson 1992, 149.

If the sages, prophets, and kings are not representative of outsiders, who do they represent? If they are not mentioned as polemical instruments, why are they mentioned at all? In the first place, these references to historic Jewish leaders should probably be taken at face value.[191] They are in no way symbolic or representative of anyone or anything outside of themselves; least of all the opponents of the Q people, including "this generation." Instead, they plainly and literally refer to the historic leaders of Israel.[192] In both the thanksgiving and the beatitude, the ultimate purpose of mentioning these leaders of old is simply to highlight how fortunate the "infants" really are to be receiving the message of Jesus.[193] The leaders of old are merely mentioned as a point of comparison and contrast, the purpose of which is to highlight the fortuity of the "infants." Both categories of differentiation, temporal and socio-economic, function to underline the privilege of the "infants" to be receiving the sapiential message of Jesus.[194] Never before has this message been proclaimed, indicating that the mere act of hearing it constitutes a unique happening in the history of Israel.[195] Moreover, the "infants" are particularly blessed by the fact that God chose *them* and not, as per usual, the privileged elite to receive the sapiential message of Jesus.[196] It follows from all this that Q 10:21, 23–24 is *solely* directed inwards[197] and is therefore most comparable to the formative stratum.

1.4 Findings

This chapter has argued that the thanksgiving and beatitude in Q 10:21–24 belong to the formative stratum, while verse 22 belongs to the main redaction. As far as the formative stratum is concerned, this means that Q 10:16 of the mission instruction was followed by Q 10:21, and that the Lord's prayer was directly preceded by Q 10:23–24.[198] As such, verse 22 is most comparable to other interpolations into Q's formative layer.[199] I have argued above that Q 10:22 was not a *Kommentarwort* but a new creation, which would make this logion most comparable to Q 6:23c and Q 10:12. Seeing as Q 10:12 was added to the document to function as a literary transition, Q 10:22 is probably most comparable to Q 6:23c. That all three of these insertions are short "one-liners"

---

[191] See Valantasis 2005, 115–116.

[192] Cf. Allison 2000, 230; Kloppenborg 2000a, 387.

[193] Cf. Marshall 1978, 438; Kirk 1998, 334; Valantasis 2005, 115.

[194] Cf. Marshall 1978, 434.

[195] Cf. Bultmann 1963, 109; Marshall 1978, 430, 438, 439; Horsley 1992, 190; Jacobson 1992, 152; Kloppenborg 2000a, 147; Fleddermann 2005a, 448.

[196] See Valantasis 2005, 110–112, 114–116; cf. Denaux 1992, 170; Horsley 1992, 190.

[197] Cf. Piper 1989, 171, 172–173.

[198] See Jacobson 1992, 149–150.

[199] Cf. Q 6:23c; 10:12, 13–15; 12:8–10.

and not extended clusters of logia[200] add additional support to the argument that Q 10:22 was created anew by the main redactor. Ultimately, it seems that Q 10:22 was added to the formative stratum (which included Q 10:21, 23–24) by the main redactor. By doing this, the main redactor ensured that the whole complex of sayings in Q 10:21–24 would henceforth (at the Q^2 level and beyond) be read together as polemic logia.[201]

---

[200] Like Q 10:13–15; 12:8–10.

[201] Cf. Dibelius 1971, 280; Kloppenborg 1986, 450.

Chapter 2

Q 11:33, 34–35, "Placed in a Hidden Place"[1]

³³οὐδεὶς καί<ει> λύχνον καὶ τίθησιν αὐτὸν ⟦εἰς κρύπτην⟧ ἀλλ᾽ ἐπὶ τὴν λυχνίαν, ⟦καὶ λάμπει πᾶσιν τοῖς ἐν τῇ οἰκίᾳ⟧. ³⁴ὁ λύχνος τοῦ σώματός ἐστιν ὁ ὀφθαλμός. ... αν ὁ ὀφθαλμός σου ἁπλοῦς ᾖ, ὅλον τὸ σῶμά σου φωτεινόν ἐστ⟦ιν⟧· ... ἂν δὲ ὁ ὀφθαλμός σου πονηρὸς ᾖ, ὅλον τὸ σῶμά σου σκοτεινόν. ³⁵εἰ οὖν τὸ φῶς τὸ ἐν σοὶ σκότος ἐστίν, τὸ σκότος πόσον.

³³No one light<s> a lamp and puts it ⟦in a hidden place⟧, but on the lamp stand, ⟦and it gives light for everyone in the house⟧. ³⁴The lamp of the body is the eye. If your eye is generous, your whole body ⟦is⟧ radiant; but if your eye is jaundiced, your whole body «is» dark. ³⁵So if the light within you is dark, how great «must» the darkness «be»!

Kloppenborg rightfully attributes the block of material in Q 11:16, 29–32, 39, 41–44, 46–52 that deals exclusively with the proclamation of judgment against "this generation," including the Pharisees and scribes, to the main redaction.[2] On the face of it, though, this block of material is rudely interrupted by Q 11:33–35.[3] The prophetic small forms, polemical content, and sombre atmosphere of this block of Q² material are visibly at odds with the sapiential small forms, practical content, and neutral tone of the two sayings in Q 11:33–35.[4] This block of material would certainly have been more cohesive, both formally and thematically, if the woes against the Pharisees followed directly after Q 11:31–32 in the tradition. In my view, the best explanation for why the main redactor would have inserted the sayings of Q 11:33–35 into this block of prophetic judgment material is because he found them in the formative layer. As such, the current chapter will re-examine the ascription of Q 11:33–35 to the main redaction.

---

[1] An earlier version of this chapter was published as an article in *Neotestamentica* 47/2 (see Howes 2013b). The chapter also draws on an article in *Acta Theologica* 35/1 (see Howes 2015b).

[2] Kloppenborg 1987, 121, 147–148.

[3] Lührmann 1994, 59–60; Sato 1994, 171; Vaage 1994, 119.

[4] Piper 1989, 127; Allison 1997, 165.

2.1 Characteristic Forms

There should be no doubt that the saying in Q 11:33, even in its present literary context, is a sapiential small form.[5] The possibility that the saying itself functioned as an eschatological or prophetic saying before being placed in its current literary context can summarily be taken off the table. It contains none of the formal features of prophetic or apocalyptic small forms, including future-tense verbs, prophetic introductory formulas, a threatening tone, and the features of the so-called "eschatological" or "prophetic correlative."[6] By the same token, the lack of imperative verbs and motive clauses clearly indicates that Q 11:33 should not be classified as an admonition.[7] The traditional and non-subversive nature of the saying also testifies against it being an aphorism.[8] Conversely, Q 11:33 contains all the formal features of a proverb.[9] Fundamentally, all the verbs of this logion appear in the indicative mood, namely καίει, τίθησιν, and λάμπει. Kirk defines a proverb as "a succinct statement in general circulation which makes an observation about a typicality in the world of experience and thereby delivers an insight about some aspect of reality and human experience."[10] A "maxim" is a proverb that is linked to a particular sage.[11] Since the Sayings Gospel attributes Q 11:33 to Jesus, it should be identified more specifically as a maxim.

Let us consider Kirk's abovementioned definition in stages. Firstly, Q 11:33 was undoubtedly "a succinct statement in general circulation." On face value, it certainly seems like a self-contained unit, with a clear and autonomous claim. Bultmann firmly believed that Q 11:33 was originally an independent secular proverb.[12] There is some evidence that Q 11:33 floated around on its own before being taken up by the Sayings Gospel Q. The original autonomy of this saying is attested by its freestanding appearances in both Mark (4:21) and the

---

[5] Piper 1989, 127.

[6] Edwards 1969, 9–20; 1976, 41, 114; Schmidt 1977, 517–522.

[7] Kirk 1998, 92. Matthew's "and it gives light to everyone in the house" (καὶ λάμπει πᾶσιν τοῖς ἐν τῇ οἰκίᾳ) should be regarded as a result clause. Luke's "so that those who come in may see the light" (ἵνα οἱ εἰσπορευόμενοι τὸ φῶς βλέπωσιν) constitutes a purpose or final clause (Fleddermann 2005a, 517). The absence of an imperative verb in the first part of the saying indicates that neither clause should technically be seen as a motive clause. Even if Luke is preferred at this point, the lack of an imperative verb still witnesses against Q 11:33 being an admonition.

[8] *Pace* Piper 1989, 127. An aphorism is a maxim or proverb that challenges and subverts traditional wisdom (Kirk 1998, 91).

[9] Bultmann 1963, 102.

[10] Kirk 1998, 90.

[11] Kirk 1998, 91.

[12] Bultmann 1963, 102.

Gospel of Thomas (33).[13] The presence of Q 11:33 in the *Gospel of Thomas* is particularly telling for a discussion of its *Mikrogattung*, since this Gospel contains only sapiential and Gnostic sayings, without any hint of apocalyptic or prophetic themes.[14] Secondly, Q 11:33 indisputably "makes an observation about a typicality in the world of experience." The saying makes a simple and straightforward observation from everyday human behaviour about what people tend to do with lamps in a domestic setting.[15] It is only from experience that one can tell what people typically do with lamps. The generality of the saying is especially indicated by the deliberate use of the word "no one" (οὐδείς), which opens the statement up to generic application.[16] The gnomic nature and applicability of this saying has been noted by others.[17] Thirdly, Q 11:33 presumably also "delivers an insight about some aspect of reality and human experience." The insight seems to be that people are naturally inclined to share what they have with others. That this application is desired by the logion itself is particularly indicated by the clause "and it gives light for everyone" (καὶ λάμπει πᾶσιν).

Verse 34 represents a separate and freestanding sapiential saying. This saying is made up of two parts, the saying proper in Q 11:34a,[18] and a further explanation in Q 11:34b–c.[19] Like verse 33, verse 34 lacks all the conventional formal indicators of prophetic and apocalyptic sayings. It further shares with the preceding verse a complete lack of imperative verbs or motive clauses. The gnomic nature of the saying also testifies against it being an aphorism.[20] The repeated use of the indicative copula (εἰμί) formally suggests that Q 11:34 should be classified as a maxim.[21] Finally, Q 11:34 subscribes to the definition of a maxim offered above in that it explains the typicality of the eye's function in relation to the rest of the body. Considered in isolation, the threatening tone of verse 35 might seem more reminiscent of prophecy than wisdom.[22] Yet verse 35 serves as the application of the freestanding sapiential maxim in the previous verse.[23] This is formally indicated by the conjunction "therefore" (οὖν). It logically follows that verse 35 should be considered as an integral part

---

[13] Kloppenborg 1987, 135; Piper 1989, 127, 246 n. 146; Roth 2018, 265.

[14] See Koester 1971, 158–204; Kloppenborg *et al.* 1990, 88, 94–95, 103.

[15] Roth 2018, 269; cf. Thurén 2014, 291.

[16] Fleddermann 2005a, 526.

[17] E.g. Schürmann 1969–1994, 2.296.

[18] "The lamp of the body is the eye" (ὁ λύχνος τοῦ σώματός ἐστιν ὁ ὀφθαλμός).

[19] Q 11:34b:" If your eye is generous, your whole body is radiant" (αν ὁ ὀφθαλμός σου ἁπλοῦς ᾖ, ὅλον τὸ σῶμά σου φωτεινόν ἐστιν). Q 11:34c: "but if your eye is jaundiced, your whole body is dark" (ἂν δὲ ὁ ὀφθαλμός σου πονηρὸς ᾖ, ὅλον τὸ σῶμά σου σκοτεινὸν).

[20] Kirk 1998, 200.

[21] Fleddermann 2005a, 525.

[22] Allison 1997, 161.

[23] E.g. Marshall 1978, 488, 489.

of the sapiential maxim in verse 34.[24] As a conditional sentence, verse 35 is a rhetorical device that is highly argumentative in nature.[25] The Sayings Gospel Q is fond of using conditional sentences to further its arguments.[26] The sapiential passage in Q 11:9–13 uses the exact same rhetorical structure as Q 11:34–35 to formulate its argument.[27] What is more, both arguments end with a conditional exclamation introduced by "if then" (εἰ οὖν).

The main purpose of the current section was to identify the *Mikrogattungen* that make up Q 11:33–35. Verse 33 represents a maxim in its most pristine form. Together, verses 34–35 represent an expanded maxim. The maxim proper appears in verse 34a. The logic of the sapiential maxim is primarily explicated and secondarily defended by two conditional clauses in verse 34b–c. Finally, the maxim and its exposition are applied to a specific social context by verse 35. That both these logia are sapiential maxims is not in any way a new discovery. In truth, that these logia are maxims has formerly been taken for granted by most.[28] Moreover, their respective designations as maxims do not necessarily indicate that they should summarily be removed from the main redaction and added to the formative stratum. There are some other proverbial sayings that suitably belong in the main redaction.[29] In fact, the two sayings in Q 11:33 and Q 11:34–35 are both held up by Kloppenborg as examples of proverbial sayings that belong in the main redaction.[30] In order to determine whether or not either of these logia should rightfully be moved to the formative stratum, a closer look at the thematic content and implied audience of each is necessary.

2.2 Characteristic Motifs

2.2.1 Q 11:33

I would like to make the novel proposal that Q 11:33, considered on its own, is primarily about the ancient social value of reciprocal sharing, especially as this pertains to natural resources at the local (village) level. If taken out of its context, there are three indicators within the maxim itself that strongly suggest this interpretation. First, the mere idea that someone would place a lit lamp in

---

[24] Viljoen 2009, 169.

[25] Betz 1995, 441.

[26] Cf. e.g. Q 4:3, 6–7, 9; 6:32, 34; 10:6, 13; 11:13, 18, 19, 20; 12:28, 39, 45–46; 15:5a, 7, [8]; 17:3, 4, 6, 23.

[27] Kirk 1998, 201–202. Allison (1997, 164) also points out the similarity between Q 11:34–35 and Q 16:13.

[28] E.g. Allison 2000, 207.

[29] Cf. Q 7:35; 11:17b–18, 20, [21–22], 23, 24–26; 12:[54–55]; 17:37.

[30] Kloppenborg 1987, 169, 239.

a hidden place, absurd as it may seem,[31] immediately brings to mind the idea of sharing. There were primarily two reasons why ancients hid things, namely to protect and safeguard them from possible theft[32] and to avoid having to share them with neighbours, friends, and family members.[33] The idea of someone hiding a lit lamp would have called to mind the image of an exceedingly stingy and selfish individual. Second, the specific mentioning of a "lampstand" (λυχνία) was probably deliberate. In the ancient world, the main purpose of a lampstand was to provide the necessary elevation so that the light would be diffused most efficiently.[34] In other words, placing a lamp on a lampstand was the most proficient way of sharing available light with as many people as possible.[35] Third, the consequence of lighting the lamp and placing it on a lampstand is expressly stated by the clause "and it gives light for everyone in the house" (καὶ λάμπει πᾶσιν τοῖς ἐν τῇ οἰκίᾳ).[36]

Taken on its own, the saying probably also has a second denotation. The key to this meaning lies with one's ability to further unlock the "light" metaphor. Unfortunately, this metaphor has so many traditional Jewish applications that one must be very careful not to rush to judgment.[37] Be that as it may, a likely application is more than suggested by the fact that the logion is a *sapiential* micro-genre. Jewish wisdom literature of the period used the image of "light" most commonly as a metaphor for wisdom itself.[38] Thus, viewed in isolation, the maxim of Q 11:33 promotes primarily the general ancient value of sharing basic necessities, like foodstuff and clothing, and secondarily the idea of sharing wisdom specifically.[39]

In its present Q context (in the main redaction), the "light" symbol of Q 11:33 is probably meant to refer to the *message* (and ministry) of Jesus.[40] This is primarily indicated by the preceding cluster of sayings (Q 11:16, 29–32), where the subject matter is also the message of Jesus, here symbolised as the "sign of Jonah."[41] This just about sums up the extent of thematic correspondence between Q 11:33 and the pericope that directly precedes it.

---

[31] Cf. Roth 2018, 266, 267, 268, 270, 273.

[32] Botha 1996, 281; cf. e.g. Q 12:33; 19:21.

[33] Cf. e.g. Q 13:21.

[34] Davies and Allison 1988, 475–476.

[35] Fleddermann 2005a, 526; cf. Roth 2018, 269.

[36] Luke's version of this clause also understands the purpose of placing the lamp on a stand as enabling it to be shared – only, in his case, it is shared with those who are still entering the house.

[37] Luz 1989, 251–252; cf. Roth 2018, 268, 269.

[38] Davies and Allison 1988, 639; cf. Job 5:12–14; 12:24–25; 22:13–14; Prov 6:23; Eccl 2:13–14; 8:1; Hos 10:12 (LXX); Wis 7:10, 26; T. Levi 4:3.

[39] Valantasis 2005, 140.

[40] Marshall 1978, 487; see Roth 2018, 271–272; *pace* Jacobson 1992, 173.

[41] See Kloppenborg 1987, 137–138; Howes 2015a, 176–181.

Upon closer examination, the superficiality of even this solitary thematic link becomes evident.[42] While Q 11:16, 29–32 is intrinsically *apocalyptic*,[43] Q 11:33 is intrinsically *sapiential*.[44] Besides the reference to Jonah,[45] the apocalyptic nature of Q 11:16, 29–32 is especially evident in its use of future-tense verbs[46] and typically prophetic-apocalyptic vocabulary.[47] Another aspect of the association between Q 11:33 and the preceding passage that showcases their dissimilarity is their underlying tones. Whereas the message of the former text is as positive, inviting, and illuminating as light itself, the message of the latter text is as negative, threatening, gloomy, and obscure as Jonah's original message of destructive condemnation.[48] As far as their respective attitudes are concerned, the two texts do not seem to be cosy bedfellows. The artificial connection between Q 11:33 and the foregoing passage is further showcased by an additional disparity. Q 11:33 sketches an image of how Jesus's message radiates from one central point, to be shared by everyone.[49] According to Q 11:29, on the other hand, Jesus expressly refuses to share a "sign" with his audience. True enough, the only exception to this refusal is the "sign of Jonah," which represents the message of Jesus.[50] As such, Q's Jesus theoretically exhibits a measure of willingness to share his message in both texts. But even so, the decidedly reserved and conditioned response of Jesus in Q 11:29 clashes with the unreserved and unconditional sharing of "light" in Q 11:33.

This uneasy thematic association of Q 11:33 with its synchronic literary context applies also to the main redaction as a whole.[51] It is just about impossible to reconcile the optimism and buoyancy of Q 11:33 with the pessimistic messages of doom and gloom that appear in most of the redactional stratum.[52] In the main redaction, flames and (other) sources of light are

---

[42] Vaage 1994, 119.

[43] Wink 2002, 91.

[44] Valantasis 2005, 140.

[45] The additional reference to Solomon should not here be taken as a reference to wisdom. Although Solomon was primarily known for his wisdom and wealth, he was also admired in the first century for his role as a staunch preacher of repentance in the face of apocalyptic judgment (Kloppenborg 1987, 133–134; Catchpole 1993, 242; cf. e.g. Wis 6:1–19). In general, contemporary wisdom often included stern messages of repentance (cf. e.g. Wis 11:23; 12:10, 19; Sir 17:24; 44:16, 48). Solomon is most likely here referenced for his role as a preacher of apocalyptic judgment.

[46] I.e. δοθήσεται, ἐγερθήσεται, κατακρινεῖ, ἀναστήσονται, κατακρινοῦσιν.

[47] I.e. ἡ γενεὰ αὕτη, πονηρός, σημεῖον, ὁ υἱὸς τοῦ ἀνθρώπου, ἐν τῇ κρίσει, κατακρίνω, ἀνίστημι, μετανοέω.

[48] Kloppenborg 1987, 138; cf. Jonah 3:4.

[49] Marshall 1978, 487; Valantasis 2005, 139–140.

[50] Kirk 1998, 199, 327.

[51] Vaage 1994, 119.

[52] Cf. Q 3:7–9, 16–17; 10:12–15; 11:39, 41–44, 46–51; 12:8–10, 46, [49], 51, 53, [54–56]; 13:29, 34–35; 17:24, 37, 26–27, 30, 34–35; 19:26.

consistently used very differently if compared to Q 11:33. They function in the main redaction not as symbols of the message of Jesus, but rather as symbols of the apocalypse.[53] In more general terms, the exact message of Q 11:33, which is that one should share indiscriminately and willingly, is contradicted by the judgmental and intolerant attitude of the main redaction.[54]

On the other side of the coin, the message of Q 11:33 echoes that of the formative layer. The high regard for the ancient social value of reciprocal sharing permeates the formative stratum.[55] In fact, there are passages in the formative layer that seem to surpass the point of mere reciprocity. Q 6:29–30 teaches that one should give selflessly, indiscriminately, and even to the point of self-deprivation. One could say that this type of contribution is like sharing one's only light source with everyone else. Quite against normal reciprocal expectations, Q 6:34 teaches that one should give to everyone, without expecting anything in return.[56] This mode of giving is like sharing one's light indiscriminately with everyone. How could one ever get it back in any case? The focus changes in Q 11:9–13 from the giver to the receiver.[57] The message of this text is that those in need somehow always manage to procure sustenance through an appeal to reciprocity.[58] This may be compared to the assurance of every family member that he or she would be allowed to share the light of the only lamp in the house. Q 11:9 reminds one that God ultimately lies behind all goods as the principal Giver and Lender.[59] According to Genesis 1:1, all things started when God said: "Let there be light!" Light was the first item created by God to be shared by mankind. Q 11:9 reminds one that God created everything else in the natural world to also be shared like light.

Normal *quid pro quo* reciprocity is sometimes also referred to as "balanced reciprocity."[60] More specifically, balanced reciprocity may be defined as barter and other (economic) exchanges that are characterised by expectations and/or obligations of equal return, in the spirit of fairness and justice.[61] In antiquity, families and neighbours cultivated and maintained reciprocal ties and relations based on mutual needs of nutrition and honour.[62] Under normal circumstances,

---

[53] Cf. Q 3:9, 17; [12:49, 54–55]; 17:24.

[54] Kloppenborg 1987, 148; cf. Q 3:9; 10:12–15; 11:23, 39, 41–44, 46–51; 12:8–9, 10, 46; 13:27, 28–29, [30], 34–35.

[55] Cf. Q 6:29–30, 31, 32, 34, 36–38, 41–42; 10:7–9, 16; 11:4, [5–8], 9–12; 12:33–34; 16:13.

[56] Horsley 1995b, 204.

[57] Cf. Betz 1995, 504.

[58] Arnal 2001, 114; see Howes 2019b, 6–11; cf. Betz 1995, 505.

[59] See Howes 2019b, 6–11; cf. Robinson 1995a, 263, 265; Kirk 1998, 181; Kloppenborg 2000a, 144; Valantasis 2005, 122.

[60] Oakman 1986, 66.

[61] Oakman 1986, 66; Horsley 1995b, 204.

[62] Freyne 1988, 154.

the social value of balanced reciprocity and the normal practice of barter exchange promoted self-sufficiency, especially at village level.[63] Goods were given to someone else with the implicit expectation of equal return. Conversely, goods were received with the full knowledge that an obligation is owed. For the most part, balanced reciprocity ensured the equal distribution of goods among the populace. During tough times, however, balanced reciprocity was occasionally replaced by expectations of "general reciprocity," which may be defined as barter and other (economic) exchanges that are characterised by the unilateral giving or receiving of something without any expectations and/or obligations of repayment, in the spirit of grace and benefaction.[64] General reciprocity was usually motivated by the claim that it would serve the common good of everyone in the community. Fundamentally, Q 11:33 has in common with much of the formative stratum this adamant endorsement of general reciprocity. Under normal circumstances, general reciprocity would be restricted to the ancient family or household internally, not the entire community.[65] This made family images and metaphors particularly applicable to the endorsement of general reciprocity at the community level.

This brings us to another thematic feature that Q 11:33 has in common with the formative stratum: family. In general, the formative stratum is somewhat ambiguous when it comes to the motif of family.[66] On the one hand, it expects its audience to sever all family ties and abandon all family relations.[67] It is extremely likely that these sayings refer to actual blood relations.[68] On the other hand, it sketches vividly romantic pictures of family life and promotes the preservation of family bonds.[69] These texts, in all probability, have the Q people in mind, who viewed themselves as the new symbolic family of God.[70] Although there is occasional mention of the family in Q's main redaction, these isolated instances are mostly incidental, functioning mainly to support the primary message of the text in question.[71] Q 12:53 could be held up as an exception, but this text nonetheless agrees with the first group of Q[1] texts (about severing patriarchal family ties), not the second (about God's new family). Hence, one of the most prominent features of the formative layer is its

---

[63] Oakman 1986, 66; Horsley 1995b, 204.

[64] Oakman 1986, 151–152; 2008, 95, 105, 138; cf. Luke 11:11.

[65] Oakman 2008, 138.

[66] Blasi 1986, 246.

[67] Cf. Q 9:59–60; 14:26.

[68] For a fuller discussion, see Jacobson 1995; Schottroff 1995; Destro and Pesce 2003; Howes 2015a, 144–149.

[69] Cf. Q 6:35, 36, 41–42; 10:5–9, 16, 21 (for the presence of Q 10:21 in the formative stratum, see chapter 1 above); 11:2–4, [5–8], 13; 12:6–7, 22–31; [15:9]; 17:3–4.

[70] For a fuller discussion, see Jacobson 1995, 374–376; Moxnes 2003, 57–58, 91; Howes 2015a, 145, 149–150.

[71] Cf. Q 7:3, 7, 31, 35; 10:22; 11:17, 19; 12:53; 13:34.

description and appreciation of the new symbolic family of God, constituted by the Q people and governed by God as the sole *paterfamilias*.[72] The "family portrait" of Q 11:33 is no less bright than those in the rest of the formative stratum. Q 11:33 explicitly features the word "house" (οἰκία) to depict the background setting.[73] The description of a lamp giving light to everyone in the house paints a vivid picture of family solidarity. The created image is one of a traditional ancient family sharing available light so that each member may perform his or her domestic duties and bond with the rest of the family before turning in. It would seem that Q 11:33 takes up not only the general theme of God's symbolic family, but also the more specific theme of solidarity within the family. The cosy image of a typical ancient family fulfilling its duties and bonding as a unit is here meant as a metaphor for God's symbolic family.[74] By combining the images of family life and sharing, this maxim is perfectly suitable as an endorsement of general reciprocity. Given that ancient domestic spaces were highly fluid and flexible,[75] involving people outside the extended family, the imagery of Q 11:33 is not just a metaphor, but also a real-life description of God's symbolic family sharing available resources. This is supported by the nebulousness of the phrase "everyone in the house" (πᾶσιν τοῖς ἐν τῇ οἰκίᾳ), which fails to identify those inside the house more specifically as a family or something else. Discussing the flexibility of ancient domestic space, Boer and Petterson state: "Flexibility leads to the need to share. We mean not some vague altruistic motive, but rather one of collective necessity: the individual would simply not survive on his or her own." Using a metaphor that draws on traditional family imagery, Q 11:33 depicts uninhibited sharing beyond the traditional (extended) family, which is precisely the point of general reciprocity.

We saw that the "light" metaphor of Q 11:33 also represents wisdom. If the themes of reciprocity and wisdom are combined, Q 11:33 could be taken to imply that people should share wisdom as easily and unreservedly as they would normally share light.[76] The same idea is expressed with very similar imagery in Q 12:2–3, which belongs to the formative stratum. Apart from the noticeable catchword connections between Q 11:33 and Q 12:2–3,[77] the two texts basically promote the same idea, which is that wisdom should not be covered up, but should instead be shared with others.[78] The idea of elevation is also repeated in Q 12:2–3 with the intentional mentioning of a "roof" or

---

[72] See Moxnes 2003, 115–122, 152; Howes 2016a, 9–33.

[73] E.g. Piper 1989, 128; cf. Thurén 2014, 291; Roth 2018, 266.

[74] Valantasis 2005, 139.

[75] See Boer and Petterson 2017, 61–68.

[76] Valantasis 2005, 140; cf. Roth 2018, 273–274.

[77] That is, οὐδείς, κρύπτη, and κρυπτός (Sato 1994, 171; Zeller 1994, 119).

[78] See chapter 10 below.

"housetop" (δῶμα). The latter word also corresponds to the "house" (οἰκία) of Q 11:33. In one important way, Q 12:2–3 develops and goes beyond Q 11:33. The wisdom that should be shared with others is specifically identified in Q 12:3 as the sapiential message of Jesus. The Q people were well aware that obedience to this instruction could have fatal consequences, as the rest of the sayings-cluster clearly indicates.[79] Similar instructions to share the message of Jesus can be found in the rest of the formative stratum,[80] but are completely lacking in the main redaction. In view of all this, one has to admit that the thematic content of Q 11:33 is in total continuity with that of the formative stratum, but seems wholly alien to that of the main redaction.

2.2.2 Q 11:34–35

Allison argues convincingly that most ancient people, including ancient Jews, favoured an extramission theory of vision, which holds that eyes are sources of light and that vision is made possible through the emission of light, not its reception.[81] Allison argues just as convincingly that Q 11:34–35 should be interpreted by means of such an extramission theory of vision, whereby the eyes reveal a person's inner light or darkness.[82] That this inner light or darkness should be understood in terms of an individual's *moral* disposition seems to be beyond serious doubt. Verse 35 draws attention to the latter by expressly mentioning "the darkness within you" (τὸ ἐν σοὶ σκότος). Most commentators mention that there are two levels of meaning to each of the adjectives used in Q 11:34 to describe one's eyes. When the adjective πονηρός is used, it literally describes an "unsound" or "jaundiced" eye.[83] Similarly, the adjective ἁπλοῦς literally means "sound" or "healthy," referring to the physical state of the human eye. On the more figurative level, the two words describe the common Jewish distinction between a "good" (ἁπλοῦς) and an "evil" (πονηρός) eye. This figurative level corresponds to the moral disposition mentioned above.[84] In other words, a person with "good" (ἁπλῷ) eyes has a "radiant" (φωτεινός) moral character, while a person with "bad" (πονηροί) eyes has a "dark" (σκοτεινός) moral character.[85]

In light of this, there is an undeniable thematic overlap between Q 11:34–35 and Q 6:43–45.[86] Both texts speculate about the ways in which a person's inner being may become visible to outside observers. According to Q 11:34–35, it is

---

[79] Cf. esp. Q 12:4–7.

[80] Cf. e.g. Q 10:2, 3, 9; 12:11–12.

[81] Allison 1997, 133–148; cf. e.g. Elliott 2011.

[82] Allison 1997, 148–167; cf. e.g. Betz 1995, 445, 450, 452, 453; Malina 1998, 71.

[83] Cf. Newman 1993 s.v. πονηρός; Thurén 2014, 292.

[84] Malina 1998, 68–72; Elliott 2011, 6; cf. Thurén 2014, 292–293.

[85] Viljoen 2009, 166–170.

[86] Kloppenborg 2000a, 394.

the eyes that betray a person's inner being. According to Q 6:43–49, a person gives herself away by means of both her mouth (verse 45) and her deeds (verses 46–47). Either way, the purpose and intent of both texts is probably the same. Both texts intend to make people question and critically re-examine the state of their own internal morality. This is particularly evident in the case of Q 11:34–35. The concluding exclamation in verse 35 forces one to take a long, hard look inside. In turn, the purpose of inducing self-examination is to motivate change and instigate positive conduct.[87] This is particularly evident in the case of Q 6:43–45, as the rhetorical question in Q 6:46 and the analogy in Q 6:47–49 clearly demonstrate.[88] The hortatory character and function of Q 11:34–35 is particularly evident in its use of second person address. It is certainly interesting that both Matthew and Luke brought out the paraenetic aspect of Q 11:34–35.[89] Matthew did so by placing the whole logion in a literary context that deals with ethical behaviour. Luke did so through his redactional doctoring of the inherited Q text.[90] The thematic overlap between Q 11:34–35 and Q 6:43–45 is not insignificant within the context of our current discussion. That Q 6:43–45 belongs to the formative stratum might be an indication that the same is true of Q 11:34–35. In more general terms, motivating positive action is an identifiable feature of the formative stratum, but not of the main redaction.

The literal and figurative levels of the adjectives in Q 11:34 were pointed out above. Yet one aspect of this standard elucidation remains unexplained: why does Q 11:34 feature the word ἁπλοῦς to describe "good" eyes, when this word does not carry the meaning "good"? By itself, this word could mean no more than "healthy" or "generous."[91] It is mostly the association of ἁπλοῦς here with its literary context, including the word πονηρός, that brings out the ethical dimension.[92] Surely, other (more conventional) Greek adjectives, like ἀγαθός, καλός, or χρηστός, would have been better suited to simultaneously bring out both the literal and figurative meanings of the "good" eye. Any of these adjectives would also have been a much better (and more conventional) opposite for πονηρός. In my view, there is a significant reason why ἁπλοῦς was

---

[87] Luz 1989, 397–398.

[88] Piper 1989, 130. Consider especially the use of ποιέω in both verse 46 and verse 47.

[89] Piper 1989, 127–130.

[90] Luke betrays deliberate redactional attempts at elaborating on the hortatory and ethical elements of Q 11:34–35 as a whole. The first of these attempts is the addition of the personal pronoun "you" (σου) to Q 11:34a (Fleddermann 2005a, 520). The second is the addition of v. 36 *in toto* after Q 11:35. For a similar view, see e.g. Jacobson 1992, 173; Betz 1995, 440; Fleddermann 2005a, 519–520, 523. However, some scholars maintain that verse 36 featured in Q and that it was simply taken over by Luke: e.g. Marshall 1978, 488, 489; Kloppenborg 1987, 137; Allison 1997, 152.

[91] Luz 1989, 396; cf. Louw and Nida 1993a s.v. ἁπλοῦς; Newman 1993 s.v. ἁπλοῦς.

[92] Davies and Allison 1988, 638.

preferred over one of the other adjectives. Although a number of commentators mention that ἁπλοῦς could also mean "generous," they fail to explain the true significance of this observation for the level of Q. Piper, for example, refers to the significance of this lexical meaning of ἁπλοῦς on the level of Matthew.[93] Unfortunately, he fails to explain why the social value of "generosity" would be important in the literary context of Q.[94] In fact, interpreters have often struggled to find any *thematic* correspondence between Q 11:33 and Q 11:34–35.[95]

Louw and Nida define ἁπλοῦς ("generous") as "pertaining to willing and generous giving."[96] Hence, ἁπλοῦς specifically recalls the social value of general reciprocity.[97] In addition, the fixed expression ὀφθαλμός πονηρός denotes the act of being "envious," "jealous," "stingy," or "selfish."[98] These attributes are the exact opposite of the "generosity" denoted by ἁπλοῦς.[99] Whereas ἁπλοῦς denotes an openhearted willingness to share with others, πονηρός denotes a stingy unwillingness to partake in reciprocal sharing.[100] Thus, it seems that the most likely reason why the saying would feature ἁπλοῦς instead of one of the other adjectives is that it refers back to the motif of reciprocal sharing in Q 11:33.[101] As such, the distinction in Q 11:34 between morally "good" and "bad" people mirrors the distinction in Q 11:33 between sharing one's light and hiding it. If the foregoing is accepted, it means that Q 11:34 includes three levels of semantic application, none of which are mutually exclusive: (1) "healthy" versus "unhealthy"; (2) "generous" versus "selfish"; and (3) "good" versus "evil." While the first level pertains to the purely physical and the second level reaches back to Q 11:33, the third level prepares for the moral application of verse 35. The placement of Q 11:34–35 in Matthew's Gospel between 6:19–21 (Q 12:33–34) and 6:24 (Q 16:13) supports the present conclusion that this logion deals with reciprocal sharing. Matthew

---

[93] Piper 1989, 128.

[94] Other examples can be added: Marshall 1978, 489; Kloppenborg 1987, 136; Davies and Allison 1988, 638–639, 640; Luz 1989, 397–398; Allison 1997, 158–161.

[95] E.g. Jacobson 1992, 173.

[96] Louw and Nida 1993b, 570.

[97] Viljoen 2009, 168–169.

[98] Davies and Allison 1988, 635; cf. Louw and Nida 1993a s.v. πονηρός.

[99] Cf. Allison 1997, 158, 160.

[100] Luz 1989, 397.

[101] It should be noted that "generous" is also one of the lexical possibilities of ἀγαθός (Louw and Nida 1993a s.v. ἀγαθός; Newman 1993 s.v. ἀγαθός; cf. Matt 20:15). The difference between the generosity of ἀγαθός and the generosity of ἁπλοῦς, though, is that the latter specifically connotes the act of "generous giving," while the former merely connotes generosity as an attribute of general goodness (Louw and Nida 1993b, 570). This slight distinction not only explains why the author of Q 11:34 would prefer the type of generosity connoted by ἁπλοῦς, but also strengthens our case that ἁπλοῦς refers back to the motif of reciprocal sharing in Q 11:33.

6:19–21 advocates against the hoarding and hiding of earthly "treasures" (θησαυρός) or possessions, while Matthew 6:24 warns against serving "wealth" (μαμωνᾶς) instead of God.[102] Three conclusions may be drawn from the current analysis. Firstly, our earlier proposition that Q 11:33 deals with the social value of reciprocal sharing is further corroborated by our current analysis. Secondly, Q 11:34–35 has the important theme of reciprocity in common with the formative layer. Thirdly, Q 11:33 and Q 11:34–35 share the motif of reciprocity. Jacobson is therefore wrong in claiming that Q 11:34–35 does not "develop further the thought of Q 11:33."[103]

There may, however, also be some indication of the possibility that Q 11:34–35 belongs with the main redaction. As its application, verse 35 directs and determines the interpretation of the maxim in verse 34. Particularly interesting is that verse 35 focuses on the negative side of the divide in verse 34.[104] Q 11:34–35 seemingly functions to underline the insight that one can spot and pinpoint evildoers by looking at their eyes. The hypothetical person with generous eyes and a radiant body is moved to the side. The spotlight is rather shone on the imagined individual with jaundiced eyes and a dark body. Q 11:34–35 becomes about one's ability to spot people with *dark* interiors and intentions. The Third Evangelist noticed this disjunction and inserted Luke 11:36 after Q 11:35 as a corrective. Verse 35 further harbours an emphatically threatening and accusatory tone. Both the focus on people's negative traits and the emphatically accusatory tone of Q 11:34–35 point to an affinity with the main redaction.[105] These negative traits go against the general intent and standpoint of the formative layer, which tends to see the good in people or at least promote being decent and helpful to others.[106]

Q 6:41–42 is very revealing when compared with Q 11:34–35. The vivid series of rhetorical questions in Q 6:41–42 also deal with eyes. The main purpose of Q 6:41–42 is to buttress the admonition against judgment in Q 6:37–

---

[102] See chapter 10 below.

[103] Jacobson 1992, 173.

[104] Fleddermann 2005a, 529.

[105] Cf. Q 3:7; 6:23c; 7:9, 25, [30], 31–32, 33–34; 10:13; 11:18, 19, 23, 29–32, 49–51; 12:9, 10, [56], 13:27, 28, 34–35. The only exceptions are when the in-group is favourably portrayed against the out-group (cf. Q 3:16; 7:6, 9, 23, 26–28, [29], 35; 11:19; 12:8, 10; [13:30; 14:11]; 22:28, 30). Regardless, the intent is still to place the latter group in an unfavourable light.

[106] Cf. Q 6:27–28, 29–30, 31, 32, 34, 36–38, 41–42; 10:9, 16; 11:9–13; 12:7; 15:4–5, 7, [8–10]; 17:3–4, 6. There are some exceptions: (1) calling earthly fathers "evil" in Q 11:13, but this is part of the larger rhetorical intent to highlight how much more giving the heavenly Father is; (2) the exclamation "you of petty faith!" in Q 12:28, but this is merely a rhetorical device; and (3) 14:26 as a whole, but this verse relates to broken family relations.

38.[107] As such, the purpose of the illustration is to promote non-judgmental attitudes. Elsewhere, I have summarised the message of Q 6:41–42 as such:

> A merciless and judgmental attitude distorts moral and spiritual vision. People who display these qualities go around looking for transgression in others, but fail to even notice their own shortcomings [...] In fact, these shortcomings are often far worse than the transgressions that were initially identified.[108]

In Q 6:41–42, the specific mentioning of an "eye" seems deliberate, but also somehow superfluous. In order for the analogy to properly fulfil its rhetorical function as an image of support for Q 6:37–38, the splinter or log could have been stuck in any human limb or orifice. For example, if I were to replace the word "eye" with the word "ear" in Q 6:41–42, the message and intent of the illustration would remain unchanged. The question, therefore, is why the text speaks specifically of an "eye" (ὀφθαλμός), as opposed to any other body part. In my view, the answer is that the common wisdom of Q 11:34 lies behind the illustration in Q 6:41–42. The author knew that people's eyes were the windows to their souls, often betraying their true intentions. By the same token, the author knew that judgment of someone else often started with what one could perceive in that person's eyes. A person that is naturally judgmental could easily go around scanning people's eyes for possible evidence of "inner darkness." In the analogy of Q 6:41–42, this type of "evidence" is represented as a "splinter" (κάρφος). When Q 11:34–35 is considered in isolation, it corresponds thematically to Q 6:41–42, since it likewise promotes self-examination rather than the judgment of others.[109] When, however, Q 11:34–35 is considered as part of the main redaction, it contradicts Q 6:41–42 by promoting the habitual judgment of others.

2.3 Implied Audience

2.3.1 Q 11:33

When compared to the material that surrounds it, Q 11:33 stands out because of what it lacks. Unlike the redactional block in Q 11:16, 29–32, 39, 41–44, 46–52, Q 11:33 seems entirely unconcerned with "this generation," including the Pharisees and scribes.[110] The point is not that this logion fails to make any express mention of this (or any other) out-group, since such silence would not necessarily rule out the possibility that the saying was still directed at them. Rather, the point is that Q 11:33 does not seem to be directed at an out-group

---

[107] Horsley 1999, 223.
[108] Howes 2015a, 249.
[109] Cf. Thurén 2014, 293.
[110] Lührmann 1994, 59–60.

at all.[111] The saying fully lacks polemical intent.[112] To be sure, it seems totally indifferent to any distinction whatsoever between us and them. One could argue that such a distinction is implied by the fact that the saying is directed at those "inside the house" (ἐν τῇ οἰκίᾳ). The same distinction might also be implied by the opposite actions of hiding and sharing the lamp, with the former then alluding to "this generation."[113] Drawing such distinctions does not, however, seem to be the intent of the logion. We saw that the logion deliberately moves beyond the confines of the traditional family to motivate sharing beyond these boundaries. The imprecision of the phrase "everyone in the house" (πᾶσιν τοῖς ἐν τῇ οἰκίᾳ) indicates both an unwillingness to demarcate the in-group precisely and an openness to outsiders. Neither explicitly nor implicitly does Q 11:33 prohibit anyone else from entering the house. In fact, Luke's version of this logion expressly states that the light is for "those still entering" (οἱ εἰσπορευόμενοι) the house. Even if this clause was not in the Sayings Gospel, it still indicates that Luke interpreted Q 11:33 as intending an openness to outsiders.[114] The First Evangelist understood this Q saying in a very similar way, as he makes clear by paring it with the saying in Matthew 5:14. In Matthew, the whole point of being "the light of the world" (τὸ φῶς τοῦ κόσμου) is to share one's light with outsiders so as to attract them to join the community.[115] Outsiders are therefore not excluded from "entering the house," neither summarily, like in the main redaction, nor incidentally. Quite the opposite: Q 11:33 seems to be inviting outsiders to enter the house and join the family.[116]

These observations are supported by the general intent and purpose of the logion. Even though the saying is not an admonition, Q 11:33 nevertheless intends to direct behaviour. Aside from what the "light" metaphor specifically represents, the rhetorical point of making the statement that *no one* places a lamp in a hidden place is to convince the audience not to hide their own light.[117] This type of injunction could not have been directed at outsiders, either directly or indirectly. The positive, optimistic, pleasant, idyllic, and inviting tone of the saying, discussed in the previous section on "characteristic motifs," also testifies against it being directed at the out-group. Finally, the social setting of the logion is perhaps most telling. As we saw, Q 11:33 deliberately invokes a family setting. Throughout the formative stratum, the symbol used most consistently and apparently as a self-designation of the Q people is the

---

[111] Jacobson 1992, 174.
[112] Vaage 1994, 115.
[113] E.g. Luz 1989, 249.
[114] Davies and Allison 1988, 478.
[115] Davies and Allison 1988, 476, 478.
[116] Valantasis 2005, 140–141.
[117] Kloppenborg 1987, 135.

family.[118] As we discussed, the Q people viewed themselves as the symbolic family of God. By uttering this maxim against the backdrop of the household, the intended audience of the logion is clearly indicated. The maxim was directed at those who saw themselves as the family of God.[119] To argue that it was in any way directed at the out-group would be to reason that the Q people applied their own self-designation to these outsiders. This seems unthinkable, particularly when the slanderous designations used elsewhere to describe these outsiders are considered.[120]

2.3.2 Q 11:34–35

Like before, our assessment of Q 11:34–35 depends on whether the saying is considered in isolation or not. When taken on its own, the saying coheres thematically with Q 6:43–45. As we saw, both maxims intend to induce not only self-examination, but also constructive conduct. In this way, the critical tone of Q 11:35 is very similar to that of Q 6:46.[121] Respectively, both of these logia follow directly upon their preceding maxims in order to instigate not only self-examination, but also positive action. Such intentionality cannot possibly have been directed at the out-group.[122] Like the rest of the formative layer, Q 11:34–35, considered by itself, strives to persuade, influence and change the conduct of the in-group. As we saw, both Matthew and Luke understood the text in this way. The division in Q 11:34–35 between those with "generous" or "healthy" (ἁπλοῦς) eyes and "radiant" (φωτεινός) bodies, on the one hand, and those with "evil," "stingy," or "jaundiced" (πονηρός) eyes and "dark" (σκοτεινός) bodies, on the other, is comparable to the division in Q 6:43–45 between "good people" (ὁ ἀγαθὸς ἄνθρωπος) and "evil people" (ὁ πονηρὸς [ἄνθρωπος]). Like the distinction in Q 6:43–45, the distinction in Q 11:34–35, regarded in isolation, is not intended as a piece of polemical boundary-marking.[123]

When read as part of its literary environs in the main redaction, however, Q 11:34–35 is chiefly concerned with boundary-marking.[124] The saying principally aims at delineating between two types of people. Within the literary

---

[118] Cf. Howes 2016a, 9–33; cf. Q 6:35, 36, 41–42; 10:5–9, 16, 21 (for the presence of Q 10:21 in the formative stratum, see chapter 1 above); 11:2–4, 9–13; 12:6–7, 22–31; [15:9]; 17:3–4.

[119] Valantasis 2005, 139.

[120] Cf. "evil generation" (γενεὰ πονηρά) in Q 11:29; "unmarked tombs" in Q 11:44 (τὰ μνημεῖα τὰ ἄδηλα). They are also accused of being murderers in Q 11:49–51 and Q 13:34–35 (Kirk 1998, 330).

[121] Piper 1989, 130.

[122] Piper 1989, 129–130; Vaage 1994, 115.

[123] Lührmann 1994, 59–60.

[124] Jacobson 1992, 174.

context of the main redaction, there should be no doubt that this distinction represents Q's characteristic demarcation between the Q people as the in-group and "this generation" as the out-group.[125] Unlike Q 11:33, the delineation seems clear-cut, self-evident, and final.[126] If Q 11:34–35 is interpreted in its current literary context as part of the Q^2 block of judgment material, it is impossible to read it as directed toward anything or anyone other than "this generation."[127] This is visibly how the main redactor intended the logion to be read. The use of the adjective "evil" (πονηρός) is particularly telling in this case. The block of material in which this logion currently appears pertinently introduces "this generation" in Q 11:29 as an "evil" (πονηρός) generation. The repetition of this epithet in Q 11:34 (five verses later) can hardly be coincidental.[128] It is worth mentioning, however, that Q 11:33–35 would in the context of the formative stratum have been preceded by Q 11:9–13, which also features the word "evil" (πονηρός), but applies it in that context to the in-group.[129] This would likewise not have been accidental.

That those with evil eyes should be identified with "this generation" is further supported by its placement directly after Q 11:33. We argued that this logion is exclusively directed at the Q people, who are evidently associated with the image of "light." When the subsequent saying continues to distinguish between those with "radiant" (φωτεινός) bodies and those with "dark" (σκοτεινός) bodies, the intention must surely be that the former group represents the radiant family of Q 11:33 and the latter group represents outsiders.[130] The demarcation of verse 34 between those who can see (Q people) and those who fail to see ("this generation") corresponds to the demarcation in verses 31–32 between those who listen (the Ninevites and the Queen of the South) and those who refuse to listen ("this generation").[131] Verse 35 spells out this demarcation by accentuating the magnitude and severity of the out-group's darkness.[132] The moral darkness and stubborn blindness of "this generation" is "worthy of judgment and condemnation."[133]

The subsequent material further confirms that, in its context in the main redaction, Q 11:34–35 has "this generation" specifically in mind.[134] The point of the association between Q 11:34–35 and the subsequent woes is that the

---

[125] Cf. Uro 1996, 93.

[126] Piper 1989, 129.

[127] Kloppenborg 1987, 138–139, 148; Piper 1989, 128; Jacobson 1992, 152, 174; Allison 1997, 160–161, 165–167; Kirk 1998, 201–202, 330; Fleddermann 2005a, 529.

[128] Allison 1997, 166; Kirk 1998, 201, 202, 330.

[129] See chapter 10 below.

[130] Kirk 1998, 201.

[131] E.g. Kloppenborg 1987, 147–148; cf. Uro 1996, 93.

[132] Piper 1989, 129.

[133] Kloppenborg 1987, 138, 148.

[134] Robinson 2005b, 592.

Pharisees and scribes have no light in them.[135] Their motives, objectives, and intentions are completely dark.[136] Yet Q's Jesus continues to expose them in the subsequent passages for who they really are. It is possible that the woes against the Pharisees also featured the adjective "evil" (πονηρία) as a description of them.[137] In addition, these Pharisees and scribes fail to perceive the true nature and value of the person and message of Jesus.[138] In Q 11:49–51, which follows directly after the woes against the Pharisees and scribes, these accusations are broadened to include all of "this generation."

2.4 Redactional Activity

The foregoing analysis reveals features of the text that are highly suggestive of redactional activity. It should be accepted without much doubt that Q 11:33 and Q 11:34–35 did not belong together originally.[139] The thematic disjunction between these two autonomous maxims has been observed by other interpreters.[140] It is certainly telling that both Matthew (5:15; 6:22–23) and *Thomas* (24, 33) separate the two sayings in their respective Gospels.[141] More significant is the fact that Mark (4:21) copies only Q 11:33, without Q 11:34–35.[142] On the other hand, there is evidence to suggest that these sayings were already joined in the pre-Lukan tradition.[143] It therefore seems likely that these two sayings were for the first time joined in Q.[144]

---

[135] Cf. esp. Q 11:39, 41, 44, 47. These verses explain that the Pharisees and scribes purify their outsides, but fail to purify their insides. Despite their best efforts, the darkness of their insides remains transparent to Jesus and his followers. This demarcation between inside and outside parallels Q 11:34–35. In general, the main redaction is extremely interested in people's interiors (cf. Q 3:16; 11:14–15, 17–20, 24–26, 39, 41, 44; [17:20–21]; Piper 1989, 129).

[136] Jacobson 1992, 174.

[137] Allison 1997, 20 n. 86, 166.

[138] Kloppenborg 1987, 148.

[139] E.g. Robinson 2005b, 592.

[140] E.g. Kloppenborg 1987, 135.

[141] Piper 1989, 128.

[142] Piper 1989, 127, 246 n. 146.

[143] Marshall 1978, 488; Zeller 1994, 119.

[144] Lührmann 1994, 59; *pace* Robinson 2005b, 591–592. Many interpreters suspect some form of redactional activity within Q 11:34–35 itself. Allison (1997, 134–135, 153) argues that verse 34a was a free-floating sapiential maxim, with the explanations in Q 11:34b–c added later (cf. Betz 1995, 441, 444). Fleddermann (2005a, 527) argues the exact opposite, namely that verse 34a was attached to the nucleus of Q 11:34b–c in order to enable a smooth transition between verses 33 and 34. Seeing as both parts of verse 34 can justifiably stand alone, it is certainly possible that either or both of them circulated independently at some stage. Against this, Luz (1989, 392–393) argues that verse 34 was a unified logion from the very beginning. Schenk (1981, 73–74) agrees with Luz, but argues that verse 34 was created

There is also evidence to suggest that Q 11:33 in particular featured between Q 11:9–13 and Q 12:2–3 at some early stage. Mark's parallel to Q 12:2 (Mark 4:22) appears directly after his parallel to Q 11:33 (Mark 4:21).[145] These two logia also appear together in the *Gospel of Thomas* (33).[146] Both of these texts are highly significant as independent evidence of the earlier presence of at least Q 11:33 directly before Q 12:2.[147] Q 11:33 follows neatly after Q 11:9–13. Both passages deal pertinently with the ancient social value of reciprocal sharing.[148] Q 12:2–3 also follows neatly after Q 11:33. Besides the obvious catchword connections,[149] both deal with the subject matter of hiding and exposing wisdom.[150] Because Q 11:33 develops both reciprocity and wisdom as motifs, it is the perfect transitional maxim between the respective Q[1] passages of Q 11:9–13 and Q 12:2–7.

These considerations suggest that those responsible for the compilation of Q's formative stratum found Q 11:33 between Q 11:9–13 and Q 12:2–3 in the pre-Q tradition, but added Q 11:33–34 after Q 11:33 due to the thematic and linguistic overlap between these two logia.[151] When the main redactor subsequently added the block of polemical material in Q 11:14–51 between Q 11:13 and Q 12:2, the logia in Q 11:33–35 were swallowed up by the added material. The main redactor purposely incorporated Q 11:33–35 into the main redaction by placing it between the section that judges "this generation" in general and the section that judges the Pharisees and scribes in particular. This decision could have been prompted by the catchword "evil" (πονηρός), which is shared by Q 11:16 and Q 11:34, as well as the thematic link between the "sign" (σημεῖον) of Q 11:16, 29–32 and the "light" (λύχνος) of Q 11:33, seeing as both were not only visible manifestations of some nature, but also identifiable images of Jesus's message.[152] In the process of being imbedded into the literary context of the main redaction, these sayings lost the meanings and applications they originally had in the formative stratum.[153] The primary focus and intent of Q 11:33 changed from the "sharing" of light by insiders to

---

entirely *ex nihilo* by the author of Q. Regarding verse 35, many see it as a redactional addition to the maxim in verse 34 (Marshall 1978, 488).

[145] Kloppenborg 1987, 215.

[146] Jacobson 1992, 173; Robinson 2005c, 438 n. 50.

[147] Robinson 2005b, 591; 2005c, 438 n. 50.

[148] See chapter 10 below.

[149] That is, οὐδείς, κρύπτη, and κρυπτός (Sato 1994, 171; Zeller 1994, 119).

[150] Valantasis 2005, 140; see chapter 10 below.

[151] Cf. Sato 1994, 171; Zeller 1994, 119.

[152] Cf. Kloppenborg 1987, 135, 137–138; Thurén 2014, 291; *pace* Jacobson 1992, 173.

[153] Even though Luz (1989, 248) maintains that "[o]ne can no longer determine for certain the original meaning of these wisdom logia [including Q 11:33]," this statement implies not only that Q 11:33 did have such an original meaning, but also that this original message was subsequently changed when placed in a new literary context by the evangelists.

the "hiding" and "ignoring" of light by outsiders. Likewise, the displacement of Q 11:34–35 had the effect of changing the logion from a paraenetic statement that encouraged self-examination and constructive conduct to a polemic statement that encouraged discrimination against the out-group. Both sayings could now function to delineate between insiders and outsiders. Additionally, both sayings also exchanged the gnomic and hortatory tone they once exhibited for a more prophetic and critical tone.[154]

2.5 Findings

This chapter reconsidered the attribution of Q 11:33–35 to Kloppenborg's main redaction. It was found that both of the logia that make up this text are best classified as traditional sapiential maxims. This finding is somewhat unremarkable, since most scholars, including Kloppenborg, view these logia as sapiential maxims. Much more significant were the criteria of "characteristic motifs" and "implied audience," which confirmed that Q 11:33–35 probably belonged to the formative stratum before being incorporated into the main redaction.[155] It would seem that Q 11:33 and Q 11:34–35 were combined for the first time by those responsible for Q's formative stratum. Some time later, these two logia were "placed in a hidden place" by Q's main redactor.

---

[154] Kloppenborg 1987, 138–139, 148; 1994, 145; Allison 1997, 166–167.
[155] Cf. Vaage 1994, 119.

Chapter 3

Q 12:39–40, "If the Householder Had Known"[1]

³⁹⟦ἐκεῖν⟧ο δὲ γινώσκετε ὅτι εἰ ᾔδει ὁ οἰκοδεσπότης ποίᾳ φυλακῇ ὁ κλέπτης ἔρχεται, οὐκ ἂν ⟦εἴας⟧εν διορυχθῆναι τὸν οἶκον αὐτοῦ. ⁴⁰καὶ ὑμεῖς γίνεσθε ἕτοιμοι, ὅτι ᾗ οὐ δοκεῖτε ὥρᾳ ὁ υἱὸς τοῦ ἀνθρώπου ἔρχεται.

³⁹But know this: If the householder had known in which watch the robber was coming, he would not have let his house be dug into. ⁴⁰You also must be ready, for the Son of Humanity is coming at an hour you do not expect.

In his analysis, Kloppenborg ascribes the cluster of sayings in Q 12:39–59 to the main redaction.[2] This cluster is introduced by the tradition about the Son of Man coming like a robber (Q 12:39–40). These two verses not only introduce a cluster of sayings ascribed by Kloppenborg to the main redaction, but are also preceded directly by material belonging to the formative stratum, namely the passages that admonish respectively against hoarding earthly treasures (Q 12:33–34) and harbouring anxiety in the face of procuring bare necessities (Q 12:22–31).[3] In other words, Q 12:39–40 appears on the boundary between a block of material attributed by Kloppenborg to the formative stratum and a block of material attributed by him to the main redaction. The two sayings in Q 12:39–40 are directly followed by the parable of the (un)faithful slave in Q 12:42–46, which forms part of Kloppenborg's block of Q² material referred to above. It will presently be argued that only the Son of Man saying in verse 40 belongs to the main redaction, while the saying about the robber in verse 39 belongs to the formative stratum.

3.1 Kloppenborg's Analysis

Kloppenborg treats the cluster of sayings in Q 12:39–59[4] together, claiming that "[t]he threat of apocalyptic judgment recurs as the formative literary and theological motif."[5] He distinguishes this cluster from the foregoing material

---

[1] An earlier version of this chapter was published as an article in *Journal of Early Christian History* 4/2 (see Howes 2014a).

[2] Kloppenborg 1987, 148–154.

[3] Cf. Kloppenborg 1994, 138–155.

[4] That is, Q 12:39–40, 42–46, 49, 51–53, (54–56), 57–59.

[5] Kloppenborg 1987, 148–154; cf. Luz 2005, 216.

(Q 12:22–34) on grounds of general tone and basic motif: "Whereas 12:22–34 is hortatory in character and sapiential in its idiom and mode of argumentation, 12:39–59 is aggressive and threatening in tone, and marked by warnings of judgment."[6] He further argues that the foregoing material is aimed at the Q people, while Q 12:39–59 breaches the boundaries of the Q people, threatening everyone with apocalyptic judgment. In other words, Kloppenborg appeals here to two of his three main criteria for distinguishing between the formative stratum and the main redaction, namely characteristic motifs and implied audience. In this instance, he also adds general tone as a criterion, but fails to consider his main criterion of form.

Kloppenborg then turns his attention specifically to Q 12:39–40.[7] He agrees with most that the combination of the two sayings in verses 39 and 40 (respectively) is secondary.[8] He points out the internal disparity between these two logia: verse 39 deals with the prevention of a robbery through foresight, while verse 40 suggests that the appearance of the Son of Man can be neither foreseen nor prevented.[9] To this internal contradiction could be added both the oddity of comparing the Son of Man (or Jesus) to a burglar[10] and the strangeness of comparing the negative happening of a burglary to the positive happening of the Son of Man's return, at least from the perspective of the Q people.[11] He rightly also points to the well-known fact that the saying in verse 39 appears in the *Gospel of Thomas* (21, 103) without the Son of Man saying in verse 40.[12] In light of these observations, Kloppenborg[13] follows other scholars[14] when he concludes that "the Son of Man saying was a secondary interpretation of the parable [in Q 12:39]." However, he goes on to argue that the addition of the Son of Man saying happened before Q 12:39–40 was attached to the subsequent parable in Q 12:42–46.[15] As evidence, he points to the strong verbal and conceptual agreement between verses 40 and 46 as the basis for the association between Q 12:39–40 and Q 12:42–46.[16]

---

[6] Kloppenborg 1987, 149.

[7] Kloppenborg 1987, 149–150.

[8] Cf. e.g. Uro 1996, 112; Luz 2005, 217, esp. n. 10.

[9] Cf. Luz 2005, 216, 217.

[10] Cf. Etchells 1998, 99.

[11] Jeremias 1963, 49. Cf., on the other hand, Fleddermann (2005a, 634), who argues against the general concensus that the combination between Q 12:39 and Q 12:40 is secondary. For other attempted harmonisations (and their refutations), see Luz 2005, 218.

[12] Cf. e.g. Jeremias 1963, 49; Crossan 1983, 57; Allison 2004, 439.

[13] Kloppenborg 1987, 149.

[14] See e.g. Koester 1994a, 38–40.

[15] Cf. Schürmann 1994, 88, 90 n. 86, 93–96.

[16] Verse 40: "the Son of Man *comes at an hour* you *do not expect*" (ᾗ οὐ δοκεῖτε ὥρᾳ ὁ υἱὸς τοῦ ἀνθρώπου ἔρχεται); verse 46: "the master of that slave will *come* on a day he *does not expect* and *at an hour* he does not know" (ἥξει ὁ κύριος τοῦ δούλου ἐκείνου ἐν ἡμέρᾳ ᾗ οὐ προσδοκᾷ καὶ ἐν ὥρᾳ ᾗ οὐ γινώσκει).

Kloppenborg makes mention of other New Testament texts where the image of a robber also occurs in connection with the expected apocalyptic event.[17] In these texts, the future apocalypse is not described as the "hour of the Son of Man," but as the "day of the Lord."[18] Fleddermann is probably correct that 1 Thessalonians 5:2, 4 does not betray Paul's literary dependence on written Q.[19] Nevertheless, this text does betray Paul's familiarity with the tradition that was responsible for Q 12:39–40.[20] Such familiarity reveals just how widespread this tradition had already become by the time Paul wrote his first known letter. Moreover, the possibility that Q had an indirect, oral influence on Paul cannot be summarily ignored or denied. The content of 2 Peter 3:10 was in all probability derivative of the letter to the Thessalonians.

Another text that betrays familiarity with this saying is Mark 13:35. Fleddermann is probably correct in his assessment that this Markan text is secondary and that it betrays Mark's familiarity with "redactional Q," as he calls it.[21] As with Paul, Mark might have made use of indirect oral traditions of Q rather than direct literary traditions – that is, if he was indeed influenced in some way by Q specifically. Revelation 3:3 and 16:15, having been written long after any of these texts, could have been influenced by any one of them. In the end, all that can be deduced with absolute certainty from these texts is that the comparison between the expected apocalypse and the intrusion of a robber was popular and widespread in the early church.[22] Even so, it is neither impossible nor unlikely that Q 12:39–40 lies behind all these traditions as a source, even if only indirectly.[23]

3.2 An Alternative Proposal

Contrary to Kloppenborg's analysis, I maintain that the Son of Man saying in verse 40 was added to the robber saying in verse 39 by the main redactor. In other words, it is my opinion that the secondary addition of verse 40 did not take place during Q's prehistory, but during Q's redaction, at the hands of the

---

[17] I.e. 1 Thess 5:2, 4; 2 Pet 3:10; Rev 3:3; 16:15; cf. Roth 2018, 170.

[18] Dodd 1958, 168; Crossan 1991, 251.

[19] Fleddermann 2005a, 630; cf. Hedrick 2014, 27.

[20] Dodd 1958, 168.

[21] Fleddermann 2005a, 630–631.

[22] Jacobson 1992, 196; Funk and Hoover 1993, 252, 342; Allison 2004, 439. As a side note, it is worth mentioning that the prevalence of Q 12:39 in the early church might be an indication of its authenticity (Bock 1996, 1171–1172; Luz 2005, 217; cf. Funk and Hoover 1993, 342). The novel act of comparing a chance robbery with the apocalyptic end is also unattested in Jewish material of the time (Allison 2004, 439).

[23] Jeremias 1963, 50.

main redactor.[24] The claim that only verse 40 was added by the main redactor would imply that the saying in verse 39 properly belongs to the formative stratum and not the main redaction. As we saw, Kloppenborg's main reason for viewing the addition of verse 40 as something that happened prior to the association of Q 12:39–40 with the subsequent material is the verbal and conceptual similarity between verses 40 and 46. This similarity, however, does not preclude other explanations of the redactional process. In fact, one could just as easily point to the strong agreement between verses 40 and 46 as a motivating factor for adding verse 40 between the saying in verse 39 and the parable in verses 42–46. Put differently, it is equally plausible that the redactor added the Son of Man saying precisely because he noted the strong agreement between this saying and verse 46. An even stronger case could be made for the likelihood that the main redactor changed the vocabulary of either verse 40 or verse 46 in order to establish an association between them. In the next chapter, it will be argued that Q 12:45–46 was also added to this complex of material by the main redactor, who found verses 42–44 already in the formative stratum. If this is correct, the correspondence between verses 40 and 46 is attributable to redactional intent. The possibility that verse 40 is a secondary formulation is supported by its nature and function as an interpolation.[25] However, if verses 45–46 were added to Q 12:42–44 by the main redactor, they were probably created *ex nihilo*. Both the widespread use of traditions akin to Q 12:40 in the early church and the probability that Q 12:45–46 was created *ex nihilo* support the conclusion that Q 12:40 was taken over as it stands from traditional material, and that Q 12:45–46 was formulated to agree with Q 12:40. Either way, the correspondence between these two texts seems to be the result of deliberate redactional activity.

One might ask why the Son of Man saying was added *between* the robber saying and the parable, instead of directly *after* the parable and its comparable conclusion in verse 46. There are three plausible reasons for the specific placement of verse 40 that support the current proposal. First, the repetition of such similar phraseology and conception in two consecutive verses would have been redundant. Second, the placement of Q 12:40 ensured that the two texts on either side of this logion would function and be transmitted as a pair of twin parables.[26] Third, by adding the Son of Man saying after the robber saying, the

---

[24] This does not necessarily mean that Q 12:40 is inauthentic (see Allison 2010, 120–125; cf. Koester 1994b, 540–541). Verse 40 could have been taken from elsewhere in the (authentic) Jesus tradition, where it circulated independently, and could merely have been added here by the main redactor (Jeremias 1963, 110; Schürmann 1994, 90–91; cf. Casey 2009, 219). Personally, I agree with the majority of scholars that Q 12:40 is inauthentic (e.g. Funk and Hoover 1993, 252, 342; Kloppenborg 1995, 293 n. 58; cf. Blomberg 1990, 278; Bock 1996, 1171). Bock's counterarguments apply only to Q 12:39.

[25] Cf. Schürmann 1994, 90–91.

[26] See Jeremias 1963, 92–94.

redactor ensured that the meaning of the latter would be transformed from a sapiential logion to an apocalyptic warning.[27] Schürmann's investigation of the Son of Man logia in Q reveal that all of them are "joined to preceding or following individual logia, serving to comment on, (re)interpret, or supplement the individual logia."[28] Due to the position of verse 40 directly after verse 39, the Son of Man saying became the lens through which the robber saying would henceforth be understood.[29] Due to the verbal agreement between verses 40 and 46, as well as the occurrence of the word "then" (ἄρα) in verse 42, the Son of Man saying *also* became the lens through which the subsequent parable would henceforth be interpreted.[30] Ironically, this diachronic analysis is reinforced by Kirk's synchronic analysis, which argues that verse 40 is the central saying or heart of the composition in Q 12:[35–38[31]], 39–40, 42–46.[32] To substantiate his proposed structure, Kirk claims that the Son of Man logion "is a discrete, self-contained pronouncement with an autonomous function."[33] He goes on to explain that the Son of Man saying acts as the hermeneutical key that unlocks both the preceding and the subsequent material. This location and function of Q 12:40 should be recognised as the brainchild of the main redactor.

The agreement between verses 40 and 46 is not the only possible reason for Q 12:39–40 and Q 12:42–46 featuring together. If the Son of Man saying in verse 40 and the second half of the parable in verses 45–46 are removed, a number of reasons remain for the robber saying in verse 39 to be attached to the first half of the parable in verses 42–44.[34] Firstly, both feature the catchwords "know" (γινώσκω) and "come" (ἔρχομαι). Secondly, both feature a householder (cf. ὁ οἰκοδεσπότης in verse 39 and ὁ κύριος ... τῆς οἰκετείας αὐτοῦ in verse 42).[35] Thirdly, both take place within a domestic setting (cf. οἰκοδεσπότης and οἶκος in verse 40 and οἰκετείας in verse 42). Fourthly, both deal in some way specifically with the householder's possessions. In verse 39, the occurrence of a robbery implies the loss of possessions, and in verses 42–44 the slave is not only put in a position of looking after his master's "household" (οἰκετεία) or "servants" (θεραπεία), both of which constitute possessions from an ancient perspective, but also promised the reward of stewardship over "all his master's possessions" (πᾶσιν τοῖς ὑπάρχουσιν αὐτοῦ). Fifthly, both

---

[27] Cf. Crossan 1983, 59, 65; Fleddermann 2005a, 630–631, 635.

[28] Schürmann 1994, 90.

[29] Cf. e.g. Valantasis 2005, 167.

[30] Cf. Zeller 1994, 119; Kloppenborg 2000a, 127.

[31] Kirk maintains that the Sondergut material in Luke 12:35–38 was also part of the Sayings Gospel. In this, he follows other scholars, like Marshall 1978, 533; Jacobson 1992, 193–196; Schürmann 1994, 87–88.

[32] Kirk 1998, 227–233.

[33] Kirk 1998, 232–233.

[34] For some of these reasons, see Fleddermann 2005a, 633–635.

[35] Funk and Hoover 1993, 341–342.

texts feature a situation where a member of the upper class is brought face-to-face with a member of the lower class. The householder suffers at the hands of a robber, while the master is forced to put his trust in one of his slaves.[36] Sixthly, both texts deal conceptually with the temporal uncertainty and unpredictability of someone's arrival. Finally, some measure of narrative progression is implied between the robber logion and the introduction to Q 12:42–44. The phrase "in which watch" (ποίᾳ φυλακῇ[37]) implies that the break-in happened during someone's watch, and that the householder might be looking to blame one of his slaves.[38] The first part of verse 42 seems to be introducing a question as to the identity of the culprit: "Who then is the faithful and wise slave whom the master put over his household…?" The adjectives "faithful" (πιστός) and "wise" (φρόνιμος) elicit sympathy from the audience, implying that the slave was not at fault, but that he[39] might nonetheless be facing his master's wrath. It is only when the sentence finishes with "…to give [them] food on time" that the audience realises that this rhetorical question[40] introduces a new passage with a different slave, who had different responsibilities. All these similarities between the robber saying and Q 12:42–44 indicate that these two texts could easily and justifiably have featured one after the other in the formative layer.

If we agree that there is a strong literary association between the robber saying and Q 12:42–44 (in the formative stratum), and if we further agree with most scholars that verse 40 was added subsequently, we are left with the likelihood that *the main redactor* added the Son of Man logion between these two texts. As we saw, Kloppenborg's main reasons for attributing all the material in Q 12:39–46 to the main redaction are the threatening tone and apocalyptic

---

[36] Robbers typically formed part of the poor in antiquity (Häkkinen 2016, 4).

[37] Luke has "in which hour" (ποίᾳ ὥρᾳ). Dodd (1958, 167) prefers the latter phrase for Q, but due to the following reasons it should probably be seen as a Lukan revision (Crossan 1983, 61; Fleddermann 2005a, 624; cf. Bock 1996, 1176): (1) Luke had just made use of the word "watch" (φυλακή) in the foregoing verse; (2) the change was probably an attempt to enhance the association between verses 39 and 40; (3) the amendation also strengthened the association between verses 40 and 46; (4) the alteration widened the application to include daytime as well; and (5) Luke prefered the more standard Christian term.

[38] On the grounds of general logic, Etchells's (1998, 99) comment that it was the householder himself who kept watch seems entirely implausble. If he was always keeping watch, he would never have time to sleep. In any case, the specific use of ποῖος, which could here either be translated as "which" or "whose," clearly indicates that the householder had slaves who took turns keeping watch (Liddell and Scott 1996 s.v. ποῖος).

[39] The gender of the slave is indicated by the Greek noun and definite article: ὁ δοῦλος.

[40] It is often assumed that a rhetorical question is a question without an answer or a question of which the answer is so obvious that it need not be given. Although this is true of many rhetorical questions, it is not true of all. A rhetorical question is better defined as any question used for rhetorical effect. Whether or not the answer is supplied by the author is mostly irrelevant when classifying a question as rhetorical.

motifs that feature therein. However, these attributes apply only to verses 40, 45–46. Taken in isolation, Q 12:39 does not harbour a threatening tone or contain the theme of apocalyptic judgment. It is only if this text is read through the lens of verse 40 that it is turned into some kind of threat about the final judgment. Without verse 40, the interpretation and application of Q 12:39 remains open for consideration.[41] If Q 12:39 is evaluated on its own terms, its proper position in the formative stratum becomes apparent.

3.3 Characteristic Forms

Kloppenborg neglects this criterion in his analysis of the material in question. If verse 39 is liberated from the shackles of verse 40, it reads not as an apocalyptic or prophetic warning, but as a piece of everyday wisdom. It lacks all the formal features of prophetic or apocalyptic small forms, including future-tense verbs, prophetic introductory formulas, a threatening tone, and the features of the so-called "eschatological" or "prophetic correlative."[42] Conversely, the saying is formally and clearly introduced as a piece of wisdom by the word "know" (γινώσκω) in the opening phrase, "but know this" (ἐκεῖνο/τοῦτο δὲ γινώσκετε ὅτι). The saying also appears to be illustrative in nature.[43]

The logion is clearly also not a *chreia*. Noticeably missing is an anecdotal introduction or, for that matter, any attempt at all to set the scene. Even though the verb "know" (γινώσκετε) in the opening phrase appears in the imperative mood and second person plural,[44] the saying proper features verbs in the indicative mood and third person singular (ᾔδει, ἔρχεται, and ἀφῆκεν). These morphologies argue against not only the possibility that this saying is an apocalyptic or prophetic warning, but also the possibility that it is a sapiential instruction or admonition.[45] Instead, these morphologies argue in favour of the saying being a sapiential maxim or aphorism, depending on whether or not the saying is judged to have been subversive.[46] The obviousness of the saying's content would seem to suggest that it is better classified as a maxim.[47] Its taxonomy as a maxim is confirmed by the fact that it draws from everyday human experience to voice a truism.[48]

---

[41] Cf. Jeremias 1963, 49, 89.
[42] Cf. Edwards 1969, 9–20; 1976, 41, 114; Schmidt 1977, 517–522.
[43] Kirk 1998, 232.
[44] Cf. Fleddermann 2005a, 624.
[45] Cf. Kirk 1998, 92.
[46] Cf. Crossan 1983, 58; Kirk 1998, 91.
[47] Cf. Bultmann 1994, 30.
[48] Cf. Murphy 1981, 4; Kloppenborg 1987, 238; Kirk 1998, 91; Howes 2012, 246.

Finally, it should also be noted that this maxim does not qualify as a parable, regardless of how colourful and imaginative the content and imagery are considered to be.[49] Kloppenborg's argument that Aristotle or Quintilian's more generic definition of "parable" (παραβολή or *similitudo*) applies to the content of Q and the Synoptics (even if not to the Jesus tradition) does not convince, regardless of the nature of these documents as literary compositions.[50] If such a general definition of "parable" were applied across the board, it would follow that traditional wisdom sayings, like the one in Proverbs 24:3–4, are also to be classified as parables. It is clear that with the parables of Jesus, even as they are presented in Q and the Synoptics, we are dealing with a distinctive micro-genre, which should be clearly distinguished from other micro-genres, like maxims, similes, and philosophic illustrations. This remains true despite the haphazard use of the word "parable" (παραβολή) by the evangelists.[51] It is only to be expected that modern scholars would be more meticulous in their methods of genre classification than ancient authors.

Scott identifies the following set of criteria for recognising and classifying the micro-genre of Jesus's parables: "[A] parable is [1] a *mashal* [or proverb] [2] that employs a short narrative fiction [3] to reference a symbol."[52] Scott adds a fourth criterion when he explains that, when it comes to the parables of Jesus, the symbol is always the kingdom of God.[53] Although Q 12:39 can be classified as a type of *mashal*, and although it might be symbolic of a deeper truth, it neither develops a narrative sequence nor references the kingdom of God.[54] Instead, the saying is only concerned with the aftermath of a robbery that had already taken place, and only one aspect thereof. One would expect a parable to concisely narrate not only the events that led up to the robbery, but also the robbery itself, the ensuing events, and the culmination. Some might argue that the text presupposes a narrative and therefore qualifies as a parable. Notwithstanding the definition offered by Scott, not all the parables of Jesus feature a narrative.[55] Even so, verse 39 is not about the kingdom of God if my interpretation in the next section of its function without verse 40 as a supporting logion in the formative stratum is accepted. Moreover, the imagery of verse 39 is also not "symbolic of a deeper truth" if my forthcoming interpretation of its function is correct. While most parable scholars of previous generations tended to view Q 12:39 as a parable,[56] a number of noteworthy scholars today skip

---

[49] Cf. Crossan 1983, 58; *pace* e.g. Bock 1996, 1172.

[50] Kloppenborg 1995, 286–287; cf. Hunter 1971, 10–11; Donahue 1988, 5.

[51] Cf. Hunter 1971, 11; Donahue 1988, 5.

[52] Scott 1989, 7.

[53] Scott 1989, 8. For the kingdom of God as a symbol, see Uro 1996, 75–78.

[54] See Scott 1989, 7–62; cf. Crossan 1974a, 31; Meier 2016, 214 n. 6.

[55] See Hunter 1971, 11; Donahue 1988, 5; cf. Dodd 1958, 18.

[56] E.g. Dodd 1958, 167–171; Jeremias 1963, 24, 48–51; Hunter 1964, 85.

over this logion in their lists and treatments of the parable tradition.[57] During his discussion of Q's redactional history, Kloppenborg dubs Q 12:39 a parable.[58] However, when turning his attention in a subsequent article to the parables in Q specifically, Kloppenborg fails to either list or discuss Q 12:39 as a parable.[59]

On the opposite side of the coin, Q 12:40 is a prophetic warning against the expected coming of the Son of Man and the implied apocalyptic turmoil that will accompany his appearance.[60] Formally, this is indicated by the imperative mood of the verb "be" (γίνεσθε), the second person plural forms of the verbs "be" (γίνεσθε) and "expect" (δοκεῖτε), and the use of the conative present verb "come" (ἔρχεται) in reference to the future coming of the Son of Man. There is no need to attribute more space arguing for the prophetic and/or apocalyptic nature of this small form, since this classification is both obvious and widely accepted. To be sure, the prophetic-apocalyptic essence of this saying is so unmistakable that it has determined the interpretation of its surrounding material for centuries.[61]

3.4 Characteristic Motifs

It is perhaps best to start with Q 12:40, since the meaning of this saying is most transparent and universally recognised. In no uncertain terms, it warns against the unexpectedness and unpredictability of the coming of the Son of Man on judgment day.[62] Although the early church identified the Son of Man's coming with the parousia of Jesus,[63] this Q text does not overtly associate Jesus with the Son of Man.[64] It seems nonetheless likely that Q 12:40 has Daniel 7:13 specifically in mind.[65] Be that as it may, the saying's chief motif is to implore its audience to be ready for the arrival of the Son of Man, seeing as it will happen unexpectedly.[66] By focusing on the theme of unexpectedness, and by

---

[57] E.g. Funk, Scott, and Butts 1988; Scott 1989; Young 1998; Bailey 2008; Crossan 2012; Levine 2014; Wright 2015; Ford 2016; Meier 2016, esp. 193, 214 n. 6. It should also be mentioned that some contemporary scholars continue to treat Q 12:39 as a parable (e.g. Blomberg 1990, 277–278; Etchells 1998, 97–100; Schottroff 2006).

[58] Kloppenborg 1987, 149.

[59] Kloppenborg 1995.

[60] Kloppenborg 1987, 148–150; cf. Q 17:23–24, 26–27, 30, 37.

[61] Cf. e.g. Dodd 1958, 168–171; Marshall 1978, 533; Donahue 1988, 97–98; Etchells 1998, 97–100.

[62] Cf. Kloppenborg 2000a, 118; Schottroff 2006, 175.

[63] Marshall 1978, 533.

[64] Jacobson 1992, 196; *pace* e.g. Bultmann 1994, 34; Valantasis 2005, 167.

[65] Allison 2000, 131; Casey 2009, 219; Howes 2013c, 10.

[66] Valantasis 2005, 167; Schottroff 2006, 175.

actually using the phrase "not expect" (οὐ δοκεῖτε), Q 12:40 makes explicit what is only implied in other Q texts, like the pericope on the sign of Jonah in Q 11:16, 29–32 and the Son of Man logia in Q 17:23–24, 26–27, 30.[67] That Q 12:40 develops one of the motifs that is distinctively characteristic of the main redaction should be accepted without much doubt.

If the maxim in Q 12:39 is read without verse 40, it enables other hermeneutical avenues and contextual associations. Both the householder and the robber are referenced in the third person, suggesting that the audience should not associate themselves with either of the two.[68] This feature underscores the artificiality of the attachment of the Son of Man saying to the robber saying. Noticing this flaw, the person or people responsible for the combination of these two sayings probably added the word "also" (καί) to the Son of Man saying, thereby enabling it to function as the hermeneutical application of the preceding maxim. In the *Gospel of Thomas* (21, 103), this maxim is elaborated in a different direction and interpreted as a directive to be watchful and "on guard" against the world.[69] In Q, however, this interpretive expansion is entirely lacking.[70] That the maxim, as it stands in Q, does not have watchfulness in mind is demonstrated by the phrase "in which watch" (ποίᾳ φυλακῇ).[71] This phrase indicates that the householder was indeed taking preventative measures and being watchful, but ended up being robbed in spite of these efforts.[72]

Rather than advising watchfulness or warning about some or other apocalyptic end, verse 39 makes the obvious point that even a cautious and watchful householder cannot protect his goods from potential robbery.[73] This is undoubtedly the most natural and uncomplicated reading of the text. The function of this truism becomes intelligible if it is read together with the material that precedes it, namely Q 12:22–31, 33–34. In my view, the pericope about anxiety (Q 12:22–31) precedes the logion about heavenly treasures (Q 12:33–34) in the

---

[67] Cf. Bultmann 1994, 27; Kloppenborg 2000a, 392.

[68] *Pace* e.g. Valantasis 2005, 167. This does not preclude the real possibility that the Q people were made up of bandits and robbers. More and more villagers were turning to a life of banditry as a result of habitual indebtedness and the subsequent loss of their smallholdings (Horsley 1995a, 43; Freyne 2000, 205; Arnal 2001, 139–140, 146; Moxnes 2003, 150; Oakman 2008, 21, 25, 104, 224, 225; Häkkinen 2016, 7; cf. Horsley 1999, 278; Reed 2000, 98).

[69] Jeremias 1963, 87–88; Crossan 1983, 62; Kloppenborg 1987, 149; Allison 2004, 439; Luz 2005, 220.

[70] Cf. Luz 2005, 218.

[71] *Pace* e.g. Hunter 1964, 85; 1971, 102–103; Blomberg 1990, 278; Zimmermann 2015, 387.

[72] Crossan 1983, 61; Nolland 2005, 995; cf. Catchpole 1993, 57–58.

[73] A similar point is made by Q 11:21–22, but the presence of this logion in Q is all but certain.

Sayings Gospel Q. The *Critical Edition of Q* features Q 12:33–34 in its Matthean placement, between Q 12:2–12 and Q 12:22–31.[74] Most scholars agree, however, that Luke represents the correct placement of Q 12:33–34, which is after Q 12:22–31 and before Q 12:39–40.[75] On the one hand, Matthew's placement is obviously determined by his heavy redaction of the Q material in his Sermon on the Mount.[76] On the other hand, Luke reproduces the sequence of his source faithfully in chapter 12 of his Gospel, which includes Q 12:33–34.[77] In the final form of the Sayings Gospel, the Lukan placement of Q 12:33–34 allows for a smooth transition from Q 12:22–31 to Q 12:39–40,[78] whereas the Matthean placement of this logion interrupts the otherwise smooth transition between Q 12:2–12 and Q 12:22–31.[79] According to Marriott, "the heavenly treasure of which they speak [in Q 12:33–34] contrasts with the fool's treasure of worldly goods [in Q 12:22–31]."[80] Q 12:22–31 follows well after Q 12:11–12, since both advise against anxiety. Q 12:33–34, on the other hand, follows well after the conclusion of Q 12:31, since the process of seeking God's kingdom enables one to disregard earthly treasures and gather heavenly treasures. There is also a natural and logical progression from the bare necessities of Q 12:22–31 (like foodstuff and clothing) to the more valuable earthly "treasures" (θησαυροί) of Q 12:33–34.

If the latter is accepted, it would mean that Q 12:39 follows after Q 12:33–34 in the Sayings Gospel.[81] That Q 12:39 reaches back to a foregoing text for interpretive meaning is indicated by the conjunction "but" or "and" (δέ) in the introduction of this maxim. The proposed sequence is further substantiated by the strong literary link between Q 12:33–34 and Q 12:39. Most visibly, this link is maintained by two catchwords, namely "robber" (κλέπτης) and "dig through/into" (διορύσσω).[82] Kloppenborg holds that these catchword connections are essentially artificial.[83] He argues firstly that the two sections[84] are radically different in tone. As we have seen, however, this is not true if Q 12:39 is considered on its own. Secondly, Kloppenborg argues that Q 12:39 deals

---

[74] Robinson, Hoffmann, and Kloppenborg 2000, 328–333; 2002, 120–121.

[75] Verheyden 2007, 58; see Johnson 2007, 18–59.

[76] Castor 1912, 85; Schweizer 1973, 101; Guelich 1982, 323–324, 364; Davies and Allison 1988, 625–626, 628; Betz 1995, 426; Kloppenborg 2007, 53; Verheyden 2007, 58; Hartin 2015, 180.

[77] Mealand 1980, 51; Kloppenborg 2007, 53; Verheyden 2007, 58; Hartin 2015, 180; Howes 2018, 156.

[78] E.g. Fleddermann 2005a, 616; see chapter 10 below.

[79] E.g. Schweizer 1973, 101–102; see below.

[80] Marriott 1925, 67; cf. Fleddermann 2005a, 616; Johnson 2007, 52.

[81] Cf. Jacobson 1992, 196–198.

[82] Jacobson 1992, 196; Sato 1994, 173; Zeller 1994, 122; Allison 1997, 29.

[83] Kloppenborg 1987, 149; 1994, 148; 1996a, 28; 2000a, 126, 129.

[84] I.e. Q 12:22–31, 33–34 and Q 12:39–40, 42–46, 49, 51, 53, 54–56, 58–59.

with the *prevention of a robbery*, while Q 12:33–34 deals with the acquisition of a treasure that *cannot be stolen*. Yet this discrepancy only applies if the heavenly treasure of Q 12:33–34 is considered to be the point of comparison. If, instead, the earthly treasure is taken as the point of comparison between the two sayings, their congruity becomes evident. Both sayings reason that earthly goods can be taken away. Thirdly, Kloppenborg argues that the robber in Q 12:33–34 represents an enemy, while in Q 12:39 it represents the Son of Man. Once again, this line of reasoning only applies if verse 40 is brought into consideration. If not, the reference to a robber only serves a functional purpose in both passages.

The earlier observation that the audience is not meant to identify with either the householder or the robber in Q 12:39 becomes significant here. In Q 12:33–34, Q's Jesus warns his audience in the second person plural not to treasure for themselves earthly treasures (μὴ θησαυρίζετε ὑμῖν θησαυροὺς ἐπὶ τῆς γῆς), since earthly treasures are in danger of being robbed, among other things. Q 12:39 then takes the argument further by claiming that even well-off householders are vulnerable to theft and loss of possessions.[85] In other words, a natural progression occurs between Q 12:33–34 and Q 12:39. Q 12:33–34 speaks about the loss of goods by those on the lower levels of society, as is indicated by the close association of this text with Q 12:22–31.[86] Q 12:39 speaks about the loss of goods by those who live in the upper strata of village society. That the householder was comparatively wealthy is indicated not only by his status as the owner of a house, but also by the fact that he had people (probably a number of slaves) keeping watch over his estate.[87] Oakman sees here a reference to "a relatively well-to-do peasant dwelling."[88] Even if the householder was relatively well-off, the verb "dig through/into" (διορύσσω) suggests that he was not exceedingly rich, since the verb assumes digging through the wall of a house that was made of clay.[89] Roth describes the householder as "a master in a nonelite house."[90] However, one should perhaps not read too much into the use of this particular verb, since it was a technical term by the time Q was written, denoting straightforwardly to "break in."[91] At any rate, the purpose of the socio-economic progression from Q 12:33–34 to Q 12:39 is to provide cumulative support for the sapiential injunction not to treasure earthly treasures, but to prefer heavenly ones. If those with means are unable to truly protect their

---

[85] Cf. Valantasis 2005, 167.

[86] Cf. Piper 1989, 26.

[87] Nolland 2005, 995. In the phrase "which watch" (ποίᾳ φυλακῇ), ποῖος can be translated as either "which" or "whose" (Liddell and Scott 1996 s.v. ποῖος). Both options clearly indicate that the householder had slaves who took turns keeping watch.

[88] Oakman 2008, 126.

[89] Roth 2018, 170–171.

[90] Roth 2018, 171.

[91] Luz 2005, 219; cf. Roth 2018, 171.

possessions, even though they seem to have preventative measures in place, how much more is this true for those without means? Hence, the maxim in Q 12:39 functions to buttress the double instruction in Q 12:33–34. In fulfilling this function, Q 12:39 acts exactly like a number of other maxims in Q.[92]

Contrasting the upper and lower levels of society might serve an additional purpose. In Q 12:33–34, the destitute are advised to gather treasures in heaven, not on earth. In Q 12:39, the relatively prosperous, with the householder as representative, are portrayed as attempting to gather earthly treasures, but ultimately failing to do so.[93] Hence, both in concept and in terms of their general fortune, the poor are elevated over the relatively prosperous. This idea that, despite appearances, the poor are blessed, finds expression in another Q text, namely the beatitudes of Q 6:20–21.[94] Since the householder does not know when the robber is coming, he is forced to maintain a constant state of vigilance and anxiety. The poor, however, are freed from anxiety through God's providential care.[95] In this sense, then, the poor are better off than the relatively wealthy of village society.[96] The less treasures one has on earth, the easier it is to have treasures in heaven and be blessed in that way.[97]

What separates the poor from the rich is not only God's providential care, but also the knowledge of such care. It is the *knowledge* of God's provision that eliminates anxiety. Such knowledge comes primarily from the wisdom of Jesus, as spelled out in the Q document.[98] Thus, the poor are blessed because they possess knowledge that the rich and important do not. The content of this knowledge is the sapiential message of Q's Jesus. This basic idea is spelled out in Q 10:21, 23–24, which also belongs to the formative stratum.[99] That the maxim in Q 12:39 has this basic concept in mind is indicated by the use of two Greek words that both mean to "know" (γινώσκω and οἶδα). The logion is firstly introduced in the second person plural with the phrase "but know this" (ἐκεῖνο/τοῦτο δὲ γινώσκετε).[100] The saying proper then goes on to describe what the householder does *not* know (εἰ ᾔδει ὁ οἰκοδεσπότης). Implied by this structure and lexical deployment is a claim that the poor, to whom the maxim is directed, are in possession of specific knowledge, while the rich, whom the

---

[92] E.g. Q 6:35, 38, 39, 43–44, 12:6, 24, 27, 28; cf. Kloppenborg 1987, 238.

[93] Cf. Nolland 2005, 995.

[94] Cf. Kloppenborg 1995, 304.

[95] Piper 1989, 30, 31; Allison 2000, 172–173; cf. Q 6:20–21; 12:22–31; 13:18–21 (see chapter 6 below).

[96] Interestingly, Kloppenborg (1995, 303–304) fosters a comparable interpretation in his treatment of the interrelation between Luke (Q?) 12:16–21 and Q 12:22–31, 33–34.

[97] Cf. Roth 2018, 175.

[98] Other wisdom traditions do, however, exist that similarly advise against anxiety (Piper 1989, 33; cf. e.g. Sir 30:24–31:2; Wis 6:15; 7:23).

[99] See chapter 1 above.

[100] Etchells 1998, 98.

householder represents, lack certain knowledge. In both cases, the content of the knowledge is not only the general message of Jesus, but also the specific wisdom that one must not gather earthly treasures. It is this knowledge that frees the poor and enslaves the rich.

On a more symbolic level, the house that was burgled might be a veiled reference to the households of the urban elite in Galilee, who controlled the ancient market through economic exploitation of the countryside.[101] Q 12:33–34 might then also be a veiled reference to the storehouses of the urban elite.[102] Not only the granaries and storehouses of ancient landowners, but also palaces and temples were occasionally in antiquity burgled and vandalised, especially by social bandits and resistance movements.[103] There is not enough space to develop this idea in full, but suffice it to say that such a reading would be even more proficient in bringing the point of Q 12:39 across. If the richest of the rich, with countless options for theft prevention at their disposal, are not even able to protect their possessions, how much less would the poorest of the poor be able to do so? Moreover, the extent of the poor's fortuity and blessedness is much greater if they are favourably contrasted with urban aristocrats, as opposed (but in addition) to village householders. The idea that the village poor were better off than the urban elite was unthinkable and revolutionary for the time. If the current symbolic reading is accepted, the saying would perhaps be better classified as an aphorism, rather than a maxim.[104] It would also follow from the current reading that this saying has thematic commonalities with Q 16:13, which also belongs to the formative layer.[105]

3.5 Implied Audience

One could easily be fooled into viewing the householder and robber in Q 12:39 as outsiders, thereby deducing that the maxim itself addresses outsiders. The exposition of this maxim offered in the preceding section could even be seen to substantiate such a view. In particular, it was argued that the audience of this logion would not have identified with either the householder or the robber. The householder in particular, it was argued, represents the relatively affluent who

---

[101] Oakman 2008, 126; cf. Herzog 1994, 156.

[102] Cf. Oakman 2008, 124, 307; Boer and Petterson 2017, 83–84. Of particular significance in this regard are the words θησαυρίζω and θησαυρός. The elite were known for extracting produce from the countryside and hoarding (θησαυρίζω) it in storehouses (θησαυροί) in the city.

[103] See Horsley 1979, 37–63; 1981, 409–432; cf. Freyne 2004, 136–139.

[104] Cf. Crossan 1979, 34; 1983, 58.

[105] Oakman 2008, 93–94, 307.

are unfamiliar with the sapiential message of Jesus.[106] However, neither the presumption that the householder and robber are outsiders, nor the deduction that the maxim therefore addresses outsiders, is accurate.

In the first place, there is no reason to assume that the Q people deliberately separated themselves from either robbers or householders. Although it seems that the Q people were mostly made up of individuals from the lower levels of village society,[107] there is no evidence that they turned more prosperous villagers away, either as a matter of principle or at all.[108] In fact, the evidence seems to suggest that the Q people also harboured individuals from the higher socio-economic strata of village life.[109] Likewise, although it seems that the Q people were for the most part constituted by hardworking, respectable, and non-violent members of village society,[110] there is no evidence that they refused membership to robbers and other bandits. Generally, ancient villagers were sympathetic and approving of bandits, especially the leaders of political rebellions and "robin hood" types.[111] It is true that robbers are usually portrayed negatively in the Old Testament,[112] but in this case it is vital to recognise that these texts represent the great tradition of the elite. This is not to say that less fortunate individuals were typically fond of thieves, especially considering that they also fell victim to thievery, perhaps even more so than wealthier individuals.[113] Instead, it is to say, firstly, that the morally despised were typically welcomed in God's kingdom and, secondly, that it would depend on the kind of robber. Someone who steals from the rich to challenge the status quo or benefit the small peasantry and poor would have been regarded positively, whereas someone who steals to enrich herself at the expense of the small peasantry and poor would have been regarded negatively. On the one hand, no political or altruistic motive is provided in Q 12:39 for the robber's actions, but, on the other hand, the robber of Q 12:39 is stealing from a fairly wealthy individual. All of this is to say that one should not assume either that the Q people would have been

---

[106] Cf. Q 10:21, 23–24.

[107] Catchpole 1993, 228; Horsley 1999, 60, 179, 260–261, 269, 296–298; Kloppenborg 2000a, 198–199; Moxnes 2003, 114–119; Oakman 2008, 112; Häkkinen 2016, 7.

[108] Cf. Crossan 2002, 251.

[109] Kloppenborg 1987, 251; Catchpole 1993, 18–19; Douglas 1995, 120; Tuckett 1996, 360, 365; Freyne 2000, 206; Reed 2000, 136–137; Arnal 2001, 150, 173.

[110] Cf. Horsley 1995a, 42; Reed 1995, 24–25; 2000, 189–199.

[111] Freyne 1988, 139; Horsley 1995a, 43; Oakman 2008, 125; Häkkinen 2016, 7. It should also be mentioned that robbery and banditry were simultaneously realities that threatened livelihood and cohesion at village level (Oakman 2008, 151–152; cf. Q 11:21–22). For most villagers, the term would only have received a negative or positive valuation once it had been established who had been robbed and what had happened with the loot.

[112] See Roth 2018, 170; cf. Ps 50:18; Prov 29:24; Jer 2:26; Joel 2:9; Zech 5:3.

[113] Kloppenborg 2014, 299; cf. Oakman 2008, 151–152.

unilaterally disapproving of robbers or that robbers were automatically excluded from the in-group.

Even if one finds that the prosperous householder and opportunist robber are in this Q text compared unfavourably with the members of Q's audience, this would not necessarily lead to the conclusion that either of them represents all outsiders, including "this generation." In fact, one of the texts that features above as a thematic comparison to Q 12:39 seems to indicate the opposite. Q 10:21, 23–24 claims that God had historically chosen to hide the wisdom of Jesus from "sages and intelligent men" (σοφοί καὶ συνετοί), as well as from "prophets and kings" (προφῆται καὶ βασιλεῖς). In chapter 1 above, the following argument was made when discussing this Q text:

> As we know, the main redaction is polemically opposed to "this generation" and, more specifically, to the Pharisees, scribes, and Jerusalem elite. Elsewhere in Q (11:49–51), these outsiders are accused of killing the "sages" (σοφοί) and "prophets" (προφῆται) of old. Here, the "sages" (σοφοί) and "prophets" (προφῆται) from Israel's history not only receive a positive valuation from the main redactor, but are also clearly distinguished from the intended out-group. That prominent figures from Israel's history could form part of the in-group, even though they had never heard the message of Jesus, is indicated by Q 13:28–29. It logically and incontrovertibly follows that the "sages," "prophets," and "kings" of Q 10:21, 23–24 cannot possibly be identified with the out-group of the main redaction.[114]

If knowledge of Jesus's wisdom was kept from the sages, prophets, and kings of old, but these figures were nonetheless seen by the Q people as forming part of the in-group, the same can be said of the householder and robber in Q 12:39. The primary function of these characters is not to be representative of any group, but to act as hypothetical examples in a maxim that exposes the ease with which earthly treasures can be taken away.

The stated audience of this maxim is clearly those listening to the wisdom of Jesus as he delivers it. This audience should in all likelihood be identified with the Q people. As we have seen, the phrase "but know this" introduces the maxim. If one asks "who should know this?," the most obvious answer is the audience of Q's Jesus, hence the Q people. As we have also seen, the conjunction "but" or "and" (δέ) in the opening phrase deliberately reaches back to the foregoing material for interpretive meaning. The complex of material in Q 12:22–31, 33–34 is introduced in verse 22 with the phrase "therefore, I tell you..." (διὰ τοῦτο λέγω ὑμῖν). Indisputably, this phrase also has the Q people in mind. However, the stated audience should not necessarily be identified with the implied audience. There are a number of passages in Q that address outsiders indirectly even though the stated audience is the Q people.[115]

---

[114] *Pace* Jacobson 1978, 140–142, 144; 1992, 152, 182; Denaux 1992, 172; Kirk 1998, 343; Valantasis 2005, 111–112.

[115] Kloppenborg 1987, 167; e.g. Q 3:7–9, 16–17; 7:31–35; 10:12–15; 11:14–15, 17–20; 11:16, 29–32, 49–51.

If neither the characters of "householder" and "robber" nor the stated audience can be used as evidence in identifying the implied audience of this maxim, whereto should one turn? In my view, the sapiential form and function of this maxim is the first real piece of evidence. Since instructional wisdom is almost always directed at the in-group, the same is probably true of Q 12:39. If we are correct in maintaining that Q 12:39 forms part of the preceding material, it would logically follow that the same audience is implied by both. Since few would contest that the wisdom in either Q 12:22–31 or Q 12:33–34 is directed at the Q people, the same must also be true of Q 12:39. The type of advice given in the former two passages is typical of instructional wisdom aimed at the in-group.[116] Specifically, there would be no reason to advise hostile outsiders like "this generation" to rid themselves of anxiety (Q 12:22–31), to seek God's kingdom (Q 12:31), or to store up heavenly treasures instead of earthly ones (Q 12:33–34). Since the maxim in Q 12:39 functions to buttress the instruction against worldly treasures with evidence from everyday experience, it should also be taken as wisdom directed at the in-group.

The latter is corroborated by what is absent from the saying. Considered in isolation, the maxim lacks any hint at a threat. If anything, it has a neutral tone. It further lacks any reference, explicit or otherwise, to "this generation." In fact, the saying seems wholly unconcerned with either boundary formation or the apocalyptic end. It has this in common with the material that precedes it.[117] I think it can be said with relative confidence that the Q people are the exclusive audience of this maxim.

3.6 Findings

This chapter began by calling into question the established position that the robber saying in Q 12:39 and the Son of Man saying in Q 12:40 were attached during the prehistory of Q's formation. Instead, it was argued that the latter saying was added to the complex of material in Q 12:22–31, 33–34, 39 by the main redactor. Room was thereby made to reconsider the usual attribution of the robber saying in Q 12:39 to the main redaction. It was found that the maxim in verse 39 rather belongs to the instructional wisdom of the formative layer, while the saying in verse 40 should retain its place in the main redaction. In the process, the original function of Q 12:39 in the formative stratum was exposed, namely to buttress the double instruction in Q 12:33–34. This conclusion substantiates a suspicion long held by other scholars. Jacobson, for example, proposed more than twenty years ago that Q 12:40 was only added to the complex

---

[116] Cf. e.g. Bultmann 1994, 30; see e.g. Piper 1989, 24–36; Allison 2000, 172–174.
[117] Cf. Kloppenborg 2000a, 129; see Piper 1989, 31–35, 103–104.

of material in Q 12:33–34, [35–38,] 39, 42–46 after this complex had already been compiled at an earlier redactional stage.[118]

---

[118] Jacobson 1992, 197–198.

Chapter 4

Q 12:42–46, "Cut in Two"[1]

⁴²τίς ἄρα ἐστὶν ὁ πιστὸς δοῦλος ⟦καὶ⟧ φρόνιμος ὃν κατέστησεν ὁ κύριος ἐπὶ τῆς οἰκετείας αὐτοῦ τοῦ δο⟦ῦ⟧ναι ⟦αὐτοῖς⟧ ἐν καιρῷ ⟦σιτομέτριον¹⟧; ⁴³μακάριος ὁ δοῦλος ἐκεῖνος, ὃν ἐλθὼν ὁ κύριος αὐτοῦ εὑρήσει οὕτως ποιοῦντα· ⁴⁴⟦ἀμὴν⟧ λέγω ὑμῖν ὅτι ἐπὶ πᾶσιν τοῖς ὑπάρχουσιν αὐτοῦ καταστήσει αὐτόν. ⁴⁵ἐὰν δὲ εἴπῃ ὁ δοῦλος ἐκεῖνος ἐν τῇ καρδίᾳ αὐτοῦ· χρονίζει ὁ κύριος μου, καὶ ἄρξηται τύπτειν τοὺς ⟦συνδούλους αὐτοῦ⟧, ἐσθί⟦ῃ⟧ δὲ καὶ πίνῃ ⟦μετὰ τῶν⟧ μεθυ⟦όντων⟧, ⁴⁶ἥξει ὁ κύριος τοῦ δούλου ἐκείνου ἐν ἡμέρᾳ ᾗ οὐ προσδοκᾷ καὶ ἐν ὥρᾳ ᾗ οὐ γινώσκει, καὶ διχοτομήσει αὐτὸν καὶ τὸ μέρος αὐτοῦ μετὰ τῶν ἀπίστων θήσει.

⁴²Who then is the faithful ⟦and⟧ wise slave whom the master put over his household to give ⟦them⟧ ⟦a ration of grain²⟧ on time? ⁴³Blessed is that slave whose master, on coming, will find so doing. ⁴⁴⟦Amen⟧, I tell you, he will appoint him over all his possessions. ⁴⁵But if that slave says in his heart: My master is delayed, and begins to beat ⟦his fellow slaves⟧, and eats and drinks ⟦with the⟧ drunk⟦ards⟧, ⁴⁶the master of that slave will come on a day he does not expect and at an hour he does not know, and will cut him to pieces and give him an inheritance with the faithless.

There is enough verbal and grammatical overlap between the Matthean and Lukan versions of this tradition to justify its place in the Sayings Gospel Q.[3] As we saw in the previous chapter, Kloppenborg treats the cluster of sayings in Q 12:39–59[4] together, claiming that "[t]he threat of apocalyptic judgment recurs as the formative literary and theological motif."[5] He distinguishes this cluster from the foregoing material (Q 12:22–34) on grounds of general tone and basic motif: "Whereas 12:22–34 is hortatory in character and sapiential in its idiom and mode of argumentation, 12:39–59 is aggressive and threatening in tone, and marked by warnings of judgment."[6] He further argues that the

---

[1] This chapter draws heavily on four articles published separately in the following journals: *Acta Classica* 58 (see Howes 2015c); two articles in *HTS Theological Studies* 71/1 (see Howes 2015d; 2015e); *Acta Theologica* Supplementum 23 (see Howes 2016b).

[2] The reason for preferring Luke's σιτομετρία ("measure/ration of corn/grain") over Matthew's τροφή ("food" or "nourishment") is explained later on in the chapter.

[3] Dodd 1958, 158; Crossan 1974a, 22; Marshall 1978, 533; Scott 1989, 208–209; Taylor 1989, 138; Funk and Hoover 1993, 253; Luz 2005, 221; see Bock 1996, 1171 n. 3; Roth 2018, 88–89.

[4] That is, Q 12:39–40, 42–46, 49, 51–53, (54–56), 57–59.

[5] Kloppenborg 1987, 148–154.

[6] Kloppenborg 1987, 149.

foregoing material is aimed at the Q people, while Q 12:39–59 breaches the boundaries of the Q people, threatening everyone with apocalyptic judgement.

Regarding the parable in Q 12:42–46, Kloppenborg rightly claims that it "gains its explicit connection with the coming Son of Man through its attachment to 12:39–40."[7] According to Kloppenborg, the parable originally addressed the delay of the parousia and functioned as a warning for leaders of the Jesus movement to be faithful and trustworthy stewards during the interim.[8] In the context of Q, however, the parable of the loyal and wise slave has been attached to Q 12:40, thereby highlighting not only the unexpectedness and suddenness of the impending parousia, but also the catastrophic consequences that will accompany it.[9] As such, the whole composition of Q 12:39–46 acts as a warning to be prepared for the Son of Man and his devastating parousia.[10]

In what follows, it will be argued that Q 12:42–44 belongs to the formative stratum and that Q 12:45–46 was added by the main redactor to redirect the message and intent of the whole pericope. Before we attend to the stratigraphy of Q 12:42–46, however, it is necessary to consider the internal make-up of this passage. Since Q 12:42–44 is presented as an intrinsic part of Q 12:42–46 in the final form of the Sayings Gospel, the proposal that it originally featured in isolation requires justification.

4.1 Exposing the Seam

Given the parable's composite nature, featuring a rhetorical question, an amen saying, a beatitude, and a conditional judgment saying, it seems likely that the content evolved over a period of time.[11] Even from a superficial reading of the parable, it is immediately evident that, on the one hand, verses 42–44 belong together, and on the other, verses 45–46 belong together. A closer look at the text supports this intuitive observation. There are a number of textual indications that betray a redactional seam between verses 44 and 45.

4.1.1 A Double Ending

The first and most obvious indication of a redactional seam between Q 12:42–44 and Q 12:45–46 is the parable's idiosyncratic double ending. The parable of the loyal and wise slave is distinctive in featuring two possible outcomes:

---

[7] Kloppenborg 1987, 150; cf. Kirk 1998, 233; Roth 2018, 175–176.

[8] Kloppenborg 1987, 150.

[9] Cf. Kloppenborg 2000a, 118.

[10] Cf. Uro 1996, 94; Allison 1997, 27; Fleddermann 2005a, 635.

[11] See Crossan 1983, 59–60; cf. Dodd 1958, 158; Scott 1989, 211; Jacobson 1992, 197; Kirk 1998, 234; Fleddermann 2005a, 633, 635; Luz 2005, 221.

one positive and one negative.[12] Without attempting to address redactional development, Fleddermann tellingly labels verses 45–46 the "negative half of the parable."[13] The only other parable of Jesus to also feature both a positive and a negative outcome is the parable of the wedding feast in Luke 12:35–38.[14] In the case of both parables, featuring a double ending is evidence of redactional development.[15] It is only logical to assume that the second ending represents redactional elaboration, not the first ending. In addition, the artificiality of featuring the same character for two opposite endings supports not only the proposal of a seam between verses 44 and 45, but also the claim that the second ending is most probably secondary.[16] In being disloyal rather than loyal and reckless rather than prudent, the second character does not fit the criteria established by the opening question, but contradicts them by veering off in a different direction.[17] As Valantasis correctly notes: "A switch has taken place in the narrative."[18]

4.1.2 Small Forms

One cannot help but notice that the first half of the parable is made up of a series of small forms. Each of the first three verses qualifies technically as a separate *Mikrogattung*.[19] Verse 42 introduces the parable with a rhetorical question.[20] Verse 43 constitutes a makarism or beatitude.[21] Verse 44 is an amen saying that functions both to buttress the beatitude in the previous verse and to conclude the train of thought.[22] In obvious contradiction to Q 12:42–44, verses 45 and 46 harbour no literary small forms whatsoever. The lack of small form indicators in Q 12:45–46 is highly suggestive of redactional invention. What is more, this shortage strongly suggests that Q 12:45–46 was added to Q 12:42–44, as opposed to the other way around.

---

[12] Cf. Donahue 1988, 98; Taylor 1989, 141; Etchells 1998, 110; Allison 2004, 439; Valantasis 2005, 168.

[13] Fleddermann 2005a, 628, 633, 635.

[14] Kirk 1998, 234. I do not consider Q 6:47–49 to be a parable (cf. Luz 2005, 221, 223).

[15] Cf. Funk 2006, 30.

[16] See Funk 1974, 53–54; cf. Jeremias 1963, 55–56; Crossan 1974a, 22; Marshall 1978, 542; Blomberg 1990, 191; Bock 1996, 1180; Luz 2005, 221, 222.

[17] Cf. Nolland 2005, 998.

[18] Valantasis 2005, 169.

[19] Jacobson 1992, 197; Fleddermann 2005a, 627, 633, 635, 636.

[20] Dodd 1958, 158; Luz 2005, 221.

[21] Crossan 1983, 59; Scott 1989, 211; Jacobson 1994, 101 n. 9; Bock 1996, 1179; Kirk 1998, 234; Luz 2005, 221; Nolland 2005, 998; Hays 2012, 50.

[22] Marshall 1978, 541; cf. Kirk 1998, 234; Scott 1989, 211.

4.1.3 Literary Emphasis

That the pericope should be dissected between verses 44 and 45 is further suggested by the fact that verse 44 features no less than two literary emphases, namely the exclamation "amen" (ἀμήν)[23] and the phrase "I tell you" (λέγω ὑμῖν). The combination of these two exclamations strongly suggests that verse 44 was the original ending of Q 12:42–44.[24] The phrase "I tell you" is particularly telling, since it is often used in Q to conclude a pericope.[25] Although intended as a synchronic rather than a diachronic observation, Fleddermann agrees that the latter phrase "brings the first half of the parable to a close."[26] If Q 12:42–44 originally ended at verse 44, it is justified to regard Q 12:45–46 as a secondary addition.

4.1.4 Narrative Mode

If emphatic exclamations betray verse 44 as the original conclusion of Q 12:42–44, a shift in narrative mode reveals a new beginning at verse 45.[27] Whereas verses 42–44 are narrated by an omniscient, third-person narrator, verse 45 introduces the protagonist's internal dialogue through first-person narration.[28] The phrase "says in his heart" (εἴπῃ ἐν τῇ καρδίᾳ αὐτοῦ) represents a familiar Semitic idiom that qualifies whatever follows as internal dialogue.[29] The change in narrative mode is therefore quite deliberate.

4.1.5 Redundant Re-identification of Character

The re-identification of characters in verses 45–46 is also fairly incriminating. The opening question introduces the main characters as a "master" (κύριος) and an appointed "slave" (δοῦλος).[30] In order to link the subsequent logion to

---

[23] Luke has "truly" (ἀληθῶς) (Marshall 1978, 541; Bock 1996, 1180; Fleddermann 2005a, 627–628; Nolland 2005, 998).

[24] Cf. Allison 2004, 440.

[25] Cf. Q 7:28 as the conclusion of Q 7:24–28; Q 10:12 as the ending of Q 10:10–12; Q 10:24 as the conclusion of Q 10:21–24; Q 11:51 as the ending of Q 11:49–51; Q 12:59 as the conclusion of Q 12:58–59; Q 13:35 as the consummation of Q 13:34–35; Q 15:7 as the application of Q 15:4–5, 7; (Q 15:10 as the application of Q 15:8–10); and Q 17:34–35 as the conclusion of Q 17:26–27, 30, 34–35. On a few occasions, the same phrase is also used to introduce a pericope (cf. Q 11:9; 12:22). Finally, the phrase "I tell you" is also sometimes used in the middle of a pericope, but in those cases it features to buttress the preceding claim (cf. Q 7:26; 12:27). Yet in not one of these latter cases does the subsequent content develop in an opposite or alternative direction, which is indeed what happens with Q 12:45–46.

[26] Fleddermann 2005a, 636.

[27] Cf. Allison 2004, 441.

[28] Scott 1989, 211; Roth 2018, 93.

[29] Marshall 1978, 542; Bock 1996, 1181; Allison 2004, 441.

[30] Roth 2018, 93.

this question, these characters are once again identified specifically as "that slave" (ὁ δοῦλος ἐκεῖνος) and "his master" (ὁ κύριος αὐτοῦ) in verse 43.[31] Such linkage is necessary to indicate continuation of the narrative and argument, although it might also be an indication of redactional development at an earlier stage.[32] With the association between verses 42 and 43 established and the characters appropriately identified, the author is free to reference both main characters in verse 44 through a verb suffix (καταστήσει) and two personal pronouns (αὐτοῦ and αὐτόν).[33] There is no longer any need to identify the characters specifically as "master" (κύριος) or "slave" (δοῦλος). One would therefore expect the author to continue using only verb suffixes and personal pronouns when referencing these characters in the rest of the parable. Yet verse 45 re-identifies the servile character unnecessarily as "that slave" (ὁ δοῦλος ἐκεῖνος), and verse 46 re-identifies the slaveholder unnecessarily as "the master of that slave" (ὁ κύριος τοῦ δούλου ἐκείνου).[34] These re-identifications seem like a deliberate, albeit artificial, literary attempt to connect these characters with the ones in verses 42–44 and to prevent confusion between the two individual characters themselves. Particularly noticeable is the repeated use of the demonstrative pronoun (ἐκεῖνος) and the wordiness of the phrase "the master of that slave" (ὁ κύριος τοῦ δούλου ἐκείνου).[35] The careful re-identification of the slave only serves to highlight the more fundamental artificiality of using "the same slave in different scenarios to depict both the good and bad behaviour."[36] Besides illuminating the seam between verses 44 and 45, these features of Q 12:45–46 betray an obsession with literary exactitude and lucidity. Such fixation strongly suggests that a redactor was responsible for these two verses.

4.1.6 On One Condition

Verse 45 begins with both the contrastive conjunction "but" (δέ) and the conditional conjunction "if" (ἐάν), thereby introducing Q 12:45–46 with a contrastive conditional clause.[37] Semantically, this beginning to verse 45 serves to indicate that the appointed slave also has a second option, which is in some way opposite to the first one.[38] It is strange, however, that the preceding verses do not also feature a conditional sentence, introduced by "if" (ἐάν). Whenever a narrative or argument features a choice with two options, each with its own consequences, it is customary to present the first option as "if ... then" and the

---

[31] Fleddermann 2005a, 636.

[32] Cf. Zeller 1994, 122.

[33] Fleddermann 2005a, 636.

[34] Cf. Fleddermann 2005a, 637.

[35] Cf. Taylor 1989, 140.

[36] Quotation from Roth 2018, 93.

[37] Cf. Fleddermann 2005a, 628, 633, 635.

[38] Bock 1996, 1180–1181; cf. Crossan 1974a, 22.

second option as "but if … then." The lack of a conditional clause in the first half of the parable therefore suggests that the author of Q 12:42–44 did not wish to introduce a choice with two options at all, even though the existence of such a choice is implied.[39] The author of verses 42–44 wanted to focus solely on a singular positive action with its consequences and had no intention of explicitly mentioning or describing a second option or its consequences. It is therefore safe to assume that the material introduced by "but if" (ἐάν δέ), meaning verses 45–46, comprise a secondary expansion of the parable.

4.1.7 The Doubling of Narrative Elements

Not only the existence of a redactional seam between verses 44 and 45, but also the probability that Q 12:45–46 represents redactional elaboration are further suggested by the fact that verses 45–46 double the elements of verses 42–44. The singular action in verse 42 of feeding the slaves is paralleled by the two actions in verse 45 of keeping improper company and beating fellow slaves.[40] Similarly, the single reward in verse 44 of being appointed over everything is mirrored by the two punishments in verse 46 of being "cut in two" (διχοτομέω) and receiving "an inheritance with the faithless" (τὸ μέρος αὐτοῦ μετὰ τῶν ἀπίστων). The text-critical principle according to which the shorter reading is more likely to be original (*lectio brevior*) could here be applied to the redaction of Q 12:42–46.[41]

The redactional acts of multiplying the desired conduct of verse 42 into two separate accusations in verse 45 and of doubling the single reward to two separate forms of punishment were likely intended to shift the parable's emphasis and reallocate its focus to the second half.[42] In the process, the spotlight was moved away from encouragement and motivation towards accusation and condemnation.[43] This tactic was highly effective, convincing not only ancient authors (like Matthew), but also modern scholars[44] that the parable's emphasis and meaning are both to be found in the parable's second half.[45]

---

[39] Cf., however, Marshall 1978, 540; Luz 2005, 222.

[40] Cf. Roth 2018, 94.

[41] Cf. Brotzman 1994, 128.

[42] See Hunter 1971, 12; Donahue 1988, 98–99; Taylor 1989, 146, 149, 150; Blomberg 1990, 192.

[43] Cf. Blomberg 1990, 191; Kloppenborg 2000a, 141.

[44] Like Taylor 1989, 146, 149, 150; Jacobson 1992, 197; Snodgrass 2008, 499; Roth 2018, 94, 96.

[45] See Donahue 1988, 98–99; cf. Hunter 1971, 12; Blomberg 1990, 192; Allison 2004, 441.

4.1.8 Abuse to the Literal Level

The punishment in verse 46 of being "cut in two" (διχοτομέω) refers to the gruesome and brutal ancient practice of "death by sawing," whereby a person was killed by being sawed into two longitudinal or latitudinal halves.[46] In Roman, Egyptian and Jewish societies, the slave's body belonged to the *paterfamilias* (and his nuclear family), who had complete control over it and could violate or abuse it as he saw fit.[47] In both societies, corporal punishment was not only permissible, but actually also encouraged as a means of promoting obedience and discipline. Being "cut in two" is only the first of two punishments. The second punishment is that the master will "give him an inheritance with the faithless" (τὸ μέρος αὐτοῦ μετὰ τῶν ἀπίστων θήσει). I have argued elsewhere that when the words in this phrase are considered against the background of ancient slavery, it is better translated as "assign his allotment of duties with the untrustworthy slaves."[48] However this second punishment is interpreted, on the literal level of the parable it requires the slave to still be alive after receiving the first punishment.[49] As such, non-fatal dismemberment appears to be the most likely meaning of διχοτομέω on the purely literal level of the parable.[50] This is not, however, the denotative lexical meaning of διχοτομέω, which does refer specifically to "death by sawing." If the second punishment requires the slave to still be alive, it is problematic on the literal level of the story that the first punishment already kills the slave. It would therefore seem as though the punishments in verse 46 were conceived from the outset because of their utility on the metaphorical level, but with disregard for the literal imagery of the parable. In other words, the logical incompatibility of the two punishments on the parable's literal level was either overlooked or ignored when verse 46 was formulated. The metaphorical reference to eternal damnation of the out-group in Gehenna or hell[51] was more important when these punishments were authored than the internal coherence and consistency of the literal story.[52] Such mutilation of the literal imagery strongly suggests secondary elaboration. As a solution, Gregg proposes that "the two punishments may very well have been intended to communicate the totality of the

---

[46] E.g. Dodd 1958, 159 n. 1; Marshall 1978, 543; Donahue 1988, 100; Taylor 1989, 143–144; Bock 1996, 1182; Luz 2005, 224–225; Nolland 2005, 1000; Hays 2012, 47 n. 32; cf. Botha 1996, 279; DuBois 2009, 55; Roth 2018, 96, 101; see Schlier 1964; cf. e.g. *Ahiqar* 8:38.

[47] Massey and Moreland 1992, 26; Hezser 2005, 204; see De Vaux 1965, 84–85; Bradley 1984, 118–123; cf. Nolland 2005, 999; Joshel 2010, 40, 114.

[48] Howes 2015c, 104.

[49] Dodd 1958, 159 n. 1; Marshall 1978, 543; Taylor 1989, 143–144; Bock 1996, 1182; Nolland 2005, 1000.

[50] See Howes 2015c, 100–101.

[51] See below.

[52] Cf. Roth 2018, 102.

judgment, both temporal and eschatological."[53] This "solution" achieves little more than proving my point, however, because it only works on the metaphorical level.

4.1.9 Technical Style

A related indication of the disunity between Q 12:42–44 and Q 12:45–46 is the technical style of each. Whereas Q 12:42–44 is syntactically succinct and compressed, Q 12:45–46 is syntactically elaborate and convoluted.[54] The former is reminiscent of not only Semitic style and syntax, but also the general style of the historical Jesus. Conversely, the latter is characteristic of not only Greek style and syntax, but also scribal activity in general. Like the aforementioned doubling of narrative elements, the syntactical disparity between the two halves of the parable tenders for a redactional application of the text-critical principle of *lectio brevior*. The wordiness of Q 12:45–46 exposes it as the redactional addition.

4.1.10 Parallelism

In its final form, the formal arrangement of Q 12:45–46 is highly suggestive of redactional intent. Verse 45 forms an antithetic parallelism with verse 43 by describing the opposite behaviour, and verse 46 forms an antithetic parallelism with verse 44 by spelling out the opposite consequences.[55] Such literary arrangement seems like a deliberate attempt to unify a pericope that is intrinsically multipart.

4.1.11 Tone

A change in tone is noticeable when the two halves of the parable are compared. We already saw that Fleddermann divides the parable into a "positive" and a "negative" half.[56] Q 12:42–44 is wholly and highly positive, not only in its ultimate conclusion of a significant reward, but also in its descriptions of the characters and their conduct. The appointed slave is described as "wise," "loyal," and "blessed." His main task to feed fellow slaves on time is also decidedly positive. The latter would have been particularly true in the estimation of ancient audiences from lower socio-economic strata. By contrast, the tone of Q 12:45–46 is intrinsically negative. The slave is imagined as keeping questionable company and resorting to physical violence against his fellow slaves. His double punishment is extremely severe. To be sure, the tone of Q 12:45–

---

[53] Gregg 2006, 216.

[54] See Fleddermann 2005a, 635–636.

[55] Crossan 1974a, 22; 1983, 59–60; Scott 1989, 211; Bock 1996, 1181; Roth 2018, 90, 91; see Taylor 1989, 141–144; cf. Allison 2004, 439; Luz 2005, 221.

[56] Fleddermann 2005a, 628, 633, 635.

46 is more than just "negative"; it is manifestly threatening. On the level of application, verse 45 was probably intended as an accusation, while verse 46 was probably intended as a threat. This explains why some scholars have described the whole parable as threatening in tone.[57] It would seem, though, that this description applies only to the second half of the parable. The accusation of verse 45 reveals the conditions under which the threat of verse 46 would be applicable. The rest of the parable is wholly and intrinsically unthreatening.

4.1.12 An Imperfect Analogy

Few scholars would disagree that Q 12:45–46 references the final judgement. Despite the apparentness of the parable's apocalyptic application, its artificial nature protrudes beneath the surface. In the process of adding verses 45–46 to the parable, the redactor created an imperfect analogy for apocalyptic judgement, especially if compared to the rest of Q. Regarding both reward and punishment, life carries on as normal for everyone except the appointed slave. This eventuality indicates that the parable does not imagine a dramatic cessation of the space-time continuum. In both the cases of reward and punishment, the consequences take place within the narrative world of the story. The narrative world is not discontinued or drastically changed. This feature differs entirely from the descriptions of apocalyptic cessation and finality in other Q texts, like Q 3:7 and Q 17:27. The parable does not seem to imagine a "next world," whether this-worldly or other-worldly, but rather a change occurring *within this world* for a specific person or group of people only.[58] Such a description of the apocalyptic end is fundamentally at odds with the rest of Q.

4.1.13 Additional Clues of Elaboration

Six additional clues point to the secondary nature of verses 45–46. The first is the general tendency of textual redactors in the early church to affix the most extensive and significant expansions to the end of Jesus's parables, generally making only smaller and lesser alterations to the beginning and middle of these parables.[59] The second is the fact that verses 42–44 are semantically independent, meaning that they could stand alone without any loss of meaning, whereas verses 45–46 are dependent upon the preceding material for the generation of its meaning. The third is the intertextual parallel with the story of Joseph in Genesis 39,[60] which coheres perfectly with verses 42–44, but is diametrically contradicted by verses 45–46, since Joseph was neither guilty of the misdeeds described in verse 45, nor punished in any way after becoming the Pharaoh's

---

[57] See e.g. Kloppenborg 1987, 148–154.

[58] Cf. Funk 2006, 46, 71.

[59] Jeremias 1963, 103; 1966, 81; cf. Crossan 1979, 31; Funk 2006, 30.

[60] See Allison 2000, 87–92; Luz 2005, 223–224; see below.

personal slave. The fourth is the near-perfect fit of the parable to the situation of the early church, which, upon closer inspection, relates particularly to verses 45–46.[61] The fifth is that the narrative complication differs in the two halves of the story, with the slave's actions in the first half being enabled solely by the master's absence and the slave's actions in the second half being motivated by the master's delayed return.[62] The second scenario relates well to the situation in the early church.[63] Finally, a number of scholars have noticed the verbal and conceptual similarities between the Son of Man saying in Q 12:40 and the second ending of the parable in Q 12:46.[64] Either the wording of verse 40 was modified to match the parable's second ending, or the wording of verse 46 was modified to fit the content of the Son of Man logion. A third possibility is that both verses were constructed at the same time to correspond to each other. Whatever the case, the similarity in wording between these two verses is highly suggestive of editorial activity and organisation.[65]

4.1.14 Findings

A rather strong case has been made for the existence of a redactional seam between verses 44 and 45 of the parable in Q 12:42–46. In the process, an equally strong case has been made for viewing the second half of this parable (Q 12:45–46) as a redactional addition to its first half (Q 12:42–44). The parable's second half is unlikely to be authentic, since it cannot possibly stand on its own and remain comprehensible, amongst other reasons. The authenticity of the parable's first half is an open question, depending to a large extent on how one interprets this earlier version of the parable.

---

[61] E.g. Marshall 1978, 534; see Bock 1996, 1171; cf. Fleddermann 1986, 26; Scott 1989, 210; Funk and Hoover 1993, 253, 342.

[62] See Roth 2018, 90–92, 103.

[63] Cf. Fleddermann 1986, 26.

[64] E.g. Kloppenborg 1987, 150; 1995, 293; Luz 2005, 223; see chapter 3 above. Verse 40: "the Son of Man *comes at an hour* you *do not expect*" (ᾗ οὐ δοκεῖτε ὥρᾳ ὁ υἱὸς τοῦ ἀνθρώπου ἔρχεται); verse 46: "the master of that slave will *come* on a day he *does not expect* and *at an hour* he does not know" (ἥξει ὁ κύριος τοῦ δούλου ἐκείνου ἐν ἡμέρᾳ ᾗ οὐ προσδοκᾷ καὶ ἐν ὥρᾳ ᾗ οὐ γινώσκει).

[65] Cf. Kloppenborg 1995, 293; see chapter 3 above.

4.2 Hermeneutical Approach

In its final form, Q 12:42–46 is clearly a parable,[66] as defined by Scott.[67] It is a *mashal* (or proverb) with a short narrative fiction that is in some way symbolic of God's kingdom. It contains all three of the elements deemed by Crossan to be essential for a narrative to be generally classified under the genre "parable": narrative form, metaphorical process, and appropriate qualifier.[68] Luz is technically correct when he points out that Q 12:42–46 only presupposes a narrative and does therefore not formally qualify as a narrative.[69] Even so, the text's clear presupposition of a narrative qualifies it as a parable. Notwithstanding the definitions offered by Scott and Crossan, not all the parables of Jesus feature, or even presuppose, a narrative.[70] In this regard, it is perhaps more significant that Q 12:42–46 coheres to Dodd's classical definition of a parable as a "metaphor or simile drawn from nature or common life, arresting the hearer by its vividness or strangeness, and leaving the mind in sufficient doubt about its precise application to tease it into active thought."[71] Notably, parable scholars all tend to include this text in their respective lists of parables.[72]

If we are correct that verses 45–46 were added by the main redactor, it would be important to try and understand verses 42–44 on their own, which would presumably reveal the earlier meaning and function of this passage in Q's formative stratum. It seems appropriate to also classify Q 12:42–44 (without verses 45–46) as a "parable," since these three verses, considered in isolation, fulfil the same criteria discussed above in relation to the whole text. Even though these verses are made up of three separate small forms, their thematic content is deliberately obscured and inherently parabolic.[73] If this is correct, how should the parable in verses 42–44 be interpreted? One's hermeneutical approach will depend largely on whether or not one believes that Q 12:42–44 deliberately recalls stock metaphors from ancient Judaism.[74] The institution of slavery was metaphorically applied to many other realities in the ancient world and Judaism in particular. Three of these metaphors are particularly relevant to Q 12:42–44. Firstly, Israel is often described as God's slave in Jewish sources

---

[66] Bock 1996, 1172.

[67] Scott 1989, 7–62.

[68] Crossan 1979, 20; 2012, 1–10.

[69] Luz 2005, 221.

[70] See Hunter 1971, 11; Donahue 1988, 5; cf. Dodd 1958, 18.

[71] Dodd 1958, 16.

[72] E.g. Dodd 1958, 158–160; Hunter 1964, 121–122; Jeremias 1966, 189–191; Donahue 1988, 234–235; Scott 1989, 207–212; Blomberg 1990, 190–193; Etchells 1998, 107–112.

[73] See Funk 2006, 29–31; cf. Marshall 1978, 532; Crossan 1979, 34.

[74] Cf. Roth 2018, 97, 100.

and was often regarded by Jews and gentiles alike as a "nation of slaves."[75] Secondly, Jewish leaders, including kings, priests, and prophets, were often described in Jewish literature as God's "special slaves," who were accountable to God and responsible for managing the people.[76] Thirdly, the same Old Testament and extra-biblical Second Temple texts that depict the nation of Israel collectively, Jewish worshippers individually, and the leaders of Israel specifically, as slaves, depict God[77] as the master of those slaves.[78] If these three stock metaphors are applied to Q 12:42–44, it would follow that the appointed slave represents Jewish leadership, the other slaves represent the nation of Israel, and the master represents God (or Jesus). A number of notable parable scholars have taken this approach when interpreting the parable.[79] One possible meaning of the parable would then be that the political, economic, and religious leaders of Israel are responsible for feeding the populace, and that God will reward those who do so.[80] The main problem with this line of interpretation is that it is allegorical.[81] The characters in the story are each related to a different entity in the "real" world through the application of a different stock metaphor. Instead, it is my contention that Jesus applied the slavery metaphor in a novel way without drawing on any of these stock metaphors.[82] This is supported by the other parables and maxims in Q, which create new metaphors instead of merely recycling existing ones. For example, the other parables in Q that deal

---

[75] Dodd 1958, 160; Bradley 1994, 65; DuBois 2009, 52, 54–66; Roth 2018, 97; see Hezser 2005, 61–63, 328–332, 341–343; 2009, 125; cf. Massey and Moreland 1992, 5, 26; Thurén 2014, 305; Boer and Petterson 2017, 176–177; De Wet 2018, 11.

[76] Dodd 1958, 160 n. 2; Jeremias 1963, 57–58; 1966, 44–45; Hunter 1964, 120; Marshall 1978, 533; Donahue 1988, 99; Bock 1996, 1183; Allison 2004, 440; Hezser 2005, 331 n. 19, 327–328; DuBois 2009, 52; see Michel 1967, 150–151; Harrill 2006, 96, 103–105, 109; cf. Josh 24:29; Judg 2:8; 15:18; 2 Sam 3:18; 7:5; 1 Kgs 11:13; 2 Kgs 9:7; 17:13; Ps 18:1; 36:1; Jer 7:25; 26:5; 29:26; 35:15; Ezek 34:23, 24; 37:24; 38:17; Hag 2:23; Zech 1:6; Mal 3:22 (4:4).

[77] Or Christ, as in the case of Paul.

[78] Cf. Bock 1996, 1183; Etchells 1998, 109; Allison 2004, 440; Roth 2018, 97; cf. Josh 24:29; Judg 2:8; 15:18; 2 Sam 3:18; 7:5; 1 Kgs 11:13; 2 Kgs 9:7; 17:13; Ps 18:1; 36:1; 119:91; Isa 41:8–9; 42:1, 19; 44:21; 65:13–14; Jer 7:25; 26:5; 35:15; Ezek 34:23, 24; 37:24; 38:17; Hag 2:23; Zech 1:6; Mal 3:22 (4:4); 1QS 11:16; 4Q264 3; 4Q421 9:3; Pss. Sol. 7:8/9; 10:4; Jos. Asen. 17:10; Philo, *Cherubim* 107; *Worse* 56; *Sobriety* 55; *Good Person* 42; Rom 1:1; 1 Cor 7:22; Gal 1:10; Phil 1:1. In the works of Philo, the estate manager (ἐπίτροπος) represents the Jewish elite, including priests, judges, and government officials, while the master represents God.

[79] E.g. Dodd 1958, 160; Jeremias 1963, 58, 166; 1966, 44–45; Hunter 1964, 79; Donahue 1988, 99; Etchells 1998, 109; Nolland 2005, 997.

[80] See Howes 2016b, 110–130.

[81] Cf. Thurén 2014, 305; Roth 2018, 98.

[82] Cf. Martinsen 2011, 138–139.

with slavery do not, at least not in my reading of them, feature the slaveholder as representative of God on the metaphorical level.[83]

It follows that the socio-historical context of slavery in ancient Judaism is probably much more relevant to the interpretation of this parable than the stock metaphors related to slavery in ancient Judaism. It is generally agreed and taken for granted that the background for the parable of the loyal and wise slave is an ancient farm, most probably a fairly large estate in rural Galilee.[84] It is, nonetheless, noteworthy that neither the opening verse nor the rest of the parable make explicit reference to agriculture or husbandry. There is not one lexis, term, or phrase that unambiguously denotes agricultural activity, animals, personnel, or implements. Even the Lukan version is not necessarily about a farm. The Lukan term σιτομετρία ("measure/ration of corn/grain") could have been used in the context of urban barter exchanges and marketplaces, and the Lukan word "manager" (οἰκονόμος) can reference the manager of either an urban household or a rural estate.[85] Even so, it remains highly likely that the parable has a rural setting in mind. If the parable derives from the historical Jesus, the Galilean countryside is the most likely setting for its original delivery, as it is for most of the Jesus tradition, especially the parables.[86] The same is true if the parable appeared for the first time in the Sayings Gospel Q, seeing as most scholars agree that it was compiled in or near Galilean villages.[87] What is more, if considering purely the quantity and percentage of material about farming in Q, the document seems somewhat preoccupied with this particular subject matter.[88] Finally, the Jewish tradition associates slavery with wealthy husbandmen and landowners, who often appointed managers to supervise their estates.[89] It follows that the parable in Q 12:42–44 should probably be read against the

---

[83] See chapters 8 and 9 below; cf. Funk 1974, 68; Thurén 2014, 305; *pace* e.g. Boer and Petterson 2017, 177.

[84] Cf. Kloppenborg 1995, 294; Bock 1996, 1179; Etchells 1998, 110; Harrill 2006, 113.

[85] Liddell and Scott 1996 s.v. οἰκονόμος; cf. Michel 1967, 150; Bock 1996, 1179; Nolland 2005, 997; Harrill 2006, 103.

[86] Cf. Dodd 1958, 21; Funk 2006, 44, 61; Oakman 2008, 118–119.

[87] Horsley 1999, 46; see Reed 1995, 21–24; 2000, 170–196; Kloppenborg 2000a, 174–175.

[88] Cf. Reed 1995, 24–25; 2000, 189–199; Park 2019, 44. These include references to the axing of fruit trees (Q 3:8–9), grain farming procedures (Q 3:17), agricultural measuring standards (Q 6:38), fruit trees bearing figs and grapes (Q 6:43–44), the ploughing of fields (Q 9:62), harvest workers (Q 10:2), sheep farming (Q 10:3; 15:4–5, 7), growing spices (Q 11:42), the process of sowing, reaping, and gathering in barns (Q 12:24; 19:21, 22), field hay used for cheap fuel (Q 12:28), a grain of mustard seeds (Q 13:19; 17:6), small plots or gardens (Q 13:19), cultivated fields (Q 14:18), the salting of dunghills (Q 14:35), millstones (Q 17:2), a sycamine tree (Q 17:6), the milling of grain (Q 17:35), and vultures circling the corpse of an animal (or human being) (Q 17:37).

[89] Hezser 2005, 299; cf. Boer and Petterson 2017, 141; cf. Gen 15:2–3; Judith 8:9–10; 16:23; T. Ab. 15:5.

background of agricultural slavery in antiquity.[90] More specifically, it seems likely that the parable presumes a farm run by slaves and overseen by a servile farm manager. That is at least how the overwhelming majority of scholars have decided to understand the parable.

Some time ago, Crossan lamented the fact that scholars are not always able to separate the literal and metaphorical levels of Jesus's parables.[91] Methodologically, he argued, one should first give full consideration to the literal or "image" part of the parable before jumping to the metaphorical or "meaning" part of the parable.[92] In order to understand any parable as it was understood by those who heard it for the first time, it is important to be familiar with the historical and narrative world of the parable itself.[93] Such familiarity is generally taken for granted by the parables, but often entirely lacking on the part of today's hearers and readers.[94] Kloppenborg speaks of a parable's "verisimilitude," which is the ability of a parable to be understood as a realistic story in its original socio-historical context.[95] When it comes specifically to the parable of the loyal and wise slave, the narrative world to which it refers is in all likelihood that of agricultural slavery.[96] Taking Crossan's observation seriously, a few general comments about ancient agriculture and slavery are in order before turning to a socio-historical interpretation of Q 12:42–44.

4.3 Ancient Agricultural Slavery

In what follows, the word "agriculture" refers primarily to crop-growing, but does not exclude possible reference to animal husbandry, while the term "(estate/farm) manager" refers to the Roman, Greek, Egyptian, and/or Jewish person who managed a farming estate during the landowner's absence. I prefer this title over English alternatives like "steward" or "bailiff."[97] It was not uncommon for the managers of slave-run farms to be slaves themselves, although they could also be day-labourers, freedmen, or freeborn citizens.[98] The Roman

---

[90] Cf. Martinsen 2011, 135–151.

[91] Crossan 1974b, 86–88; cf. Zimmermann 2009, 172.

[92] Cf. Hunter 1971, 11–12; Ukpong 2012, 190–191, 195.

[93] Via 1967, 91; see Van Eck 2015; cf. Zimmermann 2009, 163.

[94] Via 1967, 18.

[95] Kloppenborg 2006, 278; see Van Eck 2015.

[96] Cf. Harrill 2006, 113.

[97] Cf. Aubert 1994, 118 n. 3.

[98] Toutain 1951, 277; Massey and Moreland 1992, 29; Harding 2003, 241; Harrill 2006, 231 n. 4; Joshel 2010, 57; Boer and Petterson 2017, 93, 96, 109; De Wet 2018, 2, 13; Roth 2018, 99–100; see Aubert 1994, 118 n. 3, 149–157; Chandezon 2011, 100, 101, 105–106; cf. Schottroff 2006, 175; Dal Lago and Katsari 2008, 209, 210.

"estate manager" was known as a *vilicus*, although this term could refer to various types of urban managers as well.[99] The Greek "estate manager" was known by a number of terms, including οἰκονόμος (as per Luke 12:42), ἐπιμελετής/ἐπιμελητής, ἐπίτροπος, διοικητής, πραγματευτής, and χειριστής.[100] In classical Greek literature, these terms are used somewhat interchangeably for both estate managers (like the Roman *vilici*) and general administrators (like the Roman *procuratores*), although the former was most commonly designated by ἐπίτροπος and οἰκονόμος.[101] In Egyptian papyri, estate managers are for the most part referenced as φροντισταί.

In the Hebrew Old Testament, the Jewish manager is often identified by use of the technical term "over the house" (עַל־הַבָּיִת).[102] That this phrase has a manager in mind is confirmed by the Septuagint's translation thereof in each case with οἰκονόμος. Managers are also referenced in the Old Testament by longer clauses, such as the one in Genesis 24:2 (my translation): "the one who ruled over everything he had" (הַמֹּשֵׁל בְּכָל־אֲשֶׁר־לוֹ), although the latter phrase could also imply a general administrator, in the sense of a Roman *procurator*. In later Jewish tradition, the phrase "son of the house" (בֶּן־בַּיִת) and the loanword *oikonomos* (אִיקוֹנוֹס) are preferred as designations for a manager.[103] In the pre-rabbinic Jewish tradition, it is not always easy to distinguish between royal and private estate managers, or between royal estate managers and royal administrators.[104] In the Jewish tradition *in toto*, the same terms are used interchangeably for both rural estate managers and urban household managers. With each usage, the intended meaning must be determined from the literary context.

As a parable of (Q's) Jesus, the historical setting is Palestine during the first century CE.[105] Unfortunately, ancient texts from Palestine have next to nothing to say about the daily operations of farming estates, especially those cultivated primarily or entirely by slaves under the watchful eye of a farm manager. Our most direct sources for the daily management of ancient farms in the Roman provinces are the papyri from Roman Egypt, but unfortunately it seems that Egyptian estates were mostly cultivated by tenants and/or hired labourers and were not run primarily or exclusively by slaves.[106] More importantly for our

---

[99] Harrill 2006, 103; cf. Hedrick 2014, 148–149.

[100] Cf. Hedrick 2014, 148.

[101] Harrill 2006, 104; see Chandezon 2011, 102–108; cf. Michel 1967, 149.

[102] Michel 1967, 149; cf. 1 Kgs 4:6; 16:9; 18:3; 2 Kgs 18:18, 37; 19:2; Isa 36:3, 22; 37:2.

[103] See Michel 1967, 149–150.

[104] See Layton 1990.

[105] Cf. Dodd 1958, 21; Funk 2006, 44, 61, 62.

[106] Rathbone 2007, 712; see Bagnall 1993, 220–221, 229–232, 237. There is evidence, nonetheless, of smallholders owning a small number of personal slaves (see Bagnall 1993, 227–230). The absence of evidence for slave-run estates or servile managers in ancient Egypt might at least to some extent be due to the nature of the evidence (see Bagnall 1993, 224–

purposes, farm managers are only mentioned in passing in Palestinian and Egyptian texts.[107] Conversely, Greco-Roman writings discuss agricultural slavery, the management of slave-run farms, and the daily operations of farm managers directly and in some detail. It follows that most of our information about these topics come from Greco-Roman literature, especially the writings of the Greek historian Xenophon and the Latin agronomists Varro, Cato, and Columella.[108]

Bradley is certainly correct when he asserts, referring specifically to the Latin agronomists, that "these sources cannot automatically be taken to apply to the [Roman] provinces or to give evidence of provincial conditions."[109] In my view, it is nonetheless methodologically and historically appropriate to appeal to these sources when examining a parable that was told in Palestine during the first century. Sociologists have drawn our attention to the fact that a significant number of common aspects are shared by all ancient slave-owning peoples.[110] Although there were, no doubt, differences between Jewish and Greco-Roman attitudes and practices surrounding (agricultural) slavery, there were also similarities, some of which applied to the ancient world in general.[111] After comparing Jewish and Roman material on farm management specifically, Harrill speaks of "an overarching ideology on slave management diffuse through-out the ancient Mediterranean."[112] An appeal to Greco-Roman sources does not mean that Jewish and Egyptian sources will be ignored. Instead, the current analysis draws on Jewish, Egyptian, Greek, and Roman sources, depending in each case on the subject matter under discussion and the availability of information.

Needless to say, slavery in rural Palestine was not a carbon copy of its Greco-Roman counterpart.[113] Hezser explains:

225, 230). Agricultural slaves were indeed present on Egyptian farms, but typically used in combination with tenant farmers (Boer and Petterson 2017, 141).

[107] Examples of Egyptian papyri that only mention managers in passing: *P.Cair.Zen.* 2.59150; *P.Enteux.* 75; *P.Mich.* 11.620; 12.657; 15.733, 741/742; *P.Mich.inv.* 4.224; *P.Col.* 3.12; 10.280; *P.Corn.* 1; *P.Oxy.* 72.4859; 74.4998, 5014–5016; 75.5050; *P.Princ.* 2.74; *P.Ryl.* 2.169; *O.Mich.* 1.68; *P.NYU* 2.36; *P.Petaus.* 92; *P.Theon.* 13; *P.Tebt.* 3.1.773; *P.Col.* 3.20, 21; *P.Duk.inv.* 920, 983; *P.Fay.* 110–124, 248–277; *P.Wisc.* 1.1; *P.Zen.Pestm.* 6; *SB* 16.12657. A number of these Egyptian references do not indicate whether the manager was in charge of a rural estate or an urban household.

[108] See Harrill 2006, 97, 101–103; cf. Massey and Moreland 1992, 26–27; Dal Lago and Katsari 2008, 189; Joshel 2010, 171; Chandezon 2011, 100.

[109] Bradley 1994, 61; cf. Martinsen 2011, 136; Boer and Petterson 2017, xiii–xiv.

[110] Hezser 2005, 8.

[111] Cf. Martinsen 2011, 136; Boer and Petterson 2017, 96.

[112] Harrill 2006, 109; cf. Chandezon 2011, 97.

[113] Boer and Petterson 2017, 96.

Similarities may indicate to what extent Jews had adopted the customs and values of the surrounding Graeco-Roman culture; differences may be based on the particular religious and moral values and the social, economic, and political circumstances under which Jews lived.[114]

For a variety of reasons, including chiefly military and political success, there were many more slaves on Roman farms than on the farms of other nations of the first century.[115] Unlike Roman Italy, mass slavery was simply not a feature of Roman Palestine.[116] Individual Roman farms (*fundi* and *latifundia*) were generally also much larger than their Palestinian (and Greek) counterparts.[117] Yet neither of these factors imply that (agricultural) slavery was absent or insignificant in first-century Palestine.[118] Older positions and arguments to that effect are, frankly and respectfully, mistaken.[119] Nor should one conclude from a comparison with Rome that there were no wealthy landowners or large estates in Palestine.[120] The material from Roman Egypt provides evidence for the existence of wealthy landowners and large estates in Roman provinces during the relevant period.[121] Some of these papyri provide evidence of large estates existing in Palestine, including Galilee, as early as the third century BCE.[122] The Gospels themselves assume and describe the existence of large-scale farms in Palestine.[123] Josephus further tells us of large estates held by himself in Judea and the coastal plain, by Ptolemy, Herod's friend, in Samaria, by Costobar, Herod's governor, in Idumaea, by Crispus, Agrippa's former *eparch*, in the Transjordan, and by Philip, Agrippa's lieutenant, near Gamla.[124] Although archaeology suggests that there were no large estates in the area between Nazareth and the tip of the Galilean Sea, literary and archaeological evidence combine to indicate that large farming estates existed on the great plain directly south of Nazareth.[125] Ultimately, Fiensy has argued conclusively for the existence of large estates in Palestine during the Herodian period.[126]

---

[114] Hezser 2005, 3.

[115] De Vaux 1965, 80, 84; White 1970, 411; Hezser 2005, 85; see Joshel 2010, 8, 53–56, 65–69; Boer and Petterson 2017, 95–96; cf. Fiensy 1991, 90, 91.

[116] Hezser 2005, 295.

[117] Andrews 1967, 89, 137–138; Chandezon 2011, 96; cf. Joshel 2010, 56.

[118] Hezser 2005, 300; cf. Fiensy 1991, 91; Boer and Petterson 2017, 141.

[119] E.g. Mendelsohn 1949, 111–112.

[120] Cf. Fiensy 2010, 196; Chandezon 2011, 96–97.

[121] Kloppenborg 2006, 284; cf. Häkkinen 2016, 1.

[122] E.g. *Papiri Greci e Latini* 6.554; *P.Lond.* 7.1948; cf. Kloppenborg 2006, 285, 297.

[123] Cf. Fiensy 1991, 55–56; 2010, 197; Kloppenborg 2006, 279.

[124] Kloppenborg 2006, 286–287; cf. Josephus, *A.J.* 15.264; 17.289; *B.J.* 2.69; *Vita* 33, 47, 422, 429.

[125] Fiensy 2010, 196.

[126] Fiensy 1991, 21–73; cf. Boer and Petterson 2017, 96–97.

The institution of slavery was a trademark feature of Israelite society from the very beginning.[127] The Elephantine papyri indicate that certain Egyptian Jews of the fifth century BCE owned slaves.[128] The biblical patriarchs are described as wealthy nomadic animal farmers, who owned large numbers of slaves and even appointed managers.[129] Some of the legendary Israelite judges owned their own slaves and sometimes utilised them in military campaigns.[130] During the monarchic period, Israelite kings are similarly portrayed as owning huge numbers of slaves, with prominent slaves at times even owning their own slaves.[131] It is possible that war captives were utilised by David and Solomon as slaves in smelter refineries. Regardless, the Israelite kings made productive use of state slaves for a host of religious, commercial, industrial, political, and personal projects.[132] 1 Chronicles 27:25–31 indicates that king David had many farms and that he appointed managers, each of them mentioned by name, to oversee his estates. Job, the pre-eminent human symbol of Jewish wisdom (together with Solomon), is depicted as an extremely wealthy slave-owner.[133] After returning from the Babylonian exile, a census counted 7 377 slaves for 42 360 freepersons.[134] The legislative, sapiential, and prophetic traditions of the Old Testament address a number of regulations and recommendations concerning the treatment of slaves to Jewish slave-owners.[135]

Slavery continued to be an integral ingredient of Jewish society during Hellenistic and Roman times.[136] Against the estimations of Josephus and Philo that slavery was not a feature of the communities behind the Dead Sea Scrolls, the Damascus Document and Khirbet Qumran ostracon provide evidence that (some of) these groups did indeed own slaves. The apocryphal book of Judith informs us that Judith owned a number of slaves, including a manager who oversaw her property on a daily basis.[137] According to the apocryphal Book of Tobit, Raguel also owned many slaves.[138] Josephus describes on a number of occasions how Jewish leaders would enslave fellow Jews who opposed them

---

[127] Cf. DuBois 2009, 52.

[128] See Hezser 2005, 289–291.

[129] See Hezser 2005, 286–287; cf. Gen 12:16; 15:2–3; 16:4; 24:2; 26:12, 15, 19; 32:5.

[130] De Vaux 1965, 83–84; cf. Judg 6:27.

[131] See Hezser 2005, 287–288; cf. 2 Sam 6:20–22; 9:2, 10; 1 Kgs 9:22; 11:26; 2 Kgs 21:23.

[132] See De Vaux 1965, 88–90.

[133] Cf. Job 1:3; 31:13; 19:15–16; 42:12.

[134] De Vaux 1965, 84; cf. Ezra 2:64; Neh 7:66.

[135] Cf. Exod 21:7–11, 20–21, 26–27; Lev 25:44–46; Neh 5:4–5; Prov 29:19.

[136] See Hezser 2005, 94–96, 291–293, 300.

[137] Judith 8:7–10; 16:23; cf. Additions to Esther 15:2; Jos. Asen. 2:10–11.

[138] Tobit 8:9–14; 9:1; 10:10.

and who were unwilling to accept their authority.[139] The Hasmonean wars resulted in the enslavement of fellow Jews, who were undoubtedly put to work in wealthy Jewish homes and on large Jewish farmlands. Josephus also informs us that king Herod had many royal slaves. Although Philo trivialises the institution of slavery by subordinating it to Stoic paradigms, his treatment of the subject matter leaves the impression that it was common for wealthy Jews to own many slaves.[140] These sources indicate that wealthy Jewish landowners of first-century Palestine made use of Jewish and gentile slaves alike in their houses and on their estates.

Although the nature and extent of Hellenisation and Romanisation was different for the two Palestinian provinces of Judea and Galilee, there is no doubt that they were both profoundly affected by Greece and Rome. Such influence also encroached on the economic sphere, including agriculture. It goes beyond the scope of the current study to discuss the extent of Hellenisation and/or Romanisation in Palestine. One interesting archaeological find will suffice. A jar fragment found at Sepphoris in Galilee around the second century BCE bears seven Hebrew letters (אפמלסלש), of which the first five might represent a transliteration of the Greek term for "manager" or "overseer" (ἐπιμελετής or ἐπιμελητής).[141]

Starting with the establishment of the monarchy, peasant smallholdings became increasingly threatened by rich landholders.[142] By no means did this situation get any better during the Greco-Roman period.[143] Even if not widespread,[144] it is certainly possible to imagine the existence of a few agricultural estates in rural Palestine that were run *entirely* by slaves, bar the occasional visit by the urban landowner or his general administrator.[145] There might be archaeological support for the latter suggestion from excavations of rural farmsteads outside Roman Italy.[146] The Roman system of making exclusive or predominant use of slaves on agricultural estates spread all over the ancient world.[147] In fact, if one would excuse the circular argument for the moment, the parable of the loyal and wise slave in Q 12:42–46 offers evidence of the

---

[139] E.g. *Vita* 1.65, 88, 222; 4.33; *A.J.* 14.275, 429.

[140] See DuBois 2009, 63–66.

[141] Chancey 2002, 77.

[142] De Vaux 1965, 167; cf. Kloppenborg 2006, 284.

[143] See Kloppenborg 2006, 284–290; cf. Harding 2003, 241.

[144] Fiensy 1991, 91; Kloppenborg 2006, 314 n. 136; see Glotz 1926, 202–203; cf. White 1970, 411; Joshel 2010, 8, 74.

[145] Cf. Toutain 1951, 275; Kloppenborg 2006, 290, 292, 314. Although the Zenon papyri attest to the presence of slaves (together with tenants and farm managers) on some of Apollonios' estates in Egypt and Palestine (Kloppenborg 2006, 297), none of these provide evidence of farms run *entirely* by slaves, including a servile farm manager.

[146] Cf. Bradley 1994, 61.

[147] Joshel 2010, 74; cf. Toutain 1951, 275.

latter scenario for rural Galilee at least.[148] The best evidence, however, that there were indeed Palestinian estates run *entirely* by slaves comes from the Old Testament.[149] In 2 Samuel 9:10, King David confers all Saul's property on Mephibosheth, Saul's grandson, and orders Ziba, a slave, to oversee the tilling of his estates by all the slaves who used to belong to Saul.[150]

During laborious periods, especially at harvest time, large estates, including self-efficient slave-run estates, usually supplemented their workforce with day-labourers.[151] Since Palestinian farms would, on average, have been smaller than Roman farms, it is likely that some of these slave-run farms operated mostly, if not entirely, without the need for outside labour.[152] The necessity for occasional outside labour would have depended on a variety of factors, including the size of the estate, the number of slaves, and the amount of work at any given time.

One aspect of slavery that applied to all ancient peoples was the practice of deliberate desocialisation and denationalisation, which entailed the physical or representational removal of a newly enslaved person from the social group of his or her birth.[153] The traditional scholarly view that Second Temple Judaism followed biblical regulations by treating their Jewish slaves as day-labourers or debt-bondsmen and by manumitting them in the seventh or Jubilee year has not stood up to subsequent investigation.[154] In earlier times, Jews distinguished in principle (not always in practice) between Jewish and gentile slaves, treating the former more humanely and manumitting them in the seventh or Jubilee year. Yet prophetic warnings against slaveholders who abstained from manumitting their slaves indicate that these biblical rulings were not always representative of experienced reality.[155] To the extent that slaves benefitted from jubilee regulations, such benefit involved at most "a partial and selective amelioration."[156]

By the first century, due to Greco-Roman influence, the distinction between Jewish and non-Jewish slaves was underemphasised and practically replaced by a rigid distinction between slave and freeperson.[157] Evidence of this shift

---

[148] Cf. Kloppenborg 2006, 314 n. 136; Hedrick 2014, 129.

[149] See De Vaux 1965, 167.

[150] Cf. 1 Sam 8:12.

[151] Toutain 1951, 278; White 1970, 335, 348–349, 355–356; Fiensy 1991, 76; Burford 1993, 183; Aubert 1994, 163; Kloppenborg 2006, 288, 289; Boer and Petterson 2017, 93; cf. Varro, *Rust.* 1.17.2–3; Egyptian papyri *P.Cair.Zen.* 4.59748, 59827; *P.Mich.* 3.200.

[152] Cf. White 1970, 349.

[153] See Hezser 2005, 8–12, 26–54.

[154] See De Vaux 1965, 82–83, 86; Hezser 2005, 3–8, 17, 90; 2009, 131; cf. Fiensy 1991, 90, 91–92; Boer and Petterson 2017, 99; cf. Exod 21:2; Lev 25:26, 39–41; Deut 15:12.

[155] E.g. Jer 34:8–11, 14–16.

[156] Boer and Petterson 2017, 99.

[157] Hezser 2005, 93–99; 2009, 131–132.

comes not only from Josephus and Philo, but also from rabbinic literature.[158] The boundaries between Jewish and gentile slaves became blurred by certain practices, like the renaming of newly acquired slaves, the tolerance of mixed procreation, the circumcision of gentile slaves, and the requirement to adopt the master's religion and culture.[159] Due to the processes of desocialisation and denationalisation, Jewish slaves were no longer viewed as genuine members of the Jewish community, which, in turn, enabled and justified not only their permanent enslavement, but also their equally harsh treatment by Jewish masters if compared to other slaves.[160] Hence, the biblical regulations regarding the enslavement of fellow Jews and the treatment of Jewish slaves were no longer observed in the Roman period.[161] In any case, even if these regulations were indeed observed to some extent, they did not prevent the enslavement or abuse of gentile slaves, whose treatment by Jewish masters must have been similar to the treatment of slaves in the ancient world generally.[162]

4.4 Q 12:42–44: An Interpretation

Q 12:42–44 begins with a rhetorical question: "Who then is the faithful and wise slave whom the master put over his household to give them a ration of grain on time?" How one interprets the parable is perhaps more than anything else dependent on how one interprets this opening question.[163] The word translated by the International Q Project as "faithful" (πιστός) could also be translated as "trustworthy," "loyal," or "obedient."[164] I would prefer just about any translation over "faithful," because of its religious overtones.[165] It is possible that wordplay is involved on the metaphorical level,[166] but on the purely literal

---

[158] It should be noted that there are individual rabbinic traditions that advise Jews not to treat Hebrew debt-slaves harshly or unfairly (see Hezser 2005, 99). The value of these texts for the current discussion is uncertain. On the one hand, it is unlikely that the Hebrew debt-slaves referred to by these rabbis represent all Jewish slaves. In any case, the reason for and occasion of a slave's initial enslavement was presumably soon forgotten – by the slave-owner, that is. On the other hand, it is unlikely that these texts represent actual practice. The reason why rabbis would place such restrictions on Jewish slave-owners was probably that Hebrew debt-slaves were treated quite harshly in reality. These discussions should be seen as representing the theoretical ideal, with a basis in biblical tradition, rather than lived reality (cf. Hezser 2005, 117).

[159] Hezser 2005, 117; cf. Glotz 1926, 198; De Vaux 1965, 85.

[160] Hezser 2005, 94, 97; cf. Fiensy 1991, 92.

[161] Hezser 2009, 131; cf. Fiensy 1991, 92; DuBois 2009, 52.

[162] Cf. Fiensy 1991, 92; DuBois 2009, 52; cf. Lev 25:39–46.

[163] Cf. Meier 2016, 242.

[164] Donahue 1988, 99; Liddell and Scott 1996 s.v. πιστός.

[165] Cf. Funk 2006, 166.

[166] Cf. Donahue 1988, 99; Etchell 1998, 110; Valantasis 2005, 168.

level the parable wishes to call attention to the slave's loyalty and reliability. Even on the metaphorical level, πιστός does not refer exclusively to religious belief.[167] Obedient loyalty (*fides* and πιστός) was considered by ancient slave-holders as *the* most important and valued characteristic that a slave could possibly possess.[168]

This is especially true of the servile farm manager, from whom absolute, unwavering loyalty was expected.[169] Significantly, in his comedy *The Merchant*, Plautus chooses to name an estate manager Pistus, based on the Greek lexis πιστός.[170] Columella advises landholders to test the loyalty of their estate managers before appointing them.[171] If judged solely by the length at which Xenophon, Columella, and Cato discuss the selection and desired qualities of the ideal farm manager, landowners typically spent a lot of time and energy discovering and selecting the "perfect" individual for the job.[172] Other characteristics that landowners sought when choosing or buying a farm manager included, among others, a rural background, tact, devotion, firmness, dependability, honesty, integrity, diligence, prudence, literacy[173] (or an excellent memory), farming experience, and exceptional character.[174] For the most part, masters desired the estate manager to be a (servile) clone of themselves; or rather, their ideal selves.[175] It is important to reiterate that the previous list of traits were additional and complementary to the all-important and central trait of obedient loyalty.[176]

---

[167] Donahue 1988, 99; cf. Hays 2012, 49; *pace* Etchell 1998, 109, 110.

[168] Hezser 2005, 155; see Bradley 1984, 33–40, 78; Joshel 2010, 115–116; cf. Harrill 2006, 152–153; Dal Lago and Katsari 2008, 204. The loyalty of slaves is also an important topic in the New Testament (Goede 2013, 6).

[169] Michel 1967, 150–151; Marshall 1978, 541; Burford 1993, 218; Dal Lago and Katsari 2008, 210; Chandezon 2011, 117; cf. Xenophon, *Oec.* 12.5.

[170] *Merc.* 277–278; cf. Aubert 1994, 160.

[171] Columella, *Rust.* 11.1.7; cf. Aubert 1994, 160.

[172] Glotz 1926, 201; White 1970, 353, 375–376, 403; Chandezon 2011, 98; cf. Xenophon, *Oec.* 12–15; Columella, *Rust.* 1.8; 11.1; Cato, *Agr.* 5.1–5.

[173] Celsus actually preferred illiterate managers, since they would then be less likely to commit fraud (White 1970, 354). That some farm managers were indeed literate is indicated by the existence of written correspondence in the form of Egyptian papyri between landowners and managers (e.g. *P.Haun.* 2.23, 32; *P.Ryl.* 2.238; *SB* 16.12579; *P.Tebt.* 2.423; cf. *P.Oslo* 2.44; *P.Tebt.* 3.1.773; *P.Oxy.* 9.1220; *P.Mich.* 1.14; *P.Duk.inv.* 614; *P.Petr.* 1.29; see Kloppenborg 2006, 442–443).

[174] White 1970, 350–351, 354, 357, 403; Chandezon 2011, 100.

[175] See Joshel 2010, 115–116; cf. Burford 1993, 173; Harrill 2006, 87, 105; Hedrick 2014, 153; cf. Xenophon, *Oec.* 12.4.

[176] White (1970, 354) maintains that diligence was the most important trait to look for in a manager, but diligence was only possible if loyalty was already present (cf. Xenophon, *Oec.* 12.5). When agronomists discuss the qualities of estate managers, they often take obedient loyalty for granted.

The word "wise" or "prudent" (φρόνιμος) is also significant in this discussion. Beginning the pericope with the word "wise" (φρόνιμος) serves to specify its genre as wisdom.[177] The parable deliberately introduces the traditional sapiential theme of how to identify a wise slave.[178] Texts that discuss this theme were all written from the perspective of slave-owners.[179] In antiquity, "wisdom" did not just refer to cleverness, but also to morality and character, so that the traits of "loyalty" and "wisdom" overlapped.[180] The ability to adequately identify, utilise, and manage a wise slave greatly benefited the slaveholder. Educated, skilled, and intelligent slaves were much more valuable to their owners than other slaves.[181] Due to their Stoic outlooks, both Philo and Jesus ben Sirach had more respect for a wise slave than an ignorant slave-owner.[182] At the same time, Jewish slave-owners feared slaves who were too intelligent and skilled, lest they should threaten or overturn the household's "ordained" hierarchical structure.[183] To describe the slave as being simultaneously "wise" and "loyal" is therefore highly significant, since it introduces him as the ideal servile farm manager.[184] In general, "prudence" (φρόνιμος) was a quality readily associated with stewards.[185]

The word translated here with "household" (οἰκετεία) literally refers to a "household of slaves."[186] Scholars mostly agree that Matthew's οἰκετεία represents Q in this case.[187] It is, nonetheless, noteworthy that Luke exchanged this lexis for θεραπεία, which denotes a body or retinue of slaves.[188] Even if Luke changed the Q text to better suit his own social context, the alteration indicates that he correctly understood the original word "household" (οἰκετεία) as a reference to the farm's *familia* and not the master's *domus* or, more narrowly, his nuclear family.[189] In Roman literature, the term *familia* could reference only the slaves of a particular household, while the term *domus* referenced

---

[177] Edwards 1976, 66; cf. Harrill 2006, 116.

[178] Kirk 1998, 234; cf. Roth 2018, 89.

[179] See Joshel 2010, 13–14, 172; cf. Aubert 1994, 121.

[180] Cf. Harrill 2006, 116.

[181] Hezser 2005, 83; 2009, 129.

[182] Philo, *Prob.* 19; Sir. 10:25; see Hezser 2005, 95–96; cf. De Vaux 1965, 85.

[183] Hezser 2005, 150; cf. Bradley 1984, 27; Joshel 2010, 119; cf. Prov. 17:2; 30:21–23.

[184] Cf. Nolland 2005, 998.

[185] Marshall 1978, 541; see Hays 2012, 49; cf. Luke 16:8.

[186] Herzog 1994, 157; Liddell and Scott 1996 s.v. οἰκετεία.

[187] E.g. Fleddermann 2005a, 627.

[188] Marshall 1978, 541; Bock 1996, 1179; Liddell and Scott 1996 s.v. θεραπεία; Luz 2005, 221; Hays 2012, 47 n. 30.

[189] Luz 2005, 221; cf. De Wet 2018, 2. The preference here for the lexis οἰκετεία instead of οἰκίας further strengthens the case that the slave was an estate manager and not the manager of an urban household, since the phrase ὁ ἐπὶ τῆς οἰκίας was standard for the latter position (cf. Liddell and Scott 1996 s.v. οἰκίας).

the entire household.[190] The *familia* included both urban and rural slaves.[191] The *domus* included the master's nuclear and extended families, with all their slaves, and was equivalent to the Hebrew and Greek words for "house(hold)" (בַּיִת and οἰκία).[192] Elsewhere in Q, the more standard word "house" (οἰκία) is used when referring to a non-servile family or household.[193] It follows that the master did not task the slave with feeding his own (that is, the master's) family, as the English translation seems to imply,[194] but with feeding the families of slaves who lived on the farm (*familia rustica*). In all likelihood, the master's nuclear family did not even live on the farm, but rather stayed in the city with the master.[195]

The opening verse does not say anything of the master's departure or subsequent absence.[196] According to most commentators, the master's departure is implied by this verse, and it is in their view reasonable to accept that the master's departure is contemporaneous with the opening of the parable.[197] On the one hand, commentators assume that this parable follows the same structure as other parables, where the master leaves at the beginning of the narrative, only to return later.[198] On the other hand, scholars assume that the master permanently resides on his farm, leaving only sporadically, even if lengthily, for a variety of reasons, as is the case with modern farmers.[199] It is much more likely, however, that the landowner of this parable does not reside on the farm at all. When the audience is thrown into the narrative, the master is absent and the chosen slave had already been appointed manager.[200] One gets the impression that the selected slave's appointment occurred in the somewhat distant distant past and is the established state of affairs when the parable begins. The

---

[190] Hezser 2005, 125; see Saller 2003, 187–189; Dal Lago and Katsari 2008, 203–204; cf. Boer and Petterson 2017, 88, 117.

[191] White 1970, 357–358; Saller 2003, 187–188.

[192] Hezser 2005, 126.

[193] E.g. Q 11:17, 33.

[194] *Pace* e.g. Donahue 1988, 98; Bock 1996, 1179.

[195] See below.

[196] Kloppenborg 1995, 294; Luz 2005, 223; Roth 2018, 90.

[197] E.g. Crossan 1974a, 38; Taylor 1989, 142; Roth 2018, 90. According to Kloppenborg (1995, 294), the parable is silent about the master's departure and subsequent absence because it is preceded in the Sayings Gospel Q by the Son of Man logion in Q 12:40, which already introduces the departure-return scenario. Yet this preceding logion is *also* silent about the departure and absence of the Son of Man. In Q 12:40, the apocalyptic Son of Man figure does not necessarily represent Jesus (Howes 2013c, 10), so that a "departure" of some kind cannot automatically be assumed (cf. Dan 7:13).

[198] E.g. Crossan 1974a, 39; Donahue 1988, 99; Scott 1989, 208, 211; Taylor 1989, 145; Funk and Hoover 1993, 342; Roth 2018, 110–111.

[199] E.g. Jeremias 1966, 44; Taylor 1989, 143; Kloppenborg 1995, 294; Bock 1996, 1179; Etchells 1998, 110.

[200] Fleddermann 2005a, 635.

latter is technically indicated by the grammar of the word "appointed" or "put over" (κατέστησεν), which features in the aorist tense precisely to indicate that the slave received his specified task in the past.[201]

In the fictional Greek tale *Daphnis and Chloe*, written by Longus in the second century CE, the servile estate manager, Lamon, is on the verge of marriage when he faces the prospect of meeting the owner of the farm, Dionysophanus, for the first time.[202] As in the parable, the landowner is absent when the story begins. The situation of absentee landownership assumed by both narratives is representative of common farming practice in antiquity.[203] It was customary for landowners to be non-resident and mainly absent from their farms.[204] Wealthy landowners mostly lived in the city and often had multiple estates.[205] These two factors explain not only their habitual absence, but also their need for estate managers.[206] Generally, Palestinian landowners resided in Tiberias, Sepphoris, and Jerusalem, especially those who owned the most fertile land.[207] Galilean landowners were typically non-resident and mostly absent from their estates.[208] The mere fact that the parable's master appointed a manager is reasonable evidence that the master was mostly absent from the farm and therefore needed a manager,[209] although managers were, at times, also appointed because resident estate owners "preferred other activities to day-to-day supervision."[210] In other words, the parable's master did not appoint the manager because he was leaving his place of residence on some errand, only to return home later, but rather appointed the manager some time ago, possibly during one of his occasional supervisory visits to the farm.[211] The farm *was* his errand, not his home. The visit during which the manager was appointed happened during the parable's prehistory and is not recounted by the parable itself.

The practice of appointing one specific slave as the manager of an estate and its personnel was very common in antiquity, especially when the estate was

---

[201] Fleddermann 2005a, 635; Roth 2018, 95.

[202] Longus 4.6.

[203] Cf. Bradley 1994, 105; Harrill 2006, 103.

[204] White 1970, 350; Massey and Moreland 1992, 27; Fiensy 2010, 196; see Aberbach 1994, 40–42; Kloppenborg 2006, 279–280, 314–316; cf. Burford 1993, 217, 219; Chandezon 2011, 98.

[205] White 1970, 353; Herzog 1994, 156; Saller 2003, 187–188; Kloppenborg 2006, 300; Fiensy 2010, 196; Dube 2015, 5; Boer and Petterson 2017, 97–98; cf. Aubert 1994, 126; Boer and Petterson 2017, 85.

[206] White 1970, 350; Massey and Moreland 1992, 27; Joshel 2010, 57.

[207] Oakman 1986, 78; 2008, 266; Freyne 1988, 149, 151; 2000, 52, 99, 195; Dube 2015, 5; Häkkinen 2016, 7; see Fiensy 1991, 49–55; 2010, 196; cf. Horsley 1995a, 42; Boer and Petterson 2017, 141; cf. Josephus, *A.J.* 17.66; 18.36–38; *Vita* 33.

[208] Scott 1989, 207; cf. Oakman 2008, 266.

[209] Cf. Aubert 1994, 122, 199.

[210] Kloppenborg 1995, 294.

[211] Cf. Herzog 1994, 157; Kloppenborg 2006, 315.

large and the landowner was non-resident.[212] In fact, with an absent landowner the estate manager was the key person on any slave-run farm, and the success of the enterprise depended almost entirely on this individual.[213] According to White, "the slave-run establishment could only be worked profitably if the standard of supervision and work-allocation was high."[214] Since a slave was generally in antiquity viewed as an extension of his master, excluding, of course, the latter's legal and social privileges, it was possible to appoint a slave as a supervisor over other slaves.[215] Theoretically, such an overseeing slave represented his master's interests, which meant that the master controlled his slaves indirectly during his absence.[216] That rural and urban managers often acted on their masters' behalf is indicated in a number of Egyptian papyri.[217]

The appointment of a supervising slave was further enabled by the strict hierarchy under which slaves operated on the farm.[218] In both Greco-Roman and Jewish society at large, there was generally tremendous variance in the positions and statuses of individual slaves.[219] The hierarchical structure was fairly intricate on large estates.[220] Increased specialisation in agricultural and other tasks translated into greater differentiation amongst the slaves themselves.[221] Whereas the hierarchical advancement of urban slaves was fairly common in antiquity, opportunities for promotion and socio-economic betterment were few and far between for rural slaves.[222] Since the farm manager was a mediator between the farmhands and the master and acted on the latter's authority, he occupied a place at the very top of any particular farm's servile hierarchy.[223] In the master's absence, which normally was most of the time, the

---

[212] White 1970, 350; Hezser 2005, 85; 2009, 132; Harrill 2006, 87; see Varro, *Rust.* 1.16; Columella, *Rust.* 11.1; cf. Xenophon of Ephesus 2.10.

[213] White 1970, 376; Harrill 2006, 102, 103; cf. Bradley 1984, 26; cf. Egyptian papyrus *P.Tebt.* 2.423.

[214] White 1970, 374; cf. Burford 1993, 218; cf. Xenophon, *Oec.* 12.15.

[215] Hezser 2005, 11.

[216] Cf. Bradley 1984, 122–123; Hezser 2005, 102; Chandezon 2011, 99, 100.

[217] E.g. *P.Mich.* 1.14; 11.620, 625; 12.657; 15.733; *P.Oxy.* 72.4859, 4862, 4871; *P.Ryl.* 2.169; *P.NYU* 2.36.

[218] White 1970, 333; Dal Lago and Katsari 2008, 195; cf. Herzog 1994, 157; Boer and Petterson 2017, 89.

[219] Harrill 2006, 103–104, 148; see Bradley 1984, 15–16; Hezser 2005, 83–84, 94; 2009, 129.

[220] See White 1970, 353, 355, 377–383.

[221] Cf. Aubert 1994, 175.

[222] See Bradley 1994, 68–72; cf. Hezser 2009, 129.

[223] White 1970, 333; Burford 1993, 173, 185; Bradley 1994, 71; Hezser 2005, 85; Harrill 2006, 148.

manager had complete authority over the whole staff, including both day-labourers and slaves.[224] On some estates, farm managers also acted as financial managers (*actores* and, for example, πραγματευτής), which gave them complete control over every aspect of the estate's daily operation.[225] Possible direct evidence hereof appears in a papyrus from Egypt, listing a host of transactions and payments that are believed to have been made by an estate manager.[226]

The *Critical Edition of Q* prefers Matthew's τροφή ("food" or "nourishment") over Luke's σιτομετρία ("measure/ration of corn/grain") for Q 12:42. Fleddermann disagrees, pointing out that σιτομετρία "is a NT *hapax legomenon* and it does not appear in any Greek literary text."[227] Although some argue that Luke introduced the more technical term,[228] it is also possible that Matthew introduced a more generic term to increase the tradition's applicability and relevance for a wider audience. Fleddermann also points out that Matthew uses τροφή redactionally on two other occasions, namely Matthew 3:4 (cf. Mark 3:6) and Matthew 10:10b (cf. Q/Luke 10:7).[229] Even if it does not provide conclusive evidence, Luke's σιτομετρία would strengthen the case that Q 12:42–44 should be read against the background of farm management. Both servile and non-servile farm workers were often compensated in kind, with corn/grain and bread being most common.[230] Whenever possible, the personnel's food was grown and prepared on the farm itself.[231] These rations typically comprised the food these workers had to survive on.[232] It therefore makes little conceptual difference to the interpretation of this parable whether the original text spoke of "food" or a "ration of grain," but it might be important when considering the intertextual link of this parable with the story of Joseph.[233] The preference here is Luke's σιτομετρία.

In Q 12:42, the appointed slave's task to feed his fellow slaves is entirely congruent with what we know of agricultural slavery in antiquity.[234] Ancient landowners were advised and encouraged by Roman agronomists and Jewish

---

[224] White 1970, 347, 350; Massey and Moreland 1992, 29; Aubert 1994, 181; cf. Harrill 2006, 87, 103.

[225] See Aubert 1994, 170–172, 191–196; Chandezon 2011, 107, 108–117.

[226] *P.Kar.Goodsp.* 96; cf. *P.Corn.* 1; *P.Oxy.* 72.4859, 4862, 4870; 75.5050; *P.Mich.* 12.657; *SB* 14.12203.

[227] Fleddermann 2005a, 627; so too Bock 1996, 1179; Allison 2000, 238–239.

[228] E.g. Taylor 1989, 142 n. 57; cf. Luz 2005, 221.

[229] Fleddermann 2005a, 627.

[230] See Glotz 1926, 32; White 1970, 360–361.

[231] White 1970, 394; Bradley 1994, 83; see Dal Lago and Katsari 2008, 191–193; cf. Aberbach 1994, 57; Aubert 1994, 176.

[232] Glotz 1926, 32.

[233] See below.

[234] Blomberg 1990, 192.

sages alike to look after the physical wellbeing of their slaves.[235] Such advice was not born out of humanitarianism or compassion. The aim was rather to promote conscientiousness and prudence on the part of the slaveholder when it came to maintaining the condition of his assets, seeing as all slaves were considered property.[236] The same advice applied also to other forms of property, like farming implements and animals.[237] It served the slaveholder's purpose to safeguard the physical condition of his slaves, mainly because it improved productivity and increased the overall value and profitability of his property.[238] Conversely, it was irresponsible and expensive to replace slaves on a regular basis.[239] Acts of apparent generosity and kindness were also the means by which slaves were retained in a general state of relative contentment, which in turn increased productivity.[240] One of the most important tasks of an estate manager was to look after the physical nourishment and wellbeing of the other slaves.[241] By being in charge of food rationing, the estate manager had complete control over the physical welfare of the other slaves.[242]

Food and clothing were the primary means by which slaves were kept in a general state of contentment and productivity.[243] Columella advises landowners to provide their slaves with sturdy clothing, because it enabled hard work in all types of weather and prevented illness in bad weather.[244] Types of food

---

[235] E.g. Columella, *Rust.* 1.6.3, 19–20; 1.8.5, 19; 12.3.7; Varro, *Rust.* 1.17.5–7; Pseudo-Phocylides 223–227; Sir 7:20–21; Philo, *Spec.* 2.83; see Bradley 1984, 21–26; Hezser 2005, 85, 151–155; cf. Glotz 1926, 196; Dal Lago and Katsari 2008, 189.

[236] Glotz 1926, 195; De Vaux 1965, 80, 84, 86; White 1970, 359–360, 372, 374; Massey and Moreland 1992, 5; Dillon 2002, 126; Harding 2003, 221; Nolland 2005, 999; Dal Lago and Katsari 2008, 193; Martinsen 2011, 141; De Wet 2018, 2; see Joshel 2010, 7, 38–41; Boer and Petterson 2017, 114–118, 177; cf. Bradley 1984, 18, 27; cf. Cato, *Agr.* 56–57; Aristotle, *Pol.* 1253b23–54a17.

[237] Glotz 1926, 196, 207; Saller 2003, 192; Joshel 2010, 57, 113; cf. Burford 1993, 210; Martinsen 2011, 140, 141; Boer and Petterson 2017, 93; cf. Egyptian papyrus *P.Tebt.* 2.423.

[238] Bradley 1984, 22; 1994, 82; Joshel 2010, 57; see Hezser 2005, 151–155; Dal Lago and Katsari 2008, 189–194; cf. Glotz 1926, 196.

[239] Hezser 2005, 85.

[240] Yavetz 1988, 157; Massey and Moreland 1992, 44; Dal Lago and Katsari 2008, 207; Joshel 2010, 113, 126, 177; see Bradley 1984, 21–26, 40–45; cf. Seneca, *Ep.* 47.4; Xenophon, *Oec.* 12.6–7.

[241] White 1970, 354, 358; Bradley 1994, 82; cf. Dal Lago and Katsari 2008, 193.

[242] Luz 2005, 225–226 n. 23.

[243] White 1970, 374; Hezser 2005, 152; see Bradley 1994, 81–84; Joshel 2010, 57, 123–124, 177; cf. Aberbach 1994, 57; Dal Lago and Katsari 2008, 190, 193; cf. e.g. Pseudo-Phocylides 223–227; Sir 7:20–21; Philo, *Spec.* 2.83; Xenophon, *Oec.* 13.9; Cato, *Agr.* 5.2; 56–59; Justinian, *Dig.* 34.1.6.

[244] Columella, *Rust.* 1.8.9, 15; 11.1.21; see Dal Lago and Katsari 2008, 190–191; cf. Bradley 1984, 22; Joshel 2010, 124.

and portion sizes were determined by each slave's assigned tasks and respon-sibilities.[245] Providing enough food and drink was also considered to be the best means by which an owner or manager could prevent pilfering.[246] Land-holders understood that rustic slaves needed adequate amounts of foodstuff if they were to work at their optimal levels of efficiency.[247]

Productivity could further be *increased* by rewarding hard or good work with *additional* food and clothing, thereby turning bare necessities into incen-tives.[248] In Xenophon's *Economics*, Ischomachos explains that he rewards dil-igent slaves with higher quality clothes and shoes, while providing sluggish slaves with items of lower quality.[249] During periods when exceptionally gru-elling labour was needed or when punishment was deemed necessary, extra food and clothing served to ease the tension and restore general levels of satis-faction.[250] Likewise, an increase in rations during periods of rest, especially holidays, increased servile satisfaction during periods of hard labour.[251] Colu-mella even advises the estate manager to reward diligent slaves by inviting them to share dinner with him.[252] Apart from the benefits of providing slaves with food and clothing, it was also considered wise and frugal for landowners to allot only the *least* expensive and nutritious foodstuffs to their slaves.[253]

Proper living conditions, humane treatment, and adequate downtime could be added to food and clothing as incentives, but only on a secondary level.[254] While rustic day-labourers who had suffered an injury or fallen ill were mostly ignored, sick and injured slaves were at least tended to or sent to the hospital or infirmary.[255] According to Columella, such care not only improved the gen-eral condition of the master's property, but also rendered these slaves more reliable in the future.[256] Tending to sick slaves was one of the main duties of

---

[245] Harrill 2006, 106; see White 1970, 360–361; Joshel 2010, 131; cf. Aubert 1994, 180.

[246] White 1970, 358; see Joshel 2010, 154–156, 178–179.

[247] Bradley 1994, 82; Dal Lago and Katsari 2008, 189–190, 193; cf. e.g. Aristotle, [*Oec.*] 1344a35–b11.

[248] White 1970, 359; Massey and Moreland 1992, 28, 32; Burford 1993, 218; Bradley 1994, 82; Dal Lago and Katsari 2008, 198, 206–207; Joshel 2010, 124, 177; De Wet 2018, 3; cf. Harrill 2006, 92; cf. Varro, *Rust.* 1.17.7.

[249] Xenophon, *Oec.* 13.10.

[250] Bradley 1984, 23; cf. Varro, *Rust.* 1.17.5–7.

[251] Bradley 1984, 42, 44; see Cato, *Agr.* 57; cf. Solinus, *The Wonders of the World* 1.35; Macrobius, *Sat.* 1.12.7.

[252] Columella, *Rust.* 1.8.5; cf. Dal Lago and Katsari 2008, 198.

[253] See Dal Lago and Katsari 2008, 192–193; cf. Burford 1993, 209, 215; Aberbach 1994, 57.

[254] Cf. Bradley 1984, 25; De Wet 2018, 3; see Dal Lago and Katsari 2008, 189–194.

[255] White 1970, 348, 360; Joshel 2010, 174; cf. Glotz 1926, 207; cf. Varro, *Rust.* 1.17.3; Columella, *Rust.* 1.1.18; 11.1.18; Cato, *Agr.* 12; 157–158; 160.

[256] Columella, *Rust.* 1.8.9; cf. Bradley 1984, 22; Dal Lago and Katsari 2008, 193–194.

the estate manager.[257] Day-labourers also tended to get the heavy and unhealthy work, with slaves being more valuable as the landowner's acquired property.[258] By mentioning both food and loyalty in the same breath, the introductory verse of this parable aptly summarises the mutual dependency that characterised all ancient master-slave relationships. Masters depended on the loyalty of their slaves, while slaves depended on masters for physical maintenance and humane treatment.[259]

Much more important on any farm than the nourishment and happiness of the personnel was their productivity; although it is true that a higher degree of contentment translated into greater productivity.[260] On ancient agricultural estates, the manager was evaluated primarily by his ability to maintain or improve productivity and profit.[261] The general contentment of the personnel was only a means to this end, albeit the most important and effective means by which productivity was ensured.[262] The goal of profitability governed an owner's treatment of his slaves.[263] "The principle behind every operation on the farm [was] to maximize profit, and prevent waste."[264] Valantasis is certainly correct that the feeding of fellow slaves would not have been the appointed slave's only task, but it would nonetheless have been his most important task as part of establishing acceptable levels of productivity.[265]

Conversely, denying food to the other slaves could also have been a form of punishment and would have been accepted by the master as such if it improved productivity.[266] In fact, it was required of the manager to do whatever it took to maintain or even increase productivity, since all slaves were considered to be naturally unreliable, gluttonous, criminalistic, intransigent, greedy, cruel,

---

[257] Bradley 1984, 21; Dal Lago and Katsari 2008, 193.

[258] Fiensy 1991, 77, 91; Kloppenborg 2006, 307.

[259] Hezser 2005, 149; Harrill 2006, 92, 107–108, 111; see Dal Lago and Katsari 2008, 199–205, esp. 204–205.

[260] See Bradley 1984, 21–26.

[261] Cf. Burford 1993, 218; cf. Xenophon, *Oec.* 15.1. By contrast, the farm manager would often have been tempted to maintain agricultural output at a slightly lower level in order to safeguard his position and at the same time please his master (White 1970, 376).

[262] Bradley 1984, 22; cf. Seneca, *Ep.* 47.4.

[263] Massey and Moreland 1992, 27; Burford 1993, 218; Joshel 2010, 57, 123.

[264] White 1970, 358.

[265] Valantasis 2005, 168.

[266] Cf. Matz 2002, 14.

and lazy, and rural slaves were specifically considered to be difficult to man-age, prone to drunkenness, and insolent.[267] A "good" manager was able to pre-vent laxity, carelessness, and criminality through sternness.[268] Yet starving and abusing the slaves would have been unacceptable, especially if it had a negative effect on productivity.[269] Brutality against one slave, or one group of slaves, could have a demoralising effect on all the other slaves, which hindered servile productivity.[270] Maltreatment and malnourishment could also render slaves disloyal and make them rebellious.[271] Agronomists warned estate managers against abusing their authority.[272] As we will see shortly, conscientious land-owners inspected the general contentment and physical condition of their slaves whenever they visited their farms. Foremen, who usually operated di-rectly under the manager, were encouraged by agronomists to use words in-stead of whips to control the farmhands.[273]

Both Matthew and Luke qualify the provision of food as happening ἐν καιρῷ, which the *Critical Edition of Q* translates as "on time." Marshall also states matter-of-factly: "ἐν καιρῷ signifies 'at the right time,'" referencing Matthew 20:10 as comparative evidence.[274] On Roman farms, the working day was typically divided into available working hours, "including the midday meal break, followed by a short siesta."[275] From the landowner's perspective, the exact time at which the workers were fed could not have made much dif-ference, but getting fed on time must have been all-important from the workers' perspective. To illustrate this, consider the following anecdote from the Baby-lonian Talmud:

One day Rabbi Yosei from Yokrat hired day laborers to work his field. It grew late and he did not bring them food. The workers said to the son of Rabbi Yosei from Yokrat: We are starving. They were sitting under a fig tree, so the son said: Fig tree, fig tree. Yield your fruits, so that my father's workers may eat. The fig tree yielded fruit, and they ate.[276]

---

[267] See Bradley 1984, 27–30; 1994, 65, 122–125; Boer and Petterson 2017, 79, 89; cf. Bagnall 1993, 235; Burford 1993, 211; Dillon 2002, 126; cf. Egyptian papyrus *P.Stras.* 4.296; Cato, *Agr.* 2.2; 4; 5.1; 66.1; 67.2; Columella, *Rust.* 1.1.20; 1.3.5; 1.6.8; 1.7.6–7; 1.8.1–2, 15, 17, 18; 1.9.1, 4; 7.4.2; 9.5.2; 11.1.12, 14, 16, 19, 21, 23, 25, 27.

[268] Joshel 2010, 155.

[269] White 1970, 358; see Bradley 1984, 21–26.

[270] Harrill 2006, 110.

[271] Descat 2011, 213; see Joshel 2010, 57–58; cf. Massey and Moreland 1992, 57; cf. Diodorus Siculus 34.2.25–28.

[272] Kloppenborg 1995, 294–295; Harrill 2006, 109; cf. Luz 2005, 224.

[273] White 1970, 359; Harrill 2006, 107; Dal Lago and Katsari 2008, 196; Joshel 2010, 126; cf. Varro, *Rust.* 1.17.5.

[274] Marshall 1978, 541.

[275] White 1970, 363.

[276] Quotation from b.Taʻan. 24a; translation from Sefaria (https://www.sefaria.org/Taanit. 24a.3?lang=bi).

Even in a modern context, anyone who has done menial or physical labour will know the significance not only of having lunch, but also of doing so at the scheduled time. The phrase "on time" reflects the perspective of the worker and betrays the parable's derivation "from below." As explained in this book's introduction, the term "from below" refers to the vantage point of those at the bottom of society. It is highly likely that the first audiences of Jesus's parables consisted of diverse socio-economic segments of the population.[277] At the same time, it is highly likely that an overwhelming majority of these audiences were from the lower segments of society.[278] Both of these statements generally apply to the audiences of Q as well.[279] After Jesus died and the socio-economic make-up of the movement changed, it became increasingly customary to interpret his parables from above. In order to bypass such secondary interpretation, it is in the case of each individual parable necessary to ask: "What does the parable mean when viewed from the underside of Jesus' society?"[280]

According to Liddell and Scott, καιρός could also mean "due measure, proportion, fitness."[281] This meaning would fit well with Luke's σιτομετρία, which we saw means "measure/ration of corn/grain." Not everyone received the same rations of food on an ancient farm.[282] The amount of food they received was determined by each worker's tasks on the farm and position on the hierarchy. Arguing against this proposal is the fact that καιρός always seems to carry a meaning related to "time" in the New Testament.[283] Liddell and Scott also indicate that "time" is the more frequent meaning of καιρός in ancient Greek literature generally.[284] The use of ἐν before καιρῷ is also interesting. To my knowledge, ἐν καιρῷ is not a technical term or standard adverbial phrase with

---

[277] Crossan 2002, 253; Funk 2006, 37, 41.

[278] Dodd 1958, 21; Funk 2006, 44; cf. Crossan 2002, 250; Häkkinen 2016, 1. Boer and Petterson (2017, 165–168) argue that the New Testament texts do not promote reading the parables of Jesus from below, but rather reflect the vantage point of people who are not from peasant provenance. I would agree with this when it comes to the level of the New Testament, which is the focus of Boer and Petterson's investigation in chapter 6 of their book, but not when it comes to the levels of Q and the historical Jesus.

[279] See Horsley 1999, 260–261, 269, 296–298; Kloppenborg 2000a, 198–199; Reed 2000, 136–137; cf. Oakman 1986, 100; Kloppenborg 1987, 251; Douglas 1995, 120; Piper 1995, 63–64; Reed 1995, 19; Tuckett 1996, 360, 365; Freyne 2000, 206; Arnal 2001, 150, 173, 188.

[280] Oakman 2008, 268.

[281] Liddell and Scott 1996, 859.

[282] See White 1970, 360–361.

[283] Cf. Louw and Nida 1993b, 128, s.v. καιρός.

[284] Liddell and Scott 1996, 859.

one predetermined meaning. It often appears in the New Testament (and else-where) with an additional qualifier to make the meaning clear.[285] I could find only three instances in the New Testament where ἐν καιρῷ appears without such a qualifier (my translations): ἐν ᾧ καιρῷ ("at that time") in Acts 7:20; ἐν καιρῷ ("at the proper time") in 1 Peter 5:6; and καὶ (ἐν) καιρῷ ("when it was time") in Luke 20:10. In the last text, ἐν only appears in some of the manu-scripts and is not featured in recent editions of Nestle-Aland, including edition 28. Out of the three texts listed above, comparison with 1 Peter 5:6 and Luke 20:10 suggests that ἐν καιρῷ could also in Q 12:42 be understood to mean "at the proper/right time," which supports both Marshall's comment that it means "at the right time"[286] and the translation "on time" by the *Critical Edition of Q*. Another option is that ἐν καιρῷ references a specific time of the year, probably the time of harvest. One of the three texts listed above, namely Luke 20:10, uses the phrase (ἐν) καιρῷ in reference to harvest time. A number of Bible translations render καιρῷ in Luke 20:10 as "harvest time."[287] καιρός has a sim-ilar meaning in a number of other New Testament texts that do not feature ἐν with καιρός.[288] If we are correct that Q 12:42–44 is set on an ancient farm, it might not be entirely illegitimate to translate ἐν καιρῷ here with "at harvest time." Such a translation would be supported by another Q text, namely Q 10:2, 7–8, where the harvest is associated with farm workers receiving food and/or wages. Luz, for example, translates ἐν καιρῷ in Matthew 24:45 (Q 12:42) as "in season."[289] It seems unlikely, however, that the author would have omitted the word "harvest" (θερισμός; θερίζω) if harvest season was the specific refer-ent and important to the interpretation of the parable. Moreover, the land-holder's instruction to the manager could not have been to only feed the slaves during harvest time, but must have been to feed them daily. The phrase "on time" therefore makes more sense as referring to a specific time of day, to be repeated on a daily basis, than a specific time of the month or year. It is likely that the phrase "on time" was included to set up the scene for the master's return. If there were not a specified time for the lunch break, the manager would not have been guilty of anything if the slaves were working or doing something

---

[285] These are the instances I was able to source (my translations): ἐν καιρῷ τοῦ θερισμοῦ ("at the time of the harvest") in Matthew 13:30; ἐν τοῖς καιροῖς αὐτῶν ("during their sea-sons") in Matthew 21:41; νῦν ἐν τῷ καιρῷ τούτῳ ("now, during this time") in Mark 10:30; ἐν καιρῷ πειρασμοῦ ("in time of testing") in Luke 8:13; ἐν τῷ καιρῷ τούτῳ ("in this age") in Luke 18:30; ἐν τῷ νῦν καιρῷ ("at the present time") in Romans 3:26; 11:5 and 2 Corin-thians 8:14; ἐν παντὶ καιρῷ ("at all times") in Ephesians 6:18; ἐν τῷ ἑαυτοῦ καιρῷ ("in his own time") in 2 Thessalonians 2:6; ἐν ὑστέροις καιροῖς ("in the end-times") in 1 Timothy 4:1; ἐν καιρῷ ἐσχάτῳ ("at the end of time") in 1 Peter 1:5.

[286] See above.

[287] E.g. NIV, NASB.

[288] E.g. Matt 13:30; 21:41.

[289] Luz 2005, 221; cf. also KJV, NKJV, ASV.

else upon the master's return. The allocation of a specific time for the lunch break creates the conditions for the master to arrive and find his manager feeding the slaves, which then leads to the manager being rewarded.

Even though the master's departure precedes the beginning of the parable and his absence is only presumed by the narrative, his subsequent arrival on the farm is expressed by the participial phrase "on coming" or "when arriving" (ἐλθών). It made good business sense for a landowner to visit his estate regularly.[290] This did not always happen in practice. There is evidence from Egyptian papyri that landowners and managers sometimes corresponded via written mail.[291] Some wealthy landowners visited their estates very rarely, thereby increasing the import of each visit.[292] Around the turn of the first century CE, for example, the Jewish landowner Rabbi Tarfon was mistaken for a common thief by the farmers on his estate, and Rabbi Eleazar ben Harsom was seized by slaves on his own estate who had never seen him before.[293] On the one hand, it goes without saying that the less often the master visited his estate, the more freedom and independence the manager had during the interim.[294] For the most part, estate managers were allowed to go about their business as they saw fit, provided that they earned the landowner a steady and sturdy return on investment.[295] "The handling of the whole operation, including the treatment of the labour force, lay very largely within the discretion of the *vilicus*."[296] On the other hand, infrequent visits allowed time for anticipation to build on the part of both the manager and the other slaves. A master's long-anticipated visit was a big event and could fill both the manager and the slaves with much fear.[297] All slaves, even estate managers, lived under constant fear of being punished.[298] Estate managers were warned by agronomists about a day of accounting.[299] In *Daphnis and Chloe*, Lamon fears being hanged by Dionysophanes as punishment for the garden being vandalised under his watch.[300] In *The Golden*

---

[290] See Harrill 2006, 109–110; Aberbach 1994, 42–44; cf. Toutain 1951, 278; Burford 1993, 173; Aubert 1994, 122; Kloppenborg 2006, 315; cf. Xenophon, *Oec.* 11.15–18.

[291] E.g. *P.Haun.* 2.23, 32; *P.Ryl.* 2.238; *SB* 16.12579; *P.Tebt.* 2.423; cf. *P.Oslo* 2.44; *P.Oxy.* 9.1220; *P.Mich.* 1.14; *P.Col.inv.* 608; *P.Fay.* 110–124, 248–277; *P.Petr.* 1.29; cf. Kloppenborg 2006, 279–280, see 442–443.

[292] Cf. Burford 1993, 216–217, 219; Kloppenborg 2006, 315.

[293] See Aberbach 1994, 40–41.

[294] Cf. Burford 1993, 177; Bradley 1994, 105, 219.

[295] White 1970, 358; cf. Aubert 1994, 159.

[296] White 1970, 358; cf. Burford 1993, 177.

[297] See Bradley 1994, 102–104; cf. Bradley 1984, 115–116, 123, 135–137, 142; Hezser 2005, 149; Harrill 2006, 91–92; see Longus 4; cf. Egyptian papyrus *P.Princ.* 2.72.

[298] Bradley 1984, 123, 135–137, 142; Hezser 2005, 149; cf. Harrill 2006, 91–92; Joshel 2010, 116.

[299] Harrill 2006, 109.

[300] Longus 4.7–9.

Ass, Apuleius tells of a servile manager whose master punished him by smearing him with honey and allowing ants to devour him.[301] According to Schottroff, servile managers "could assure themselves of a great deal of power and influence, but always remained in the unconditional dependent state of slavery, with their bodies at the owner's disposal."[302] There is no small number of ancient reports about slaves who were so scared of facing their masters' punishment that they would rather commit suicide.[303] Filling slaves with fear was an efficient and deliberate method to ensure that they did what was expected of them, even in the absence of their masters.[304] At the same time, infrequent visits could endorse and generate different types of laxity and opportunistic behaviour from both the slaves and the manager.[305] A number of Jewish landowners complained about tenant farmers stealing from them or in some other way doing them in.[306] For these reasons, agronomists advised absent landowners to visit their estates regularly and unexpectedly.[307] Jewish rabbis also advised landowners to visit their estates regularly, even as much as daily or twice daily, although this was not followed in practice by most Jewish landowners.[308]

Upon such visits, all operations on the farm were inspected, including especially the progress of the labour.[309] One of the most important factors that was taken into consideration during inspection was the slaves' general physical condition and level of contentment.[310] Of particular interest was the state of the slaves' food and clothing. The watchful master would allow his slaves to express any and all grievances that they might have against the manager. Ideally, the master would ascertain the reason(s) behind each and every punishment, so that he could evaluate the degree of appropriateness.[311] In addition to inspecting the condition and contentment of the slaves, landholders inspected every aspect of the farm's general condition during their visitations, including the crops, the farm animals, and the finances, thereby scrutinising the farm's levels

---

[301] Apuleius, *Metam.* 8.22; cf. Aubert 1994, 173.

[302] Schottroff 2006, 175.

[303] E.g. Plutarch, *Cat. Maj.* 10.5; Seneca, *Ep.* 4.4; see Bradley 1994, 111–112.

[304] Bradley 1984, 136; cf. Joshel 2010, 116, 178.

[305] Bradley 1994, 105; Kloppenborg 1995, 295; 2006, 316.

[306] See Aberbach 1994, 43–47.

[307] Burford 1993, 173; Kloppenborg 1995, 295 n. 61; Harrill 2006, 109; Joshel 2010, 175; Chandezon 2011, 101; cf. e.g. Xenophon, *Oec.* 11.15–18.

[308] See Aberbach 1994, 42–44.

[309] Cf. Egyptian papyrus *P.Princ.* 2.72.

[310] Bradley 1984, 24; 1994, 82, 104; Dal Lago and Katsari 2008, 204; Joshel 2010, 175; cf. Columella, *Rust.* 1.8.16–18; Pliny, *Ep.* 5.14.8.

[311] Harrill 2006, 110; cf. Dal Lago and Katsari 2008, 197.

of profitability and waste.[312] Estate managers usually had a host of responsibilities, of which workforce management was only one.[313] A good example of such responsibility is reflected in a papyrus from Egypt, containing over 1 200 transactions, believed to have been kept by an estate manager.[314]

It is very difficult to determine the extent to which farm managers did what was expected of them and how they actually treated their subordinates. The advice of agronomists often reflect ideal conditions from a landowner's perspective, which do not necessarily represent a one-to-one relation with common practice.[315] In Roman comedies and elsewhere, the farm manager is often portrayed negatively as a stereotyped regal tyrant, who terrorises and brutalises everyone under his yoke.[316] In fact, it was so common in the Roman world for a manager to physically and emotionally torment his fellow slaves that the term itself (*vilicus*) became synonymous with servile brutality in popular culture. The redactional addition of Q 12:45–46 probably draws on this caricature when depicting the appointed slave as beating his fellow slaves while eating and drinking with drunkards.

Individual slaves on the same farm generally had separate religious, ethnic, social, and educational backgrounds.[317] No less distinctive were their agricultural tasks and functions, as well as their living conditions.[318] In general, a slave's background determined her[319] task(s), which in turn determined her rank, which in turn determined her living conditions.[320] For the most part, such internal differentiation thwarted the development of group solidarity among

---

[312] Bradley 1994, 104; cf. Pliny, *Ep.* 9.20.2; Longus 4.13.

[313] See Aubert 1994, 170–172; cf. Fleddermann 2005a, 627; Valantasis 2005, 168.

[314] *P.Kar.Goodsp.* 96; cf. *P.Tebt.* 2.423.

[315] Cf. Fisher 1998, 194.

[316] See Harrill 2006, 104–105.

[317] Burford 1993, 211; Dillon 2002, 125; Hezser 2005, 116; cf. Glotz 1926, 193.

[318] White 1970, 333.

[319] The use here of inclusive language in the form of a feminine pronoun is not illegitimate or anachronistic. Due to the desexualisation of slaves in antiquity, some female slaves were expected to work as farmhands, while some male slaves were expected to perform household chores (Hezser 2005, 84; cf. Joshel 2010, 66, 170). Even some of the estate managers were women, although this was extremely rare (see Aubert 1994, 140–141, 193; Chandezon 2011, 99). The same fluidity in labour applied to non-servile peasant farming, where the tasks of men and women overlapped quite significantly (see Boer and Petterson 2017, 66–67). There was, nonetheless, on most ancient farms a broad division between female domestic labour and male agricultural (and other outside) labour (see Saller 2003, 199–201; Mouritsen 2011, 133–134).

[320] Cf. Bradley 1984, 16; Harrill 2006, 148.

slaves and prevented rebellion against the master.[321] For this reason, slaveholders deliberately established and upheld internal dissention among slaves.[322] Much more common than servile solidarity was dissention, jealousy, and competition for hierarchical advancement. Such antagonism was even greater between slaves and their manager.[323] The fact that the manager was also a slave, but had the authority to boss his fellow slaves around and even discipline them as he saw fit, made him the object of intense envy, resentment, and defiance. Rural slaves would often compete with the manager for the master's favour, which would foster a working environment replete with mutual hostility, distrust, and anxiety. The manager was therefore caught between a rock and a hard place, having to deal with the envy of fellow workers and the expectations of the landholder. At the same time, the position carried with it a certain amount of power, which could be used to selfishly promote one's own situation or to selflessly improve the living conditions of all the farmhands. No doubt, the staff would be very grateful for the latter, so that jealousy and envy would make way for appreciation and respect, which would ultimately increase productivity and profitability to the satisfaction of the landholder.

In verses 43–44, the conduct proposed by verse 42 is motivated by the promise of future reward in the form of a promotion.[324] A number of commentators have objected to an apparent internal contradiction in the parable.[325] In verse 42, the chosen slave is appointed over the master's entire "household" (οἰκετεία). As we saw, this refers to the servile manager's position at the top of the estate's hierarchy. In verse 44, however, that slave's reward is to be appointed "over all his [the master's] possessions" (ἐπὶ πᾶσιν τοῖς ὑπάρ-χουσιν αὐτοῦ). How can it be seen as a promotion to place a servile manager in charge of everything and put him at the top of the hierarchy if he was already in charge of everything and at the top of the hierarchy before the master had left? Commentators have attempted to explain this difficulty in a number of ways. Donahue reasons that the slave was initially only in charge of food distribution, but was subsequently set over all his master's possessions.[326] Allison holds that the chosen slave was initially only appointed over the other slaves, but was subsequently promoted to authority over all his master's possessions, not just his slaves.[327] Taylor argues that the slave did not, at the beginning of the narrative, enjoy the formal title of "manager," since his supervision was only a temporary arrangement, but was indeed formally appointed as a permanent

---

[321] Bradley 1984, 16; Burford 1993, 212; Hezser 2005, 11–12; De Wet 2018, 2.

[322] Burford 1993, 212; Joshel 2010, 57; cf. Dal Lago and Katsari 2008, 211; DuBois 2009, 57; cf. Plato, *Leg.* 6.777c–d; Aristotle, [*Oec.*] 1344b17–20.

[323] Bradley 1994, 72.

[324] Taylor 1989, 143; Etchells 1998, 110; cf. Crossan 1974a, 25–26, 38.

[325] E.g. Marshall 1978, 541.

[326] Donahue 1988, 98.

[327] Allison 2004, 440.

"manager" when his master witnessed his satisfactory performance.[328] Bock similarly maintains that the reward entails a promotion from temporary to permanent management.[329] Marshall reasons that servile estate managers were symbols of service and subordination in the early church, so that the appointed slave's initial authority is only partial and temporary, while his eventual authority would be complete and permanent.[330] Nolland explains the difficulty from a diachronic standpoint: the original text, which Matthew follows, does not feature the appointed slave as an estate manager when the parable commences, since he only becomes one at the end, and Luke was simply wrong in introducing the appointed slave as a "manager" (οἰκονόμος).[331] Like Donahue, Nolland argues that the slave was initially only put in charge of food distribution, not comprehensive management. Like Taylor, Nolland holds that a temporary arrangement gives way to a more permanent arrangement. These explanations are all inadequate and erroneous, failing to fully consider the social background of agricultural slavery.

The simple solution is that the selected slave was initially indeed at the top of the hierarchy of that individual estate, but not of the master's entire fortune.[332] Q 12:44 portrays the master as an extremely wealthy man, owning more than one estate.[333] In verse 44, the entrusted slave is promoted as manager over the other estates as well. We argued earlier that the "household" (οἰκετεία) of verse 42 does not reference the owner's entire household (*domus*) or nuclear family, but the families of slaves who lived and worked on that particular farm (*familia rustica*). This interpretation is confirmed by the content of verse 44. It was not uncommon for a landowner who owned multiple estates to appoint an administrator (*procurator* and, for example, πραγματευτής) to supervise all the different estates and estate managers.[334] If Kloppenborg and others are correct that the word βαιτανῶτα in the Egyptian papyrus *P.Lond.* 7.1948 refers to Beth Anath in Galilee, we have direct evidence of such a general administrator visiting a large farm in Galilee to inspect its progress before returning to his employer, Apollonios, in Alexandria.[335] According to Boer and Petterson, slaves "preferred to be owned by a wealthy and powerful master with many slaves, especially if they could make it to the top of the servile pecking order."[336] De

---

[328] Taylor 1989, 139–140, 143.

[329] Bock 1996, 1180.

[330] Marshall 1978, 541.

[331] Nolland 2005, 997–998; cf. Fleddermann 2005a, 627.

[332] Cf. Chandezon 2011, 102, 107.

[333] Cf. Fiensy 1991, 56; 2010, 197.

[334] White 1970, 353, 355, 379; Harrill 2006, 103–104; see Aubert 1994, 137, 141–144, 183–186; cf. Hedrick 2014, 148–149; Boer and Petterson 2017, 89–90, 124; cf. Columella, *Rust.* 1.6.7, 23; Egyptian Papyrus *SB* 16.12607.

[335] Kloppenborg 2006, 368–369.

[336] Boer and Petterson 2017, 89.

Wet further mentions that "some managerial slaves seized opportunities for upward mobility, which at times afforded them much authority."[337]

The all-inclusivity of the phrase "over all his [the master's] possessions" (ἐπὶ πᾶσιν τοῖς ὑπάρχουσιν αὐτοῦ) implies that the slave was not only put in charge of all the other estates, but also placed in charge of the entire *familia*, including the master's urban slaves.[338] Such a promotion would entail liberation from the confinements of one particular farm.[339] In fact, it would entail a movement from the farm to the master's urban household, where he would henceforth reside with his family, although it would still be expected of him to visit the different estates for inspection.[340] Since urban slaves were normally seen as hierarchically superior to rural slaves, this jump in rank would not at all have been insignificant.[341] What is more, conditions were generally much better for urban than for rural slaves.[342] In fact, urban household slaves were at times threatened with being sent to some or other rural estate as punishment for extreme misdeeds.[343] Whereas rural managers mostly shared the unfortunate socio-economic conditions of their inferiors, urban slaves could improve their socio-economic conditions dramatically.[344] To top it all off, manumission might have accompanied the promotion of the slave in the parable, since "[o]nly freeborn or manumitted *procuratores* are recorded in sources."[345]

In the parable, the promoted slave is placed at the very top of the slave hierarchy, second only to the master and his family.[346] One gets the impression that the slave was promoted to being the master's right-hand man and confidant.[347] Both Greco-Roman and Jewish masters could develop highly intimate and/or respectful relationships with one or two of their slaves.[348] Roman and Jewish stories of ideal master-slave relationships give expression to the latter

---

[337] De Wet 2018, 11; cf. Schottroff 2006, 175.

[338] Cf. Aubert 1994, 173; Saller 2003, 187–188.

[339] Cf. Aubert 1994, 118.

[340] Cf. Herzog 1994, 157; Chandezon 2011, 102, 107; cf. Egyptian papyri *P.Princ.* 2.72; *SB* 16.12607.

[341] Cf. Bradley 1994, 70; Schottroff 2006, 175.

[342] Yavetz 1988, 159; see White 1970, 362–363, 365; Massey and Moreland 1992, 27–28. It should nonetheless be noted that urban domestic slaves were more visible and spent more time in the vicinity of their masters, which made them more vulnerable (Bradley 1984, 123; Scheidel 2008, 110).

[343] White 1970, 358; Massey and Moreland 1992, 50; cf. Hezser 2005, 153 n. 13; cf. Plautus, *Asin.* 342; *Bacch.* 365; *Most.* 19; cf. *Vid.* 31.

[344] See Bradley 1994, 68–72.

[345] Aubert 1994, 185; cf. Burford 1993, 185, 220; Herzog 1994, 157; Mouritsen 2011, 137; *pace* Allison 2004, 440.

[346] Cf. White 1970, 355; Fleddermann 2005a, 636.

[347] Cf. Marshall 1978, 541; Herzog 1994, 157.

[348] De Vaux 1965, 85; Andrews 1967, 134; Burford 1993, 217; Aubert 1994, 159; Hezser 2005, 100, 141, 292, 301.

phenomenon.[349] As one would expect, the most important trait of the ideal slave was unmoving loyalty to the master, sometimes unto death.[350] Due to the physical distance between rural managers and urban landowners, as well as the infrequency with which they saw each other, it is extremely unlikely that land-owners would have pursued or fostered cherished relationships with farm man-agers.[351] Urban household slaves were by far the more likely recipients of such favour.[352] In the literature, such slaves are often described by their masters as true confidants or even friends. Funeral inscriptions indicate that at least some of these "privileged" slaves had the same high regard and genuine love for their masters.[353] It is doubtful, however, that the same would have been true of all, or even most, of these "prominent" slaves. At its core, the master-slave rela-tionship was typified by inequality and disproportion. Like an abusive mar-riage, the slave-master relationship could be characterised by the simultaneous presence of both intimacy and exploitation, both affinity and submission.[354] Even so, these individual slaves were usually granted a lot of autonomy and responsibility. It follows that the promotion of which verse 44 speaks entails more than just an advancement of status and an increase in responsibility.[355] In addition to the movement from the farm to the city, it entails a highly honour-able movement from the master's blind spot to his right-hand side.[356] This new position would have afforded the (manumitted) slave plenty of opportunities for significant wealth creation.[357] The particular promotion described here would have been extremely significant and life-changing for the appointed slave. He would have been put in charge of all the landowner's different es-tates.[358] In effect, he would have been second in command, subordinate only to the landowner (and his family). Such a promotion reminds one of the story of Joseph.[359]

One aspect of verses 43–44 that seems extraordinary is the imbalance and disproportion here between achievement and reward. The magnitude of the

---

[349] Andrews 1967, 138; Yavetz 1988, 158; see Matz 2002, 17–18; Hezser 2005, 155–162; 2009, 127–128.

[350] Yavetz 1988, 158; Hezser 2005, 155; 2009, 127; see Joshel 2010, 116–117; cf. Harrill 2006, 146, 152–153.

[351] Bradley 1994, 105; cf. Massey and Moreland 1992, 27, 32.

[352] Dillon 2002, 125–126.

[353] Aubert 1994, 159–160; see Hezser 2005, 162–166; cf. Fiensy 1991, 92.

[354] Hezser 2005, 149.

[355] Cf. Allison 2004, 440; Valantasis 2005, 169.

[356] Cf. Chandezon 2011, 102, 107.

[357] Cf. Herzog 1994, 157.

[358] See Aubert 1994, 137, 141–144, 183–186; Howes 2015c, 90–93; cf. White 1970, 353, 355, 379; Harrill 2006, 103–104; Chandezon 2011, 102, 107; cf. Columella, *On Agriculture* 1.6.7, 23.

[359] Luz 2005, 223–224; see below.

manager's reward seems exaggerated given the nature of the actual achievement. This exaggeration is doubly augmented by the exclamation "amen" (ἀμήν)[360] and the emphatic phrase "I tell you" (λέγω ὑμῖν).[361] In the Sayings Gospel Q, the latter phrase often precedes an exaggerated, subversive, and/or implausible statement by Q's Jesus, as if the audience needs convincing of the claim's validity.[362] For an estate manager to be promoted to administrator was no small achievement, and this reward is totally atypical for the simple and straightforward task of feeding farmhands. Yet one should not overlook the possibility that the act of feeding slaves was representative of the manager's entire managerial function. Even so, it would, even in general terms, have been exceptional for a farm manager to be promoted to administrator. The imagined promotion was within the realm of possibility, but was at the same time exceptional, especially if feeding fellow slaves was the manager's only or main accomplishment.[363]

According to Funk, the parables of Jesus are all characterised by an uncomfortable mix of "everydayness" (or vividness) and strangeness (or incongruity).[364] On the one hand, they portray everyday reality truthfully, causing the audience to agree: "That's the way things are!" On the other, they distort and overturn everyday reality through one or more narrative elements that are exaggerated, implausible, or unusual, causing the audience to ask: "What's wrong with this picture?" The interplay between "everydayness" and peculiarity gives birth to the meaning of each parable.[365] From all the contextual information in this section it would seem that most if not all of the details in Q 12:42–44 are historically reliable. It is safe to say that the parable displays a very high degree of verisimilitude. On the level of "everydayness," the parable is entirely congruent with the practice of agricultural slavery in antiquity, so that the original audience would have identified the narrative and imagery as highly familiar and true-to-life.[366] On the level of strangeness, one is hard-pressed to find an element of incongruence with agricultural slavery in antiquity. Only one feature of the parable could possibly fall into this category, namely the extent of the servile manager's reward, especially if compared to his actual achievement. That a servile farm manager would be rewarded handsomely for the simple act of feeding others is surprising and incredible. The reward is not so much incongruent as it is unusual; it is exaggerated beyond any reasonable expectation.

---

[360] Luke has "truly" (ἀληθῶς) (Marshall 1978, 541; Bock 1996, 1180; Fleddermann 2005a, 627–628; Nolland 2005, 998).

[361] Cf. Kirk 1998, 234.

[362] Cf. Q 7:26, 28; 10:12, 24; 11:9, 51; 12:22, 27, 59; 13:35; 15:7, [10]; 17:34.

[363] Nolland 2005, 997; cf. Schottroff 2006, 175.

[364] Funk 2006, 43–51.

[365] Cf. Crossan 1974c, 98; 1979, 28; Kloppenborg 1995, 278.

[366] Cf. Park 2019, 44.

One should not overlook the specific task of feeding others as both the precondition for the handsome reward and the factor that highlights the incongruence of the reward.[367]

The importance of feeding others as the specific task of the manager is further supported by the intertextual link between Q 12:42–44 and the story of Joseph in Genesis. There is a rich scholarly history of reading this parable in the light of Genesis 39, especially verses 4–5, where Joseph is appointed as overseer over Pharaoh's "house"[368], which included not only the royal household, but also the entire Egyptian kingdom[369].[370] Allison makes a very compelling case for seeing Genesis 39:4–5 as a legitimate intertext for our parable.[371] Most significantly, the vocabulary, grammar, and word order of two specific phrases in Q 12:42–46 are almost identical to two corresponding phrases in the Septuagint's version of Genesis 39:4–5. The first parallel concerns the phrase "put over his household" (κατέστησεν […] ἐπὶ τῆς οἰκετείας αὐτοῦ) in Q 12:42 and LXX Genesis 39:4–5.[372] Nowhere else in the Septuagint does καθίστημι ("put" or "appoint") precede ἐπί + οἰκ- ("over" + "house"). This very distinctive phrase is commonly used in the Jewish tradition in contexts where the story of Joseph is specifically being referenced.[373] The second parallel concerns the phrase "over all his possessions" (ἐπὶ πᾶσιν τοῖς ὑπάρχουσιν αὐτοῦ) in Q 12:44 and LXX Genesis 39:5.[374] As with the first phrasal parallel, the vocabulary, grammar, and word order of the latter phrase are highly distinctive. Its only other occurrence in the Septuagint is in Judith 8:10, but there it occurs not only without the preposition "over" (ἐπί), but also without the preceding verb "put" or "appoint" (καθίστημι). In any case, the story of Joseph was much better known and much easier to recall than the more obscure tale of Judith. In the remainder of the parable, a number of keywords further strengthen the connection between Q 12:42–44 and the story of Joseph: (1) κύριος ("master" or "lord")[375]; (2) φρόνιμος ("wise," "sensible," or "prudent")[376]; and (3) δοῦλος

---

[367] Cf. Luz 2005, 223.

[368] MT: בַּיִת; LXX: οἶκος.

[369] The latter is indicated by verse 6, where it clearly states that Joseph was put in charge of every aspect of the Egyptian kingdom, even to the extent that the Pharaoh's only concern was feeding himself. See also Gen 41:40–41, where Joseph is reinstated as the overseer over all of Egypt, subject only to the Pharaoh himself.

[370] Allison 2000, 87 n. 61; Luz 2005, 223 n. 22.

[371] Allison 2000, 87–92.

[372] Luz 2005, 223; LXX Gen 39:4: κατέστησεν αὐτὸν ἐπὶ τοῦ οἴκου αὐτοῦ; LXX Gen 39:5: τὸ κατασταθῆναι αὐτὸν ἐπὶ τοῦ οἴκου αὐτοῦ.

[373] Allison (2000, 88–89) lists the following examples: LXX Ps 104:21; Jub. 39:3; 40:7; Philo, *Joseph* 37; 38; 117; T. Jos. 2:1; 11:6; Josephus, *Ant.* 2.39; Jos. Asen. 4:7; 20:9; Acts 7:9–10.

[374] LXX Gen 39:5: ἐπὶ πᾶσιν τοῖς ὑπάρχουσιν αὐτῷ.

[375] Q 12:42, 43 // LXX Gen 39:3, 4, etc.

[376] Q 12:42 // LXX Gen 41:33, 39; cf. LXX Ps 104:21.

("servant" or "slave")[377]. Allison also points to the keyword "ration of grain" (σιτομετρία) as a link with Q 12:42.[378] The word σιτομετρία features twice in the story of Joseph, who happens to be the acting subject in both cases.[379] Additionally, the noun σιτοδοσία ("gift / gratuitous distribution of grain/corn") appears twice in the story of Joseph as a reference to him specifically.[380] This noun was commonly and fondly applied to Joseph in the subsequent Jewish tradition.[381] Finally, the story of Joseph is replete with references to "grain" or "corn" (σῖτος).[382]

The degree of overlap between the narrative of Joseph and the parable in Q 12:42–44 surpasses mere verbal correspondence.[383] In both cases, a wise servant becomes an overseer. In both cases, the promotion happens by means of official appointment. In both cases, the newly appointed overseer is in charge of rationing out food to his subjects, placing their sustenance and survival in his hands. In both cases, faithfulness during an initial appointment is rewarded by a promotion in the form of a second, more important appointment. In Genesis 45:5, 7, Joseph's hardships and eventual appointment as the Pharaoh's right-hand man are revealed as part of God's plan to ensure the survival of Joseph's brothers; with the word "brothers" here referring to both his biological brothers and his kinsmen.[384] Just like the ultimate goal of Joseph's appointment was the nutritional provision and physical survival of his fellow kinsmen, the ultimate goal of the slave's appointment in Q 12:42–44 is the nutritional provision and physical survival of his fellow slaves.[385] The following quotation from the pseudepigraphical *Testament of Joseph* (3:5), written in the first person from Joseph's perspective, indicates just how important this aspect of Joseph's role had become in contemporary Jewish tradition: "If my master was absent, I drank no wine; for three-day periods I would take no food but give it to the poor and ill."[386] For Philo, eating and storing food (as well as accumulating possessions) are preoccupations of the body and therefore subordinate to acts that feed the soul. This paradigm causes him at times to judge negatively

---

[377] Q 12:42, 43 // LXX Gen 39:17, 19; 41:12. Even if LXX Gen uses παῖς (also "slave" or "servant") instead of δοῦλος, many subsequent Jewish texts do indeed feature δοῦλος in reference to Joseph (Allison 2000, 90 n. 74).

[378] Allison 2000, 89.

[379] LXX Gen 47:12, 14; cf. Marshall 1978, 541; Hays 2012, 47 n. 29.

[380] LXX Gen 42:19, 33.

[381] Jos. Asen. 4:8; 25:6; 26:3, 4; Josephus, *Ant.* 2.124, 189.

[382] Cf. LXX Gen 41:35, 49; 42:2, 3, 25, 26; 43:2; 44:2; 47:12, 13, 14.

[383] Allison 2004, 440; Luz 2005, 223–224.

[384] Cf. Hunter 1971, 109.

[385] See Hays 2012, 49–50; cf. Allison 2004, 440.

[386] Translation from Kee 1983, 820.

the person of Joseph, who accumulated wealth and stored food to feed the people.[387] Despite this caricature, Philo's writings provide evidence of the proclivity in first-century Jewish tradition to associate Joseph with the act of feeding the populace. Other examples can be added.[388]

In my view, the specific nature of the slave's task to feed his fellow slaves is crucial to the interpretation of this parable. It is highly significant that the appointed slave is charged specifically with feeding his fellow slaves.[389] Previous studies have tended to disregard the content of the task itself.[390] The specific description of the slave's task and the explicit naming of the recipients thereof become redundant and unintelligible if the parable is read from above. A reading from above associates with the master and evaluates the slave's actions from the master's vantage point.[391] Considered from above, the slave's obedience becomes the focal point.[392] Succinctly put, "[r]eward awaits the slave acting in the manner expected of him by the master."[393] Considered from below, however, the slave's obedience is little more than the eventuality that brings about his reward. Much more important in a reading from below is how the hypothetical slave treats his fellow slaves.[394] In a reading from above, the appointed slave's specific task could have been just about anything, since it is his (non)compliance that is hermeneutically important.[395] Viewed from above, it has no impact whatsoever on the parable's metaphorical meaning if the task is changed to, say, scrubbing the floor. In a reading from below, however, the appointed slave's specific task is paramount, since it impacts the fellow slaves and their nutritional wellbeing directly, while his (non)compliance is only important inasmuch as it relates to the task in question.[396]

Q 12:42–44 is the story of an unlikely character, the servile farm manager, who provides for the corporeal needs of others and gets rewarded for it. This focus is not very different from stories in the New Testament of tax collectors and sinful women who surprise everyone by doing the will of God and who are then welcomed by Jesus into the kingdom of God.[397] But more than just "doing the will of God," the parable specifically encourages people to take care of each other's physical and dietary needs to the benefit of all. In this story, a

---

[387] Cf. esp. *Names* 89–91, 215; *Dreams* 1.78–79, 219–220; 2.46–47, 65–66.

[388] Cf. T. Jos. 3:4; 10:1; Philo, *Alleg. Interp.* 3.179; *Agriculture* 55–58; *Migration* 203–204; *Names* 89–90; *Dreams* 2.46.

[389] Cf. Fleddermann 2005a, 635; Valantasis 2005, 168.

[390] E.g. Blomberg 1990, 192.

[391] See Valantasis 2005, 170–171; cf. Oakman 2008, 266, 267.

[392] Cf. Blomberg 1990, 190; Nolland 2005, 998.

[393] Roth 2018, 94.

[394] Cf. Bock 1996, 1170; Valantasis 2005, 168, 170.

[395] Cf. Blomberg 1990, 190, 192.

[396] Cf. Bock 1996, 1179; Oakman 2008, 268.

[397] Cf. e.g. Luke 7:36–50; 19:1–10.

landholder does not visit his estate in the first place to inspect the productivity of his slaves and the profitability of his land, but the physical wellbeing of his slaves and the ability of his land to provide food. Moreover, the landholder rewards the manager specifically for feeding his slaves. The story is a snapshot of what society might look like if people made the material welfare of others their main priority. Essentially, the parable depicts someone attending to the physical needs of his fellow human beings. In this sense, it may be regarded as an "example parable."[398] Even on the literal level, the parable is a depiction of God's kingdom in action. As such, the parable functions in a similar way to other Q parables, including especially Q [11:5–8],[399] Q 14:16–21, 23,[400] and Q 19:12–13, 15–24.[401] It imagines a world where landowners actually reward kindness and the middleman looks out for the interests of the small peasantry and poor. It promotes a world very much unlike the world of rich landowners, where productivity and profitability are the be all and end all of one's existence in this life. Instead, it promotes a world where the sustenance and survival *of others* are foremost in people's minds and the focus of all economic operations. In the kingdom of God, a rich landholder and a despised farm manager can be the source of people's subsistence. In the kingdom of God, people get rewarded for helping others economically. Such reward, in turn, has the potential to benefit even more people.[402] One must assume that if the slave manager was kind and generous to his fellow slaves when left to his own devices on a rural farm, he would continue such behaviour in his new position as overseer of other farms and people. He would undoubtedly expect the same behaviour from other farm managers. What is more, if his master rewarded kind and generous behaviour on one farm, that same master would be likely to expect the same kind of behaviour from the manager and his managerial staff going forward. Hence, the kindness of one slave manager expands exponentially, so that ever-increasing numbers of people receive food and other material needs as a result of his benevolence. And so, the kingdom of God grows.

Ultimately, the parable promotes general reciprocity against not only balanced reciprocity, but also the political economy of the rich.[403] In the kingdom of God, the bottom-line is not the bottom-line. Normally, general reciprocity occurred only within the family.[404] Yet, when portions of the populace were suffering, especially at village level, they would often expect acts of general reciprocity from *other* families. They wanted those with more to continually

---

[398] Cf. Scott 1989, 189–202; Funk 2006, 155; Crossan 2012, 29–44.

[399] See chapter 10 below.

[400] See chapter 8 below.

[401] See chapter 9 below.

[402] Cf. Allison 2004, 440.

[403] See Hays 2012, 49–50, 52; cf. Crossan 2002, 258; Oakman 2008, 97.

[404] Oakman 2008, 138.

give to those with less for the common good of all.[405] This differentiation between general and balanced reciprocity mirrors the typical distinction between
grace and justice in the parables of Jesus.[406] As a corollary, the implementation
of general reciprocity throughout society would include tax exemption and debt
remission.[407] If applied consistently and exhaustively, such an arrangement
would practically entail the application of a domestic economy to society at
large, in replacement of the existing political economy.[408] Similar expectations
appear in the Old Testament.[409] Economically speaking, this transformation
would turn all of Israel into "one big, happy family," often referred to by Jesus
as the "kingdom of God."[410] Q 12:42 implies that consistent application of such
expectations would give birth to God's kingdom.[411]

The fact that the parable features two characters who fulfil leadership roles
introduces the question of whether or not ancient Jewish leadership is a theme
that the parable intends to address. The likelihood that the audiences of Jesus's
parables were mostly made up of those from the lower echelons of society suggests that the parable is not directed in the first instance to Jewish leaders.[412]
Instead, the parable is directed at the populace, pressing them to reconsider the
world in which they live.[413] Just like a reading from above associates primarily
with the master, as opposed to the appointed slave, a reading from below does
not in the first place identify with the appointed slave, but with the fellow
slaves, who were nourished and fed.[414] However, it would not be unreasonable
to regard leadership as a motif in this parable. The story does portray two characters on different levels of authority taking responsibility for feeding those
under them. Essentially, the parable imagines a world where leaders make the
provision of food their first priority.[415] Stated negatively, the parable claims
that leaders who fail to feed their followers are disloyal and foolish. The subversive and seditious nature of such a claim is fully apparent. Yet the claim
was by no means novel. In Palestine, popular protests against the rule of certain
high priests continued throughout the first century CE.[416] There might be a
suggestion that Q's Jesus regards those from the lower strata of society as more

---

[405] Oakman 1986, 151–152.
[406] See Funk 1974, 64–66.
[407] Oakman 2008, 271–272, 282; cf. Q 11:4.
[408] Oakman 2008, 105.
[409] Lev 25:35–46; Deut 15:2; Neh 5:6–13.
[410] Cf. Crossan 2002, 258; Oakman 2008, 105, 264, 271–272; Park 2019, 47.
[411] Cf. Oakman 2008, 105, 264.
[412] Luz 2005, 223; *pace* e.g. Allison 2004, 440.
[413] Cf. Dodd 1958, 158; Crossan 2002, 250; 2012, 63, 95.
[414] See Valantasis 2005, 170–171; cf. Oakman 2008, 268.
[415] See Hays 2012, 49–50, 52; cf. Crossan 2002, 253, 258.
[416] Horsley 1995b, 136.

appropriate candidates for leadership. Elsewhere in Q, socio-economic under-lings are described as being wiser and more knowledgeable than the educated and political elite.[417] The word "wise" in Q 12:42 could therefore be a veiled reference to the less fortunate.[418] Moreover, the cryptic and open-ended nature of the opening question might suggest that anyone who feeds his/her fellow (wo)man automatically becomes a leader in society.[419] Roth comments: "With its query of 'who is...,' this question [in Q 12:42] breaks through the bounda-ries of the text and draws the addressees directly into the realm of the inquiry and its question involving conduct."[420] Such a reading is supported by the fact that the identity of "that slave" (ὁ δοῦλος ἐκεῖνος) is not specifically disclosed in verse 43, inviting anyone in the audience to insert herself into that position of "blessedness."[421] According to Marshall, the phrase ὁ δοῦλος ἐκεῖνος in verse 43 gives the impression of "that sort of slave."[422] Hence, the parable ad-dresses everyone in ancient Israel, encouraging them to take deliberate action and start feeding each other.[423] The slavery metaphor itself, in featuring slaves as characters, suggests that lower levels of leadership were also included in the parable's purview. The exact same instructions are also directed at servile lead-ers, who constitute the very bottom of any ancient socio-economic hierarchy. As such, the parable's metaphorical meaning is not only to be found on its metaphorical level, but also on its literal level. What is expected of society at the metaphorical level is also expected of slaves at the literal level, so that the parable becomes a microcosm of society at large, with all its socio-economic strata, including slaves.[424]

4.5 Characteristic Forms

We concluded above that Q 12:42–44, considered in isolation, should be re-garded as a parable. Even so, Q 12:42–44 is itself made up of a series of small forms. As we saw, each of the first three verses qualify technically as a separate literary small form, with verse 42 being a rhetorical question, verse 43 being a makarism or beatitude, and verse 44 being an amen saying. Significantly, these are all sapiential small forms, commonly used in wisdom literature.[425] More

---

[417] That is, Q 10:21, 23–24.

[418] Cf. also Q 7:35.

[419] Cf. Donahue 1988, 98; Luz 2005, 223; Nolland 2005, 997; Hays 2012, 47.

[420] Roth 2018, 94.

[421] Cf. Fleddermann 2005a, 635; Luz 2005, 223; Valantasis 2005, 169, 170; Roth 2018, 90.

[422] Marshall 1978, 541.

[423] Cf. Hunter 1971, 12–13.

[424] Cf. Crossan 2012, 9, 32.

[425] Cf. Scott 1989, 211.

specifically, these micro-genres are all typical of instructional wisdom and function deliberately to identify each individual verse as a piece of instruction. This taxonomy is substantiated by the deliberate use of the words "wise" (φρόνιμος) and "loyal" or "faithful" (πιστός) to describe the slave in verse 42.[426] The first three verses address two classical themes of traditional wisdom. Firstly, they address the sapiential theme of how to distinguish between wise and foolish slaves.[427] Secondly, they address the theme of trusty and wise household management.[428]

In addition, Q 12:42–44 lacks all the formal features of prophetic or apocalyptic small forms, including prophetic introductory formulas, a threatening tone, and the features of the so-called "eschatological" or "prophetic correlative."[429] One could point to the future tense verb "will appoint" (καταστήσει) in verse 44 as an indication of apocalyptic or eschatological intent, but this singular literary feature is wholly overshadowed by the evidence that Q 12:42–44 is intrinsically sapiential. In any case, the appearance of a verb in the future tense is not necessarily an indication that the author has an eschatological or apocalyptic future specifically in mind.

On the other side of the coin, Q 12:45–46 features no small forms. As we saw, there are no textual indicators that would qualify either verse as a micro-genre of some kind. On the one hand, these verses are not marked by textual markers as sapiential small forms. On the other hand, they are not clearly marked as prophetic or apocalyptic small forms either. For instance, Q 12:45–46 lacks not only prophetic introductory formulas, but also the textual features of the so-called "eschatological" or "prophetic correlative."[430] It follows that Q 12:45–46 does not *formally* function as either a prophetic or an apocalyptic warning. On the interpretive level, however, verse 46 does indeed seem reminiscent of a prophetic warning.[431] It is worth noting that verse 46 features no less than three future tense verbs, namely "will come" (ἥξει), "will cut in two" (διχοτομήσει), and "will give" (θήσει). As with verse 44, these verbs are not necessarily indications that an apocalyptic or eschatological future is intended. The single aspect of verse 46 that is most telling in the current discussion is its unmistakable threatening tone.[432] In fact, the final verse is not merely threatening in tone, but in essence. Irrespective of its precise interpretation, the content of verse 46 can easily and without much controversy be classified as a threat.

---

[426] Edwards 1976, 66.

[427] Kirk 1998, 234.

[428] Kirk 1998, 230; cf. Prov 31.

[429] Cf. Edwards 1976, 41, 114.

[430] Cf. Edwards 1969, 9–20; 1976, 41, 114; Schmidt 1977, 517–522.

[431] Jeremias 1966, 45; cf. Jacobson 1994, 104 n. 32.

[432] Blomberg 1990, 191.

4.6 Characteristic Motifs

As a whole, the parable has traditionally been interpreted as highlighting some aspect of the apocalyptic event, whether it be its unexpectedness, severity, or delay. Yet these interpretations are exclusively dependent on verses 45–46. As we saw, other interpretations are made possible if verses 42–44 are considered on their own. If I am correct that Q 12:42–44 represents an earlier version of this passage, none of the traditional interpretations would apply to this earlier version. Q 12:42–44, if considered in isolation, is not about the unexpectedness, severity, or delay of some or other future event.

The most obvious links between Q 12:42–44 and the preceding material in the formative stratum[433] were listed in the previous chapter and do not require repetition here. The current discussion will rather expand on those links. Both Q 12:22–31 and Q 12:42–44 are about the kingdom of God.[434] To the extent that Q 12:42–44 can be labelled a parable, it is a metaphor or symbol for God's kingdom.[435] Q 12:31, on the other hand, encourages its audience to actively seek God's kingdom, which in this context means to firstly consider and survey the natural world for clues about God's rule and to secondly implement these discoveries in their daily lives. This coheres with Crenshaw's estimation of wisdom's general intent: "wisdom is the reasoned search for specific ways to assure wellbeing and the implementation of those discoveries in daily existence."[436] It is something of a truism that ancient wisdom tended to draw its inspiration and evidence from, above all else, both nature and human conduct.[437] The same is true of the parables of Jesus.[438] Whereas Q 12:22–31 looks at nature to learn about the kingdom of God, Q 12:42–44 looks at human behaviour. Whereas Q 12:22–31 asks what we can learn about God's rule from ravens and lilies, Q 12:42–44 asks what we can learn about God's rule from agricultural slaves.

The passage in Q 12:22–31 advises against anxiety over basic necessities. The instruction not to be anxious is buttressed by the promise that God will feed and clothe his children.[439] Q 12:42–44 then gives an example of God feeding his children. Whereas Q 12:22–31 gives examples of God feeding animals, Q 12:42–44 gives an example of God feeding humans.[440] Although it is not

---

[433] That is, Q 12:33–34, 39.

[434] Bock 1996, 1170; Marshall 1978, 532; cf. Oakman 2008, 105.

[435] Cf. Dodd 1958, 33; Hunter 1971, 10; Crossan 1979, 20, 31; 2012, 111; Scott 1989, 51–62, 211; Nolland 2005, 997; Funk 2006, 59, 158; Oakman 2008, 266. For the kingdom of God as a symbol, see Uro 1996, 75–78.

[436] Crenshaw 2010, 16.

[437] Howes 2012, 246.

[438] Dodd 1958, 22; Hunter 1971, 10; Jacobson 1994, 104; cf. Funk 2006, 43, 48.

[439] Piper 1989, 30.

[440] Cf. Oakman 2008, 105.

spelled out, the implication is that God is behind all human acts that lead to the feeding of other humans, including those of slaves on a farm. Q 12:42–44 contributes to this key theme by offering one specific example of how God provides for his children. This is supported by the possibility that Q 12:42 recalls Psalm 103:27 in the Septuagint: πάντα πρὸς σὲ προσδοκῶσι, δοῦναι τὴν τροφὴν αὐτοῖς εὔκαιρον ("all wait for you to give them food on time / in season"). Its literary context in this LXX Psalm makes clear that this verse refers to God feeding all of his creation.[441] In chapter 6 below, the same Psalm is indicated as an important intertext for Q 13:18–19, underscoring the material provision of God for humans and animals alike. The same meaning might be suggested in Q 12:42, hinting at the idea that God's provision of food is carried out through human acts of benevolence. To a certain degree, the thematic overlap between Q 12:42–44 and Q 12:22–31 extends further to Q 11:2–4, [5–8], 9–13.[442] Ultimately, both Q 12:22–31 and Q 12:42–44 centre around the relationship between material support and the kingdom of God.[443]

Q 12:33–34, 39 then continues to warn against the gathering of perishable and transient worldly treasures in neglect of imperishable and enduring heavenly treasures.[444] At first sight, the content of Q 12:42–44 might seem to contradict the derision of earthly possessions in Q 12:33–34. This is particularly true of verse 44, where the appointment over more possessions acts as a reward. In truth, however, Q 12:33–34, 39 is not against possessions *per se*, but against the "gathering" or "hoarding" (θησαυρίζω) of possessions. This motif is wholly reconcilable with Q 12:42–44. If the two texts are read together, they advocate that those who are in a position to help should not be stingy with their possessions, but should provide for the basic needs of those around them.[445] In the parable of Q 12:42–44, the reward of being appointed over even more possessions is a blessing, not only because of the slave's increased honour,[446] but also because it places that slave in a position to address the needs of even more slaves.[447] The distinction in Q 12:33–34, 39 between "earthly" and "heavenly" treasures relates well to the distinction in Q 12:42–44 between the slave's initial and ultimate appointment, especially if the latter is somehow representative of a "heavenly reward."[448] Whereas the passage in Q 12:22–31 relates to the

---

[441] Cf. Roth 2018, 100. The LXX text is from Brenton 1870, and the English translation is mine.

[442] See Howes 2019b, 6–11.

[443] Cf. Hays 2012, 51–52; Häkkinen 2016, 8.

[444] Cf. Q 16:13.

[445] Cf. Hays 2012, 49.

[446] Cf. Kloppenborg 1995, 294.

[447] Cf. Allison 2004, 440.

[448] Cf. Hays 2012, 49, 51.

fellow slaves in Q 12:42–44, the passage in Q 12:33–34, 39 relates to the appointed slave. As such, Q 12:42–44 is thematically linked to both preceding Q[1] pericopes.

Besides the thematic linkage of Q 12:42–44 with its immediate literary context in the formative stratum, this text relates to a number of other themes that feature prominently in the rest of the formative stratum. Firstly, it develops the motif of general reciprocity that recurs often in the formative stratum,[449] but is spelled out explicitly in Q 6:30, 34.[450] Secondly, Q 12:42–44 relates to the tendency in the formative stratum to contemplate the different kinds of relationships between the elite and less fortunate members of society.[451] Unlike the main redaction, the elite are not here or in the rest of the formative stratum either portrayed as outsiders or condemned as a matter of principle.[452] Instead, the complicated and nuanced relationship between the elite and the populace is accurately depicted in Q 12:42–44. Finally, Q 12:42–44 corresponds to the topic of daily sustenance and survival,[453] which is arguably the most important, repeated, and central topic of Q's formative stratum.[454] In general, the formative stratum is heavily concerned with people's basic needs, like food, clothing, and housing.[455] In these texts, the focus is on physical survival, and basic needs are mentioned for their own sake, as the means for survival. By contrast, when food, clothing, or housing is mentioned in the main redaction (and final recension), they unfailingly serve some larger rhetorical purpose.[456] It is interesting that both Q 6:20–23 and Q 12:43 make use of beatitudes to address the ruling socio-economic situation.[457] Q 12:42–44 has thematically a lot in common with

---

[449] E.g. Q 11:2–4 (see chapter 5 below); Q [11:5–8] (see chapter 10 below); Q 11:33 (see chapter 2 above).

[450] Cf. Oakman 2008, 95, 105; Hays 2012, 49, 50; see chapter 5 below.

[451] Cf. Q 6:22–23, 27–28, 29–30; 10:3, 10–11, 21, 23–24 (see chapter 1 above); 11:3–4; 12:4–5, 11–12; 13:25 (see chapter 7 below); 14:16–21, 23 (see chapter 8 below); 16:13; 17:1–2; 19:12–13, 15–24 (see chapter 9 below).

[452] E.g. Q 7:24–28; 11:39, 42–44, 46–52; 13:34–35. Horsley (1992, 191; 1995a, 49; 1999, 299) argues that the term "this generation" refers in Q to the Jewish elite (cf. Jacobson 1992, 169).

[453] Or in the words of Schulz (1972, 91), "*das notwendige Existenzminimum*" (cf. Catchpole 1993, 224).

[454] Cf. Kloppenborg 1987, 240–241; Piper 1995, 62, 64; Vaage 1995a, 89; Robinson 1997a, 237, 238; cf. Q 6:20–21, 29–30, 34; 9:58; 10:2, 5–9, 16; 11:3–4, [5–8], 9–13, 33 (see chapter 2 above); 12:22–31, 58–59 (see chapter 5 below); 13:18–19, 20–21 (see chapter 6 below); 13:24–25 (see chapter 7 below); 14:16–21, 23 (see chapter 8 below); 15:4–5, 7, [8–10]; 19:12–13, 15–24 (see chapter 9 below).

[455] For examples of texts about food, see the previous footnote. Clothing: Q 6:29; 12:22–31. Housing: Q 6:47–49 (in my view, this text is not merely symbolic); 9:58; 13:18–19 (see chapter 6 below); 13:24–25 (see chapter 7 below).

[456] E.g. Q 3:8–9, 16–17; (4:3–4); 7:25, 33–34; 11:17, 42, 51; 13:28–29, 35; 17:27, 35.

[457] Hays 2012, 50.

the first few lines of the inaugural sermon.[458] The first two beatitudes claim
that the poor and hungry are blessed, because they will eat anyway.[459] This
initial claim is clarified by the remainder of the Sayings Gospel, which explains
that God provides for the poor in a variety of ways, sometimes in rather unexpected ways. One way in which God provides is through other people. The poor
are further blessed because they are free, not only from the stress,[460] but also
from the responsibility and accountability[461] that comes with having a lot.[462]

Moving on to verses 45–46, the thematic link between the Son of Man logion in Q 12:40 and the redactional ending of the parable in Q 12:46 is not only
legitimate, but also completely unavoidable.[463] The main intention of Q 12:40
is to stress the unexpectedness of the Son of Man's apocalyptic return, in order
to promote preparedness on the part of the listeners.[464] As such, verse 46, and
so the parable as a whole, has understandably often been taken by scholarship
as a reference to the apocalyptic end.[465] Like the Son of Man saying, verse 46
explicitly and emphatically singles out the unexpectedness of the apocalyptic
event, dedicating no less than two temporal clauses to this purpose: "on a day
he does not expect" (ἐν ἡμέρᾳ ᾗ οὐ προσδοκᾷ) and "at an hour he does not
know" (ἐν ὥρᾳ ᾗ οὐ γινώσκει).[466] Like the Son of Man logion, the harshness
of the dual punishment seems to be an attempt at endorsing preparedness in the
face of apocalyptic judgment.[467] A master punishing his slave is in itself appropriate as an image of apocalyptic judgment.[468] One could finally argue that
the punishment of verse 46, including especially the clause "give him an inheritance with the faithless" (τὸ μέρος αὐτοῦ μετὰ τῶν ἀπίστων θήσει), connotes
eternal damnation in Gehenna[469] or hell.[470]

---

[458] Cf. Allison 2004, 441; Luz 2005, 225.

[459] Q 6:20–21.

[460] Q 12:22–31, 33–34, 39.

[461] Q 12:42–44.

[462] Cf. Hunter 1964, 120; Allison 2004, 440.

[463] Kloppenborg 1995, 294; cf. Sato 1994, 173.

[464] Cf. Hunter 1964, 84; Jeremias 1966, 40, 50; Allison 1997, 27; Kloppenborg 2000a,
118.

[465] E.g. Jeremias 1963, 57–58, 63, 165; 1966, 45, 50; Hunter 1964, 79; Donahue 1988,
99; Jacobson 1994, 114; Allison 1997, 27; 2000, 131–132; Etchells 1998, 109; Luz 2005,
223.

[466] Kloppenborg 1987, 150; Taylor 1989, 142–143 n. 58, 146; Funk and Hoover 1993,
253, 342; Bock 1996, 1182; Fleddermann 2005a, 637; Luz 2005, 221.

[467] Kloppenborg 1987, 150; 1995, 294; Blomberg 1990, 191; Fleddermann 2005a, 635;
Valantasis 2005, 168, 169; cf. Marshall 1978, 534; Jacobson 1994, 114; Allison 1997, 27.

[468] Cf. Blomberg 1990, 191.

[469] Cf. Q 12:5.

[470] Jeremias 1963, 57; 1966, 44; Allison 2004, 441, 442; Nolland 2005, 1000; Hays 2012,
47; see Bock 1996, 1183–1184; cf. Kloppenborg 1987, 150–151; Blomberg 1990, 191–192;
Luz 2005, 223.

If verse 45 is read through this apocalyptic lens, the parable's master should be associated with the Son of Man.[471] The logion in Q 12:40 is not clear about the specific identity of this Son of Man,[472] but if read in conjunction with the parable, it does seem to point to Jesus.[473] This inference is particularly suggested by the intimate and explicit nature of the phrase "my master is delayed" (χρονίζει ὁ κύριος μου), which most scholars have taken as a deliberate reference to the delay of the parousia.[474] In any case, it does indeed seem likely that Q 12:40 and Q 12:45–46 both point to the apocalyptic return of the same individual, even if the former describes him as "the Son of Man" (ὁ υἱὸς τοῦ ἀνθρώπου) and the latter as "the master" (ὁ κύριος).[475]

Past and present scholars have justly noticed a great degree of thematic overlap between Q 12:46 and other texts in the main redaction that likewise deal with the apocalyptic end.[476] Such thematic overlap is both obvious and inescapable if Q 12:46 is read in light of Q 12:40, as it should be on the level of the main redaction. The idea that the apocalyptic event will occur abruptly and unexpectedly is a central theme of the main redaction.[477] The appeal for preparedness, sometimes in the form of repentance, is also a central motif for the main redaction.[478] The harsh and unforgiving imagery with which verse 46 of the parable describes apocalyptic punishment fits very well with similar images in the rest of the main redaction.[479]

Out of these Q² texts, one or two may be singled out for specific discussion. The image in Q 3:9 of an "axe" (ἀξίνη) corresponds well to the image in Q 12:46 of being "cut in two" (διχοτομέω). In Q 3:9, the axe is used to chop down trees in order to separate the good ones from the bad ones. In the context of Q 3:7–9, this image symbolises the separation between good and bad people in the face of apocalyptic destruction.[480] Although the image in Q 12:46 is of a

---

[471] Jeremias 1963, 56, 58; 1966, 44, 45; Marshall 1978, 533; Kloppenborg 1995, 294; Kirk 1998, 233; Nolland 2005, 997; cf. Scott 1989, 207; Allison 1997, 27.

[472] Marshall 1978, 534.

[473] See Robinson 2005d, 407–408; cf. Marshall 1978, 533, 534; Bock 1996, 1171; Kirk 1998, 233; cf. Q 6:46.

[474] Kloppenborg 1995, 293; see Allison 2000, 131–132; 2004, 441; Valantasis 2005, 169–170; e.g. Jeremias 1963, 56; 1966, 44; Marshall 1978, 542; Taylor 1989, 147; Blomberg 1990, 192; Funk and Hoover 1993, 342; Etchells 1998, 108; Fleddermann 2005a, 623, 637.

[475] Jeremias 1963, 56, 58; 1966, 44, 45; Fleddermann 2005a, 635; Luz 2005, 223; Nolland 2005, 997, 998; cf. Blomberg 1990, 192; Allison 1997, 27; Roth 2018, 98, 104.

[476] E.g. Jacobson 1994, 114. Kloppenborg (1987, 150–151) lists the following texts: Q 3:9, 17; 11:24–26, 34–36; 13:26–27, 28–29; 17:26–27, 30.

[477] Cf. Q 17:23–24, 26–27, 30, 34–35.

[478] Cf. Q 3:8; 10:13; 17:26–27, 30.

[479] E.g. Q 3:9, 17; 10:12, 14–15; 13:28; 17:24, 26–27, 30, 34–35, 37.

[480] Kloppenborg 1987, 102–103; Reiser 1990, 247–248; Horsley 1992, 206; 1995a, 40; 1999, 87, 261; Kirk 1998, 369; see Fleddermann 1990, 9; 2005a, 228–231; Catchpole 1993, 8–12; Valantasis 2005, 44–48.

single individual being cut into two pieces, some scholars have argued that the word "dissect" or "cut in two" is purposely used here as a symbol for being cut from the midst of God's chosen people, whether it be Israel or the hypothetical Q community.[481] However the image of being cut in two is interpreted, the second leg of the punishment in Q 12:46 certainly points to a separation between the "loyal" or "faithful" (πιστός) and "disloyal" or "unfaithful" (ἄπιστος) slaves. It is finally possible that both the phrases "thrown on the fire" (εἰς πῦρ βάλλεται) and "give him an inheritance with the faithless" (τὸ μέρος αὐτοῦ μετὰ τῶν ἀπίστων θήσει) refer to eternal damnation in Gehenna or hell.

Whether to describe guilty misconduct, oblivious unpreparedness, or joyful camaraderie, the phrase "eating and drinking" appears in literary contexts of the main redaction that deal specifically with the apocalyptic event. Q 12:45 shares this characteristic with Q 17:27 and Q 13:26, 29.[482] In Q 12:45, eating and drinking are part of the misdeeds of the untrustworthy slave. More specifically, he is not merely accused of eating and drinking, but of eating and drinking "with the drunkards" (μετὰ τῶν μεθυόντων). It is for this transgression, among others, that he is being punished. In Q 17:27, describing people as eating and drinking is a symbolic way of saying that these people were going about their daily lives in the normal fashion, when they were suddenly hit by a catastrophic flood.[483] The suddenness of the apocalyptic event is also a theme of Q 12:42–46 in its final form.[484] In Q 13:26, the expression "eat and drink" (ἐφάγομεν καὶ ἐπίομεν) appears again, but in this case it features with the phrase "in your presence" (ἐνώπιόν σου) to express former camaraderie with the householder.[485] The text goes on to claim that such amity will not necessarily be of assistance at the apocalyptic end.[486] Irrespective of their precise interpretations, it is noteworthy that these texts, including Q 12:45, all deal in some way with the apocalyptic end.[487]

4.7 Implied Audience

That Q 12:42–44 is neither directly nor indirectly aimed at an out-group is confirmed by four factors. Firstly, there is no explicit mention of an out-group,

---

[481] Dodd 1958, 159 n. 1; Taylor 1989, 144 n. 60; Allison 2004, 441; Hays 2012, 47 n. 32; see Bock 1996, 1182–1184; e.g. Marshall 1978, 543; Donahue 1988, 100; Etchells 1998, 108; cf. Blomberg 1990, 191.

[482] Cf. Jacobson 1992, 197; Allison 2004, 441.

[483] Kloppenborg 1987, 157; Catchpole 1993, 250; Kirk 1998, 261; Allison 2010, 35; Howes 2012, 156.

[484] Jeremias 1966, 40.

[485] Cf. Uro 1996, 109.

[486] See chapter 7 below.

[487] Cf. Kloppenborg 1987, 150.

including "this generation," either in the parable itself or in its immediate literary context.[488] Secondly, Q 12:42–44 operates within the closed system of the "household of slaves" (οἰκετεία). The parable does not feature any other characters in addition to the master, the appointed slave, and his fellow slaves. What is more, within the narrative world of Q 12:42–44, the master only features when he is within the closed system. His existence is only relevant in as far as it relates to the "household of slaves."[489] We do not follow him when he leaves this space. The reason for his departure is not even mentioned, being entirely irrelevant to the story, which operates within the confines of a closed system.[490] It is hard to imagine a spatial depiction such as this being directed at outsiders, whether directly or indirectly. Thirdly, the sapiential aim of Q 12:42–44 to direct behaviour is reminiscent of wisdom for insiders. As mentioned in chapter 2 above, motivating positive action is an identifiable feature of the formative stratum, but not of the main redaction. In our pericope, the intention to motivate positive action is particularly indicated by the opening clause, which introduces the parable as pertaining to the "loyal" (πιστός) and "wise" (φρόνιμος) slave.[491] It is highly unlikely that Q would introduce a text aimed at an out-group with these epithets.[492] Lastly, the master in the parable instructs the appointed slave to feed *fellow slaves*.[493] From this, it is hard to avoid the conclusion that on both the literal and metaphorical levels of the parable people are invited to behave in a certain way towards fellow members of the same group.[494] Given the nature of the task to tend to the physical needs of others, it is all the more likely that Q 12:42–44 is aimed at the in-group. Conversely, it is extremely unlikely that this text would have hostile outsiders in mind as either the givers or the receivers of such kindness.[495]

Even a cursory glance reveals that verse 45 centres around accusation and verse 46 around threat. The positive, constructive aims of Q 12:42–44 are moved to the background in order to make room for the negative characterisation and threatening condemnation that occurs in verses 45–46.[496] Whatever

---

[488] That is, Q 12.

[489] Cf. Dodd 1958, 159; Funk 1974, 68.

[490] Cf. Dodd 1958, 159.

[491] Cf. Oakman 2008, 271–272; *pace* Crossan 1983, 60.

[492] Cf. Jacobson 1992, 197.

[493] Luke exchanged this phrase for "the male and female slaves" (τοὺς παῖδας καὶ τὰς παιδίσκας) (Nolland 2005, 999; cf. Scott 1989, 209; Taylor 1989, 140). He probably did so to specify the socio-economic context more clearly (Luz 2005, 221) and render the text inclusive of both genders. Fleddermann (2005a, 628) argues in favour of the Lukan phrase for Q. Regardless, on a semantic level the Lukan text also features fellow slaves of the same household (Luz 2005, 221).

[494] Allison 2004, 440.

[495] Cf. Scott 1989, 210; *pace* Kloppenborg 2000a, 141.

[496] Cf. Dodd 1958, 160; Crossan 1983, 60.

the metaphorical function of the accusations in verse 45 might be, the content clearly accuses the implied audience of gross misconduct and does so by cari-caturing them.[497] Such rhetoric is certainly reminiscent of socio-religious dis-crimination and demarcation. Jacobson points out that the beating of fellow slaves calls to mind the violence meted out by "this generation" against God's prophets and sages in Q 11:49–51.[498] The debauchery of the disloyal slave is further comparable to the actions of "this generation" in Q 17:27.[499] What is more, both the slave's internal dialogue and his revelry point to a careless dis-regard for Q's message about the Son of Man's unexpected return.[500] Con-versely, it seems extremely unlikely that the author of Q would feature descrip-tions of violent and licentious behaviour to depict the conduct and general at-titude of the in-group.[501] If the two forms of punishment in Q 12:46 are con-sidered together, they seem like purposeful attempts at socio-religious segre-gation.[502] The probability of such intentionality is enhanced if verse 46 is read together with the Son of Man saying in verse 40, as intended by the main re-dactor. However one interprets verse 46, it clearly foresees the implied audi-ence receiving severe punishment for their misdeeds.[503] One may conclude with reasonable confidence that the implied audience of verses 45–46 consti-tutes outsiders.[504]

4.8 Findings

This chapter reconsidered the redactional make-up of the parable in Q 12:42–46. In the process, the parable of the loyal and wise slave was "cut in two," with each half considered separately. On the one hand, it was argued that verses 42–44 properly belong to Q's formative layer. On the other hand, it was argued that verses 45–46 were added by the main redactor in order to adjust the mean-ing of the parable as a whole, thereby aligning it with the overall message of the main redaction. Q 12:42–46 is but one example of how, in the Sayings Gospel Q, the parables of Jesus were "coopted to serve the compositional ends of the document [and] to embellish and dramatize the destablizing [*sic*] of the

---

[497] Dodd 1958, 160.

[498] Jacobson 1992, 197.

[499] Jacobson 1992, 197.

[500] Kloppenborg 1987, 150; see Fleddermann 2005a, 637; Luz 2005, 223; cf. Bock 1996, 1182.

[501] Jacobson 1992, 197.

[502] Cf. Kloppenborg 1987, 150–151.

[503] Donahue 1988, 99.

[504] Cf. Kloppenborg 2000a, 141.

cosmos by the Day of the Son of Man."[505] Matthew and Luke took this editorial process further, each in its own direction.[506]

---

[505] Kloppenborg 1995, 289.

[506] See Jeremias 1963, 56–57, 104; 1966, 44; Donahue 1988, 96–101; Scott 1989, 209; Taylor 1989, 138–150; Blomberg 1990, 123–124, 190–193; Funk and Hoover 1993, 253; Etchells 1998, 107–109; Allison 2004, 439–442; Luz 2005, 225; Nolland 2005, 996–1001; Hays 2012, 45–53.

Chapter 5

Q 12:58–59, "You Will Not Get Out of There!"[1]

⁵⁸⟦ἕως ὅτου⟧ ... μετὰ τοῦ ἀντιδίκου σου ἐν τῇ ὁδῷ, δὸς ἐργασίαν ἀπηλλάχθαι ἀπ' αὐτοῦ, μήποτε σε παραδῷ ⟦ὁ ἀντίδικος⟧ τῷ κριτῇ καὶ ὁ κριτὴς τῷ ὑπηρέτῃ καὶ ⟦ὁ <ὑπηρέτης> σε⟧ β⟦α⟧λ⟦εῖ⟧ εἰς φυλακήν. ⁵⁹λέγω σοι, οὐ μὴ ἐξέλθῃς ἐκεῖθεν, ἕως τὸ⟦ν⟧ ἔσχατον ⟦κοδράντην⟧ ἀποδῷς.

⁵⁸⟦While⟧ you «go along» with your opponent on the way, make an effort to get loose from him, lest ⟦the opponent⟧ hand you over to the judge, and the judge to the assistant, and ⟦the <assistant>⟧ throw ⟦you⟧ into prison. ⁵⁹I say to you: You will not get out of there until you pay the last ⟦penny⟧!

There is widespread scholarly agreement that the primitive saying about avoiding the courts in Matthew 5:25–26 and Luke 12:58–59 featured in the Sayings Gospel Q.[2] Kloppenborg ascribes this saying to the main redaction.[3] As an alternative, this chapter will argue that Q 12:58–59 belongs to the formative stratum.

---

¹ An earlier version of this chapter was published as an article in *Pharos Journal of Theology* 98 (see Howes 2017a). The chapter also draws on an article in *Acta Theologica* 35/1 (see Howes 2015b).

² Burkett 2009, 144; Roth 2018, 341; e.g. Marshall 1978, 546; Davies and Allison 1988, 519, 521; Funk and Hoover 1993, 142, 344; Sato 1994, 160, 173; Luz 2007, 233, 234; cf. Hunter 1964, 82, 121; Carlston 1982, 110, 113, 115; Kloppenborg 1987, 152; 1995, 309; 2000a, 194; 2001, 165; Piper 1989, 105–107; 1995, 60–61; 2000, 250; Jacobson 1992, 201–203; 1994, 114; Catchpole 1993, 150; Bultmann 1994, 26, 27, 30; Cotter 1995, 127; Horsley 1995a, 40, 43–45; Robinson 1995a, 273; 1998a, 240; 1998b, 135; Vaage 1995, 89; Tuckett 1996, 433; Allison 1997, 26; Koester 1997, 143, 145, 147; Kirk 1998, 238–241; 2016, 196; Arnal 2001, 94, 171, 173, 194; Denaux 2001, 432; Fleddermann 2005a, 652–658; 2014, 160; Johnson-DeBaufre 2005, 103–104; Valantasis 2005, 174–176; Joseph 2012, 29, 86; Batten 2014, 82; Park 2014a, 77; 2014b, 4; Rollens 2014a, 93–113; Zimmermann 2014, 11, 28; Bazzana 2015, 308; Oakman 2015, xi, 72, 75, 81; Ra 2016, 224–225. For the opposite minority position that Matthew 5:25–26 and Luke 12:58–59 do not derive from Q, see e.g. Bock 1996, 1189–1190.

³ Kloppenborg 1987, 101, 102, 166, 169; 2000a, 144.

5.1 Kloppenborg's Analysis

Kloppenborg acknowledges that Q 12:58 used to be a sapiential admonition, but argues that verse 59 "is more typical of a prophetic judgment statement."[4] According to him, the formula λέγω ὑμῖν (σοι)· οὐ μὴ ... ἕως/μέχρις[5] occurs predominantly in apocalyptic and prophetic announcements.[6] Moreover, the first part of this formula (λέγω ὑμῖν/σοι[7]) often "serves as an assertive introducing [a] solemn statement concerning punishment, reward and judgment."[8] According to Kloppenborg, the adverb ἐκεῖθεν ("from there" or "out of there") indicates that verse 59 could not have circulated independently, but must have been conceived with verse 58 in mind. Hence, a saying that used to be a straightforward admonition (verse 58) was turned into an apocalyptic-prophetic logion when a climactic exclamation (verse 59) was subsequently added to it.[9] Kloppenborg continues to argue that verse 59 must already have been added to verse 58 before the logion was incorporated into Q, since the addition of verse 59 was motivated by "the theme of judgment and punishment which runs through [Q] 12:39–56."[10] Hence, Kloppenborg finds that Q 12:58–59 belongs with the material on apocalyptic judgment in Q's main redaction.[11] More than anything, this finding relies on a prophetic-apocalyptic reading of verse 59.[12]

Kloppenborg is in all likelihood correct that Q 12:58–59 was a complete saying when it was added to Q. Whether or not verse 58 ever existed without verse 59 is more difficult to determine. There is no reason why Q 12:58–59 could not have existed more or less as it appears in Q from inception.[13] The forceful climax to the logion would then be a way of emphasising the horrific conclusion of a process that started with going to court, thereby supporting the

---

[4] Kloppenborg 1987, 152–153. Kloppenborg assumes that verse 57 also featured in Q. Whether or not it did has little impact on the content of his case. I follow both the *Critical Edition of Q* and the majority of scholars in viewing verse 57 as a Lukan addition (e.g. Jacobson 1992, 202; Amon 1997, 318; Johnson 1997, 319).

[5] My translation of the "formula": "I say to you [singular or plural]: 'certainly not ... until [ἕως/μέχρις].'"

[6] Cf. also Fleddermann 2005a, 657.

[7] "I say to you [singular or plural]."

[8] Kloppenborg 1987, 153; cf. Luz 2007, 241.

[9] Cf. Carlston 1982, 110, 112–113, 114–115; Kirk 1998, 238.

[10] Kloppenborg 1987, 153; cf. Koester 1997, 143, 145, 147.

[11] Kloppenborg 1987, 101, 102, 166, 169; cf. 2000a, 144; 2001, 165; cf. Jacobson 1994, 114.

[12] Howes 2015a, 75.

[13] Davies and Allison 1988, 519.

central command not to go to court.[14] If so, there is reason to doubt the prophetic and eschatological nature of verse 59 in the first place, which in turn would jeopardise the finding that this logion belongs in Q's main redaction.[15] Kloppenborg is correct that the theme of eschatological judgment features strongly in the preceding Q material, but according to his own stratigraphical model this material was only added during the main redactional process. If Q 12:58–59 was a unit when incorporated into Q, and if the logion is not particularly prophetic, then the saying could easily have featured in the formative stratum before being incorporated into the main redaction. In this regard, it is important to notice that Q 12:58–59 appears on the border between Q[1] and Q[2] material. The two sayings that follow Q 12:58–59 belong to the formative stratum.[16]

Kloppenborg further fails to consider the Matthean placement of this logion. Matthew situates the logion between Q 16:17 and Q 16:18 in his Gospel.[17] If this is correct, there would be little reason to regard Q 12:58–59 as a prophetic logion.[18] It is true that the two logia that would probably have preceded Q 12:58–59 directly in this context, namely Q 16:17 and Q 16:16, belong to the final recension and the main redaction respectively, according to Kloppenborg's stratigraphy.[19] Out of these two, Q 16:16 in particular discusses a prophetic and/or eschatological subject. It is worth mentioning, though, that the placement of Q 16:16 is itself in question, with some scholars preferring its Matthean position after Q 7:24–28.[20] More importantly, most of the sayings that surround Q 12:58–59 in this context are wisdom logia that belong to the formative stratum,[21] including those sayings that would have followed Q 12:58–59 directly.[22] In other words, Q 12:58–59 is also in this literary context on the border between Q[1] and Q[2] material. Furthermore, the same argument made above with regard to the Lukan placement applies in this context as well: if Q 12:58–59 was a unit when incorporated into Q, and if the logion is not particularly prophetic, then the saying could easily have featured in the formative stratum before being incorporated into the main redaction.[23]

These factors warn against appealing to the literary context of Q 12:58–59 when trying to determine whether it belongs to the formative stratum or the main redaction. The position of this logion in Q is not entirely certain, and in

---

[14] Cf. Betz 1995, 228–229.

[15] See below.

[16] That is, Q 13:18–19, 20–21; see chapter 6 below.

[17] See Howes 2018.

[18] Howes 2015a, 75, 113.

[19] See Kloppenborg 1987, 112–115; 2000a, 152–153.

[20] See Kloppenborg 1987, 112–114.

[21] E.g. Q 14:26, 27; 17:33; 14:34–35; 16:13, 18; 17:1–2.

[22] That is, Q 16:18; 17:1–2.

[23] Cf. Horsley 1999, 65.

the case of both its Matthean and Lukan placement, the logion is on the border between Q^1 and Q^2 material.

5.2 Characteristic Forms

Q 12:58–59 has often been taken as a parable.[24] If this were true, the sapiential nature of the saying would be immediately evident, since parables were above all sapiential small forms, even if they at times happened to discuss prophetic, eschatological, and/or apocalyptic motifs.[25] On the other hand, the Sayings Gospel seemingly had a propensity for turning sapiential parables into eschatological material.[26] It follows that if Q 12:58–59 were indeed a parable, an eschatological interpretation might already have been bestowed upon it by the time the evangelists found it in Q.[27] Despite the fact that these arguments cancel each other out, they should also be disregarded simply because Q 12:58–59 is not a parable.[28] Rather than invite contemplation by comparing God's kingdom (or something else) to some corporeal reality in daily life, the saying tries to convince through logic and argumentation. In the words of Foster: "The situation envisaged in this tradition is presented more as a hypothetical possibility, than the type of fictionalized reality that is often assumed in the narrative world of certain types of parables."[29] More crucially, the imperative mood of the verb δός immediately disqualifies Q 12:58–59 as a parable. As a rule, verbs never appear in the imperative mood in the narrative of a parable.[30] The only exception is when a character within the parable gives a command.[31] In such cases, the command with the imperative verb is separated from the rest of the narrative by featuring as part of direct speech. It is only with the (secondary) parable applications that the *narrator* of a parable might use an imperative

---

[24] E.g. Weiß 1878, 452; Bultmann 1968, 96, 149; Marshall 1978, 551, 552; Bock 1996, 1190; Amon 1997, 318–319; Zimmermann 2015, 102, 215.

[25] See Kirk 1998, 234, 246–248; cf. Edwards 1976, 74; Howes 2015a, 203, 220, 292–293.

[26] Cf. Carlston 1982, 112–113; cf. e.g. Q 12:42–46 (see chapter 4 above); 13:24–29 (see chapter 7 below); 14:16–21, 23 (see chapter 8 below); 19:12–13, 15–24, 26 (see chapter 9 below).

[27] Carlston 1982, 112–113, 114–115.

[28] Luz 2007, 234; Foster 2014a, 261, 278; Wright 2015, 81–82; cf. Kloppenborg 1995.

[29] Foster 2014a, 278.

[30] Bultmann (1968, 96) acknowledges the problem of the imperative, but continues to treat Q 12:58–59 as a parable – or a similitude, in his case.

[31] E.g. Q 13:27; 14:23; 19:24.

verb. Supporting these observations is the fact that very few contemporary parable scholars actually consider Q 12:58–59 to be a parable.[32]

Few would protest the fact that Q 12:58–59 is a sapiential admonition.[33] Taken literally, the saying is an unadulterated piece of advice to make amends with one's legal opponent before going to court.[34] The saying consists of a temporal clause,[35] a central command in the imperative mood,[36] and a lengthy final or motive clause[37].[38] The emphatic statement of verse 59 functions to underline and strengthen the force of the foregoing motive clause, thereby providing additional support to the central command.[39] Causality is central to the rhetorical approach of the logion, which argues that if you fail to make amends with your legal opponents (the cause), you will be at the mercy of the legal system and end up in prison (the effect).[40] Once set in motion, the judicial process is unstoppable and the outcome inevitable.[41] Verse 59 is the emphatic finale to this cause-and-effect chain of reasoning.[42] Such rhetoric is intrinsically sapiential and particularly at home with instructional wisdom.[43] In all, the saying uses logic and argumentation to convince its audience. These features are all conventional for a sapiential admonition.[44]

Despite the instructional nature of the logion, it still has a gnomic application, much like a maxim.[45] In other words, although the saying is technically

---

[32] See Foster 2014a, 255–285, esp. 275, 281; cf. Kloppenborg 1995. It has been suggested that Q 12:58–59 is a special kind of parable, namely an "aphoristic parable," which presupposes a fictional narrative, but lacks the formal features of a parable (e.g. Crossan 1992a, 148; Rollens 2014a, 105, esp. n. 32). This suggestion, apart from being entirely unhelpful in classifying the logion, is in fact little more than an acknowledgement that the saying fails to conform to the formal features of a parable.

[33] Cf. Zeller 1977, 66–67; Piper 1989, 102, 106, 157; Jacobson 1992, 202; Allison 1997, 42; Kirk 1998, 238; Luz 2007, 234.

[34] Kirk 1998, 238; Valantasis 2005, 175; Foster 2014a, 261; Wright 2015, 81–82; cf. Luz 2007, 241.

[35] "[While] you «go along» with your opponent on the way" ([ἕως ὅτου] … μετὰ τοῦ ἀντιδίκου σου ἐν τῇ ὁδῷ).

[36] "make an effort to get loose from him" (δὸς ἐργασίαν ἀπηλλάχθαι ἀπ' αὐτοῦ).

[37] "lest [the opponent] hand you over to the judge, and the judge to the assistant, and [the <assistant>] throw [you] into prison" (μήποτε σε παραδῷ [ὁ ἀντίδικος] τῷ κριτῇ καὶ ὁ κριτὴς τῷ ὑπηρέτῃ καὶ [ὁ <ὑπηρέτης> σε] β[α]λ[εῖ] εἰς φυλακήν).

[38] Cf. Zeller 1977, 65; Jacobson 1992, 202; Kirk 1998, 238; Fleddermann 2005a, 656, 657.

[39] Roth 2018, 342.

[40] Valantasis 2005, 175; cf. Jacobson 1992, 202.

[41] Nolland 2005, 234; Rollens 2014a, 105; cf. Dodd 1958, 138; Robinson 1995a, 273.

[42] Cf. Marshall 1978, 551; Betz 1995, 226, 228.

[43] Cf. Howes 2015a, 230.

[44] Cf. Kirk 1998, 92.

[45] Cf. Kirk 1998, 238.

presented as a command, it is intended as a piece of sapiential advice.[46] As Kirk explains, the line between a maxim and an admonition is easily crossed and often merely an aspect of technical classification.[47] The generic second person address allows the audience to insert themselves into the described situation and apply the saying to their own lives.[48] Taken at face value, Q 12:58–59 is a sapiential admonition that addresses the typical and commonsensical subject of avoiding (at all costs) any form of judicial procedure.[49] Significantly, there are logia from contemporary sapiential texts that are not merely comparable, but remarkably similar to Q 12:58–59.[50]

As we saw, Kloppenborg acknowledges that verse 58 used to be a sapiential admonition, but argues that verse 59 "is more typical of a prophetic judgment statement."[51] According to him, the formula λέγω ὑμῖν (σοι)· οὐ μὴ ... ἕως/μέχρις occurs predominantly in apocalyptic and prophetic announcements.[52] Yet none of the texts held up by Kloppenborg as examples of this prophetic and/or apocalyptic "formula"[53] match the phrase in Q 12:59 word for word. Kloppenborg argues further that λέγω ὑμῖν/σοι[54] commonly introduces a statement about punishment, reward, and judgment.[55] Yet, while discussing a different occurrence of the phrase λέγω ὑμῖν in Q,[56] Kloppenborg admits that it occurs frequently in sapiential material.[57] In fact, during his discussion of Q 6:27–30, Kloppenborg argues fiercely *against* the notion that the phrase λέγω ὑμῖν in verse 27[58] functions as a prophetic formula, maintaining instead that the formula introduces a sapiential admonition and calling the idea that the logion is prophetic "entirely conjectural."[59] Other examples could have been

---

[46] Cf. Hunter 1964, 82; Betz 1995, 227; Valantasis 2005, 175; Luz 2007, 241.

[47] Kirk 1998, 92.

[48] Roth 2018, 343.

[49] See Piper 1989, 105–107; Kirk 1998, 238–239; cf. Edwards 1976, 129; Marshall 1978, 551; Kloppenborg 1987, 152–153; 2000a, 194; Piper 2000, 250; Luz 2007, 241; Foster 2014a, 261; Roth 2018, 347, 350–351.

[50] Piper 1989, 106; Betz 1995, 228, esp. n. 248; Luz 2007, 237, 241; cf. Prov 6:1–5; 25:7–10; Sir 8:14, 19–20; 22:24; 34:21–22; 2 Enoch 44:3; *Didache* 1:5; 3:2; Qumran Scrolls 4Q416 2, II:4–6; *idem.* 4Q417 1, II:6–8; *idem.* 4Q418 8:3–5; Sent. Sextus 39; Eliezer ben Hyrcanus, *Derek Ereṣ* 10.

[51] Kloppenborg 1987, 152–153.

[52] Cf. also Fleddermann 2005a, 657.

[53] That is, Mark 9:1; 13:30; 14:25; Matt 5:18; Luke 13:35.

[54] "I say to you [singular or plural]."

[55] Cf. Luz 2007, 241.

[56] I.e. Q 12:4–5.

[57] Kloppenborg 1987, 210, esp. n. 164.

[58] Although the phrase "but I say to you" (ἐγὼ δὲ λέγω ὑμῖν // ἀλλ' ὑμῖν λέγω) appears in both the Matthean (5:44) and Lukan (6:27) versions of this text, the International Q Project chose not to feature it in the *Critical Edition of Q* (6:27).

[59] Kloppenborg 1987, 178–180, quotation from page 178.

added.[60] Betz sees the phrase λέγω σοι as evidence that Matthew 5:26 (i.e. Q 12:59) derives from "a proverb taken out of the oral tradition of wisdom sayings."[61] In general, the Sayings Gospel Q uses the phrase λέγω ὑμῖν in both the proverbial logia of the formative stratum[62] and the prophetic-eschatological *chreia* of the main redaction.[63] This observation is particularly significant in the current case, where the sapiential nature of the isolated logion is so apparent.[64] As it stands, Q 12:59 does not need to be read as a prophetic or eschatological saying at all.[65] Davies and Allison, who are generally fond of eschatological readings, view Q 12:59[66] as a saying that does "not directly pertain to eschatology."[67]

To be sure, Q 12:58–59 lacks all the formal features of prophetic, apocalyptic, and eschatological small forms, including prophetic introductory formulas, a threatening tone, and the features of the so-called "eschatological" or "prophetic correlative."[68] More importantly, the logion is not introduced as a *chreia*. In other words, there is no narrative introduction that contextualises the logion as an anecdote. It is further significant that the verb "get out" (ἐξέλθῃς) is in the aorist tense and subjunctive mood, not the future tense and indicative mood as one would expect from a prophetic or eschatological saying. The subjunctive mood fits better with logical reasoning and rhetorical argumentation. One could perhaps point to the adjective ἔσχατος ("last" or "final") in verse 59, which is the Greek word from which the English term "eschatology" derives, but its usage here is purely coincidental, functioning in the syntactical context as a description of the noun κοδράντης ("penny").[69] Given these considerations, it is justified to conclude that Q 12:58–59 is an admonition.[70]

---

[60] E.g. Kloppenborg 1987, 209–210, 218–219.

[61] Betz 1995, 228.

[62] Cf. Q 11:9; 12:22, 27; 15:10.

[63] Cf. Q 3:8; 7:26, 28; 10:12, 24; 12:44; 13:35; 17:34.

[64] See above.

[65] See Foster 2014a, 261–262; cf. Schulz 1972, 423; Zeller 1977, 66–67; Piper 1989, 106; Howes 2015a, 113.

[66] They mistakenly reference Q 12:59 as "Mt 5.26 = Lk 12.29."

[67] Davies and Allison 1988, 488.

[68] See Edwards 1969, 9–20; 1976, 41, 142; Schmidt 1977, 517–522; cf. Horsley 1999, 65.

[69] *Pace* Fleddermann 2005a, 657.

[70] Cf. Luz 2007, 234.

5.3 Characteristic Motifs

5.3.1 Q 12:58–59

On the surface of the literal text, no mention is made of the eschatological end. Particularly conspicuous is that neither God nor the Son of Man fulfil the function of "judge."[71] Instead, the judge appears to be a human person. Moreover, the direct subordinate of the judge is a human "assistant" (ὑπηρέτης),[72] not the celestial being one would expect in an apocalyptic-type saying. The punishment is prison (φυλακή), as opposed to eternal damnation. The same basic arguments also speak against the classification of this logion as prophetic. Piper explains when he says that the warning in this logion "remains couched in the imagery set by the saying as a whole, dealing as it does with an accuser, a judge, an officer. It never emerges into a direct identification of the addressees or into a direct confrontation, such as would be more characteristic of prophetic speech."[73] Even if one were to read the saying allegorically, it is not clear who the different characters would represent.[74] If the judge represents God, it portrays God not only in an unflattering light, but also as a supporting character whose only function is to contribute to the main character's demise as one link in the judicial chain.[75] Instead, the logion's message is to reconcile with your legal opponent, before ending up in jail, where you will not leave before your obligation has been met.[76] Considered on its own, Q 12:58–59 fails to treat apocalyptic, eschatological, or prophetic motifs.[77] Neither are there any features that could be described as "polemical."[78] Although verse 59 might surreptitiously condemn juridical injustice,[79] the saying is not formulated as criticism directed at the powers that be, but rather as advice directed at the powerless.[80]

The absence of any ethnic references indicates that both hypothetical parties were probably understood to be Jewish. The Sayings Gospel Q typically points out the ethnicity of someone if that person is not Jewish.[81] The clause "until

---

[71] Piper 1989, 106–107; cf. Bazzana 2015, 308.

[72] Luke has πράκτωρ (Marshall 1978, 551; Davies and Allison 1988, 520; Bock 1996, 1199).

[73] Piper 1989, 106.

[74] Thurén 2014, 306; cf. Roth 2018, 344, 350.

[75] Cf. Roth 2018, 344.

[76] See Prov 6:1–5; cf. Piper 1989, 106; Luz 2007, 241; Foster 2014a, 261.

[77] See Foster 2014a, 261–262.

[78] Piper 1989, 106, 114; cf. Horsley 1999, 65.

[79] See below.

[80] Rollens 2014a, 102, 105, 107, 108; cf. Horsley 1995a, 43; Park 2014b, 4–5.

[81] Howes 2015a, 250; e.g. Q 7:3; 11:30–32.

you pay the last penny" (ἕως τὸν ἔσχατον κοδράντην ἀποδῷς) in verse 59 contextualises the legal proceedings of verse 58 as pertaining specifically to the
issue of debt or indebtedness.[82] In the Lukan context, the term πράκτωρ ("bailiff," "court official," or "officer of the court") confirms that the saying has to
do with some economic or financial dispute, since this office was associated
with a debtors' prison.[83] This indicates that the ἀντίδικος ("legal opponent") of
verse 58 should be understood as a creditor.[84] Likewise, the addressee (represented by the second person singular throughout the logion[85]) should be understood as a debtor.[86] These observations are supported by the clause "make an
effort to get loose from him" (δὸς ἐργασίαν ἀπηλλάχθαι ἀπ' αὐτοῦ). On the
one hand, the verb translated here as "get loose" (ἀπαλλάσσω) could in legal
contexts refer specifically to forgiving or discharging debt.[87] On the other hand,
the clause as a whole indicates that the addressee would have been under the
control of the ἀντίδικος, as would indeed have been the case if the addressee
owed him a substantial amount of money. The likelihood that they are going to
an urban court[88] suggests that the debt must have been substantial.

In general, the noun ἀντίδικος could refer either to a plaintiff or to a defendant,[89] but the context of indebtedness suggests that the ἀντίδικος of Q 12:58
would have been the plaintiff, while the addressee would have been the defendant.[90] The clause "make an effort to get loose from him" (δὸς ἐργασίαν
ἀπηλλάχθαι ἀπ' αὐτοῦ) supports the identification of the ἀντίδικος as the plaintiff. If the addressee were the plaintiff, he[91] would not have needed to make
any effort in this regard; he could simply have cancelled the debt and dropped
the lawsuit. Conversely, the defendant would have been the one needing to
make a real effort to avoid court, since he would have been bound by the debt
and incapable of simply dropping the charges. In any case, it seems logical to

---

[82] Jacobson 1992, 202; Valantasis 2005, 175; Oakman 2008, 225; 2015, xi, 72; Howes
2015a, 257; Roth 2018, 346; cf. Dodd 1958, 138; Hunter 1971, 90; Davies and Allison 1988,
521; Betz 1995, 226; Robinson 1995a, 273; Kloppenborg 2000a, 200; Arnal 2001, 94, 173;
Fleddermann 2005a, 657; Luz 2007, 241; Thurén 2014, 306.

[83] Marshall 1978, 551; Bock 1996, 1199; cf. Oakman 2015, xi; see below.

[84] Piper 2000, 250; Howes 2015a, 257; Oakman 2015, 81; cf. Hunter 1971, 90; Jeremias
1972, 43; Reiser 1990, 278; Kloppenborg 2006, 126; Luz 2007, 241; cf. Luke 18:2–5.

[85] See Roth 2018, 342–343.

[86] Marshall 1978, 551; Jacobson 1992, 202; cf. Hunter 1971, 90; Davies and Allison 1988,
521; Reiser 1990, 278; Piper 2000, 250; Kloppenborg 2006, 126; Luz 2007, 241.

[87] Liddell and Scott 1996, 176.

[88] See below.

[89] Liddell and Scott 1996, 155.

[90] Cf. Blair 1896, 286; Klostermann 1909, 190; Rengstorf 1936, 168.

[91] The defendant would in all likelihood have been male, taken to court as head and representative of his family.

suppose that the creditor would have been the plaintiff.[92] The saying also presumes that the debtor was not able to pay off the debt, as indicated not only by the fact that they are going to court in the first place, but also by the fact that the debtor is encouraged to reconcile with the creditor rather than pay him.[93]

A number of factors indicate that the court of Q 12:58–59 is envisioned as an urban court: (1) the description of being summoned to court as being "handed over to the judge" (παραδῷ τῷ κριτῇ); (2) specifically calling the arbiter a "judge" (κριτής); (3) the result of being thrown into "prison" (φυλακή); and (4) the specific context of indebtedness, since matters of indebtedness between the underclass and elite were resolved in higher-level urban courts, even if local disputes involving lending and borrowing between underlings were handled by local courts.[94] It has sometimes been argued that the ὑπηρέτης of Matthew 5:25 was a Jewish official in the synagogue during the first century CE, whereas the πράκτωρ of Luke was an official of the Greco-Roman court during that time.[95] Marshall has indicated, however, that "ὑπηρέτης was a term used in Hellenistic practice as well as Jewish to describe the court official who executed the sentence imposed by the court, while πράκτωρ had the more restricted sense of the official who dealt with debts and was in charge of the debtors' prison."[96] "Hellenistic" here implies not only Greek, but also Roman influences and institutions. Egyptian papyri likewise show that both terms were used in Roman provinces of the time.[97] Even if ὑπηρέτης is compatible with a Jewish setting, both terms are compatible with a Hellenistic setting.[98] Scholars are in agreement that a Hellenistic court is in view here, since imprisonment for debt was not a feature of Jewish law.[99] Betz follows Jackson in pointing out that the description of the plaintiff "handing over" (παραδίδωμι) the defendant to the judge probably reflects a Roman court.[100] A Hellenistic setting is further indicated by the fact that the two legal opponents meet in advance, since legal procedure in the ancient Greco-Roman world enabled creditors to coerce their

---

[92] Cf. Blair 1896, 286.

[93] Roth 2018, 343.

[94] Cf. Kloppenborg 2000a, 256; Reed 2000, 193; Joseph 2012, 86; Zimmermann 2014, 11; Howes 2015a, 256, esp. n. 239.

[95] E.g. Jeremias 1972, 26–27, esp. n. 10.

[96] Marshall 1978, 551; cf. Bock 1996, 1199; Fleddermann 2005a, 655; Roth 2018, 345.

[97] Kloppenborg 2006, 345–346, esp. n. 264; cf. *P.Col.* 3.54.47.

[98] It follows that if Luke was responsible for changing ὑπηρέτης to πράκτωρ, it was probably not to Hellenise the saying, but rather to identify the legal post with greater specificity (cf. Marshall 1978, 551; Fleddermann 2005a, 655). Luke might have had a better knowledge of the urban court system than those responsible for Q.

[99] Marshall 1978, 551; Davies and Allison 1988, 520; Nolland 2005, 234; Luz 2007, 241; Roth 2018, 346; cf. Oakman 2015, 35, 75.

[100] Jackson 1972, 144; Betz 1995, 226–227.

debtors to accompany them to court.[101] This is supported by the Lukan version of the saying, which uses the verb κατασύρω ("drag" or "carry off") to describe the act of being taken to court, instead of Matthew's παραδίδωμι ("hand over" or "deliver up"), thereby denoting coercion and possible violence.[102] Bock translates Luke's κατασύρω as being "dragged by force."[103] Since Q 12:58–59 originated somewhere in Palestine and Hellenistic courts were almost exclusively concentrated in Palestinian *cities*, the court can confidently be identified as an urban court.

As far as the verb κατασύρω is concerned, there are in fact reasons to favour this Lukan word for Q over Matthew's παραδίδωμι. The lexeme κατασύρω is a *hapax legomenon* in the New Testament. More importantly, it correctly portrays the act of taking a debtor to court as one of coercion and violence.[104] Matthew could have softened the imagery to suit his context of brotherly reconciliation.[105] On the other hand, the verb παραδίδωμι could also presuppose violence, since it was sometimes in antiquity used to describe the act of handing someone over to authorities or even enemies for severe punishment, including the act of handing over a slave for torture.[106] However, the violence would in this case follow after being handed over and would not form part of the process of being handed over. In any case, the most common usage of the verb παραδίδωμι did not suggest violence or coercion.[107] By contrast, κατασύρω was a monolithic term that always denoted force and possible violence. If Matthew replaced κατασύρω with παραδίδωμι, the multiple meanings of the latter term would have allowed him to stay true to both his source and his literary context at the same time.[108] It is true that Luke also features the verb παραδίδωμι as part of the next clause,[109] but the two different actions of the legal opponent (κατασύρω) and the judge (παραδίδωμι) might be reflective of ancient practice and therefore explicable on the level of Q. Fleddermann argues that Luke introduced κατασύρω to reflect a Hellenistic setting, but the current analysis has shown that the Q saying already presupposes a Hellenistic urban court.[110] Luke could, however, have been responsible for introducing the verb to provide a more accurate description of actual practices.

---

[101] Kloppenborg 2006, 345; cf. Rollens 2014a, 105.

[102] Cf. Louw and Nida 1993a, 205; Liddell and Scott 1996, 915; Fleddermann 2005a, 655.

[103] Bock 1996, 1199; cf. Marshall 1978, 551.

[104] Cf. Louw and Nida 1993a, 205; Liddell and Scott 1996, 915; Batten 2014, 82.

[105] Cf. Matt 5:21–24; cf. Dodd 1958, 136–139; Hunter 1964, 82.

[106] Louw and Nida 1993a, 485; Liddell and Scott 1996, 1308.

[107] See Liddell and Scott 1996, 1308.

[108] Cf. Kirk 2016, 112, 117.

[109] Matt 5:24 // Luke 12:58 (ESV): "and the judge to the guard" (καὶ ὁ κριτὴς τῷ ὑπηρέτῃ) // "and the judge hand you over to the officer" (καὶ ὁ κριτής σε παραδώσει τῷ πράκτορι).

[110] Fleddermann 2005a, 655.

It should be obvious at this stage that an unequal relationship between the two participants is assumed by the logion, with the debtor lower and the creditor higher on the socio-economic scale.[111] Although the logion does not specify the vocation of either party, an involvement in agriculture seems most likely in both cases.[112] It was typical for eighty to ninety percent of agrarian societies like first-century Palestine to be involved in agriculture. The creditor was in all likelihood a wealthy landowner who resided in the city.[113] That he was wealthy is indicated not only by the fact that he had a significant amount of money to lend in the first place, but more so by the fact that he had recourse to a higher level court.[114] That he was a landowner is suggested by his wealth, since control over land was the primary means of wealth creation in antiquity.[115] That he resided in the city is indicated by his appeal to an urban court. As we saw in the previous chapter, it was typical for wealthy landowners to be largely absent from their farms.[116] These landowners mostly lived in the city and owned multiple estates.[117] Palestinian landowners, especially those who owned the most fertile land, therefore resided in cities like Tiberias, Sepphoris, and Jerusalem.[118] These observations are further supported by the description of the plaintiff "handing over" (παραδίδωμι) the defendant to the judge. This act betrays not only the immense socio-economic superiority of the plaintiff, but also the existence of an established relationship with the urban judge of this higher level court.[119] If the logion featured κατασύρω,[120] there would be even more reason to accept these findings.

The debtor was in all likelihood from the lower echelons of society.[121] He was also probably involved in agriculture.[122] His relationship with a wealthy creditor makes more sense on the assumption of agriculture than some other vocation. Due to unreasonable demands from above, small peasants were much more likely to borrow from wealthy creditors than people from other backgrounds, like fishermen or potters.[123] What is more, an overwhelming majority

---

[111] Cf. Piper 2000, 250; Arnal 2001, 173; Batten 2014, 82.

[112] Cf. Kloppenborg 2000a, 194; Howes 2015a, 257.

[113] Howes 2015a, 257.

[114] Cf. Batten 2014, 82.

[115] Arnal 2001, 102, 139; Häkkinen 2016, 2.

[116] Freyne 2000, 99, 195; see Kloppenborg 2006, 279–280, 314–316.

[117] Herzog 1994, 156; Kloppenborg 2006, 300; Ukpong 2012, 200; Dube 2015, 5; Boer and Petterson 2017, 97–98.

[118] Oakman 1986, 78; Freyne 2000, 52, 99, 195; Park 2014a, 85; Dube 2015, 5; Häkkinen 2016, 7; cf. Horsley 1995a, 42; Boer and Petterson 2017, 141.

[119] Cf. Valantasis 2005, 175.

[120] See above.

[121] Cf. Arnal 2001, 173; Batten 2014, 82; Rollens 2014a, 107, 108, 113.

[122] Cf. Kloppenborg 2000a, 194; Howes 2015a, 257.

[123] Cf. Horsley 1999, 222.

of Q's audiences were from the lower segments of society, including especially the small peasantry.[124] In ancient Palestine, especially in the first century under Roman occupancy, significant percentages of agricultural goods were taken from the peasantry through various kinds of taxes, tithes, and rents, and were then redistributed among the rich to use as they saw fit.[125] If Oakman's estimations are correct, taxes and rents could amount to between one half and two thirds of a small peasant's overall harvest, leaving much less produce for daily survival.[126] If a small peasant was unable to meet existing obligations, that peasant was forced to borrow from wealthier individuals.[127]

In antiquity, borrowing from wealthy individuals initiated a patron-client relationship between the two parties, which was skewed in favour of the patron and typically resulted in foreclosure on land due to the client's inability to pay off debts.[128] In fact, debt accumulation was the primary means by which the wealthy confiscated ancestral land from small peasants.[129] Consistent indebtedness was therefore very important to the economic goals of the largescale landowner, but was diametrically opposed to the reciprocal economic values of the peasant, who sought to cancel out debt as soon as possible.[130] To ensure lasting indebtedness, the affluent charged excessive and usurious interest rates on debt.[131] The content of contemporaneous loan documents indicate that foreclosure was the chief motivating factor behind lending.[132] Some landowners in Jerusalem made use of debt contracts for the sole purpose of squeezing and wrestling land from small peasants.[133] As a result, many small peasants were forced into indebtedness, which initiated a downwards spiral of control by creditors, loss of land, starvation, and ending up as day-labourers, beggars, or

---

[124] There is widespread agreement on this: see Horsley 1995a, 44; 1999, 260–261, 269, 296–298; Kloppenborg 2000a, 198–199; Reed 2000, 136–137; Rollens 2014a, 96; cf. Oakman 1986, 100; Kloppenborg 1987, 251; Douglas 1995, 120; Piper 1995, 63–64; Reed 1995, 19; Tuckett 1996, 360, 365; Freyne 2000, 206; Arnal 2001, 150, 173, 188; Häkkinen 2016, 7.

[125] Herzog 1994, 161; Van Eck 2011, 5, 7; Park 2014a, 85, 86; see Howes 2015a, 137–138; cf. Horsley 1999, 222–223; Boer and Petterson 2017, 93.

[126] Oakman 1986, 72; cf. Ukpong 2012, 200; Häkkinen 2016, 2.

[127] Oakman 1986, 72; 2008, 24; Horsley 1995b, 215, 219; Van Eck 2011, 7.

[128] Herzog 1994, 161; see Boer and Petterson 2017, 97–100.

[129] Oakman 1986, 149; 2008, 33; Ukpong 2012, 200; see Boer and Petterson 2017, 97–100.

[130] Cf. Drake 2014, 237.

[131] Ukpong 2012, 200; cf. Drake 2014, 237; Häkkinen 2016, 3.

[132] Arnal 2001, 140.

[133] Oakman 1986, 75; see Boer and Petterson 2017, 97–100.

bandits.[134] Some of these peasants were allowed to remain on their smallhold-ings as tenant farmers, with ownership of the land and its produce reverting to the landlord.

Given this state of affairs, foreclosure was a much more likely result than imprisonment for small peasants being summoned to court by a creditor.[135] This circumstance seems to be contradicted by the content of Q 12:58–59, where imprisonment is put forward as a foregone conclusion.[136] Hence, the inevitability of imprisonment might speak against the identification of the log-ion's addressee as a small-scale farmer. If this is correct, should we rather view him as a beggar, bandit, day-labourer, or tenant farmer? Debtors without land as security could be sold as slaves or wind up in prison if they were unable to repay their loans.[137] The options of beggar and bandit may be eliminated by virtue of the fact that the debtor was successful in borrowing from the creditor in the first place.[138] The option of tenant farmer also seems unlikely, given the verdict of imprisonment. For the sake of profitability and convenience, the landowner would presumably not have desired the imprisonment of someone who farmed on one of his plots. The inevitability of imprisonment rather seems to suggest that the debtor could have been a farm worker. He would then have worked either as a day-labourer or on a more permanent basis. This would make him one of "the poor," which constituted all those ranked below the peas-antry, including women without patriarchs, children without parents, and fam-ilies without land, as well as "beggars, robbers, bandits, prostitutes and other despised people."[139] It is even possible that he laboured as a mere worker on the smallholding that he used to own and probably grew up on. This would imply that the debtor incurred the debt when he still had a smallholding, but that the smallholding was eventually seized in partial repayment of the debt. Without a smallholding, the debtor was unable to repay the rest of his debt, despite working as a farmhand on his former or a different smallholding, and was eventually imprisoned for his outstanding debt.[140]

However, it is also possible to read the inevitability of imprisonment differ-ently. Q's Jesus could merely be holding up the worst possible outcome as an inevitability to support his argument that courts should be avoided at all costs.[141] Stated differently, Q's Jesus could be exaggerating the consequences of going to court in order to drive home his point that the courts should be

---

[134] Horsley 1995a, 43; 1995b, 60, 215–216, 219; Freyne 2000, 205; Arnal 2001, 139–140, 146; Moxnes 2003, 150; Oakman 2008, 21, 25, 224; Häkkinen 2016, 3, 7.

[135] See Oakman 2015, 35–36.

[136] Cf. Dodd 1958, 138; Kloppenborg 2000a, 194; Rollens 2014a, 107.

[137] Oakman 2008, 27; 2015, 36; cf. Matt. 18:23–35.

[138] Cf. Oakman 2015, 35–36.

[139] Häkkinen 2016, 4.

[140] Cf. Oakman 2015, 35–36.

[141] Cf. Rollens 2014a, 107.

avoided.[142] This interpretation is supported by the programmatic opening clause "I tell you" (λέγω σοι) at the beginning of verse 59. In the Sayings Gospel Q, the clause "I tell you"[143] often precedes an outlandish, exaggerated, subversive, and/or implausible statement by Q's Jesus, as if the audience needs convincing of the claim's validity.[144] This observation supports the earlier case that verse 59 was never intended as a prophetic or eschatological exclamation. Instead, the function of the clause λέγω σοι in the context of the isolated logion is to lend credence to the outlandishly subversive claim that going to court will necessarily result in imprisonment.[145] The credibility of the claim in verse 59 is supported by the authority of Jesus.[146] Even if the final supporting argument in verse 59 might seem exaggerated or incredible, the authority of Jesus is invoked to legitimise its inherent accuracy. If verse 59 is understood in this sense, it remains possible (and probable) to view the debtor of this logion as a small peasant or tenant farmer.[147]

Urban courts were biased and geared towards the servicing of wealthy and "respected" citizens against the lower classes.[148] Traditional Jewish law forbade the charging of interest and demanded that all debts be released during the Sabbath year and Jubilee.[149] As such, ancestral lands were traditionally regarded as the permanent properties of the historical clans and, if sold, had to be redeemed during Jubilee.[150] By the first century, however, Jewish aristocrats and landlords controlled the courts and manipulated the law, bypassing these "outdated" commandments in order to grant loans against immovable property, enforce the foreclosure thereof, and so obtain land from the small peasantry.[151] Since the courts were controlled by the rich, land foreclosure was a near certainty.[152] Some Jerusalem elites even bypassed *Roman* law and defrauded small peasants out of their land.[153] It is no wonder that lower-level citizens were

---

[142] Cf. Davies and Allison 1988, 520; Thurén 2014, 306.

[143] Albeit in the plural: λέγω ὑμῖν.

[144] Howes 2015c, 94; see Smith 2006, 104–108; cf. Q 7:26, 28; 10:12, 24; 11:9, 51; 12:22, 27, 44, 59; 13:35; 15:7, [10]; 17:34.

[145] Cf. Smith 2006, 105, 106.

[146] Cf. Davies and Allison 1988, 490; Carruth 1995, 98–115, esp. 108–110; Thurén 2014, 306.

[147] Cf. Kloppenborg 2000a, 194.

[148] Horsley 1996, 120; Kloppenborg 2000a, 194; 2006, 126; Rollens 2014a, 108; cf. Robinson 1995a, 273; Oakman 2015, 75.

[149] Lev 25; Deut 15:1–2; see Drake 2014, 235–236; Bazzana 2015, 177–180; cf. Tuckett 1996, 430.

[150] Lev 25; Oakman 2015, 74; cf. Jacobs 2018, 125.

[151] See Arnal 2001, 140–141; Oakman 2008, 139–140, 225–227; 2015, 72–74; Boer and Petterson 2017, 97–100; cf. Drake 2014, 236–237; Ford 2016, 21, 30, 32, 36; Häkkinen 2016, 3; see Rabbi Hillel's prozbul in Mishnah tractate Šhebi'it 10.

[152] Cf. Horsley 1995a, 45; 1996, 120; Robinson 1995a, 273; Oakman 2008, 139.

[153] Oakman 2008, 24.

mostly suspicious of higher-level courts.[154] The interests of the small peasantry and poor were not protected by these judges and lawmakers.[155] In a word, ancient courts were merciless.[156] We saw above that the verb παραδίδωμι (or κατασύρω) implies an existing relationship with the judge on the part of the plaintiff. The presumed existence of such a relationship is confirmed by the inevitability of the guilty verdict.[157] The assumption of a guilty verdict further supports the likelihood that the debtor was from a low social location.[158]

It is noteworthy that the debtor is not advised to settle his debt, but rather to "make an effort to get loose from him" (δὸς ἐργασίαν ἀπηλλάχθαι ἀπ' αὐτοῦ). We saw that the verb translated here as "get loose" (ἀπαλλάσσω) could in legal contexts refer specifically to forgiving or discharging debt, but it could also in legal contexts mean to "throw up one's case" or "give up a prosecution."[159] What is more, in more generic terms the same verb could also mean to be "liberated," "released," "delivered," or "set free" from something.[160] Given the description of the two parties being "on the way" (ἐν τῇ ὁδῷ) to court, it is likely that the verb here denotes the legal case being dropped. Yet, in light of the reference to money in verse 59,[161] it is at the same time also likely that, on a secondary level, the verb denotes the debt being forgiven.[162] The one would anyway presuppose the other, since there would be no reason to drop the lawsuit if the creditor had no intentions of forgiving the loan, or vice versa. Finally, on a third semantic level, the verb probably connotes its more generic meaning of liberation. In other words, the advice to "make an effort to get loose from him" (δὸς ἐργασίαν ἀπηλλάχθαι ἀπ' αὐτοῦ) means to petition the creditor to jettison the lawsuit by forgiving the debt, which would completely liberate the debtor from the creditor's control.[163] Such advice coheres with everyday practice at the time. Papyrus contracts from antiquity indicate that people typically made contractual arrangements outside the law and attempted to resolve matters between themselves before going to court.[164] Evidence from Egypt in fact shows that people from the lower classes only appealed to the courts as an absolute last resort and that such appeals only happened when former attempts

---

[154] Horsley 1995a, 45; 1996, 120; Rollens 2014a, 107, 108.
[155] See Garnsey 1970; cf. Robinson 1995a, 273; Kloppenborg 2000a, 194; 2006, 126; Oakman 2015, 75.
[156] Funk and Hoover 1993, 344; cf. Roth 2018, 343.
[157] Cf. Dodd 1958, 138; Robinson 1995a, 273; Valantasis 2005, 175; Rollens 2014a, 105.
[158] Rollens 2014a, 107, 108; cf. Robinson 1995a, 273.
[159] Liddell and Scott 1996, 176.
[160] Liddell and Scott 1996, 176.
[161] Cf. Thurén 2014, 306.
[162] Cf. Jacobson 1992, 202.
[163] Cf. Luz 2007, 241.
[164] See Piper 1995, 61.

at arbitration and coercion had been unsuccessful.[165] It is, however, questionable to what extent the elite would have done the same, especially if their ultimate goal was foreclosure. Yet, if foreclosure was not their ultimate goal, they might have been motivated to settle out of court in the hope of actually getting repaid.[166] The imprisonment of a debtor would not have guaranteed repayment of the loan (by the debtor's family and/or friends), but would instead have rendered such repayment more difficult and less likely.[167] Also, the act of relinquishing one's legal rights was a norm of contemporary Jewish ethics.[168] On the other hand, imprisonment pressurised the debtor's family to somehow come up with the outstanding amount and impelled the debtor to fork over hidden currency or treasure.[169]

The particular phrasing of the clause "make an effort to get loose from him" (δὸς ἐργασίαν ἀπηλλάχθαι ἀπ' αὐτοῦ) is interesting.[170] The part that says "make an effort" (δὸς ἐργασίαν) qualifies the act specifically as an *attempt*, implying that the attempt would in all likelihood be unsuccessful. Such pessimism squares well with the desperate situation of Palestinian small peasants in the first century CE. Once caught up in the cycle of indebtedness, small peasants were extremely unlikely ever to escape.[171] Even so, the elite ensured that the myth of eventual repayment was kept alive so that tenant farmers would continue labouring on these estates in the hope of one day escaping their debt.[172] As we saw, the saying implies that the creditor forced the debtor to appear in court. We also saw that those from the lower classes tended to only go to court as a last resort, suggesting that the scenario depicted in Q 12:58–59 represents the end of a lengthy process.[173] Under such circumstances, it is unlikely that any attempt at convincing the creditor to write off the debt would have been successful. The pessimistic tone is sustained throughout the saying, which depicts the small peasant being handed over from one person to the next, totally at the mercy of other role players.[174] Pessimism reaches its pinnacle at the conclusion of the saying.[175] The peasant ends up in prison, where he is told: "You will not get out of there until you pay the last penny!" (οὐ μὴ ἐξέλθῃς ἐκεῖθεν, ἕως τὸν ἔσχατον κοδράντην ἀποδῷς). The debtor might have reckoned

---

[165] Kloppenborg 2000a, 194.

[166] See below.

[167] Luz 2007, 241; see below.

[168] Betz 1995, 227–228.

[169] Oakman 2015, 36, 75, 78–80; cf. Josephus, *J.W.* 2.273.

[170] Cf. Bock 1996, 1199.

[171] Cf. Drake 2014, 237.

[172] Boer and Petterson 2017, 99.

[173] Kloppenborg 2000a, 194; Rollens 2014a, 104.

[174] Betz 1995, 226; Rollens 2014a, 102; Roth 2018, 343, 344; cf. Kloppenborg 2000a, 194; Nolland 2005, 234.

[175] Cf. Funk and Hoover 1993, 344.

that at least he had some chance of reprieve during the juridical proceedings.[176] There is documentary evidence from the first two centuries CE to show that the lower classes at times petitioned the "chief magistrate" (στρατηγός) and other ancient administrators.[177] In this regard, the saying in Q 12:58–59 is a reality check and wake-up call, expressing the view that a debtor is much more likely to end up in prison than receive any form of clemency when going to court.[178] In fact, the saying articulates the conviction that a guilty verdict, followed by imprisonment, would be inevitable.[179] Better to avoid the risks involved by attempting to settle out of court.[180] Although there is documentary evidence of the non-elite petitioning the courts,[181] there is also documentary evidence of the non-elite attempting to evade the courts altogether, usually by hiding at the time of the trial.[182]

The closing statement is steeped in irony. The debtor is expected to repay his debt from prison.[183] The adjective "last" (ἔσχατος) in verse 59 indicates that settling the entire debt was the only possible avenue that would enable release from prison.[184] Rollens explains: "Prisons in antiquity, as papyri indicate, often functioned as holding cells until certain obligations were met instead of a punishment or ultimate sentence."[185] Although the temporal conjunction "until" (ἕως) suggests that the prisoner could look forward to someday being released from prison, the condition that follows indicates that such release was practically impossible. In the first place, small peasants who incurred debt with wealthy patrons typically remained in debt forever. In the second place, it would be practically impossible for a small peasant to produce a harvest, make payments towards his debt, or work off his debt while in prison.[186] In the ancient world generally, there was virtually no hope of being released from a debtors' prison.[187] The final exclamation is in effect a death sentence. The peasant will never be able to settle his debt, which means that he will never

---

[176] Cf. Piper 1995, 64.

[177] Piper 1995, 61; see Rollens 2014a, 101–105; cf. Boer and Petterson 2017, 99; e.g. *P.Tebt.* 2.278; *SB* 4.7376; *P.Mich.* 3.173.

[178] Kloppenborg 2006, 126; cf. Betz 1995, 226.

[179] Cf. Robinson 1995a, 273; Kloppenborg 2000a, 194; Rollens 2014a, 105, 107.

[180] Marshall 1978, 551; Funk and Hoover 1993, 344; Betz 1995, 228; Bock 1996, 1199; Piper 2000, 250; Valantasis 2005, 175; Foster 2014a, 261; Kirk 2016, 196; Roth 2018, 347; cf. Nolland 2005, 234; Oakman 2015, 35.

[181] See above.

[182] See Rollens 2014a, 106–107; e.g. *P.Mich.* 1.57; 9.534; *P.Tebt.* 1.5; *P.Col.* 10.266.

[183] Jacobson 1992, 202; Bock 1996, 1199; Rollens 2014a, 108; cf. Valantasis 2005, 175; Oakman 2015, 75.

[184] Cf. Ra 2016, 225.

[185] Rollens 2014a, 107. Rollens (2014a, 107 n. 43) holds up Egyptian papyrus *P.Cair.Zen.* 4.59628 as an example.

[186] Cf. Rollens 2014a, 107, 108; cf. Egyptian papyrus *P.Cair.Zen.* 3.59520.

[187] Bock 1996, 1200.

be released from prison. Adding insult to injury, imprisoned debtors were often physically beaten to incentivise their families and friends to settle their debts.[188] In addition to torture, the poor conditions in ancient prisons meant that death was a likely outcome, and not as a result of old age.[189]

The logion is therefore an ironic portrayal of the plight of small peasants in the first century.[190] It further highlights the link between the ancient judicial system and the struggle of the average small peasant to secure and preserve food and clothing.[191] The saying exposes the ancient judicial system for what it really is: a means of stealing the livelihood of the small peasantry by facilitating their exploitation. This is supported by the conditional temporal clause "until you pay the last penny" (ἕως τὸν ἔσχατον κοδράντην ἀποδῷς), emphasising that the main concern of both the creditor and the court is to extract as much money as possible from the debtor.[192] In addition to financial ruin, the small peasant would have suffered a significant loss of honour as a result of both his inability to repay his debts and his imprisonment.[193] One should also not forget that the women and children who formed part of the peasant's extended family were also faced with hardships and starvation because of the actions of ancient creditors, lawmakers, and judges.[194] As a piece of social commentary that exposes the status quo, Q 12:58–59 can be viewed as satire – only that the saying is not funny, but dead serious.

5.3.2 The Formative Stratum

The motifs implied and treated by Q 12:58–59 are characteristic of Q's formative layer. Q 12:58–59 has thematically a lot in common with Q 6:29–30.[195] In the inaugural sermon, Q 6:29–30 follows directly after the programmatic instruction to love one's enemies and pray for one's persecutors,[196] providing practical examples of how to achieve this daunting task in everyday life.[197] The second example in verse 29 suggests that if someone threatens to take you to court to get your "shirt" or "tunic" (χιτών), you should offer him your "coat" or "cloak" (ἱμάτιον) as well. The tunic was a fairly inexpensive inner garment,

---

[188] Bock 1996, 1200.

[189] Rollens 2014a, 107; cf. Egyptian papyrus *P.Mich.* 1.85.

[190] Cf. Park 2014b, 4; Oakman 2015, 75.

[191] Cf. Horsley 1995a, 43–44.

[192] Cf. Roth 2018, 347.

[193] Häkkinen 2016, 4.

[194] Park 2019, 53; see Oakman 2015, 76–83.

[195] Cf. Piper 1989, 107; 2000, 250; Horsley 1999, 96; Arnal 2001, 194; Johnson-DeBaufre 2005, 104; Kloppenborg 2006, 126; Batten 2014, 82; Park 2014b, 4; Rollens 2014a, 93–94, esp. n. 3, 108–109; Howes 2015a, 256, esp. n. 239.

[196] That is, Q 6:27–28, 35.

[197] Piper 1989, 111; Horsley 1992, 184; Allison 2010, 316; Ra 2016, 34; see Kirk 1998, 159–160; cf. Tuckett 1996, 303; Fleddermann 2005a, 329; Howes 2015a, 243, 245, 258.

while the cloak was an expensive outer garment.[198] This example probably has strictly Jewish partakers in mind.[199] The text presupposes a debtor's trial, during which it was customary for a creditor to demand the debtor's tunic as collateral to ensure repayment.[200] Documentary papyri from Egypt confirm not only that garments were often used as surety against loans, but also that garments were often retrieved by legal force.[201] According to traditional Jewish law, a tunic taken from a poor debtor as security had to be returned to him before nightfall so that he would have something to sleep in.[202] Whether this regulation was followed in practice is impossible to know, but the regulation itself does presuppose the existence of poverty and exploitation.[203] That the debtor only had clothing to offer as collateral indicates that he must have counted among the poor.[204] This corresponds to the opening beatitudes in Q 6:20–21, which overtly address "the poor" (οἱ πτωχοί) and "the hungry" (οἱ πεινῶντες).[205]

It is unlikely that a wealthy urban creditor would have gotten involved in lending to such a poor person. However, the debt might still have been left over from previous dealings, when the debtor was in a better situation. Hence, the creditor could have been from any superior social location, including the middle-to-high peasantry or the elite, with the latter being more probable.[206] Egyptian papyri indicate that garments were typically taken by the elite from lower class citizens.[207] Whatever the case, the relationship between the creditor and the debtor was an unequal one.[208] The supposition of inequality corresponds to the programmatic statement in Q 6:27–28, where the persecuted are instructed

---

[198] Piper 1995, 57; see Rollens 2014a, 102–103.

[199] Howes 2015a, 250; cf. Horsley 1999, 220–223.

[200] Piper 1995, 57; Luz 2007, 272; see Aberbach 1994, 52–53; cf. Catchpole 1993, 24–25, 110; Betz 1995, 290; Tuckett 1996, 304; Batten 2014, 82; Rollens 2014a, 100; Oakman 2015, 102; Ra 2016, 34.

[201] See Rollens 2014a, 101–105; e.g. *P.Tebt.* 2.331; 3.1.784, 802; *SB* 4.7376; *P.Duk.inv.* 739; *P.Mich.* 3.173.

[202] Piper 1995, 57; Horsley 1999, 221; Kloppenborg 2000a, 194, 199; Ra 2016, 34; cf. Catchpole 1993, 24–25, 110; Tuckett 1996, 304; cf. Deut 24:10–13, 17; Exod 22:24–27. It is interesting that the two examples of verse 29 also appear together as examples of serious insults in Jewish literature (Catchpole 1993, 25, 111; Tuckett 1996, 305; i.e. m. B. Qam. 8:6).

[203] Rollens 2014a, 101 n. 21.

[204] Kloppenborg 2000a, 194; Ra 2016, 35; cf. Batten 2014, 82; Rollens 2014a, 100–101, 104, 113.

[205] Ra 2016, 35; see Kloppenborg 2001, 183–184; cf. Horsley 1992, 184, 186; 1995a, 43; 1999, 223; Cotter 1995, 120.

[206] Cf. Piper 2000, 250; Batten 2014, 82.

[207] See Rollens 2014a, 99–105; cf. esp. *P.Tebt.* 2.278.

[208] Cf. Piper 2000, 250; Batten 2014, 82; *pace* Valantasis 2005, 59.

how to treat their persecutors.[209] According to Rollens, the imagery of Q 6:29 is symbolic of exploitative injustice and "would have had particular resonance with an especially vulnerable part of society."[210]

Hence, Q 6:29 advises someone with only the clothes on his back, who is asked to give up his tunic as collateral for a loan, to sacrifice both his tunic and his much more expensive cloak just to avoid going to court.[211] Such advice would have been counter-intuitive and unconventional, especially considering the evidence from documentary papyri that people often formally petitioned for the return of garments.[212] Following such advice would leave the debtor naked.[213] The suggestion seems like poor legal advice and might be an example of exaggeration.[214] But why exaggerate? I suggest that the reason is to underline the importance of avoiding the ancient legal system entirely. Q 6:29 is not merely about avoiding court, but about doing so at all costs.[215] The suggestion to give the creditor much more than what he is asking for relates to the suggestion in Q 12:58 to "make an effort to get loose from him." The purpose of both is to avoid going to court at all costs.[216]

In all likelihood, Matthew 5:41 stood in Q between verses 29 and 30.[217] The verb ἀγγαρεύω ("conscript") has a very specific reference (comparable to

---

[209] Cf. also Q 6:22–23; see Kloppenborg 2001, 183–184; cf. Horsley 1992, 184. Some scholars argue for discontinuity between the two examples of Q 6:29 (as they appear in Matthew 5:40 and later in the *Critical Edition of Q*), since the first example (of being slapped) addresses the *offended* party and the second example (of being sued for clothing) addresses the *offending* party (e.g. Catchpole 1993, 110; Tuckett 1996, 304–305). This is a clear example of reading the text from above instead of from below (cf. Rohrbaugh 1993, 33, 35; Van Eck 2011, 5). From a small peasant perspective, the offending party would be the exploitative and litigious creditor, not the exploited and persecuted debtor (cf. Robinson 1993, 1–2). Both examples of verse 29 (as well as Matt 5:41) presuppose abusive maltreatment by a superior party, and all the examples of Q 6:29–30 reflect the everyday struggle of the small peasantry and poor to live and survive in a context of subjugation (Vaage 1994, 52; Piper 2000, 250; see Rollens 2014a, 99–105; Ra 2016, 34–35; cf. Valantasis 2005, 59).

[210] Rollens 2014a, 104; cf. Robinson 1993, 1–2; Kloppenborg 2001, 183–184; Park 2014b, 4–5.

[211] Kloppenborg 2000a, 194; 2006, 126; Piper 2000, 250; Arnal 2001, 194; Valantasis 2005, 59–60.

[212] See Rollens 2014a, 101–105, esp. 104; cf. Funk and Hoover 1993, 145; e.g. *P.Tebt.* 2.331; 3.1.784, 802; *SB* 4.7376; *P.Duk.inv.* 739; *P.Mich.* 3.173.

[213] Funk and Hoover 1993, 144; Betz 1995, 291; Horsley 1999, 222.

[214] See Funk and Hoover 1993, 144–145.

[215] Piper 1995, 60; Kloppenborg 2000a, 194, 199.

[216] Kloppenborg 2000a, 194; see Piper 1995, 60–61.

[217] See Robinson, Hoffmann, and Kloppenborg 2000, 60–65; 2002, 84–85; cf. Funk and Hoover 1993, 145. Allison (2010, 344) holds that it is not possible to reach a decision on this matter due to insufficient evidence.

French *corveé*), denoting the authority of Roman soldiers in first-century Palestine to force Jewish civilians to carry any type of load for a distance.[218] The
same verb is used in Mark 15:21, where Simon of Cyrene is forced by Roman
soldiers to carry Jesus's cross.[219] The noun ἄγγαρος ("mounted courier") derives from the same stem as the verb ἀγγαρεύω and was sometimes used as a
"term of abuse."[220] Despite the literal meaning of ἀγγαρεύω, it is not impossible that the same verb was applied to exclusively Jewish contexts, like when a
Jewish farm worker or day-labourer was forced by a Jewish master or employer
to carry something.[221] Important currently is that the "enforcer" or "abuser" is
in all these cases protected by law. Despite running the risk of immediate (violent) retaliation by the soldier or employer, the inferior party also ran the risk
of being taken to court for disobedience or even insurrection, which could result in imprisonment or death. The advice of Matthew (Q) 5:41 is therefore to
do twice as much as one is compelled to do, in an effort to avoid both immediate (physical) and deferred (legal) retaliation.[222] If this is correct, part of the
advice would again be to avoid the courts at all costs.[223] It needs to be reiter-
ated, however, that this logion might not have featured in Q, since it appears
only in Matthew.[224]

The example in Q 6:30 continues with the topic of debt and indebtedness.[225]
Unlike Q 12:58–59 (and Q 6:29), the examples in verse 30 are from the perspective of the lender.[226] Even so, the two directives are in all likelihood aimed
at the lower classes.[227] The fact that the lender instead of the borrower is addressed need not imply that the lender was socially well off, especially since
the amount is left unspecified.[228] To be sure, the programmatic saying in Q
6:27–28 contextualises the examples in Q 6:29–30 as aimed at the persecuted,
not the persecutors.[229] The hypothetical lender can therefore not be the type of
urban landowner described earlier, but is more likely to be a rural peasant or
craftsman.[230] The hypothetical borrower must therefore be lower on the socio-

---

[218] Louw and Nida 1993a, 476; 1993b, 2; Betz 1995, 291; Valantasis 2005, 60; Oakman
2015, 102; cf. Aberbach 1994, 41; Kloppenborg 2000a, 194, 198, 235; 2001, 183.

[219] Louw and Nida 1993a, 476; cf. Betz 1995, 291.

[220] Liddell and Scott 1996, 7.

[221] Cf. Horsley 1999, 220–223; Howes 2015a, 249–250.

[222] Valantasis 2005, 59, 60.

[223] Cf. Piper 1995, 60; Kloppenborg 2000a, 194; 2006, 126.

[224] Cf. Betz 1995, 291; Park 2019, 44.

[225] Tuckett 1996, 304; Kloppenborg 2000a, 200; 2001, 178, 184.

[226] Cf. Tuckett 1996, 304; Kloppenborg 2001, 184.

[227] Piper 2000, 254; cf. Horsley 1992, 184, 186; 1999, 220.

[228] Piper 1995, 63; 2000, 250; cf. Kloppenborg 2000a, 198–199; *pace* Arnal 2001, 42–
43, 173.

[229] Cf. Cotter 1995, 120; Kloppenborg 2001, 183–184.

[230] Cf. Horsley 1999, 222–223.

economic scale, or at least in a worse position than the lender, suggesting someone from the ranks of the poor, perhaps a former peasant. This is confirmed by
the rest of Q, where the accumulation of wealth is frowned upon and real-life
examples feature insignificant numismatic denominations.[231] The text instructs
the lender to give freely to the one who asks, without expecting anything in
return.[232] The saying therefore promotes the replacement of balanced reciprocity with general reciprocity at village level.[233] Tuckett points out that the verb
"lend" or "give" (δανίζω/δανείζω) in Q 6:30 may presuppose the Sabbath year
and Jubilee,[234] in which case it promotes widespread debt remission and abolition.[235] However, if Oakman is correct in translating the saying according to
Luke's version, with the verb "take away" (ἀείρω) instead of "lend" or "give"
(δανίζω/δανείζω), the second instruction in verse 30 takes on an entirely different meaning: "and if anyone takes away your goods, do not ask for them
again."[236] Instead of advocating generous giving and general reciprocity among
social equals on village level, the saying would then advocate relentless economic submission to the powers that be. This actually corresponds better to the
preceding logia that infer submission to a socio-economic superior. Yet the
first instruction in verse 30 would still advocate general reciprocity together
with generous giving to beggars and the poor. It follows that at least the first
instruction of verse 30 (but perhaps both of them) is consistent with certain
sapiential traditions that likewise advocate generous giving, especially to the
poor.[237] According to Kloppenborg, Q 6:30 promotes activity that is "designed
to overcome victimization."[238] Q 6:34 develops these themes further and directs its audience to lend to anyone who asks, not just those who are in a position to repay the loan.[239]

Q 6:30 also presupposes the legal system by advising the lender not to attempt recovery of the loan if and when it defaults.[240] In other words, verse 30
advises the lender not to appeal to the legal system to recuperate a defaulted
loan. Whereas verse 29 advises the *debtor* or potential defendant to avoid a

---

[231] See Kloppenborg 2000a, 198–199; cf. Valantasis 2005, 176; Howes 2015a, 257; e.g.
Q 12:6, 33–34, 59; [15:8–9].

[232] Valantasis 2005, 60.

[233] Cf. Douglas 1995, 124–125; Horsley 1995a, 43; Allison 2010, 368.

[234] Cf. Lev 25; Deut 15; see above.

[235] Tuckett 1996, 430; cf. Catchpole 1993, 113; Horsley 1999, 221; Piper 2000, 250;
Kloppenborg 2001, 178; Valantasis 2005, 60; Park 2014b, 4.

[236] Oakman 2015, 102.

[237] Catchpole 1993, 112; cf. Horsley 1999, 221; cf. Ps 37:26; Prov 19:17; Sir 20:15; 29:1–
2.

[238] Kloppenborg 2001, 184.

[239] Allison 1997, 83; 2010, 320, 368; cf. Funk and Hoover 1993, 145; Kirk 1998, 161;
Kloppenborg 2001, 184; Valantasis 2005, 175; Howes 2015a, 250.

[240] Piper 1995, 59; 2000, 250; Kloppenborg 2000a, 194.

court hearing at all costs, verse 30 advises the *creditor* or potential plaintiff to avoid legal action as well.[241] Like Q 12:58–59, the examples in Q 6:29–30 deal with the intersection and interdependence of three social phenomena, namely the problem of indebtedness, the ancient legal system, and the corporeal survival of the lower classes.[242] In all cases, the advice seems to be to avoid going to court, whatever it takes.[243] Piper is undoubtedly correct that these texts "reflect at least a profound lack of confidence among the Q people regarding the social and judicial institutions active in their sphere."[244] Such a lack of confidence squares well with the attitude of pessimism detected in Q 12:58–59.[245] Rollens finds that a crucial connective between Q 6:29–30 and Q 12:58–59 is "a shared perception of injustice in the world."[246]

The second text that deserves scrutiny in the current context is the Lord's prayer in Q 11:2–4. In Q's version of this famous prayer, the petitions "give us today our day's bread" (τὸν ἄρτον ἡμῶν τὸν ἐπιούσιονδὸς ἡμῖν σήμερον) and "cancel our debts for us" (ἄφες ἡμῖντὰ ὀφειλήματα ἡμῶν) once again associate the issues of corporeal survival and indebtedness.[247] Scholars are in overwhelming agreement that Matthew's "debt" (ὀφείλημα) should be preferred over Luke's "sin" (ἁμαρτία) in Q 11:4.[248] Perpetual indebtedness at the hands of wealthy aristocrats is probably at issue here.[249] Owing your fellow peasant a few coins or a measure of wheat would presumably not have been urgent enough to require mention in a prayer. This is particularly true for Q's version of the Lord's prayer, which contains only three requests related to the needs of the petitioners, or "we" (ἡμεῖς) requests, in addition to the two requests related

---

[241] Piper 1995, 60, 61; 2000, 250; Kloppenborg 2000a, 194; Arnal 2001, 194.

[242] Cf. Horsley 1995a, 43–44.

[243] Kloppenborg 2000a, 194; cf. Horsley 1995a, 45; Arnal 2001, 194.

[244] Piper 1995, 60, 63, 66; 2000, 250, quotation from Piper 1995, 60. Piper (1995, 60) argues further: "It can hardly be accidental that the next section of the Q sermon (Q 6:37–38) continues the very vocabulary of warning against judicial procedures" (cf. Kloppenborg 2000a, 194). I agree that the motif of "judgment," understood in its broadest possible sense, might link Q 6:29–30 with Q 6:37–38, but I have argued at length elsewhere that Q 6:37–38 presupposes not judicial or eschatological judgment, but moral-sapiential judgment (see Howes 2015a, 221–283, esp. 258–259).

[245] Kloppenborg 2000a, 194; Piper 2000, 250; Rollens 2014a, 108.

[246] Rollens 2014a, 108; cf. Park 2014b, 4–5.

[247] Horsley 1999, 219, 278; Kloppenborg 2000a, 195; 2001, 176–177; Oakman 2008, 104; 2015, 71; Rollens 2014a, 97; Bazzana 2015, 187; cf. Drake 2014, 234, 237; Joseph 2014, 21; Park 2014a, 77; 2014b, 4; 2019, 44.

[248] See Carruth and Garsky 1996, 145–155; cf. Bazzana 2015, 166; e.g. Funk and Hoover 1993, 149; Fleddermann 2005a, 458–459; Drake 2014, 234, 239, 242. It is true that the Aramaic word underlying the Greek "debt" (ὀφείλημα) was sometimes used as a metaphor for "sin" (Robinson 1995a, 155), but it is debatable the extent to which this etymology has any bearing on the Q text (*pace* e.g. Jospeh 2014, 21; Ra 2016, 70).

[249] Cf. Drake 2014, 237; Park 2014a, 77, 87.

to the kingship of God, or "you" (σύ) requests.[250] In fact, the term ὀφείλημα denoted not only private debt owed to individual creditors and landlords for loans and leases, but also public debt owed to the royal treasury for taxes, leases, and rents.[251]

Bazzana argues that the Lord's prayer presupposes political debt relief by the royal house.[252] Considering the reference to God's "kingdom" or "kingship" (βασιλεία) in verse 2, this seems likely.[253] Such officially sanctioned debt acquittals were not uncommon in the ancient world, including ancient Israel.[254] Bazzana explains that these political pardons included also the absolution of debts between private individuals.[255] As we saw, this was also true for ancient Israel, who traditionally commanded debt abolition during the Sabbath year and Jubilee.[256] The clause "and proclaim liberty throughout the land to all its inhabitants"[257] in Leviticus 25 indicates that debt abolition was supposed to be sanctioned and decreed by the political authorities during Jubilee, even if it might only have been an informal, non-official arrangement or expectation during other Sabbath years.[258] Joseph deliberately links Q 11:4 with Jubilee,[259] and Kloppenborg describes Q 11:4 as pertaining to "a sabbatical or jubilee debt release."[260] Oakman observes that the verb "cancel" (ἀφίημι) in Q 11:4 features also in Deuteronomy 15:3, discussed above in connection with sabbatical debt release.[261] Interestingly, the verb "cancel" (ἀφίημι) has very similar semantic options as the verb "get loose" (ἀπαλλάσσω) in Q 12:58–59. While one of the most prominent meanings of ἀπαλλάσσω is to "get loose," one of the most prominent meanings of ἀφίημι is to "loose" or "let go."[262] Like ἀπαλλάσσω, ἀφίημι could refer in legal contexts to being acquitted or released from debt.[263] Like ἀπαλλάσσω, ἀφίημι carried the more general meaning of being liberated,

---

[250] Kloppenborg 2001, 175, 176; Fleddermann 2005a, 469, 470; Bazzana 2015, 167; cf. Oakman 2015, 50–51; Du Toit 2016, 70, 71.

[251] Bazzana 2015, 168.

[252] Bazzana 2015, 167–180.

[253] Cf. Oakman 2015, 80–81; Van Eck 2016, 176.

[254] See Bazzana 2015, 176–180; Van Eck 2016, 173, 175–176, 180.

[255] Bazzana 2015, 170, 174; cf. Van Eck 2016, 175, 181.

[256] See above.

[257] ESV; MT: וּקְרָאתֶם דְּרוֹר בָּאָרֶץ לְכָל־יֹשְׁבֶיהָ; LXX: καὶ διαβοήσετε ἄφεσιν ἐπὶ τῆς γῆς πᾶσιν τοῖς κατοικοῦσιν αὐτήν.

[258] Cf. Deut 15:1–2.

[259] Joseph 2014, 21.

[260] Kloppenborg 2001, 177; cf. 179. He relates the forgiveness of debts to the forgiveness of sins, appealing to intertexts from Qumran (i.e. 1Q22 III:5–7; 11Q13 II:1–6).

[261] Oakman 2015, 75.

[262] Liddell and Scott 1996, 290.

[263] Liddell and Scott 1996, 290.

with translation possibilities like "set free" and connotations of manumission.[264] Bazzana shows from documentary papyri that the verb ἀφίημι implies debt relief in the Lord's prayer, especially considering its appearance with ὀφείλημα in the text.[265]

The second petition qualifies the request with the following clause: "as we too have cancelled for those in debt to us" (ὡς καὶ ἡμεῖς ἀφήκαμεν τοῖς ὀφειλέταις ἡμῶν). Oakman distinguishes between the two clauses as the "vertical" and "horizontal" aspects of the petition.[266] Even if the main (vertical) clause references unequal indebtedness, it is likely that the subordinate (horizontal) clause has small debts between lower-level equals in mind.[267] It is unlikely that someone praying for release from debt in the context of daily survival would have been wealthy enough to subdue others by lending them significant amounts of money. As such, this petition is reminiscent of the parable of the unmerciful servant in Matthew 18:23–35.[268] The forgiveness of a massive debt by a vastly superior role player motivates the recipient to apply the same grace to his equals by also forgiving *their* debts.[269] Like the parable, the petition in Q 11:4 encourages its audience with *imitatio Dei* logic to treat others with the same forgiveness and grace that they receive from God.[270] Like the parable, this saying promotes general reciprocity at village level, while beseeching God for relief from perpetual indebtedness.[271] In fact, the comparative preposition "like" (ὡς) assumes that the Q people are *already* forgiving each other's debts and perhaps even the debts of outsiders.[272] As such, it features an *imitatio Dei* argument "in reverse," depicting the Q people as already practicing general reciprocity and asking God to do the same.[273] Petitioning God for relief from economic debt should not be seen as strange, since the ancient Jewish notion of a theocratic monarchy qualified political debt relief as a decree from God.[274] Knowledge of political debt relief in antiquity further informs the association in the Lord's prayer between "bread" and "debt," since royal par-

---

[264] Liddell and Scott 1996, 290.

[265] Bazzana 2015, 170–177. Bazzana's investigation focuses on two papyri, namely *SB* 20.14106 and *P.Köln* 7.313.

[266] Oakman 2015, 75; cf. Drake 2014, 234.

[267] Cf. Horsley 1999, 267.

[268] See Drake 2014, 241–242; cf. Oakman 2015, xi, 34–36, 72.

[269] Drake 2014, 241; cf. Kloppenborg 1987, 206; 2000a, 190; Valantasis 2005, 118; Van Eck 2016, 181–182.

[270] Cf. Kloppenborg 1987, 206, 241; Robinson 2001b, 39–40; 2003, 38; Fleddermann 2005a, 470; Drake 2014, 234.

[271] Cf. Valantasis 2005, 118; Ra 2016, 70; Van Eck 2016, 181–182.

[272] Howes 2016a, 21; see Valantasis 2005, 118–120, 175.

[273] Howes 2016a, 21; see Valantasis 2005, 118–120, 175.

[274] Bazzana 2015, 177; cf. Valantasis 2005, 117–118.

dons were seemingly often accompanied by the provision of foodstuffs, especially during times of hardship.[275] If private individuals were expected to write
off existing debt during political pardons, they might also have been expected
at such times to provide nourishment to those in need. Such benefaction was
certainly not unprecedented in antiquity.[276] In addition to debt relief and the
provision of food, taxes were also sometimes remitted, which is what Herod
the Great did during times of famine.[277]

The *Critical Edition of Q* translates the last request in the Lord's prayer as
follows: "and do not put us to the test" (καὶ μὴ εἰσενέγκῃς ἡμᾶς εἰς πειρασμόν).
Bazzana considers the use of the word πειρασμός (together with πεῖρα and
πειρά[ζ]ομαι) in the Septuagint, Ben Sirach, and documentary papyri, arguing
that it should here be understood as an educational, intellectual, and/or moral
test.[278] His analysis is intended to dispel the scholarly notion that the word
denotes eschatological temptation or violent persecution in the midst of dangerous (apocalyptic) events.[279] Although his case against these latter avenues
of interpretation is commendable and convincing, Bazzana's own interpretation is questionable. It seems implausible that the prayer would move from
concrete, tangible issues like subsistence and indebtedness to an abstract, generic issue like moral-intellectual assessment.[280] Bazzana attempts to show that
his understanding fits the rest of Q, looking specifically at Q 4:1–13, but ultimately his interpretation is discordant with the material concerns of the Lord's
prayer and most of the formative stratum.[281] More crucially, his interpretation
of the final petition is incongruous with his own analysis of the Lord's prayer,
which correctly reads the passage as pertaining to the provision of actual nourishment and the relief of actual debt.[282] In my view, interpreters like Oakman
and Horsley are closer to the truth, reading the noun πειρασμός as a reference
to actual judicial trials.[283] Like the English word "trial," Greek words with the
stem πειρα could denote not only an evaluative ordeal like a test or temptation,

---

[275] Bazzana 2015, 189–191. According to Häkkinen (2016, 4), Roman acts of feeding the
populace benefitted the community, not the poor.

[276] See Bazzana 2015, 191–193; Lampe 2016, 1–28; Van Aarde 2016, 150–175; cf. Häkkinen 2016, 4.

[277] Häkkinen 2016, 5.

[278] Bazzana 2015, 194–199.

[279] Cf. Valantasis 2005, 119.

[280] Cf. Horsley 1995a, 44; 1999, 266–268; Drake 2014, 234; Oakman 2015, 81, 84. This
does not mean that the Lord's prayer could not have communicated abstract ideas on a secondary level (cf. Valantasis 2005, 119, 120; Howes 2015a, 281). If it did, however, these
ideas would have been subordinate to the text's primary literal inclination.

[281] Bazzana 2015, 199–202.

[282] Cf. Horsley 1999, 266–268; Oakman 2015, 81, 84.

[283] Horsley 1995a, 45; 1999, 271–272, 297; Oakman 2008, 104; 2015, 84; cf. Howes
2015a, 257, 281.

but also a court proceeding.[284] The same is true of the Hebrew word מַסָּה, which is translated with πειρασμός in the Septuagint. Translation possibilities for this Hebrew noun include both "test" and "trial."[285] Like the first two "we" petitions in the Lord's prayer, the last one is about a tangible feature of ancient life related directly to physical survival.[286] In this case, it is about judicial trials.

Like all the texts considered up to this point, Q 11:4 seems fearful and pessimistic about appearing in court, beseeching God to assist in avoiding such a conclusion. This petition is separated from the preceding one about the cancellation of debts with a semi-colon, indicating some kind of relationship between the two petitions. Likewise, the petition about indebtedness is separated from the preceding one about daily sustenance with a semi-colon. Hence, the syntax of Q 11:2–4 deliberately associates daily sustenance, indebtedness, and appearance in court.[287] This implies not only a link between court appearances and indebtedness, but also between court appearances and corporeal survival.[288] Like all the foregoing texts, Q 11:2–4 deals with the intersection and interdependence of three social phenomena, namely the problem of indebtedness, the ancient legal system, and the corporeal survival of the lower classes. In fact, these three motifs represent each of the three "we" petitions in the Lord's prayer. The associations in question are further strengthened by the subsequent section, that is, Q 11:[5–8], 9–13, which deals specifically with material subsistence and provision.[289] In addition to its obvious treatment of subsistence, a number of scholars understand Q 11:9–13 as pertaining to the issue of debt as well.[290]

---

[284] See Liddell and Scott 1996, 1355; Oakman 2015, 83–84; cf. Valantasis 2005, 119.

[285] Holladay 1971, 203; Brown, Driver, and Briggs 1977, 650; Swanson 2001, domain 4999; Oakman 2015, 84; cf. e.g. Job 9:23–24. In my view, מַסָּה should be translated as "trial" in the problematic case of Job 9:23 and not as "calamity" or "despair" (cf. Swanson 2001, domain 5000; see most English translations). This is supported by the judicial terms and images in the literary context of Job 9:13–24.

[286] Oakman 2015, 81, 84; cf. Horsley 1999, 266–268.

[287] Cf. Horsley 1999, 219, 260, 267, 271–272, 295–296, 297; Howes 2015a, 257; Oakman 2015, 84, 90.

[288] Cf. Piper 1995, 62; Oakman 2008, 104; 2015, 84, 90; Howes 2015a, 257.

[289] Horsley 1999, 296; Arnal 2001, 46–47; see Piper 1989, 22–23; 2000, 246–247; Catchpole 1993, 223–225; Robinson 1998b, 138–139; 1999, 192; 2001a, 16; 2001b, 32, 49; 2003, 30; 2005a, 117–118; Kloppenborg 2000a, 125, 195; 2001, 177–178; Robinson and Heil 2001, 18; Fleddermann 2005a, 467–468, 473; Howes 2019b, 6–11; cf. Kirk 1998, 179; Rollens 2014a, 97; Howes 2015a, 281; Oakman 2015, 67; *pace* Tuckett 1996, 152–155.

[290] E.g. Horsley 1999, 260; Kloppenborg 2001, 178; Kaden 2014, 104 n. 21; Rollens 2014a, 97.

As mentioned in the previous chapter, daily sustenance and survival is arguably the most important, repeated, and central topic of Q's formative stratum.[291] It was argued above that Q 12:58–59 is similarly concerned with issues of daily sustenance and survival. Instead of appealing to earthly courts for survival in the face of poverty and persecution, the Q people are advised to trust in God for their survival.[292] In practice, this entailed keeping their heads down and satisfying their persecutors beyond expectation in order to avoid going to court.[293] Regardless of the extent of exploitation, "redress for personal injury seems to be viewed as dangerous, counterproductive, or simply wrong."[294]

Another important topic for the formative stratum is the different kinds of relationships between the elite and the weaker members of society.[295] Especially relevant are those texts that expose the vulnerability of the small peasantry and poor in the face of deliberate exploitation by the elite.[296] Q 12:4–7, 11–12 indicates that persecution and repression were realities facing the Q people and that it involved "having to appear in front of judges."[297] These verses further indicate that a meeting with judicial and other authorities could very well end up being fatal.[298] A link between subsistence and persecution (or ex-

---

[291] Cf. Kloppenborg 1987, 240–241; Piper 1995, 62, 64; Vaage 1995a, 89; Robinson 1997a, 237, 238; Park 2019, 52; cf. Q 6:20–21, 29–30, 34; 9:58; 10:2, 5–9, 16; 11:3–4, [5–8], 9–13, 33 (see chapter 2 above); 12:22–31, 42–44 (see chapter 4 above); 13:18–19, 20–21 (see chapter 6 below); 13:24–25 (see chapter 7 below); 14:16–21, 23 (see chapter 8 below); 15:4–5, 7, [8–10]; 19:12–13, 15–24 (see chapter 9 below).

[292] Piper 1995, 62; 2000, 234, 256; Robinson 1995a, 265; 1997a, 238, 246; Howes 2015a, 257; cf. Kloppenborg 1987, 241; 2000a, 195, 372, 386; Douglas 1995, 124–125; Allison 2000, 52, 190; 2001, 399; Jacobson 2000, 195; Valantasis 2005, 120; Joseph 2014, 157–158; Rollens 2014a, 109.

[293] Piper 1995, 62; 2000, 250; Arnal 2001, 194; cf. Kloppenborg 1987, 252; 2000a, 194; Horsley 1995a, 43; Valantasis 2005, 59; Rollens 2014a, 99, 104–105, 109, 110; Ra 2016, 34; *pace* Cotter 1995, 120–121.

[294] Piper 1995, 62; cf. Horsley 1995a, 45; Arnal 2001, 194.

[295] Cf. Q 6:22–23, 27–28, 29–30; 10:3, 10–11, 21, 23–24 (see chapter 1 above); 11:3–4; 12:4–5, 11–12; 12:42–44 (see chapter 4 above); 13:25 (see chapter 7 below); 14:16–21, 23 (see chapter 8 below); 16:13; 17:1–2; 19:12–13, 15–24 (see chapter 9 below).

[296] See Piper 1995, 61–62; cf. Park 2014a, 77; Jacobs 2018, 124–125; i.e. Q 6:22–23, 27–28, 29–30; 10:3; 11:4; 12:4–5, 11–12; 13:25 (see chapter 7 below); 17:1–2; 19:12–13, 15–24 (see chapter 9 below).

[297] Ra 2016, 216–217, 224, quotation from p. 224; so too Horsley 1995a, 45; 1999, 147, 245, 271–272, 297; Verheyden 2001, 712; Smith 2006, 140, 142; Joseph 2014, 158; cf. Kloppenborg 1987, 232, 235; 2000a, 372, 386; Piper 1989, 53; Jacobson 1992, 187; Robinson 1999, 185; Fleddermann 2005a, 593; Howes 2015a, 142, 256; *pace* Piper 2001, 348–349.

[298] Horsley 1999, 272; Fleddermann 2005a, 593; Howes 2015a, 256; Ra 2016, 217; cf. Piper 1989, 53, 60; Allison 1997, 174; Kirk 1998, 208, 213; Kloppenborg 2000a, 372; Valantasis 2005, 154–155, 160; Smith 2006, 121. Tuckett (1996, 315–320) argues at some length that the references to death and appearances before synagogues in Q 12:4–5, 11–12

ploitation) in the context of court appearances is further suggested by the position of Q 12:4–7, 11–12 directly before Q 12:22–31 in the sequence of the Sayings Gospel.[299] Exegetes often associate Q 11:2–4, [5–8], 9–13 and Q 12:22–31, mainly due to their overlapping themes of survival and subsistence.[300] Less frequently recognised is the linkage between Q 11:2–4 and Q 12:4–7, 11–12 based on the theme of court appearances before authorities.[301] If the reference to "wolves" in Q 10:3 is understood in terms of its traditional association with "rulers," this passage confirms both that the Q people faced persecution by authorities and that death was a possible outcome of meeting with these rulers.[302] There is an obvious conceptual overlap between the vulnerability of lower class citizens in the face of elite exploitation and the advice to avoid official systems of (in)justice.[303] In general, Q's formative stratum betrays a sustained fear of authorities and an intrinsic suspicion of administrative procedures.[304] More specifically, the content of Q's formative stratum reveals distrust in the institutionalised legal system, resulting in the promotion of habitual and deliberate avoidance of institutional courts.[305] Q 12:58–59 relates directly to these matters.[306] In fact, Q 12:58–59 is the text *par excellence* when it comes to the topic of avoiding the ancient legal system.

It is interesting and perhaps telling that Piper, while considering largely the same thematic issues that we have considered here, adds a footnote that seems

---

do not reflect the actual situation of the Q people and that one should therefore not deduce from this tradition that the Q people were judicially, physically, or violently persecuted. His argument has failed to convince scholars and remains a minority opinion.

[299] Kloppenborg 1987, 250–251; 2000a, 195; Howes 2015a, 257; cf. Allison 1997, 23–24.

[300] E.g. Robinson 1995a, 263–265; 1997a, 238, 246, 248–249; 1999, 192; 2001a, 16; 2001b, 32–33, 49; Horsley 1999, 260; Jacobson 2000, 195; Piper 2000, 234, 245, 247, 252, 256, 258; Kloppenborg 2001, 178; Robinson and Heil 2001, 18–19; Rollens 2014a, 97; Howes 2015a, 118 n. 105.

[301] Horsley 1999, 297.

[302] Howes 2015a, 142, esp. n. 151, 256–257; see Horsley 1999, 96, 244–245, 249, 272; Valantasis 2005, 97–98; cf. Jacobson 1982, 422; Joseph 2012, 90; cf. Prov 25:15 (LXX); Ezek 22:23–27; Zeph 3:1–3; 1 Enoch 89:13–27; Pss. Sol. 8:23; 4 Ezra 5:18.

[303] Piper 1995, 62; 2000, 250; cf. Horsley 1995a, 43–45; Kloppenborg 2000a, 194; Park 2014a, 77; Rollens 2014a, 107, 108.

[304] Piper 1995, 63; 2000, 250.

[305] Piper 1995, 60, 63, 66; 2000, 250; Kloppenborg 2000a, 194, 198, 199; Rollens 2014a, 110. Arnal (2001, 194–195) argues that Q does not advocate a wholesale avoidance of legal institutions, but rather a wholesale avoidance of combative and confrontational interactions. These positions are not mutually exclusive, and both were probably advocated simultaneously. Considering the evidence for institutional and juridical exploitation from both the ancient world and the Sayings Gospel (e.g. Q 10:3; 12:4–7, 11–12, 58–59), the advice to avoid judicial proceedings as much as possible makes absolute sense.

[306] Horsley 1995a, 45; Kloppenborg 2000a, 194; Piper 2000, 250; Howes 2015a, 257; cf. Park 2014a, 77; Rollens 2014a, 107, 108, 110.

to express dissatisfaction with Kloppenborg's attribution of Q 12:58–59 to the main redaction.[307] In fact, Q 12:58–59 represents the only instance where the sapiential clusters identified by Piper do not correspond to Kloppenborg's formative stratum.[308] Likewise, it is not insignificant that Rollens, in her study of justice in Q, initially follows Kloppenborg in attributing Q 12:58–59 to the main redaction,[309] but later treats the same logion as part of the formative stratum.[310] This seems to be more than the scholarly version of a Freudian slip. According to Rollens's larger case, the formative stratum presumes that the actions of people can improve the world, but the main redaction has been disillusioned to the point that it accepts divine intervention as the only means through which improvement is possible.[311] As part of this discussion, Rollens claims that "some material such as Q 6,29–30 and 12,58–59 still bears markers of self-help strategies [typical of the formative stratum]."[312] The operative word in this sentence is "still," betraying the conviction by Rollens that Q 12:58–59 was part of the formative stratum before being incorporated into the main redaction, which is exactly what the current chapter argues.[313]

5.4 Implied Audience

It is noteworthy that Kloppenborg does not explicitly invoke his own criterion of "implied audience" when considering the redactional placement of this logion in Q.[314] As indicated above, the logion's addressee (σου) is someone from the lower classes of society. We also saw that Q's audiences were for the most part made up of people from the lower segments of society, including especially the (dispossessed) small peasantry.[315] As a sapiential instruction, Q

---

[307] Piper 2000, 250 n. 115, cf. 257.

[308] Kloppenborg 1996a, 51.

[309] Rollens 2014a, 94 n. 4, 105.

[310] Rollens 2014a, 110.

[311] See Rollens 2014a, 109–113.

[312] Rollens 2014a, 111.

[313] Cotter (1995, 127) claims that the logion belongs in the main redaction because the directive to settle before going to court is motivated by the rationale "that it will be less expensive to do so." Not only is this claim contradicted by the text itself, where (lifelong) imprisonment is the ultimate consequence, but the socio-historical context of the logion considered in this chapter also speaks strongly against it. Clearly, Cotter's anachronistic observation is not informed by the socio-historical realities of indebtedness and judicial praxis in first-century Palestine.

[314] Howes 2015a, 75.

[315] There is widespread agreement on this: see Horsley 1995a, 44; 1999, 260–261, 269, 296–298; Kloppenborg 2000a, 198–199; Reed 2000, 136–137; Rollens 2014a, 96; cf. Oakman 1986, 100; Kloppenborg 1987, 251; Douglas 1995, 120; Piper 1995, 63–64; Reed 1995,

12:58–59 attempts to direct the behaviour of these underprivileged insiders.[316] Its main intent is to offer practical advice for the in-group.[317] Assuming the Lukan placement of Q 12:58–59, it presents serious problems if one reads the logion as directed against outsiders. If the "opponent" is a reference to the out-group, the saying would contradict the preceding material[318] by advocating reconciliation with outsiders. Likewise, if the fate of the person in verse 59 is symbolic of the fate of outsiders, it is not clear why Q's Jesus would address this hypothetical person directly in verse 58, attempting to direct his behaviour. In the remainder of Q, such instructions are reserved for the in-group. If the Matthean placement of Q 12:58–59 is followed, the supposed function of the logion to address outsiders is even more dubious, especially if the subsequent logion in Q 16:18 is taken into consideration.

Few would doubt that Q 12:58–59 addresses the Q people directly. The question, however, is whether or not the saying *indirectly* condemns outsiders. We saw that the saying could be understood as a veiled critique of the official legal system and those who partake in its daily operation. Yet such critique is at most implied in a very subtle and oblique way. The saying primarily and overtly addresses those who often fall victim to the judicial system, not those who make a living (and a killing!) out of their involvement with it.[319] The saying is not formulated as criticism directed at the powers that be, but rather as advice directed at the powerless.[320] The internal workings of the judicial system is exposed as a wake-up call to the recipients of this logion. Instead of condemning *people* in an *obvious* way, the saying critiques the *system* in a *clandestine* way. More importantly, the judicial system is not exposed for the sake of separating between insiders and outsiders. Lawyers, judges, and other courtroom officials, though mentioned, are not identified as outsiders or condemned with eternal damnation – not even implicitly.[321] In fact, the language of Q 12:58–59 is not at all polemical.[322] The saying seems unconcerned with

---

19; Tuckett 1996, 360, 365; Freyne 2000, 206; Arnal 2001, 150, 173, 188; Häkkinen 2016, 7.

[316] See Valantasis 2005, 174–175; cf. Kloppenborg 2006, 126; Rollens 2014a, 109–110; *pace* Kirk 1998, 237.

[317] Howes 2015a, 75, 76; cf. Horsley 1995a, 40, 43.

[318] That is, Q 12:42–46, [49], 51, 53, [54–56].

[319] Cf. Piper 1989, 106; Horsley 1995a, 43; Rollens 2014a, 102, 105, 107, 108.

[320] Rollens 2014a, 102, 105, 107, 108.

[321] Piper 1989, 106; cf. Horsley 1999, 65. This is despite the fact that these people were in all likelihood outsiders, especially if scholarship is correct about the court being located in the city. Valantasis (2005, 175) argues that the presumption of debt identifies the creditor as an outsider, since insiders ostensibly practiced general reciprocity – that is, if they actually followed their own teachings. Even so, the point of the saying is neither to isolate any of these people as outsiders, nor to earmark them for condemnation.

[322] Piper 1989, 106, 114; cf. Horsley 1999, 65.

matters of boundary demarcation and very concerned with the fate of its recipients.[323]

5.5 Findings

Kloppenborg's case that Q 12:58–59 belongs to the main redaction might have made it seem as though this logion "would not get out of there." Kloppenborg's main reason for locating Q 12:58–59 in the main redaction, however, is that he views verse 59 as a prophetic-eschatological addition that was added on the basis of preceding Q^2 material. I have argued here that verse 59 featured as an intrinsic part of the logion from the beginning, underlining the importance and urgency of the sapiential directive to avoid litigation. Much weight should not be placed on the syntagmatic literary context of Q 12:58–59 when attempting to determine its stratigraphical placement, since it appears on the border between Q^1 and Q^2 material in both its Matthean and Lukan positions. If the logion is considered in isolation, as it should be, its proper place in Q's formative stratum is revealed. When measured against Kloppenborg's three main criteria for distinguishing between Q^1 and Q^2, the logion qualifies as a tradition of Q's formative stratum.[324] Like the rest of Q's formative stratum, Q 12:58–59 advocates avoiding the official legal system, mainly because of its contribution to continual indebtedness and starvation.

---

[323] Cf. Kloppenborg 2006, 126.

[324] This finding would remain valid even if my proposals about the vocations of the two parties were off the mark and the background had nothing to do with agriculture.

Chapter 6

Q 13:18–21, "The Birds of the Sky Nested"[1]

[18]τίνι ὁμοία ἐστὶν ἡ βασιλεία τοῦ θεοῦ καὶ τίνι ὁμοιώσω αὐτήν; [19]ὁμοία ἐστὶν κόκκῳ σινάπεως, ὃν λαβὼν ἄνθρωπος ἔβαλεν εἰς [[κῆπ]]ον αὐτοῦ· καὶ ηὔξησεν καὶ ἐγένετο εἰς δένδρον, καὶ τὰ πετεινὰ τοῦ οὐρανοῦ κατεσκήνωσεν ἐν τοῖς κλάδοις αὐτοῦ. [20][[καὶ πάλιν]]· τίνι ὁμοιώσω τὴν βασιλείαν τοῦ θεοῦ; [21]ὁμοία ἐστὶν ζύμη, ἣν λαβοῦσα γυνὴ ἐνέκρυψεν εἰς ἀλεύρου σάτα τρία ἕως οὗ ἐζυμώθη ὅλον.

[18]What is the kingdom of God like, and with what am I to compare it? [19]It is like a seed of mustard which a person took and threw into his [[garden]]. And it grew and developed into a tree, and the birds of the sky nested in its branches. [20][[And again]]: With what am I to compare the kingdom of God? [21]It is like yeast, which a woman took and hid in three measures of flour until it was fully fermented.

The parables of the mustard seed and leaven each include a number of elements that may be relevant to their application, which explains not only why they have received such different interpretations over the years, but also why a number of scholars have argued that they each have more than one application. Funk, for example, describes these parables as "plurisignificative," by which he means that they highlight more than one aspect of God's kingdom.[2] Scholars overwhelmingly agree that these parables stem from Q.[3] Scholars also agree that both parables derive from the historical Jesus.[4] Since the two parables probably featured together in Q, the current discussion will also treat them together.[5] This is neither to ignore the differences between them,[6] nor to deny that they probably circulated separately before being joined in Q.[7]

---

[1] An earlier version of this chapter was published as an article in *Neotestamentica* 53/2 (see Howes 2019c).

[2] Funk 2006, 39–43, 96–98, 103, 108; cf. Meier 2016, 233.

[3] See Foster 2014a, 255–285. Virtually all parable, Jesus, and Q scholars can be listed here as examples. For the minority opinion that these parables do not derive from Q, see e.g. Burkett 2009, 54.

[4] Virtually all parable and Jesus scholars can be referenced as examples. Meier (2016, 239–240) accepts the parable of the mustard seed as one of only four authentic parables. Bultmann (1968, 172) regards the parable of the leaven as a "secondary accretion" to the parable of the mustard seed.

[5] See Kloppenborg 1995, 305–308.

[6] Cf. e.g. Hunter 1971, 44; Snodgrass 2008, 219, 233.

[7] See Scott 1989, 322–323.

6.1 Kloppenborg's Analysis

In *The Formation of Q*, Kloppenborg is unclear about Q 13:18–21. Although he seems to attribute it to the formative layer,[8] he fails to treat the two logia as part of his exegetical discussion. He devotes only one footnote to this text, claiming that it relates better to Q 12:2 than his sixth block of logia.[9] In a subsequent publication, Kloppenborg confirms that he regards Q 13:18–21 as part of the formative stratum and argues that it featured at the end of his fifth block of material[10] in the formative stratum.[11] He points out that the two parables in Q 13:18–21 concern the kingdom of God, just like his fifth block.[12] In particular, the parables expand on the themes of the spreading of the kingdom (Q 12:3, 31) and the fruition of the kingdom from something hidden (Q 12:2). Noteworthy here is the appearance of the catchword "kingdom" (βασιλεία) in both Q 12:31 and Q 13:18. One could add to Kloppenborg's observations that both Q 13:18–21 and Q 12:22–31 argue from nature, referencing not only flora, namely "mustard" (σίναπι) in Q 13:18 and "lilies" (κρίνα) and "grassland" (χόρτος) in Q 12:27–28, but also birds, namely "ravens" (κόρακες) in Q 12:24 and "birds" (πετεινά) in general in both Q 12:24 and Q 13:19. The latter reference to "birds" (πετεινά) is in fact a second catchword link between these two texts. Since Kloppenborg (like me) attributes Q 13:18–21 to the formative stratum, this chapter will focus on the interpretation of this text rather than its redactional placement, although the latter will also receive some attention at the end. Even though I agree with Kloppenborg that Q 13:18–21 relates to the rest of the formative stratum by considering the initial hiddenness and subsequent expansion of God's kingdom, I argue that these concerns are only tangential to the meaning and intent of the parable. As a result of my particular interpretation of these parables, I highlight different reasons for attributing Q 13:18–21 to the formative stratum.

6.2 The Impurity Angle

A number of interpreters mention that mustard and leaven were impure items in ancient Judaism.[13] Some of them make the professed impurity of these items

---

[8] Kloppenborg 1987, 236.

[9] Kloppenborg 1987, 223 n. 214.

[10] That is, Q 12:22–31, 33–34.

[11] Kloppenborg 1995, 305–311.

[12] Kloppenborg 1995, 311.

[13] E.g. Dodd 1961, 143; Donahue 1988, 67–68; Scott 1989, 324, 381; 2001, 25; 2007, 101; Crossan 1991, 280; Jacobson 1992, 205; Funk and Hoover 1993, 195, 347, 523; Vaage

the most important key to unlocking the meaning of one or both of these parables.[14] Not only was the mustard plant, according to these scholars, considered to be a weed in the ancient Jewish world, but to plant mustard in a garden would violate the Jewish law that prohibited two types of crop from being planted in the same plot of land. For further support, they typically reference Kil'ayim 3.2 in the Mishnah, arguing that mustard was supposed to be planted in fields, not gardens. The word "garden" (κῆπος) in Q 13:19 is therefore fundamental to this avenue of interpretation.[15] As far as leaven is concerned, these scholars typically point out that leaven was banned during certain religious festivals, including especially Passover. Likewise, ancient sources, including the Bible, often use the image of leaven negatively, mostly to express the idea of a corrupting influence.[16] Scott describes the culinary reasons why leaven came to have this negative association: "Leaven is made by taking a piece of bread and storing it in a damp, dark place until mold forms. The bread rots and decays, unlike modern yeast, which is domesticated."[17] Apart from the actual leaven, the fermentation process itself was also off-putting. The process is vividly described by Levine: "the idea of sour smell combined with a bubbly mixture created by the process of fermentation – that is, enzyme decay – does not immediately strike me as palatable. To the contrary, there's an 'ick' factor at play."[18] The obvious conclusion for these interpreters (not Levine: see below) is that the parables associate the kingdom of God with the uncontrollable and undesirable defilement that usually results from mustard and leaven. In more clinical terms, the argument is that these two parables compare the kingdom of God to an impure element that is introduced to an otherwise neutral or positive source, with the inevitable result of contaminating the whole source.[19] The mustard shrub does this to the garden and the leaven does this to the flour. As Scott cleverly paraphrases, God's kingdom is likened to a rotten apple that spoils the barrel.[20] Hence, the kingdom of God is to be found at those instances where the introduction of a contaminant, in the ancient Jewish sense, causes purity and normativity to be

---

1994, 64, 65; 2001, 486; Allison 2000, 136–137; Valantasis 2005, 177–180; Funk 2006, 102–105; Beutner 2007a, 60–61; Ford 2016, 59, 62; Ra 2016, 160; Van Eck 2016, 81–82.

[14] E.g. Scott 1989, 321–329, 373–387; 2001, 21–34; 2002, 21–23, 24–25; Crossan 1991, 276–279, 280–281; Van Eck 2016, 81–82. Funk and Crossan interpret only the parable of the leaven as a parable about defilement, but they do regard the mustard plant to be a weed.

[15] Roth 2018, 306.

[16] E.g. Matt 16:6; Mark 8:15; Luke 12:1; 1 Cor 5:6–8; Gal 5:9; Plutarch, *Quaest. rom.* 289F; Ignatius, *Magn.* 10; Justin, *Dial.* 14.2; Pseudo-Clement, *Hom.* 8.17.

[17] Scott 1989, 324.

[18] Levine 2014, 122.

[19] E.g. Scott 2001, 28–29, 33–34; Oakman 2008, 116.

[20] Scott 1989, 324; 2001, 26; 2002, 23.

wholly displaced by impurity and undesirability.[21] This understanding of the parables is then taken one step further by relating it to what is otherwise known about the ministry of Jesus,[22] including not only the attitude of Jesus towards socially undesireable figures like tax collectors and prostitutes,[23] but also the likelihood that Jesus proclaimed his kingdom message specifically to the small peasantry and poor,[24] who were generally in the ancient world regarded with contempt by the socio-economic and politico-religious well-to-do.[25] Thus, according to these readings, the vision of God's kingdom subverts traditional Jewish expectations and conceptions of God's rule on earth, which included most fundamentally the Temple system of the great tradition, with its division of reality into hierarchies of religious purity and socio-economic class.[26] Instead of being holy and pure, God's kingdom is inherently defiled.

True as these more general observations about the ministry of Jesus may be, scholars like Liebenberg, Schellenberg, and Levine have argued convincingly against the association between impurity and the items discussed in the parables of the mustard seed and leaven.[27] As we saw, in the case of the parable of the mustard seed, the word "garden" (κῆπος) is crucial to interpretations that regard the mustard plant as impure. Yet this word is arguably the least secure aspect of the parable, since it occurs only in Luke.[28] If Luke introduced it, he did not do so to import any message related to Jewish purity regulations, since his audience was in all likelihood predominantly non-Jewish and regarded mustard to be a standard garden plant.[29] According to Matthew, the seed was sown in a "field" (ἀγρός). Luke might have changed it to a garden for the sake of his urban and/or non-Jewish audience.[30] Oakman, for example, argues that Matthew's "field" goes back to the historical Jesus.[31] Yet Matthew might have introduced the "field" to create a catchword link with the preceding parable of the weeds in Matthew 13:24–30.[32] Generally, Matthew seems to have an affinity for the phrase "in the field" (ἐν τῷ ἀγρῷ).[33] The *Critical Edition of Q*

---

[21] Funk 1996, 157.

[22] E.g. Scott 1989, 329, 386–387; 2001, 34; Funk and Hoover 1993, 60, 484–485; Vaage 1994, 64, 65; Funk 2006, 103, 104, 118–119; West 2009, 411.

[23] Cf. e.g. Matt 21:31.

[24] Cf. Q 6:20.

[25] Häkkinen 2016, 4.

[26] See Funk 1996, 157; 2006, 103, 105–107; Van Eck 2016, 77–78, 81–82.

[27] Liebenberg 2001, 318–321, 336–339; Schellenberg 2009, 527–543; Levine 2014, 117–137, 165–182.

[28] Bock 1996, 1227.

[29] Liebenberg 2001, 311, 313.

[30] Schellenberg 2009, 534 n. 37; Levine 2014, 176.

[31] Oakman 2008, 114.

[32] Nolland 2005, 550; cf. Scholtz 2015, 2–3, 6.

[33] See Scott 1989, 375.

opts for the word "garden," but it flags this choice as uncertain by featuring the word between double square brackets.[34] Whatever the case, an interpretation of this parable on the levels of Q and the historical Jesus should be careful of reading too much into the specific use of the word "garden" instead of "field."

Even if the Q parable did speak of a garden, it is not clear that Jews would necessarily have associated this with impurity, whether in the first place or at all. As we saw, the rabbinic tradition in Kil'ayim 3.2 is used by scholars to argue that mustard was not allowed in a garden. Danby translates the text as follows: "Not every kind of seed may be sown in a garden-bed, but any kind of vegetable may be sown therein. Mustard and small beans are deemed a kind of seed and large beans a kind of vegetable."[35] The text starts off by saying that not "every kind" (כֹּל מִין) of seed may be planted. It then goes on to say that mustard is considered a seed. The nature of the link between the initial prohibition and the subsequent statement is not clear in this translation. It is only if one assumes that the regulation names mustard as an example of the type of seed not permitted that the same interpretation follows. However, the passage nowhere says that mustard may not be planted. Moreover, the regulation has to do with a "garden-bed" (עֲרוּגָה), which is not necessarily equavelent to Q's "garden" (κῆπος).[36] The former Hebrew word differs from the word that is usually used for a "garden" in the Old Testament, namely גַּנָּה, indicating that something different and more specific than a normal garden is in view here. The Septuagint uses κῆπος to describe a generic garden, often as a translation of the Hebrew גַּנָּה, adding words like λαχανεία/λάχανον ("vegetable") and καρύας ("nut") when it wants to indicate the type of garden more specifically.[37] A better translation of Kil'ayim 3.2 is perhaps the one by Sefaria: "They may not sow different species of seeds in one bed, but they may sow different species of vegetables in one bed. Mustard and small polished peas are a species of seed; large peas are a species of vegetable."[38] As this translation makes clear, the issue is not with sowing mustard seed in a garden, but with sowing different species or kinds of seed in the same garden bed.[39] Unlike seeds, it is permitted to sow more than one kind of vegetable in the same garden bed. In this context, the word "seeds" refers to plants cultivated specifically for their dried seeds.[40] This distinction between seeds and

---

[34] Robinson, Hoffmann, and Kloppenborg 2000, 400–401; 2002, 128–129; see also Crossan 1992b, 48; Hoffmann and Heil 2013, 132.

[35] Danby 1933, 31.

[36] Liebenberg 2001, 319; Snodgrass 2008, 220; Schellenberg 2009, 535; Levine 2014, 177.

[37] See Liebenberg 2001, 320 incl. n. 166.

[38] Available online: https://www.sefaria.org/Mishnah_Kilayim.3.2?lang=bi&with=all&lang2=en.

[39] See Schellenberg 2009, 533–536.

[40] Scott 1989, 383.

vegetables has the potential to cause confusion, since there are some individual plants that may legitimately be classified in either category. To clear up the confusion, Kil'ayim 3.2 continues to explain that mustard and small peas should be classified as seeds, while large peas should be classified as vegetables.

These observations are confirmed by the larger literary context of Kil'ayim 3.2 in the Mishnah. Kil'ayim 2.8 says the following: "They may not flank a field of grain with mustard or seed of safflower, but they may flank a field of vegetables with mustard or seed of safflower."[41] According to this text, it is the presence of mustard in a *field* of *grain* (specifically) that Kil'ayim 2.8 flags as potentially problematic.[42] Scott explains that "the tall mustard plants with their yellow flowers would look too much like ripened stalks of grain."[43] Conversely, the presence of mustard in a vegetable garden or plantation is not just acceptable, but standard practice.[44] According to Schellenberg, Kil'ayim 2.5 "explicitly permits surrounding the vegetables in a garden bed with mustard or safflower."[45] In Kil'ayim 2.9, the rabbis debate about how many patches of field with mixed plants may include mustard as well, with opinions ranging from no more than three to no more than nine.[46]

Hence, the version of the parable that speaks of a "field" is actually more relevant in the context of purity regulations.[47] As in English, the word "field" (ἀγρός) could refer both to an agricultural piece of land and to an open field, including the countryside more generally.[48] Seeing as the man in the parable of the mustard seed actively plants the seed, the former possibility is more likely, but only if the "garden" option is dismissed. Oakman actually makes this argument, maintaining that the original parable spoke of a "field," which he then regards as a cultivated field of grain.[49] This interpretation, however, reads elements into the parable that are not present. To begin with, one must assume that the seed ended up in the field either without human involvement or by mistake to make sense of the parable, which is precisely what Oakman argues.[50] Yet, in Matthew, Luke, and Q, there is no doubt that the seed is sown deliberately by a person. Mark does not mention the sower, but his twofold use of the verb "sow" (σπείρω) does imply deliberate human activity.[51] It is only

---

[41] Translation from Danby 1933, 30.

[42] Cf. Oakman 2008, 114.

[43] Scott 1989, 382.

[44] Levine 2014, 176.

[45] Schellenberg 2009, 536.

[46] Levine 2014, 176.

[47] Cf. Oakman 2008, 114–115.

[48] Liddell and Scott 1996, 15–16, s.v. ἀγρός.

[49] Oakman 2008, 113–115.

[50] See also Crossan 1991, 278.

[51] *Pace* Crossan 1991, 278; Kloppenborg 1995, 306.

in the *Gospel of Thomas* where the verb "fall" (πίπτω) and the absence of a human actor imply that the seed ended up in the field without human intention. More importantly, regardless of which version you follow, nothing at all is said of there being any other seed or plant, in addition to mustard, in the field (or garden).[52] There is no indication that the sower is mixing two different types of seed in the same piece of land, if it is an agricultural piece of land to begin with.[53] This would be an important piece of information to include if the intention is to introduce impurity as a motif. Also, there is no indication that a field of *grain* is specifically in view. Even if Jews strictly followed the law that different types of seed should not be planted as part of the same crop, violating this law would not mean that the mustard is intrinsically corrupt, but rather that the act of mixing two types of seed in the same field introduces impurity. As Levine indicates, mustard itself is totally kosher, then as now.[54] It carries "no greater threat to purity and order than any other seed."[55] Adding mustard to gardens or fields does not seem to be an issue at all for ancient Jews, provided that it is not done too much or in combination with grain. Snodgrass is therefore correct when he says: "Halakhic regulations have no relevance for this parable."[56] Finally, the tradition in Kil'ayim 3.2 post-dates the ministry of Jesus, representing a later time when traditional purity laws were elaborated by specifying and regulating minutiae.[57]

The idea that Jesus used the image of mustard because it was regarded as a weed in antiquity is also spurious.[58] If Jesus wanted to tell a parable about weeds, he would undoubtedly have used the term "weed" (ζιζάνιον), as he does in the parable of the weeds in Matthew 13:24–30.[59] Scholars usually reference the following comment by Pliny the Elder on mustard:

though it will grow without cultivation, [it] is considerably improved by being transplanted; though, on the other hand, it is extremely difficult to rid the soil of it when once sown there, the seed when it falls germinating immediately.[60]

Pliny does not call the mustard plant a "weed" in this text, but merely points out that the plant is not easy to control.[61] This interpretation is supported by two considerations. Firstly, the comment about mustard growing without cultivation is probably intended as a positive attribute, as indicated by the fact

---

[52] Levine 2014, 177.
[53] Cf. Liebenberg 2001, 324.
[54] Levine 2014, 168, 176.
[55] Schellenberg 2009, 534.
[56] Snodgrass 2008, 221.
[57] Levine 2014, 175.
[58] Schellenberg 2009, 537; Roth 2018, 306.
[59] Levine 2014, 172.
[60] *Nat.* 19.54; translation by Bostock 1855, 4197.
[61] Schellenberg 2009, 532; Roth 2018, 306.

that the next part of the sentence starts with "though, on the other hand" and then continues to describe its negative aspect of being difficult to remove from the soil. In a different context, Pliny praises the mustard seed for its durability.[62] Secondly, Pliny assumes that the mustard would have been sown or transplanted deliberately, which is not the case with weeds. Pliny is concerned here with the intentional domestication of mustard plants, not their eradication as a nuisance.[63] As we will see, the positive attributes of mustard, which Pliny discusses at much greater lengths in the same writing, by far outweigh this one comment about mustard being difficult to remove from the soil.[64]

Leaven was also not intrinsically corrupt. It is true that Exodus 12:15 instructs Jews to remove leaven from their homes during Passover, but that just goes to show that leaven, far from being impure during the rest of the year, was a staple ingredient in Jewish houses.[65] This is supported by traditions in the Hebrew Scriptures that instruct people to bring *leavened* bread to the Temple, the most holy place in Judaism, as thanksgiving and first-fruit offerings to God.[66] Levine takes this argument one step further: "If yeast [or leaven] were impure, bread would be too; that very point should demostrate why purity is the wrong category."[67] Snodgrass likewise says: "Leaven is not to be used with burnt offerings, but neither is honey. No ones concludes that honey is negative."[68]

The negative metaphorical references to leaven in the Gospels specify the *type* of metaphorical leaven that is bad.[69] For example, Matthew 16:6 warns against "the leaven of the Pharisees and Sadducees" (τῆς ζύμης τῶν Φαρισαίων καὶ Σαδδουκαίων), specifying the type of leaven that is bad.[70] In verse 12, this "bad leaven" is associated with "the teaching" (τῆς διδαχῆς) of the Pharisees and Sadducees. The conclusion necessarily follows that there is good leaven as

---

[62] *Nat.* 19.58.

[63] Schellenberg 2009, 532, 537; Levine 2014, 177; Roth 2018, 306.

[64] It is nonetheless possible that the image of the mustard plant hints at the kingdom as something that spreads easily and automatically, that is, without requiring much effort or interference from humans (cf. Carlston 1975, 161; Liebenberg 2001, 296, 329; Schellenberg 2009, 532; Zimmermann 2015, 253; Van Eck 2016, 81, 83). The same idea might be present in the image of leaven, which ferments the flour/dough spontaneously and automatically once introduced (Ford 2016, 55, 57, 62; cf. Dodd 1961, 144). This accent is not, however, the main point of the parable. At most, it is merely implied as a recognisable attribute of God's kingdom.

[65] Levine 2014, 126; cf. Luz 2001, 262; Ra 2016, 160.

[66] Liebenberg 2001, 337; Snodgrass 2008, 233; Roth 2018, 316; see Levine 2014, 126–127; cf. Lev 7:13; 23:17; Amos 4:5.

[67] Levine 2014, 126.

[68] Snodgrass 2008, 233.

[69] Levine 2014, 124.

[70] Davies and Allison 1991, 588–589; Liebenberg 2001, 338.

well, which is most obviously associated with the teaching of Jesus.[71] This conclusion is supported by the following statement of Ignatius: "Set aside then, the evil leaven, old and sour, and turn to the new leaven, that is, Jesus Christ."[72] There are in fact a number of positive references to leaven in Jewish literature that balance out the negative references mentioned above.[73] In *Special Laws* 2.184, Philo speaks of leaven as the "most perfect and entire food, than which one cannot, among all the things of daily use, find any which is better and more advantageous."[74] It is hard to imagine a more positive description. In particular, the references to leaven being the "most perfect and entire" (ἐντελεστάτης καὶ ὁλοκλήρου) staple food seems to describe the exact opposite of being unholy or impure. Philo continues to say in the next passage (2.185) that "everything that is leavened rises, and joy is the rational elevation of the soul."[75] It is hard to square these positive references with the idea that leaven was unilaterally associated with impurity in ancient Judaism.[76] Instead, it seems that although leaven could be used as a negative metaphor in some cases (as Philo also does[77]), it was understood in literal terms as a (or perhaps, *the*) staple food necessary for survival, which partly explains why it also sometimes functioned as a positive metaphor.[78] Schellenberg's comment is apposite: "Leavening is an unambiguously positive process when concrete food is discussed."[79] Metaphorical openness is a feature of leaven in both Judaism and the ancient world generally, where it was used both positively and negatively to describe a variety of phenomena. A number of interpreters regard the reference to leaven in the parable of the leaven as a positive metaphor.[80] Discussing this parable, Luz rightly states: "Jesus is speaking not of the Passover but of baking bread."[81] As such, impurity would have been the furthest thing from the minds of the first Jewish audience(s). This is not to deny that mustard and leaven were atypical and non-traditional items to use as metaphors about God's kingdom, which is probably part of the reason why these parables were remembered and preserved.[82]

---

[71] Levine 2014, 130; cf. Bock 1996, 1228.

[72] *Magn.* 10.2; translation from Liebenberg 2001, 338.

[73] See Liebenberg 2001, 337–339; Schellenberg 2009, 538–541.

[74] Translation from Yonge 1995, 585; cf. also Der. Er. Zuṭ on Lev 26:6.

[75] Translation from Snodgrass 2008, 229.

[76] Levine 2014, 128.

[77] E.g. *QE* 1.15.

[78] Cf. Schottroff 2006, 205–206.

[79] Schellenberg 2009, 539.

[80] E.g. Bock 1996, 1228; Fleddermann 2005a, 671; Schellenberg 2009, 542; Gathercole 2014, 547.

[81] Luz 2001, 262.

[82] Cf. Funk and Hoover 1993, 59, 194, 484; Bock 1996, 1227; Scott 2001, 37; Levine 2014, 122; Zimmermann 2015, 247–248, 256; Roth 2018, 305.

6.3 The Growth Angle

Growth and development are often emphasised as important themes in the interpretation of the parable of the mustard seed.[83] Snodgrass goes as far as to say that "for the meaning of the parable all characteristics of the mustard seed are irrelevant except that it grows so high from such a small seed."[84] Within this camp, opinions differ about whether the emphasis is on the developmental process itself or on the contrast between the beginning and end of that process.[85] Recently, there has been a tendency to include both of these accents as part of the same interpretation.[86]

How valid is this avenue of interpretation? In Mark (4:31), Matthew (13:32), and the *Gospel of Thomas* (20), Jesus explicitly states that the mustard seed is the smallest of all existing seeds. In Mark (4:30–32) and Matthew (13:31–32), Jesus further states that the mustard plant is the largest of all garden shrubs. The *Gospel of Thomas* does not include these comments, but does call the resulting plant "large" (μέγας). Interpreting the parable of the mustard seed as a parable of growth or contrast is therefore valid when considering its performances in Mark, Matthew, and *Thomas*.[87] The same is not necessarily true for Luke or earlier versions of the parable, like those on the levels of Q and the historical Jesus.[88] The side-line comment that the mustard seed is the smallest seed is most likely an elaboration by Mark, which was then followed by the Gospels of Matthew and *Thomas*.[89] The reference to the smallness of

---

[83] E.g. Hedrick 2014, 138. See the summary of scholarship in Van Eck 2016, 64–66.

[84] Snodgrass 2008, 220.

[85] See e.g. Hunter 1964, 43–45; Jeremias 1972, 147–149; Carlston 1975, 28, 161; Davies and Allison 1991, 415–417, 419, 421–424; Bock 1996, 1225, 1228; Robinson 2003, 31; Snodgrass 2008, 222, 225, 233.

[86] Snodgrass 2008, 225; e.g. Fleddermann 2005a, 669, 670; Meier 2016, 232–233; Roth 2018, 303, 310.

[87] Schellenberg 2009, 542; e.g. Carlston 1975, 26–28, 157–159; Zimmermann 2015, 251–258.

[88] See Scott 1989, 322–323; Crossan 1991, 276–277; Van Eck 2016, 71–75.

[89] See Scott 1989, 323, 373, 378, 379; 2001, 36–37, 40; Fleddermann 2005a, 665–666; Van Eck 2016, 71–75, 79–80. Although the *Gospel of Thomas* probably includes authentic traditions, it was also subsequently influenced by the canonical Gospels (Howes 2014b, 226). Fleddermann (2005a, 666–668) argues convincingly that Thomas was influenced by the Synoptic traditions in the parables of the mustard seed and leaven (so too Davies and Allison 1991, 421, 424). The fact that the *Gospel of Thomas* uses the Matthean term "kingdom of heaven" (βασιλεία τῶν οὐρανῶν) in his version of the parable of the mustard seed suggests that it was here influenced by Matthew in addition to Mark (Fleddermann 2005a, 667). After a fairly detailed discussion of the relationship between the *Gospel of Thomas* and the Synoptics, Meier (2016, 111–115, 231) finds that the *Gospel of Thomas* represents a conflation of all three Synoptic Gospels. Scott (1989, 323, 377) argues that the parables of the mustard seed and leaven in the *Gospel of Thomas* are not dependent on the canonical Gospels, but rather on oral tradition

the mustard seed was not in Q.[90] Matthew gets it from Mark and Luke does not include it. It is unlikely that the historical Jesus interrupted his telling of the parable to make a botanical remark about the size of the mustard seed.[91] The same is true of the comment in Mark and Matthew that mustard is the largest of all garden plants. Both of these comments should be seen as secondary elaborations by Mark, through which he determined the interpretation of the parable, making it about growth from small to large.[92] When adding these parentheses, Mark used an insertion technique that is typical of him and easy to spot.[93]

Since the comments about the smallness of the mustard seed and the largeness of the mustard plant are not present in Luke or Q, some scholars look for ways to import the same interpretation to these texts. To substitute the comment of the mustard seed's smallness, on the one hand, scholars claim that the mustard seed was *proverbially* known in antiquity and Judaism for its smallness.[94] Even if Luke and Q make no mention of the mustard seed being small, this is assumed to have been common knowledge at the time and implied by these two texts.[95] It is also sometimes pointed out that the sower, oddly enough, sowed only a single mustard seed into his garden, which adds to the "smallness."[96] To substitute the comment of the mustard plant's largeness, on the other hand, some interpreters point out that in Luke and Q the mustard seed grows into a "tree" (δένδρον).[97] The word "tree" is emphasised here, since the

---

that was influenced by the proverbial smallness of both mustard seeds and leaven (see also Liebenberg 2001, 349). This is unlikely, since the smallness of the mustard seed, though recognised, was not proverbial and leaven was not known for its smallness at all (see below).

[90] Scott 1989, 323; 2001, 40; Crossan 1992b, 48; Roth 2018, 311; see Dodd 1961, 141–142.

[91] Luz 2001, 258.

[92] See Scott 1989, 322–323, 373, 378, 379–380; 2001, 35–36; Van Eck 2016, 71–75, 79–80.

[93] Dodd 1961, 142 n. 11; Van Eck 2016, 73 incl. n. 42; see Scott 1989, 378; 2001, 36; Crossan 1992b, 45–46. Liebenberg (2001, 302–304) discusses some of the practical and theological reasons why Mark might have repeated the phrases "when sown" (ὅταν σπαρῇ) and "on the earth" (ἐπὶ τῆς γῆς). Although some of these reasons are convincing, they do not disprove the likelihood that the clumsy language results from Mark adding material to his inherited tradition.

[94] Virtually all scholars who discuss this parable mention the proverbial smallness of mustard seeds in (Jewish) antiquity. Examples often cited include Matt 17:20 // Luke (Q) 17:6; m. Naz. 1:5; m. Nid. 5.2; m. Ṭehar. 8.8; y. Ber. 5, 8, 36; b. Ber. 31; Antigonus of Carystus 91; Diodorus Siculus 1.35.2.

[95] E.g. Liebenberg 2001, 313–314; Fleddermann 2005a, 665; Snodgrass 2008, 222.

[96] E.g. Jacobson 1992, 204; Luz 2001, 261; Nolland 2005, 550.

[97] E.g. Jacobson 1992, 204; Bock 1996, 1225–1226; Fleddermann 2005a, 669–670; Meier 2016, 233; Van Eck 2016, 82; Roth 2018, 307.

mustard shrub was not in antiquity (nor is it today) classified as a tree,[98] even if it could grow to be quite large.[99] Thus, the use of the word "tree" is deliberately provocative, contrasting the insignificant beginning with the unexpected end result.[100] According to Zimmermann, the traditional idea of reaping what one sows is here turned on its head: a comparably small seed produces a comparably large tree.[101] This contrast is ultimately related to the kingdom of God, which started out small and inconspicuous, but then grew (and continues to grow) into something that is larger than life.[102] For some of these interpreters, the function of the birds in the narrative is little more than to confirm the plant's extravagant size.[103]

These arguments are not as convincing as they might seem at first. The extra-biblical *Jewish* texts used by scholars to show that the mustard seed was associated particularly with smallness in antiquity post-date the ministry of Jesus.[104] *Non-Jewish* authors like Antigonus of Carystus (91) and Diodorus Siculus (1.35.2) did indeed make reference to the smallness of the mustard seed before the ministry of Jesus, but apart from the fact that these references are not Jewish, they are not very common. As we will see, other observations about the mustard seed were much more prevalent in the ancient world. In no unclear terms, Levine states: "the smallness of the mustard seed is not proverbial in Greek, Roman, or Jewish culture – at least as far as we know."[105] Mark's parenthesis, placed in the mouth of Jesus and duplicated by Matthew, that the mustard seed is the smallest of all seeds, is precisely what one would expect if the smallness of the mustard seed was *not* proverbial in the ancient world, having to be pointed out by the author.[106] By the same token, the fact that Mark deliberately points out that mustard is the largest garden plant speaks against the size of the mustard plant being proverbial in antiquity.[107] Finally, the reference to only one seed need not represent much more than a turn of phrase, since the parable is ultimately about one plant that grew from one seed.[108] Besides, focusing on only one seed does not say anything about the size of that seed.

---

[98] Hedrick 2004, 93; see Scott 1989, 376–377, 383–384; 2001, 37, 38; Liebenberg 2001, 311–312.

[99] Jeremias 1972, 148; Etchells 1998, 62; Oakman 2008, 114; Snodgrass 2008, 220; Zimmermann 2015, 246, 247; Van Eck 2016, 76.

[100] Allison 2000, 136.

[101] Zimmermann 2015, 248–249, 252.

[102] E.g. Tuckett 1996, 143; Kirk 1998, 303; Järvinen 2001, 521.

[103] E.g. Etchells 1998, 64; Snodgrass 2008, 224.

[104] Schellenberg 2009, 537; see Levine 2014, 170–171.

[105] Levine 2014, 170.

[106] Cf. Liebenberg 2001, 297.

[107] *Pace* Liebenberg 2001, 298, 300, 329; Zimmermann 2015, 247.

[108] Snodgrass 2008, 221; Roth 2018, 302.

The only Jewish reference to the smallness of the mustard seed that does not post-date the ministry of Jesus appears in Q 17:6, which has been reconstructed by the International Q Project as follows: "If you have faith like a mustard seed, you might say to this mulberry tree: Be uprooted and planted in the sea! And it would obey you." It is not a given that the association is with the smallness of the mustard seed, since the attribute of smallness is not mentioned explicitly. Yet smallness does seem to be the most obvious point of comparison in this particular saying.[109] This implies that the smallness of the mustard seed was indeed one of its identifiable features in ancient Judaism, like it was in the ancient world generally.[110] Yet this is not the same as saying that the smallness of the mustard seed was *proverbial*. Being small does not seem to have been the most important or commonly recognised feature of mustard in either Judaism or antiquity, as we will see. Recognising that Q 17:6 alludes specifically to the smallness of the mustard seed does not require such smallness to be a proverbial quality of the mustard seed in ancient Judaism. Instead, it requires a proper understanding of the saying *in toto*. An important clue in the text assisting the audience to make the connection with smallness is the fact that faith is here the referent of the mustard seed.[111] Yet it needs repeating that this interpretation might be wrong. The saying could be about quite a different feature of mustard, like its ability to grow rapidly,[112] in which case it is rapid-growing faith that can move mountains. Oakman maintains that the Matthean version of this logion hints at mustard plants that destroy city walls by growing in the crevaces of these walls.[113] He goes on to paraphrase the logion: "If you have the faith to act in concert, [then you can have the same power as the mustard plant growing in the cracks]" (square brackets original).[114] I would admit that these latter interpretations are less likely, but they do caution one against using this single logion as evidence that the smallness of the mustard seed was proverbial in ancient Judaism.

If the mustard seed is not chosen in Q 13:18–19 because of its smallness, what about the fact that it grows into a "tree" (δένδρον)? The first important factor to consider here is that the word "tree" does not appear in all versions of the parable. Mark 4:32 features the word "shrub" (λάχανον) instead of "tree."

---

[109] Kloppenborg 1995, 316; Kirk 1998, 300; Fleddermann 2005a, 670; Roth 2018, 307; see Schellenberg 2009, 536–537.

[110] Scott 1989, 381; Etchells 1998, 62; Meier 2016, 233; Roth 2018, 311.

[111] See Ra 2016, 233–234.

[112] Cf. Kloppenborg 1995, 316; Liebenberg 2001, 296.

[113] Oakman 2008, 116–117.

[114] Oakman 2008, 117.

A number of scholars maintain that Mark is more original at this point.[115] The *Gospel of Thomas* (20) likewise features "shrub" or "branch" (κλάδος) instead of "tree." Matthew features both "shrub" (λάχανον) and "tree" (δένδρον). The only Gospel that features only a "tree" is Luke. As such, interpretations of the parable on the level of the historical Jesus should not place too much stock in the specific word "tree," since the word might not have been part of the original telling(s) of the parable.[116] Being deliberate about describing a shrub erroneously as a tree is highly unusual for the parables of Jesus, which are deliberately realistic and true to life.[117] Surprising turns in the parables are not unexpected because they are impossible, but precisely because they fall within the realm of possibility and have been set up by the preceding events or information.[118] Yet it seems likely that Q featured only the word "tree," considering not only that the word is shared by Matthew and Luke, but also that Matthew's version is an obvious amalgamation of Mark's "shrub" and Q's "tree."[119] Even so, the use of the word "tree" might not be intended to say anything about its size. There are other possible reasons for using the word "tree" instead of "shrub." For example, the (likely rural) authors or compilers of Q might have been more familiar with large mustard plants, simulating trees, than they were with mustard shrubs. More likely, a tree might have been regarded as a more appropriate image to describe the nesting of birds, especially under the influence of Jewish tradition and Scripture.[120] In any case, the Greek word δένδρον was sometimes used loosely to refer to a large plant.[121]

A number of interpreters take the significance of the word "tree" a step further by recalling Ezekiel 17:22–24, where the future kingdom of Israel is likened to the cedar of Lebanon, a traditional Jewish symbol of mighty earthly empires.[122] The same metaphor is used to describe the Egyptian and Assyrian empires in Ezekiel 31:1–9 and the Babylonian empire in Daniel 4. According to some, the mustard shrub is a burlesque of the cedar, deliberately substituting

---

[115] E.g. Jeremias 1972, 147; Scott 1989, 387; Crossan 1991, 277; 1992b, 48; Funk 2006, 101, 108, 115; Zimmermann 2015, 245–246. For the opposite view that Q's "tree" is original, see Davies and Allison 1991, 416; Fleddermann 2001, 29 n. 27; 2005a, 665; Luz 2001, 258.

[116] Crossan 1992b, 48.

[117] McArthur 1971, 210; cf. Crossan 1992b, 47.

[118] McArthur 1971, 210; cf. Meier 2016, 234.

[119] Perrin 1967, 157; Carlston 1975, 26, 158; Donahue 1988, 36. Scholars generally agree that Matthew conflated Mark and Q to produce his version of the parable: e.g. Dodd 1961, 141–142; Bultmann 1968, 172; Marshall 1978, 560; Scott 1989, 322, 373, 379; 2001, 36; Davies and Allison 1991, 416, 418; Horsley 1999, 90; Liebenberg 2001, 325; Oakman 2008, 113; Snodgrass 2008, 218, 222; Meier 2016, 232, 233; Roth 2018, 299–300.

[120] See below; cf. Crossan 1992b, 48; Jacobson 1992, 204.

[121] Scott 2001, 37; cf. Snodgrass 2008, 220.

[122] For the kingdom of God as a symbol, see Uro 1996, 75–78.

it with an unimpressive (and unclean) plant as a more appropriate metaphor of God's subversive kingdom.[123] Hence, the kingdom of God ends up being a complete reversal of expectations.[124] Instead of being mighty, forceful, and violent like earthly kingdoms, it is insignificant, peaceful, and accommodating.[125]

In my view, it is entirely likely that the audience would have noticed an allusion to the so-called "world tree" when hearing the parable of the mustard seed. Even if the verbal overlap between Q 13:18–19 and the Jewish texts mentioned above is not extensive,[126] the ideational overlap is quite strong.[127] All of these texts refer to birds nesting in the branches of a tree as a metaphor for a kingdom.[128] Granting that the lower classes might in general not always have been familiar with official traditions of the Hebrew Scriptures or the so-called "great tradition,"[129] the idea that earthly kingdoms are comparable to massive trees could easily have been a stock image of popular culture or the "little tradition."[130] In the absence of literature from these illiterate groups, we should be careful of speculating about what they might or might not have known from their own scriptural tradition. In the parable of the mustard seed, it is likely that Jesus is deliberately comparing his vision of God's kingdom with former earthly kingdoms and/or traditional expectations of Israel's future kingdom.[131] In fact, the opening of the parable seems to imply that the kingdom of God is here being compared to other kingdoms: "What is the kingdom of God like, and with what am I to compare it?"[132]

However, to call this comparison a "burlesque" or "parody" is perhaps going too far.[133] Although it would not have been uncharacteristic for the historical Jesus to be controversial or subversive, I do not get the impression from this parable that Jesus is trying to mock earthly kingdoms. Instead, it seems to me

---

[123] E.g. Funk 1966, 203 n. 7; 1996, 157; 2006, 101–102, 117; Scott 1989, 385–387; 2001, 39; 2007, 105; Vaage 1994, 64; 2001, 486; Zimmermann 2015, 256–258. Funk (1996, 157) also regards the parable of the leaven as "a burlesque of the old standard – the unleavened – that used to be associated with the sacred."

[124] Valantasis 2005, 178; Ra 2016, 160; see Allison 2000, 136–137, 221–222.

[125] See Scott 2001, 30–31, 39; Zimmermann 2015, 250–251, 256–258.

[126] Snodgrass 2008, 224; Meier 2016, 235, 236. According to Allison (2000, 134–135), Daniel 4 (LXX and Theodotion) provides the closest *verbal* parallel to Q 13:19, while Ezekiel 17 provides the closest *thematic* parallel.

[127] Dodd 1961, 142; Kloppenborg 2006, 220; Roth 2018, 309.

[128] Heil 2001, 657 n. 50; Scott 2001, 38; Roth 2018, 309.

[129] Oakman 2008, 112, 113; Meier 2016, 235; Van Eck 2016, 80; cf. Thurén 2014, 309.

[130] Cf. Häkkinen 2016, 8; Roth 2018, 305, 308. Being a small peasant or poor is not the same as being ignorant or obtuse, even if it is true that many poor people are often uneducated (Rollens 2014b, 192 n. 181).

[131] Cf. Dodd 1961, 142; Snodgrass 2008, 224; Roth 2018, 308, 323.

[132] Van Eck 2016, 77–78.

[133] Snodgrass 2008, 224.

that the parable is merely implying that the kingdom of God envisioned by Jesus differs from past, present, and future kingdoms. This is an attribute of the kingdom accurately portrayed by the parable. To understand how this attribute is relevant to the interpretation of the parable, one needs to know *in what way* God's kingdom differs from other kingdoms. My current argument is that impurity should not be seen as the answer, and neither should growth.

The parable of the leaven is also interpreted by many scholars as a parable of growth or contrast. Although there is no comment about the smallness or insignificance of leaven in the parable, this is assumed due to its proximity to the parable of the mustard seed in Matthew, Luke, and Q.[134] It is only the *Gospel of Thomas* (96) that specifies the amount of leaven as "little" (μικρός) and then contrasts it with the resultant "large" (μέγας) loaves of bread.[135] These elaborations make sense if one considers that the two parables are separated from each other in the *Gospel of Thomas*. Without the parable of the mustard seed to influence the interpretation of the parable of the leaven, *Thomas* was compelled to make these changes if he wanted the latter to be about growth.[136] This observation should already caution one that the parable of the leaven is not necessarily about growth or contrast when considered in isolation.

Yet, just like we saw with the parable of the mustard seed, certain elements in the parable of the leaven are highlighted to argue that it was indeed about growth or contrast. In particular, a number of scholars emphasise the fact that the woman initially "hid" (ἔκρυψεν/ἐνέκρυψεν) the leaven and that the flour was ultimately "fully" (ὅλον) fermented.[137] The peculiarity of the verb "hide" is particularly noticeable in this context.[138] It would be unusual for someone to "hide" leaven in flour and not expect it to ferment, as opposed to merely "placing" the leaven in the flour with the deliberate intention of effecting fermentation.[139] Under normal circumstances, "placing" leaven in flour would be followed by "kneading."[140] The reference to hiddenness was particularly important to those responsible for the Sayings Gospel Q.[141] Other passages in Q likewise associate the kingdom of God with hiddenness.[142] In particular, Q describes the message of Jesus about God's kingdom as formerly being hidden

---

[134] E.g. Kloppenborg 1987, 223 n. 214.

[135] See Scott 1989, 322–323; 2001, 22–23, 24, 37; Liebenberg 2001, 345–347.

[136] Cf. Scott 2001, 23, 37, 40.

[137] E.g. Marshall 1978, 561; Crossan 1991, 281; Funk 1996, 156; 2006, 100–101; Scott 2001, 27–28, 32; Valantasis 2005, 180; Snodgrass 2008, 231.

[138] Scott 1989, 326; 2001, 27–28; Jacobson 1992, 204; Fleddermann 2005a, 671; Snodgrass 2008, 231; Roth 2018, 312, 313, 317, 318.

[139] Funk and Hoover 1993, 195; Luz 2001, 262; Valantasis 2005, 180; Funk 2006, 100.

[140] Scott 1989, 326; Luz 2001, 262; cf. e.g. Gen 18:6.

[141] Fleddermann 2005a, 671.

[142] E.g. Q 10:21; 11:33; 12:2–3; [17:20–21]; 19:21; see Fleddermann 2005a, 664, 671–672.

(Q 10:21; 12:2–3), but subsequently being proclaimed openly by the followers of Jesus (Q 11:33; 12:2–3). Whereas Jesus originally shared his kingdom message in secret and ambiguity, the followers of Jesus are expected to share that same message in public with lucidity after his death.[143] In other words, the development is from something that starts out hidden to something that ends up permeating everything.[144] This line of interpretation can then be associated with the kingdom of God, which starts out obscure, but inevitably ends up as something that permeates the whole ancient world.[145] It is sometimes argued that the parable of the mustard seed also implies hiddenness, since the seed would have been concealed in the ground.[146]

A word of caution is warranted. Although ἐγκρύπτω typically means "hide," it was on rare occasions used to simply mean "put into."[147] According to Liebenberg, this verb is used merely because it accurately portrays what happens to leaven when it is worked into dough: it becomes invisible.[148] Moreover, hiddenness is not the same as smallness. Apart from the accretions in the *Gospel of Thomas*,[149] the parable says nothing about the initial smallness of the leaven. This is because the leaven is probably not small at all. According to Luz, almost four pounds of leaven would be required to ferment three measures or fifty pounds of flour.[150] As such, it is unlikely that contrast between small and large is the focus of the parable.[151] In my view, the reference to "hiding" the leaven is probably deliberate, especially on the level of Q, but the foregoing observations should alert one against reading too much into this verbal choice.

Another feature of the parable highlighted in this context is the express mention of "three measures" (σάτα τρία) of flower at the end of the parable. The "three measures" equate to about fifty pounds of flour, which would have produced enough bread for over a hundred people.[152] The massive amount of fermented flour is therefore equavalent in metaphorical meaning to the massive size of the tree in the parable of the mustard seed.[153] As I will continue to argue, the references to the "three measures" of flour and the flour being "fully" fermented probably have a different emphasis than the massiveness or all-encompassing nature of God's kingdom, although these aspects of the kingdom

---

[143] Cf. Bultmann 1994, 28; Robinson 1998c, 21.

[144] Vaage 1994, 64; Luz 2001, 261, 263; cf. 1 Cor 5:6; Gal 5:9.

[145] See Dodd 1961, 142–144; Liebenberg 2001, 341–345.

[146] E.g. Ra 2016, 159; cf. Tuckett 1996, 421.

[147] Davies and Allison 1991, 423; Funk 2006, 100.

[148] Liebenberg 2001, 339–340; cf. Vaage 1994, 64; Etchells 1998, 64.

[149] See above.

[150] Luz 2001, 262.

[151] Liebenberg 2001, 342.

[152] Jeremias 1972, 147; Park 2019, 52; see Snodgrass 2008, 231–232.

[153] Nolland 2005, 554.

might also be implied. At any rate, scholars ultimately conclude that both parables treat growth as a factor of God's kingdom, contrasting small, humble, clandestine beginnings with massive, magnificent, all-pervasive endings.[154]

Viewing the parables as being about growth or contrast can be taken one step further. Some scholars have emphasised that both parables envision something impossible occuring.[155] According to these scholars, the parable of the leaven implies that only a small amount of leaven was hidden in the flour, even if the exact amount is left unexpressed.[156] Just like the mustard seed unexpectedly and impossibly grows into a "tree," the hidden leaven unexpectedly and impossibly ferments a massive amount of flour.[157] Even the idea that a mustard shrub is a good example of a tree in which birds nest is hyperbolic,[158] albeit within the realm of possibility and observed experience.[159] Likewise, the basic idea that a woman would ever need to prepare such a large amount of bread is an exaggeration of everyday reality in ancient life.[160] It follows for a number of these interpreters that something miraculous is taking place.[161] By itself, the idea of a dead seed germinating to produce a live plant was regarded as mysterious and miraculous in antiquity.[162] Likewise, the idea of flour fermenting as a result of the mere introduction of leaven would have been regarded as mysterious and miraculous.[163] If this is correct, it would mean that this sense of wonderment is pushed even further to surpass these normal

---

[154] Most interpreters reach this conclusion. An interesting variation to this traditional interpretation appears in Jacobson (1992, 204), Robinson (2003, 31–32), and Snodgrass (2008, 216–235), who argue that these parables are not in the first place about either growth or contrast, but about the (surreptitious) kingdom being already present and underway in the earthly ministry of Jesus (cf. Vaage 1994, 63–64; Tuckett 1996, 128, 144, 210, 421; Allison 2000, 137; Heil 2001, 653, 656; Hoffmann 2001, 282; Joseph 2014, 198–199). Eschatological and teleological aspects of the parable are not in the process denied by these scholars (see Foster 2014a, 283–284; cf. Funk and Hoover 1993, 346; Tuckett 1996, 143–144, 210, 421; Allison 1997, 183; 2000, 136, 137; Hoffmann 2001, 282; Järvinen 2001, 521; Joseph 2012, 29; Bazzana 2015, 264 incl. n. 3; Ra 2016, 159–160, 224).

[155] E.g. Jeremias 1972, 147.

[156] E.g. Jeremias 1972, 148; Jacobson 1992, 204–205; Roth 2018, 319.

[157] Jacobson 1992, 204–205; Tuckett 1996, 144; Scott 2001, 38; Roth 2018, 321, 324–325.

[158] Jeremias 1972, 147; Jacobson 1992, 203; Liebenberg 2001, 311–312, 313, 314; Fleddermann 2005a, 665; Funk 2006, 116, 118; Roth 2018, 308.

[159] Liebenberg 2001, 313; Luz 2001, 261; Nolland 2005, 551 n. 90; Zimmermann 2015, 246.

[160] Hunter 1971, 44; Jeremias 1972, 147; Nolland 2005, 554; Funk 2006, 102.

[161] E.g. Jeremias 1972, 147; Davies and Allison 1991, 416; Tuckett 1996, 144; Robinson 2003, 31–32.

[162] See Jeremias 1972, 148–149; Crossan 1992b, 49–51; Etchells 1998, 62–63.

[163] Robinson 2003, 31; Schottroff 2006, 206; see Etchells 1998, 62–63. For the opposite view that germination and fermentation were not regarded as miraculous by ancients, see Liebenberg 2001, 297, 340.

expectations of "everyday miracles."[164] The "typical miracle" of germination is amplified to produce a tree from the seed of a plant, and the "typical miracle" of fermentation is enlarged to produce a massive amount of food from only a small amount of leaven.

That the parables of the mustard seed and leaven mention growth and hiddenness is accurate.[165] In fact, growth and hiddenness are indisputable components of these parables, as indicated by the mere presence of the verbs "grow" (αὐξάνω), "develop" (γίνομαι), "leaven" (ζυμόω), and "hide" (ἐγκρύπτω).[166] There may even be the suggestion of something miraculous or mysterious taking place. However, this does not mean that the emphasis is on these elements or that the applications of the parables lie "hidden" in them. The parables also feature the verbs "take" (λαμβάνω) and "throw" (βάλλω), but interpreters are not queueing up to extract the message of the parables from these latter verbs. One could actually argue that these verbs are more important, given (1) that the verb "take" (λαμβάνω) is repeated in both parables;[167] (2) that the verb "throw" (βάλλω) is unusual to describe sowing;[168] and (3) that the two verbs appear (and sound) so similar in their grammatical forms in the parable of the mustard seed (i.e. λαβών and ἔβαλεν). I am not making this argument here. Instead, I point this out to indicate that one should be wary of reading too much into the specific choices of verbs. That is not to say that these accents are irrelevant, as we will see, but rather that they are subordinate to (and supportive of) the central message.[169] The oft-repeated claim that the earliest versions of these parables place particular emphasis on the minuteness of the initial stage and the massiveness of the end result seems untenable. On the level of Q, the parable of the mustard seed merely mentions growth as an aspect of the kingdom, just as the parable of the leaven merely mentions hiddenness as an aspect of the kingdom. These are hardly shocking or surprising observations about the kingdom of God.[170] Given what we know

---

[164] Tuckett 1996, 143–144; Nolland 2005, 554.

[165] Crossan 1992b, 38, 50; Levine 2014, 181.

[166] Cf. Jacobson 1992, 203; Vaage 1994, 63; Kloppenborg 1995, 307–308, 310; Fleddermann 2005a, 670; Meier 2016, 232–233; Roth 2018, 300, 303, 315; *pace* Van Eck 2016, 74.

[167] Jacobson 1992, 203; Kloppenborg 1995, 307; Roth 2018, 312.

[168] Roth 2018, 301.

[169] Cf. Bock 1996, 1226; Levine 2014, 120.

[170] According to Levine (2014, 118–119, 169, 171, 181), interpretations that view growth as the central message of these parables are watered down and banal (cf. Funk 2006, 99). I tend to agree, even if I find her rhetoric a bit heavy handed. Moreover, although Levine's interpretations of the parables of the mustard seed and leaven are innovative and convincing, one or two of her conclusions may equally be criticised for being banal, including, for example, her conclusions that "the kingdom will come if we nurture it" (p. 136); that the kingdom "is present, inchoate, in everything, and it is available to all" (p. 137); that "some things need to be *left alone*" (p. 182, emphasis original); and that "sometimes we need to *get out of the way*" (p. 182, emphasis original). In tone and significance, these generalised conclusions

about the historical Jesus (as well as Q's Jesus), it is unlikely in my view that he would have told these parables in order to make the obvious point that the kingdom grows. Instead, my contention is that the key to understanding these parables lies in their endings,[171] to which we now turn.

6.4 The Provision Angle

The parable of the mustard seed ends with the image of birds nesting in the branches of the "mustard tree." This ending has been the cause of much speculation and doubt.[172] In particular, it seems to lend itself to allegory. Some scholars, for example, postulate that the reference to birds nesting in the branches might have been a veiled reference to the presence of gentiles in the kingdom of God.[173] Nolland doubts that Matthew intended the birds to be associated with gentiles, because the evangelist has failed to retain the word "all" (כֹּל; πᾶς, πᾶσα, πᾶν) from Ezekiel 17:23 (and 31:6).[174] In general, though, the idea that the references to birds has gentiles in mind is unnecessarily allegorical and transgresses beyond the parameters set up by the parable itself.[175] Allison is also correct that in Jewish tradition "the image of a large tree with birds resting in it or under it does not always have to do with Gentiles."[176] Crossan and Oakman see the birds as an agricultural nuisance, eating produce and destroying plantations.[177] This reading also transgresses beyond the imagery of the parable, where birds are depicted as nesting in the mustard plant, not as destroying the garden or field.[178] Some have also regarded the words "of heaven" (τοῦ οὐρανοῦ) in the term "birds of heaven" (τὰ πετεινὰ τοῦ οὐρανοῦ) as having some spiritual, religious, or metaphorical significance.[179] This idea is refuted by the popularity of the term "birds of

---

are very similar to the ones that Levine criticises, like that the kingdom grows or that it is mighty. In the case of the first example above, Levine's association of the leaven with a child in the womb might be considered interesting, but the ultimate application that "the kingdom will come if we nurture it" (p. 136) is not really that interesting.

[171] Cf. Dodd 1961, 142, 143.

[172] Scott 1989, 383.

[173] Many examples could have been listed here, but the following will suffice: Hunter 1961, 44; 1971, 24, 45; Perrin 1967, 157; Carlston 1975, 27, 28, 159, 160, 161; Marshall 1978, 561; Uro 1996, 86; Scholtz 2015, 6; Zimmermann 2015, 255–256.

[174] Nolland 2005, 551 n. 92.

[175] See Bock 1996, 1226–1227; Liebenberg 2001, 293–295, 299, 301–302, 326–327.

[176] Allison 1997, 183.

[177] Crossan 1991, 278; Oakman 2008, 116.

[178] Roth 2018, 304.

[179] E.g. Zimmermann 2015, 244–245, 254; Roth 2018, 305.

heaven" in the Hebrew Bible, wider Jewish literature, and the New Testament as a straightforward reference to literal birds.[180]

When considering the rest of Q, it becomes clear that the image of nesting birds must be understood differently.[181] On the level of Q, the most important intertext for this imagery is the saying in Q 9:58: "Foxes have holes, and birds of the sky have nests; but the son of humanity does not have anywhere he can lay his head." Crucially, the two traditions share not only the phrase "birds of the sky" (τὰ πετεινὰ τοῦ οὐρανοῦ), but also the word "nest" (κατασκήνωσις/κατασκηνόω).[182] The latter word is striking, since the more usual and technically appropriate term for birds "nesting" is νοσσεύω.[183] In Q 9:58, the literary context makes clear that κατασκήνωσις is used deliberately because the analogy is with human housing or accommodation.[184] In ancient literature, the Greek word "nest" (noun: κατασκήνωσις; verb: κατασκηνόω) is typically used of people and carries the meaning "dwell."[185] Liddell and Scott offer translation possibilities like "take up one's quarters," "encamp," and "occupy."[186] In the Septuagint, the verb κατασκηνόω often translates the Hebrew word שָׁכַן, which literally means to "settle," "abide," or "dwell."[187] Only one of these occurances relates to birds, namely Psalm 104:12.[188] The other occurances of κατασκηνόω in the Septuagint all relate to people.[189] In Q 9:58, the image of birds nesting is indisputably used to make the point that animals have a place to stay, as the rest of the logion indicates.[190] By contrast, the Son of Man often does not have a place to stay. In this Q context, the term "son of humanity" or "Son of Man" (ὁ υἱός τοῦ ἀνθρωποῦ) refers to the earthly Jesus, while the saying *in toto* implies that his followers might have to share in his homelessness.[191] Yet the saying also hints at the homelessness of humanity

---

[180] See Liebenberg 2001, 293–295; Levine 2014, 179–180. E.g. Gen 2:20; 7:3; 1 Sam 17:44, 46; 2 Sam 21:10; 1 Kgs 14:11; Ps 79:2; Jer 7:33; Job 12:7; Ps 8:8; Judith 11:7; Q 9:58; Matt 6:26. Zimmermann (2015, 244) and Roth (2018, 305) acknowledge these Jewish intertexts, but still argue that the reference to "heaven" has some metaphorical significance.

[181] Cf. Bock 1996, 1226–1227; Levine 2014, 179–180.

[182] Liebenberg 2001, 327; Zimmermann 2015, 243 n. 14.

[183] Zimmermann 2015, 243; cf. Liddell and Scott 1996, 1169, s.v. νεοσσεία.

[184] Cf. Liebenberg 2001, 327.

[185] Davies and Allison 1991, 420; Nolland 2005, 551; Snodgrass 2008, 224; Zimmermann 2015, 244; Roth 2018, 303; cf. Acts 2:26; 1 Clem. 58.1.

[186] Liddell and Scott 1996, 912.

[187] Brown, Driver, and Briggs 1977, 1014–1015, s.v. שָׁכַן; Zimmermann 2015, 243–244.

[188] Zimmermann 2015, 243–244. LXX Ps 103:12: "By them shall the birds of the sky lodge [κατασκηνώσει]: they shall utter a voice out of the midst of the rocks" (translation from Brenton 1870).

[189] Zimmermann 2015, 244.

[190] See Van Aarde 2002, 1641–1649; 2004, 434–438; 2009, 540–541.

[191] See Howes 2015a, 170–171; cf. Uro 1996, 108.

in general.[192] In other words, the term κατασκήνωσις is used in Q 9:58 to compare animals with one or more humans in the context of lodging.[193]

It seems likely that κατασκηνόω is similarly used in Q 13:19 to say something about lodging in relation to animals and humans.[194] Roth is therefore spot-on when he says the following about the nesting birds in Q 13:19: "The mimetic component is related to their 'dwelling,' that is, not simply perching but 'taking up abode' in the tree."[195] Roth continues to say that "the focus here is on the provision of a habitat for the birds."[196] It is not a coincidence that the *Gospel of Thomas* (20) uses the noun "shelter" (σκέπη) instead of the verb "nest" (κατασκηνόω) to describe the benefit of the mustard plant to the birds in his version of the parable.[197] The main difference between the two Q texts is that Q 9:58 *explicitly contrasts* the "housing" of animals and humans, while Q 13:19 *implicitly relates* the "housing" of animals and humans. The reason for this difference is that Q 9:58 describes reality in the world, while Q 13:19 describes reality in the kingdom of God.[198] In the former, animals are better off than humans, but in the latter God provides for humans as he does for animals. Referring specifically to the connection between Q 9:58 and Q 13:19, Fleddermann remarks: "God provides a home in the kingdom, though, to replace the home the disciple abandoned."[199] The point here is not to argue that Q 13:19 compares humans to animals – although such a comparison might be implied – but to illustrate that Q 13:19 is like Q 9:58 in that it uses the image of nesting birds to say something about human accommodation.

These associations also find expression in the Hebrew Scriptures. Proverbs 27:8 explicitly relates birds' nests with human houses: "Like a bird that strays from its nest is a man who strays from his home."[200] Conversely, Isaiah 16:2 describes those without houses and lodging by comparing them to birds without nests: "Like fleeing birds, like a scattered nest, so are the daughters of Moab at

---

[192] Casey (2009) argues that the historical Jesus used the term Son of Man in an idiomatic way to say something about humanity in general, but with implied specific relevance to the speaker, the speaker and others, or another person indicated by the literary context. This usage would also make sense for Q 9:59. For the claim that the expression Son of Man originally referenced humanity in general, see Crossan 1983, 241; Robinson 1991, 189; 1994a, 321; Horsley 1999, 239; Rollens 2014b, 157. For arguments to the contrary, see Marshall 1978, 410; Nolland 2005, 365–366; Joseph 2012, 61–63.

[193] Liebenberg 2001, 327.

[194] Cf. Zimmermann 2015, 255.

[195] Roth 2018, 303; cf. Liebenberg 2001, 315, 322; Meier 2016, 233–234.

[196] Roth 2018, 304. Although Roth places equal emphasis on other aspects of the parable, like growth, he does interpret this accent of the parable accurately.

[197] Cf. Jeremias 1972, 31; Scott 1989, 378; Crossan 1992b, 49; Funk 2006, 115; Snodgrass 2008, 219; Gathercole 2014, 297; cf. LXX Isa 16:3.

[198] Liebenberg 2001, 315 n. 146, 327.

[199] Fleddermann 2005a, 671.

[200] In this chapter, all translations of the Bible are from the ESV.

the fords of the Arnon." The passage continues in verse 4 to instruct its readers and listeners to let these outcasts "sojourn" or "dwell" (MT: גּוּר; LLX: παροικέω) among them and be a "shelter" (MT: סֵתֶר; LXX: σκέπη) for them (see also Hos 11:10–11). Ancients must have been fascinated, mesmerised even, by the fact that simple creatures like birds have the ability to build their own "houses." Even today – all our scientific knowledge notwithstanding – the fact that birds build their own nests from twigs and other material remains a natural wonder. Ancient fascination at this natural wonder finds poetic expression in Psalm 104:16–17: "The trees of the Lord are watered abundantly, the cedars of Lebanon that he planted. In them the birds build their nests; the stork has her home in the fir trees." Particularly noteworthy for the current discussion is the poetic synonymisation of the word "home" (MT: בַּיִת; LXX: οἰκία) with the idea of birds building nests in the two parallel lines of verse 17. Speaking about mountain springs, the same Psalm says in verse 12: "Beside them the birds of the heavens dwell; they sing among the branches." Taken together, these verses contain a number of terms that also feature in the parable of the mustard seed, including "tree" (MT: עֵץ; LXX: ξύλον), "birds of heaven" (MT: עוֹף־הַשָּׁמַיִם; LXX: τὰ πετεινὰ τοῦ οὐρανοῦ), "nest/dwell" (MT: שָׁכַן; LXX: κατασκηνόω), and "branches" (MT: עֳפָאיִם; "rocks" in the LXX: πετρῶν). In particular, the combination of the term "birds of heaven" with the verb "nest/dwell" is strikingly similar to the conclusion of the parable. Liebenberg argues: "The text from Ps 104:12 is listed in a context of the wonder of creation and JHWH's care for all creatures and is not seriously to be considered as an Old Testament allusion [to the parable of the mustard seed]."[201] Liebenberg misses the point that the "wonder of creation" and "JHWH's care for all creatures" are precisely the components of Psalm 104 that apply to the parable of the mustard seed. The imagery of birds nesting is used in both texts to describe God as the provider of accommodation. Crossan dismisses Ezekiel and Daniel as intertexts, but concludes his discussion on the intertextuality of the parable by saying that "*if* there is any Old Testament allusion behind the original version of Mark 4:31, it is no more and no less than an allusion to God's loving providence in the pastoral scene of Psalm 104:12."[202] Texts like Proverbs 27:8, Isaiah 16:2, and Psalm 104:12 indicate that the image of birds

---

[201] Liebenberg 2001, 292; see also Meier 2016, 236. Snodgrass (2008, 224) argues that Psalm 104:12 could not have been an intertext, because (1) "it has no reference to a king-dom"; and (2) "[i]t merely describes the provision available in water God supplies." The first argument ignores the similarities that do exist between Psalm 104 and Q 13:18–19. The second argument fails to recognise that divine provision is precisely the point. Both texts describe God providing the bare necessities required to survive and do so with the imagery of birds nesting in trees.

[202] Crossan 1992b, 46–47, quotation from p. 47, emphasis original; see also Donahue 1988, 37. Crossan repeats the same opinion on p. 48.

nesting was sometimes used in ancient Judaism to say something about the presence or provision of lodging and shelter.[203]

The same is true of other texts from the Hebrew Scriptures.[204] This includes Ezekiel 17 and 31, discussed above.[205] In the midst of the cedar metaphor, Ezekiel 17:23 says: "On the mountain height of Israel will I plant it, that it may bear branches and produce fruit and become a noble cedar. And under it will dwell every kind of bird; in the shade of its branches birds of every sort will nest." Also as part of the cedar metaphor, Ezekiel 31:6 says: "All the birds of the heavens made their nests in its boughs." Daniel 4:12, 14, 21 could also have been quoted here. Understood as part of the cedar metaphor, these birds represent the people or subjects being sheltered by the empire in question.[206] The intent is to depict an earthly kingdom that provides abundantly for its populace. In my view, the exact same meaning lies behind the imagery of nesting birds in the parable of the mustard seed.[207] In this parable, the intent with the image is to depict God's kingdom as a place where God provides lodging and shelter for people as he does for birds.[208] This is the point of the comparison between the parable of the mustard seed and the cedar of Lebanon: both describe empires that are able to provide shelter and lodging for people, and both do so by using the metaphor of nesting birds.[209] Rather than alluding to one particular Jewish intertext, the parable alludes to the general idea that an earthly kingdom is comparable to a tree with nesting birds, especially in its function and ability to provide.[210] Whether those who receive shelter include

---

[203] Apart from Jewish intertexts, this interpretation is also supported by literature and art from the ancient world more generally. Consider, for example, the description of Calypso's cave in Homer's Odyssey (Book V), where images of trees, plants and nesting birds symbolise domesticity and paradise. Consider also the following sentence from the Gilgamesh Epic, while discussing human mortality: "Ever do we build our households, ever do we make our nests" (Standard Version, X.308–309; trans. George 2003, 87). Consider finally the relief sculpture in the Lateran Museum in Rome of Ino feeding the infant Dionysus, where life, provision and lodging are symbolised by a tree and/or vine with nesting birds (cf. Harris and Platzner 2012, 247).

[204] Bock 1996, 1226; Levine 2014, 178.

[205] Bock 1996, 1226.

[206] Dodd 1961, 142; Donahue 1988, 37; Funk and Hoover 1993, 194; Fleddermann 2005a, 670; *pace* Liebenberg 2001, 291–293.

[207] Bock 1996, 1226, 1227, 1229; Meier 2016, 234, 236.

[208] Levine 2014, 181; Meier 2016, 234, 236; cf. Von Gemünden 1993, 201–202.

[209] Hunter 1971, 45; Meier 2016, 234, 236.

[210] Snodgrass 2008, 224; Roth 2018, 309; see Meier 2016, 234–236, esp. 236. Liebenberg (2001, 289–295, 299–300, 312, 326–327) argues at some length that the parable of the mustard seed does not allude to a Jewish intertext at all. Although I agree that this parable does not have one specific intertext in mind, I do believe that it alludes to the general idea in Hebrew Scriptures that a kingdom is comparable to a tree, specifically in its ability to provide. All texts that develop this metaphor are therefore relevant to the parable as intertexts,

gentiles or other nations is not the point of the parable, although this possibility is not precluded either.[211] Rather, the point is that the kingdom of God provides shelter to all those included under its shadow.

There are also suggestions that such provision might include more than just accommodation. Luz points out that "birds like to eat mustard seeds,"[212] and Zimmermann remarks that "[m]ustard seed was also used as bird feed."[213] Moreover, mustard shrubs were also a food source for humans in the ancient world, who cooked its leaves as greens and used its kernels as spice.[214] Oakman reads the Lukan version as saying "that the mustard is sown for the purpose of raising a condiment."[215] The only other occurance (in addition to Q 9:58) of the collective term "birds" (πετεινά) in the Sayings Gospel, namely Q 12:24, states: "Consider the ravens: They neither sow nor reap nor gather into barns, and yet God feeds them. Are you not better than the birds?" The link with food is further supported by the description of the "world tree" in Daniel 4:12, which in that context represents king Nebucadnezzar and his Babylonian kingdom: "Its leaves were beautiful and its fruit abundant, and in it was food for all. The beasts of the field found shade under it, and the birds of the heavens lived in its branches, and all flesh was fed from it." These words, repeated in verse 21, clearly associate the ability of the tree to provide shelter with its ability to feed those who depend on it. Another text that is at least interesting in this regard is Numbers 24:5–7:

> How lovely are your tents, O Jacob, your encampments, O Israel! Like palm groves that stretch afar, like gardens beside a river, like aloes that the Lord has planted, like cedar trees beside the waters. Water shall flow from his buckets, and his seed shall be in many waters; his king shall be higher than Agag, and his kingdom shall be exalted.

This passage is suggested as an intertext by the words "cedar" (MT: אֶרֶז; LXX: κέδρος), "seed" (MT: זֶרַע; LXX: σπέρμα), "garden" (MT: גַּנָּה; LXX: παράδεισος), and "kingdom" (MT: מַלְכוּת; LXX: βασιλεία). While making reference to cedar trees, the kingdom of Israel is here associated with the abundant provision of water; although, in this case, it is the cedar that is being fed by the water. God supports the kingdom of Israel. Similar imagery appears

---

even if the parable does not allude to any one of them in particular. For his reaction to this line of reasoning, see Liebenberg 2001, 312 incl. n. 139.

[211] Cf. Allison 1997, 183–184; Fleddermann 2005a, 670–671.

[212] Luz 2001, 261.

[213] Zimmermann 2015, 247; cf. Davies and Allison 1991, 420; Funk 1996, 157; Liebenberg 2001, 298–299; Valantasis 2005, 178; Oakman 2008, 116.

[214] Scott 1989, 380; Crossan 1991, 278; Liebenberg 2001, 296; Luz 2001, 261; Schellenberg 2009, 532; Zimmermann 2015, 247; Van Eck 2016, 76, 81. Cf. t. Maʿaś. 3.7; b. B. Meṣ. 86; b. Ḥul. 133; b. Ber. 40; Pliny, *Nat.* 19.40, 54, 61.

[215] Oakman 2008, 115.

in verse 16 of Psalm 104, discussed above.[216] It is worth quoting Psalm 104:16–17 again here: "The trees of the Lord are watered abundantly, the cedars of Lebanon that he planted. In them the birds build their nests; the stork has her home in the fir trees." The Septuagint's version of this text uses the verb χορτάζω to describe how God provides for the cedars of Lebanon.[217] This verb is more commonly used to describe the act of feeding humans or animals and specifically denotes feeding them until they are full.[218] The verb is also sometimes used to describe a feast.[219] The connotation of a feast relates well not only to the parable of the leaven,[220] but also to other texts in the Sayings Gospel that describe banquets, like Q 13:29 and Q 14:16–21, 23.[221]

In addition to being a food source for animals and humans alike, the mustard plant was highly regarded for its medicinal value in the ancient world.[222] In fact, this was arguably its most popular characteristic in the ancient world, in addition to its sharp taste and smell.[223] Pliny the Elder goes on and on about the medicinal and gastronomical benefits of mustard.[224] *Natural History* 20.87 is particularly relevant, describing mustard, sometimes in combination with other resources, as a cure or suppressant for numerous ailments, including snake bites, tooth-ache, stomach problems, asthma, epilepsy, dropsy, body pains, leprosy, and bruising – to mention only a few. Referring specifically to this text by Pliny, Scott remarks: "From his description, there appears to be no illness that mustard will not cure."[225] Rather than being known for its smallness, mustard was known for its healing power. Given both its culinary and medicinal benefits, mustard was precisely the type of plant ancients would have wanted in their gardens or fields.[226] Far from being an impure weed, it was a useful resource. Given these attributes of mustard, the parable might be hinting at the provision of food and healing in addition to shelter as features of God's kingdom.[227] Q 12:6–7, 22–24 associates birds particularly with God's all-inclusive providential care, which includes at least the provision of food as well. As Zimmermann states, the mustard shrub "becomes a source of life for

---

[216] Cf. Snodgrass 2008, 224.

[217] LXX: Ps 103:16–17.

[218] See Liddell and Scott 1996, 1999–2000, s.v. χορτάζω.

[219] Liddell and Scott 1996, 1999–2000, s.v. χορτάζω.

[220] See below.

[221] Cf. Kirk 1998, 304; Hoffmann 2001, 282.

[222] Schellenberg 2009, 532, 543; Roth 2018, 306; see Levine 2014, 169, 170, 177, 181.

[223] Cf. Liebenberg 2001, 296; Schellenberg 2009, 532–533, 543.

[224] E.g. *Nat.* 16.60; 19.54; 20.13, 50, 87; 21.89; 27.113; 28.46, 62; 29.34; cf. Zimmermann 2015, 247.

[225] Scott 1989, 380.

[226] Levine 2014, 178.

[227] Cf. Scott 1989, 380; Järvinen 2001, 521.

other creatures."[228] To the extent that people are worth more to God than birds (cf. Q 12:7, 24), God's kingdom promises to be a place where God provides more abundantly for people than he does for animals (cf. Q 12:22–31).[229] It is probably no coincidence that two of the three features most commonly associated with God's kingdom in Q, namely food and healing,[230] are also two of the features for which the mustard plant was best known in the ancient world.[231] The third of the three features most commonly associated with God's kingdom in Q, namely shelter,[232] is brought out in the parable through the image of the nesting birds. Although the association with food and healing might be implied by the choice of mustard in particular, it is the provision of accommodation that is explicitly mentioned in the parable when using the verb "nest" (κατασκηνόω).

Given the discussion up to this point, it would be fair to conclude that the imagery of birds nesting in a tree is appropriate to depict God's kingdom as a place where God provides. The appropriateness of the mustard plant in particular, even if it is not specified as a "world tree" anywhere in the Hebrew Scriptures, lies in the fact that birds were especially attracted to the abundant seeds and shade of mustard plants.[233] Nonetheless, this image might be the unexpected turn in the parable.[234] The telling starts off with a mustard seed, as opposed to the seed of a cedar, oak, or maple, so that the last thing the audience expects is that the comparison will draw on birds nesting in its branches.[235] The potential of the insignificant socio-economic movement intiated by Jesus, otherwise referred to as "the kingdom of God," to feed people of the world

---

[228] Zimmermann 2015, 242.

[229] Peters 2016, 39, 40; Cf. Valantasis 2005, 178.

[230] For food and healing as central to Q's understanding of God's kingdom, see Robinson 1993, 15; 2001a, 16; 2001b, 33; 2002, 15; Vaage 1994, 63; Uro 1996, 79–82, 87–89; Horsley 2003, 30–33, 35; 2012, 127; Howes 2015a, 123–124; 2019b, 4–11; cf. also Piper 2000, 241, 251, 259; Järvinen 2001, 521; Kloppenborg 2001, 166; Park 2019, 44.

[231] It might also not be coincidental that Luke precedes the parable of the mustard seed with a story of healing (see Etchells 1998, 64–65; cf. Liebenberg 2001, 309–310; Snodgrass 2008, 218, 219–220). In fact, Luke presents Jesus as telling the parable in the synagogue where people had just witnessed this healing (Etchells 1998, 65; Liebenberg 2001, 309). The parable's literary context in Luke is otherwise difficult to explain (Snodgrass 2008, 219–220).

[232] For shelter as central to Q's understanding of God's kingdom, see Howes 2019b, 4–6.

[233] Perrin 1967, 157; Crossan 1992b, 48; Liebenberg 2001, 298–299, 300, 303, 313; Funk 2006, 116; Snodgrass 2008, 220. However, some scholars question whether birds actually built nests in mustard plants (e.g. McArthur 1971, 198–201; cf. Crossan 1992b, 48).

[234] Roth 2018, 308, 309–310, 321, 324–325; cf. McGaughy 2007, 12; Zimmermann 2015, 243.

[235] Allison 2000, 136.

might likewise be one of its surprising aspects.[236] This is how the kingdom of God envisioned by Jesus differs from other kingdoms, whether Egyptian, Assyrian, Babylonian, Roman, or Herodian.[237] From the perspective of socio-economically struggling Palestinians, these earthly kingdoms, including Israel, exploited the populace in various ways, confiscating bare necessities like food and shelter from the most vulnerable members of society.[238] One might have here a veiled criticism of former and existing earthly kingdoms, especially in their tendency to exploit the lower classes. Instead of explicitly mocking these kingdoms, Jesus is implicitly criticising them. They did not and do not live up to the metaphor of the cedar, which was traditionally depicted as providing for birds and animals. The kingdom of God is different, providing instead of extracting resources.[239]

Additional support for the interpretation advocated here is provided by the elements of the parable that remain constant across different versions of the parable of the mustard seed. While these different versions disagree on whether the seed was sown or thrown, whether it ended up in a garden or a field, whether it grew into a plant or a tree, and whether the birds found shelter in its branches or its shade, they agree that a mustard seed grew into something that provided shelter to birds.[240] It would be sensible to locate the key to understanding the parable not in these variables, but in the elements that remain constant.[241] Far from being a later interpolation into the parable, as some scholars have suggested,[242] the detail about the birds nesting was part of the original parable.[243] More than that, it was probably the parable's most important element.[244] Interestingly, Carlston finds the meaning of the parable *as it appears in Mark* to be about the provision of shelter, with Daniel 4 indicated as the most important intertext.[245] It is worth pointing out that the interpretation proposed here would remain valid even if Q 13:18–19 did not allude to any text in the Hebrew Bible whatsoever, given that the parable ends with a description

---

[236] Cf. Vaage 1994, 63; Tuckett 1996, 128; Allison 2000, 136, 137; Valantasis 2005, 178. Bultmann (1968, 200) is virtually alone in maintaining that the kingdom of God should not be understood as a "human community." Jacobson (1992, 204) makes explicit what most scholars assume: "The Q people are probably the mustard seed which will become a tree; they are the kingdom."

[237] Cf. Valantasis 2005, 178; Roth 2018, 323.

[238] Herzog 1994, 161; Horsley 1995a, 43; 1995b, 60, 215–216, 219; Freyne 2000, 205; Arnal 2001, 139–140, 146; Moxnes 2003, 150; Oakman 2008, 21, 25, 224; Van Eck 2011, 5, 7; 2016, 78, 79; Park 2014a, 85, 86.

[239] Cf. Scott 2001, 30–34; Valantasis 2005, 178; Van Eck 2016, 78, 79, 82–83.

[240] Van Eck 2016, 72; see Levine 2014, 165–166, 173, 181.

[241] Cf. Dodd 1961, 142; Snodgrass 2008, 222.

[242] E.g. Carlston 1975, 160; Vaage 2001, 487; Howes 2015f, 329–330.

[243] Dodd 1961, 142; Scott 1989, 378, 379–380; see Van Eck 2016, 74–75.

[244] Bock 1996, 1226; cf. Dodd 1961, 142; Carlston 1975, 159.

[245] Carlston 1975, 158.

of birds nesting/dwelling in trees. Whether or not the ancient lower-classes knew the intertexts listed above, they could (and probably would) have understood the analogy between birds' nests and human houses.

As we saw, the parable of the leaven ends with a massive amount of bread. This one observation would have been central to any ancient Jewish interpretation of the parable: "At that time and in that society bread was the basic staff of life. The word bread can represent all the food on the table or all the nourishment people need."[246] The baking anticipates a very large meal or, as Funk puts it, "a festive occasion of significant proportions."[247] According to Levine, "[t]he image is one of extravagance, or hyperbole."[248] The fact that this food is shared particularly at a feast or other festive occasion is certainly not irrelevant, depicting God's kingdom in terms of a cheerful communal event.[249] Whereas the parable of the mustard seed ends with people having a place to stay, the parable of the leaven ends with people having more than enough to eat.[250] What is more, the chronological progression from farming in the parable of the mustard seed to baking in the parable of the leaven would have seemed altogether natural and familiar to an ancient audience, especially peasants.[251] The anticipated outcome of both these activities is food. In fact, the parable of the leaven is about food from beginning to end. As Luz states: "The image of the leaven comes from the kitchen."[252] Yet the ending is particularly vivid, depicting the kingdom of God as a place where people have abundant food.[253] Throughout Q, the kingdom of God is particularly associated with food.[254] Using "bread" (ἄρτος) as an image of God's provinence is an important motif in Q. In this regard, the most important intertext for the parable of the leaven is arguably Q 11:2–4, [5–8], 9–13, which speaks about "bread" in the context of daily survival.[255] Robinson also noticed this intertextual linkage:

Die Auslegung der Bitte „Deine Königsherrschaft komme!" im Vaterunser selbst, nämlich: „Unser Brot für den Tag gib uns heute!", wurde nicht durch vom Himmel gefallenes Manna erfüllt, sondern durch Frauen, die, nach dem Rezept von Q 13,21, Sauerteig in drei Sat

---

[246] Schottroff 2006, 205–206.

[247] Funk 2006, 101; cf. Park 2019, 52.

[248] Levine 2014, 133; so too Nolland 2005, 554; Funk 2006, 102.

[249] Park 2019, 53.

[250] Cf. Luz 2001, 263; Levine 2014, 136–137.

[251] Cf. Schottroff 2006, 206; Oakman 2008, 112; Park 2014a, 78; Thurén 2014, 194.

[252] Luz 2001, 262; cf. Schottroff 2006, 207; Park 2019, 47.

[253] Cf. Levine 2014, 136–137.

[254] See Valantasis 2005, 190–191; cf. Vaage 1994, 63, 64; Park 2019, 46, 47, 52; cf. Q 6:20–21; 10:8–9; 11:2–3, 11–13; 12:22–31, 42–46; 13:18–19, 20–21, 28–29; 14:16–21, 23.

[255] Cf. Vaage 1994, 63; Schottroff 2006, 206–207; Levine 2014, 119, 136–137; Howes 2016a, 18–20; 2019b, 6–13; see chapter 5 above.

Weizenmehl verbargen, bis es ganz durchsäuert war, im Backofen in Brot verwandelt zu werden.[256]

Unfortunately, limited space does not allow me to unpack the question of how exactly Q envisions the kingdom of God providing accommodation and food, but Robinson is correct that it in no small way involves human action,[257] which is then interpreted as indirect divine providence.[258]

This line of interpretation is further supported by the intertextual link with Genesis 18:6–8, where Abraham provides food to three mysterious visitors from "three measures" (MT: שְׁלֹשׁ סְאִים; LXX: τρία μέτρα) of flour.[259] This narrative was the prime example of hospitality in ancient Judaism. Hunt writes: "The paradigm for hospitality in Jewish thinking is, of course, Abraham, who went out of his way to receive three special visitors in Genesis 18."[260] The meal that Abraham prepared included not only three measures of "breadcakes" (MT: עֻגוֹת; LXX: ἐγκρυφίας), but also milk, curds, and a calf. To say that this feast was too much for three visitors is a gross understatement.[261] The deliberate link with Genesis 18 reinforces the parable's emphasis on abundant food, while also evoking the motif of generous hospitality. Rather than associating leaven negatively with impurity, the parable associates it positively with food.[262]

It is true that the imagined feast is not recounted by the parable, but the parable does include the comment that the flour ended up being "fully fermented" (ἐζυμώθη ὅλον). In fact, these two words conclude the parable.[263] According to Dodd, on the level of Q, "the emphasis must lie upon the completion of the process of fermentation."[264] And as any peasant would have told you, "the completion of the process of fermentation" translates into bread.[265] I cannot imagine any ancient listener hearing this parable and not thinking about bread.

The introduction of leaven turns the massive amount of flour into a staple food.[266] Similarly, when the kingdom of God is introduced, it produces plenty

---

[256] Robinson 1998c, 20.

[257] Cf. Q 6:29–32, 34, 46–49; 10:5–9, 16; 11:4, [5–8], 9–12; 11:33; 12:31, 42–44, 58–59; 14:16–21, 23; 16:13; 19:12–13, 15–24.

[258] See Howes 2019b:6–11; cf. Kloppenborg 1995, 308, 311; Bazzana 2015, 263–313, esp. 277–279; cf. Q 6:20–21, 35, 36; 10:9; 11:2–3, 13; 12:6–7, 22–31.

[259] See Levine 2014, 133–134; cf. e.g. Ryle 1921, 206; Jeremias 1972, 147; Ford 2016, 58–59; Roth 2018, 319; cf. Judg 6:19; 1 Sam 1:24. For the view that Genesis 18 should not be regarded as an intertext for the parable of the leaven, see Snodgrass 2008, 234.

[260] Hunt 2012, 88; cf. also Nolland 2005, 554; Ford 2016, 59.

[261] Cf. Davies and Allison 1991, 423.

[262] Cf. Roth 2018, 317.

[263] Hunter 1971, 44; Fleddermann 2005a, 672.

[264] Dodd 1961, 143.

[265] Cf. Etchells 1998, 62–63; Robinson 1998c, 20; Scott 2001, 25; Valantasis 2005, 179.

[266] Jacobson 1992, 205.

of food.[267] Choosing specifically the ingredients for making bread as the metaphor is no coincidence.[268] Schottroff is therefore absolutely correct when she says about the parable of the leaven: "A dualistic parable theory that interprets this image 'from the kitchen' as purely illustrative of something completely different does not do justice to the materiality of our experiences with bread."[269] If the idea that God's kingdom will (inevitably) spread throughout the ancient world is present, the specific nature of the metaphor draws attention to the ability of the kingdom to create food for people throughout the world. Liebenberg comments: "The end result is that the dough acquires the most distinctive trait of the leaven – it becomes *leavened*, all of it."[270] In the same way, the world – probably all of it – acquires the most distinctive trait of the kingdom according to Q, which is that it provides for people, especially by feeding them. However, the latter accent is at most only implied, requiring one to regard the flour or dough somewhat allegorically as the world. Instead, the main focus is plainly on the function of the kingdom to produce a lot of food for a lot of people. Like the parable of the mustard seed, it is worth pointing out that the interpretation proposed here would remain valid even if the parable of the leaven did not allude to any Old Testament text, and even if we are mistaken in viewing "three measures" as a large quantity.[271] Intrinsically and essentially, the parable is about a process that ends in bread, the most important staple food in antiquity.[272] Since the festive occasion implied by the parable would typically take place in someone's house,[273] the baking metaphor might also imply lodging. In the Sayings Gospel Q, gaining entry into someone's house is regarded as an important way of procuring sustenance.[274] This suggestion is strengthened by the intertextual link to Genesis 18, which depicts the most famous example in Jewish antiquity of hospitality in action. Yet this facet is at most only implied, since the parable is primarily and explicitly about food. Although the two parables in Q 13:18–21 emphasise two different aspects of divine providence in God's kingdom (i.e. accommodation and food, respectively), both aspects are present in both parables – what is expressly stated by the one is implied by the other. The subsequent material in the final form of Q (i.e. Q 13:24–29) makes this association between food and lodging explicit. As Levine rightly notes, the

---

[267] Cf. Ford 2016, 64–65.

[268] Cf. Robinson 1998c, 20.

[269] Schottroff 2006, 207.

[270] Liebenberg 2001, 341, emphasis original; cf. Etchells 1998, 63; Fleddermann 2005a, 672.

[271] Cf. Snodgrass 2008, 231–232, 234.

[272] Cf. Robinson 1998c, 20; Schottroff 2006, 205–206.

[273] Park 2019, 53.

[274] Cf. Q 10:5–9; 11:9–10; 13:25–26; 14:16–21, 23; see Howes 2019b, 4–11.

parables of the mustard seed and leaven "are both about the necessities of life: bread and shelter."[275]

On the level of Q, the main point of the parable of the mustard seed is that God's kingdom provides shelter to everyone, and the main point of the parable of the leaven is that God's kingdom provides more than enough food for everyone. These parables might hint at the inclusivity of God's kingdom to "everyone" with the image of the "world tree," as well as the use of a man and a woman as main characters to form one of Q's famous gender-pairs.[276] These parables might further hint at the unassuming and unusual (but not impure) nature of God's kingdom when compared to other kingdoms, or its humble, clandestine beginnings, rapid growth, and anticipated magnitude, but these features are not what the parables are ultimately about. Like the rest of Q, these parables associate the kingdom of God with bare necessities like food and shelter – maybe even healing. Surprisingly, these necessities are made available not through an impressive Roman or Jewish empire, but through an obscure and unassuming social movement, called the "kingdom of God" by its (mostly) lower-class proponents.[277] But still, this is incidental to the main point that the kingdom of God will house and feed its members. To my mind, this line of interpretation brings us very close to the message and intent of the historical Jesus.

6.5 Findings

The interpretation of the parables proposed here goes a long way towards explaining the logic behind the specific placement of Q 13:18–21 in the Sayings

---

[275] Levine 2014, 174. In relation to Levine's critique in an earlier footnote that readings focusing on growth or contrast are banal, some might want to argue that the reading proposed here is no less banal. Firstly, having something to eat would not have been a trivial matter for the first audience(s) of this parable. It would certainly have been more important to them than the abstract idea that God's kingdom grows or that it starts out small and ends up big. Anyone who regards the current proposal as dull or trivial does not know what it is like to worry about lodging and food on a daily basis – year in, year out. Secondly, given the exploitative nature of concurrent earthly empires, promoting a kingdom that existed primarily or exclusively to benefit the small peasantry and poor by feeding and housing them would have been not only novel and surprising, but also subversive.

[276] See e.g. Batten 1994, 47–49; Park 2019, 47–48, 51–54; cf. Peters 2016, 41.

[277] Cf. Hunter 1964, 43–44; Carlston 1975, 161; Donahue 1988, 37; Scott 1989, 387; Jacobson 1992, 204; Vaage 1994, 63; Tuckett 1996, 128; Allison 2000, 137; Heil 2001, 656; Fleddermann 2005a, 670; Valantasis 2005, 178; Snodgrass 2008, 221, 222, 225, 235; Van Eck 2016, 78, 82–83.

Gospel, which a number of scholars have otherwise found peculiar.[278] A number of texts in the immediate literary context of Q 13:18–21 in the formative stratum explicitly discuss food and accommodation.[279] Interpreters often miss concrete links and motifs like these, tending to over-theologise and abstractify texts. When one focuses narrowly on the religious aspects of a text, one loses sight of its economic and political dimensions.[280] The thematic overlap between Q 13:18–21 and its immediate literary context in the formative stratum is therefore extensive and involves specifically food and shelter as the means to physical survival. A thoroughgoing thematic analysis is not necessary to appreciate this thematic overlap. That takes care of the criterion of characteristic motifs. When it comes to the criterion of characteristic forms, identifying Q 13:18–19, 20–21 as two parables of Jesus suffices to indicate that these traditions should be regarded as sapiential logia. Their sapiential essence is particularly noticeable in their appeal to nature and daily life, as well as their intent to stimulate intellectual reflection. Although the parables draw on both sapiential *and* prophetic traditions in the Hebrew Bible, the images are used in Q 13:18–21 to depict God's kingdom as a present reality that provides for people's material needs in this life. As God's kingdom grows in this world, more and more people benefit from God's providential care. There is no need for an apocalyptic cessation of the current world to establish God's kingdom. As far as the criterion of implied audience is concerned, the parables of the mustard and leaven are not on any level intended to threaten or ostracise outsiders. Instead, these parables describe God's kingdom for consideration by insiders, but do so by imagining everyone sharing in God's bounty. It is no coincidence that Q 13:18–19 draws on traditional Jewish imagery that are inclusive of gentiles. The two parables in Q 13:18–21 are essentially all-inclusive. Ultimately, the focus of Q 13:18–21 on food and shelter as attributes of God's kingdom situates it squarely within the formative stratum.

---

[278] E.g. Schürmann 1982, 161; Kloppenborg 1987, 92; 1995, 308–311; Sato 1994, 173; Vaage 1994, 119–120; Liebenberg 2001, 317. For the opposite opinion that Q 13:18–21 fits well in its literary Q context, see Jacobson 1992, 204; Kirk 1998, 303–304; Horsley 1999, 87–88 incl. n. 92; Fleddermann 2005a, 673. Kirk (1998, 303–304), for example, finds the connection of Q 13:18–21 with its literary surroundings in the small/few-large/many contrast.

[279] I.e. Q 12:22–31, 39, 42–44; 13:24–25; 14:16–21, 23; cf. Kloppenborg 2000b, 93; Park 2019, 53. I will argue in the next chapter that Q 13:26–27, 28–29 belongs to the main redaction. It is true that Q 13:26–27 also speaks about eating (ἐσθίω) and drinking (πίνω), but in this context the point of these images is to recall the communion of Jesus with his followers during his ministry, not to say anything about daily survival (see chapter 7 below; cf. Uro 1996, 109). Likewise, it is true that Q 13:28–29 discusses a banquet (with food) to depict the eschatological kingdom of God, but the intent here is to promote exclusion of the out-group, not material survival through inclusion as in Q 14:16–21, 23 (see chapters 7 and 8 below).

[280] Cf. Oakman 2008, 117.

Chapter 7

Q 13:24–27, "I Do Not Know You!"[1]

²⁴εἰσέλθατε διὰ τῆς στενῆς θύρας, ὅτι πολλοί ζητήσουσιν εἰσελθεῖν καὶ ὀλίγοι ⟦εἰσὶν οἱ <εἰσερχόμενοι δι'> αὐτῆ<ς>⟧. ²⁵ἀφ' οὗ ἂν ⟦ἐγερθῇ⟧ ὁ ⟦οἰκοδεσπότης⟧ καὶ κλείς⟦ῃ τ⟧ὴ⟦ν⟧ θύρα⟦ν καὶ ἄρξησθε ἔξω ἑστάναι καὶ κρούειν τὴν θύραν⟧ λέγοντες· κύριε, ἄνοιξον ἡμῖν, καὶ ἀποκριθεὶς ἐρεῖ ὑμῖν· οὐκ οἶδα ὑμᾶς, ²⁶τότε ἄρξεσθε λέγειν· ἐφάγομεν ἐνώπιόν σου καὶ ἐπίομεν καὶ ἐν ταῖς πλατείαις ἡμῶν ἐδίδαξας· ²⁷καὶ ἐρεῖ λέγων ὑμῖν· οὐκ οἶδα ὑμᾶς· ἀπόστητε ἀπ' ἐμοῦ ⟦οἱ⟧ ἐργαζόμενοι τὴν ἀνομίαν.

²⁴Enter through the narrow door, for many will seek to enter and few ⟦are those who <enter through> it.⟧ ²⁵When the ⟦householder has arisen⟧ and locked the door, ⟦and you begin to stand outside and knock on the door⟧, saying: Master, open for us, and he will answer you: I do not know you, ²⁶then you will begin saying: We ate in your presence and drank, and it was in our streets you taught. ²⁷And he will say to you: I do not know you! Get away from me, ⟦«you» who⟧ do lawlessness!

Although the reconstruction of Q 13:25–27 faces a number of difficulties, there is enough verbal and conceptual overlap between Luke 13:25–27 and Matthew 7:22–23; 25:10–12 to justify its place in the Sayings Gospel Q.[2] Kloppenborg ascribes Q 13:25–27 in its entirety to the main redaction.[3] As an alternative, it will presently be argued that verses 25 belongs to the formative stratum, while verses 26–27 belong to the main redaction.

7.1 Kloppenborg's Analysis

Kloppenborg is doubtful about the original presence of verse 25 in Q's version of this passage. At times during his discussion, he features verse 25 between brackets to indicate his uncertainty, but for the most part he features only verses 26–27. In a footnote, Kloppenborg explains that although Luke 13:25 and Matthew 25:10–12 probably drew on the same source, it is all but certain that this source text featured in the Sayings Gospel as an introduction to Q 13:26–27.[4]

---

[1] An earlier version of this chapter was published as an article in *Journal of Theological Studies* 67/2 (see Howes 2016c).

[2] Marshall 1978, 563; Davies and Allison 1988, 714; 1997, 393; Luz 2005, 228.

[3] Kloppenborg 1987, 234–237.

[4] Kloppenborg 1987, 224 n. 217.

In fact, Kloppenborg suggests that Matthew 7:22a provides a better introduction to verses 26–27. He clearly believes that the Third Evangelist relocated verse 25 from elsewhere in Q (or the wider Jesus tradition[5]) to its subsequent position in the Gospel of Luke between verses 24 and 26.[6]

Kloppenborg regards verse 24 as a wisdom saying.[7] He follows Zeller in claiming that Q 13:24 is comparable to the sapiential logic and logia of Proverbs 1–4. As in the rest of the formative stratum, this logion calls for devotion to the radical expectations of discipleship.[8] To show that Q 13:24 and Q 13:[25], 26–30 were originally two separate units, Kloppenborg draws attention to the abrupt shift from a narrow door in verse 24 to a locked door in verse 25.[9] He also points out that the focus shifts from the "few" (ὀλίγοι) in verse 24 to the "many" (πολλοί) in verse 29.[10] According to him, the two units were superficially combined by means of both catchword connection, with the words "many" (πολλοί) and "door" (θύρα)[11] featuring in both units, and "the common motif of successful and unsuccessful attempts to enter (the kingdom)." Kloppenborg further holds that both Q 13:[25], 26–27 and Q 13:28–30 are prophetic in form and theme, being "prophetic pronouncements" that turn away from the topic of discipleship to speak about "judgment and exclusion from the kingdom."[12] Within the Sayings Gospel, Q 13:[25], 26–27 functions as a prophetic threat against those who would not respond to the preaching of early Christians,[13] even including some of the Q people. This threat is semantically very similar to other sayings in the main redaction. The threat of eschatological denial encapsulated by the phrase "I do not know you!" (οὐκ οἶδα ὑμᾶς) in Q

---

[5] Kloppenborg fails to mention whether the source common to Luke 13:25 and Matthew 25:10–12 was Q or not. His larger discussion certainly suggests that he viewed it as part of Q. Most scholars agree that Luke 13:25 and Matthew 25:10–12 draw upon Q as a common source (Fleddermann 2005a, 680).

[6] Cf. e.g. Mussner 1967, 117, 120, 121.

[7] Kloppenborg 1987, 234–235.

[8] Cf. Davies and Allison 1988, 696.

[9] Kloppenborg 1987, 235; cf. Bultmann 1963, 130; Marshall 1978, 565; Funk and Hoover 1993, 347.

[10] Cf. Crossan 1983, 144.

[11] Kloppenborg (1987, 223–224, 235) accounts for the possibility that Q featured the "road" (ὁδός) and "city gate" (πύλη) of Matthew 7:13–14 and not the "door" (θύρα) of Luke 13:24, as well as the possibility that both evangelists altered the original wording of Q (cf. Marshall 1978, 563; Betz 1995, 524; Bovon 2001, 288; Luz 2007, 370–371). These options introduce the possibility that the word "door" (θύρα) did not feature in Q 13:24 and could therefore not have functioned as a catchword connection between Q 13:24 and Q 13:25–27. Nonetheless, the *Critical Edition of Q* is in all probability correct in preferring Luke's "door" (θύρα) for Q 13:24 (see Jacobson 1992, 206–207; Tuckett 1996, 189–190; Fleddermann 2005a, 677–679; cf. Funk and Hoover 1993, 156, 347).

[12] Kloppenborg 1987, 235–237.

[13] "Christians" is Kloppenborg's term.

13:[25], 27 overlaps extensively with Q 12:9. Also, the veiled application of the threat to Galilean settlements in Q 13:26 with the phrase "you taught in our streets" (ἐν ταῖς πλατείαις ἡμῶν ἐδίδαξας) overlaps extensively with Q 10:13–15. Kloppenborg further relates Q 13:[25], 26–27 to the mission discourse, that is, Q 10:4–10, 16. Although the latter text belongs to the formative stratum, Q 13:[25], 26–27 presumably perceives the efforts and subsequent failure of the Q preachers from a temporal distance. Finally, Kloppenborg points to an overlap with the pronouncements of condemnation that fall upon those who reject the Q message in Q 3:7–9 and Q 11:31–32.

Kloppenborg's analysis is for the most part convincing. I agree not only that Q 13:24 qualifies formally and thematically as a wisdom saying that belongs to the formative stratum,[14] but also that Q 13:26–27 qualifies at least thematically as a prophetic threat that belongs to the main redaction. The point of contention is with verse 25. Whereas Kloppenborg argues that the Third Evangelist was responsible for relocating this saying to its subsequent position in the Gospel of Luke between verses 24 and 26, I follow the *Critical Edition of Q* in preferring the Lukan position of verse 25 for Q.[15] Kloppenborg's arguments against the Lukan placement of verse 25 for Q draw exclusively on the editorial activity of Luke. The shifts from a narrow door in verse 24 to a locked door in verse 25 and from "the exclusion of latecomers" in verse 25 to "the rejection of evildoers" in verses 26–27 suggest to him that verse 25 represents a redactional interpolation, presumably by Luke. Yet the former shift would be entirely explicable if these were two individual logia, merely placed one after the other on account of the catchword "door" (θύρα).[16] Equally, the latter shift could be explicable as a redactional addition on the level of Q itself. Kloppenborg further estimates that the comprehensive usage of second person plural verbs could be Lukan.[17] As Jacobson correctly notes, however, the very difficulty of Luke's second person verbs testifies to their probable origination in Q.[18] Even if Luke's second person verbs were a result of his editing, such editorial activity would not qualify as an argument against either the Lukan placement of verse 25 in his source or the presence of this logion in Q. Finally, he points out that the whole passage in Luke 13:22–30 is structured around the

---

[14] Even if it might or might not develop the theme of discipleship.

[15] At times it seems that Kloppenborg also acknowledges the likelihood that Q 13:25 stood in its Lukan position in Q. We have already seen that he occasionally features verse 25 in brackets when discussing Q 13:25–30. Perhaps more significant is Kloppenborg's (1987a, 235) argument that a shift in *Bildlogik* takes place after Q 13:24, where he not only considers as part of his argument the reference to a locked door in verse 25, but also refers explicitly to Q "13:25–30." In references to this text appearing after 1987, Kloppenborg explicitly adds Q "13:25–27" to his lists of Q² material (e.g. Kloppenborg 1988, 5 n. 1).

[16] Cf. Funk and Hoover 1993, 347; Bovon 2001, 288.

[17] Cf. Bovon 2001, 286.

[18] Jacobson 1992, 207.

metaphor of a festive meal. Since only the introduction of this passage in Luke 13:22–23 does not derive from Q,[19] the same claim could (and should) be made on the level of Q.[20] To Kloppenborg's arguments could be added the fact that Q 13:25 is the only text that interrupts the common order between Matthew and Luke in the larger complex of logia in Q 13:24, 25, 26–27, 28–29, [30,] 34–35[21].[22] Yet there is no reason why Matthew could not have been responsible for relocating Q 13:25 to the end of his parable of the ten virgins, especially considering Matthew's general tendency to displace Q logia.[23] Matthew did, after all, separate all the sayings that make up this complex,[24] reapplying them to different contexts within his Gospel.[25]

There are a number of positive reasons for accepting Luke's position of Q 13:25. The mentioning of a "householder" (οἰκοδεσπότης) links the tradition in Q 13:25–27 with the parable in Q 14:16–21, 23.[26] This might have been a deliberate attempt at linking these two parables through catchword connection. Conversely, if Luke were responsible for adding Q 13:25 to its current Lukan position, he could not have done so for the same reason, since the two units are separated by a lot of material in Luke's narrative sequence. This renders quite inexplicable Luke's motivation for adding Q 13:25 between Luke 13:24 and Luke 13:26–27. Also, when considering the complex of sayings in Q 13:24–30 as a whole, the structural harmony of the passage supports its unity in Q.[27] At any rate, if the overlap in vocabulary, syntax, and content between Matthew 25:10–12 and Luke 13:25 are sufficient to postulate their origination in Q, as is generally agreed,[28] then Luke provides the only Synoptic clue for its place in Q, since its Matthean position is obviously secondary.[29] Finally, Luke's propensity to treat Q 13:25–29 as a single unit suggests that he already had access to it as a unified text in his source, even if, and precisely because, internal connections between the constitutive sayings are fairly artificial.[30] We may

---

[19] Jacobson 1992, 206; Bovon 2001, 287; see Fleddermann 2005a, 676–677.

[20] Cf. Jacobson 1992, 208; Fleddermann 2005a, 679.

[21] That is, Matt 7:13–14 // Luke 13:24; Matt 25:10–12 // Luke 13:25; Matt 7:22–23 // Luke 13:26–27; Matt 8:11–12 // Luke 13:28–29; [Matt 20:16 // Luke 13:30].

[22] Piper 1989, 108; cf. Kirk 1998, 241; Fleddermann 2005a, 694.

[23] Tuckett 1996, 192; Davies and Allison 1997, 392; cf. Via 1967, 123.

[24] Except possibly for Q 13:34–35, which Luke might have relocated (see below).

[25] Jacobson 1992, 208; Tuckett 1996, 189; Bovon 2001, 287; cf. Funk and Hoover 1993, 160, 225.

[26] Kirk 1998, 247 n. 357.

[27] See Fleddermann 2005a, 694–695; *pace* Hoffmann 1967, 188–214; Mussner 1967, 113–124.

[28] Fleddermann 2005a, 680.

[29] Via 1967, 123; Donahue 1988, 104.

[30] Davies and Allison 1991, 26; Jacobson 1992, 208; cf. Marshall 1978, 564.

therefore conclude that Matthew and Luke had access to a unified pericope in Q, which included verse 25 in its Lukan position.[31]

Once it is accepted that Luke's position of verse 25 represents Q, it needs to be determined whether this logion belongs to the formative stratum or the main redaction. Even if between brackets, Kloppenborg features verse 25 when discussing verses 26–27 and not when discussing verse 24, suggesting that he would have added verse 25 to the main redaction if he had accepted its Lukan position in Q.[32] This is confirmed by his discussion of the shift in *Bildlogik* between Q 13:24 and the rest of the passage, since the content of verse 25 forms for Kloppenborg an integral part of this shift.[33] It is further confirmed by references to this text in subsequent publications, where he explicitly includes Q "13:25–27" to his list of Q^2 material.[34]

Kloppenborg is certainly correct that verses 24 and 25 were originally separate, but this inference does not necessarily support his stratigraphy. The two texts could just as easily have been combined during Q's complex prehistory,[35] or they could have been placed one after the other by those responsible for the final structure of the formative stratum. The practice of placing contradictory logia side-by-side was common and often intentional in ancient wisdom.[36] Moreover, despite the near certainty that Q 13:24 and Q 13:25 were originally separate, they do not necessarily contradict each other.[37] A narrow door can easily be locked. In fact, if the narrow door remained open indefinitely, it would contradict the claim in verse 24 that only a few would enter through it. This claim is made not because some of these individuals are overweight, but probably because entry is restricted by the householder.[38] Verse 25 confirms this interpretation by admitting that the householder has a tendency to lock the door.[39] According to Kirk, the shift from a narrow door to a closed door represents "a clever development" in the overall narrative sequence.[40]

---

[31] Cf. Tuckett 1996, 189, 193.

[32] Kloppenborg 1987, 224–225, 235–236.

[33] Kloppenborg 1987, 235.

[34] E.g. Kloppenborg 1988, 5 n. 1.

[35] Cf. Tuckett 1996, 71.

[36] Cf. Kloppenborg 1996a, 28; Kirk 1998, 211, 346; Piper 2000, 248; Allison 2010, 90; Meier 2011, 321.

[37] Marshall 1978, 565; cf. Bock 1996, 1235, 1236; Tuckett 1996, 145; Fleddermann 2005a, 695.

[38] Valantasis 2005, 181; cf. Tuckett 1996, 192.

[39] Jeremias 1963, 96; cf. Tuckett 1996, 145, 191, 192.

[40] Kirk 1998, 247 n. 357, 249; cf. Jacobson 1992, 207.

7.2 An Alternative Proposal

I propose that verses 24 and 25 featured in the formative stratum as two individual logia and that the main redactor added verses 26–27 after verse 25 as a secondary interpretation, altering its meaning in the process. This is in many respects the direct opposite of Kirk's suggestion that "13:25 may be a redactional creation of the Q-editor which does triple duty: connecting 13:26–27 with 13:24, preparing for the banquet-hall imagery of 13:28–29, and establishing a cross-cluster connection with the other banquet parable in 14:16–24."[41] Even so, Kirk and I do share the impression that Q 13:25 and Q 13:26–27 were combined secondarily. Bovon tables a very similar proposal to mine, but attributes the combination of verse 25 with verses 26–27 to Lukan redaction, as opposed to Q redaction.[42] The same is true of Funk and Hoover, who claim that "Luke has linked the closed door saying [Q 13:25] with the non-recognition sayings [Q 13:26–27] that occur in Matthew in a different context (Mat. 7:22–23)."[43] Tuckett claims that verses 26–27 cannot have been a later addition at all, since the identity of the addressees and the reason for their exclusion are for the first time revealed in these subsequent verses, not having been specified in verse 25.[44] Tuckett's logic is flawed here. In the development of the Jesus tradition, additions were made precisely to clarify, alter, and dictate the respective interpretations of otherwise obscure, ambiguous, and open-ended material.[45] The very fact that verses 26–27 elucidate an aspect of verse 25, thereby directing and controlling its meaning, qualifies as evidence of expansion.

My proposal is substantiated by a number of textual features. The exclamation "I do not know you!" (οὐκ οἶδα ὑμᾶς) at the end of verse 25 is an appropriate conclusion and entirely sufficient to communicate the point of the saying.[46] Even on the face of it, verses 26–27 appear to be an elaboration of the concluding exclamation in verse 25. Although Fleddermann intends it as a synchronic observation, he agrees that a "brief initial dialogue" is enlarged by a "more expanded second dialogue" or "fuller exchange."[47]

A compelling piece of evidence supporting the original independence of verse 25 is the conspicuous use of the second person plural. Valantasis might be correct that the narrator of Q 13:25–27 "observes the action from a distance,"[48] but the utilisation of the second person plural inappropriately shatters

---

[41] Kirk 1998, 247–248 n. 357.
[42] Bovon 2001, 288–289.
[43] Funk and Hoover 1993, 348.
[44] Tuckett 1996, 192.
[45] Funk 2006, 30.
[46] Vaage 2001, 487.
[47] Fleddermann 2005a, 680, 682, 697; cf. Bovon 2001, 286.
[48] Valantasis 2005, 181.

the facade of distance and separation between the characters of the story and the audience listening to the story.[49] On the one hand, it is customary for the parables of Jesus to remain within the constructed narrative world for the duration of the narrative itself, which is why characters within that world are typically referenced in the third person, as separate from the audience listening to the parable. On the other hand, it is normal for individual logia to address an audience directly in the second person. Both the presence of the second person plural and the failure to identify the narrative characters behind the second person plural strongly suggest that Q 13:25–27 was turned into a parable when the individual saying of verse 25 was elaborated by the addition of verses 26–27.[50]

Another weighty indication that verses 26–27 were secondarily added to verse 25 is the clumsiness of the syntax in Q 13:25–26. A number of commentators and translators have struggled with this difficulty.[51] A popular solution has been to regard the last clause of verse 25[52] as the apodosis and conclusion of the sentence, so that the adverb "then" (τότε) at the beginning of verse 26 introduces a new sentence.[53] Even the Nestle-Aland has followed suit, placing a full stop at the end of verse 25. Yet the combination of τότε in verse 26 and καὶ in the final clause of verse 25 indicates that verse 26 should be taken as the apodosis of a longwinded sentence.[54] Marshall is probably correct that the clumsiness is not attributable to Luke, but to his source.[55] This corroborates the International Q Project's decision to feature Luke's troublesome syntax in the *Critical Edition of Q.* Even so, these syntactical difficulties suggest not only that verse 25 used to be an independent sentence, with its final clause featuring as the apodosis, but also that this sentence was elaborated by the addition of verse 26, at which time the final clause of verse 25 was turned into a protasis (probably by replacing an original τότε with καὶ) and verse 26 was turned into the apodosis of this newly-created sentence. If the *Critical Edition of Q* is correct that the clumsy sentence was already a feature of Q in its final form, then the development sketched above must have happened at some earlier stage, probably at the occasion of Q's main redaction.

If Q 13:25 were indeed an independent logion at an earlier stage, how should we interpret it? The fact that the householder is addressed as "master" (κύριε) indicates that the people knocking on his door are inferiors, most likely slaves, day-labourers, or household staff.[56] Taken on its own, Q 13:25 claims that if a

---

[49] Bovon 2001, 286; cf. Jacobson 1992, 207.

[50] Cf. Jeremias 1963, 95–96.

[51] Bock 1996, 1241; e.g. Jacobson 1992, 207.

[52] That is, "and he will answer you: I do not know you!" (καὶ ἀποκριθεὶς ἐρεῖ ὑμῖν· οὐκ οἶδα ὑμᾶς πόθεν ἐστέ).

[53] E.g. Marshall 1978, 565–566.

[54] Cf. Bock 1996, 1241.

[55] Marshall 1978, 566; cf. Jacobson 1992, 207.

[56] Cf. Herzog 1994, 157.

worker arrives at his master's house after the door has been locked, that worker will not be allowed inside. Would this have been a truism for a first-century Jewish audience? Or, would the master's reply have been somewhat shocking and unexpected? I suspect that the former is closer to the truth,[57] since ancient masters were notoriously callous.[58] Harsh treatment was not only directed at slaves, but often also at non-servile workers.[59] As a truism, the saying would have been well-suited to substantiate the preceding logion. Hence, the catch-word "door" (θύρα) might not have been the only factor that motivated the attachment of these two sayings. Taken together, the two sayings instruct its audience to enter or face the possibility of being locked out.[60] The fact that Q 13:24 references a "narrow" (στενός) door in particular should not necessarily be taken to indicate that it is being favoured over a wider alternative, as Matthew (7:13–14) has it. In Q, as in Luke (13:24), there is no mention of either a wide door or a choice between two doors. The narrow door might be all that is available, and the audience is encouraged to enter through it or risk being locked out. Admittedly, describing the door as "narrow" does complicate the imagery somewhat, damaging the overall argument,[61] but such imprecise logic is exactly what one would expect from the attachment of two previously independent logia.[62]

Whether or not the reading proposed above is on target, verse 25 is concerned with the uncomplicated topic of the master-worker relationship. There are no signs in the saying itself to indicate or even suggest that it requires to be read non-literally. Nor are there any signs to suggest that the master is a veiled reference to Jesus.[63] It is only after the introduction of verses 26–27 that the saying is turned into a Christological parable of sorts.[64] Bock unintentionally reinforces the latter with his commentary on verse 26: "It is significant that Jesus' identity as the householder is made clear by their appeal."[65] What is more, it is only after the introduction of verses 26–27 that the saying is turned into a parable about the eschatological end.[66] Tuckett inadvertently supports the previous claim when he states that "the continuation [after Q 13:25] makes it clear that the eschatological future is in mind [at Q 13:25]."[67] The statement

---

[57] Cf. Thurén 2014, 311.

[58] See Bradley 1984, 18, 121–123, 137, 140–141; Yavetz 1988, 158–159; Hezser 2005, 58, 94, 97; Joshel 2010, 40, 122–123, 152.

[59] Cf. White 1970, 348, 360; Joshel 2010, 174.

[60] See Tuckett 1996, 191–192.

[61] Tuckett 1996, 192.

[62] *Pace* Tuckett 1996, 192.

[63] Cf. Dormeyer 2014, 192.

[64] Cf. Jeremias 1963, 95–96; Uro 1996, 118.

[65] Bock 1996, 1236.

[66] Cf. Crossan 1979, 34; Etchells 1998, 172.

[67] Tuckett 1996, 192.

"we ate and drank in your presence" (ἐφάγομεν ἐνώπιόν σου καὶ ἐπίομεν) might still be consistent with the literal imagery of verse 25, but the statement "it was in our streets you taught" (ἐν ταῖς πλατείαις ἡμῶν ἐδίδαξας) transgresses beyond that imagery.[68] No longer is verse 25 to be understood as a corporeal saying about the relationship between masters and their workers, but it is now to be applied unfittingly to the context of public instruction. The imagery changes without warning from the private sphere of an individual's house to the public sphere of communal streets. The activity changes without precedence from knocking on a master's house to teaching in the streets. Funk and Hoover agree that Q 13:25 fits awkwardly in its literary context before Q 13:26–27.[69] The changes in narrative background and activity represent a superficial attempt to redirect the meaning of verse 25. There should be little doubt that the intent was to associate the householder with Jesus.[70] The phrase "it was in our streets you taught" clearly recalls Jesus as a public teacher.[71] As a result, the imagery of Q 13:25 is turned into an allegorical parable.[72] The master becomes Jesus, and the excluded workers become either polemical outsiders or certain members of the Q people, depending on one's interpretation.[73]

The clear intent behind the introduction of the phrase "it was in our streets you taught" suggests that a similar intent lay behind the introduction of the phrase "we ate and drank in your presence," even if the latter phrase is to some extent consistent with the literal imagery of verse 25. Firstly, table-fellowship was one of the most identifiable features of the public ministry of Jesus.[74] That the Q people were aware of this is indicated most clearly by Q 7:34, where Jesus is accused of being a glutton and a drunkard, while associating with tax collectors and sinners. Secondly, it seems unlikely that a master would have eaten with his workers, especially the callous and pitiless type of master described in verse 25. Conversely, Jesus was known for extending his table-fellowship to include all kinds of "undesirables." If the images of someone who teaches in public and eats with social inferiors are combined, the obvious result is a depiction of Jesus during his earthly ministry.[75]

---

[68] Cf. Etchells 1998, 172.

[69] Funk and Hoover 1993, 348.

[70] Cf. Jacobson 1992, 207–208; Kirk 1998, 247–248.

[71] Bock 1996, 1237.

[72] Cf. Kloppenborg 1995, 282, 289–290, 317, 319; Bovon 2001, 291.

[73] Cf. Robinson 1991, 189; 1994a, 318; Jacobson 1992, 207–208; Hoffmann 2001, 275 n. 59.

[74] See e.g. Borg 1998, 88–134.

[75] Bock 1996, 1237; cf. Uro 1996, 94.

Instead of the dialogue in Luke 13:26, Fleddermann argues that the dialogue in Matthew 7:22[76] represents Q.[77] If this is correct, it would strengthen the current case that Q 13:26–27 represents a redactional addition, since the claims in Matthew 7:22 are even more disconnected from the imagery in Q 13:25 and even more obvious as references to the ministry of Jesus and his followers.[78] For the following reasons, however, the reconstruction in the *Critical Edition of Q* is preferable in this case: (1) Matthew's version is much more clearly connected to his community situation than Luke's version is to the situation of *his* community; (2) Matthew's version describes behaviour typical of the early church; (3) Christological elaboration is decidedly apparent in Matthew's version, but less so in Luke's version; (4) Luke's version is closely related in theme to Q 10:13–15, whereas Matthew's version has no thematic connection to the rest of Q; and (5) Luke's version seems to be more archaic.[79] It is widely agreed by scholarship that Luke's version of the dialogue in verse 26 represents Q.[80]

Few would disagree that verse 27 is a more forceful repetition of the phrase "I do not know you" in verse 25.[81] As a repetition, it is semantically redundant.[82] Yet its presence is necessitated by the introduction of verse 26. The main redactor correctly intuits that the exchange needs to end with the master's response, since this was the original climax of the saying in verse 25.[83] The main redactor's solution is to repeat the master's response after verse 26, but to add the following words: "Get away from me, you who do lawlessness!" The purpose behind this addition is twofold. Firstly, it elaborates on the master's initial response so as to augment its potency and conceal the fact that it is a repetition.[84] Secondly, it explains the master's harsh response as a reaction to the workers' "lawlessness" (ἀνομία) in particular.[85] Yet this explanation contradicts the content of verse 25, where the workers are denied entry for the simple reason that the door has already been locked.[86] Given that the master

---

[76] ESV: "Lord, Lord, did we not prophesy in your name, and cast out demons in your name, and do many mighty works in your name?" (Nestle-Aland 28: κύριε κύριε, οὐ τῷ σῷ ὀνόματι ἐπροφητεύσαμεν, καὶ τῷ σῷ ὀνόματι δαιμόνια ἐξεβάλομεν, καὶ τῷ σῷ ὀνόματι δυνάμεις πολλὰς ἐποιήσαμεν;).

[77] Fleddermann 2005a, 683–684; cf. Vaage 2001, 487.

[78] Cf. Davies and Allison 1988, 701–702; Bock 1996, 1237; Bovon 2001, 289.

[79] Davies and Allison 1988, 714; Luz 2007, 376; see Catchpole 1993, 41–43; Bovon 2001, 289; cf. Funk and Hoover 1993, 158.

[80] Tuckett 1996, 192; e.g. Crossan 1983, 142.

[81] Bovon 2001, 292; cf. Roth 2014, 383.

[82] Cf. Bock 1996, 1237.

[83] Cf. Bock 1996, 1241.

[84] Cf. Jacobson 1992, 208; Bovon 2001, 286.

[85] Roth 2014, 383; cf. Betz 1995, 544; Tuckett 1996, 193.

[86] Kloppenborg 1987, 224 n. 217; cf. Etchells 1998, 175.

has been turned into an allegory for Jesus, the main redactor judged it necessary to explain the master's unflattering behaviour. By adding this explanation, the main redactor changed the characterisation of the householder from a cold and heartless master to a just and impartial judge.[87] Ultimately, the expansion of Q 13:25 resulted in the creation of an eschatological parable about the final judgment.[88]

The changes made by the main redactor also assisted in linking verse 25 to the redactional material that follows. Q 13:28–29[89] has long been regarded as a redactional addition.[90] The present proposal submits that Q 13:26–27 formed part of the same editorial activity in an attempt to iron out the transition between Q 13:25 and Q 13:28–29.[91] Jacobson also allows for such editorial activity in the following statement: "The addition of 13:28–29 may have been accompanied by alterations in 13:25–27 and its attendant problems."[92] As a result of such redaction, the logion in Q 13:28–29 now functions on the level of Q's final form as a parable application.[93] The workers denied entry are to be associated with those outsiders who will be condemned at the final judgment.[94] Conversely, the workers allowed entry are to be associated with those who will recline with the Jewish patriarchs at the eschatological feast.[95] Depending on how one reads Q 13:28–29, the workers allowed entry are to be understood as either gentiles[96] or diaspora Jews.[97] Similarly, the workers denied entry are to be understood as either Israel *in toto* or the inhabitants and leaders of the geo-

---

[87] Cf. Betz 1995, 552–556; Bock 1996, 1237.

[88] Cf. Crossan 1979, 34; Funk and Hoover 1993, 347–348; Kloppenborg 1995, 289–290, 317, 319; Etchells 1998, 172.

[89] [29][[And many]] shall come from Sunrise and Sunset and recline [28]with Abraham and Isaac and Jacob in the kingdom of God, but [[you will be]] thrown out [[into the]] out[[er darkness]], where there will be wailing and grinding of teeth ([29][[καὶ πολλοὶ]] ἀπὸ ἀνατολῶν καὶ δυσμῶν ἥξουσιν καὶ ἀνακλιθήσονται [28]μετὰ Ἀβραὰμ καὶ Ἰσαὰκ καὶ Ἰακὼβ ἐν τῇ βασιλείᾳ τοῦ θεοῦ, [[ὑμ<εῖ>ς]] δὲ ἐκβλ[[ηθής<εσθε>]] εἰς τὸ σκότος τὸ]] ἐξώ[[τερον]]· ἐκεῖ ἔσται ὁ κλαυθμὸς καὶ ὁ βρυγμὸς τῶν ὀδόντων).

[90] E.g. Jacobson 1992, 208; cf. Tuckett 1996, 194; Etchells 1998, 172.

[91] Cf. Etchells 1998, 172.

[92] Jacobson 1992, 208.

[93] Cf. Etchells 1998, 172.

[94] Piper 1989, 108; cf. Tuckett 1996, 193; Hoffmann 2001, 283; Zeller 2001, 353.

[95] Kirk 1998, 248–249.

[96] *À la* Jeremias 1963, 96; Marshall 1978, 568; Tuckett 1996, 194, 197, 394, 396, 400; Etchells 1998, 173; Kloppenborg 2000a, 192–193; 2001, 168; Arnal 2001, 177; Luz 2001, 9, 11; Robinson 2001a, 8; 2001b, 38–39; Fleddermann 2005a, 698–699; Smith 2006, 148; Bork 2014, 8, 9.

[97] *À la* Davies and Allison 1991, 27–28; Horsley 1995a, 38; 1999, 65, 69, 94–95, 97, 229, 242, 283; Allison 1997, 176–191; 2000, 166–169; Verheyden 2001, 702. Valantasis (2005, 184) makes room at the banquet for *both* gentiles *and* Jews (cf. Bock 1996, 1232–1233, 1239; Nolland 2005, 357).

political centre.[98] The content of Q 13:34–35 would suggest the latter under-standing in each case.[99] Interestingly, the reference to "our streets" (ταῖς πλατείαις ἡμῶν) in Q 13:26 links to the woes against Jerusalem in Q 13:34–35. This association remains valid even if the phrase also references the Galilean towns of Q 10:13–15.[100]

There is, of course, the genuine possibility that Q 13:34–35 appeared in its Matthean (23:34–39) context in the Sayings Gospel, that is, after Q 11:49–51.[101] The latter is supported not only by the presence of the catchword "house" (οἶκος) in both Q 11:51 and Q 13:35, but also by the presence of the deuteron-omistic theme in both texts.[102] If the Matthean context of Q 13:34–35 is ac-cepted, it would mean that both the reference to Galilean towns in Q 10:13–15 and the reference to Jerusalem in Q 13:34–35 preceded Q 13:24–27 in the over-all sequence of Q. Hence, both the Matthean and the Lukan positions of Q 13:34–35 support an association between "our streets" and Jerusalem, probably in addition to the Galilean towns of Q 10:13–15. The Lukan position does so by mentioning Jerusalem within the same pericopal complex of logia.[103] The Matthean position does so by mentioning Jerusalem before Q 13:25–27 (and after Q 10:13–15) in the overall sequence of Q. The strong thematic and struc-tural linkage between Q 10:13–15 and Q 13:34–35 supports the likelihood that the phrase "our streets" in Q 13:26 references both of these texts.[104] The link-age between "our streets" and Jerusalem supports not only the claim that the main redactor formulated verse 26 in light of other Q material, but also the claim that Q 13:28–29 understands the distinction to be between diaspora Jews and those Jews at the geo-political centre.[105]

In addition to being a parable application, Q 13:28–29 is turned into the conclusion of a short narrative sequence.[106] The quasi-narrative starts with a narrow door that allows entry (Q 13:24), continues with the door being closed (Q 13:25–27), and concludes with a banquet behind closed doors (Q 13:28–

---

[98] Etchells 1998, 173; cf. Jacobson 1992, 208.

[99] Cf. Jacobson 1992, 212; *pace* Luz 2005, 164.

[100] Cf. Funk and Hoover 1993, 348; Robinson 1998a, 257.

[101] Lührmann 1969, 48; Marshall 1978, 502, 573; Neirynck 1982, 66; 2001, 62, 63; Rob-inson 1988, 121; Allison 2010, 85. For a more detailed discussion of this possibility, see Jacobson 1992, 209–210; Bock 1996, 1243–1244; Tuckett 1996, 173–174; Davies and Alli-son 1997, 312; Robinson 1998a, 225–260; Luz 2005, 158–159; Nolland 2005, 949.

[102] See Robinson 2001b, 36–39; cf. Carlston 1982, 105; Crossan 1983, 138–139; Vaage 2001, 484; Smith 2006, 102.

[103] That is, Q 13:24, 25–27, 28–29, [30,] 34–35.

[104] See Catchpole 1993, 277–278.

[105] See Davies and Allison 1991, 27–29.

[106] Cf. Etchells 1998, 172.

29).[107] Yet three features of Q 13:25 indicate that it did not originally deal with the image of *guests* in particular arriving at a banquet. Firstly, it would have been wholly inappropriate for guests at a banquet to address their host as "master" (κύριε), especially if we consider that ancient people typically invited dinner guests of equal or higher social standing.[108] Secondly, identifying the character who locked the door as a "householder" (οἰκοδεσπότης) is unnatural in the setting of a banquet, since the other guests would presumably also have owned houses. For this type of setting, it would have been much more appropriate to introduce the character as "a certain person" (ἄνθρωπός τις), as in Q 14:16, where the other characters are likewise dinner guests.[109] Thirdly, it would not make sense for the householder to invite guests to a banquet and then turn them away as soon as they arrive. Even if there might be some hint in the story that (a lot of) food lies waiting on the other side of the door,[110] the people whose arrival is narrated and who are denied entry by the householder are not his guests.

One final feature of the main redactor's activity deserves mention. By quoting the Septuagint's version of Psalm 6:9[111] word for word in Q 13:27, the main redactor strengthened the linkage with the subsequent material, since Q 13:29 quotes LXX Psalm 106:3[112] verbatim and Q 13:35 quotes LXX Psalm 117:26[113] verbatim.[114] In fact, the presence in Q 13:26–27 of a direct quotation from the Septuagint is in itself suggestive of redactional activity.[115]

At this point, it seems justified to conclude that the generic saying in verse 25 was secondarily elaborated by the addition of verses 26–27, thereby turning it into a parable about Jesus.[116] In the process, the meaning of verse 25 was

---

[107] Kirk 1998, 249; cf. Jacobson 1992, 207–208. One could start the narrative earlier, with the preparation of a meal before the door is opened (Q 13:20–21); or even earlier still, with the cultivation of ingredients before the meal is prepared (Q 13:18–19).

[108] Cf. Luz 2005, 235; Nolland 2005, 1009.

[109] Cf. Funk 2006, 123. The character is only identified as a "householder" (οἰκοδεσπότης) at Q 14:21, 23, where his relationship to his slave and the homeless is in view.

[110] See below.

[111] Psalm 6:8 in English translations.

[112] Psalm 107:3 in the Masoretic Text and English translations.

[113] Psalm 118:26 in the Masoretic Text and English translations.

[114] See Allison 2000, 163–164, 165–171. It is widely acknowledged by commentators that these Q texts quote the identified Psalms: Marshall 1978, 567, 577; Davies and Allison 1988, 717, 718; 1991, 26; 1997, 322, 323; Jacobson 1992, 211; Funk and Hoover 1993, 349; Betz 1995, 544, 552; Bock 1996, 1250–1251; Tuckett 1996, 175, 193, 204–205, 423; Etchells 1998, 173–174; Horsley 1999, 282; Bovon 2001, 289; Vaage 2001, 484, 486–487; Fleddermann 2005a, 685; Johnson-DeBaufre 2005, 110; Luz 2005, 160, 162–164; 2007, 376, 380; Nolland 2005, 341; Valantasis 2005, 187.

[115] Cf. Jeremias 1963, 31–32; Vaage 2001, 487.

[116] Cf. Uro 1996, 118.

forcefully delimited.[117] Significantly, verse 25 appears on the boundary between a cluster of sayings from the formative stratum (Q 13:18–19, 20–21, 24)
and a cluster of sayings from the main redaction (Q 13:26–27, 28–29, [30,] 34–
35). The proposal that verses 26–27 were secondarily added to verse 25 supports my claim that verse 25 featured in the formative stratum before being
incorporated into the main redaction. The rest of this chapter will defend the
claim that verse 25 belongs to the formative stratum.

7.3 Characteristic Forms

There are no formal indicators of genre in Q 13:25. Even so, four non-formal
features seem to support the identification of this logion as a sapiential micro-
genre. Firstly, the saying is "parabolic" in nature, even if it does not seem to
qualify as a parable when considered in isolation. Secondly, like most sapiential logia, verse 25 deals with an aspect of everyday life. Thirdly, despite the
master's harsh response, the saying is very neutral and matter-of-fact in tone.
Lastly, the saying follows directly after a series of wisdom sayings.[118] These
four features not only support the identification of this logion as a sapiential
small form, but also speak against it being a prophetic small form. In other
words, to the extent that the logion is not straightforward, hyperbolic, threatening, or preceded by prophecy, it fails to qualify as a prophetic micro-genre.
Considered on its own, there is no indication whatsoever that verse 25 deals
with the prophetic, eschatological, or apocalyptic future of Israel.[119] The future-tense verb "will say" (ἐρεῖ), which appears after the pleonastic participle
"answering" (ἀποκριθείς), is probably not used to reference future time, but
rather to indicate that the act of the apodosis, namely the master's reply, happens *after* the acts of the protasis, namely the locking of the door and the plead-
ing of the workers. Taken at face value, Q 13:25 is not about Israel at all, but
about a master and some of his workers. In essence, this is an entirely appropriate topic for sapiential consideration, but not really for prophetic application. Perhaps more importantly, Q 13:25 qualifies as a maxim or aphorism,
depending on how typical or subversive the saying is deemed to be. Either way,
the saying is of the sort commonly featured in ancient instruction collections.
By the same token, the saying is not a *chreia*.[120] Unlike *chreiai*, the saying is
not uttered in response to a specific situation.

---

[117] Cf. Funk 2006, 30.

[118] That is, Q 13:18–19, 20–21, 24.

[119] *Pace* Tuckett 1996, 155.

[120] Cf. Hock and O'Neil 1986, 26; Robbins 1996, 61; Alexander 2006, 24; Hedrick 2014,
3 n. 12.

7.4 Characteristic Motifs

Superficially considered, Q 13:25 links thematically with both the preceding logion and the subsequent material. Both verses 24 and 25 are about gaining access through a "door" (θύρα). Verse 25 might also have been intended as motivation for the instruction in verse 24.[121] Narrative progression links Q 13:25 with the subsequent material. The initial exchange between the householder and the workers leads into another exchange.[122] Both exchanges begin with the workers trying to convince the householder to open the door for them and end with the master rudely refusing to do so. Most visibly, both exchanges feature the master's phrase: "I do not know you!" (οὐκ οἶδα ὑμᾶς). We have further seen that there are discontinuities between Q 13:25 and both its preceding and subsequent material. Thus, as far as thematic continuity is concerned, the syntagmatic context of Q 13:25 is not very helpful in determining the redactional placement of this logion – at least not on a superficial level.

A more promising endeavour is to consider Q 13:25 in isolation and search its *paradigmatic* context for thematic continuity. I have suggested elsewhere that the formative stratum's mission discourse (Q 10:2–11, 16) is not in the first place directed at missionaries, but at non-servile farm workers and day-labourers.[123] Whether or not this is correct, both Q 13:25 and Q 10:2–11, 16 deal on the most literal semantic level with workers. Significantly, like the logion currently under discussion, Q 10:5–6 is about gaining entry to a house.[124] The same topic is also treated in Q 11:9–10.[125] Interestingly, Q 13:25 functions to describe circumstances opposite to those of Q 10:5–9 and Q 11:9–10. In the latter texts, householders welcome workers and the needy into their houses. By contrast, the householder of Q 13:25 refuses to open the door for his workers, even disavowing any knowledge of their identity. Crucially, signs of the potentiality of such opposite behaviour also feature in the foregoing texts, especially in Q 10:3, 6b, 10–11 and Q 11:[8a,] 11–12. One should also not overlook the possibility that those outside the door are in fact strangers and that the householder speaks the truth when he claims not to know them.[126] The mission discourse in Q 10:2–11 would seem to support the latter proposal, since it describes a stranger in particular either being allowed or not being allowed into

---

[121] See above.

[122] Bovon 2001, 286; Fleddermann 2005a, 680, 682, 697.

[123] See Howes 2015a, 80–81, 103, 171–172.

[124] See Howes 2019b, 4–6.

[125] See Howes 2019b, 6–11; cf. Etchells 1998, 171. It should perhaps be noted that Q 11:52, which belongs to the main redaction, also treats the topic of "entry" (cf. Borg 1998, 131). Yet in this case the topic does not reference entry into someone's house.

[126] Cf. Thurén 2014, 311.

someone's house to receive hospitality and food.[127] Whether the outsiders are the master's own subordinates or unknown strangers, the scenario would still have been a familiar and typical one.[128]

It is important to realise that entry into someone's house equals survival for those at the bottom of the socio-economic ladder. It goes without saying that a house offers not only refuge from the elements, but also the possibility of receiving lodging, clothing, and food.[129] This was even more true in antiquity, since the ancient social value of hospitality required people to offer such things to those who came knocking, even if everyone did not always oblige.[130] The householder's negative response gives expression and form to the invisible boundary between the honourable and the honourless. In this respect, Q relates to those on the lower levels of the socio-economic hierarchy. Deliberately excluded from the resources in the house are those socio-economic underlings who need it the most. I can imagine Q's audience nodding their heads in recognition of the typical scenario of a householder locking out the less fortunate.[131] The theme of daily corporeal survival appears throughout the formative stratum,[132] but is almost entirely absent from the main redaction[133] and final recension.[134] The following generic statement by Robinson about redactional development in Q applies particularly to the elaboration of Q 13:25 with the addition of verses 26–27 and 28–29: "The Q people had been led to expect that trust in the coming of the kingdom would involve daily bread, a hope which was ultimately reduced to the eschatology of the Messianic banquet."[135]

I argued in the previous section that there is no reason to read Q 13:25 non-literally. This is surely true when considering the logion by itself, but the immediate literary context of Q 13:24–25 must now also be contemplated. Even if I am correct that Q 13:24–25 belongs to the formative stratum, these two sayings would still follow directly after two parables on the kingdom of God (Q 13:18–19, 20–21), indicating that they might deal in some way with the

---

[127] Cf. Q 11:9–13; cf. Valantasis 2005, 190, 191.

[128] Thurén 2014, 311.

[129] Cf. Q 10:5–9; see Howes 2019b, 4–6; cf. Robinson 1995a, 265.

[130] Cf. Q 10:5–9; 11:[5–8], 9–10; cf. e.g. m. 'Abot 1.5: "Let your house be wide open, and let the poor be the companions of your house" (Schottroff 2006, 52).

[131] Cf. Funk 1966, 191, 194; Thurén 2014, 311.

[132] Cf. Q 6:20–21, 29–30; 9:58; 10:2–11, 16; 11:2–4, 9–13; 12:4–7, 22–31, 42–44 (see chapter 4 above); 13:18–21 (see chapter 6 above); 15:4–5, 7, [8–10].

[133] Cf. Q 7:22. Yet here the themes of healing the sick and evangelising the poor do not feature for their own sake, but rather to prove that Jesus is the "coming one" (ὁ ἐρχόμενος).

[134] Cf. Q 4:2–4. Yet here the theme of eating bread does not feature for its own sake, but rather in the midst of a forty-day fast as the content of a temptation. In fact, the claim in verse 4 that a person is not to live from bread alone contradicts the preoccupation of the formative stratum with the procurement of daily bread.

[135] Robinson 1995a, 264; cf. 2003, 31; cf. Jacobson 1992, 208.

non-literal topic of entering God's kingdom.[136] Even so, one does well to remember that the "kingdom of God" refers in Q to tangible, corporeal circumstances that enable and constitute the healing of the sick[137] and the feeding of
the poor[138].[139] As such, the proposed literal meaning of Q 13:25 is not harmed
by its association with the metaphor of God's kingdom. One way for the poor
to be fed is for them to gain entry into someone's house, probably as a slave or
a worker, and to then rely on the householder's hospitality.[140] When this happens in the literal, tangible sense, the kingdom of God comes into being. The
same association between the metaphor of God's kingdom and actual, literal
events is made throughout the rest of Q. For example, in Q 11:2–4, 9–13, the
metaphor of God's kingdom is related to actual sustenance through hospitality,[141] and in Q 11:20 the metaphor of God's kingdom is linked to actual healing through exorcism.[142] The best example is actually the two parables in Q
13:18–21 that precede Q 13:25. It was argued in the foregoing chapter that
these parables relate God's kingdom specifically to accommodation and food.
The thematic link between Q 13:18–21 and Q 13:24–25 is therefore very
strong, especially with regards to the importance of lodging as a means of material survival. Using the metaphor of birds nesting (together with the metaphor
of a woman baking bread), Q 13:18–21 discusses entry to a house as the reali-
sation of God's kingdom.[143] Without similar appeal to a metaphor, Q 13:24–
25 describes a situation where entry is denied and the kingdom of God prevented from realising.[144] Speaking of concrete events in terms of the kingdom
metaphor does not turn the events themselves into metaphors. For Q, God's
kingdom appears wherever and whenever people are actually being fed. At any
rate, the setting of verse 25 is in itself appropriate for discussing God's kingdom, since the elite household was in antiquity a microcosm for the larger kingdom.[145] In this regard, the literal imagery of Q 13:25 may be regarded as a
symbolic example of life as it is for socio-economic underlings in existing
earthly kingdoms. Thematically, Q 13:18–21 and Q 13:24–25 may therefore be

---

[136] Jacobson 1992, 206; cf. Hoffmann 2001, 283.

[137] Cf. Q 10:9; 11:20.

[138] Cf. Q 6:20–21; 10:8–9; 11:2–3; 12:31; 13:18–19, 20–21 (see chapter 6 above); 13:28–
29.

[139] Robinson 1993, 15; 2001a, 16; 2001b, 33; 2002, 15; see Uro 1996, 79–82, 87–89; cf.
Piper 2000, 241, 251, 259; Järvinen 2001, 521; Kloppenborg 2001, 166; Horsley 2003, 30–
33, 35; 2012, 127; Van Aarde 2014, 2.

[140] Cf. Herzog 1994, 157.

[141] See Howes 2019b, 7–11.

[142] See Uro 1996, 79–82. For an African perspective on the miracles and healings performed by Jesus, see Dube 2015.

[143] Cf. Q 10:5–9; 11:[5–8], 9–10.

[144] Cf. Q 10:3, 6b, 10–11; 11:[8a,] 11–12.

[145] Bradley 1994, 81; Herzog 1994, 156; Hezser 2005, 129; Joshel 2010, 113, 128.

regarded as an antithetic parallelism, contrasting existence in God's kingdom with existence in worldly kingdoms. The focus will shift again to existence in God's kingdom in Q 14:16–21, 23, which probably followed Q 13:25 directly in the formative stratum.[146]

As we saw, the parable of the leaven anticipates a very large meal or large dinner party.[147] When this element of the parable is brought to bear on the logion that directly follows it in Q 13:24, the meaning of the latter logion is augmented to involve access to food and perhaps even a large meal.[148] Thus, the preceding parable hints at what lies beyond the narrow door once it is traversed, namely food and maybe even a banquet. Such background information is only suggested, so that Q 13:24 might still be mainly about the difficulties of discipleship.[149] In fact, these two features of Q 13:24 complement each other. If radical discipleship is likened to entering through a narrow door, then participating in the celebrations of God's kingdom is the reward of such effort.[150] While Q 13:24 treats both the possibilities of entering and not entering a house, Q 13:25 considers only the possibility of not entering. This is then followed in the formative stratum by Q 14:16–21, 23, where the opposite case of entering a house is depicted. In this way, Q 13:24 constitutes an appropriate opening logion for the material that follows in the formative stratum, imagining both the negative possibility of not entering a house that is developed in Q 13:25 and the positive possibility of entering a house that is developed in Q 14:16–21, 23. Moreover, the unstated assumption of Q 13:24–25 that entry to a house might lead to food is made explicit in Q 14:16–21, 23. Despite the implication of food in Q 13:24–25, one does well to remember that these two logia deal primarily and explicitly with gaining entry to a house, so that the topic of lodging represents the most direct link between Q 13:18–21 and Q 13:24–25. Q 13:25 is ultimately a description of a householder refusing to allow socio-economic inferiors entry into his house. As such, this logion vividly depicts the tendency of those with means to selfishly withhold resources from those who need it.

7.5 Implied Audience

When considering Q 13:25 in isolation, there is not much evidence to assist in determining its implied audience. If verses 24 and 25 were originally two separate and autonomous logia that appeared back-to-back, it stands to reason that

---

[146] See chapter 8 below.

[147] Cf. Davies and Allison 1991, 423; Scott 2002, 22.

[148] Cf. Kirk 1998, 304.

[149] Cf. e.g. Kloppenborg 1987, 235; Davies and Allison 1988, 696.

[150] Cf. Scott 1989, 172; Kirk 1998, 304, 305.

they were directed at the same audience. Seeing as verse 24 has a decidedly positive intent to direct the behaviour of insiders,[151] the same audience may be assumed for verse 25, especially if the latter operated as justification for the former. Although verse 24 features in the imperative mood and verse 25 in the indicative mood, both logia are "parabolic" in essence, inviting further contemplation as to their precise meanings.[152] In this way, they cohere with the preceding two parables (Q 13:18–19, 20–21).[153] In antiquity, such "parabolic" wisdom is characteristically aimed at the in-group. If we are correct that Q 13:25 was originally about workers, then it is justified to view the second person plural as directed at those in the audience who were workers themselves. Such rhetoric must have been aimed at insiders. When verse 25 is read together with verses 26–27, however, the implied threat is certainly aimed implicitly at outsiders.

These considerations suggest that Q 13:25 was originally intended for contemplation by insiders, but was subsequently elaborated to serve a polemical purpose against outsiders as part of a process of boundary demarcation.[154] This is supported by the three scriptural quotations in Q 13:27, 29, 35,[155] since the Sayings Gospel Q typically employs tacit direct quotations of Scripture in support of its polemic.[156] The resultant metaphor of Q 13:25–27 (together with Q 13:28–29) is essentially divisive, creating a definite boundary between "inside" and "outside."[157] True enough, verse 25 also creates this boundary between "inside" and "outside," without the help of verses 26–27. Even so, one gets the distinct impression when reading verse 25 in isolation that this boundary is only meant spatially and literally, as opposed to polemically and metaphorically. It is the addition of verses 26–27 that turns the imagery into a polemical metaphor that distinguishes between flawless insiders and lawless outsiders. Verses 28–29 make the distinction between insiders and outsiders even more rigid and final.[158] Here, the final punishment of outsiders is deliberately contrasted with the final reward of insiders.[159]

Some have taken Q 13:25–27 as a whole to be directed inwardly at certain members of the Q people.[160] However, the statements that Jesus ate and drank with the addressees and that he taught in their streets are not to be taken as

---

[151] See Piper 1989, 109–110.

[152] See Valantasis 2005, 182–183.

[153] Cf. Jacobson 1992, 206.

[154] Cf. Jacobson 1992, 208; Kloppenborg 1995, 319; Tuckett 1996, 194, 203–207.

[155] See above.

[156] Vaage 2001, 487.

[157] See Smith 2014, 52–54; cf. Funk and Hoover 1993, 254; Bovon 2001, 286.

[158] See Valantasis 2005, 183–184.

[159] Verheyden 2001, 713; cf. Jeremias 1963, 67.

[160] E.g. Roth 2014, 395; cf. Davies and Allison 1988, 696; Uro 1996, 94; Kirk 1998, 247–248.

evidence of membership in the Q group. During his ministry, Jesus shared his table with many people, not all of whom became part of the Jesus movement or the Q people in particular.[161] Likewise, residing in close proximity to the streets where Jesus taught does not a disciple of Jesus make.[162] Rather, exclusion from the eschatological banquet in verse 28, the excessiveness of the punishment in verses 28–29, and the content of the accusations in verses 34–35 strongly suggests that the addressees referenced throughout by the second person plural are outsiders.[163] In fact, the whole purpose of this pericope seems to be to draw a clear boundary between members and non-members of the Q people by disqualifying illegitimate claims of familiarity with Jesus.[164] Thus, in its final form in the main redaction, Q 13:25–27 has much in common with the woes in Q 10:13–15, since the addressees of the latter text also reside in geographical proximity to the locus of Jesus's earthly ministry, but are nonetheless taken to be outsiders due to their rejection of that ministry.[165] Having shared the table of Jesus and having heard him teach during his earthly ministry do not qualify people for eschatological salvation.[166]

In Matthew's (7:21–23) reading of Q 13:26–27, future deliverance is only achieved when responding to the ministry of Jesus by putting his teachings into

---

[161] Bock 1996, 1237; cf. Marshall 1978, 566.

[162] Matthew's version of the saying is indeed directed at fellow Christians (Davies and Allison 1988, 696; Betz 1995, 540; Luz 2007, 372–373), but even these Christians are not necessarily part of the in-group that is the Matthean community (see Catchpole 1993, 40–41; *pace* Luz 2007, 372–373). If Matthew's version is accepted for Q, the same logic would apply (cf. Fleddermann 2005a, 697).

[163] Cf. Etchells 1998, 173; Bovon 2001, 292; Vaage 2001, 481; Valantasis 2005, 183. If Bovon (2001, 289) is correct that ἐνώπιόν σου should be translated as "in front of you" instead of "with you," the identification of these individuals as outsiders would be even more apparent. In fact, the descriptions of these people as "eating and drinking in front of Jesus" and as claiming to own the streets in which Jesus taught (cf. "our streets" [ἐν ταῖς πλατείαις ἡμῶν]), taken together, portray them as upper-class snobs. This would imply that a distinction between rich and poor was important to the boundary concerns of the Q people. Even though this line of reasoning would support my larger case, there are good reasons to doubt it. Firstly, Bovon's translation removes the rhetorical heart of the appeal for the master to open the door. Why would the master open the door if those begging him to do so ate in front of him at an earlier stage? Why would this be a good argument? Secondly, the phrase "our streets" (ἐν ταῖς πλατείαις ἡμῶν) is much better understood as a geographical reference than a reference to ownership.

[164] Jacobson 1992, 208; cf. Hoffmann 2001, 283; Kloppenborg 2001, 169.

[165] Catchpole 1993, 42; Uro 1996, 94; cf. Verheyden 2001, 713; Zeller 2001, 353. This is not to say that the Sayings Gospel did not foresee the future punishment of individual insiders (cf. Q 12:9).

[166] Jeremias 1963, 175; Marshall 1978, 562–563; Bock 1996, 1237; Etchells 1998, 173; Bovon 2001, 291; Hoffmann 2001, 283; Zeller 2001, 353; Valantasis 2005, 182.

practice.[167] Three features of our text strongly suggest that the same is true for Q: (1) the "narrow door" metaphor in Q 13:24; (2) the imperative mood of "enter" (εἰσέλθατε) in Q 13:24; and (3) the reference to "lawlessness" (ἀνομία) in Q 13:27.[168] It seems reasonable to assume that the Q people originated as a group of people who wanted to put the teachings of Jesus into practice in their daily lives, suggesting that the two concepts of Q membership and practicing the message of Jesus were for them closely related. Hence, the people accused of "lawlessness" in the face of chance encounters with the earthly Jesus would naturally have qualified as outsiders.[169] Ultimately, the parable's literal outsiders are wholly rejected as the community's metaphorical outsiders.[170]

7.6 Findings

This chapter has argued, firstly, that Q 13:25 was elaborated by the addition of Q 13:26–27 and, secondly, that Q's main redactor was responsible for this addition. The former case was built on textual features that betray the original independence of verse 25, the artificiality of verses 26–27, and the discontinuity between verse 25 and the material that immediately follows it in Q 13:26–27, 28–29. As in the other chapters, the latter case was built on Kloppenborg's three main criteria for delineating between the formative stratum and the main redaction. It was found that Q 13:25 initially belonged to the formative stratum as an independent sapiential logion, but that the main redactor added verses 26–27 (together with verses 28–29) to create a parable that proclaims the eschatological judgment of outsiders.

---

[167] Nolland 2005, 341; see Davies and Allison 1988, 716–717; Donahue 1988, 97–98; Betz 1995, 540–541, 546–548, 550–551; Luz 2007, 372–373, 380–381. Luke's larger literary context similarly deals with the topic of human responsibility as a corollary to divine action (Bovon 2001, 285, 293; cf. Jeremias 1963, 175; Bock 1996, 1234–1235, 1237; Etchells 1998, 172, 174–175, 176).

[168] Tuckett 1996, 193, 294; Kirk 1998, 248–249; Hoffmann 2001, 269; Kloppenborg 2001a, 169; Zeller 2001, 353; Fleddermann 2005a, 696–697; Valantasis 2005, 182; cf. Jeremias 1963, 175, 194–195; Betz 1995, 521, 523, 534, 541; Bock 1996, 1234–1235; Luz 2007, 380; cf. Q 6:43–46; 14:27.

[169] Jacobson 1992, 208; cf. Hoffmann 2001, 283.

[170] Cf. Valantasis 2005, 183; see Etchells 1998, 175–177.

Chapter 8

Q 14:16–21, 23, "Whomever You Find, Invite"[1]

[16]ἄνθρωπός τις ἐποίει δεῖπνον ⟦μέγα, καὶ ἐκάλεσεν πολλοὺς⟧ [17]καὶ ἀπέστειλεν τὸν δοῦλον αὐτοῦ ⟦τῇ ὥρᾳ τοῦ δείπνου⟧ εἰπεῖν τοῖς κεκλημένοις· ἔρχεσθε, ὅτι ἤδη ἕτοιμά ἐστιν. [18]... ἀγρόν, ... [?19?] ... [?20?] ... [21]«καὶ < > ὁ δοῦλος < > τῷ κυρίῳ αὐτοῦ ταῦτα.» τότε ὀργισθεὶς ὁ οἰκοδεσπότης εἶπεν τῷ δούλῳ αὐτοῦ· [23]ἔξελθε εἰς τὰς ὁδοὺς καὶ ὅσους ἐὰν εὕρ<ῃς> καλέσ<ον>, ἵνα γεμισθῇ μου ὁ οἶκος.

[16]A certain person prepared a ⟦large⟧ dinner, ⟦and invited many⟧. [17]And he sent his slave ⟦at the time of the dinner⟧ to say to the invited: Come, for it is now ready. [18]«One declined because of his» farm. [?19?]«Another declined because of his business.» [?20?]«A third declined because of his wedding.[2]» [21]«And the slave, <on coming, said> these things to his master.» Then the householder, enraged, said to his slave: [23]Go out on the roads, and whomever you find, invite, so that my house may be filled.

Although the reconstruction of Q 14:16–21, 23 faces tremendous difficulties, most contemporary scholars agree that there is enough verbal and conceptual overlap between Matthew 22:2–10 and Luke 14:16–23 to justify its place in the Sayings Gospel Q.[3] Kloppenborg ascribes Q 14:16–24 to the main redaction.[4] As an alternative, it will presently be argued that this passage

---

[1] An earlier version of this chapter was published as an article in *Neotestamentica* 49/2 (see Howes 2015f).

[2] This sentence represents my own addition to the *Critical Edition of Q*. Although the Q version almost certainly featured a third excuse (cf. Funk 1966, 186; Scott 1981, 35; Crossan 1985, 41), it is difficult to reconstruct this third excuse, given the complete lack of verbal overlap. In my view, some version of the Lukan excuse of a wedding is most probable, not only because it is likewise attested in Gos. Thom. 64, but also because the theme of a wedding appears throughout Matt 22:2–14, albeit not as the third excuse (cf. Scott 1981, 35; 1989, 161, 167, 170). At any rate, commentators agree that Matthew's third excuse is obviously secondary.

[3] Davies and Allison 1997, 194; Fleddermann 2005a, 722; see Tuckett 1996, 92–93; Roth 2018, 129–130; e.g. Donahue 1988, 93–94; Kloppenborg 1995, 292; cf. Funk 1966, 163; Scott 1981, 32; Foster 2014a, 275; Roth 2014, 384. There are scholars who doubt the attribution of this text to the Sayings Gospel Q: e.g. Marshall 1978, 584; Davies and Allison 1997, 194; Allison 2000, 232; Luz 2005, 47; Meier 2016, 253–260, 270; cf. Dodd 1958, 121; Blomberg 1990, 237; Snodgrass 2008, 310; Foster 2014a, 275. One has to disagree with Schottroff (2006, 53): "How the parable was told in the tradition available to the Gospels (Q and the historical Jesus) is something we can no longer reconstruct."

[4] Kloppenborg 1987, 229–230; cf. 1995a, 290.

appeared in the formative stratum before being incorporated into the main redaction.

8.1 Kloppenborg's Analysis

Kloppenborg's attribution of Q 14:16–21, 23 to the main redaction depends on two interdependent considerations, namely its literary context in Q and its consequent interpretation.[5] Kloppenborg argues that, given its position after Q 13:24–35, the parable functions allegorically in Q, with the large dinner representing the eschatological banquet, those who declined the initial invitation representing greater Israel, and those who end up being invited representing gentiles.[6] The Synoptic Gospels clearly assimilated and developed this line of interpretation.[7] Some have argued that Q 13:28–29 does not pertain to the eschatological ingathering of gentiles at all, but rather to the eschatological return of diaspora Jews.[8] If so, there is reason to doubt that the parable in Q 14:16–21, 23 distinguishes between Israel and gentiles.[9] Rather, the distinction would then be between the diaspora, on the one hand, and the leaders and/or inhabitants associated with the geo-political centre of Jerusalem (including perhaps greater Judaea and/or Palestine), on the other.[10] It is also not impossible that both geo-political and ethnic distinctions were intended at the same time, even if this complicated the internal logic of the final text.[11]

The foregoing geo-political distinction hints at a concomitant socio-economic distinction as well, between the Jewish elite and the *'am ha-'areṣ* or "people of the land."[12] However, as Kloppenborg points out, the initial invitation is to all of Israel, not some sub-group within Israel.[13] Following the

---

[5] Kloppenborg 1987, 229–230; cf. Zimmermann 2009, 173.

[6] Cf. Uro 1996, 86–87; Kirk 1998, 251; Kloppenborg 2000a, 121; Piper 2000, 237; Valantasis 2005, 191; Roth 2018, 139–140, 142–143. In Jewish tradition, it was standard to describe the eschatological kingdom of Israel in terms of a great banquet (Dodd 1958, 121; Hunter 1971, 93; Blomberg 1990, 233–234; Luz 2001, 9; 2005, 50, 52; see Bryan 2002, 77–81; Bailey 2008, 310–311, 318–319; cf. Scott 1989, 172–173; Snodgrass 2008, 300, 301–302, 311; cf. Isa 25:6; 1 Enoch 62:14; 2 Enoch 42:3–14).

[7] Lührmann 1994, 61.

[8] E.g. Davies and Allison 1991, 27–28; Horsley 1995a, 38; 1999, 65, 69, 94–95, 97, 229, 242, 283; Allison 1997, 176–191; 2000, 166–169; Verheyden 2001, 702; cf. Jacobson 1992, 204. I tend to agree (see chapter 7 above).

[9] Cf. Allison 1997, 188.

[10] Cf. Etchells 1998, 186, 188–189; Horsley 1999, 86, 88, 92; Snodgrass 2008, 308; Meier 2016, 271–272; see chapter 7 above.

[11] See footnote below.

[12] Cf. Roth 2018, 139–140.

[13] Kloppenborg 1987, 230.

logic of the parable, a socio-economic distinction within the confines of Israel would imply that the *'am ha-'areṣ* were not initially invited to the eschatological banquet.[14] This goes against the Jewish *Heilsgeschichte*, according to which all of Israel were liberated from Egypt and included in the great covenant between God and Israel, especially the poor. By the same token, the ultimate open invitation is to those who were not initially invited, meaning that if the initial invitation was to Israel, the final invitation can only include gentiles.[15] It needs to be stressed, however, that these arguments are only valid if the parable is read allegorically, with the initial invitees representing (a subgroup within) Israel and the subsequent feast representing the eschatological banquet.[16] It follows that the parable could have been intended as a non-allegorical story at an earlier stage, during which socio-economic concerns could have been intended, perhaps even exclusively so.[17]

Be that as it may, Kloppenborg is undoubtedly correct that the parable needs to be read allegorically if its immediate literary context in the main redaction is considered. Conversely, if read allegorically, the parable fits perfectly in its literary context in the main redaction. The parable is also thematically very similar to the rest of the main redaction, where Israel's rejection of Q's message is likewise met with anger and disbelief.[18] If the parable has gentiles in mind as the ultimate guests, the story's surprising ending is further comparable to the measure of astonishment described in the rest of the main redaction at the positive reaction of gentiles to the message of Q's Jesus.[19] Like the rest of the

---

[14] Marshall 1978, 585; cf. Funk 1966, 189–190; Jacobson 1992, 219; Snodgrass 2008, 315.

[15] Cf. Bultmann 1968, 175. The same arguments pertain equally to the distinction between Jerusalem and the diaspora. In other words, if the parable of the great supper were intended to be understood along the lines of a geo-political distinction in the final form of Q, it would necessitate the misguided conclusion that Jews living outside Jerusalem, Judaea, and/or Palestine were not included in the covenant unless and until they accepted some sort of second invitation, and neither were their ancestors. On the other hand, Q 13:34–35, which immediately precedes the parable of the great supper in the final form of Q, clearly speaks against Jerusalem and requires the subsequent parable to be read along the lines of a geo-political distinction (cf. Kloppenborg 1995, 292). These two observations expose a disjunction in the logic of Q 13:28–29, [30], 34–35; 14:16–21, 23. The main redactor was either unaware of this disjunction or untroubled by it. It is possible that the main redaction understood this cluster of material to imply both a geo-political and an ethnic distinction at the same time, even though the combination of these two features introduced internal tensions. These distinctions could in any case not have been clear-cut, since the good news of God's kingdom was rejected neither by all the Jews nor by all the elite (cf. Snodgrass 2008, 314–315, 321). This is true for both the ministry of Jesus and the ministry of the Q people.

[16] Cf. Marshall 1978, 585.

[17] Cf. Jeremias 1972, 69; Luz 2005, 51.

[18] Cf. Q 7:31–35; 10:13–15; 11:49–51; 13:34–35.

[19] Cf. Q 7:1–10; 11:31–32; cf. Robinson 1994b, 252–253.

main redaction, the parable functions as a piece of polemic against greater Israel. Israel's position of privilege over against the nations is not automatically guaranteed.[20] In fact, the literary context in Q 13:25–27, 28–29 indicates that the parable deliberately attempts to portray (a portion of) greater Israel as outsiders, unseated by gentiles and/or the diaspora.[21] By discussing the typical Q[2] motifs of Jewish rejection and gentile acceptance, and by implying outsiders as the projected audience, the passage complies with two of Kloppenborg's three criteria for attribution to the main redaction, namely "characteristic motifs" and "implied audience."[22]

Although I agree with Kloppenborg's analysis of Q 14:16–21, 23 on the level of the main redaction, there is no comparable analysis of this text on the level of the formative stratum. The question has to be raised: what would be the result if the parable's literary context in the formative stratum were to be considered? Since the parable's literary context drives its interpretation for Kloppenborg, which in turn drives its allocation to the main redaction, it stands to reason that a different literary context, say that of the formative stratum, would foreseeably alter not only the parable's interpretation, but also its redactional placement.[23]

8.2 Q 14:16–21, 23 in the Formative Stratum

It was argued in chapter 7 above that Q 13:25 belongs to the formative stratum, while Q 13:26–27 constitutes an addition by Q's main redactor. If this is correct, it would mean that the parable of the great supper followed directly after Q 13:24, 25 in the formative stratum. Significantly, both Q 13:24–25 and Q 14:16–21, 23 are about gaining entrance to a house.[24] Noticeable are also the following catchword connections: (1) "many" (πολύς) in Q 13:24 and Q 14:16; (2) "master" (κύριος) in Q 13:25 and Q 14:21; and (3) "householder" (οἰκοδεσπότης) in Q 13:25 and Q 14:21.[25] Whereas Q 13:25 is about a householder excluding the needy from his house and its resources, Q 14:16–

---

[20] Cf. Q 3:7–9; 13:28–29; 22:28, 30; cf. Hunter 1964, 57; Perrin 1967, 114; Etchells 1998, 188–189; Bryan 2002, 81; Nolland 2005, 889–890; Snodgrass 2008, 306, 308, 314, 317, 322.

[21] See Smith 2014, 52–53; cf. Catchpole 1993, 282; Bultmann 1994, 32; Joseph 2012, 89.

[22] Allison (1997, 20 n. 85) claims that the parable's literary context in Q's final form is instead suggestive of its function as "paraenesis for insiders." This claim is not substantiated by supportive argumentation and it is hard to imagine how this could be the case. If anything, the literary context of Q 14:16–21, 23 in the main redaction and final form of Q indicates that the parable needs to be understood as an attempt at boundary demarcation (see Smith 2014, 52–53; cf. Kloppenborg 1995, 292; Bryan 2002, 79–80).

[23] Cf. Zimmermann 2009, 173.

[24] Cf. Johnson-DeBaufre 2005, 104.

[25] Cf. Marshall 1978, 566; Kirk 1998, 247 n. 357; Fleddermann 2005a, 724, 736, 737.

21, 23 is about a householder including the needy at a banquet in his house. Moreover, Q 13:24, 25 is preceded by the parables of the mustard seed and leaven in Q 13:18–19, 20–21. It was argued in chapter 6 that these parables relate specifically to God's provision in the form of lodging and food. Whereas Q 13:24–25 explicitly treats lodging and presumes a banquet, Q 14:16–21, 23 explicitly treats a banquet and presumes lodging. That lodging is implied by Q 14:16–21, 23 is particularly indicated by the concluding clause: "…so that my house may be filled." Although these thematic links are clear enough not to require much elaboration, it is worthwhile to delineate how the parable in Q 14:16–21, 23 would have been interpreted on the level of the formative stratum.

After exposing the typicality of societal norms and customs in Q 13:25, Q's Jesus creates the unfamiliar and unusual scenario of a householder who invites random strangers to his banquet, including especially the *'am ha-'areṣ*.[26] This happens only after the host of the parable had initially invited his peers, who declined the invitation. That those who were initially invited represent the upper class is indicated not only by the content of their excuses,[27] but also by the fact that a slave is sent to summon them.[28] Thomson compares the details of the parable to persisting Oriental customs and determines that the practice of sending out a slave to summon guests, especially with a formula like "come, for the supper is ready," is a hallmark of an event "confined to the wealthy."[29] One could argue against the latter by pointing out that the "street people" are also summoned by the householder's slave, but the whole aim of the parable is precisely to sketch a scenario in which the poor end up being treated like the rich normally would be. It seems reasonable to assume that the first round of guests were of the same social standing as the householder, who is portrayed as being wealthy.[30] To be sure, the mere fact that these guests decline an invitation to a large dinner with plenty of food is reason enough to assume that they were people of means.

That the feast ended up being attended mostly by the needy, and that this was deliberate, is a legitimate deduction to make from the fact that the slave

---

[26] Cf. Jeremias 1972, 178; Bock 1996, 1276; Kirk 1998, 253; Luz 2005, 49, 50, 51; Bailey 2008, 319.

[27] Even though the excuses are difficult to reconstruct precisely, both Matthew and Luke feature excuses that would apply typically to the wealthy.

[28] Jeremias 1972, 176–177; Marshall 1978, 585–586; Scott 1981, 35–36; 1989, 169; Bock 1996, 1272, 1274; Kirk 1998, 252–253; Horsley 1999, 284; Luz 2005, 52; Schottroff 2006, 52; Snodgrass 2008, 313; Van Eck 2013, 9–10; *pace* Young 1998, 177.

[29] Thomson 1859, 178–179 in Young 1998, 179–180.

[30] Scott 1981, 35; 1989, 169; Kirk 1998, 253; Schottroff 2006, 52, 53; Van Eck, Renkin, and Ntakirutimana 2016, 6; cf. Hezser 2005, 175; Van Eck 2013, 10; Bork 2014, 5; Roth 2014, 384–385; 2018, 135; *pace* Young 1998, 177.

was instructed to find people "on the roads" (εἰς τὰς ὁδοὺς).[31] In Q 13:24–25, "many" (πολλοί) tried to enter the house, but only a privileged "few" (ὀλίγοι) were allowed inside, because the householder restricted the access of those at the lower levels of society.[32] In Q 14:16–21, 23, by contrast, the householder deliberately tells his slave to invite "as many as you can find" (ὅσους ἐὰν εὕρῃς), so that everyone and anyone who wants to participate in the lavish banquet may do so.[33] It is precisely the contrast between Q 13:24–25 and Q 14:16–21, 23 that highlights the peculiarity and shock value of the parable's unexpected ending. The socio-economic boundary created by the householder's response in Q 13:25 is shattered by another householder's reaction in Q 14:23.[34] The system of honour affirmed by the householder of Q 13:25 is subverted by the householder of Q 14:23.[35] The parable could even be poking fun at the very institutions and practices that validate and enable social distinctions, including banquets.[36]

The point of narrating the individual instances of initial rejection in the parable is to provide the realistic background against which the invitation of random people off the streets is ultimately made.[37] The foregoing statement is intended as an argument against the claim by a small number of scholars that the initial rejection of the invitation is just as surprising and shocking as the decision to invite random people, if not more so.[38] People are inherently

---

[31] Marshall 1978, 590; Etchells 1998, 187; Kirk 1998, 253; Young 1998, 171; Bryan 2002, 80; Schottroff 2006, 52; Van Eck, Renkin, and Ntakirutimana 2016, 7; see Roth 2018, 139–142; cf. Scott 1989, 168; Bock 1996, 1275, 1276; Young 1998, 181, 185; Van Eck 2013, 10.

[32] Cf. Fleddermann 2005a, 738; Smith 2014, 52–53.

[33] Cf. Crossan 1991, 262; Kirk 1998, 247; Nolland 2005, 888; Valantasis 2005, 192. It has to be noted, even if only in a footnote, that despite the householder's charity, the slave is not emancipated and we are not told whether or not he was allowed to participate in the feast. Slaves were at times allowed to join the master's table (Harding 2003, 223; Joshel 2010, 126; cf. Massey and Moreland 1992, 52), but during important events they were utilised to serve and entertain guests (Massey and Moreland 1992, 27, 38–39, 52; Bradley 1994, 57, 64, 87–88; Matz 2002, 20; Harding 2003, 222–223; Hezser 2005, 140, 175; Joshel 2010, 133–134, 146–148). Although they were on occasion allowed to eat some of the leftovers (Bradley 1994, 83; Joshel 2010, 146–148), they were also subject to elevated levels of mistreatment and punishment during these events (Massey and Moreland 1992, 27, 52; Matz 2002, 20; cf. Bardley 1994, 64).

[34] Cf. Funk 1966, 194; Bork 2014, 5; Van Eck, Renkin, and Ntakirutimana 2016, 7.

[35] Scott 1989, 173–174.

[36] Scott 1981, 38; cf. Funk 1966, 190, 195–196; Bryan 2002, 79–80.

[37] Cf. Hunter 1971, 11–12; Roth 2018, 132.

[38] E.g. Perrin 1967, 114; Blomberg 1990, 234; Young 1998, 171, 172, 180; Luz 2005, 50; cf. Funk 1966, 188–189; Funk and Hoover 1993, 352, 353, 510. This is not to claim that the specific content of the excuses was thematically insignificant for Q, especially in the document's final form (cf. Fleddermann 2005a, 740; Johnson-DeBaufre 2005, 104; Snodgrass 2008, 307; cf. Q 12:33–34; 16:13; 17:26–27, 30; 19:26).

untrustworthy, and arranging a social gathering that ends up being unattended is an experience to which many people can relate.[39] Having said this, I am in agreement with Van Eck, who reads the parable in its proper socio-historical context and argues convincingly that the invitees did not merely fail to attend a social gathering, but that the community as a whole ended up rejecting the host and his appeal to honour and status.[40] After the initial invitation, which should be seen as a challenge of honour, the host's peers gossip about him, the purpose of which is to reach consensus about his lack of honour and social standing. Their lame excuses are the result of the latter process: the host and his appeal to peer-recognition are rejected across the board.[41]

Whereas such rejection was perhaps somewhat uncommon in ancient societies, it was certainly not unprecedented. By contrast, inviting every Tom, Dick, and Harry off the streets to one's house for a party was unheard of. It is true that in the ancient Greco-Roman world ordinary citizens were often included in the symposia and comparable festivities of the elite.[42] In first-century Rome, for example, a certain Marcus Licinius Crassus apparently hosted suppers on a daily basis that were open to "anyone and everyone" at his house.[43] Yet the extent to which such activities were also a feature of Jewish life in ancient Palestine is debatable.[44] More importantly, whereas the Greco-Roman symposia and similar events targeted *ordinary citizens* for the sake of boosting the honour of the host, the householder of Q 14:16–21, 23 deliberately targets *riff raff off the streets* to challenge the ancient system of honour distribution. Inviting strangers to a large celebration is much less radical as an act of benefaction for the sake of increased honour than it is as a deliberate attempt to erase social and other boundaries for the sake of improving the livelihoods of those at the bottom.[45] It follows that the gathering of street people to attend a large banquet is the aspect of the story that shatters the expectations and experience of everyday reality and proposes an alternative in its place.[46] The emphasis of the story and the heart of the metaphor is the host's

---

[39] Cf. Blomberg 1990, 234.

[40] Van Eck 2013, 1–14; cf. Bailey 2008, 314–316; Wright 2015, 114; Van Eck, Renkin, and Ntakirutimana 2016, 6.

[41] See Young 1998, 183–184; Bailey 2008, 314–316; cf. Wright 2015, 115.

[42] Schottroff 2006, 40, 50; see Fisher 1998, 213–218.

[43] Joshel 2010, 50.

[44] Cf. Thomson 1859, 178–179 in Young 1998, 179–180; Schottroff 2006, 50. Similar stories appear in Jewish literature that post-date the ministry of Jesus (see Young 1998, 180–182; Schottroff 2006, 51), but it is likely that these traditions were in the first place modelled on Jesus's parable of the great supper.

[45] Crossan 1991, 262.

[46] See Funk 2006, 43–51, 134–135, 172, 173; cf. Funk and Hoover 1993, 352; Kirk 1998, 253; Bailey 2008, 313; Zimmermann 2009, 175; Thurén 2014, 315; Van Eck, Renkin, and Ntakirutimana 2016, 6–7.

decision to invite unknown street people to his house.[47] This is supported by certain literary characteristics in verse 21 that signify Q 14:21, 23 as the parable's crisis-denouement: (1) the temporal particle "then" (τότε); (2) the description of the householder as being "enraged" (ὀργίζω); and (3) the closer identification of the protagonist as a "householder" (οἰκοδεσπότης) after initially only introducing him as "a certain person" (ἄνθρωπός τις).[48]

Young expresses the opinion of many other interpreters when he writes: "By inviting the beggars and the homeless to his banquet, he brought honor to himself and put the rest of the people to shame."[49] It is not clear to me how this act could have restored the host's honour with the original guests, who had decided as a unified group to reject his honour across the board. If anything, his actions would in my view have been perceived by the original guests as a spiteful attempt at retaliation, "to demonstrate to those first invited that the banquet can happen without them."[50] This would only have added to their gossip and his shame. The mere act of eating and drinking with social outcasts would have had the same result. Consider, by analogy, the defamatory gossip about Jesus preserved in Q 7:34: "Look! A person «who is» a glutton and drunkard, a chum of tax collectors and sinners!" At any rate, nothing is said of either the original guests' reaction or the host's subsequent honour. It is not even clear whether or not the original guests knew about the "replacement banquet." The host's actions are much better understood as a challenge of social values like honour and shame than an attempt to reclaim personal honour. It seems unlikely that the host would attempt to reclaim his own honour with those who had just snubbed him and would do so at the very moment that he was "angry" (ὀργισθείς) with them.

Significantly, the parable of the great supper likens the kingdom of God to an event at which everyone receives food, including especially the poor.[51] For Q, God's kingdom has to do with the feeding of the poor[52] and the healing of the sick[53].[54] This emphasis on feeding the poor corresponds to the cultural context: "The Middle Eastern culture highly values food and recognizes the

---

[47] Marshall 1978, 589; Van Eck 2013, 12; *pace* Perrin 1967, 114.

[48] See Funk 2006, 122–124; cf. Funk 1966, 166; Funk and Hoover 1993, 510; Roth 2014, 384–387.

[49] Young 1998, 184; cf. e.g. Wright 2015, 114, 115, 163, 165; Ford 2016, 109–110; Meier 2016, 270.

[50] Schottroff 2006, 50, cf. also 55–56.

[51] Cf. Funk 1966, 191; Kirk 1998, 253; Horsley 1999, 284–285; Valantasis 2005, 190–191, 192; Van Aarde 2014, 2.

[52] Cf. Q 6:20–21; 10:8–9; 11:2–3; 12:31; 13:18–21 (see chapter 6 above); 13:28–29.

[53] Cf. Q 10:9; 11:20.

[54] Robinson 1993, 15; 2001a, 16; 2001b, 33; 2002, 15; Vaage 1994, 63, 64; see Uro 1996, 79–82, 87–89; Horsley 2003, 30–33, 35; cf. Piper 2000, 241, 251, 259; Järvinen 2001, 521; Kloppenborg 2001, 166; Valantasis 2005, 190–191; Horsley 2012, 127.

needs of the less fortunate. Food is precious."[55] By convincing the wealthy to feed the poor, this parable follows the rest of the formative stratum in promoting general reciprocity at all societal levels as a replacement of balanced reciprocity.[56] Like the parables in Q 13:18–21, the growth and expansion of God's kingdom is at most a *peripheral* motif in the parable of the great supper. In Q 14:16–21, 23, the contrast between the kingdom's beginning and its end might be relevant, seeing as the affair starts out lacking a single guest, but ends up with a house filled to the brim.[57] As with the parables of the mustard and leaven, though, the emphasis is not on the expansion of God's kingdom, but on the depiction of God's kingdom as a place where people receive food (and perhaps even lodging). All three parables seem to promote social transformation through the replacement of existing socio-economic-religio-political patterns with an alternate reality dubbed "the kingdom of God."[58] Piper correctly observes that the parable of the great supper is not primarily concerned with the categories of rich and poor in Q's main redaction, but it does seem that these categories were in focus at the level of Q's formative stratum.[59] Ultimately, "[t]he outcome of the unusual events brought food to the hungry."[60] What is more, the deliberate use of the word "house" (οἶκος) in verse 23 recalls the family metaphor of Q's formative stratum, so that the banquet for the needy becomes an expression of God's symbolic family.[61] Once again, general reciprosity is the means by which the kingdom of God is established, since it applies the socio-economic dealings usually reserved for the biological family to society at large, thereby turning society into God's symbolic family.[62] In practice, the historical Jesus implemented God's kingdom through inclusive meal practices and open commensality.[63] According to Schottroff, these meal practices signified "the feeding of the hungry, the realization of solidarity within the people of God, and an experience of the kingdom of God."[64] She continues:

That banquets are to be made a locus of solidarity means that hunger among the people requires the opening of the houses of those who have enough to eat. In this way the hosts

---

[55] Young 1998, 184.

[56] Van Eck 2013, 12, 13; Van Eck, Renkin, and Ntakirutimana 2016, 7; cf. Ford 2016, 117; see chapter 4 above.

[57] Cf. Kirk 1998, 246–247.

[58] Vaage 1994, 56; 2001, 486; Kloppenborg 2001, 169; cf. Borg 1984, 96; Funk and Hoover 1993, 485, 352; Kloppenborg 2000b, 81, 108; Zimmermann 2009, 175; Van Eck 2013, 12, 13; Van Eck, Renkin, and Ntakirutimana 2016, 7.

[59] Piper 2000, 236.

[60] Young 1998, 185.

[61] Cf. Young 1998, 186.

[62] Cf. Ford 2016, 117–118.

[63] See Schottroff 2006, 50–51; cf. Bailey 2008, 318; Wright 2015, 35.

[64] Schottroff 2006, 51.

become siblings of the poor. Because the experience of being the people of God together with the poor is made possible through eating together, such a festive meal was understood as the beginning of the reign of God.[65]

Roth doubts that this parable is about the householder's altruistic behaviour, arguing that his narrated anger determines how one should understand his subsequent behaviour.[66] True as this may be, it is my contention that even if anger motivated the householder, his actions still contributed positively to the establishment of God's kingdom.[67] Likewise, even if interpreters are correct that the householder's actions were motivated by a spiteful and selfish attempt to increase his own honour, his actions would still have contributed positively to the establishment of God's kingdom. His intentions are relevant as an explanation for why he ended up inviting street people to his banquet, but irrelevant as far as the end result is concerned. The poor still receive food. In this way, his actions are comparable to those of the host in Q 11:[5–8].[68] Despite their intentions not being entirely commendable, both characters still end up contributing to the establishment of God's kingdom. Like the slave manager of Q 12:42–44 and the city slaves of Q 19:12–13, 15–24,[69] the *angry* householder of Q 14:16–21, 23 is an unlikely candidate when it comes to establishing God's kingdom, which is probably why all of them were chosen as main characters. Besides, there are other ways of interpreting his anger as well. Instead of seeing it as evidence that the householder invited these "undesirables" out of pure spite, one could interpret it as a motivating factor for doing good. His internal reasoning would then have sounded something like this: "I am so angry at my wealthy friends for rejecting me that I will now concentrate my efforts on those who actually stand to benefit from these efforts." Anger at one group does not necessarily imply apathy towards another. One of the aims of the parable might even be to advocate anger by those who are more fortunate against their peers for doing so little to address the concurrent socio-economic situation. If we are correct that the rejection of the householder was holistic, then it stands to reason that his anger would not just have been against particular individuals who rejected him, but against the whole social game that relied on the recognition of honour and status by others. If so, his anger motivated the replacement of a negative social system with a

---

[65] Schottroff 2006, 55.

[66] Roth 2018, 135–136; cf. Schottroff 2006, 50, 55–56; Wright 2015, 116; Ford 2016, 110–112. It is further significant that Roth regards the Gospel traditions about the deliberate exclusion of the initial invitees as going back to Q (cf. Young 1998, 186). If these elaborations are transferred to Q, it is indeed almost impossible to maintain that the host's intentions were positive in Q.

[67] Cf. Schottroff 2006, 50, 55–56; Bailey 2008, 313, 316–317; Ford 2016, 110; Roth 2018, 143.

[68] See chapter 10 below.

[69] See chapter 4 above and chapter 9 below.

positive one that makes room for everyone. By the same token, his anger might have been at society at large, so that his actions were motivated by a need to challenge the whole hierarchy operative in society. Anger at both the honour-game and society at large are two sides of the same coin, requiring radical and rebellious behaviour to effect change.

In addition to catchword connections and thematic continuity, the internal links between the individual traditions that make up Q 13:18–19, 20–21, 24–25; 14:16–21, 23 are strengthened by some form of chronological development: (1) ingredients are cultivated in Q 13:18–19; (2) food is prepared in Q 13:20–21; (3) the door is opened in Q 13:24; (4) entry is restricted in Q 13:25; (5) invited guests are summoned in Q 14:16–17; (6) the invited guests decline in Q 14:18–20; and (7) all restrictions are lifted so that anyone may enter in Q 14:21, 23. The catchword, thematic, and chronological connections suggested in this section go some way towards explaining the ostensibly inappropriate position of Q 13:18–21 in the main redaction.[70] Seemingly, the main redactor inserted material between Q 13:18–19, 20–21, 24–25 and Q 14:16–21, 23, thereby changing the meaning of both, but at the same time weakening and eliminating internal linkage between them.[71]

If the parable of the great supper is considered in its context in the formative stratum, it is best interpreted as an illustration of God's kingdom as a place where everyone receives food. By contrast, the following aspects that were important for the parable's interpretation in the main redaction are not on the table at all if it is interpreted as part of the formative stratum: (1) a distinction between insiders and outsiders;[72] (2) any indication that the parable should be read allegorically; and (3) any indication that the parable is about an eschatological banquet.[73] In fact, the literary context on the level of the formative stratum seems to speak against and rule out these avenues of interpretation. Significantly, Jeremias blames the source shared by Matthew and Luke (referring to Q) for introducing these interpretive avenues into the parable of the great supper.[74] At present, we can say with greater specificity that Q's main redactor was in all likelihood the responsible party.

---

[70] See chapter 6 above and chapter 10 below.

[71] At the same time, the main redactor created new possibilities for linking Q 13:18–21 to surrounding material, even if these new links were weaker and subtler than the original links in the formative stratum (cf. Kloppenborg 1995, 309–311).

[72] Such a distinction remains valid irrespective of whether the distinction is between Israel and gentiles or between those at the geo-political centre, like the Jerusalem elite, and those on the geo-political periphery, like the diaspora.

[73] Cf. Young 1998, 184.

[74] Jeremias 1972, 67–69; cf. Donahue 1988, 94.

8.3 A "Formative" Context: Open Invitation

If the parable in Q 14:16–21, 23 is considered in isolation, there is reason to argue that its content is more conducive to its place in the formative stratum than in the main redaction. On the one hand, the interpretation of the parable in its Q[1] context is already suggested by the content of the parable itself. One does not need to go outside the parable itself to see the imagined scenario as one where food is made available to those who need it most. On the other hand, the themes developed by the parable in its Q[2] context, as outlined by Kloppenborg, are not inherent to the parable itself, but require a literary context to enforce the desired interpretation.[75] In other words, the story as it unfolds in the parable itself says nothing about the exclusion of Israel or those at the geo-political centre from eschatological merriment in favour of gentiles or the diaspora.[76] As with all allegory, this theme is introduced into the parable from outside its own boundaries. It follows that if one interprets the parable in isolation, its inherent themes fit much better with its context in the formative stratum than in the main redaction. As such, one can make a strong case that the parable has more claim for placement in the formative stratum if measured against Kloppenborg's criterion of characteristic motifs.

The same applies to his criterion of characteristic form. Q 14:16–21, 23 is one of only a few proper narrative parables in Q, with most of the other examples qualifying rather as similitudes.[77] In its capacity as a parable, Q 14:16–21, 23 qualifies formally as a piece of wisdom.[78] Even if the content of any particular parable happens to feature eschatological, apocalyptic, or prophetic themes and/or small forms, that parable still operates as part of the teaching experience to incite reflection and contemplation. In this regard, the following comment by Funk is informative: "*What* the parable says cannot be simply divorced from the *way* it says. Form and content are wedded."[79] In the case of Q 14:16–21, 23, where the content is only eschatological and/or prophetic if so interpreted, the formal classification of the parable as wisdom is even more definite and determinative.

That only leaves the criterion of implied audience. Since boundary demarcation is one of the themes necessitated by the Q[2] context, but not inherent to the parable itself, it follows that the parable, if considered on its own, fails to develop this theme in particular. In fact, the parable's content actually seems to contradict and prohibit any manner of division between

---

[75] Thurén 2014, 315.

[76] Young 1998, 184; Thurén 2014, 315.

[77] Cf. Davies and Allison 1991, 416; Funk 2006, 31.

[78] See Kirk 1998, 234, 246–248; cf. Edwards 1976, 74.

[79] Funk 2006, 104, emphasis original.

insiders and outsiders.[80] The parable ends with the doors being flung wide open so that everyone and anyone may enter the feast, without distinction.[81] A private event is transformed into an extended bash that permeates all segments of society, almost like hidden leaven would transform and permeate massive amounts of flour.[82] The purpose of the transformation is precisely to break down established boundaries, not to invert, create, or strengthen them.

On the logic of the parable itself, even those who initially declined the invitation would presumably be welcome should they change their minds and arrive at the party anyway.[83] These individuals would then be included in the banquet. As the motive clause "so that my house may be filled" (ἵνα γεμισθῇ μου ὁ οἶκος) makes clear, the householder's intent is to fill his house with guests.[84] As far as this objective is concerned, banning people from his party would be counterproductive, including anyone who initially declined the invitation. To be sure, the Q parable nowhere asserts expressly that the first group of invitees were to be excluded as a matter of principle.[85] True enough, the parable *also* fails to mention expressly that the first group of invitees would have been *included* if they showed up anyway. Yet its failure to explicitly address the fate of the original invitees at all goes to show how unimportant their inclusion or exclusion was to the parable's original function in Q. Conversely, the indiscriminate inclusion of "whomever you find" is indeed mentioned explicitly.[86] It is nonetheless unlikely that (m)any of the initial

---

[80] *Pace* Crossan 1985, 51–52.

[81] Crossan 1991, 262; Nolland 2005, 888; Wright 2015, 116; cf. Valantasis 2005, 191. Although the parable of the great supper should not at the level of the formative stratum be interpreted in terms of futurist eschatology, its indiscriminate inclusivity is comparable to similar visions of broad inclusivity in traditional descriptions of the eschatological banquet (cf. Bryan 2002, 78, 81; Bailey 2008, 310–311, 318–319; Wright 2015, 116–117; Roth 2018, 140–141, 142; cf. Isa 25:6–8).

[82] Cf. Scott 2002, 23.

[83] *Pace* Funk 1966, 190; Jeremias 1972, 179–180; Borg 1984, 220; Jacobson 1992, 218; Bock 1996, 1270.

[84] Jeremias 1972, 177; Valantasis 2005, 192; cf. Bock 1996, 1277.

[85] *Pace* Piper 2000, 236; Bryan 2002, 77. One could point to the householder's angry reaction to argue that he would not have welcomed the first round of invitees if they pitched up anyway (cf. Funk 1966, 165; Bryan 2002, 77, 80; Roth 2018, 135–136). Yet the house-holder's emotive response is featured in Q to motivate his unorthodox reaction of inviting random people to his house (see Thurén 2014, 316–317; cf. Crossan 1974c, 85). Most people would get upset under similar circumstances (cf. Crossan 1985, 45; Thurén 2014, 316; Ford 2016, 109), but most people would also get over it pretty soon. What is more, Scott (1989, 168) argues that the reference to the householder's anger is a later addition to the parable and that the absence of such a reference in Gos. Thom. 64 is more original (cf. Funk 1966, 167; Crossan 1985, 45, 48). If so, Q's main redactor could very well have been responsible for this addition, so that it was absent from the formative stratum.

[86] Cf. Young 1998, 186; Wright 2015, 116.

invitees would have attended, even if they were otherwise welcome. If they attended, they would have subjected themselves to the same processes of gossip and rejection by their peers.[87] To some extent, it may therefore indeed be appropriate to refer to Q 14:16–21, 23 as a "parable of reversal,"[88] but not as a "parable of exclusion," so that comprehensive and complete reversal is imposed. This is particularly true for the historical Jesus, who should in no way be associated with the programmatic promotion of social exclusion, not even of the corrupt Jewish leadership or well-to-do.[89] Q's formative stratum seems to have understood this message well. I find it at best interesting and at worst baffling that so many scholars interpret this parable in terms of reversal across the board, instead of inclusivity across the board.[90] The former is common enough in ancient literature and ends up with the exact same boundaries, only with the representatives of the two groups swapped around. Conversely, the latter is intrinsically subversive and fundamentally revolutionary, promoting an entirely novel constitution of reality, which Jesus called the "kingdom of God."[91] Socio-economic categories, though important, do not function as a means of distinguishing between insiders and outsiders.[92] If they did, the householder would not have been welcome at his own party. Instead, socio-economic categories function to emphasise that all people are welcome and that the destitute are sure to attend in abundance for that very reason.[93] The final invitation is ultimately "completely unlimited and universal."[94]

It is the evangelists who were guilty of adding explicit reference to the deliberate exclusion of the initial invitees. In Matthew 22:8, the narrative's protagonist explicitly says that "those invited [initially] were not worthy."[95] In verse 10, the narrator goes on to say that "the wedding [hall] was filled" (ἐπλήσθη ὁ γάμος). Luz correctly deduces from this information that the opportunity for attending had by that stage expired, so that those who initially declined the invitation were thereby excluded as a matter of principle.[96] It would in any case have been impossible for these people to attend, since they had according to verse 7 already been annihilated.[97] The mistake Luz makes is

---

[87] Cf. Van Eck 2013, 1–14.

[88] Cf. e.g. Crossan 1974c, 85; 1974d, 205, 214.

[89] Criticism is not the same as exclusion.

[90] There are exceptions, including most notably Crossan 1991, 262.

[91] Cf. Zimmermann 2009, 175.

[92] Cf. Bork 2014, 5; Van Eck, Renkin, and Ntakirutimana 2016, 7; *pace* Funk 1966, 192.

[93] Cf. Crossan 1974c, 85; Van Eck, Renkin, and Ntakirutimana 2016, 7.

[94] Quotation from Young 1998, 186, although he reads the parable on the level of Luke, whose version of the parable ultimately excludes the initial guests.

[95] NRSV; Bock 1996, 1276.

[96] Luz 2005, 51–52; cf. Scott 1981, 37; Etchells 1998, 186; Bork 2014, 5.

[97] Cf. Jeremias 1972, 33; Young 1998, 171–172, 174.

to apply this line of reasoning to the level of the historical Jesus.[98] Young explains why this is a mistake:

Matthew places the parable in Jesus' ministry. [...] Reading this parable anachronistically does a terrible injustice to his life and ministry by imposing a later setting for the parable that envisions the sharp separation between the church and the synagogue. The allegorical interpretation that views the invited guests as the Jewish people and the others who accepted the invitation from the highways and thoroughfares as the Gentiles must be rejected. For the historical Jesus there was only the synagogue.[99]

Like Matthew, Luke refuses to allow the initial invitees a place at the banquet and has Jesus overtly state at 14:24 that "none of those who were invited will taste my dinner."[100] These Synoptic emphases obscure the original intent of the parable, which was to advocate the breaking down of boundaries through practices like open commensality in order to feed the hungry and desperate.[101]

Yet the evangelists should not in this instance be blamed for polluting the tradition.[102] Liability rather falls on Q's main redactor. As we have seen, the parable ends in Q with the motive clause "so that my house may be filled" (ἵνα γεμισθῇ μου ὁ οἶκος), which supports the likelihood that those who initially declined would have been welcome had they attended anyway. The parable's literary context in the formative stratum does little to contradict this scenario, and the focus remains on indiscriminate admittance. By contrast, the parable's literary context in the main redaction complicates the scenario to such an extent that one has to assume the exclusion of the initial invitees.[103] Hence, the source critic can witness before her very eyes the evolution of the tradition along these lines: (1) the historical Jesus tells a parable that imagines the kingdom of God as a place where everyone receives food and access is not restricted;[104] (2) Q's formative stratum links this parable to other parables with overlapping themes; (3) Q's main redactor adds further material that obscures the openness of the original parable and introduces the motif of demarcation between insiders and outsiders;[105] (4) the evangelists make explicit the motif of condemning outsiders that was only implied by the literary context in the final form of Q.[106] Similar evolutionary steps could be isolated for other components of our parable, including most notably its growth from a non-allegorical, non-

---

[98] Cf. Etchells 1998, 188, 190.

[99] Young 1998, 175.

[100] NRSV; Funk, Scott, and Butts 1988, 43; Funk and Hoover 1993, 352; Bock 1996, 1268, 1278; Etchells 1998, 186; Young 1998, 186; Snodgrass 2008, 305; Thurén 2014, 317; see Funk 1966, 165, 173–175, 182–183, 186–187; Neirynck 1982, 63–64, 67.

[101] Cf. Van Eck 2013, 12.

[102] Cf. Jeremias 1972, 69.

[103] Cf. esp. Q 13:26–27, 28.

[104] Cf. Van Eck 2013, 12.

[105] Cf. Kloppenborg 1995, 292, 300; Kirk 1998, 251; Smith 2014, 52–53.

[106] Cf. Scott 1989, 168.

eschatological narrative to a fiercely allegorised eschatological parable.[107] The initial transition to allegory seems to have happened first during the inception of Q's main redaction. If the parable is considered in isolation, Kloppenborg's criteria of characteristic forms, characteristic motifs, and implied audience almost demand a position for it in the formative stratum.

8.4 Findings

This chapter has argued that the parable of the great supper featured in the formative stratum before it was incorporated into the main redaction. With Kloppenborg, I have little doubt that the parable stood in the main redaction at that stage of the document's diachronic development. Its literary context in the main redaction is just too conveniently appropriate to be coincidental or irrelevant. Even so, an equal or greater measure of appropriateness in the context of the formative stratum strongly suggests that the main redactor inherited this tradition from the formative stratum and changed its former meaning. Brilliantly, this was achieved without changing the content of the parable at all, but by merely adding different material in front of it.

---

[107] See e.g. Schottroff 2006, 45–48.

Chapter 9

Q 19:12–13, 15–24, 26, "Reaping Where You Did Not Sow"[1]

¹²ἄνθρωπός τις ἀποδημῶν ¹³ἐκάλεσεν δέκα δούλους ἑαυτοῦ καὶ ἔδωκεν αὐτοῖς δέκα μνᾶς ⟦καὶ εἶπεν αὐτο<ῖ>ς· πραγματεύσασθε ἐν ᾧ ἔρχομαι.⟧ ¹⁵ ... ⟦μετὰ⟧ ... ⟦πολὺν χρόνον⟧ ἔρχεται ὁ κύριος τῶν δούλων ἐκείνων καὶ συναίρει λόγον μετ' αὐτῶν. ¹⁶καὶ ⟦<ἦ>λθ<εν>⟧ ὁ πρῶτος λέγων· κύριε, ἡ μνᾶ σου δέκα προσηργάσατο μνᾶς. ¹⁷καὶ εἶπεν αὐτῷ· εὖ, ἀγαθὲ δοῦλε, ἐπὶ ὀλίγα ἦς πιστός, ἐπὶ πολλῶν σε καταστήσω. ¹⁸καὶ ἦλθεν ὁ ⟦δεύτερος⟧ λέγων· κύριε, ἡ μνᾶ σου ἐποίησεν πέντε μνᾶς. ¹⁹εἶπεν ⟦αὐτ⟧ῷ· ⟦εὖ, ἀγαθὲ δοῦλε ἐπὶ ὀλίγα ἦς πιστός,⟧ ἐπὶ πολλῶν σε καταστήσω. ²⁰καὶ ἦλθεν ὁ ἕτερος λέγων· κύριε, ²¹⟦ἔγνων⟧ σε ὅτι σκληρὸς εἶ ἄνθρωπος, θερίζων ὅπου οὐκ ἔσπειρας καὶ συνάγων ὅθεν οὐ διεσκόρπισας, καὶ φοβ⟦ηθεὶς ἀπελθὼν⟧ ἔκρυψα ⟦<τὴν μνᾶν> σου⟧ ἐν ⟦τῇ γῇ⟧· ἴδ⟦ε⟧ ἔχεις τὸ σόν. ²²λέγει αὐτῷ· πονηρὲ δοῦλε, ᾔδεις ὅτι θερίζω ὅπου οὐκ ἔσπειρα καὶ συνάγω ὅθεν οὐ διεσκόρπισα; ²³⟦ἔδει σε οὖν βαλεῖν⟧ μου τ⟦ὰ⟧ ἀργύρι⟦α τοῖς⟧ τραπεζ⟦ίταις⟧, καὶ ἐλθὼν ἐγὼ ἐκομισάμην ἂν τὸ ἐμὸν σὺν τόκῳ. ²⁴ἄρατε οὖν ἀπ' αὐτοῦ τὴν μνᾶν καὶ δότε τῷ ἔχοντι τὰς δέκα μνᾶς· ²⁶τῷ ⟦γὰρ⟧ ἔχοντι παντὶ δοθήσεται, τοῦ δὲ μὴ ἔχοντος καὶ ὃ ἔχει ἀρθήσεται ἀπ' αὐτοῦ.

¹²A certain person, on taking a trip, ¹³called ten of his slaves and gave them ten minas ⟦and said to them: Do business until I come⟧. ¹⁵ ... ⟦After a long time⟧ the master of those slaves comes and settles accounts with them. ¹⁶And the first ⟦came⟧ saying: Master, your mina has produced ten more minas. ¹⁷And he said to him: Well done, good slave, you have been faithful over a pittance, I will set you over much. ¹⁸And the ⟦second⟧ came saying: Master, your mina has earned five minas. ¹⁹He said to ⟦him: Well done, good slave, you have been faithful over little,⟧ I will set you over much. ²⁰And the other came saying: Master, ²¹⟦I knew⟧ you, that you are a hard person, reaping where you did not sow and gathering up from where you did not winnow; and, scared, I ⟦went «and»⟧ hid ⟦your <mina>⟧ in ⟦the ground⟧. Here, you have what belongs to you. ²²He said to him: Wicked slave! You knew that I reap where I have not sown, and gather up from where I have not winnowed? ²³⟦Then you had to invest⟧ my money ⟦with the⟧ money ⟦changers⟧! And at my coming I would have received what belongs to me plus interest. ²⁴So take from him the mina and give «it» to the one who has the ten minas. ²⁶⟦For⟧ to everyone who has will be given; but from the one who does not have, even what he has will be taken from him.

Although the reconstruction of Q 19:12–13, 15–24, 26 faces tremendous difficulties, most contemporary scholars agree that there is enough verbal, structural, and conceptual overlap between Matthew 25:14–29 and Luke 19:12–26

---

[1] An earlier version of this chapter was published as an article in *Journal of Early Christian History* 6/2 (see Howes 2016d).

to justify its place in the Sayings Gospel Q.[2] In particular, Denaux has argued comprehensively and convincingly that the parable of the entrusted money belongs in Q.[3]

9.1 Kloppenborg's Analysis

In his *Formation of Q*, Kloppenborg does not examine the parable of the entrusted money in any detail. It was sufficient for his purposes to draw upon Lührmann's redactional observations about this text.[4] Accordingly, Kloppenborg maintains that both Q 19:12–27 and Q 22:28–30 fit well in their literary context in the Sayings Gospel after Q 17:23–35, since all three of these texts "deal with the subject of [eschatological] judgment."[5] Like Q 17:23–35, the parable of the entrusted money treats the negative side of eschatological judgment. Q 22:28–30 concludes the Sayings Gospel on a high note by treating the positive side of such judgment. Although Kloppenborg does not spell it out for his readers in his 1987 publication, the obvious consequence is that the parable of the entrusted money belongs to the main redaction, since it deals with the same theme as the rest of this layer, namely eschatological judgment.[6] It is worth mentioning that Kloppenborg appeals only to his criterion of "characteristic motifs" when he attributes this parable to the main redaction, thereby failing to draw upon his criteria of "characteristic forms" and "implied audience."

Kloppenborg's case is very convincing, and there is no reason to doubt his analysis of the parable on the level of the main redaction. In fact, the current author has proposed similar avenues of interpretation in earlier publications when considering the parable synchronically as part of Q's final form.[7] Even

---

[2] E.g. Donahue 1988, 105; Piper 1989, 144–145; Funk and Hoover 1993, 256, 374, 375; Funk 1996, 133; Tuckett 1996, 147; Denaux 2001, 429–460; Fleddermann 2005a, 837–838; Smith 2006, 124; Van Eck 2011, 1–3; Park 2014a, 84; Roth 2018, 108–109; cf. Scott 1989, 223 Roth 2014, 388. Some scholars doubt the attribution of this text to the Sayings Gospel Q: e.g. Dodd 1958, 146; Crossan 1974a, 23; Jacobson 1992, 244; Luz 2005, 247–248; Snodgrass 2008, 531; Wright 2015, 75, 170. A small number of scholars maintain that Matthew and Luke each used a different version of Q when copying this parable: e.g. Marshall 1978, 702; Crossan 1983, 199; Bock 1996, 1528; Nolland 2005, 1013. Schottroff (2006, 187) holds that Matthew 25:14–30 and Luke 19:11–27 are "two completely different parables" (see also Meier 2016, 278–288). For a good overview of scholarly opinion on this matter, see Van Eck 2011, 2–3.

[3] Denaux 2001, 429–460.

[4] Lührmann 1969, 75.

[5] Kloppenborg 1987, 164–165, quotation from page 164; cf. Lührmann 1994, 64; Kloppenborg 1995, 298–299; Piper 2000, 239; Smith 2006, 126.

[6] Cf. Robinson 1991, 185–186 n. 38; 1995a, 260–261 n. 4; Vaage 1994, 107; Kloppenborg 1995, 290; 2000a, 118 Kirk 1998, 299.

[7] E.g. Howes 2014c, 6; 2015a, 214.

so, there are indications suggesting that the parable featured in the formative stratum before it was incorporated into the main redaction.

9.2 The Most Primitive Form of the Parable

There should be little doubt that Q 22:28, 30 was added after the parable by Q's main redactor.[8] It follows that this logion was not associated with the parable before the formation of the main redaction. In addition, parable scholars are in agreement that the application in Q 19:26 was added to the parable secondarily.[9] The latter is confirmed by the fact that Q 19:26 was a free-floating maxim in the early Jesus tradition.[10] A number of scholars have commented that the maxim does not correspond perfectly to the parable's content.[11] Anyone wanting to determine the parable's meaning at an earlier stage needs to consider it without this application (Q 19:26) or the subsequent logion (Q 22:28, 30).

Recently, a number of scholars have investigated and interpreted the parable of the entrusted money on the level of the historical Jesus by seriously considering its social, economic, historical, cultural, political, and religious contexts in first-century Palestine.[12] Out of these, the most convincing interpretation is arguably the one put forward by Van Eck, who draws on Rohrbaugh and Herzog.[13] Unfortunately, Van Eck takes the minority position that the throne

---

[8] *Critical Edition of Q* 22:28, 30 (Matt 19:28 // Luke 22:28, 30): "You who have followed me will sit ... on thrones judging the twelve tribes of Israel." (ὑμεῖς οἱ ἀκολουθήσαντές μοι ... καθήσεσθε ἐπὶ θρόν[ους]] κρίνοντες τὰς δώδεκα φυλὰς τοῦ Ἰσραήλ.)

[9] Luz 2005, 249; e.g. Dodd 1958, 148–149; Via 1967, 46, 114; Jeremias 1972, 62, 111; Crossan 1974a, 24; Scott 1981, 40; 1989, 224; Donahue 1988, 105; Taylor 1989, 165; Funk and Hoover 1993, 375; Kloppenborg 1995, 296; Davies and Allison 1997, 410; cf. Hunter 1964, 19; Crossan 1979, 31; Piper 1989, 146; Funk 2006, 30, 109–110; Hedrick 2014, 134–135.

[10] Hunter 1964, 120; Via 1967, 114; Jeremias 1972, 106; Crossan 1974a, 24; 1983, 201; Scott 1981, 40; 1989, 224; Donahue 1988, 105; Taylor 1989, 165; Jacobson 1992, 241; Funk and Hoover 1993, 375; Herzog 1994, 151–152; Kloppenborg 1995, 296; Luz 2005, 249; Nolland 2005, 1019; Van Eck 2011, 6; cf. Snodgrass 2008, 535; cf. Matt 13:12; Mark 4:25; Luke 8:18; Gos. Thom. 41.

[11] E.g. Dodd 1958, 149; Bultmann 1968, 176; Crossan 1974a, 24; Davies and Allison 1997, 410; Luz 2005, 249. Although he also sees Q 19:26 as a secondary addition, Jeremias (1972, 62) claims that the addition "is an entirely relevant explanation of the command [in Q 19:24]" (cf. Derrett 1970, 30). The current author agrees with Jeremias on this point against most scholars.

[12] E.g. Scott 1989, 217–235; Jacobson 1992, 239–244; Rohrbaugh 1993, 32–39; Herzog 1994, 155–168; Oakman 2008, 53–55, 68–69; Van Eck 2011, 1–11; Crossan 2012, 98–106; Park 2014a, 84–88; cf. Ukpong 2012.

[13] Van Eck 2011, 1–11; cf. Rohrbaugh 1993, 32–39; Herzog 1994, 155–168.

claimant narrative in Luke 19:12b, 14, 15b, 27[14] was part of the most primitive form of the parable.[15] In other words, he accepts the Lukan form of the parable in more or less its existing structure (but without verses 11 and 25–26) as the form that goes back to the earliest layer of the Jesus tradition. This is curious, since he acknowledges that the parable probably stems from Q.[16] To my mind, it is not sound methodology to argue that the Lukan form of a text is more primitive than the Q form of that same text. If Q is accepted as Luke's source for the parable, Luke's version cannot possibly predate that of Q. One might want to argue that the Lukan form goes back to Q, but this would have to be done by engaging other reconstructions of the Q text, including especially the *Critical Edition of Q.* Unfortunately, Van Eck fails to consider the parable and its reconstruction on the level of Q. Whether on the level of Q or the historical Jesus, scholars overwhelmingly agree that the parable initially featured without the elements of the throne claimant in Luke 19:12b, 14, 15b, 27.[17]

Van Eck's main reason for including these elements is that they accurately reflect the social, economic, and political situation of Palestine around the time of Jesus's public ministry.[18] In fact, the description recalls a historical event: In 4 BCE, Archelaus travelled to Rome in order to have his kingship over Judea confirmed, but was opposed in Rome by a Jewish embassy of 50 people.[19] In the end, he received his kingship and took revenge on those who had opposed him. Even so, identifying a text as historically reliable or socio-scientifically accurate does not qualify as sufficient evidence for accepting it as authentic. As an ancient person, one would expect Luke to have knowledge of the ancient world, so that he would reflect it accurately in his own material.[20] On the one hand, Luke could have been familiar with the historical incident described

---

[14] Luke 19:12b, 14, 15b, 27 (ESV): "[12b]A nobleman went into a far country to receive for himself a kingdom and then return. [14]But his citizens hated him and sent a delegation after him, saying, 'We do not want this man to reign over us.' [15b]...having received the kingdom... [27]But as for these enemies of mine, who did not want me to reign over them, bring them here and slaughter them before me.'"

[15] Van Eck 2011, 6–7; cf. Schottroff 2006, 187; Wright 2015, 83, 142.

[16] Van Eck 2011, 1, 3.

[17] Marshall 1978, 701; Jacobson 1992, 241; Denaux 2001, 431; Snodgrass 2008, 530, 537; e.g. Hunter 1964, 19, 79–80; Bultmann 1968, 176; Jeremias 1972, 58–59, 95; Crossan 1974a, 22; Piper 1989, 144–145; 2000, 238; Scott 1989, 220, 223; Funk and Hoover 1993, 374; Kloppenborg 1995, 295; Davies and Allison 1997, 402; Fleddermann 2005a, 838–839; Luz 2005, 248; Meier 2016, 298–301.

[18] Van Eck 2011, 6; cf. Funk 2006, 44, 61; Wright 2015, 140.

[19] Jeremias 1972, 59; Marshall 1978, 701, 703–704; Scott 1989, 223; Blomberg 1990, 218; Funk and Hoover 1994, 374; Bock 1996, 1525–1526, 1532; Snodgrass 2008, 521, 537; Van Eck 2011, 6; see Schottroff 2006, 182–184; Wright 2015, 55, 138–140; cf. Taylor 1989, 153–155; Thurén 2014, 339; see Josephus, *J.W.* 2.80–100, 111; *Ant.* 17.208–249, 299–314.

[20] Cf. Funk 2006, 156.

above and could easily have changed the parable of Jesus to recall this histori-cal event.[21] On the other hand, featuring a recognised historical event as part of a parable was not typical of the historical Jesus,[22] and even went against his rhetorical strategy in the telling of parables.[23] Even if Luke received the story of the throne claimant as part of the tradition that came down to him, he might have been responsible for conflating it with the parable of the entrusted money.[24] To be sure, scholars overwhelmingly agree that the story of the throne claimant and the parable of the entrusted money were conflated by Luke.[25] This means that the two stories did not feature together before their conflation by Luke. Van Eck argues that "the parable cannot portray its core purpose without the throne claimant story to make its point."[26] Against this claim, it will be argued in what follows that the broad strokes of Van Eck's reading are not only possible, but also likely, if the parable is interpreted without the throne claim-ant story.

9.3 Socio-Economic Background

To repeat what was said in chapter 5, significant percentages of agricultural goods were taken from the peasantry in first-century Palestine through various kinds of taxes, tithes, rents, and loan repayments, and were then redistributed among the rich to use as they saw fit.[27] If Oakman's estimations are correct, taxes and rents could amount to between one half and two thirds of a small peasant's overall harvest, leaving much less produce for daily survival.[28] The small peasantry naturally viewed such appropriation of their produce as intrin-sically unfair and immoral.[29] They understood the world as consisting of "lim-ited goods."[30] According to the ancient social value of "limited goods," social

---

[21] Davies and Allison 1997, 402.

[22] Scott 1989, 223.

[23] Funk 2006, 62, 172.

[24] See Taylor 1989, 155–157; cf. Jeremias 1972, 59, 95; Crossan 1974a, 22; 1983, 199; Snodgrass 2008, 530.

[25] Blomberg 1990, 217; Jacobson 1992, 241; Bock 1996, 1528; Snodgrass 2008, 530; e.g. Bultmann 1968, 176; Crossan 1974a, 22; Scott 1981, 40; 1989, 221, 223; Donahue 1988, 105; Piper 1989, 144–145; 2000, 238; Funk and Hoover 1993, 374; Herzog 1994, 150; Klop-penborg 1995, 295; Tuckett 1996, 147; Fleddermann 2005a, 838; Nolland 2005, 1013; Snod-grass 2008, 537.

[26] Van Eck 2011, 8.

[27] Herzog 1994, 161; Van Eck 2011, 5, 7; Park 2014a, 85, 86; Häkkinen 2016, 3; cf. Rohrbaugh 1993, 34; Boer and Petterson 2017, 93.

[28] Oakman's 1986, 72; cf. Ukpong 2012, 200; Häkkinen 2016, 2.

[29] Cf. Crossan 2002, 252.

[30] Rohrbaugh 1993, 33; Herzog 1994, 152; Van Eck 2011, 5, 9; cf. Oakman 2008, 54–55.

and economic realities were closed systems and resources were always in short supply.[31] Available resources could be neither increased nor created *ex nihilo*, but could only be distributed and apportioned. One could only attain *additional* goods by depleting the resources of someone else, who probably needed those resources for survival.[32] This explains why the predominant type of economic exchange amongst small peasants was balanced reciprocity.[33] Any economic endeavour aimed at gaining profit or accumulating wealth was therefore regarded as inherently devious and socially damaging.[34] "Those who seemed to be slightly better off were tolerated insofar as their 'wealth' was seen to benefit the village as a whole."[35]

Yet earning profit and accumulating wealth were exactly what motivated the rich.[36] Most important for wealth creation was control over land and its produce.[37] Similarly, the most important concern of small peasants was control of their own smallholdings, but for a different reason altogether. Whereas the elite saw "land" as an opportunity for wealth creation, small peasants saw it as an indispensable means for daily survival.[38] From a small peasant perspective, the first and most important function of the land was the immediate need to assure family sustenance.[39] Whereas the political economy of the elite was aimed at earning a profit, the domestic economy of small peasants was aimed at maintaining necessary levels of subsistence.[40] If a small peasant was unable to meet existing obligations, that peasant was forced to borrow from wealthier individuals.[41] Such borrowing instigated a patron-client relationship between the two parties, which was skewed in favour of the patron and often resulted in foreclosure of land due to an inability to pay off debts.[42] In other words, small peasants were often forced into indebtedness, which initiated a downward spiral that included control by creditors, loss of land, starvation, and becoming

---

[31] Rohrbaugh 1993, 33; Douglas 1995, 122–123; Ford 2016, 21.

[32] Rohrbaugh 1993, 33, 35; Crossan 2002, 252; Van Eck 2011, 5; Häkkinen 2016, 4; Tönsing 2019, 131; cf. Ukpong 2012, 200.

[33] Oakman 1986, 66; Horsley 1995b, 204; see chapter 2 above for a definition of balanced reciprocity.

[34] Crossan 2002, 252; Van Eck 2011, 5; Tönsing 2019, 131; see Rohrbaugh 1993, 33–34; cf. Kyrtatas 2002, 151.

[35] Boer and Petterson 2017, 67.

[36] Cf. Ford 2016, 26.

[37] Herzog 1994, 162; Arnal 2001, 102, 139; Häkkinen 2016, 2.

[38] Arnal 2001, 139; see Oakman 1986, 49–52; cf. Jacobs 2018, 124–125.

[39] Rohrbaugh 1993, 33–34; Van Eck 2011, 5.

[40] Park 2014a, 85; see Oakman 2008, 56–57; cf. Jacobs 2018, 124–125.

[41] Oakman 1986, 72; 2008, 24; Horsley 1995b, 215, 219; Van Eck 2011, 7.

[42] Herzog 1994, 161; Ukpong 2012, 200; see Boer and Petterson 2017, 97–100; cf. Oakman 2008, 69; Van Eck 2011, 7; Ford 2016, 21, 32; see chapter 5 above.

day-labourers, slaves, beggars, and bandits.[43] Apart from the economic implications, this would have entailed a tremendous loss of honour, which was obviously a big deal in antiquity.[44] From a small peasant perspective, the process of exploitation was to a large extent aided by the existence of physical money, the symbols of the elite, which is why many small peasants used physical coins "only when they were forced to do so."[45] Such a negative view of actual coinage is an undercurrent of the parable when viewed from a small peasant perspective.

Some of these peasants were allowed to remain on their smallholdings as tenant farmers, with ownership of the land and its produce reverting to the landlord.[46] As we saw in chapter 4, it was typical for such landlords and landowners to be non-resident and largely absent from their farms.[47] Wealthy landowners and landlords mostly lived in the city, usually owning multiple estates.[48] Palestinian landowners therefore resided in cities like Tiberias, Sepphoris, and Jerusalem,[49] especially those who owned the most fertile land.[50] It is safe to say that the economic system of the day enabled rich and powerful individuals to exploit the small peasantry by extracting produce from them and eventually appropriating their smallholdings through indebtedness and foreclosure.[51] The households of these city-dwelling elite functioned like businesses, controlling rural smallholdings by collecting, storing, redistributing, selling, and exporting significant percentages of their produce.[52] The elite often used skilled city slaves to take care of the daily operations of their "commercial

---

[43] Herzog 1994, 162, 166; Horsley 1995a, 43; 1995b, 60, 215–216, 219; Freyne 2000, 205; Arnal 2001, 139–140, 146; Moxnes 2003, 150; Oakman 2008, 21, 25, 224; Van Eck 2011, 7; Park 2014a, 86; Häkkinen 2016, 3, 7.

[44] Häkkinen 2016, 4.

[45] Boer and Petterson 2017, 121; cf. Q 16:13.

[46] See chapter 5 above.

[47] White 1970, 350; Massey and Moreland 1992, 27; Freyne 2000, 99, 195; Fiensy 2010, 196; see Kloppenborg 2006, 279–280, 314–316; cf. Burford 1993, 217, 219; Chandezon 2011, 98.

[48] White 1970, 353; Herzog 1994, 156; Saller 2003, 187–188; Kloppenborg 2006, 300; Fiensy 2010, 196; Ukpong 2012, 200; Dube 2015, 5; Boer and Petterson 2017, 97–98; cf. Aubert 1994, 126; Van Eck 2011, 5.

[49] Some of these landowners might also have lived in Rome (Oakman 1986, 78; cf. Häkkinen 2016, 1), although the fact that Palestine was not *ager publicus populi Romani* before 70 CE would seem to speak against this.

[50] Oakman 1986, 78; Freyne 1988, 149, 151; 2000, 52, 99, 195; Park 2014a, 85; Dube 2015, 5; Häkkinen 2016, 7; cf. Horsley 1995a, 42; Boer and Petterson 2017, 141.

[51] Ukpong 2012, 200; Ford 2016, 21, 32; Häkkinen 2016, 3; see Boer and Petterson 2017, 97–100; cf. Drake 2014, 237.

[52] Herzog 1994, 156.

households," which included making loans and collecting rents from the peasantry.[53] In other words, the elite made use of one oppressive system (slavery) to implement and maintain another oppressive system (economic exploitation of the peasantry).[54] It is no wonder that small peasants saw rich people as thieves who were insatiably greedy and inherently evil.[55]

9.4 A Response to Economic Exploitation

The parable of the entrusted money presupposes the situation described in the previous section.[56] With the narrative setting being that of a wealthy urban household, the story plays out against the backdrop of a political economy, located in the city and motivated by profit and self-improvement.[57] The reference in Q 19:23 to earning "interest" (τόκος) with "money changers" (τραπεζῆται) reflects an urban economic system built on the appropriation of rural produce and land.[58] In the narrative, city slaves further the economic interests of their master, who is portrayed as a powerful landowner. That the master should be seen as a landowner is particularly indicated when he is described with agricultural terminology as someone who "reaps where he did not sow, and gathers up from where he did not winnow."[59] That he is a wealthy man is indicated by the fact that he owns slaves and land, by the fact that he is "taking a trip" (ἀποδημῶν), by the fact that he has a lot of money on hand to entrust to his slaves, and by the fact that he is willing to risk his money in such

---

[53] See Bradley 1994, 75–76; cf. Van Eck 2011, 5; Park 2014a, 86. A number of Jewish parables feature a king or master who assigns management over his belongings to his slaves before leaving on some or other extended trip (Snodgrass 2008, 531; see Derrett 1970, 29; Davies and Allison 1997, 404; Luz 2005, 249–250; cf. Yal. 267a; b. Šabb. 152b; Tanna debe Eliyyahu 53; Cant. Rab. 7.14.1; Pesiq. Rab Kah. 14.5; Mek. Baḥodeš 5; Sem. 3.3; Mek. on Exod 20:2; ʾAbot R. Nat. A 14).

[54] Cf. Hezser 2005, 11; Schottroff 2006, 185; Ukpong 2012, 200, 201; Ford 2016, 25, 30; Boer and Petterson 2017, 72.

[55] See Rohrbaugh 1993, 34–35; cf. Schottroff 2006, 223; Ukpong 2012, 201; Ford 2016, 20, 21.

[56] Funk and Hoover 1993, 374; see Ukpong 2012, 199–201. Roth (2018, 116–118) argues that exploitation is not necessarily a topic developed by the parable, since exploitation is not expressly mentioned in the narrative and the high return might have been accrued by other means if the master was away for an extended period of time. The latter is, however, not the only feature that betrays the master's exploitation. This chapter has argued that there are many elements in the narrative that reveal the master's exploitative nature, not least of all the unproductive slave's description of him, which he does not deny.

[57] Herzog 1994, 155; Park 2014a, 85; cf. Van Eck 2011, 5; Ford 2016, 26; Roth 2018, 122–123.

[58] Joseph 2012, 86; Park 2014a, 86; Häkkinen 2016, 3; cf. Herzog 1994, 165–166.

[59] Q 19:21, 22; cf. Jacobson 1992, 242; Van Eck 2011, 7.

a way.[60] Even though Matthew's talents constituted a much higher currency than the minas of Luke and Q,[61] these minas still represented much more money than the average small peasant would have been familiar with.[62]

The master is depicted *negatively* as a "hard" (σκληρός) man.[63] Scott explains that σκληρός refers to a person who is "merciless in his dealings with others."[64] Park adds that the term σκληρός functions in the tradition of Israel to portray "cruel foreign kings" (Isa 19:4) and "stubborn Israelites standing against God's will" (Isa 48:4).[65] She also points out that the term "hard-hearted" (σκληροκαρδία) features in the history of Israel to describe stubborn and disobedient individuals.[66] From a small peasant perspective, the description of the master as someone who reaps where he did not sow and gathers up from where he did not winnow would have been categorically negative and immoral at its core.[67] According to Marshall, the master is here being described as "a grasping person who wants money without the labour of earning it."[68] According to Jeremias, the master is portrayed as "a rapacious man, heedlessly intent on his own profit."[69] According to Scott, the master's characterisation is "of an absentee landlord who bleeds the land dry."[70] According to Ukpong, the master is presented as "one who enriches himself at the expense of others, practically a thief."[71] And from the perspective of Israel as a whole, elite and non-elite alike, the master's comment about earning interest would have been dis-

---

[60] Cf. Jacobson 1992, 242; Herzog 1994, 158; Ukpong 2012, 197; Wright 2015, 170.

[61] Cf. Ukpong 2012, 197; Tönsing 2019, 129.

[62] Scott 1989, 224; Park 2014a, 85; cf. Blomberg 1990, 218; Botha 1996, 281; Snodgrass 2008, 528; Wright 2015, 170. One talent equalled about 6,000 denarii – or 6,000 dragma in Greek currency, with the Roman and Greek currencies being roughly the same – and one mina equalled about 100 denarii, with a denarius being equivalent to one day's wage (Scott 1989, 224; Bock 1996, 1533, 1534; Davies and Allison 1997, 403; Snodgrass 2008, 528; Crossan 2012, 98–99, 100–101; cf. Hunter 1971, 96; Jeremias 1972, 27; Marshall 1978, 704; Blomberg 1990, 218; Funk and Hoover 1993, 256; Kloppenborg 1995, 296; Fleddermann 2005a, 841; Nolland 2005, 1014; Ukpong 2012, 197; Wright 2015, 139, 170).

[63] Scott 1989, 228; Luz 2005, 252; Oakman 2008, 54–55; Van Eck 2011, 5, 6; Park 2014a, 86; Roth 2014, 389, 390; 2018, 115; Ford 2016, 35.

[64] Scott 1989, 229 n. 57; cf. Rohrbaugh 1993, 36; Herzog 1994, 164; Luz 2005, 252 n. 49; Nolland 2005, 1017.

[65] Park 2014a, 86; cf. Luz 2005, 252 n. 49.

[66] Park 2014a, 87; cf. LXX Deut 10:16; Jer 4:4; Matt 19:8; Mark 10:5.

[67] Park 2014a, 87; Ford 2016, 20, 30, 35; Jacobs 2018, 132–133; cf. Scott 1981, 42, 44; Herzog 1994, 160–161, 164; Luz 2005, 252; Van Eck 2011, 5; Crossan 2012, 100; Ukpong 2012, 201; Roth 2018, 115.

[68] Marshall 1978, 707; cf. Jacobson 1992, 242; Bock 1996, 1538; Valantasis 2005, 221.

[69] Jeremias 1972, 60; cf. Roth 2018, 112.

[70] Scott 1989, 230; cf. Herzog 1994, 164.

[71] Ukpong 2012, 198; cf. Bailey 2008, 404; Ford 2016, 20.

graceful and abominable, since it was absolutely forbidden in concurrent Judaism.[72] The master's reference to earning interest could in fact be an indication
that the master is depicted as a *non-Jewish* landowner, which was not entirely
uncommon in Palestine during the first century.[73]

Snodgrass points out that the noun δοῦλος can mean either "slave" or "servant."[74] According to him, "slave" is the more likely option, even if it is impossible to know with certainty which option is intended. Following Derrett,[75]
Scott claims that the stewards in our parable were not slaves but servants.[76]
Derrett's influential claim is simply wrong that "the wide powers needed for
commercial enterprise and to protect the capital belong to a fully competent
agent, which a slave never can be."[77] In antiquity, a slave could indeed function
as "a fully competent agent" on the authority of the slaveholder,[78] and using a
slave as business agent was a *more* effective way to "protect the capital" than
using a free person. Even if free persons could also function as business
agents,[79] it made much better legal sense to use slaves. According to Hezser,
neither the slave nor the master could be sued by third parties for the slave's
actions.[80] Slaves could also not take legal action against their masters.[81] Using
slaves for business therefore protected the master from all kinds of legal action.
The same was not true of servants. Moreover, there was certainly security for
slaveholders in knowing that their slaves were under their complete control,
which included measures of control like physical torture.[82] Using slaves also

---

[72] Bailey 2008, 406; Oakman 2008, 69; Ukpong 2012, 198; Park 2014a, 87; Tönsing
2019, 131; see Crossan 2012, 103–105; cf. Herzog 1994, 166; Crossan 2002, 252; Luz 2005,
252, 253; Snodgrass 2008, 528; Ford 2016, 30; Roth 2018, 124. Cf. Exod 22:25; Lev 25:35–
37; Deut 15:7–11; 23:19–20; Ps 15:5; Jer 15:10; Ezek 18:8–9, 13, 17; 22:12; 4 Macc 2:8.
Charging interest was allowed in economic dealings with gentiles (Snodgrass 2008, 528; cf.
Deut 23:20).

[73] Luz 2005, 253.

[74] Snodgrass 2008, 527.

[75] Derrett 1970, 18–24.

[76] Scott 1989, 226; cf. Marshall 1978, 704.

[77] Derrett 1970, 19.

[78] Ukpong 2012, 197; see Hezser 2005, 275–284; Boer and Petterson 2017, 89–90, 124–
126.

[79] Bradley 1994, 76; Herzog 1994, 157; see Derrett 1970, 18–24.

[80] Hezser 2005, 275, 281; 2009, 132. Boer and Petterson (2017, 126) claim that people
could indeed sue masters if slaves performed transactions on behalf of their masters. It is
possible that the latter pertains to Greco-Roman practices, whereas Hezser focuses on Jewish
practices in particular.

[81] Hezser 2005, 11; cf. Ford 2016, 30.

[82] Schottroff 2006, 175. Derrett (1970, 22) points out that, according to Talmudic law,
non-servile agents had to become *ad hoc* servants of the investor, because "the independent
business man would not often be as attractive as the servant over whom P [the investor] had
ultimate control." This practice supports my argument that slaves would have been more
attractive business agents than free persons.

protected the master's honour by concealing his practice of usury and amassing wealth at the expense of others in a "limited goods" context.[83] According to Boer and Petterson, "slaves undertook most of the exchange activities in markets."[84] The restriction was that slaves could legally not do business or own money in *their own* capacity, but with their masters' money (including the *peculium*) they could perform all tasks a free person could, as long as it carried the approval of their masters.[85] Herzog argues that the δοῦλοι were household retainers, not slaves.[86] He defends his position by drawing on the hierarchy presupposed by the Matthean phrase "to each according to his ability/power/status" (ἑκάστῳ κατὰ τὴν ἰδίαν δύναμιν). On the one hand, as Herzog admits, this phrase is widely seen as Matthean redaction and is therefore not relevant to an interpretation of the parable at an earlier stage. On the other hand, even if the phrase were part of the parable at an earlier stage, it could just as easily refer to the abilities and/or hierarchy of *slaves* in the household.

There are a number of very good reasons to conclude that our parable intended the stewards to be understood as slaves. Firstly, the lexis δοῦλος is used almost exclusively of slaves, as is indicated by the fact that most Greek-English dictionaries do not even list "servant" as a translation possibility.[87] Secondly, there were a number of Greek words available if the author wanted to indicate that the stewards were free servants, including θεράπων, ὑπηρέτης, διάκονος, οἰκέτης, οἰκετεία, θεραπεία, and λειτουργός. Thirdly, the scenario sketched by the parable fits the ancient context best if the stewards were slaves, considering the landholder's actions towards the stewards, which include controlling, commanding, and rewarding or punishing them. Fourthly, the word δοῦλος is characteristically used by the Sayings Gospel Q to denote slaves.[88] Fifthly, the parables of Jesus are typically about slaves, not servants. Sixthly, both Matthew and Luke retained the lexis δοῦλος, which indicates that they probably also understood the stewards to be slaves. Finally, Luke (19:14) deliberately distinguishes the δοῦλοι in the parable of the entrusted money from the πολῖται in the story of the throne claimant.[89] Although the latter lexis should be translated as "citizens" in the context of the throne claimant narrative, it also denotes "free persons."[90] Given these considerations, it is extremely likely that the

---

[83] Ukpong 2012, 200, 201.

[84] Boer and Petterson 2017, 124.

[85] See Hezser 2005, 275–284; Boer and Petterson 2017, 124–126.

[86] Herzog 1994, 158.

[87] E.g. Louw and Nida 1993b, 67, s.v. δοῦλος; Liddel and Scott 1996, 447, s.v. δοῦλος; cf. De Wet 2018, 1.

[88] Cf. Q 7:8; 12:42–46; 14:17, 21.

[89] Taylor 1989, 158; cf. Blomberg 1990, 219, 220; Herzog 1994, 162.

[90] Cf. Liddel and Scott 1996, 1434–1435, s.v. πολίτης.

δοῦλοι in our parable are intended to be understood as slaves, and the onus rests on those wanting to argue that they were servants.[91]

By "doing business" (πραγματεύομαι) for the master, the productive slaves in the narrative were actively contributing to the exploitation of the small peasantry.[92] That the productive slaves were in all likelihood exploiting the small peasantry is indicated by their exceptionally high returns.[93] Such high returns could only have been gained through usurious loans, produce extraction, land speculation, commodities trading, maritime speculation, or political extortion.[94] For the first audiences, the first three options would have come immediately to mind.[95] On a secondary level, these three activities would have made commodities trading possible.[96] To be sure, one would expect the slaves to speculate in the same economic ventures as their master, who is portrayed primarily as a landowner.[97] It was not unprecedented for ancient slaves to make and receive loans.[98] Certainly, the productive slaves were not merely investing at financial institutions to earn interest.[99] On the one hand, the returns on investment would in that case not nearly have been so high. On the other hand, earning interest at such institutions is mentioned in Q 19:23 as an alternative

---

[91] Cf. Martinsen 2011, 317–318.

[92] Crossan 2002, 252; Schottroff 2006, 185; Van Eck 2011, 5, 7; Park 2014a, 86; see Herzog 1994, 160–161, 163; cf. Hezser 2005, 11; Luz 2005, 252.

[93] Jacobson 1992, 243; Van Eck 2011, 5; see Rohrbaugh 1993, 35; cf. Marshall 1978, 705; Scott 1989, 226 n. 41; Taylor 1989, 163; Herzog 1994, 161; Bock 1996, 1535, 1537; Nolland 2005, 1015. The oft-repeated claim by Derrett (1970, 24) that such high returns were "not unusual by the standards of the day" is simply incorrect (Rohrbaugh 1993, 35). Even Matthew's one hundred percent is high by ancient standards, not to even mention Luke and Q's five hundred percent and one thousand percent for the first two slaves respectively.

[94] Jacobson 1992, 243; Herzog 1994, 161; Kloppenborg 1995, 296–297; Piper 2000, 240; Luz 2005, 251–252.

[95] Herzog 1994, 162.

[96] Herzog 1994, 161.

[97] See Bradley 1994, 75–76; cf. Hezser 2005, 275. Piper (2000, 240) argues that agricultural loans could not have incurred such great returns on investment and offers as alternatives "maritime speculation or political extortion." This is unlikely, since the master is portrayed as a landowner and both of these options seem to fall outside the boundaries of the parable itself. Moreover, the parable was probably told and retained in an interior (non-maritime) Palestinian setting by average people (non-politicians). Certainly, the master is not depicted as either a politician or a maritime business man. It is not impossible, however, that he dabbled in other business ventures. We know from rabbinic literature that landowners did at times get involved in business outside agriculture (see Aberbach 1994, 39–54). For example, Rabbi Eleazar ben Harsom was both a landowner and a shipping magnate, Rabbi Hiyya was both a landowner and a silk and linen merchant, and Rab Hisda was both a landowner and a beer manufacturer. Regardless, the present parable focuses exclusively on the agricultural dimension of the master's business practices.

[98] Boer and Petterson 2017, 125.

[99] Luz 2005, 252.

to whatever the slaves were doing with the money.[100] Ultimately, the master and his productive slaves represent the immoral and unfair economic system of the elite, who exploit the small peasantry in their never-ending search for profits.[101]

It is important to note that both the starting capital and the profits gained belong to the master, not the slaves.[102] The master did not loan capital to his slaves, but entrusted them with his own money, to deal with on his behalf.[103] On the one hand, we know this because the money is entrusted to *slaves*, who could not do business with borrowed capital like free persons.[104] On the other hand, we know this because the parable indicates as much in a number of ways: (1) all the slaves speak of "your [the master's] mina" (ἡ μνᾶ σου) in their replies;[105] (2) the master also speaks of "my money" (μου τὸ ἀργύριον);[106] (3) both the master and the unproductive slave declare that the money "belongs to" (ἔχεις τὸ σόν and τὸ ἐμόν) the master;[107] and (4) the description of the master as someone who reaps where he did not sow implies that the master used his slaves to advance himself.[108] Thus, when the master instructs the unproductive slave to hand over his mina to the most productive slave, the mina still belongs to the master. The master only commands this exchange because he wants to earn as much profit as possible and the first slave in the narrative seems to be his most lucrative minion.[109] Regardless of their levels of productivity, the slaves would not have been rewarded financially.[110] Instead, they would have been rewarded with additional responsibilities, additional privileges, and opportunities to share in the lavish lifestyle of their masters. In our parable, the

---

[100] Luz 2005, 252; cf. Nolland 2005, 1018.

[101] Cf. Jacobson 1992, 243; Herzog 1994, 160–161, 163; Luz 2005, 250; Schottroff 2006, 185; Van Eck 2011, 7; Häkkinen 2016, 3; Jacobs 2018, 131; Tönsing 2019, 130.

[102] Luz 2005, 251; see Hezser 2005, 276–278, 284; 2009, 132; cf. Massey and Moreland 1992, 40; Joshel 2010, 128.

[103] Jacobson 1992, 242; Luz 2005, 251; Ukpong 2012, 197; see Bradley 1994, 75–76, 85–86; Boer and Petterson 2017, 125–126; cf. Hezser 2005, 11, 102; 2009, 132; Nolland 2005, 1014; Joshel 2010, 41.

[104] Luz 2005, 251; see Hezser 2005, 276–278, 284; 2009, 132; cf. Massey and Moreland 1992, 40; Joshel 2010, 41.

[105] Q 19:16, 18, 21.

[106] Q 19:23.

[107] Q 19:21, 23.

[108] Cf. Van Eck 2011, 7; Tönsing 2019, 130.

[109] Cf. Derrett 1970, 30–31; Rohrbaugh 1993, 36; Wright 2015, 140.

[110] See Hezser 2005, 276–278, 284; 2009, 132; cf. Nolland 2005, 1014; *pace* Marshall 1978, 704; Scott 1989, 226; Herzog 1994, 157, 160; Meier 2016, 309. Such profits, despite belonging to the master, could enable slaves to eventually "buy" their freedom, in addition to other privileges, and slaves could even receive a share of these profits upon their release from slavery (Massey and Moreland 1992, 32, 41; Hezser 2005, 277; Joshel 2010, 128).

first option, namely that of additional responsibilities (with possibly an increase in status and honour), seems to have been the main and perhaps exclusive reward, as is indicated by the master's response to the productive slaves: "...you have been faithful over little, I will set you over much."[111] Ultimately, all the rewards and punishments in the parable are driven primarily by the master's greed, not his benevolence or annoyance.[112] As Roth observes, "the labor of the slave is the gain of the master."[113]

If the socio-economic context of the parable is taken into consideration, it is impossible to understand any of the characters allegorically. The image of the master is decidedly negative and could not have represented Jesus or God.[114] If the master were depicted as a gentile, his association with Jesus or God would have been even more unthinkable. Similarly, the productive slaves participated in the unfair dealings of their master and could therefore not have represented the Q people, the disciples of Jesus, or people in general.[115] We therefore have to strongly disagree with Marshall, who accurately expresses the sentiment of most other scholars when he claims that "the original form [of our parable] could not but have an allegorical significance for the hearers."[116]

---

[111] Q 19:17, 19; Jeremias 1972, 61; Luz 2005, 252; Nolland 2005, 1014; Bailey 2008, 403; Ukpong 2012, 197; cf. Scott 1981, 44; 1989, 225; Herzog 1994, 163; Kloppenborg 1995, 294; Bock 1996, 1533, 1536, 1637, 1640; Wright 2015, 141, 171.

[112] Ukpong 2012, 197–198; cf. Rohrbaugh 1993, 36; Jacobs 2018, 131.

[113] Roth 2018, 116.

[114] Rohrbaugh 1993, 38; Ukpong 2012, 201–202; Park 2014a, 86; Wright 2015, 75, 83, 86, 140–141; cf. Jeremias 1972, 59–60; Funk 1974, 68; 2006, 155; Tuckett 1996, 218; Nolland 2005, 1018; Beutner 2007b, 36; Verhoeven 2007, 49; Crossan 2012, 106; Ford 2016, 35; *pace* e.g. Blomberg 1990, 216; Catchpole 1993, 160; Luz 2005, 253; Nolland 2005, 1020; Snodgrass 2008, 535; Roth 2018, 118–119. This is not to say that the master of this and other Q parables did not represent Jesus and/or God in the *final form* of Q. Roth (2014, 391–396) argues convincingly that one should not refuse to identify the master characters in Q with Jesus and/or God just because they are portrayed as violent and vicious characters in some Q texts. Although such characterisations are negative from a (post-)modern perspective, they accurately represent ancient images of the divine and support the polemical expectation in Q of severe eschatological judgment against unresponsive outsiders and lax insiders, which was a positive expectation from the perspective of the Q people (cf. Blomberg 1990, 216; Snodgrass 2008, 535–536, 540–541). Such reasoning is certainly correct, but it has to be separated from the argument made in this chapter that oppressed peasants would not have identified an abusive landowner with either Jesus or God (cf. esp. Rohrbaugh 1993, 38). The landowner in the parable of the entrusted money represents everything that is wrong with the world from the perspective of the small peasantry (cf. Herzog 1994, 160–161). Moreover, Jews would have found it almost impossible to identify someone who invests for the sake of interest with God. Yet such a view of God might have been possible for the Q people at a later stage, after they had broken away from greater Israel (and some of her laws).

[115] Park 2014a, 86.

[116] Marshall 1978, 702; cf. Dodd 1958, 151.

If the "original form" of the parable was not allegorical, then there is no reason to presume an eschatological reading either.[117]

Like other interpreters, Marshall approaches the parable from above.[118] Against this tendency, the current interpretation approaches the parable from below.[119] Both on the level of the historical Jesus and on the level of Q's formative stratum, audiences would have identified with the unproductive slave.[120] Against the sensibilities and intuition of those who read the parable from above, which includes not only the evangelists, but just about every single interpreter thereafter, the hero of the story is the unproductive slave.[121] He is the only character in the narrative portrayed positively from a small peasant perspective. Against the exploitative behaviour of the productive slaves, the unproductive slave acts according to the standards and norms of a domestic economy, associated with the countryside and motivated by subsistence and self-preservation.[122] The unproductive slave's act of hiding the money in the ground would have been sensible and prudent according to ancient standards, so that the first audiences would have identified with this narrative character.[123]

The parable of the entrusted money sketches a scenario of a slave who refuses to participate in the economic exploitation of lowly smallholders and tenant farmers.[124] His actions might have brought about the disfavour of his master, but the audience would have understood that it also brought about the favour of God. In the process, the slave exposes the master for who he really is: a money-hungry bully and tyrant.[125] The unproductive slave does so by accusing the master directly of economic exploitation in Q 19:21, and the master not only accepts this description of himself,[126] probably viewing it as a compliment

---

[117] Cf. Jacobson 1992, 242.

[118] Cf. Rohrbaugh 1993, 35; Bailey 2008, 397; Ford 2016, 35.

[119] Cf. Rohrbaugh 1993, 33; Van Eck 2011, 5; Ukpong 2012, 191. As this chapter continues to argue, Luz (2005, 253) is mistaken when he claims that the parable of the entrusted money "was not formulated from the perspective of poor people," that it was not interested in questioning prevailing economic practices, and that it was "not socially subversive."

[120] Donahue 1988, 107; Rohrbaugh 1993, 36, 38; Oakman 2008, 68; cf. Scott 1981, 42; Crossan 2002, 253.

[121] Rohrbaugh 1993, 33, 35, 38; Herzog 1994, 153, 167; Oakman 2008, 55; Van Eck 2011, 1, 5; Ford 2016, 27, 35; *pace* Wright 2015, 141.

[122] Crossan 2002, 252; cf. Herzog 1994, 152; Jacobs 2018, 123–124.

[123] Scott 1989, 227, 228, 230, 232; Rohrbaugh 1993, 36, 38; Davies and Allison 1997, 408; Oakman 2008, 68–69; Van Eck 2011, 5; cf. Herzog 1994, 164; Crossan 2002, 253; *pace* Wright 2015, 141; see below.

[124] Crossan 2002, 252; Schottroff 2006, 223; Van Eck 2011, 10; Ukpong 2012, 197.

[125] Herzog 1994, 164, 165, 167; Van Eck 2011, 5; Park 2014a, 87; cf. Luz 2005, 252; Funk 2006, 46.

[126] Ukpong 2012, 199; cf. Roth 2018, 115.

instead of the accusation that it is, but even repeats it verbatim in Q 19:22.[127] As a narrative character, the master embodies economic exploitation. He is a tragic character, who is unable to perceive his own faults and accountability.[128] The slave stood up against his master's evil ways and, because of clever rhetoric, is no worse off at the end of the narrative than he was at the beginning.[129] His "punishment" is to give his mina to the slave with ten minas, but this is really a reward, since it releases him from having to participate in any economic endeavours in the foreseeable future.[130] His master has one less minion to rely on in his abusive activities. Part of the parable's intent is to illustrate how one can stand up against prevailing exploitation and in the process contribute to the establishment of God's kingdom.[131] The parable is a response to the economic exploitation of the small peasantry in first-century Palestine.[132]

9.5 Cunning Trickery in the Face of Fear

One could argue that the unproductive slave is not characterised as a humanitarian. The text clearly describes him as burying the money because he was "scared" (φοβέω), not because he wanted to make an impact on society.[133] This explanation is also highly believable, since fear was by far the most important strategy used by ancient (and modern) slaveholders to control their slaves.[134] For the most part, such fear was instilled through severe physical punishment, used in combination with emotional torment. All forms of slavery presupposed

---

[127] Donahue 1988, 107; Valantasis 2005, 221; Crossan 2012, 100; Wright 2015, 141, 171; cf. Fleddermann 2005a, 862; Luz 2005, 247, 253; Nolland 2005, 1018, 1019; Van Eck 2011, 5; Ford 2016, 22; Tönsing 2019, 136; *pace* Bailey 2008, 405.

[128] Cf. Beutner 2007a, 62.

[129] Park 2014a, 87.

[130] Cf. Snodgrass 2008, 535; Park 2014a, 87; *pace* Via 1967, 120.

[131] Cf. Van Eck 2011, 8; Wright 2015, 40.

[132] Cf. Jacobson 1992, 239–244; Oakman 2008, 36, 54–55, 68–69, 252; Park 2014a, 84–88. Piper (2000, 241; cf. 255–256) concludes his analysis of the parable by claiming that it corresponds to the rest of Q in that "concern to present a socio-economic critique of *oppressive structures* of the day is not high on the agenda for the Q people in their attitudes towards wealth and poverty" (emphasis original). His analysis considers the parable as it appears in the final form of Q, and I would agree that on that redactional level the parable is not presented as "a socio-economic critique of oppressive structures." However, this chapter argues that the parable did indeed level such a critique at an earlier stage in the formation of Q and that this critique is in continuity with the socio-economic concerns expressed in the rest of the formative stratum.

[133] Cf. Bock 1996, 1538; Davies and Allison 1997, 409.

[134] See esp. Bradley 1984, 113–143.

fear, and all slaves lived under constant fear of being punished or even killed.[135] Yet there are a number of good reasons to conclude that fear was not the true factor that motivated his actions.[136] One should not assume that the slave's description to the master of his own internal motivation is entirely truthful. It is important to realise that, unlike the Matthean parable, the Q parable, following Luke, only narrates what the slave *told* his master, not what he actually did or how he actually felt.[137] It is likely that the slave did bury the mina, as he claims, but unlikely that he did so because he was scared, as he claims.[138] This does not mean that the slave was not afraid of his master, which he must have been, but merely that fear did not motivate his actions.[139] In my view, the slave's words represent shrewd rhetoric aimed at deceiving the master.[140] A closer look at the content of the unproductive slave's response will reveal just how calculating and sneaky his utterances were.

The slave's response begins with the description of the master as "a hard person, reaping where he did not sow and gathering up from where he did not winnow." We have seen that the description of the master as a "hard" (σκληρός) man is a decidedly negative one. It paints the master as a merciless, cruel, stubborn, and perhaps even godless individual. From the master's perspective, however, the term could easily have come across as a positive reflection on him as an astute and solid business man.[141] Even today, being tough and emotionally neutral are considered positive traits in the business world, promoting "objective" decision-making and "professional" conduct. When it comes to earning a profit, whether in antiquity or today, being "ruthless" and "tough" are regarded as positive attributes. Being "hard" could further easily have been taken as a compliment by a man who lived in a patriarchal society that valued "hard" masculinity over "soft" femininity.[142] Similarly, the unproductive slave's description of the master as someone who reaps where he did not sow and gathers up from where he did not winnow is decidedly negative if

---

[135] Bradley 1984, 123, 135–137, 142; Hezser 2005, 149; Martinsen 2011, 139–140; see Howes 2015c, 101–104; cf. Harrill 2006, 91–92; Joshel 2010, 116. Valantasis (2005, 221) asks: "If the story vindicates the slave's perspective, why should he fear?" The answer is: because he is a slave and severe punishment is always just around the corner (cf. e.g. Martinsen 2011, 139–140). Even if the slave was the hero of the story, there is enough evidence given in the story itself to indicate that the slave had reason to fear his master (Rohrbaugh 1993, 36; Roth 2014, 390; Wright 2015, 171; cf. Kloppenborg 1995, 297).

[136] Ford 2016, 26; cf. Luz 2005, 253.

[137] Roth 2018, 111; see Denaux 2001, 439–440; cf. Crossan 1974a, 23; Marshall 1978, 704; Scott 1989, 221; Davies and Allison 1997, 406; Luz 2005, 247, 249; Nolland 2005, 1015, 1017; Wright 2015, 172; *pace* Fleddermann 2005a, 842–843.

[138] Cf. Luz 2005, 253.

[139] Cf. Rohrbaugh 1993, 36, 37; Ford 2016, 26.

[140] Ford 2016, 26, 30, 38.

[141] *Pace* Tönsing 2019, 134–135.

[142] Cf. e.g. Dreyer 2005, 740; Helena Visser 2017, 352.

viewed from the perspective of the socio-economic underclass, but fairly positive if viewed from the perspective of the socio-economic upper class.[143] To the small peasantry, it depicts the master as a ruthless exploiter, but to the master, it depicts him as a good business man who is able to procure a harvest and make money from enterprises in which he did not even invest.[144] For someone motivated by greed and profit, the ability to make money off the sweat of others is often something to boast about, comparable to the tendency of con-men to brag about their ability to get one over on their victims.[145] Ancient groups like the Gauls and the Bedouins prided themselves in their abilities to steal from others.[146] Such attitudes were not restricted to non-Jews. Without any hint of irony or contradiction, the Babylonian Talmud depicts David as a pious king who nonetheless viewed plundering and exploitation as acceptable forms of economic enterprise.[147] By combining the verbs "gather up/in" (συνάγω) and "winnow" (διασκορπίζω), the same phrase was probably also intended as a criticism of the master's lavish and wasteful lifestyle.[148] The latter criticism would have come across as a compliment to the master, since wasteful living was one of the ways in which the ancient elite showcased their wealth and increased their honour.[149] Hence, the slave characterises the master negatively by accusing him of economic exploitation and profligate living, but does so in a way that not only conceals the negative characterisation, but also presents it as a positive characterisation from the master's perspective.

Within the context of the slave's rhetoric, the description is made to convince the master that he was afraid of him and to explain why.[150] By describing the master as a hard man, the slave ultimately convinces his master that he hid the mina out of fear.[151] This implies that the master is an effective slaveholder, knowing when and how to utilise the "fear factor," which would have come across as a type of compliment to the master. From the master's perspective, the slave's description of him can be paraphrased as: "you are the kind of person who deserves to be feared…" From the slave's hidden perspective, however, the description means something entirely different and may be paraphrased as: "you are the kind of person who takes food from those less fortunate…" The master accepts the slave's description of him as someone who

---

[143] Van Eck 2011, 5; cf. Luz 2005, 252; Park 2014a, 87; *pace* Tönsing 2019, 134–135.
[144] Cf. Schottroff 2006, 223.
[145] Cf. Bailey 2008, 405; McGraw 2012, 21, 69.
[146] Bailey 2008, 404.
[147] Bailey 2008, 405.
[148] Herzog 1994, 164–165; cf. Luke 15:13.
[149] Herzog 1994, 164–165.
[150] Bock 1996, 1538; Luz 2005, 252; cf. Van Eck 2011, 10.
[151] Cf. Rohrbaugh 1993, 36; Ford 2016, 26.

reaps where he did now sow and even repeats it verbatim in Q 19:22.[152] It is interesting that the master fails to repeat the slave's description of him as a "hard" man.[153] Perhaps this is an indication that the master was suspicious of the slave's reply, knowing on some level that the slave's description of him was actually a veiled insult.[154] Schottroff writes: "The third slave tells the truth. He accuses the slaveowner of theft. And the slaveowner does not feel insulted by it."[155]

The second half of the slave's response is no less astute: "Scared, I went and hid your mina in the ground. Here, you have what belongs to you." The slave's reference to hiding the money in the ground recalls Jewish tradition, according to which someone could not be held liable for the loss of money if it had been buried in the ground by the responsible party.[156] According to Jewish tradition (and ancient practice in general), burying money was the most secure way for an average person to hide and protect it against theft.[157] The slave makes a case for his own innocence by appealing to Jewish tradition, despite having disobeyed his master deliberately.[158] By burying the money, the slave absolves himself from any additional responsibility or accountability.[159] The deliberate use of the verb "hide" (κρύπτω) may also be relevant here.[160] On a connotative level, the verb probably symbolised the slave's sly interaction with his master. Hence, the slave's act of hiding the mina symbolises his larger activity of concealing not only his true valuation of the master, but also the true intent behind his actions. Through clever wordplay, the slave both hints at and conceals his own cleverness, slyness, and intentionality by describing his own actions with the verb "hide." Finally, attempting to give the master his money back is an important part of the slave's attempt to excuse his own behaviour and save his

---

[152] Fleddermann 2005a, 862; Valantasis 2005, 221; Crossan 2012, 100; Wright 2015, 141, 171; cf. Luz 2005, 247, 253; Ford 2016, 22; *pace* Bailey 2008, 405.

[153] Davies and Allison 1997, 409; Nolland 2005, 1018–1019. That is, if Matthew is followed in this case, since the term does appear in Luke's version of the master's response (cf. Fleddermann 2005a, 852).

[154] Cf. Tönsing 2019, 136.

[155] Schottroff 2006, 223.

[156] Jeremias 1972, 61 n. 51; Scott 1989, 227; Davies and Allison 1991, 436; 1997, 406; Rohrbaugh 1993, 36; Herzog 1994, 164; cf. b. B. Meṣ. 42a; 42b; m. B. Bat. 4.8.

[157] Jeremias 1972, 61 n. 51; Scott 1989, 227; Blomberg 1990, 215; Rohrbaugh 1993, 36; Herzog 1994, 164; Botha 1996, 281; Davies and Allison 1997, 407; Luz 2005, 252; Tönsing 2019, 132; cf. Marshall 1978, 706; Funk and Hoover 1993, 256; Bock 1996, 1538; Nolland 2005, 1015; Miller 2007, 69; Snodgrass 2008, 528; cf. 2 Enoch [J] 51:2; Josephus, *J.W.* 6.5.2; m. B. Meṣ. 3.10–11; b. Šabb. 102b; b. Ketub. 67b.

[158] Cf. Scott 1989, 227, 230.

[159] Scott 1989, 228, 230; Tönsing 2019, 132.

[160] Cf. Funk 2006, 100–101, 104.

own skin.[161] It gives the impression that the slave was genuinely trying to protect the master's economic interests. In truth, however, the phrase "you have what belongs to you" implies that the master does not deserve more than what he had to begin with.[162] In other words, the phrase is a veiled criticism of earning profit through economic dealings.[163] It obliquely promotes the subsistence economy of the small peasantry over the profit-seeking economy of the elite.

There is one feature of the text that strongly suggests trickery in the slave's claim that he hid the mina because he was scared, namely the suspicious use of the participial form for the verb "scared" (φοβηθείς).[164] If his aim was merely to convince his master, it would have been much more effective rhetorically for the slave to use the indicative mood and state emphatically: "I was scared" (ἐφοβήσαμην). In my view, the participle is employed to be deliberately ambiguous. The use of the participle makes it seem as if fear motivated the slave's decision to hide the money, especially if the participle is read together with the foregoing description of the master.[165] The translation "because I was scared" expresses this meaning of the participle well. Grammatically, when used in this way, the adverbial participle is known as a causal participle. Yet the adverbial participle in verse 21 can just as easily be read in a number of other ways. If it is read as a circumstantial participle, it means that the act of "being scared" merely happened in addition to the act of hiding the mina in the ground.[166] If it is taken as a concessive participle, it means that the slave hid the mina "despite being scared." If it is taken as a modal participle, it is merely an expression of the slave's emotional state of mind when burying the mina. If it is taken as a temporal participle (in the aorist tense), it simply means that the slave hid the mina "after being scared." In my view, the slave chose his words in such a way that the master took φοβηθείς to be a causal participle, even though the slave secretly intended it as one of the other options above. Any of the options listed would work in the sentence as the slave's hidden meaning, but the concessive participle seems most apposite. This means that the slave hid the mina *despite* being scared of his master, with an attitude of bold defiance and considered rebelliousness.[167] In other words, the slave spoke in such a way that the master would understand his fear as a motivating factor for his act of hiding the mina,

---

[161] Derrett 1970, 25; Scott 1981, 44; Herzog 1994, 165; Van Eck 2011, 5.
[162] Luz 2005, 252; cf. Scott 1981, 42; 1989, 231–232.
[163] Cf. Ukpong 2012, 198.
[164] Cf. Ukpong 2012, 198.
[165] Cf. Rohrbaugh 1993, 36.
[166] Cf. Ukpong 2012, 198.
[167] Cf. Rohrbaugh 1993, 37.

even if he secretly meant that the act of hiding the mina was part of his deliberate disobedience.[168] As before, the slave employs clever wordplay (or "gram-
mar-play," in this case) to bring about deliberate misunderstanding.[169] In the
process, the slave manages to conceal the true meaning behind his words and
his deeds without technically speaking a lie. The slave was indeed afraid, but
fear was not the factor that motivated his actions.[170]

An important indication that the unproductive slave was not being entirely
truthful is that his argument is illogical.[171] Fear would have motivated the slave
to obey his master, not to disobey him.[172] More realistically, fear would have
motivated the slave to conjure up as many tactics as possible to make at least
some profit. Even if the slave ended up being unsuccessful in his economic
activities, the master would surely have preferred an attempt at earning profit
over a "cowardly" refusal to do so. The master tasks his slaves with "doing
business" (πραγματεύομαι) and not with "earning a profit." Even though the
intent of "earning a profit" is implied by the command to "do business,"[173]
failing to do the latter is a direct and deliberate violation of the task, while
failing to do the former could be blamed on incompetence or bad luck.[174] As
such, harsh punishment would more likely have followed intentional non-compliance than unintentional failure, especially since loyal obedience was the
foremost attribute expected from slaves in antiquity.[175] Hence, the slave's excuse that he was hiding the mina "because he was scared" defies logic, since
this very act would have induced the wrath of his master – something that his
master points out to him.[176] The unstated assumption is that the slave was
scared of losing the money because of the risks involved in economic undertakings.[177] Yet the master acknowledges the irrationality of the slave's reasoning when he tells the slave that he could have invested the money with money
changers for virtually no risk.[178] By investing the money, the slave would have
earned at least some return in the form of interest, without having to take the

---

[168] Ford 2016, 26.

[169] Cf. Ford 2016, 26, 38.

[170] Cf. Rohrbaugh 1993, 36, 37; Ford 2016, 26.

[171] Scott 1981, 42; Wright 2015, 140.

[172] Cf. Scott 1989, 232; Bock 1996, 1539; Ford 2016, 25; Roth 2018, 125.

[173] Bock 1996, 1533; Roth 2014, 390; 2018, 123.

[174] Cf. Bailey 2008, 400, 403.

[175] Hezser 2005, 155; see Bradley 1984, 33–40, 78; Joshel 2010, 115–116; cf. Harrill
2006, 152–153; Bailey 2008, 400, 403; Dal Lago and Katsari 2008, 204.

[176] Via 1967, 118; Bock 1996, 1539; Wright 2015, 140; Roth 2018, 115; cf. Jeremias
1972, 61; Scott 1981, 42; 1989, 232; Ford 2016, 25.

[177] Jacobson 1992, 242–243; Nolland 2005, 1018; cf. Dodd 1958, 152; Via 1967, 120;
Marshall 1978, 707.

[178] Via 1967, 118; Scott 1981, 42; cf. Donahue 1988, 107; Bock 1996, 1539–1540; Luz
2005, 253; Nolland 2005, 1018; Wright 2015, 140; Roth 2018, 113.

risks that go with more adventuresome financial dealings.[179] Understood from the master's perspective, who regards fear as the motivating factor, the slave's excuse is illogical. However, understood from the slave's perspective, who secretly intends defiance as the motivating factor, the slave's excuse is entirely rational, since the slave must have known that the master would punish disobedience, but decided to hide the mina anyway.[180] The description of the master as a cruel person who takes food out of the mouths of those less fortunate explains why the slave would intentionally disobey the master's command and hide the money despite being scared of him.[181] In other words, in addition to explaining on the surface level of the parable why the slave was scared, the foregoing description of the master also explains on the hidden level why the slave acted as he did, despite being afraid.[182] In truth, the slave's actions were motivated by the master's ruthless and heartless economic approach, not by his own fear.[183]

The slave's strategy was a gamble and the outcome uncertain. In most circumstances, his disobedience would have invited severe (physical) punishment. The slave must have been extremely anxious and fearful when he confronted the slaveholder, which makes his actions all the more courageous.[184] Fortunately, his cunning and considered response, which he must have rehearsed more than once, literally saved his skin.[185] Because of the slaveholder's privileged station and judgmental stance, he failed to recognise that the slave's exhibited stupidity and cowardice were in actual fact his concealed astuteness and courage.[186] If he did suspect some form of chicanery in the slave's response,[187] he was left quite powerless by the slave's masterful guile.[188] By pulling the wool over his master's eyes, the slave managed not only to evade severe (physical) punishment, but also to induce a form of punishment that was actually a reward from his own perspective.[189] Most importantly, the slave managed to frustrate and impede, to some extent at least, an evil and unfair process of economic exploitation.

Here is an overview of the unproductive slave's ambiguous and misleading response:

---

[179] Derrett 1970, 26; cf. Roth 2018, 117.
[180] Cf. Rohrbaugh 1993, 37.
[181] Cf. Valantasis 2005, 221.
[182] Rohrbaugh 1993, 37.
[183] Ford 2016, 26.
[184] Cf. Rohrbaugh 1993, 36, 37.
[185] Ford 2016, 26.
[186] Cf. Ford 2016, 35–36, 38.
[187] Cf. Herzog 1994, 165.
[188] Cf. Scott 1989, 230.
[189] Cf. Snodgrass 2008, 535; Park 2014a, 87; *pace* Crossan 1974a, 25–27, 38–39.

Part 1: Honouring the Master

The slave's actual words:	"Master, I knew you, that you are a hard (σκληρός) person, reaping where you did not sow and gathering up from where you did not winnow…"
What the master heard:	"Master, I knew you, that you are a solid (σκληρός) person [compliment], who earns money all over the place and induces fear in your subordinates [compliment]…"
The slave's hidden message:	"Master, I knew you, that you are a harsh and cruel (σκληρός) person [insult and accusation], seizing agricultural produce from the blood, sweat, and tears of others [insult and accusation]…"

Part 2: Explaining His Actions

The slave's actual words:	"…and, scared (φοβηθείς), I went and hid your mina in the ground."
What the master heard:	"…and, *because* I was scared (φοβηθείς), I went and hid your mina in the ground."
The slave's hidden message:	"…and, *despite* being scared (φοβηθείς), I went and hid your mina in the ground anyway."

Part 3: Returning the Mina

The slave's actual words:	"Here, you have what belongs to you."
What the master heard:	"I protected your interests, and I am now returning your property back to you exactly as I found it."
The slave's hidden message:	"I am giving you exactly what you deserve, which is no more than what you had to begin with, since you have no right to exploit people for the sake of earning a profit."

In the ancient Greco-Roman world, slaves were commonly viewed by their masters as being lazy, intransigent, and unreliable.[190] We also saw that slaveholders were well aware that their slaves were afraid of them and made "good" use of such fear to control their slaves.[191] The unproductive slave in our parable knew how his master viewed him. To explain away his deliberate insubordination and thereby avoid harsh (physical) punishment, the slave drew upon his master's perception of him and presented himself as unintelligent, lazy, inefficient, and, most importantly, fearful.[192] Instead of explaining to his master the real reasons for hiding the mina, he told his master that he did it out of fear.[193] This was a very clever rhetorical ploy, explaining his actions in a way that

---

[190] Howes 2015c, 96.
[191] Bradley 1984, 136; cf. Joshel 2010, 116, 178.
[192] Cf. Luz 2005, 252.
[193] Ford 2016, 26; cf. Luz 2005, 253.

would be plausible and believable from the master's perspective. His explanation was also not a straight-out lie, since the slave must indeed have been afraid of his master, as all slaves of antiquity were, but this was not his reason for hiding the mina.[194]

Van Eck also interprets the unproductive slave's response as deliberately deceiving.[195] According to him, the master would have heard the following: "Master, I have so much respect for you (I am honouring you), that I did not want to take a chance with your money. I did what I thought was the honourable thing to do, that is, to protect what belongs to you." Yet, according to Van Eck, the peasant audience of Jesus would have heard the following: "You are a thief, and I am not willing to be part of what you are doing!" With these paraphrases, Van Eck captures the heart of the cunning exchange as I have tried to explain it above. Other interpreters have also noticed some measure of ambiguity and pretence in the slave's response. Rohrbaugh considers how the unproductive slave's answer leaves a more favourable impression if heard with peasant ears.[196] Luz says intuitively: "The [unproductive] slave's speech sounds unbalanced; it fluctuates among defiance, protest, and fear."[197] Scott is moved by the narrative to ask: "Whom do I trust? Where does the truth lie?"[198] Although offering a variant explanation of the truth behind the slave's words, Derrett also reckons that the slave was lying about being scared.[199] Ford summarises the unproductive slave's response to the master as follows: "Appearing inept, he is hiding behind a facade of cowardliness in order to effect a covert opposition."[200] It is surely significant that the unproductive slave's feedback, together with the master's reply, carry a much higher degree of verbal overlap between Matthew and Luke than any other part of this narrative.[201] Such conformity strongly suggests that the two evangelists instinctively understood that the exact wording of the slave's response was important to the story. And indeed, they were correct, seeing as the heart of the slave's deceit lies in those exact words.

Although the slave is characterised as being sly,[202] such characterisation would not have been judged negatively from the perspective of socio-economic underlings. Misleading one's master or landlord would have been acceptable and even commendable if it enabled one to evade severe (physical) punishment or if it assured one's daily survival. Such deceit was part of the so-called

---

[194] Cf. Rohrbaugh 1993, 36, 37.
[195] Van Eck 2011, 10.
[196] Rohrbaugh 1993, 37.
[197] Luz 2005, 252.
[198] Scott 1989, 232.
[199] Derrett 1970, 25–26.
[200] Ford 2016, 30.
[201] Piper 1989, 145; Scott 1989, 229; Crossan 2012, 102.
[202] Ford 2016, 26.

"weapons of the weak" employed by small peasants to protect themselves against the exploitation of the elite.[203] Like the other parables of Jesus, behaviour that might seem morally questionable to some is not condemned or even commented upon.[204] Instead, such behaviour seems to be encouraged.[205]

9.6 Humour and Surprise

The first audiences would probably have found the misunderstanding between the master and his unproductive slave amusing. Derrett sees humour specifically in the slave's words: "Here, you have what belongs to you" (ἴδε ἔχεις τὸ σόν).[206] The parables of Jesus were certainly not immune to humour.[207] In two ways, then, the parable of the entrusted money functioned as a satire of sorts: (1) by exposing the status quo; and (2) by doing so in a humorous way.[208] Generally speaking, satires were (and are) ironically comical, exposing the status quo by poking fun at it. As a form of social commentary, satires functioned across cultures as "weapons of the weak."[209] As a satirical narrative featuring a slave, the story of the entrusted money is comparable to the comedies of Plautus. On the surface level, the parable seems to follow a tragic plot, leading to catastrophe,[210] but on the covertly intended level, the parable follows a comic plot, leading to triumph.[211]

It is important to point out, though, that the story was not in the first place told as a satire, but as a parable.[212] In my view, Funk is on the money, so to speak, when he argues that the parables of Jesus were generally not intended to fulfil the mere satirical role of exposing the status quo.[213] Instead, their ultimate intent was to conjure up an alternative reality and call people to action in

---

[203] See Van Eck 2011, 10; cf. Park 2014a, 87.

[204] See Hedrick 2014, 135; cf. Wright 2015, 171. The unproductive slave is not "punished" or criticised by the master for being sly, but for failing to try and make a profit.

[205] Luz 2005, 250; Van Eck 2011, 10; cf. Matt 10:16b; 13:44; Luke 16:1–8; 18:2–8a; Gos. Thom. 39:3.

[206] Derrett 1970, 25.

[207] See Beutner 2007a, 59–63; 2007b, 33–34; cf. Funk 2006, 117–118, 158, 174; 2007, 90–91.

[208] Park 2014a, 84, 87–88.

[209] Park 2014a, 87.

[210] See Via 1967, 113–122; cf. Blomberg 1990, 214.

[211] Cf. Scott 1981, 39–40, 46–47; Beutner 2007a, 59–63.

[212] *Pace* Park 2014a, 87–88; Wright 2015, 141, 172.

[213] Funk 2006, 43–51, 173.

the establishment of that reality.[214] His ultimate intent was not to reveal the existing kingdom of man, but to reveal the imagined kingdom of God. Likewise, none of the parables in the formative stratum – or the main redaction, for that matter – operate as satires. Even if some of these parables do illuminate ancient socio-economic conditions and disparities in various ways, they fulfil larger rhetorical roles within their respective literary contexts.[215]

The latter is not to say that the parable was uninterested in exposing the economic status quo operative in first-century Palestine.[216] Surely, exposing the economic exploitation of the small peasantry was part of the parable's intent, but it was not the parable's *main* intent. The parable's main intent was to illustrate how one can stand up against the reigning economic system of the elite without severely jeopardising one's livelihood, thereby contributing to the establishment of God's kingdom on earth.[217] As a result of his actions, the unproductive slave is perhaps worse off than his fellow slaves, who might have enjoyed certain privileges as a result of their productivity, but those small peasants who stood to lose from his exploits are better off. In this way, the unproductive slave's actions do not merely expose the status quo, but also changes it.[218] The slave has made a real difference by refusing to participate in a corrupt and evil system.[219] By refusing to "do business" (πραγματεύομαι), and by burying the coin, the slave was not "doing nothing," but was actively resisting an abusive and exploitative economic system.[220] As a narrative character, the unproductive slave personifies non-violent resistance.[221]

One could argue that the unproductive slave did not accomplish much in the end, since his coin was eventually handed over to the most proficient slave, who would ostensibly have been able to produce another tenfold return. Firstly, the latter should not be presumed, since it is at least possible that the most productive slave had by that time depleted his economic resources. Secondly, the unproductive slave was able to curb any business to be done with his mina for at least the period of his master's absence, which could indeed have made a noticeable difference in the lives of individual smallholders, especially since the master was away for "a long time" (πολὺν χρόνον).[222] Thirdly, his actions

---

[214] See Funk 2006, 35, 38, 48–51, 62, 63, 86, 106–107, 158, 172, 175; 2007, 90–91; McGaughy 2007, 12–13; Scott 2007, 117–118; cf. Hunter 1964, 12–13; Rohrbaugh 1993, 33; Verhoeven 2007, 49; Zimmermann 2009, 175; Park 2019, 47.

[215] Kloppenborg 1995, 300.

[216] Cf. Funk 2006, 46, 172; Wright 2015, 40.

[217] Cf. Van Eck 2011, 8; Wright 2015, 40.

[218] Cf. Beutner 2007b, 36.

[219] Cf. Schottroff 2006, 223; Van Eck 2011, 5; Ford 2016, 26.

[220] See Ford 2016, 25–26; cf. Rohrbaugh 1993, 38; *pace* Roth 2018, 123, 126–127.

[221] Cf. Crossan 2012, 127–131; Ford 2016, 23–25.

[222] Herzog 1994, 167; cf. Luz 2005, 249. It should be noted that the phrase "after a long time" (μετὰ πολὺν χρόνον) appears only in the Matthean version of the parable and is printed

do succeed in exposing an alternative reality – one where it is possible to completely sidestep economic dealings for the sake of profit and so hamper to some extent the economic exploitation of others.[223] Lastly, he did prevent the master from earning profits that, from a peasant viewpoint, did not belong to him.[224]

The surprising feature of the narrative is not the unproductive slave's deceit, though, but the master's reaction.[225] After the first two slaves in the narrative give their feedback, the audience expects the last slave's response to be different, as was the convention in ancient storytelling and in the parables of Jesus.[226] The audiences of Q had even more reason to expect a different response from the last slave, since Q typically features a "broken third."[227] A lower-class audience would intuitively have understood the deceit as it has been explained and would probably have tipped their hats (metaphorically) to the slave's guile, but would not have found it surprising.[228] Given both the characterisation of the master and the content of the third narrated response, however, the audience would have expected the unproductive slave to be punished harshly.[229] Instead, he is merely called a "bad" (πονηρός) slave and released from a duty he did not want to begin with.[230] The surprising feature of the parable is that the disobedient slave manages to evade punishment altogether.[231] The slave manages this because of his sly (but technically true) response, not because of his actions, which would otherwise have invited severe punishment. The unproductive slave manages not only to act exactly how he wants, being deliberately disobedient to his master, but also to procure the exact outcome that he wants, namely to avoid harsh punishment and be dismissed from any participation in the exploitation of others. Even the insult that he was a "bad" slave would probably have been taken by the unproductive slave as a compliment, considering the

---

in double square brackets in the *Critical Edition of Q*. A number of scholars view it as a Matthean addition to reference the delayed parousia: e.g. Davies and Allison 1997, 407; Luz 2005, 256; Nolland 2005, 1016; Van Eck 2011, 3; cf. Jeremias 1972, 63; Herzog 1994, 151. Yet the final form of Q could also have referenced the delayed Parousia with this term. Also, the temporal reference is explicable and perhaps even necessary as a narrative feature to allow enough time for the productive slaves to earn a return on investment (Dodd 1958, 150; Via 1967, 121; Blomberg 1990, 220; Snodgrass 2008, 532). In any case, Denaux (2001, 440–441) has argued convincingly for its inclusion in Q.

[223] Cf. Herzog 1994, 167.

[224] Cf. Luz 2005, 252; Ford 2016, 22.

[225] Van Eck 2011, 8.

[226] Crossan 2012, 100, 108–109; *pace* Herzog 1994, 164.

[227] See Fleddermann 2005a, 86–87, 861.

[228] Cf. Crossan 2002, 253.

[229] Wright 2015, 172; cf. Jacobson 1992, 243; Roth 2014, 390.

[230] Cf. Scott 1989, 222; Van Eck 2011, 3, 8, 10.

[231] Van Eck 2011, 8; *pace* Crossan 1974a, 25–27, 38–39.

source.[232] Conversely, the master ends up indicting himself in more than one way. Firstly, as we saw, he repeats the slave's characterisation of him, thereby acknowledging his own insatiable greed and heartless exploitation. Secondly, he instructs the remaining mina to be handed over to the most productive slave – an act that would have characterised him as profoundly unjust to a peasant audience subscribing to balanced reciprocity.[233] The master's concluding act functions as a symbol and microcosm of the inherently unjust process through which the wealthy wrestle land, produce, and sustenance from the small peasantry and poor.[234] At its heart, the story of the entrusted money is a "challenge parable" – as this term has been defined by Crossan[235] – challenging the existing economic system that enabled the perpetual and aggressive exploitation of the small peasantry and poor, and daring them to stand up against that system.[236]

As a challenge parable, it cannot be taken as a mere example story.[237] The situation of the unproductive slave is not directly transferrable to the situation of the parable's first (and later) audiences. These first hearers were (for the most part, as far as we can tell) not slaves, so they could not act exactly (or even approximately) how the unproductive slave did. Instead, the parable confronts the audience with the question: how can I, in my own situation, boycott the existing economic system that exploits the weak, without facing the consequences of such purposeful behaviour? In some sense, the parable poses a *qal wahomer* argument for contemplation: if a slave can accomplish so much, how much more should a free person, even a small peasant, not be able to accomplish in the struggle against economic oppression? On a secondary level, the parable of the entrusted money also operates like the parable of the Samaritan, portraying a stereotypically negative character in a positive light. Peasants dealt with privileged city slaves and retainers on a regular basis and must have despised these parasitic exploiters.[238] Against the backdrop of this stereotype, the unproductive slave is a troubling figure.[239]

---

[232] Cf. Rohrbaugh 1993, 38; Beutner 2007a, 62; Ukpong 2012, 199; Wright 2015, 142, 171; Jacobs 2018, 132–133.

[233] Scott 1981, 44; 1989, 232–233; Rohrbaugh 1993, 38; Oakman 2008, 69; cf. Funk and Hoover 1993, 256; Kloppenborg 1995, 297, 298; Roth 2014, 390; Ford 2016, 26.

[234] Cf. Kloppenborg 1995, 298; Ukpong 2012, 199, 200.

[235] See Crossan 2012, 45–112.

[236] Ukpong 2012, 202; cf. Wright 2015, 40.

[237] See Crossan 1974c, 63–104; 2012, 29–44; cf. Funk 2006, 48, 85–86.

[238] Herzog 1994, 160, 161, 167, 168.

[239] Herzog 1994, 162. Scott (1981, 44–47) provides a similar reading, but sees the master as the negative stereotype who ends up being portrayed in a positive light.

9.7 Counter-Arguments

Some scholars have reacted against the line of interpretation followed here.[240] Kloppenborg holds that "the parable cannot be meant as black irony, condemning the rapacity of the rich."[241] He supports this claim by arguing that the description of the unproductive slave as "bad" (πονηρός) and the productive slaves as "good" (ἀγαθός) and "faithful" (πιστός) dictate how the parable should be interpreted, even if sympathy is otherwise evoked for the unproductive slave.[242] Although Kloppenborg interprets the parable on the level of Q's main redaction, his observation would apply equally to the formative stratum, since the master's valuation of his slaves appears as part of the narrative on that level as well. Yet the current analysis has shown, hopefully with some degree of success, that the parable presumes two levels of interaction.[243] On a surface level, as understood from above by the master and more fortunate interpreters, the unproductive slave is scared, fails to gain a profit, and gets punished. On a hidden level, as secretly intended by the unproductive slave and understood by less fortunate listeners, the slave is courageous, deliberately refuses to gain a profit, and actually gets rewarded. On the surface level, the master's valuation of the unproductive slave is negative, but on the hidden level, the exact same valuation is positive.[244] According to Jacobs, the audience "is left questioning who are truly good, and who are truly wicked."[245] Herzog intuits correctly that the master's reply "is not to be taken at face value."[246] Being called "bad" by a bad person is ultimately a compliment. The first audiences would not have placed much stock in the master or his viewpoint anyway, since his character stood for the economic exploitation of small peasants.[247]

Luz comments that the master did not necessarily agree with the slave's characterisation of him in Q 19:21.[248] It seems unlikely to me that the master would have repeated the slave's description word for word if he did not agree with its content. If the master disagreed with the statement, he could easily have begun the exact same counter-argument with words like, "if you thought that of me…" or "let us say for argument's sake that I am like that…" Instead, he chose to repeat the same characterisation exactly. The repetition drips of

---

[240] E.g. Roth 2018, 116–122.

[241] Kloppenborg 1995, 298.

[242] Cf. also Roth 2018, 119–120, 125. According to Rohrbaugh (1993, 38), Scott's approach is similar to the one described here for Kloppenborg.

[243] Cf. Van Eck 2011, 10.

[244] Cf. Jacobs 2018, 133.

[245] Jacobs 2018, 132.

[246] Herzog 1994, 165; cf. Rohrbaugh 1993, 38; Wright 2015, 142.

[247] Wright 2015, 142, 171; cf. Herzog 1994, 160–161.

[248] Luz 2005, 253.

pompous boasting and self-aggrandisement. Scott argues more definitively than Luz that the master in fact did not accept the slave's characterisation of him, since he not only acted kindly towards the productive slaves, but also refused to take the unproductive slave's coin for himself, giving it to the most productive slave instead.[249] These arguments betray Scott's erroneous conviction that the stewards were not slaves but servants.[250] Snodgrass applies the same observation of the master's "kind" treatment of the productive slaves to argue that the master is not characterised as "harsh" in the narrative at all and that the unproductive slave's description of him is unwarranted.[251] Both Scott and Snodgrass fail to notice that it is wrong to read much about the master's character into his specific punishments and rewards, since the money belonged to the master regardless. Ultimately, both the productive slaves' "reward" and the unproductive slave's "punishment" are motivated by the master's greed, not his kindness.[252]

Snodgrass is perhaps the most vehement opponent of the line of interpretation advocated here, claiming that "it is more of a usurpation of the parable than an interpretation."[253] He states: "If this [parable of the entrusted money] is a warning about mistreating the poor, it is cryptic in the extreme."[254] First of all, this statement betrays his proclivity to read the parable from above, since a "warning about mistreating the poor" would still be directed at the rich, not the poor. To be fair, Snodgrass is here reacting to Rohrbaugh, who did indeed argue that the parable should be understood as "a warning ... to those who mistreat the poor."[255] The present chapter has argued instead that the parable is a challenge aimed primarily at the small peasantry and poor, who made up the majority of Jesus's first audiences. Second of all, to the extent that the parable was also aimed at the rich, it challenged these members of Jesus's first audiences to rethink the economic system of which they were part, which constitutes a much more subversive challenge than merely warning against mistreating the poor.[256] Third of all, Snodgrass is absolutely correct that the parable is "cryptic in the extreme," but only if read both from above and from a Western standpoint.[257] Rohrbaugh rightly says: "The fact that we western capitalists find the peasant reading so difficult to imagine may be little more than a function of our socialization in a world where amassing wealth is the accepted

---

[249] Scott 1981, 43–47; 1989, 233–234; cf. Donahue 1988, 107–108.

[250] See above.

[251] Snodgrass 2008, 534. See Herzog 1994, 154 for more examples of scholars who refuse to see truth in the unproductive slave's description of the master.

[252] Ukpong 2012, 197–198; cf. Rohrbaugh 1993, 36; Jacobs 2018, 131.

[253] Snodgrass 2008, 534.

[254] Snodgrass 2008, 534.

[255] Rohrbaugh 1993, 32.

[256] See Crossan 2002, 252–253; 2012, 105–106; cf. Rohrbaugh 1993, 38.

[257] See Ford 2016, 35–36; cf. Bailey 2008, 397, 403.

norm."[258] By contrast, it is very likely that the first audiences would have immediately and intuitively understood the unproductive slave's reply as a skilful and deliberate attempt to deceive the master by being cryptic. In this regard, it is simply wrong to assume that interpretations like the one in this chapter "imputes too much cunning to the slave."[259] In any case, all the parables of Jesus were cryptic in essence.[260] By contrast, Snodgrass's interpretation of the current parable is straightforward to the extreme. Worse yet, his interpretation is inherently allegorical, even if he delimits the number of allegorical applications to only a few features in the text.

Snodgrass argues further that the unproductive slave's words "are merely the basis on which he is judged," thereby attempting to negate finding any relevance in these words to the parable's interpretation.[261] Yet the fact that Matthew and Luke feature these words with such a high degree of verbal overlap indicates that the unproductive slave's response must have been important to the story.[262] The same is indicated by the sheer length of the unproductive slave's response.[263] The exposition offered above indicates that every word in the slave's response was measured and deliberate. The slave's words were indeed "the basis on which he was judged," but his words were also the weapons he used to indict the master, as well as the reason why he did not receive a harsher punishment. Snodgrass continues to argue that "the rule of end stress places the emphasis on the master's verdict, not on the actions of the third servant."[264] This is a false dichotomy, since the rule of end stress applies to the entire interaction between the master and the unproductive slave, as the current exposition has indicated and as commentators unfailingly confirm.[265] Even so, the surprising turn in the parable is indeed the master's verdict, as I have argued above, but it is only possible to appreciate the unexpectedness of the master's actual verdict if one is able to perceive the insolence and critique hidden in the unproductive slave's response.

Snodgrass argues further that audiences "would hardly identify with the third servant and his fear, which leads him to hide the money."[266] This is the

---

[258] Rohrbaugh 1993, 38.

[259] Roth 2018, 121.

[260] Cf. Beutner 2007b, 34; Funk 2007, 90; Wright 2015, 47.

[261] Snodgrass 2008, 534.

[262] Piper 1989, 145; Scott 1989, 229; Crossan 2012, 102; cf. Roth 2018, 113.

[263] Herzog 1994, 164; cf. Tuckett 1996, 147–148; Nolland 2005, 1017.

[264] Snodgrass 2008, 534; cf. Dodd 1958, 150; Wright 2015, 172.

[265] E.g. Hunter 1964, 81; 1971, 97; Donahue 1988, 106; Piper 1989, 145; Herzog 1994, 164; Davies and Allison 1997, 401–402; Luz 2005, 247; Nolland 2005, 1020; Crossan 2012, 102; cf. Jeremias 1972, 61; Tuckett 1996, 147–148.

[266] Snodgrass 2008, 534.

typical impression when approaching the parable from above, failing to recognise or consider the true plight of a slave in antiquity.[267] Fear was a necessary part of being a slave, and such fear should not make it more difficult to identify with the slave, but easier, since fear is a condition we all share, especially those on the bottom of society.[268] Snodgrass also claims that the unproductive slave's actions "are hardly defiance of an oppressive system."[269] Indeed, the slave could have acted more aggressively, blaming the master in unambiguous language for oppressing those less fortunate and explaining in clear terms that he refused to be party to such conduct. If he did, he would probably have found himself whipped or dead – and who would that have served? The "weapons of the weak" were in use precisely because the poor and defenceless needed ways of standing up against the rich and powerful without having to face the usual consequences of such insolence. Ford explains it as follows:

> Should the slave register his protest with anything even slightly more obvious, he would provoke, instead of disappointment and puzzled anger, only a smoothly rationalized scorn – followed, of course, by retaliation. His indirectness gives this subordinate not only his best chance to register his voice but also his best chance to survive.[270]

Snodgrass continues to claim that the unproductive slave's act of burying the money "is not a commendable action."[271] Once again, the question is: from whose perspective? As argued above, the slave's behaviour represents a crafty way of drawing on Jewish tradition to sidestep both accountability and blame. Ancient peasant audiences would have seen the unproductive slave's actions as commendable and the master's punishment as arbitrary.[272] The preceding claim is confirmed by Luke's editorial activity.[273] Firstly, Luke struggled to find guilt in the unproductive slave's act of burying the money and therefore changed it to an act that was more deserving of punishment according to Jewish tradition, namely that of hiding the money in a cloth.[274] Secondly, Luke (19:25)

---

[267] Cf. Rohrbaugh 1993, 35, 38; Ukpong 2012, 198; see above.

[268] Cf. Wright 2015, 142.

[269] Snodgrass 2008, 534.

[270] Ford 2016, 26.

[271] Snodgrass 2008, 534.

[272] Rohrbaugh 1993, 38. This remains true even if the punishment was more like a reward for the unproductive slave.

[273] Cf. Davies and Allison (1997, 408) claim that "perhaps Jesus' hearers and Matthew's readers would have thought him [the unproductive slave] prudent" (cf. Roth 2014, 390).

[274] Scott 1989, 222, 228; Herzog 1994, 151; Luz 2005, 248, 252; cf. Derrett 1970, 24; Jeremias 1972, 61, esp. n. 51; Marshall 1978, 706; Blomberg 1990, 218; Rohrbaugh 1993, 36; Herzog 1994, 164; Fleddermann 2005a, 852; *pace* Davies and Allison 1997, 407; Nolland 2005, 1015.

added a statement of disbelief on the part of Jesus's first audience at the injustice of the punishment.[275] To Lukan redaction can be added the amendment of this parable in the *Gospel of the Nazoreans* (18), according to which the slave who buried his money is either joyfully accepted or mildly rebuked, depending on how one reads the parable, but with the former option being much more likely.[276] In that version, punishment is reserved for a slave who squandered his money with prostitutes and flute girls. Snodgrass supports his claim that the slave's act was not commendable by pointing out that the money was left with the slave not for safekeeping, but for investment.[277] This is true, but only highlights the fact that the slave found a cunning way of boycotting the master's direct instruction while maintaining his own innocence. Snodgrass is certainly correct that "[t]he presumption of the parable is that failure to invest the money was a dereliction of duty."[278] The question, however, is whether such "dereliction of duty" should be viewed as positive or negative. Viewed from above, it is surely negative, but viewed from below, it is decidedly positive, since it not only benefits others, but also represents opposition against oppression.[279] I share Schottroff's emotive reaction when she says: "He [the third slave] has refused to be a henchman in the dispossession of small farmers. To see this third slave as the embodiment of people who reject God's righteousness and God's Torah is simply unbearable to me."[280] This section provides additional support to Van Eck's observation that the parable of the entrusted money is itself a "hidden transcript," validating the status quo if read from above, but surreptitiously challenging the same status quo if read from below.[281] Rather than the present interpretation being a usurpation of the parable, the parable is a protest against all forms of usurpation.

9.8 Characteristic Forms

Q 19:12–13, 15–24 is clearly a parable. In fact, it is one of the few proper narrative parables in Q, with most of the other options qualifying instead as

---

[275] Jeremias 1972, 62; Piper 1989, 147; Scott 1989, 228; Taylor 1989, 165; Fleddermann 2005a, 853; Luz 2005, 253; cf. Marshall 1978, 708; Davies and Allison 1997, 402, 403; Roth 2014, 389.

[276] Jeremias 1972, 58, 63; Donahue 1988, 107; Piper 1989, 147; Scott 1989, 232–233; Herzog 1994, 152; Kloppenborg 1995, 297; Luz 2005, 248–249; Oakman 2008, 55; see Crossan 1986, 11; 2002, 252; 2012, 102–103; Rohrbaugh 1993, 36–37.

[277] Cf. Blomberg 1990, 215.

[278] Snodgrass 2008, 534.

[279] Cf. Rohrbaugh 1993, 38; Ford 2016, 35–36.

[280] Schottroff 2006, 223; cf. Ford 2016, 21–22, 28, 35.

[281] Van Eck 2011, 10; cf. Rohrbaugh 1993, 38; Ford 2016, 35–36, 38–39.

similitudes.[282] In its capacity as a parable, Q 19:12–13, 15–24 qualifies formally as a piece of wisdom.[283] As a sapiential form, Q 19:12–13, 15–24 belongs to the formative stratum.

9.9 Characteristic Motifs

Like much of the formative stratum, the parable of the entrusted money deals with a socio-economic matter and does so from the perspective of the underprivileged.[284] The formative stratum promotes general reciprocity at all societal levels over both balanced reciprocity and exploitative economic dealings.[285] General reciprocity was usually in antiquity reserved for exchanges between family members, but Q's formative stratum promotes it for society at large. The parable of the entrusted money contributes to this social vision by exposing and criticising economic endeavours that threaten both balanced and general reciprocity at village level.[286]

The formative stratum's radical vision included economic practices like loan acquittal (Q 6:30) and debt release (Q 11:4).[287] With such expectations, the formative stratum confronts economic practices that promote perpetual indebtedness head on.[288] As we saw, it was through systemic and systematic indebtedness that members of the upper class were able to appropriate the smallholdings of individual small peasants and in the process force these peasants into becoming tenant farmers, day-labourers, slaves, beggars, and bandits. In the spirit of texts like Q 6:30 and Q 11:4, the parable of the entrusted money takes a stand against the abusive practice of loaning money to small peasants at outrages interest rates in order to compound their debts and steal their livelihoods.[289] This parable features people who participate in those economic dealings that ultimately result in the indebtedness of small peasants, but continues to tell about one character who refused to be party to such dealings.[290] This

---

[282] Cf. Funk 2006, 31.

[283] Beutner 2007c, 4; see Kirk 1998, 298, 234, 246–248; cf. Edwards 1976, 74.

[284] See Van Eck 2015, 6–7; cf. Fleddermann 2005a, 862–863; Van Eck 2011, 10; cf. Q 6:20–23a, 27–28, 29, 30; [Matt 5:41]; 11:2–4, 9–13; 12:6–7, 11–12, 22–31, 42–44 (see chapter 4 above), 58–59 (see chapter 5 above); 13:18–21 (see chapter 6 above); 13:24–25 (see chapter 7 above); 14:16–21, 23 (see chapter 8 above), 34–35; 16:13; 15:4–5, 7, [8–10].

[285] Cf. Q 6:27–28, 35, 29–30, 31, 32, 34; 11:33 (see chapter 2 above); 12:42–44 (see chapter 4 above); 14:16–21, 23 (see chapter 8 above).

[286] Van Eck 2011, 10; cf. Funk 2006, 46, 106–107.

[287] See chapter 5 above.

[288] Cf. Van Eck 2011, 10; Park 2014a, 87.

[289] Cf. Rohrbaugh 1993, 38; Oakman 2008, 36; Häkkinen 2016, 3.

[290] Crossan 2002, 252; Schottroff 2006, 223; Van Eck 2011, 5; Ukpong 2012, 197; see Ford 2016, 19–28; cf. Valantasis 2005, 221.

stubborn character might have incited the wrath of his master, but he also prompted the favour of God. The same strategies of passive resistance and employing the weapons of the weak might be reflected in Q 6:29 (incl. Matt 5:41), where the audience is implored to shame the abuser by offering the other cheek when assaulted, handing over additional clothing when sued, and walking twice as many miles when conscripted.[291] Like the conduct of the unproductive slave, the actions promoted by Q 6:29 are both brave and comical.[292]

In thematic content, the parable of the entrusted money overlaps further with the logion in Q 16:13.[293] By refusing to participate in the economic exploitation of others, the unproductive slave has illustrated through his actions how one can practically choose to serve God instead of mammon.[294] In the conduct of the unproductive slave, there is no middle ground. In choosing not to "do business," the slave deliberately chooses for God and against mammon. His so-called "punishment" was to be released completely from any financial responsibilities,[295] so that he could from that moment on focus all his attention on serving God. Although the parable of the entrusted money should not in the first place be seen as an example story, the unproductive slave does feature as an exemplary character.[296] He provides a practical example of someone who chose for God and against wealth in his daily life. Conversely, the master and his other slaves provide examples of people who chose for wealth and against God in their daily financial dealings.

The same thematic overlap extends to Q 12:22–31 and Q 12:33–34.[297] In the former text, Q's Jesus instructs his disciples to seek God's kingdom instead of earthly needs. If God's kingdom is understood as a place where everyone receives food[298] as part of God's family[299],[300] then Q 12:31 instructs its hearers to contribute to the establishment of such a place before selfishly scrambling to address one's own needs. This is exactly what the unproductive slave in the parable of the entrusted money does. Unlike the other slaves in this parable,

---

[291] See chapter 5 above.

[292] Cf. Funk 2006, 174.

[293] Cf. Kloppenborg 1995, 299; Piper 2000, 260; Park 2014a, 87.

[294] Schottroff 2006, 223; cf. Fleddermann 2014, 152.

[295] Wright 2015, 141, 171.

[296] Cf. Van Eck 2011, 8.

[297] Cf. Fleddermann 2005a, 858 n. 540.

[298] Q scholars agree that the Sayings Gospel associated God's kingdom with the feeding of the poor: e.g. Robinson 1993, 15; 2001a, 16; 2001b, 33; 2002, 15; Uro 1996, 87–89; Piper 2000, 241, 251, 259; Järvinen 2001, 521; Kloppenborg 2001, 166; Horsley 2003, 30–33, 35; 2012, 127; Howes 2015a, 123–124; Park 2019, 46.

[299] Q scholars agree that the Sayings Gospel understood God's kingdom as a new symbolic family: e.g. Jacobson 1995, 374–376; Freyne 2000, 206; Piper 2000, 264; Arnal 2001, 174; Vaage 2001, 486; Moxnes 2003, 105, 115–121, 152; Fleddermann 2014, 149; Park 2014a, 73, 78, 88–91; 2014b, 7–8, 9; 2019, 47; Howes 2015a, 144–150.

[300] Cf. Fleddermann 2014, 144.

the unproductive slave puts the economic needs of others ahead of his own wellbeing. In the process, he establishes the kingdom of God in the most unlikely of places.[301] In Q 12:33–34, people are told to accumulate heavenly treasures instead of earthly treasures.[302] Once again, the unproductive slave does exactly that: he wins the favour of God by devaluing earthly treasures like money and profit.

Piper argues that the parable of the entrusted money (in the final form of Q) commends the behaviour of the *productive* slaves and promotes taking economic risks instead of trying to preserve material possessions (including presumably money).[303] He sees the latter as the point of thematic overlap between the parable of the entrusted money and the texts in Q 12:22–31 and Q 12:33–34. Firstly, I strongly doubt that the parable, as it appears in the main redaction or final form of Q, addresses economic matters at all. Instead, it seems that an allegorical interpretation reinforcing eschatological judgment completely overshadows any economic message that the parable might have had at an earlier stage. Secondly, the main thrust of the passages in Q 12 is to redirect focus away from material concerns and towards heavenly and "kingdom" concerns. The economic behaviour being discouraged as resulting from material concerns seem to include not only an obsessive focus on the preservation of money and possessions,[304] but also an obsessive focus on economic undertakings as such, whether these be risky or not.[305] By contrast, the parable of the entrusted money, according to Piper's reading, promotes economic activity for the sake of profit. It follows that Piper's reading of the parable introduces a contradiction between Q 12 and Q 19, not an overlap.

Like our parable, the parable of the loyal and wise slave in Q 12:42–46 is about the activities of slaves during their master's absence, ultimately leading to a moment of reckoning at the master's visit or return.[306] It was argued in chapter 4 above that Q 12:42–44 originally appeared in the formative stratum, to which Q 12:45–46 was added by Q's main redactor. In this earlier version, the parable features a slave who uses his position of privilege to feed his fellow

---

[301] Cf. Beutner 2007b, 34.

[302] The comparison between someone who buries money to selfishly hoard it (Q 12:33–34) and someone who buries money to unselfishly protect the small peasantry (Q 19:21) is also interesting (cf. Oakman 2008, 36, 68).

[303] Piper 2000, 240, 259–260.

[304] Cf. the phrases "gather into barns" (συνάγουσιν εἰς ἀποθήκας) in Q 12:24 and "treasure treasures" (θησαυρίζετε θησαυροὺς) in Q 12:33.

[305] Cf. the phrases "neither sow nor reap" (οὐ σπείρουσιν οὐδὲ θερίζουσιν) in Q 12:24 and "neither work nor spin" (οὐ κοπιᾷ οὐδὲ νήθει) in Q 12:27.

[306] Kirk 1998, 298; Nolland 2005, 1012–1013; Snodgrass 2008, 526, 531; Roth 2018, 110–111; see Smith 2006, 124–126; cf. Jeremias 1972, 58; Crossan 1974a, 18–20; Donahue 1988, 109; Jacobson 1992, 244; Catchpole 1993, 99; Piper 2000, 255; Fleddermann 2005a, 858, 862.

slaves. According to my interpretation of Q 12:42–44, Q's Jesus views those who take care of the physical and nutritional needs of others as the true leaders of Israel. God expects those in privileged positions to address the needs of their underlings. Whereas the parable of the loyal and wise slave in Q 12:42–44 features a slave who contributes to the economic survival of others, the parable of the entrusted money in Q 19:12–13, 15–24 features a slave who refuses to participate in the economic starvation of others. Both are exemplary characters, working towards a world that is unperturbed by debt and starvation – a world otherwise referred to by Q's Jesus as the "kingdom of God."

9.10 Implied Audience

If my proposed interpretation of the parable is correct, it would be difficult to read it as aimed either directly or indirectly at outsiders. In portraying the kingdom of God as a place where contemporary economic endeavours have no place, the parable intends to direct the behaviour of insiders.[307] In the context of the Q movement, the parable envisages the in-group operating outside the economic affairs of existing society as God's family. This does not mean that the Q movement functioned from the start as a breakaway Jewish movement, aiming to create a sectarian community outside of Judaism. Rather, it means that the early Q movement wished to convince all their fellow Jews of the kingdom message, thereby establishing a new Israel operating on kingdom principles as part of God's new family.[308] They wished to revive Israel, but only succeeded in creating yet another Jewish reform movement, which ultimately operated outside the boundaries of contemporary Judaism.[309]

It was during the latter stage that those responsible for the main redaction changed the meaning of the parable to focus on the eschatological judgment of outsiders at the return of Jesus as the Son of Man.[310] This was achieved through clever redactional work and seemingly without changing the parable itself. First, the main redactor added a whole complex of eschatological material directly before the parable. Second, the main redactor added Q 19:26 after the parable as its application in order to generalise its meaning.[311] Unfortunately,

---

[307] Cf. Davies and Allison 1997, 403–404; Kirk 1998, 298, 300; Piper 2000, 255–256; Johnson-DeBaufre 2005, 184.

[308] See Howes 2015a, 253–255; cf. Park 2019, 47.

[309] Howes 2015a, 144.

[310] Cf. Crossan 1979, 34; Robinson 1994a, 317–318; Smith 2006, 170.

[311] Cf. Dodd 1958, 147–148; Hunter 1964, 19; Jeremias 1972, 36–37, 62, 110; Piper 1989, 144; Taylor 1989, 165; Funk and Hoover 1993, 375; Herzog 1994, 150–151; Davies and Allison 1997, 410. This claim goes against my earlier intuition that "this addition [referring to Q 19:26] was probably made before the parable as a whole was incorporated into the Sayings Gospel Q" (Howes 2015a, 213). The current more detailed investigation of the text

this addition caused a direct contradiction with the themes of socio-economic and eschatological reversal that appear throughout the rest of Q.[312] Third, the main redactor added Q 22:28, 30 after the generalising application to not only refocus and control its meaning, but also explain away the contradiction caused by its addition. Elsewhere, I have explained the development in logic from Q 19:26 to Q 22:28, 30 as follows:

> While the Q people, who already has [*sic*] the kingdom, will be afforded the additional priv-ilege of judging the rest of Israel at the final judgment, Israel, who currently lacks the king-dom, will also be robbed of their privileged status as "sons of Abraham" at the final judg-ment.[313]

Interestingly, such a change in the parable's meaning strongly suggests that those behind the main redaction were socio-economically better off than those behind the formative stratum. Thanks to the efforts of Q's main redactor, a path was cleared for the evangelists to further refine and emphasise the parable's eschatological allegory through their own redactional efforts.[314]

9.11 Findings

This chapter argued that the parable of the entrusted money in Q 19:12–13, 15–24 featured in Q's formative stratum before it was incorporated into the docu-ment's main redaction. If the parable's context in first-century Palestine is taken into account, its message and intent fit the formative stratum much better than the main redaction. Moreover, if all three criteria used by Kloppenborg to separate Q^1 and Q^2 from each other are applied to Q 19:12–13, 15–24, the orig-inal position of this text in the formative stratum is revealed. Finally, it is pos-sible to retrace the steps through which the parable was redacted by Q's main redactor. Some time ago, Jeremias noticed that the process of turning the par-ables into allegories had already started with pre-Synoptic traditions, including

has obliged me to adjust my view in this regard. If Luke's phrase "I tell you" (λέγω ὑμῖν) featured in Q, it would also be an indication that the logion was probably added by Q's main redactor (Neirynck 1982, 55, 56, 67; cf. Bultmann 1968, 326; Marshall 1978, 708; Kloppen-borg 1995, 296, esp. n. 65).

[312] Jacobson 1992, 244; Howes 2015a, 213; see Piper 1989, 149–153; cf. Funk and Hoo-ver 1993, 257, 374; cf. Q 6:20–22; 10:21; 11:9–10, 19, 31–32; 12:22–31, 45–46; 13:28–29; [30], 34–35; 14:[11], 16–21, 23.

[313] Howes 2014c, 6; cf. Reiser 1990, 249; Kirk 1998, 297–298; Vaage 2001, 480; Fledder-mann 2005a, 869; Valantasis 2005, 222; Kloppenborg 2011, 265; Roth 2018, 127.

[314] See Dodd 1958, 152–153; Jeremias 1972, 59–60, 62–63; Herzog 1994, 151; Luz 2005, 255–258; cf. Via 1967, 114; Bultmann 1968, 176, 195–196; Scott 1989, 220, 223–224; Ja-cobson 1992, 241, 242; Funk and Hoover 1993, 256; Kloppenborg 1995, 297; Funk 1996, 192; Piper 2000, 239; Denaux 2001, 459; Fleddermann 2005a, 842, 848, 854.

the tradition common to Matthew and Luke (referring to Q).[315] It is now possible to say with greater specificity that, pertaining to the parable of the entrusted money at least, this process was started by Q's main redactor. By changing the meaning of an earlier parable into an allegory about the final judgment, the main redactor was also "reaping where he did not sow."

---

[315] Jeremias 1972, 67, 89.

Chapter 10

The Literary Unity of Q[1]

In 1982, Arland D. Jacobson wrote an article titled "The Literary Unity of Q," arguing that the Sayings Gospel Q can be shown to have existed as a literary whole.[1] In 1994, the article was included in *The Shape of Q: Signal Essays on the Sayings Gospel*, a publication featuring ten of the most influential articles on Q ever to appear.[2] In this chapter, I consider *not* the literary unity of Q as a whole, but rather the literary unity of Q's formative stratum. According to Kloppenborg, one can reach the following conclusion from the research of other scholars on Q's redactional development: "Conscious literary organization and deliberate theological stylizing can be seen not only at the level of final redaction, but at earlier stages as well."[3] Hence, the literary unity of Q as a whole is not a legitimate argument against the existence of an earlier version like the formative stratum.[4] One would expect a capable editor like the main redactor of Q to introduce new connections between individual traditions, thereby creating a unity that differs in content and structure from the original unity in the document or tradition that s/he inherited. If both the Sayings Gospel Q in its final form and the formative stratum, respectively, show strong signs of unity, it would provide compelling evidence that the formative stratum existed as a separate tradition, most likely a written document, before it was enlarged by the main redactor.

One of the arguments against Kloppenborg's proposed stratigraphy is that the formative stratum might not have been a unified document before it was combined with the main redaction.[5] According to these scholars, it would negate Kloppenborg's proposal if the formative stratum was not already a unified document in its own right before the main redaction was added to it. Instead, editorial activity would then consist merely of assembling a host of disparate

---

[1] Jacobson 1982; see also Hoffmann 2001, 271–285; cf. Kloppenborg 1996a, 8–9; Uro 1996, 75.

[2] Jacobson 1994.

[3] Kloppenborg 1996a, 27. Kloppenborg refers here to the formation of Q clusters, which would strictly have happened *before* the compilation of the formative stratum, but the statement applies equally to the formative stratum as such.

[4] *Pace* e.g. Kirk 1998; Hoffmann 2001, 255–288.

[5] E.g. Hoffman 1995, 187; Tuckett 1996, 71–74; Horsley 1999, 67; Dunn 2003, 156–157.

sayings (and/or clusters of sayings) into one document.[6] In other words, the compositional process proposed by these scholars would basically entail collecting individual sayings (and clusters) attributed to Jesus and compiling them into one document. If this is correct, the postulation of more than one compositional layer would be unnecessary and unjustified. These critics do make a valid point. Dunn, for example, claims that Kloppenborg fails to show that the formative stratum "ever functioned as a single document or stratum."[7] Tuckett elaborates:

In this context, the question arises whether it is justified to regard the "Q^1" material as a literary unity, existing as a self-contained entity at some stage in the pre-history of Q. [...] In fact, as we shall see, Kloppenborg's sapiential layer is rather multi-faceted. This applies at the level of the individual alleged "speeches", or "blocks", of Q^1 material as well as the whole. Some of the alleged "collections" turn out to be extremely fragmentary. [...] One may have different collections (plural) which were never united prior to their use by Q^2.[8]

Hoffmann develops this line of argumentation in more detail.[9] In this chapter, I will argue not only that it is indeed possible to view the formative stratum as a literary unity, but also that my slightly revised version of the formative stratum produces a more cohesive unity than Kloppenborg's version. If the fragmentary nature of the formative stratum is a legitimate objection to Kloppenborg's stratigraphy, then a less fragmentary version of the formative stratum would be more probable as a solution to the stratifigraphy of Q. Moreover, if the unity of Q in its final form is a legitimate argument for the existence of Q, then the literary unity of the formative stratum is also a legitimate argument for its prior existence.

10.1 General Considerations

It should be mentioned at the outset that the fragmentary nature of the formative stratum does not in and of itself refute the idea that this layer existed as a literary unity at some earlier stage. Some ancient writings were indeed internally disparate and fragmentary, but physical copies of these collections prove that they were in fact complete literary writings at the time. This is particularly true of collections of logia. The *Gospel of Thomas*, for example, shows very little internal coordination and coherence, but is known to have existed as a physical document. Compared to the *Gospel of Thomas*, the Sayings Gospel Q is much more coherent and cohesive.[10] It is further pertinent to consider the

---

[6] Cf. Kloppenborg 1996a, 27.

[7] Dunn 2003, 156–157.

[8] Tuckett 1996, 71–72; cf. Hoffmann 2001, 267.

[9] Hoffmann 2001, 255–288.

[10] Cf. Horsley 1991, 202; 1995a, 41.

nature of the inherited material itself. Collecting available sayings and stories attributed to the same sage does not guarantee that these individual traditions will address the same themes with the same vocabulary and rhetoric. The compliers and editors are at the mercy of their inherited material. If the individual logia and/or clusters of logia relate poorly and the redactors refrain from adding literary links, the final product will by definition be fragmentary. This explains why sapiential literature is typically more fragmentary than other literary productions. Unconnected and dissimilar logia frequently appear side-by-side in ancient sapiential texts. This phenomenon is readily observable in the book of Proverbs. Superficially, some of the logia in Proverbs may seem disparate and unrelated, but closer scrutiny reveals attentive composition, particularly when the structural, rhetorical, and thematic similarities within the corpus are taken into account.

Different techniques are used by ancient authors to smooth over the staccato nature of such writings. The goal of these techniques is to produce cohesive writings that flow well from beginning to end. The mention of "flow" is important here and closely related to the larger issue of uniformity and cohesion. The notion of "flow" expresses the degree to which logia, clusters, and speeches are able to move effortlessly from the one to the next. In other words, "flow" addresses the question of how well individual logia, clusters, and speeches follow from preceding items and prepare for subsequent items. The better the overall flow, the more uniform the writing will be. The most basic and important technique applied in antiquity was to group logia with the same, similar, or related themes together, creating extended "blocks" or "speeches" of thematically overlapping traditions.[11] Even if some individual traditions are different or even contradictory, they are linked thematically.[12] Another popular technique, especially in extended collections of proverbs, was "catchword connection," which entailed the linking of sayings, clusters, and speeches that featured the same lexemes.[13] Some of the techniques applied in the Sayings Gospel Q include thematic, catchword, grammatical, and small-form connection, as well as narrative, logical, and rhetorical progression. According to Kloppenborg, the following techniques account for the connections and units in Q: (1) catchwords; (2) common structures and formal elements; (3) common themes; (4) syntactical devices that create a subordination, a sequence, or an inference between disparate traditions; (5) rhetorical organisation of larger units; and (6) presenting disparate units as the same communicative event.[14] Out of these, thematic and catchword connections are the most obvious and arguably the most popular in Q.

---

[11] See Kirk 2016, 131–134.
[12] Cf. Kloppenborg 1996a, 28.
[13] Kloppenborg 1996a, 28; 2000a, 125.
[14] Kloppenborg 2000a, 125–128.

It is important to point out that the formative stratum as a whole does indeed show obvious signs of conscious, deliberate, and sophisticated composition.[15] Apart from the internal parallels regarding characteristic forms, characteristic motifs, and implied audience, a great number of rhetorical and structural characteristics in the formative stratum also suggest that the sapiential blocks of the formative stratum were simultaneously edited by the same hands.[16] Furthermore, the structure, genre, and style of the formative layer is rather conventional when compared to contemporary Instructions, like Pseudo-Phocylides and Sirach.[17] Finally, the various methods used to interpose materials from the main redaction into the formative stratum suggest that the different sapiential blocks were already in written form when the main redactor made use of them.[18] These factors strongly suggest not only that two separate redactors were responsible for Q's two main layers, but also that the same redactor was responsible for the six blocks of Q¹ material.

10.2 Kloppenborg's Formative Stratum

Initially, Kloppenborg's formative stratum constituted the following six blocks of material:

1. Q 6:20–49 (minus Q 6:23c)
2. Q 9:57–62; 10:2–16, 21–24 (minus Q 10:12, 13–15, 21–24)
3. Q 11:2–4, 9–13
4. Q 12:2–12 (minus Q 12:8–9, 10)
5. Q 12:22–31, 33–34 (plus Q 13:18–19, 20–21)
6. Q 13:24–14:34 (minus Q 13:25–27, 28–30, 34–35; 14:16–24)[19]

In another publication, he argues for the inclusion of a number of additional traditions in the formative stratum, namely Q 15:4–10; 16:13, 16, 18; 17:1–4.[20] Kloppenborg also considers the possibility that Q 10:23–24 belongs to the same layer, but fails to make a final determination in this regard.[21] Hence, his ultimate version of the formative stratum constitutes the following blocks of material:

---

[15] Cf. Kirk 1998, 38; 2016, 181–182.

[16] See Kloppenborg 1987, 242–243; Piper 1989, 35–36, 61–63, 72–73, 139; Kirk 1998, 61–62, 269.

[17] Cf. Kirk 1998, 269.

[18] Cf. Kloppenborg 1987, 244; Kirk 1998, 269.

[19] Kloppenborg 1987, esp. 238, 243–244.

[20] Cf. Kloppenborg 2000a, 146 n. 62.

[21] Kloppenborg 2000a, 145, 147 n. 63.

1. Q 6:20–23b, 27–35, 36–45, 46–49
2. Q 9:57–60, (61–62[22]); 10:2–11, 16, (23–24?)
3. Q 11:2–4, 9–13
4. Q 12:2–7, 11–12
5. Q 12:22–31, 33–34; 13:18–19, 20–21
6. Q 13:24; 14:26–27; 17:33; 14:34–35; 16:13, 16, 18; 17:1–2; 15:4–7, 8–10; 17:3–4, 6[23]

Excluding consideration of Q 10:23–24 for the moment, scholars generally agree that each of the first five blocks listed above are cohesive and well-structured entities in their own right.[24] If careful attention is paid to their individual structuring techniques, constitutive themes, literary features, and rhetorical strategies, the unity of each block becomes not only apparent, but undeniable. It is not difficult for scholars to accept that these respective blocks were unified traditions before their incorporation into the Sayings Gospel Q or the canonical Gospels. Although each individual block is clearly composed of separate logia, the logic behind the combination of these logia betrays deliberate compilation. Each of these extended speeches flows effortlessly from beginning to end. To be sure, the speeches still betray redactional seams, indicating that the constitutive logia had a prior existence, but this does not take away from the probability that they were combined into speeches at an early stage during a process of deliberate redaction.

The same is not necessarily true of the sixth block, though.[25] The sayings that make up this block have typically been regarded as loose-standing traditions. As we have seen, it has also been questioned by scholarship whether the six blocks deserve to be unified under the same umbrella as constituting the same compositional layer. In order to argue that the formative stratum existed as a unified entity, one would therefore have to indicate (1) that the six blocks were connected to each other; and (2) that the logia that make up the last block were likewise connected to each other. The remainder of this chapter addresses these two matters.

---

[22] For the current analysis, Q 9:61–62 is not taken into consideration. The International Q Project does not regard this text as part of the Sayings Gospel, since it is lacking from Matthew (Robinson, Hoffmann, and Kloppenborg 2000, 156–157; 2002, 96–97; cf. Jacobson 1992, 133; 2000, 192 n. 11; Funk and Hoover 1993, 160; Fleddermann 2005a, 395–396). It is not impossible, however, that the saying appeared in Q (Marshall 1978, 408; see Crossan 1983, 238–239; Bock 1996, 975–976; cf. Jacobson 2000, 192, incl. n. 11).

[23] Kloppenborg 2000a, 146. In the case of the sixth block, the sequence of the *Critical Edition of Q* is followed for the added material, unless otherwise indicated.

[24] See e.g. Vaage 1995a, 87–88.

[25] Cf. Tuckett 1996, 71–72.

10.3 The Transition from Block 1 to Block 2

Although Q 6:20–49 should be seen as a literary unit in its own right,[26] it does flow effortlessly into Q 9:57–60. The inaugural sermon is introduced in Q 6:20 by deliberately mentioning that Jesus addressed "his disciples" (οἱ μαθηταὶ αὐτοῦ // τοὺς μαθητὰς αὐτοῦ).[27] On the level of Q, it is unlikely that this reference has "the twelve" in mind. Not once in the rest of Q is a numerical value attached to the term "disciples" (μαθηταί),[28] nor are any of the individual disciples ever named.[29] Instead, Q uses the term "disciples" (μαθηταί) in the more inclusive sense of the "general followers" of Jesus (and John).[30] The "disciples" of Q 6:20 are the general followers of Jesus listening to his wisdom message.[31] In its totality, Q 6:20–49 should be viewed as a pericope that deals with the theme of what it practically means to be a disciple of Jesus.[32]

Yet discipleship becomes the specific and deliberate topic of discussion at the end of the sermon. Verses 43–45 use examples from nature and agriculture to argue that one's deeds reveal one's heart.[33] Thus, a good person will do good deeds and a bad person will do bad deeds.[34] That people's *deeds* are being addressed is indicated not only by the Q text itself, but also by the familiar metaphorical use of the word "fruit" (καρπός) as a traditional reference to deeds (as well as words).[35] The passage ends with the statement: "For from exuberance of heart one's mouth speaks" (ἐκ γὰρ περισσεύματος καρδίας λαλεῖ τὸ στόμα αὐτοῦ), connecting words (in addition to deeds) with one's inner being.[36] This creates a decent segue to Q 6:46–49, where the relationship between

---

[26] Robinson 1982, 391; see Allison 1997, 67–95, 96–103; Fleddermann 2005a, 266–335.

[27] Cf. Casey 2009, 169–170.

[28] Cf. Horsley 1999, 262.

[29] Cf. Lührmann 1969, 97.

[30] Cf. Q 6:40; 7:18; 10:2; 14:26, 27; cf. Kloppenborg 1996b, 327 n. 88. According to Van Aarde (2004), "the twelve" were representative of Judean Christianity, not Galilean Christianity.

[31] See Catchpole 1993, 18–19; cf. Nolland 2005, 180, 191–192.

[32] See Catchpole 1993, 18–19; cf. Kloppenborg 1987, 184–185.

[33] See Bock 1994, 615–616; Betz 1995, 628–635; Kirk 1998, 173–175; Horsley 1999, 215, 224; Nolland 2005, 337–338; Valantasis 2005, 74–75; see chapter 2 above.

[34] Bock 1994, 617; Valantasis 2005, 75; Zimmermann 2014, 9; see Robinson 1997b.

[35] Marshall 1978, 140, 271, 272; Davies and Allison 1988, 305, 706; Horsley 1999, 198, 224; cf. Bock 1994, 617; *pace* Betz 1995, 634–635; cf. Ps 1:3; 58:11; Prov 1:31; 31:16, 31; Isa 3:10; Jer 6:19; 17:8–10; Hos 10:1, 13; Mic 7:13; Wis 3:13–15; Sir 23:25; 27:6; 2 Enoch 42:14; 2 Bar. 32:1; Apoc. Adam 6:1; Josephus, *Ant.* 20.48; John 15:2–17; Rom 6:22; Gal 5:19–23; Jas 3:10–12, 18; b. Ber. 48a; b. Qidd. 40a.

[36] Marshall 1978, 273; Piper 1989, 50; Bock 1994, 616, 617; Kirk 1998, 174–175; Horsley 1999, 198; Luz 2001, 210; Fleddermann 2005a, 333; Valantasis 2005, 75; Ra 2016, 108; see Betz 1995, 634–636.

words and deeds is the topic of discussion.[37] In this latter text, people are directed to put into *action* the words contained both in the teachings of Jesus and their own confessions.[38] In short, the passage teaches against "deedless discipleship," which is doomed to failure.[39] A rhetorical question unites the argument in Q 6:46–49: "Why do you call me: Master, Master, and do not do what I say?" (τί με καλεῖτε· κύριε κύριε, καὶ οὐ ποιεῖτε ἃ λέγω;). The reference to Jesus as "master" (κύριος) makes sense in a traditional discipleship context as a respectful address to a teacher.[40]

The first two logia of the second block (Q 9:57–60) also discuss the theme of discipleship.[41] The word "follow" (ἀκολουθέω), which is a usual indicator that discipleship is in view,[42] appears not only in verse 57, but also in verse 60.[43] Matthew deliberately adds the lexeme "disciple" (μαθητής) in 8:21 to make explicit that the theme of discipleship is in view. Lührmann also comments on the potent "discipleship" link between Q 6:46–49 and Q 9:57–60.[44] Out of the audience, someone interrupts Jesus's delivery of the inaugural ser-

---

[37] Marshall 1978, 273–274; Catchpole 1993, 98; Bock 1994, 618; Allison 1997, 94; 2000, 37; Valantasis 2005, 77; Ra 2016, 109; see Johnson-Debaufre 2005, 102–103.

[38] Kloppenborg 1987, 185; 2000a, 142; Jacobson 1992, 106; Catchpole 1993, 97, 99; Robinson 1993, 4, 16; 1998b, 137; Horsley 1999, 224; Fleddermann 2005a, 333, 334; Luz 2007, 386; Ra 2016, 39, 109, 110; see Marshall 1978, 273–275; Davies and Allison 1988, 719–724; Funk and Hoover 1993, 158–159, 299; Bock 1994, 618–624; Johnson-Debaufre 2005, 102–103; Nolland 2005, 342–344; Valantasis 2005, 77–80; Joseph 2012, 89; 2014, 207–210, 228; Foster 2014a, 282; 2014b, 25–26; Hartin 2015, 170–171.

[39] Catchpole 1993, 99; see Betz 1995, 557–567, 636–639.

[40] Marshall 1978, 274; Robinson 1991, 189; 1994a, 318; Funk and Hoover 1993, 158, 299; Bock 1994, 618; Joseph 2014, 207.

[41] Davies and Allison 1991, 39; Bock 1996, 974, 976–977; Verheyden 2001, 712; Tuckett 2014, 61; see Fleddermann 2014, 148–150; cf. Edwards 1976, 101; Marshall 1978, 408; Kloppenborg 1987, 190; Allison 1997, 11; Kirk 1998, 347; Luz 2001, 17; Fleddermann 2005a, 389, 400; Nolland 2005, 364. According to Fleddermann (2001, 21 n. 8), Q 9:57–60 is also linked to the subsequent material (Q 10:2–16, 21–24; 11:2–4, 9–13) by the theme of discipleship. It is especially noteworthy that Q 10:2 features the term "disciple" (μαθητής) (Fleddermann 2001, 32 n. 32).

[42] See Kingsbury 1978, 56–75; cf. Verheyden 2001, 712. Horsley (1999, 230, 262) problematises the link between the concept of "following" and the theme of discipleship, but his critique is based on a false dichotomy between "individualistic" discipleship and participation in "a movement based in local communities." Obviously this movement would have been made up of individuals who decided to "follow" Jesus as "disciples" by joining the Q group.

[43] Crossan 1983, 239; Fleddermann 2005a, 399; 2014, 148–149; Nolland 2005, 180, 365; Ra 2016, 58.

[44] Lührmann 1969, 58; cf. Marshall 1978, 408. Unfortunately, Lührmann includes Q 7:1–10, which is more about gentile faith than discipleship.

mon to enthusiastically declare her willingness to follow Jesus and be a disciple.[45] In a way, this is an attempted answer to the rhetorical question in Q 6:46. Vaage states: "The question asked in 6:46 ('Why do you call me, "Lord, Lord," but not do what I say to you?') is answered not only by the parable that follows in 6:47–49 but even more directly in 9:59–60."[46] By responding, the person attempts to illustrate her willingness to implement the teachings of Jesus. Jesus's response, however, is unexpected.[47] Instead of congratulating the eager listener for her compliant response, Jesus underlines the cost of discipleship.[48] The person seems to have underestimated the degree of commitment involved.[49] Discipleship might even include the abandonment of house and home.[50] A second person gets the same response from Jesus, requiring him to abandon family obligations.[51]

The reactions of the two individuals are not recorded, and their silence suggests non-compliance.[52] As such, the interaction between Jesus and his audience in Q 9:57–60 becomes a real-life example of people saying the right things, but not following through with committed action. Q 6:46 is brought to life by Q 9:57–60. Incidentally, the same thematic link would be applicable if the two individuals of the latter text responded compliantly, in which case it would be an example of saying the right things and following through with committed action. If the "teacher" (διδάσκαλε) of Matthew 8:19 featured in Q 9:57, the link would be even stronger.[53] On the one hand, the title "teacher" would be particularly appropriate as a response to the sapiential message of Jesus in the inaugural sermon.[54] In this regard, Fleddermann's observation is apt: "Obviously, the title ['teacher'] refers to the Sermon which presents Jesus' teaching."[55] On the other hand, it would illustrate the truth of Q 6:46 even better, since Q 9:57–60 would then feature people who call Jesus "teacher," but struggle to actually implement his teachings. In fact, the second response in Q 9:59–60 does indeed address Jesus in the vocative mood directly as "master" (κύριε), forming not only an unmistakeable catchword link with the same word

---

[45] Cf. Marshall 1978, 408; Jacobson 1992, 135; Kirk 1998, 394; Fleddermann 2005a, 398.

[46] Vaage 1995a, 89.

[47] Jacobson 1992, 133, 135–136; Ra 2016, 79; cf. Marshall 1978, 409; Bock 1996, 979.

[48] See Fleddermann 2005a, 389, 400–402; cf. Marshall 1978, 408; Luz 2001, 17.

[49] Marshall 1978, 408; Nolland 2005, 365; cf. Fleddermann 2005a, 399.

[50] Cf. Jacobson 1995, 361–362; Schottroff 1995, 354; Moxnes 2003, 54–55.

[51] Funk and Hoover 1993, 161, 317; Vaage 1994, 90; Allison 2000, 142, 143; Downing 2001, 204; cf. Marshall 1978, 411–412; Kloppenborg 1987, 191; Davies and Allison 1991, 53, 55; Bock 1996, 979–982; Tuckett 1996, 424; Arnal 2001, 93, 176; Nolland 2005, 367–368; Rollens 2014b, 167, 169; Ra 2016, 206.

[52] Cf. Ra 2016, 205.

[53] Cf. Marshall 1978, 409–410, 411; Bock 1996, 978; Fleddermann 2014, 150.

[54] Cf. Joseph 2014, 207.

[55] Fleddermann 2005a, 400.

(repeated twice) in Q 6:46, but also an exact illustration of Q 6:46.[56] It should be apparent from this description that the link between Q 6:43–49 and Q 9:57–60 is not only thematic, but also narratological. When the audience verbally responds to the message of Q's Jesus in the inaugural sermon, it creates narrative progression from the inaugural sermon to Q 9:57–60.

The thematic link between Q 6:46–49 and Q 9:57–60 extends beyond discipleship to include the topic of homelessness, which for Q is related to discipleship.[57] That Q 9:57–60 deals with the topic of homelessness (and its relation to discipleship) is often acknowledged.[58] However, scholars often fail to recognise the same topic in Q 6:46–49, where two houses are built, but only one remains standing.[59] Jesus continues to say in Q 9:57–60 that the Son of Man is also without a house. In this Q context, the term "Son of Man" refers to the earthly Jesus, while the saying *in toto* implies that his followers might have to share in his destitution.[60] In Q 6:47–49, Jesus compares acting on his message

---

[56] Cf. Robinson 1991, 189; 1994a, 318; Horsley 1999, 2; Nolland 2005, 339, 367; Joseph 2014, 207 n. 70; Roth 2014, 391. Although the term κύριε appears only in Matthew (Davies and Allison 1991, 54), the *Critical Edition of Q* is followed here.

[57] Uro 1996, 108. Homelessness is also a topic of the subsequent mission discourse (Uro 1996, 108; Fleddermann 2001, 32; Smith 2014, 36; Tuckett 2014, 63).

[58] E.g. Marshall 1978, 408, 410; Jacobson 1992, 135–136; 2000, 191; Funk and Hoover 1993, 161; Vaage 1994, 89; Bock 1996, 978–979; Tuckett 1996, 182–183, 255, 288–289, 366, 367; 2014, 62–63; Uro 1996, 108; Allison 1997, 13; Kirk 1998, 356; Robinson 1999, 194; Piper 2000, 219, 244; Arnal 2001, 176; Järvinen 2001, 519; Luz 2001, 17–18; Fleddermann 2005a, 400; 2014, 149, 161; Nolland 2005, 366–367; Joseph 2012, 61; Smith 2014, 36; Hartin 2015, 223.

[59] Cf. esp. Deut 28:15, 30. One or two interpretations come close to recognising the "homelessness" motif in Q 6:46–49. Kloppenborg (2014, 305), for example, comments that Q 6:46–49 and Q 13:26–27 imply "that being an erstwhile follower of Jesus or a kinsman or fellow villager is not enough to guarantee safety or entry into the 'house.'" Somewhat related is also Smith's (2014, 49–50) observation that Q 6:43–45 and Q 6:48–49 presuppose the traditional "house-as-self metaphor" that compares individual people to houses (cf. Q 11:24–26).

[60] Marshall 1978, 410; Kloppenborg 1987, 192; Davies and Allison 1991, 42; Robinson 1991, 189; 1999, 194; Funk and Hoover 1993, 161, 317; Vaage 1994, 89; Bock 1996, , 978, 979; Tuckett 1996, 183, 255, 288–289, 366; 2001a, 373, 374, 380 n. 38; 2014, 62; Horsley 1999, 71; Allison 2000, 160, 162; 2010, 294 n. 307; Jacobson 2000, 191; Meyer 2000, 154; 2003, 21; Arnal 2001, 92–93, 176; Järvinen 2001, 519; Luz 2001, 17–18; Fleddermann 2005a, 400; 2014, 149, 161; Casey 2009, 168–178; Park 2014a, 78–79; Ra 2016, 57, 58, 104; cf. Uro 1996, 108; see Nolland 2005, 365–367; Howes 2015a, 170–171. As a side note, if the Son of Man saying does on some level hint at the homelessness of humanity in general, it relates well to the depiction in Q 6:46–49 of the constant human struggle to avoid homelessness. For the claim that the expression Son of Man originally referenced humanity in general, see Bultmann 1963, 28 n. 3; Crossan 1983, 241; Davies and Allison 1991, 52; Robinson 1991, 189; 1994a, 321; Funk and Hoover 1993, 161; Horsley 1999, 239; Allison 2000,

to building an indestructible house, but in Q 9:57–60 Jesus warns that acting on his message might result in homelessness.[61] Ironically, building the symbolic house of God's kingdom might entail abandoning one's actual home.[62] Likewise, inclusion in God's symbolic family might entail abandonment of (or by[63]) one's biological family.[64] This is a central topic for the rest of the Sayings Gospel.[65] The catchword "master" (κύριος) might also be relevant in the context of homelessness and discipleship, hinting at the status of Jesus as head of the symbolic household, whose expectations trump those of actual householders.[66] It goes without saying that the abandonment of family ties would have had severe socio-economic effects.[67] Such homelessness and associated poverty relate well to the remainder of block 2 (Q 10:2–11, 16), where appealing to the hospitality of others is put forward as a means of receiving accommodation and sustenance.[68] As often noted, the link between Q 9:57–60 and the mission discourse is also based on the theme of discipleship.[69]

It is perhaps also worth noting that all the relevant passages reference nature in some way as part of their sapiential argumentation.[70] Particularly noticeable is the association between "rain" (βροχή) in Q 6:48–49 and "sky" (οὐρανός) in Q 9:57–58. Ultimately, we are left with a very strong linkage between blocks 1 and 2 by means of catchword connection (κύριος), thematic overlap (discipleship, homelessness), narrative progression (speech followed by audience reaction), and rhetorical strategy (arguing from nature). Despite his minority opinion that "discipleship" is not a theme in Q, Horsley makes the following statement: "An obvious sequel to the covenant renewal discourse in 6:20–49 is

---

160–163; Arnal 2001, 92, 176, 177; Casey 2009, 168–178; Rollens 2014b, 157. For arguments to the contrary, see esp. Marshall 1978, 410; Nolland 2005, 365–366; Joseph 2012, 61–63.

[61] Cf. Kloppenborg 1987, 185; Jacobson 1995, 361–362; Schottroff 1995, 354; Kirk 1998, 356; Moxnes 2003, 54–55.

[62] Cf. Piper 2000, 244; Luz 2001, 19; Moxnes 2003, 114, 140.

[63] Tuckett (2014, 61–64, 68) argues that Q 9:57–60 does not advocate abandonment of one's family or house as much as it legitimises the Q people's existing situation of homelessness and family rejection.

[64] Cf. Kirk 1998, 343; Jacobson 2000, 191; Fleddermann 2014, 149; Ra 2016, 206.

[65] See esp. Moxnes 2003; Howes 2015a, 144–150; cf. esp. Q 12:[49], 51, 53; 14:26; 17:33.

[66] Valantasis 2005, 77; cf. Robinson 1994a, 318.

[67] Piper 2000, 252; see Howes 2015a, 147–148; cf. Park 2014a, 77.

[68] Horsley 1999, 240; see Howes 2019b, 4–6; cf. Tuckett 1996, 183, 288–289; 2001a, 374, 386, 387; 2014, 62, 63; see below.

[69] E.g. Kloppenborg 1987, 200–201.

[70] Ra 2016, 130. Q 6:43–45: "tree" (δένδρος); "fruit" (καρπός); "thorn" (ἄκανθα); "fig" (σῦκον); "thistle" (τρίβολος); "bunch of grapes" (σταφυλή). Q 6:47–49: "bedrock" (πέτρα); "rain" (βροχή); "flash-flood" (ποταμός); "wind" (ἄνεμος); "sand" (ἄμμος). Q 9:57–60: "fox" (ἀλώπηξ); "cave" (φωλεός); "bird" (πετεινός); "sky" (οὐρανός); "nest" (κατασκήνωσις).

the mission discourse in Q 9:57–10:16."[71] This strong connection is quite remarkable if one considers that a lot of Q^2 material features between these two blocks. This provides good evidence in support of Kloppenborg's stratigraphy.

10.4 The Transition from Block 2 to Block 3

Kloppenborg initially excluded Q 10:21, 23–24 from his second block,[72] but subsequently considered the possibility that verses 23–24 in particular were attached after the mission discourse (Q 10:2–11, 16) at the end of block 2.[73] I argued in chapter 1 that not only verses 23–24, but also verse 21 featured in the formative stratum. Hence, in this section we consider the linkage between the three successive passages in Q 10:2–11, 16, Q 10:21, 23–24, and Q 11:2–13.[74] The corporeal concerns of the socio-economic underclass are a definite priority for these passages, which are written from the perspective of these underlings.[75] Seeking out hospitality is promoted as a survival strategy in the mission discourse.[76] Particularly relevant is the phrase "eat what is set before you" (ἐσθίετε τὰ παρατιθέμενα ὑμῖν).[77] Other indications of poverty and destitution (whether voluntary or not) include the reference to agricultural "workers" (ἐργάται), the identification of the listeners as "sheep in the midst of wolves" (πρόβατα ἐν μέσῳ λύκων), and the imagery of travellers who "carry no purse, nor knapsack, nor shoes" (μὴ βαστάζετε βαλλάντιον, μὴ πήραν, μὴ ὑποδήματα).[78] In the latter clause, "knapsack" (πήρα) may equally refer to the bag of a traveller or a beggar.[79] To be without such a bag would mean that no food could be taken along, and to be without a purse would mean that no food could be bought – the combination of which would make one dependent on the hospitality of others (and, by extension, the providence of God).[80] Similarly, to

---

[71] Horsley 1999, 297. In line with his own understanding of Q, Horsley (1999, 297) bases this linkage on the theme of Israel's renewal.

[72] Kloppenborg 1987, 197–203.

[73] Kloppenborg 2000a, 145, 147 n. 63.

[74] Interestingly, Allison (1997, 11–15, 30–36; 2000, 190) regards Q 9:57–11:13 not only as a literary unit, but also as part of the first layer that originally constituted Q (together with Q 12:2–32).

[75] Cf. Horsley 1999, 82.

[76] See Howes 2019b, 4–6; cf. e.g. Robinson 1995a, 265; 2001a, 16.

[77] Robinson 1999, 199.

[78] Marshall 1978, 418; Kloppenborg 1987, 194; Davies and Allison 1991, 171, 173, 180; Catchpole 1993, 182; Horsley 1999, 96, 244–245, 249, 272; Arnal 2001, 50; Rollens 2014b, 156; Ra 2016, 61, 63.

[79] Nolland 2005, 418; cf. Catchpole 1993, 183; Tuckett 1996, 387.

[80] Robinson 1993, 6; 1995a, 270; 1997a, 225; 2001a, 16; 2003, 35; Allison 1997, 14, 15; 2000, 52; Horsley 1999, 246; Jacobson 2000, 195; Meyer 2000, 149; Piper 2000, 243;

be without sandals was to be regarded as poor in the ancient Jewish world.[81] According to Tuckett, the instructions in Q 10:4 would have created "a visual appearance of extreme poverty."[82] In Q 10:21, 23–24, the word "children" (νήπιοι) is used to reference socio-economic underlings in particular.[83] Fleddermann associates these "children" with "the poor of the Sermon," referring to Q 6:20.[84] This association is strengthened by the fact that the rich and powerful of society are also mentioned, namely "sages" (σοφοί), "intellectuals" (συνετοί), "prophets" (προφῆται), and "kings" (βασιλεῖς).[85] These elite figures are deliberately contrasted with feeble "children."[86] Similarly, the mission discourse contrasts feeble farm workers with superior householders.[87] If Horsley is correct that the "wolves" (λύκοι) of Q 10:3 refer to ancient rulers, then this saying also juxtaposes the vulnerable underclass with the ruthless elite.[88]

These passages are followed by Q 11:2–13, which primarily deals with the daily survival of socio-economic underlings.[89] I have been convinced by scholars like Catchpole and Kirk that Luke 11:5–8 featured in the Sayings Gospel

---

Fleddermann 2005a, 431, 433; see Valantasis 2005, 98–100; cf. Joseph 2012, 88; Ra 2016, 61–62; cf. Judith 10:5; 13:10; b. Beṣah 32b.

[81] Bock 1996, 997; cf. Catchpole 1993, 183; Ra 2016, 61; cf. b. Šabb. 152a.

[82] Tuckett 1996, 387; cf. also Vaage 1994, 18, 24–25; Valantasis 2005, 99; Ra 2016, 61.

[83] Marshall 1978, 434, 439; Kloppenborg 1987, 198; Catchpole 1993, 197–198; Bock 1996, 1010; Luz 2001, 163; Howes 2016a, 21; see Nolland 2005, 470–471; cf. Davies and Allison 1991, 274–276; Johnson-DeBaufre 2005, 77, 167.

[84] Fleddermann 2005a, 453. Interestingly, Ra (2016, 63, 69) associates the kingdom message in Q 10:9 and the petition for God's kingdom to come in Q 11:2 with the same saying in Q 6:20 (cf. Horsley 1999, 219). Ra (2016, 69) further associates the request for bread in Q 11:2 and the description of bread and fish being provided in Q 11:11–13 with the promise of food provision in Q 6:21 (cf. Horsley 1999, 218–219, 221; Park 2014a, 84). Meyer (2000, 154) associates the saying that prohibits taking a purse on the way in Q 10:4 with Q 6:20. Schröter (2001, 49, incl. n. 54) links the beatitude of Q 10:23 to the beatitudes of Q 6:20–21.

[85] Horsley 1999, 99, 116, 118; see Luz 2001, 162–163; cf. Rollens 2014b, 165; Ra 2016, 131.

[86] Marshall 1978, 432, 439; Kloppenborg 1987, 198; Robinson 1998a, 247; Horsley 1999, 96, 99, 116, 118, 292; Luz 2001, 163; Fleddermann 2005a, 450, 453; 2014, 154–155; Valantasis 2005, 111–112; Rollens 2014b, 165, 166; Bazzana 2015, 272–273; Ra 2016, 130.

[87] Cf. Piper 2000, 254; Ra 2016, 62.

[88] Horsley 1999, 96, 245–246, 272.

[89] Kirk 1998, 179; see Catchpole 1993, 211–228; cf. Piper 1989, 20; 2000, 245, 256; Horsley 1999, 219, 221, 260, 295–296; Nolland 2005, 289; Luz 2007, 324.

between Q 11:2–4 and Q 11:9–13.[90] If Luke 11:5–8 were in Q, it would originally have formed part of the formative stratum.[91] There is no need to doubt the internal unity of Q 11:2–13,[92] which is itself made up of three smaller passages, namely Q 11:2–4, Q 11:5–8, and Q 11:9–13. All three of these sub-units deal explicitly and primarily with subsistence.[93] According to Kirk,

cultivation of patronage relations (11:2–4), cooperative friendship between households (11:5–8), and cooperative relations within the patriarchal household (11:11–13) constitute a complete list of survival strategies resorted to by subsistence-level peasants in agricultural societies.[94]

The theme of subsistence is particularly emphasised with the catchwords "bread" (ἄρτος) and "give" (δίδωμι), both of which appear in all three sub-units.[95]

---

[90] Catchpole 1993, 201–228; Kirk 1998, 177–180; cf. also Schürmann 1968, 119; Piper 1989, 24; Tuckett 1996, 152 n. 43. Q 11:5–8 qualifies when measured against Kloppenborg's (1996a, 5) criteria for including Sondergut traditions in Q: "(a) if it is a component of a text already clearly belonging to Q, (b) if it coheres stylistically and formally with other Q pericopae, (c) if it reflects the material emphases and ethos of other portions of Q, and provided that (d) there are grounds for supposing that the evangelist who preserved the pericope did not in fact create it and (e) there are good reasons for the other evangelist to have omitted the pericope."

[91] Q 11:5–8 features in the midst of Q¹ material. The content of this passage is thematically similar to the rest of the formative stratum, but not at all comparable to the main redaction. The rhetoric of Luke 11:5–8 is deductive rather than polemical. None of the typical imagery or terminology associated with apocalyptic and/or prophetic literature appear in Luke 11:5–8. Insiders represent both the intended and actual audiences of this passage. Finally, the structure of Q 11:2–13 is almost identical to other passages that belong to the formative stratum, including Q 6:27–35, Q 6:37–42, and Q 12:22–31 (Kirk 1998, 177).

[92] Cf. Kloppenborg 2000a, 125.

[93] Kirk 1998, 179; see Catchpole 1993, 211–228, esp. 218, 222, 225; cf. Kloppenborg 1987, 205; Piper 1989, 20, 23, 24; 2000, 245, 256.

[94] Kirk 1998, 179, cf. 324, 325.

[95] Kirk 1998, 179; cf. Marshall 1978, 463; Kloppenborg 1987, 205; 2000a, 125; 2001, 177; Piper 1989, 23, 24; 2000, 245, 252; Scott 1989, 88; Jacobson 1992, 153; Catchpole 1993, 225; Allison 1997, 14; Fleddermann 2005a, 467, 470, 471; Rollens 2014b, 148; Ra 2016, 71, 73; Van Eck 2016, 232. I disagree with Rollens (2014b, 147–151, 192) that the passage in Q 11:2–4, 9–13 (including, in my case, verses 5–8) has either partially or completely abandoned its former focus on the concerns of small peasants for subsistence and functions in the final form of Q to emphasise "the more abstract exhortation to retain confidence in God in spite of obstacles" (quotation from Rollens 2014b, 151). The instructions and examples in Q 11:2–13 remain very concrete and specific, dealing as they do with "bread" and "fish." The fact that Q 11:2–13 follows after Q 10:2–24 does not take away from this focus on subsistence, seeing as the mission discourse itself deals with the topic of subsistence in the context of hospitality. Even if Rollens is correct that Q 11:2–13 was writ-

As these catchwords indicate, prayer is overshadowed by subsistence as the main theme of these three sub-units. This goes against mainstream scholarship,[96] which regards the main thematic link between these units to be the topic of prayer.[97] Also against mainstream scholarship[98] is the case I made elsewhere that the three verbs in Q 11:9 do not *in the first place* reference prayer, but rather three different ways in which the ancient poor and small peasantry secured food and other basic necessities.[99] Likewise, the example in Q 11:5–8 is about human interaction long before it is about prayer.[100] It functions to buttress the instruction in Q 11:9–10 to ask other people for basic necessities.[101] As Bock rightly observes: "The point of comparison [in Luke 11:5–8] is not between the neighbor and God but between the petitioner and the disciple."[102] Unfortunately, Bock continues like most scholars to interpret this text in relation to prayer, when it is actually about human interaction in the context of securing basic needs like food. Kirk remarks that the whole pericope in Q 11:2–13 is directed at people who "are poor to the point of being threatened with hunger, for supply of daily bread is a recurring matter for prayer."[103] I agree with Kloppenborg that "the association of the prayer in 11:2–4 with 11:9–13 [and, in my case, 11:5–8] is not due to a mechanical clustering of similar sayings, but shows signs of the attempt to form an argument for confidence in the ethos expressed in the Lord's prayer."[104] In my view, this argument revolves around corporeal survival and subsistence living, not prayer. Within the context of *this* rhetorical focus, religious, political, social, and economic practices like general reciprocity, debt forgiveness, (the avoidance of) court proceedings, and, yes, prayer all have a role to play.[105]

The "bread" (ἄρτος) of verses 3, 5, and 11 should be understood as representative of food in general.[106] Verse 12 also mentions "fish" (ἰχθῦς), which

---

ten from a scribal perspective that fails to adequately address small-peasant concerns regarding subsistence, it would still not take away from the fact that this passage deals with the *topic* of subsistence. Whether it does so adequately is another question.

[96] E.g. Huffard 1978, 154; Kloppenborg 1987, 203; Tuckett 1996, 152–155; Allison 1997, 14, 15.

[97] Allison 2000, 242; see Van Eck 2016, 227–232.

[98] E.g. Marshall 1978, 467; Kloppenborg 1987, 204; Fleddermann 2005a, 471.

[99] Howes 2019b, 6–8.

[100] Van Eck 2016, 252; *pace* e.g. Huffard 1978, 154; Snodgrass 1997, 512–513; see below.

[101] Cf. Catchpole 1993, 222; Kirk 1998, 180; Oakman 2008, 94.

[102] Bock 1996, 1060.

[103] Kirk 1998, 324.

[104] Kloppenborg 2000a, 125.

[105] See Horsley 1999, 266–267, 295–296; cf. Kloppenborg 2001, 176–179; Valantasis 2005, 117–120.

[106] Catchpole 1993, 212; Bock 1996, 1053; Horsley 1999, 266–267; Piper 2000, 245; Fleddermann 2005a, 470; Bazzana 2015, 191.

was also a staple food in antiquity and would have been particularly common around the Sea of Galilee.[107] One cannot overlook the link between "eat" (ἐσθίω) in Q 10:7, 8 and "bread" (ἄρτος) plus "fish" (ἰχθῦς) in Q 11:3, 5, 11, 12.[108] Other such necessities are mentioned in the preceding mission discourse, namely "harvest" (θερισμός) in Q 10:2 and "sheep" (πρόβατα) in Q 10:3. The latter two terms represent the two avenues of farming that ultimately produce food, namely crop growing and animal husbandry.[109] Moreover, chronological development is assumed by the movement from "harvest" (θερισμός) in Q 10:2 to "bread" (ἄρτος) in Q 11:3. Interestingly, Luz relates the petition for "bread" in the Lord's prayer to "the situation of a day-laborer," which obviously calls to mind the "workers" (ἐργάται) of the mission discourse.[110] To summarise, the three passages in Q 10:2–11, 16, Q 10:21, 23–24, and Q 11:2–13 are in the first place linked by their concern for the daily needs of socio-economic under-lings.[111] This linkage is not trivial, since the topic of survival and sustenance is not only a golden thread that runs through the whole formative stratum, but also a central concern for blocks 3–5.[112]

A less obvious theme that links all three passages is the deliberate correla-tion between human and divine conduct.[113] According to Bazzana, Q 10:9 im-plies human involvement in the establishment of God's kingdom.[114] The mis-sion discourse ends in verse 16 with the notion that hospitality shown to hu-mans is the same as hospitality shown to Jesus and God, which is reminiscent

---

[107] Davies and Allison 1988, 682, 683; Betz 1995, 505; Horsley 1999, 267, 296; Luz 2007, 358.

[108] Robinson 1998d, 147–148; 1999, 199; Fleddermann 2005a, 431.

[109] Cf. Nolland 2005, 409.

[110] Luz 2007, 321; cf. Valantasis 2005, 118; Rollens 2014b, 156.

[111] Allison (1997, 15) also sees "the activity of God the Father on behalf of his children" as a theme that links all three of these passages. Although this is no doubt true for Q 10:21, 23–24 and Q 11:2–13 (see Park 2014a, 88–91), it is much more difficult to isolate this theme in Q 9:57–60; 10:2–11, 16. God is here neither identified as "Father" nor portrayed as taking care of his children. In fact, the possibility of not receiving hospitality (Q 10:6, 10–11), not having "a place to lay one's head" (ποῦ τὴν κεφαλὴν κλίνῃ) (Q 9:58), and being exposed to "wolves" (Q 10:3) do not bode well for God's providential care. The acts of hospitality that are received may indeed be evidence of God's care (Valantasis 2005, 99, 118), but the text does not explicitly bring this out. It is only if the mission discourse is read together with Q 11:2–13 that the latter inference becomes justified, but this does not mean that Q 9:57–60; 10:2–11, 16 addresses the topic of God's care.

[112] Cf. Kloppenborg 1987, 206; Catchpole 1993, 211–228, esp. 227–228; Robinson 1997a, 225, 236–237, 246–249; 2001a, 15–16, 32–33; 2003, 35; Jacobson 2000, 195; Piper 2000, 243–249; Schröter 2001, 49 n. 55; Park 2014a, 84, 90; Rollens 2014a, 97, 112; 2014b, 147.

[113] Cf. Kloppenborg 1987, 206; Bazzana 2015, 273–276.

[114] Bazzana 2015, 275–276.

of Genesis 18,[115] where Abraham shows hospitality to angelic visitors.[116] Q 10:21, 23–24 then correlates the divine acts of "hiding" (ἀποκρύπτω) and "disclosing" (ἀποκαλύπτω) to the human acts of "seeing" (βλέπω) and "hearing" (ἀκούω). This line of reasoning ultimately receives its fullest development in Q 11:2–13. Betz argues that the plural forms of the personal pronouns "our" (ἡμῶν) and "us" (ἡμῖν) in the Lord's prayer presuppose human involvement and generosity in the sharing of available resources.[117] Receiving food from God and receiving food from fellow human beings are therefore two sides of the same coin.[118] This relates well to the association drawn between divine and human action in the subsequent petition about forgiving debts.[119] Marshall likewise understands the petition to keep God's name holy in Q 11:2 as implying both divine and human activity. Associating divine and human action is also a chief intention of Q 11:5–13,[120] where the argument moves seamlessly from human to divine activity. Verses 5–8 and 9–10 focus on the human response to someone in need, while verse 13 focuses on the divine response.[121] Verses 11–12 represent a sort of segue, continuing the exclusive focus on the human response in verses 5–10, but doing so in order to prepare for the divine response in verse 13.[122] This means that the pericope in Q 11:2–13 is introduced by material on prayer in verses 2–4 and concluded by material on prayer in verse 13, with the material in-between dealing with human activity.[123] Divine activity functions as an *inclusio*, sandwiching the discussion on human activity.[124] Regarding both human and divine activity, subsistence is the topic of concern. It is finally worth mentioning that all three passages are linked not only by the words "kingdom" (βασιλεία) and "king" (βασιλεύς) in Q 10:9, 24; 11:2, but also by the topic of God's kingdom.[125]

---

[115] Cf. Heb 13:2.

[116] Jacobson 1992, 146; cf. Herzog 1994, 211–212.

[117] Betz 1995, 379–380, 399–400; cf. Luz 2007, 316.

[118] Cf. Kloppenborg 1987, 206.

[119] Marshall 1978, 461; Kloppenborg 1987, 206, 241; Davies and Allison 1988, 611; Bock 1996, 1055; Horsley 1999, 267; Robinson 2001b, 39–40; 2003, 38; Fleddermann 2005a, 470; Nolland 2005, 291; Luz 2007, 322; Oakman 2015, 75; Howes 2016a, 23; Ra 2016, 70; see Betz 1995, 400–404; cf. Sir 28:1–4. The "debt" (ὀφείλημα) of Q 11:4 might reach back to the "purse" (βαλλάντιον) of Q 10:4.

[120] Marshall 1978, 457; cf. Davies and Allison 1988, 678.

[121] Cf. Betz 1995, 504, 506; Kirk 1998, 182.

[122] Piper 1989, 17–18, 19; cf. Catchpole 1993, 212; Robinson 1995a, 263; Kirk 1998, 181; Kloppenborg 2000a, 125; Valantasis 2005, 123.

[123] Kirk 1998, 181.

[124] Kirk 1998, 182; cf. Kloppenborg 2000a, 125; Fleddermann 2005a, 473; Ra 2016, 73, 129.

[125] Cf. Catchpole 1993, 185, 201; Tuckett 1996, 148–149; Allison 1997, 15; Horsley 1999, 16–17, 87, 88, 147, 219, 266–267, 295; Fleddermann 2005a, 437, 470; Valantasis 2005, 103–104, 115–118; Joseph 2014, 198 n. 13; Ra 2016, 69.

Let us now take a closer look at the transition from Q 10:2–11, 16 to Q 10:21, 23–24. The Sayings Gospel presents the hospitality scene of the mission discourse in two parts: (1) in Q 10:5–9, hospitality is received; and (2) in Q 10:10–11, hospitality is denied.[126] Receiving hospitality culminates in the sick being cured and the kingdom message being shared, while being denied hospitality culminates in "shaking the dust from one's feet" (ἐκτινάξατε τὸν κονιορτὸν τῶν ποδῶν ὑμῶν).[127] Q 10:21, 23–24 develops this line of thought further by arguing that people more important than the householders of the mission discourse have likewise failed to receive the message of God's kingdom.[128] According to Q 10:9, the workers should say to those who offer them hospitality: "God's kingdom has reached unto you" (ἤγγικεν ἐφ᾽ ὑμᾶς ἡ βασιλεία τοῦ θεοῦ).[129] However, those who refuse hospitality will not receive this message.[130] They are like the prophets and kings of Q 10:24 who "[wanted] to hear what you hear, but never heard it" ([ἐπεθύμησαν/ἠθέλησαν] ἀκοῦσαι ἃ ἀκούετε καὶ οὐκ ἤκουσαν).[131] Q 10:9 further instructs the workers to "heal the sick there" (θεραπεύετε τοὺς ἐν αὐτῇ ἀσθενοῦντας).[132] Those who refuse hospitality will therefore never see these wonders.[133] They are like the prophets and kings of Q 10:24 who "wanted to see what you see, but never saw it"

---

[126] See Valantasis 2005, 101–106; cf. Marshall 1978, 414; Jacobson 1992, 142; Catchpole 1993, 187; Vaage 1994, 19; Bock 1996, 998, 1005; Tuckett 1996, 184, 287, 288; Horsley 1999, 248; Kloppenborg 2000a, 147–148; Hoffmann 2001, 270; Fleddermann 2005a, 432, 434; Nolland 2005, 419–420; Ra 2016, 61–64. The possibility that hospitality might be denied is already preempted in Q 10:6 by the clause "…but if not, let your peace return upon you" (εἰ δὲ μή, ἡ εἰρήνη ὑμῶν ἐφ᾽ ὑμᾶς ἐπιστραφήτω) (Vaage 1994, 19, 33; Fleddermann 2005a, 432, 433; Valantasis 2005, 101).

[127] Bock 1996, 999–1000, 1001, 1005; Tuckett 1996, 287; Horsley 1999, 246–247; Robinson 1999, 188; Fleddermann 2005a, 434; see Valantasis 2005, 103–106. For an explanation of the symbolic gesture to "shake the dust from one's feet," see Davies and Allison 1991, 178; Robinson 1993, 6; Vaage 1994, 36–37; Bock 1996, 1001–1002; Tuckett 1996, 287–288; Kloppenborg 2001, 167; Fleddermann 2005a, 434; Nolland 2005, 420; Valantasis 2005, 105–106.

[128] Cf. Marshall 1978, 439; Davies and Allison 1991, 277; Zeller 1994, 126; Kirk 1998, 344.

[129] Robinson 1983, 31; 2001a, 16; Catchpole 1993, 186; Kloppenborg 2001, 167; Schröter 2001, 49; Fleddermann 2005a, 434; 2014, 155; Johnson-DeBaufre 2005, 65; Ra 2016, 63. The fact that receiving the kingdom is a consequence of extending hospitality indicates that the hosts could not already have been disciples or followers of Jesus, forming part of an "established community" or network to be contrasted with the missionaries or "wandering radicals" (cf. Marshall 1978, 420).

[130] Marshall 1978, 420, 423; Bock 1996, 1002.

[131] Cf. Davies and Allison 1991, 277, 394; Luz 2001, 247; Fleddermann 2005a, 453 Valantasis 2005, 111.

[132] Catchpole 1993, 186; Fleddermann 2005a, 434; 2014, 155; Johnson-DeBaufre 2005, 65; Ra 2016, 63.

[133] Valantasis 2005, 111, 115; cf. Johnson-DeBaufre 2005, 190.

(ἐπεθύμησαν/ἠθέλησαν ἰδεῖν ἃ ὑμεῖς βλέπετε καὶ οὐκ εἶδαν).[134] Conversely, Q 10:23 says that those who do offer hospitality will indeed be able "to see what you see..." (οἱ βλέποντες ἃ βλέπετε).[135] In the second half of the hospitality scene, the householders reject the workers and thereby unwittingly preclude themselves from receiving the kingdom message or seeing the kingdom miracles.[136] Q 10:21, 23–24 justifies this eventuality by explaining that the sages, prophets, and kings of old have likewise been precluded from receiving the kingdom message or seeing the kingdom miracles.[137] Yet the unassuming followers of Jesus have heard the message and seen the wonders, which is what the demonstrative pronoun ταῦτα ("these things") refers to in Q 10:21.[138] The word "children" (νήπιοι) in Q 10:21, 23–24 therefore refers both to the workers and to the hospitable householders in Q 10:5–9.[139] Likewise, the mentioning of "sages" and "prophets" in Q 10:21, 23–24 relates well to the phrase "the one who sent me" (τὸν ἀποστείλαντά με) in Q 10:16.[140] In the present dispensation, Jesus and the workers fulfil the function that used to be fulfilled by the sages

---

[134] Cf. Marshall 1978, 438; Davies and Allison 1991, 277, 394; Luz 2001, 247; Fleddermann 2005a, 453; Valantasis 2005, 111. For the link between teaching and healing as two ways of proclaiming God's kingdom, see Du Toit 2016, 67.

[135] Cf. Nolland 2005, 537.

[136] Marshall 1978, 423; cf. Jacobson 1992, 137, 147, 149; Bock 1996, 1002; Tuckett 1996, 280; Allison 1997, 14–15; 2000, 82; Horsley 1999, 242; Kloppenborg 2000a, 124; Fleddermann 2005a, 434, 449; Ra 2016, 131. Most interpreters maintain that the inhospitable householders reject the message of God's kingdom, but if proclamation of the message is a precondition for receiving the message in the first place, it follows that these inhospitable householders did not receive the message to begin with and could therefore not have rejected the message. Instead, they rejected the messengers; or rather, they failed to offer them hospitality, which might have been interpreted by the messengers as rejection. The link in Q 10:9 between healing and proclaiming or receiving God's kingdom is reminiscent of Q 11:20 (Uro 1996, 80).

[137] Jacobson 1992, 149; Zeller 1994, 126; Kirk 1998, 344; Kloppenborg 2000a, 387; Valantasis 2005, 111; cf. Piper 1989, 172. It should be noted that the focus is not in any of these texts on "reception" or "acceptance" of the kingdom message as a human act or decision, but rather on God's agency in revealing the kingdom. In other words, although "receiving the kingdom message" (through word and deed) is a theme that links the mission discourse to Q 10:21, 23–24, this theme is discussed from the perspective of God, Jesus and the workers, not the recipients. The issue is never whether or not certain people would accept the message, but whether or not they will receive the message in the first place. Of course, the latter depends on whether or not they receive the workers by showing them hospitality.

[138] Marshall 1978, 434, 439; Kloppenborg 1987, 197; 1990, 79; 2000a, 372; Jacobson 1992, 149; Tuckett 1996, 280; Kirk 1998, 344; Valantasis 2005, 111, 112; see Allison 1997, 14–15; Fleddermann 2014, 155–156; cf. Piper 1989, 172; Bazzana 2015, 310; Ra 2016, 133, 134.

[139] Zeller 1994, 126; Allison 1997, 14; Kirk 1998, 344; cf. Tuckett 1996, 280.

[140] Jacobson 1992, 146.

and prophets of old, which is to act as the recipients and messengers of God's revelation, including most importantly the message of God's kingdom.[141]

Another link worth mentioning here is the catchword "father" (πάτερ) that Q 10:21, 23–24 shares with Q 9:57–60.[142] Both passages therefore deal with the family as topic to form a sort of *inclusio* around the mission discourse.[143] Yet the passages differ in that Q 9:59–60 deals with the biological family and Q 10:21, 23–24 with the symbolic family. This seems like an appropriate *inclusio* for the mission discourse, so that hospitality is by virtue of this prolegomenon and postscript identified as the means through which biological family relations are to be replaced by symbolic family relations in the establishment and expansion of God's kingdom. One may therefore observe some measure of chronological progression from the abandonment of biological family obligations, including to one's earthly father, and being without shelter in Q 9:57–60 to receiving hospitality and shelter from others in Q 10:2–11, 16 to establishing a supportive network of symbolic siblings, with God as Father, in Q 10:21, 23–24 and Q 11:2–13.[144]

There is another connection between Q 9:57–60 and Q 10:21, 23–24 that is perhaps less obvious. The "foxes" (ἀλώπεκες) and "birds" (πετεινά) of Q 9:57–60 represent land and sky animals respectively, thereby signifying creation in its totality.[145] It is therefore no coincidence that God is described in Q 10:21 as "Father, Lord of heaven and earth" (πάτερ, κύριε τοῦ οὐρανοῦ καὶ τῆς γῆς), expressing the totality of God's authority over his creation.[146] When this connection is further read together with the title "Father from heaven" (ὁ πατὴρ ἐξ οὐρανοῦ) in Q 11:13, the net result is a depiction of God as the creator who takes care of the physical needs of his whole creation, including especially his human children.[147] In addition to the catchword "father," Q 10:21, 23–24 has the catchword "lord" (κύριος) in common with Q 10:2 in the mission discourse.[148]

---

[141] See Valantasis 2005, 115–116; cf. Tuckett 1996, 209, 280; Allison 1997, 15; Horsley 1999, 96, 310; Kloppenborg 2000a, 372–373; Fleddermann 2005a, 448, 450, 453; 2014, 155.

[142] Cf. Fleddermann 2001, 32 n. 32.

[143] Kirk 1998, 340.

[144] Cf. Tuckett 1996, 288–289; Kirk 1998, 343, 347, 357; Fleddermann 2005a, 449–450; Valantasis 2005, 109.

[145] Kirk 1998, 342; cf. Ra 2016, 130.

[146] Fleddermann 2005a, 430, 450; 2014, 143–144; Valantasis 2005, 111; Ra 2016, 130; cf. Hartin 2014, 39; Bazzana 2015, 309, 310.

[147] Cf. Allison 1997, 14, 15; Robinson 2001a, 16; Fleddermann 2005a, 450; 2014, 144; Valantasis 2005, 123; Hartin 2014, 39–40; Park 2014a, 90.

[148] Catchpole 1993, 160, 161; Robinson 1994a, 317; Bock 1996, 995, 1009; Fleddermann 2005a, 430, 450; 2014, 143; Dormeyer 2014, 192; Joseph 2014, 207 n. 70.

Let us move on to the linkage between Q 10:21, 23–24 and Q 11:2–4. "Prayer" is the obvious theme that links these two passages.[149] Both Q 10:21 and Q 11:2 make use of the vocative "father" (πάτερ) in the context of a prayer to God.[150] The difference between the two texts is that Q 10:21 is a prayer of Jesus to his heavenly Father, whereas Q 11:2 is a model prayer to be used by others.[151] While Jesus is the subject speaking to God in Q 10:21, all followers of Jesus are the potential subjects of Q 11:2. Yet this distinction is somewhat artificial. On the one hand, Q 10:21, 23–24 was also a model prayer uttered in public and was therefore no less capable of being copied by the followers of Jesus.[152] On the other hand, the Lord's prayer was also an example of Jesus speaking directly to God with performative language.[153] Both prayers are public demonstrations of speaking to God in a direct and intimate fashion.[154] According to Kirk, Q 11:2–13 "begins to unfold the meaning of the blessing of 10:23–24, setting forth as it does the privileged access to God and paternal care which is bestowed by Jesus' revelation."[155] The catchword "father" (πατήρ) is again repeated in Q 11:13.[156] Also in this case, the intention of the word "father" is to underscore the intimacy of God's relationship with his children, which extends to his corporeal provision and care for his children.[157] Even more impressive than the catchword "father," though, is the fact that both Q 10:21 and Q 11:13 use the words "father" (πατήρ) and "heaven" (οὐρανός) in combination.[158] These observations are further reinforced by the association between "children" (νήπιοι) in Q 10:21 and "children" (τέκνα) in Q 11:13.[159] This association presumes a chronological development from the "infants"

---

[149] Allison 1997, 13–14; Kirk 1998, 344–345; Valantasis 2005, 110. If one regards the phrase "ask the Lord" (δεήθητε οὖν τοῦ κυρίου) in Q 10:2 as an instruction to pray, the topic of prayer is already introduced here (Allison 1997, 14; Fleddermann 2005a, 430, 447; Ra 2016, 124; cf. Horsley 1999, 233–234; Luz 2001, 65; Nolland 2005, 408).

[150] Jacobson 1992, 149, 153; Allison 1997, 14; Fleddermann 2001, 32 n. 32; 2005a, 466; Valantasis 2005, 110; Joseph 2014, 224; Ra 2016, 67, 68, 129; see Luz 2001, 156, 161–162; 2007, 314–316; cf. Marshall 1978, 456.

[151] Allison 1997, 13–14; Fleddermann 2005a, 430, 447, 466; Valantasis 2005, 110, 117; Ra 2016, 129; cf. Jacobson 1992, 159; Betz 1995, 373; Nolland 2005, 285, 470.

[152] Nolland 2005, 470; cf. Marshall 1978, 433; Valantasis 2005, 110–112.

[153] Betz 1995, 349, 373, 377, 382; Luz 2007, 324.

[154] Cf. Marshall 1978, 433; Bock 1996, 1009, 1011, 1051–1052; Valantasis 2005, 110–112; Ra 2016, 68.

[155] Kirk 1998, 326; cf. Jacobson 1992, 159.

[156] Scott 1989, 88; Jacobson 1992, 153; Catchpole 1993, 225; Allison 1997, 14; Kirk 1998, 182; Kloppenborg 2000a, 125; 2001, 177; Fleddermann 2001, 32 n. 32; 2005a, 467, 473; Nolland 2005, 327; Ra 2016, 73, 129.

[157] Bock 1996, 1062; Kirk 1998, 180; Kloppenborg 2000a, 125; 2001, 178; Valantasis 2005, 123; cf. Vaage 1995a, 89; Piper 2000, 258.

[158] Cf. Jacobson 1992, 153.

[159] Jacobson 1992, 153; cf. Park 2014a, 88.

(νήπιοι) that initially receive the message of Jesus to the "toddlers" or pre-adolescent children (τέκνα) that ultimately support each other in God's symbolic family. When combining the internal cohesion of Q 11:2–13, outlined above, with the present survey of the transition from Q 10:21, 23–24 to Q 11:2–13, one cannot but agree with Jacobson that there is "a particularly strong linkage" between these traditions.[160]

It is not coincidental that Q 10:21, 23–24 is introduced with the clause: "at that time he said" (ἐν ἐκείνῳ τῷ καιρῷ εἶπεν // ἐν αὐτῇ τῇ ὥρᾳ εἶπεν). The narrative introduction indicates both that Jesus interrupted himself to introduce a new topic and that the new topic was somehow related to the previous teaching.[161] In fact, Jesus is depicted here as some kind of charismatic who starts talking audibly to God in the midst of giving a speech.[162] Luke picks up on this portrayal of Jesus, adding to the narrative introduction that Jesus "rejoiced exceedingly in the Holy Spirit" (ἠγαλλιάσατο ἐν τῷ πνεύματι τῷ ἁγίῳ).[163] Q's Jesus is probably inspired to start praying to God by the phrase "the one who sent me" (τὸν ἀποστείλαντά με) at the end of his speech in Q 10:16.[164] The connection between the latter phrase and the divine titles "Lord" (κύριος) and "Father" (πάτερ) in Q 10:21 is therefore another feature that links the mission discourse with Q 10:21, 23–24. However strange the spectacle might have seemed, both the act of praying and the content of the prayer relate thematically to the previous material by addressing the topic of gaining access to God and his kingdom.[165] Just as unexpectedly as the prayer was started, Jesus ends the prayer and turns back to his audience.[166] The Lord's prayer follows perfectly after the charismatic display as a lesson on how anyone can speak directly to God.[167] Luke makes the switch to instruction explicit with an introductory verse in 11:1.[168] After giving a live demonstration of prayer in Q 10:21, 23–24, Jesus empowers and encourages his audience in Q 11:2–4 to do it themselves.[169] According to Ra, "the literary flow [from Q 10:21, 23–24, although

---

[160] Jacobson 1992, 153. Although Jacobson is here speaking specifically about Q 10:21–22, Q 11:2–4, and Q 11:9–13, which differs slightly from our corpus by including Q 10:22 and excluding Q 11:5–8, he points to many of the same catchword and thematic connections.

[161] Kloppenborg 1987, 197; 2000a, 128; Fleddermann 2005a, 449; 2014, 153, 156; Nolland 2005, 470; cf. Marshall 1978, 430, 432; Allison 1997, 14.

[162] Cf. Valantasis 2005, 110–112.

[163] Marshall 1978, 433; Bock 1996, 1009, 1010; cf. Van Eck 2016, 233.

[164] Cf. Valantasis 2005, 111.

[165] Cf. Tuckett 1996, 153; Kirk 1998, 319; Fleddermann 2005a, 470.

[166] Cf. Fleddermann 2005a, 467.

[167] Jacobson 1992, 159; cf. Marshall 1978, 454; Betz 1995, 382; Fleddermann 2005a, 466; Ra 2016, 129.

[168] Bock 1996, 1049–1050; Robinson 1996, 96; cf. Kloppenborg 1987, 192; Van Eck 2016, 233.

[169] Cf. Marshall 1978, 454; Betz 1995, 349, 373.

Ra includes Q 10:22, to Q 11:2–4] is natural in that Jesus had once prayed to God and then gave his disciples an example of prayer."[170] Jesus is therefore depicted as a passionate charismatic with a sound pedagogy. Hence, in addition to the catchword "father" (πάτερ), both Q 10:21, 23–24 and Q 11:2–4 deal with the topic of intimate and unmediated prayer.[171] In fact, the vocative catchword "father" (πάτερ) and the theme of intimate, unmediated prayer are two sides of the same coin.[172]

Hospitality can further be discerned as a thematic link between Q 10:2–11, 16 and Q 11:2–13. As we saw, hospitality is a main theme of the mission discourse. Hospitality is also a major theme of Q 11:5–8.[173] I have argued elsewhere that the verb "knock" (κρούετε) in Q 11:9–10 references hospitality.[174] If this is correct, the two sub-units in Q 11:5–8 and Q 11:9–13 are linked by the topic of hospitality, which is itself directly related to the larger theme of subsistence.[175] This link is strengthened by the combination of the catchwords "knock" (κρούετε) and "bread" (ἄρτος) in both Q 11:5–8 and Q 11:9–13.[176] It follows that the theme of hospitality links the two outer passages of the complex considered here – that is, Q 10:2–11, 16 and Q 11:2–13 – forming a type of thematic *inclusio*. Although the verb "search" (ζητέω) in Q 11:9 should in the first place be understood as a reference to one's pursuit for food and other bare necessities,[177] it might on a secondary level also connote one's pursuit for wisdom and knowledge.[178] In antiquity, the verbs "search" and "find" were often used in reference to truth, wisdom, philosophy, and knowledge.[179] In the *Gospel of Thomas* (92), the saying "seek and you shall find" is used in the context of seeking revelation and knowledge.[180] If the verb "search" does connote a person's pursuit for wisdom and knowledge, Q 11:9–13 is also in this way thematically linked to Q 10:21, 23–24.[181]

---

[170] Ra 2016, 129.

[171] Cf. Arnal 2001, 198, 257 n. 65.

[172] Betz 1995, 382; Bock 1996, 1009, 1011, 1051–1052; Arnal 2001, 198, 257 n. 65; Ra 2016, 68; see Davies and Allison 1988, 601–602; cf. Jacobson 1992, 159.

[173] Betz 1995, 504; Bock 1996, 1057, 1058; Kirk 1998, 179–180; Snodgrass 2008, 441; see Jeremias 1972, 157–159; Scott 1989, 86–92; Catchpole 1993, 201–210; Herzog 1994, 199–214; Van Eck 2016, 227–253, esp. 235–236.

[174] Howes 2019b, 7; cf. Valantasis 2005, 121.

[175] Catchpole (1993, 222) maintains that all three verbs in Q 11:9–10 (i.e. "ask," "search," and "knock") reach back to Q 11:5–8.

[176] Cf. Scott 1989, 88; Van Eck 2016, 233.

[177] See Howes 2019b, 7.

[178] Davies and Allison 1988, 679; Betz 1995, 501; Valantasis 2005, 121; Luz 2007, 358; cf. Prov 1:28; 8:17; Wis 6:12.

[179] Davies and Allison 1988, 679, 682; Luz 2007, 358; see Betz 1995, 501–502; cf. Allison 2000, 242; Valantasis 2005, 121.

[180] Kloppenborg 1987, 204; Piper 1989, 23; Horsley 1999, 267; Gathercole 2014, 537.

[181] Piper 1989, 23; cf. Johnson-DeBaufre 2005, 65.

Before summarising, a few words are in order regarding the way in which the relationship between Jesus and God is portrayed here. The phrase "the one who sent me" (τὸν ἀποστείλαντά με) in Q 10:16 might hint at a special relationship between Jesus and God, which is also implied by the vocative "father" (πάτερ) in Q 10:21 and Q 11:2.[182] Yet these traditions do not seem to teach that the relationship between Jesus and God is somehow better or holier than other people's relationships with God.[183] In fact, the whole point of the logion in Q 10:16 is that the presence of Jesus is not a requirement for gaining direct access to God.[184] People can receive God (and Jesus) in their homes by showing hospitality to the followers of Jesus.[185] The workers are themselves emissaries of God, able to share the kingdom message without Jesus's help.[186] By the same token, the point of the Lord's prayer is to teach people how to pray to God directly without the mediation or intercession of Jesus or anyone else.[187] Hence, even though these texts do reveal a special relationship between Jesus and God, the point is that anyone can access God without mediation and so develop the same kind of relationship with God.[188] In the new symbolic family that Q advocates, all those who accept the kingdom message become sons and daughters of God the Father, which automatically grants them unbrokered access to the divine.[189] In fact, the kingdom message and the symbolic family of God are two sides of the same coin: "Experiencing God as Father means experiencing the kingdom; experiencing the kingdom means learning to live as children of the Father."[190] In both prayers, addressing God directly as "Father" (πάτερ) presupposes participation in God's symbolic family, which includes

---

[182] Cf. Marshall 1978, 432; Davies and Allison 1991, 226; Catchpole 1993, 161; Bock 1996, 1009, 1011; Kloppenborg 2000a, 375, 393; Luz 2007, 315.

[183] Cf. Betz 1995, 389; Tuckett 1996, 280; *pace* Catchpole 1993, 188.

[184] Cf. Tuckett 1996, 280; Valantasis 2005, 109; *pace* Ra 2016, 66, 128.

[185] Vaage 1994, 38; Johnson-DeBaufre 2005, 112; Valantasis 2005, 109; Ra 2016, 65; cf. Fleddermann 2005a, 436–437.

[186] Vaage 1994, 38; Tuckett 1996, 280; 2001a, 374–375; cf. Marshall 1978, 426; Kloppenborg 1990, 79; 2000a, 372; Davies and Allison 1991, 170, 226; Bock 1996, 1005; Horsley 1999, 301; Luz 2001, 75, 120; Schröter 2001, 45; Nolland 2005, 417, 443–444.

[187] Jacobson 1992, 159; Betz 1995, 382; Arnal 2001, 257 n. 65 Luz 2007, 325; Ra 2016, 68; cf. Marshall 1978, 456.

[188] Marshall 1978, 456; Jacobson 1992, 159; Bock 1996, 1060; Arnal 2001, 198, 257 n. 65; Luz 2007, 315, 325; see Betz 1995, 386–389; cf. Tuckett 1996, 280; Fleddermann 2005a, 449, 468–469.

[189] Kirk 1998, 325–326; Howes 2016a, 19; cf. Park 2019, 47; cf. Q 6:35.

[190] Fleddermann 2005a, 470; cf. Park 2019, 47.

direct access to God.[191] It is true that Jesus and the workers mediate the kingdom message initially,[192] but to those who then accept the message, God and his kingdom become directly accessible.[193] These observations should not be seen as negating the historical role or significance of Jesus, since it is not only the message and practices of *Jesus* that are adopted by the workers, but also *Jesus* who was initially sent by God.[194]

In sum, all three passages are linked by the themes of daily survival, access to God, exposure to God's kingdom, and the relationship between human and divine action.[195] The catchwords "kingdom" (βασιλεία) and "king" (βασιλεύς) also link all three passages. A number of additional themes further facilitate the transition from Q 10:2–11, 16 to Q 10:21, 23–24, including especially socio-economic juxtaposition and receipt of the kingdom message (in word and deed). The connection is strengthened by the catchword "lord" (κύριος). Then, the theme of intimate, unmediated prayer and the catchword "father" (πατήρ) facilitate the transition from Q 10:21, 23–24 to Q 11:2–4.[196] The topic of hospitality further links Q 10:2–11, 16 and Q 11:2–13 (esp. verses 5–8, 9–10). The overarching flow is strengthened by narrative and rhetorical progression from a *speech* about receiving access to God and his kingdom (Q 10:2–11, 16) to a *demonstration* of praying to God directly (Q 10:21, 23–24) to a *lesson* on how to pray to God directly (Q 11:2–4). Importantly, the links identified in this section between the three relevant passages would remain valid if Q 11:5–8 were taken out of the equation. It should finally be recognised that, with the exception of the interpolated Johannine thunderbolt in Q 10:22 and the interpolated woes in Q 10:13–15, the sequence suggested here for the formative stratum is also the sequence of the Sayings Gospel Q.[197] In other words, except for the interpolated sayings in Q 10:13–15, 22, the exact same sequence proposed here also represents the final version of Q (as it has been reconstructed by the International Q Project).

---

[191] Jacobson 1992, 159; Betz 1995, 382; cf. Tuckett 1996, 153, 280; Kirk 1998, 319, 325–326; Arnal 2001, 198, 257 n. 65; Fleddermann 2005a, 449–450, 468–469; Nolland 2005, 326; Ra 2016, 68, 129.

[192] Tuckett 1996, 280; see Ra 2016, 65–66, 128; cf. Bock 1996, 1005; Allison 1997, 15; Kirk 1998, 326; Horsley 1999, 301; Smith 2006, 119; see above.

[193] Cf. Jacobson 1992, 159; Arnal 2001, 198, 257 n. 65.

[194] Kloppenborg 2000a, 393; cf. Horsley 1999, 301; Fleddermann 2005a, 454; Smith 2006, 119; Hartin 2015, 133; Ra 2016, 65, 128.

[195] Cf. Allison 1997, 11–15.

[196] Cf. Bock 1996, 1009, 1011, 1051–1052.

[197] Cf. Luz 2001, 157.

10.5 The Transition from Block 3 to Block 4

Before considering the flow between blocks 3 and 4, a closer look at Q 11:5–8 is necessary. As mentioned in the previous section, it is my contention that Luke (Q) 11:5–8 is not even in its Lukan (or Q) context about prayer. I am not aware of any other scholar who makes this argument. The certainty with which scholars hold that Luke 11:5–8 is about prayer in its Lukan context may be illustrated by two quotations, although many others could have been added. In his commentary on Luke, Marshall states: "There is no essential connection between the parable [in Luke 11:5–8] and the Lord's Prayer. The parable itself, however, must be about prayer, although it contains no application, and there is a catchword connection between 11:3 and 11:5 (ἄρτος)."[198] In his book on the parables of the historical Jesus, Van Eck states: "From the above it is clear that the majority of parable scholars see the parable as a teaching of Jesus on prayer. When one reads the parable in its literary context [in Luke], one can hardly come to a different conclusion."[199] Despite such scholarly unanimity, I am convinced that the three sub-units in Q 11:2–13 are in the first place linked by the topics of subsistence and reciprocity, both of which are supported by the only two catchwords that appear in all three units, namely "bread" and "give." When considering only the literary context of Q 11:2–13, the references to prayer in Q 11:2–4 and Q 11:13 function primarily (if not exclusively) to illuminate the part that God plays in the human activities of subsistence living and reciprocal exchange.[200]

Q 11:5–8 is introduced in verse 5 with the verb "lend" (χρῆσόν), which indicates that the initial request is for an act of balanced reciprocity.[201] By using this verb, the neighbour at the door is promising the neighbour inside the house that he will repay him for the bread. It is true that expectations of balanced reciprocity were sometimes replaced by expectations of general reciprocity at village level, especially when ancient villages struggled economically.[202] The

---

[198] Marshall 1978, 463.

[199] Van Eck 2016, 232.

[200] Cf. Kloppenborg 2000a, 125; Valantasis 2005, 118, 123.

[201] I disagree with Herzog (1994, 208) and Van Eck (2016, 249) that the imperative verb "lend" (χρῆσόν) in verse 5 expresses "the mutuality involved in their friendship" rather than normal lending (cf. Marshall 1978, 464; Liddell and Scott 1996, 955, s.v. κίχρημι). Moreover, Herzog (1994, 200–201) assumes incorrectly that the request would necessarily have been for a gift instead of a loan just because the entire village was responsible to show hospitality. Even though hospitality was the responsibility of the entire village (Arnal 2001, 178–179, 180; Van Eck 2016, 236), the transaction could (and probably would) under normal circumstances still be regarded as a loan, since exchanges operated at village level according to balanced reciprocity. This explains the deliberate use of the verb "lend" instead of "give" in verse 5.

[202] See Oakman 2008, 252–253; Howes 2015a, 145; Van Eck 2016, 239.

typical form of economic exchange at village level, however, was balanced reciprocity.[203] It is therefore not strange that the neighbour would initially appeal to balanced reciprocity, even if they were friends. The least he could do would be to repay the three loaves at a future date, especially considering that he woke up his friend at such an inconvenient time. Oftentimes, a request to borrow something from a friend or family member is made with the hope that the loan will be forgiven. The same might have been the case here. Regardless, the initial request is for a loan. After complaining about the inconvenience of getting up at midnight in verse 7, the neighbour inside the house is portrayed in verse 8 as handing over to his friend and neighbour "whatever he needs" (ὅσων χρῄζει). Crucially, this gracious act is described using the verb "give" (δίδωμι) instead of "lend" (κίχρημι). A request for balanced reciprocity has resulted in an act of general reciprocity.[204] Instead of acting in such a way that his friend becomes indebted to him, the neighbour inside the house acts in such a way that neither party ends up being indebted to the other.[205] The standard form of economic exchange at village level gives way to a much more unusual form. The latter is further confirmed by the shift from the very specific "three loaves" (τρεῖς ἄρτους) in verse 5 to the unspecified "whatever he needs" (ὅσων χρῄζει) in verse 8. When operating on the principles of balanced reciprocity, it is crucial to keep track of the specific values involved, but not when operating on the principles of general reciprocity. In this way, the phrase "whatever he needs" bears a striking resemblance to the phrase "whomever you find" (ὅσους ἐὰν εὕρητε) in the parable of the great supper (Q 14:16–21, 23).[206] In both cases, the altruistic act is unrestricted.[207]

Sure enough, their friendship would have been enough reason for the neighbour to act in such an altruistic way,[208] but Jesus claims that the actions of this

---

[203] Oakman 1986, 66; 2008, 137–138; Horsley 1995b, 204; see Malina 1993, 99–103.

[204] I disagree with Oakman (2008, 94) and Van Eck (2016, 250–251) that the neighbour inside the house ends up opting for balanced reciprocity over general reciprocity. It seems odd to me that the story would provide an example of someone insisting on balanced reciprocity in order to promote general reciprocity. As Van Eck (2016, 252) acknowledges, "Jesus did *not* advocate balanced reciprocity" (italics original). This forces Van Eck to find that the parable "criticizes nonkingdom behavior." In other words, the parable gives an example of someone doing something (i.e. the neighbour practicing balanced reciprocity) in order to promote the exact opposite (i.e. the followers of Jesus practicing general reciprocity). To me, this seems counterproductive and counterintuitive.

[205] *Pace* Oakman 2008, 94–95.

[206] Herzog (1994, 214) similarly compares the hospitality shown by the village in Q 11:5–8 to "the great banquets of the elites," even if it were "little more than a poor imitation" thereof.

[207] See chapter 8 above. Cf. also the similarity between "off the road" (ἐξ ὁδοῦ) in Q 11:6 and "on the roads" (τάς ὁδούς) in Q 14:23. Could both be an indication of the destitution of the ultimate recipient(s) of altruism (cf. Herzog 1994, 209–211)?

[208] See Scott 1989, 90–91; Proctor 2019, 449–450.

neighbour was not motivated by friendship.[209] Instead, it was motivated by
ἀναίδεια. Against most interpreters, I agree with Huffard, Jeremias, Marshall,
Scott, Oakman, and Van Eck that the word ἀναίδεια refers to the actions of the
neighbour inside the house, not the neighbour at the door.[210] The term ἀναίδεια
literally means "shamelessness" or "impudence," not "persistence" or "impor-
tunity."[211] Herzog and Van Eck explain that ἀναίδεια is most commonly used
to express attitudes that challenge and disrupt social boundaries and prescribed
behavior.[212] According to Snodgrass, the term "refers to people who have no
proper sense of shame and willingly engage in improper conduct."[213] Malina
and Rohrbaugh likewise indicate that ἀναίδεια is "the negative quality of lacking sensitivity (as sense of shame) to one's public honor status."[214] Snodgrass
argues convincingly that ἀναίδεια must be regarded as a negative attribute.[215]
Van Eck explains further that the neighbour's complaints and refusal to help in
verse 7 are "a veiled way [of] saying that he does not consider himself a friend
of the host."[216] The same is probably also indicated by the fact that the neighbour inside fails to reciprocate by also greeting the neighbour outside as
"friend" (φίλος).[217] It follows that friendship is indeed entirely off the table as
a motivating factor.[218] The behaviour of the neighbour inside the house is motivated entirely by ἀναίδεια.[219]

Given these considerations, the neighbour inside the house is not portrayed
in a very positive light.[220] First, he rudely denies or swears off any friendship
with his neighbour. Second, his actions are motivated by a desire to be socially
disruptive and countercultural. Despite such negative characterisation, however, he acts in accordance with the principles and message of God's kingdom.

---

[209] Jeremias 1972, 159; Huffard 1978, 157, 158; Schottroff 2006, 189.

[210] Jeremias 1972, 158, 159; Huffard 1978, 156–157; Marshall 1978, 465; Scott 1989,
89–90; Oakman 2008, 94; Van Eck 2016, 240–245, 250–251; cf. Catchpole 1993, 202.

[211] Huffard 1978, 155; Marshall 1978, 465; Scott 1989, 88–89; Herzog 1994, 202–203;
Malina and Rohrbaugh 2003, 273; see Johnson 1979, 125–127; Snodgrass 1997, 506, 511–
512; cf. Catchpole 1993, 203–206.

[212] Herzog 1994, 213; Van Eck 2016, 245.

[213] Snodgrass 1997, 506.

[214] Malina and Rohrbaugh 2003, 273.

[215] Snodgrass 1997, 506–510.

[216] Van Eck 2016, 249.

[217] Cf. Marshall 1978, 464.

[218] Huffard 1978, 157, 158.

[219] Proctor (2019, 449–450) argues that the εἰ καί condition in Luke 11:8 should be translated as "even if" instead of "even though." This would make little difference to the current
interpretation. It would merely leave open the question of whether or not the two neighbours
truly are friends, but still regard ἀναίδεια as the real reason for the actions of the neighbour
inside the house.

[220] Thurén 2014, 67; cf. Catchpole 1993, 208; *pace* Schottroff 2006, 189.

Instead of saying the right things, he actually does the right things.[221] In this way, the negative portrayal of the sleeping neighbour as "impudent" bears some resemblance to the description in Q 11:13 of earthly fathers as "evil" (πονηρός) even though they do the right thing by feeding their children.[222] The neighbour inside the house acts in the way he does not because of his friendship with the neighbour at the door (which would be typical behaviour that abides by existing social norms[223]), but rather because he deliberately wants to challenge societal norms and accepted practice.[224] In this case, he challenges balanced reciprocity as the common manner of economic exchange among villagers. One should not be surprised to find a countercultural, subversive group like the Jesus movement using socially negative concepts like ἀναίδεια to describe the in-group positively.[225] The Jesus movement often used imagery that was negative according to societal standards to make positive claims about themselves.[226] Stereotypically negative characters are often used as positive examples for correct behaviour in the kingdom of God. Consider, for example, the association of God's kingdom with drunkards and tax collectors in Q 7:34, with farm managers in Q 12:42–44,[227] with city slaves in Q 19:12–26,[228] and with Samaritans in Luke 10:25–37. Often, it is precisely the fact that the character in question is viewed negatively by society that makes it a positive symbol for a socially subversive group like the early Jesus movement.

This interpretation is bolstered by the fact that verse 8 is introduced with the phrase: "I tell you" (λέγω ὑμῖν). In the Sayings Gospel Q, the formula "I tell you" often precedes an outlandish, exaggerated, subversive, and/or implausible statement by Q's Jesus, as if the audience needs convincing of the claim's validity.[229] Provided only with the information in verses 5–7, one would not expect the rude person in the house to respond by fulfilling his neighbour's request.[230] Yet Q's Jesus surprises his audience by claiming that even this rude person would act altruistically if he lives according to the subversive principles of God's kingdom. That such a socially insensitive person would perform such an altruistic act might seem outlandish, but in the kingdom of God it is often

---

[221] Thurén 2014, 67; cf. Q 6:46–49.

[222] Cf. Piper 1989, 20; Scott 1989, 89; Valantasis 2005, 123.

[223] See Huffard 1978, 157–160; Scott 1989, 90–91.

[224] Cf. Scott 1989, 91–92; Fleddermann 2005b, 281.

[225] See Herzog 1994, 194–214; cf. Huffard 1978, 155; *pace* Van Eck 2016, 243–245, 250–251.

[226] Cf. Davies and Allison 1991, 424.

[227] See chapter 4 above.

[228] See chapter 9 above.

[229] See Smith 2006, 104–108; cf. Kloppenborg 2000b, 79 n. 15; Thurén 2014, 232; cf. Q 7:26, 28; 10:12, 24; 11:9, 51; 12:22, 27, 44, 59; 13:35; 15:7, [10]; 17:34.

[230] Hedrick (2014, 127), who reads the story without verse 8, finds that the petition for bread was unsuccessful.

"undesirables" who truly commit to the teachings of Jesus.[231] Also, that someone would be motivated by a desire to challenge societal norms instead of
friendship or biological family connections to show kindness and practice general reciprocity might seem farfetched, but that is what Q's Jesus is claiming.
The vision of God's kingdom is stronger and more important than friendship
or family ties.[232]

Having considered the meaning of Q 11:5–8, we are now in a position to
discuss the transition between blocks 3 and 4. Kloppenborg's fourth block (Q
12:2–7, 11–12) follows very poorly after his third block (Q 11:2–4, 9–13). The
main theme of Q 11:2–13 is subsistence living, whereas the main theme of Q
12:2–7, 11–12 is bold proclamation of Jesus's message. Given its theme, the
fourth block would have followed better after the mission discourse. The only
connection between these two passages is the reference to God as "Father"
(πατήρ) in both Q 11:2, 13 and Q 12:6. Yet this connection is grossly overshadowed by the abrupt change in topic. The likelihood that Q 12:2 was not introduced by a formula like "I tell you" (λέγω) or "he said" (εἶπεν) suggests that it
did not introduce a new topic, but followed after closely related material. In
chapter 2, I argued that the two logia in Q 11:33–35 featured in the formative
stratum before they were incorporated into the main redaction. If this is correct,
these logia would have stood between blocks 3 and 4 in the sequence of the
formative stratum.[233]

It was argued in chapter 2 that Q 11:33 promotes general reciprocity by
sketching the image of a household that shares available light with everyone in
the house. The topic of general reciprocity is also central to Q 11:2–13. In Q

---

[231] Cf. Luke 18:9–14; 19:1–10 vs. Mark 10:17–22 // Matt 19:16–22 // Luke 18:18–23.

[232] Cf. Q 9:57–60; 14:26.

[233] It is possible that Q 11:17b ("Every kingdom divided against itself is left barren, and
every household divided against itself will not stand" [πᾶσα βασιλεία μερισθεῖσα καθ'
ἑαυτῆς ἐρημοῦται καὶ πᾶσα οἰκία μερισθεῖσα καθ' ἑαυτῆς οὐ σταθήσεται]) could have featured between Q 11:9–13 and Q 11:33–35 in the formative stratum (see Howes 2017b). Finding Q 11:17b in this position, the main redactor would then have incorporated this logion
into the Beelzebul pericope. It is, however, also possible that this saying was taken up (during the prehistory or main redaction of Q) from outside as an established sapiential maxim.
The rhetorical function and embeddedness of Q 11:17b in the Beelzebul pericope (Q 11:14–
15, 17–20) might support the latter conclusion. On the other hand, the thematic overlap of
this isolated logion with the formative stratum might support its original position in the
formative stratum. Due to such uncertainty, I have opted not to discuss its potential presence
in the formative stratum here. Suffice it to say that if it were included, it would fit in with
the intent of both Q 11:2–13 and Q 11:33–35 to depict the kingdom of God as a cohesive
symbolic family that shares available resources by practicing general reciprocity. Particularly noticeable would be "house" or "household" (οἰκία) as a catchword connection between
Q 11:17b and Q 11:33.

11:2–4, the petition about cancelling debts promotes general reciprocity at village level, while beseeching God for relief from perpetual indebtedness.[234] Q 11:5–8 links up with both the topic of general reciprocity and the topic of indebtedness.[235] In the literary context of the Sayings Gospel, Q 11:5–8 functions as a rhetorical example rather than a parable, which is why it is presented in the form of a (protracted and syntactically awkward) rhetorical question (verses 5–7) with a concluding explanation (verse 8).[236] Virtually the exact same structure is repeated in Q 11:11–13.[237] Jacobson views Q 11:11–13 as "an exposition of the Lord's Prayer," which means that it fulfils a similar function in the pericope as Q 11:5–8.[238] In both cases, the rhetorical question(s) is/are introduced by the phrase "which of you" (τίς ἐξ ὑμῶν).[239] Q 11:5–8 exemplifies not only a life without indebtedness, but also a life determined by general reciprocity.[240] In essence, these are two sides of the same coin, since general reciprocity can never lead to relations of indebtedness. If everyone distributed available resources without expecting a return, no one would ever be indebted to anyone else.[241] Finally, Q 11:11–13 uses the imagery of earthly fathers providing for their children as a metaphor to illustrate how the heavenly Father provides for his children in the symbolic family of God.[242] These earthly fathers are depicted as sharing available resources with their children.[243] In the symbolic family of God, all people share their resources with one another for the benefit of all.[244] Q 11:33 uses another image from daily life to also illustrate how people share available resources in the symbolic family of God. That the word "house" (οἰκία) often functions in the Sayings Gospel as a metaphor for the symbolic family of God is certainly relevant for the interpretation of this logion.[245] Hence, the material in Q 11:2–4, 5–8, 9–13, 33 are constituted by a chain of images that promote the sharing of available resources and the practicing of general reciprocity: (1) people forgiving each other's economic debts in Q 11:2–4; (2) friends and neighbours sharing bread, even at inconvenient times,

---

[234] See chapter 5 above; cf. Kloppenborg 2001, 176–179; Johnson-DeBaufre 2005, 104; Valantasis 2005, 118; Park 2014a, 77, 87; Ra 2016, 70; Van Eck 2016, 181–182.

[235] Cf. Oakman 2008, 94–95.

[236] Kirk 1998, 179; cf. Jeremias 1972, 158; Marshall 1978, 464; Catchpole 1993, 203, 209–210; Herzog 1994, 196; Bock 1996, 1057.

[237] Catchpole 1993, 211; Kirk 1998, 181; cf. Kloppenborg 1987, 204; 2000a, 125; Piper 1989, 16, 21; Rollens 2014b, 148–149.

[238] Jacobson 1992, 159.

[239] Catchpole 1993, 217.

[240] Cf. Kirk 1998, 325; *pace* Oakman 2008, 94–95.

[241] Cf. Johnson-DeBaufre 2005, 104; Valantasis 2005, 118–119.

[242] Piper 1989, 20; Kirk 1998, 181, 325; Robinson 1998b, 138; 2001a, 16; Kloppenborg 2001, 178; Valantasis 2005, 123; Park 2014a, 84; Ra 2016, 73.

[243] Piper 1989, 18; Kirk 1998, 325.

[244] Kirk 1998, 325; see Valantasis 2005, 122–123.

[245] Valantasis 2005, 139; Smith 2014, 46–47; Ra 2016, 140; cf. Zimmermann 2014, 27.

in Q 11:5–8;[246] (3) fathers giving bread and fish to their children in Q 11:9–13; and (4) family members sharing light and shelter in Q 11:33. There might even be a degree of progression from the forgiving of debts in Q 11:2–4 to the implementation of general reciprocity in Q 11:5–8 to the sharing of food in Q 11:8, 9–13 to the provision of other needs like shelter and light in Q 11:33. Each of the images in these texts function like snapshots of God's kingdom, where society at large operates like an extended family that shares available resources without expecting anything in return.[247] The movement from Q 11:9–13 to Q 11:33–35 might also be motivated by the logical connection between searching for something and using a source of light like a lamp to do so,[248] as well as the progression from knocking at someone's door to the lamp of the house being lit. Let it also be said that although the inclusion of Q 11:5–8 adds force to the proposed transition from Q 11:2–13 to Q 11:33, the proposal would not be much weaker without Q 11:5–8.

The connection between Q 11:33 and Q 11:34–35 is fairly obvious. The logia were most visibly attached on the basis of the catchword "lamp" (λύχνος).[249] In addition, the two logia both speak about light, highlighting its wide reach with phrases like "everyone in the house" (πᾶσιν τοῖς ἐν τῇ οἰκίᾳ) and "the whole body" (ὅλον τὸ σῶμά).[250] With limited biological knowledge, the eyes were believed to brighten the body internally in the same way that a lamp brightens a house.[251] Also, with an extramission theory of vision,[252] both the lamp and the eye were regarded as objects that emit light to their environments.[253] Kloppenborg regards verses 34–35 as a commentary word on verse

---

[246] Cf. Schottroff 2006, 189.

[247] Cf. Kirk 1998, 325; Park 2019, 47.

[248] Cf. Q 15:[8].

[249] Kloppenborg 1987, 135; Piper 1989, 128; Jacobson 1992, 173; Robinson 1998a, 254; Ra 2016, 80, 139, 140.

[250] Kloppenborg 1987, 135; Fleddermann 2005a, 526–527, 530; cf. Funk and Hoover 1993, 332; Lührmann 1994, 59; MacEwen 2015, 155.

[251] Marshall 1978, 489; Kloppenborg 1987, 136; Funk and Hoover 1993, 151; Kirk 1998, 200; 2016, 208; Fleddermann 2005a, 527; Valantasis 2005, 141; *pace* Ra 2016, 141.

[252] See chapter 2 above.

[253] Davies and Allison 1988, 636–637. The idea that the eye emits light to the outside world and that it also emits light into the body might seem like a contradiction, but if one considers that the eye is round (not unlike a lamp), it can certainly be understood as emitting light in all directions (also not unlike a lamp), including both outwards from the body and inwards into the body (cf. Kloppenborg 1987, 136; Allison 1997, 153, on Jerome and Plato; Nolland 2005, 300–301). The latter is not the same as an intromission theory of vision, which regards the source of light as existing outside the eye (and the body) (*pace* Davies and Allison 1988, 638; Allison 1997, 153–161, although their interpretation is not currently excluded, according to which the condition of the eye provides evidence of the light/darkness within).

33, "directing attention away from the objective fact of 'light' to the precondi-
tions for subjective appropriation of that light."[254] Despite this focal shift, it
would be wrong to assume that verses 34–35 fail to develop the thought of
verse 33 further.[255] Drawing on Piper's observation that general maxims in Q
often give way to illustrative maxims that apply the former to a more specific
context, Kirk describes verse 34 as "a self-contained illustrative unit with a
concretizing function, specifying and beginning to apply to the human realm
the general maxim of 11:33."[256] Importantly, Kirk also points out that Q 11:33–
35 is structurally identical to Q 11:9–13, since it "enacts the sequence of a
general maxim, followed by a two-part illustrative unit, concluded by an ex-
clamatory application introduced by εἰ οὖν."[257] This observation significantly
strengthens our current claim that Q 11:33–35 followed Q 11:9–13 directly in
the sequence of the formative stratum. The linkage between these two units is
further strengthened by the catchword "evil" (πονηρός) in both Q 11:13 and Q
11:34. In both cases, the word seems to refer to the in-group,[258] notwithstanding the many scholarly interpretations of the latter logion at least as a reference
to outsiders on the level of the main redaction or final form of Q.[259] Finally and
perhaps most importantly, we saw in chapter 2 above that the word ἁπλοῦς in
Q 11:34 denotes generosity, which links to the topic of general reciprocity expressed not only in Q 11:33, but also by the entire sequence of preceding material in Q 11:2–13, 33. This interpretation is supported by Matthew's placement of Q 11:34–35 in his Gospel, where the saying is sandwiched between
the logion that speaks against hoarding treasures on earth (Matt 6:19–21, from
Q 12:33–34) and the logion that speaks against serving mammon (Matt 6:24,
from Q 16:13).[260] This placement clearly indicates that Matthew understood
the "generous eye" (ἁπλοῦς ὀφθαλμός) in Q 11:34–35 as the opposite of economic greed, which, in turn, is associated with the "evil eye" (πονηρός
ὀφθαλμός).[261] Greed was indeed one of the traits associated with the evil eye
in antiquity.[262] While considering the interpretation of Q 11:34–35 within its
Matthean literary context, Kirk explains that "desire towards possessions,

---

[254] Kloppenborg 1987, 138; cf. Kirk 1998, 200–201; Robinson 1998a, 254; Valantasis
2005, 141. The quotation continues: "…and to the fearful prospects which await those who
do not respond adequately" (Kloppenborg 1987, 138). This part of Kloppenborg's statement,
however, is determined by the logion's context in the main redaction, as his subsequent discussion demonstrates.

[255] *Pace* Jacobson 1992, 173.

[256] Kirk 1998, 200; cf. Fleddermann 2005a, 524.

[257] Kirk 1998, 201–202; cf. Allison 1997, 152, 164; Fleddermann 2005a, 524–525.

[258] Johnson-DeBaufre 2005, 184; cf. Piper 1989, 129–130; Zeller 1994, 128.

[259] E.g. Allison 1997, 165–167.

[260] Cf. Kirk 2016, 209.

[261] Davies and Allison 1988, 635; Piper 1989, 128; cf. Luz 2007, 334.

[262] Luz 2007, 333.

which quite literally involves the eye, is a defect of moral perception sympto-
matic of a moral disposition."[263] For Q's formative stratum, giving up an affinity for possessions and money enables people to act out the generosity and altruism promoted by Q 11:2–13, 33–35, so that general reciprocity may increasingly replace balanced reciprocity in society.

Q 11:33–35 prepares sufficiently for the opening of the fourth block in Q
12:2–3. The latter text is linked to Q 11:33 by the catchwords "hidden" (κρυπτή
and κρυπτός) and "no one" or "nothing" (οὐδείς).[264] Catchwords also link Q
12:2–3 to Q 11:34–35, namely "dark" (σκότος, σκοτία and σκοτεινόν) and
"light" (φῶς and φωτεινός).[265] Particularly noticeable about these catchwords
is that a saying about concealment (Q 11:33; 12:2) is followed by a saying
about light and darkness (Q 11:34–35; 12:3) in the case of each respective text
(i.e. Q 11:33–35 and Q 12:2–3). That both Q 11:33–35 and Q 12:2–3 begin
with a general maxim (Q 11:33 and Q 12:2) that is then followed by a maxim
that narrows the opening maxim's application (Q 11:34 and Q 12:3) also connects these texts structurally.[266] Another lexical link between these two texts is
the reference to an "eye" (ὀφθαλμός) in Q 11:34 and the reference to an "ear"
(οὖς) in Q 12:3. Far from being coincidental, this combination reflects the ancient tendency to consider "the functioning and malfunctioning of the eyes,
especially in comparison with the ears."[267] Q 11:34–35 is also linked to the
logia in Q 12:4–5 by both the catchword "body" (σῶμα) and the idea of the
"soul" (ψυχή).[268] Even if the latter is not mentioned expressly in Q 11:34–35,
it is almost certainly presupposed, perhaps specifically by the phrase "the light
within you" (τὸ φῶς τὸ ἐν σοί).[269]

Thematically, both of these texts apply light and darkness as metaphors.[270]
Moreover, the notions of concealment and disclosure are central to the message
of both Q 11:33 and Q 12:2–3.[271] These ideas are probably also implied in the
somatology of Q 11:34–35, in the sense that the eyes of a person betray her
attitudes and intentions. These notions of concealment and disclosure reveal
some measure of logical progression from Q 11:33–35 to Q 12:2–3. Whereas
the former text deals with concealment, both in the form of someone trying to
hide a lamp and in the form of a bad person trying to conceal her inner darkness,

---

[263] Kirk 2016, 209.

[264] Sato 1994, 171.

[265] Sato 1994, 171; Zeller 1994, 119.

[266] Cf. Piper 1989, 57; Funk and Hoover 1993, 172, 336; Kirk 1998, 200, 206–207.

[267] Betz 1995, 438.

[268] Sato 1994, 171; Zeller 1994, 119; cf. Ra 2016, 215.

[269] Cf. Betz 1995, 439, 443, 445, 452; Allison 1997, 154 n. 117, 154–155; Kirk 2016,
209.

[270] Fleddermann 2005a, 524, 528, 529, 530, 586.

[271] Cf. Kloppenborg 1987, 210; Kirk 1998, 206; Nolland 2005, 436.

the latter text claims that such attempts at concealment will in any case be exposed. Oakman summarises the meaning of the latter text in four words: "Nothing can remain secret."[272] The progressive argument culminates in Q 12:3 with the conclusion that it is wise to share secrets openly.[273] If all attempts at concealment will be exposed, the emphatic conclusion of Q 12:3 to "speak in the light" (εἴπατε ἐν τῷ φωτί) and "proclaim on the housetops" (κηρύξατε ἐπὶ τῶν δωμάτων) logically follows.[274] It seems probable, although verse 3 is not explicit in this regard, that the advice about sharing secrets is a deliberate attempt at counteracting deception. Verse 2 in particular seems to imply one or more forms of deception. Luke (12:1) expressly links Q 12:2–3 to the hypocrisy of the Pharisees.[275] For an ancient audience, the topic of deception would have been a very natural follow-up after a discussion of the human eye. In ancient literature, deliberations about blindness and compromised vision often involved the topic of deception.[276] Similarly, the negative moral associations with the "evil eye" (πονηρός ὀφθαλμός) in Q 11:34–35, which included traits like "malice, greed, envy, and calculating behaviour,"[277] as well as "selfishness, covetousness, an evil and envious disposition, [and] hatred of others,"[278] would have been a fitting prelude to the deception implied by the terms "covered up" (κεκαλυμμένον) and "hidden" (κρυπτόν) in Q 12:2.

The themes of Q 11:33–35 and Q 12:2–3 overlap in yet another way. As we saw in chapter 2, both texts deal with the topic of concealing and sharing the sapiential message of Q's Jesus.[279] Although the imagery of Q 11:33 is in the first place about the sharing of available corporeal resources, it is also about sharing the wisdom of Jesus, especially when read against the backdrop of Q 12:2–3. Fundamentally, this dual meaning is why Q 11:33–35 constitutes such a good transition between Q 11:2–13, which promotes general reciprocity, and Q 12:2–3, which promotes sharing the message of Jesus. One should also not overlook the linkage between the image of a house in Q 11:33 and the mentioning of "housetops" (δώματα) in Q 12:3. Although the noun δῶμα undoubtedly means "housetop" in the context of Q 12:3, where the phrase "proclaim

---

[272] Oakman 2008, 293; cf. Marshall 1978, 512; Piper 1989, 57; Kloppenborg 1994, 147; Bock 1996, 1134; Valantasis 2005, 153; Ra 2016, 149.

[273] Cf. Fleddermann 2005a, 584.

[274] Cf. Kloppenborg 1994, 147.

[275] Marshall 1978, 509, 510, 512; Kloppenborg 1987, 210; Piper 1989, 57; Funk and Hoover 1993, 172, 336; Zeller 1994, 119; Bock 1996, 1134; Robinson 1998a, 256–257; Fleddermann 2005a, 567.

[276] Betz 1995, 452.

[277] Luz 2007, 333; cf. Thurén 2014, 293.

[278] Davies and Allison 1988, 640; *idem.* Allison 1997, 160; cf. Nolland 2005, 302.

[279] Cf. Marshall 1978, 512; Kloppenborg 1987, 135, 137–138; Davies and Allison 1991, 205; Robinson 1993, 6, incl. n. 47; 1995b, 32; Bock 1996, 1100; Allison 1997, 165; Ra 2016, 140.

on the housetops" (κηρύξατε ἐπὶ τῶν δωμάτων) denotes public preaching,[280] it could also carry the more general meaning of "house."[281] The noun has the sense of "habitable roof space."[282] The intimate space of the household in Q 11:33 is therefore not totally abandoned by the content of Q 12:2–3, even if it promotes public preaching. At any rate, the movement from one house in Q 11:33 to a number of housetops in Q 12:3 communicates a logical progression from intimately sharing the sapiential message of Jesus with those *few* who are *already* part of Q's symbolic family to publicly sharing it with those *many* who might also soon *become* members of this family. In contrast to the main redaction, the boundaries between inside and outside are deliberately blurred here.[283]

Q 11:33–35; 12:2–3 reminds of the parables of the mustard seed and the leaven (Q 13:18–19, 20–21), which also portray the expansion of God's kingdom with memorable imagery,[284] although this was not the main message of these parables.[285] That the second of these parables features the verb "hide" (ἐγκρύπτω) might also be significant when compared to our text.[286] It is worth noting that Q 10:21, discussed earlier, also deals with the ideas of concealment and disclosure, sharing the words "hide" (κρύπτ-) and "reveal" (ἀποκαλύπτω) with Q 12:2.[287] In both texts, the object being either hidden or revealed is the kingdom message, with Q 10:21 focusing on the transmission of the message from God to his children and Q 12:2–3 focusing on the transmission of the same message from God's children to others. The phrases "you [God] hid these things" (ἔκρυψας ταῦτα) in Q 10:21 and "I [Jesus] say to you in the dark" (ὃ λέγω ὑμῖν ἐν τῇ σκοτίᾳ) in Q 12:3 indicate that the kingdom message was originally communicated by Jesus in secret.[288] Yet, according to Q 12:2–3, the message that the Q people received in secret should now be shared in public.[289]

The imagery of Q 11:33–35; 12:2–3 is further reminiscent of the mission discourse (esp. Q 10:7–9), where the message of God's kingdom, which is the

---

[280] Marshall 1978, 512; Louw and Nida 1993b, 89, 343, domains 7.51 and 28.64; Robinson 1995b, 32; cf. Piper 1989, 58; Bock 1996, 1135; Kirk 1998, 206–207; Luz 2001, 101; Fleddermann 2005a, 585.

[281] Liddell and Scott 1996, 464, s.v. δῶμα.

[282] Logos Bible Software, n.p.

[283] Valantasis 2005, 140, 153; cf. Fleddermann 2005a, 585.

[284] Kloppenborg 1995, 311.

[285] See chapter 6 above.

[286] Cf. Luz 2001, 263; Fleddermann 2005a, 584–585, 586; Levine 2014, 131–132; see chapter 6 above.

[287] Ra 2016, 81, 140, 141, 148; cf. Levine 2014, 132.

[288] Robinson 1998c, 21. This might also be an allusion to the deliberate ambiguity and obscurity of Jesus's logia and parables (cf. Robinson 1998c, 21; Levine 2014, 132; cf. Matt 13:35, which references Ps 78:2 [LXX 77:2]). In fact, the saying in Q 11:33 is perhaps a prime example of such ambiguity (Funk and Hoover 1993, 140; Bultmann 1994, 28).

[289] Marshall 1978, 512; Robinson 1995b, 32; 1998c, 21; Fleddermann 2005a, 585; see Valantasis 2005, 152–154; cf. Levine 2014, 131–132; Ra 2016, 140.

mainstay of Jesus's wisdom, is shared in a household setting.[290] Two additional features of this intertextual comparison are interesting here. Firstly, in both texts the sharing of daily needs (like food and light) overlap and coincide with the sharing of Jesus's message. Secondly, in both texts the house becomes the setting where private and public spaces overlap and coalesce, enabling the sharing of Jesus's message. For that reason, the intimate family setting of Q 11:33 could also be understood as a potential locale for sharing the kingdom message with individuals who are not (yet) part of the biological and/or symbolic family.[291] We saw in chapter 2 that ancient domestic spaces were highly flexible,[292] catering to more than just the traditional (extended) family, so that the involvement of outsiders might also be implied by the imagery in Q 11:33. In his interpretation of Q 11:33, Bock, for example, remarks that "Jesus' teaching is not secretly disseminated, it is openly proclaimed."[293] Such an understanding of Q 11:33 brings this logion very close in meaning to Q 12:2–3.[294] For example, the foregoing quotation about Q 11:33 is almost identical in meaning to Fleddermann's interpretation of Q 12:2–3: "What the disciples have heard in secret they should preach in public."[295] Despite such extensive semantic overlap, the proclamation is more public and less restricted in Q 12:3 than in Q 11:33, providing for the logical progression from Q 11:33 to Q 12:3 discussed above.

In sum, the inclusion of Q 11:33–35 in the formative stratum allows for a smooth transition between Kloppenborg's third and fourth blocks, accompanied by catchword and thematic connections. Q 11:33 is most obviously linked to the preceding material in Q 11:2–4, 5–8, 9–13 by the theme of general reciprocity. Q 11:33 represents the pinnacle of a sequence of snapshots depicting the real-life implementation of general reciprocity in the kingdom of God. The theme of general reciprocity also extends to Q 11:34–35, although the most obvious links between Q 11:33 and Q 11:34–35 are the catchword "lamp" (λύχνος) and the fact that both logia speak about light, highlighting its wide reach with phrases like "everyone in the house" (πᾶσιν τοῖς ἐν τῇ οἰκίᾳ) and "the whole body" (ὅλον τὸ σῶμά). In addition to the catchword "evil" (πονηρός), Q 11:9–13 and Q 11:33–35 are further linked by their identical syntactical structures. Q 11:33–35 is then linked to Q 12:2–5 by a host of catchwords, including "hidden" (κρυπτή and κρυπτός), "no one" or "nothing"

---

[290] Ra 2016, 140; cf. Kloppenborg 1987, 210–211; Robinson 1993, 6, incl. n. 47; Fleddermann 2005a, 585. Matthew features Q 12:2–3 as part of his version of the mission discourse (Marshall 1978, 510–511; Piper 1989, 57; Funk and Hoover 1993, 172; Fleddermann 2005a, 566).

[291] Valantasis 2005, 139–140; cf. Kloppenborg 1987, 137–138; Ra 2016, 140.

[292] See Boer and Petterson 2017, 61–68.

[293] Bock 1996, 1100; cf. Kloppenborg 1987, 135, 138; Valantasis 2005, 140.

[294] Cf. Valantasis 2005, 139–140, 152–153.

[295] Fleddermann 2005a, 585.

(οὐδείς), "dark" (σκότος, σκοτία, and σκοτεινόν), "light" (φῶς and φωτεινός) and "body" (σῶμα). More important than these catchwords, however, are the thematic links, especially the use of light and darkness as metaphors for disclosure and concealment (in addition to deception), which relates in both traditions to the theme of sharing the kingdom message of Jesus. These links are further strengthened by structural similarities and logical progression.

10.6 The Transition from Block 4 to Block 5

Kloppenborg's fifth block follows well after his fourth block. The strong connection between Q 12:2–7, 11–12 and Q 12:22–31 is obvious and widely acknowledged by scholars.[296] This connection does therefore not require a detailed analysis, which is why only the most apparent and important aspects of this connection will be considered in what follows. The central theme of both blocks is anxiety, which explains the linking catchword "anxious"

---

[296] See e.g. Vaage 1995a, 87–88; Allison 1997, 21–25; Kirk 1998, 294–297; Fleddermann 2005a, 565–623. Kloppenborg (1987, 216 n. 182; 1995, 311; 2007, 53) argues that the Sondergut material in Luke 12:13–14, 16–20 featured in the Sayings Gospel between Q 12:2–12 and Q 12:22–31. The vocabulary, themes, and style of this tradition are certainly reminiscent of Q, so that this possibility cannot be summarily ruled out. As part of his case, Kloppenborg (2007, 53) claims that the connective διά τοῦτο ("therefore") in Q 12:22 does not really make sense after Q 12:11–12, "since the issue of offering *apologiae* before councils has nothing to do with basic subsistence" (cf. Verheyden 2007, 59). This, however, seems to overlook the very real correlation between the ancient judicial system and corporeal survival in the ancient world, as discussed at some length in chapter 5 above. Moreover, the content of Luke 12:13–14, 16–20 does not in my opinion offer a better context for the use of διά τοῦτο in Q 12:22. It does not make sense to me that a saying aimed at the rich about not accumulating wealth would offer any consolation to the poor about daily subsistence, which is what διά τοῦτο would mean if it were preceded by Luke 12:13–14, 16–20. The claim that the Holy Spirit will assist people when they appear before the courts would have been much more reassuring to the poor when discussing daily subsistence, given the link between court appearances and survival in antiquity. The life-threatening nature of ancient courts is probably the reason why Q 12:22 advises people not to be anxious about their lives (τῇ ψυχῇ ὑμῶν) before the saying even addresses the topic of daily needs. This linkage to the word "life" (ψυχή) in Q 12:22 is much more appropriate to the topic of anxiety in the face of death than the link offered by the abstract and esoteric use of the word "life" (ψυχή) in Luke 12:19–20, even if the latter would be a catchword. It finally seems odd to me that the Q author would feature a request by an audience member about inheritance in the context of a discussion about life-and-death matters. Granted, the request (as well as the response by Jesus) relate to legal matters, which links to the courtroom setting of Q 12:11–12, but the topic draws attention away from the very serious and relevant discussion of anxiety in the context of life-threatening circumstances.

(μεριμνάω).[297] Whereas Q 12:2–7, 11–12 deals with anxiety in the face of opposition to the kingdom message, Q 12:22–31 deals with anxiety in the face of securing bare necessities.[298] Both of these represent life-threatening situations for the Q audience. As such, a related thematic link further connects the two blocks, namely survival. Q 12:4–5 contemplates the possibility of death, expressed graphically with the phrase "those who kill the body" (τῶν ἀποκτεινόντων τὸ σῶμα). The verb ἀποκτείνω often refers to being condemned or put to death as the result of a legal hearing.[299] This meaning is confirmed by verses 11–12, where people are brought "before synagogues" (ἐπὶ τὰς συναγωγὰς). The reference to sparrows "falling to the earth" (πεσεῖται ἐπὶ τὴν γῆν) is also intended as a visual description of death. Whereas Q 12:2–7, 11–12 contemplates the possibility of death as a result of sharing the kingdom message, Q 12:22–31 contemplates the possibility of death as a result of failing to procure bare necessities. Even if death is not expressly mentioned as an outcome in Q 12:22–31, the anxiety over food and clothes only makes sense if consequences like starvation and hypothermia are actual possibilities, if not realities. This link is strengthened by the catchword ψυχή ("life" or "soul") featuring in Q 12:4–5 and Q 12:22, which further links up with πνεῦμα ("spirit") in Q 12:12. Also, the mentioning of "life" (ψυχή) in Q 12:22 contrasts well with the mentioning of "death" (ἀποκτείνω) in Q 12:4.

Both passages argue from nature. Particularly striking is the use of particular species of birds as part of an *a minore ad maius* argument in each rhetorical context, namely "sparrows" (στρουθία) in Q 12:6–7 and "ravens" (κόρακες) in Q 12:24.[300] This connection is strengthened by the mentioning in Q 12:24 of "birds" (πετεινοί) in general. In each case, the point of the argument is that the heavenly Father protects and provides for his children.[301] This thematic and rhetorical link is strengthened by the catchwords "your Father" (ὁ πατὴρ ὑμῶν) in Q 12:6 and Q 12:30.[302] In both cases, acknowledgment of such nurturing care is held up as an antidote against anxiety.[303] Divine providence and general reciprocity are perhaps the most important aspects of Q's kingdom message. Although the "kingdom of God" (βασιλείαν αὐτοῦ) is overtly mentioned for the first time at the end of the fifth block (Q 12:31), it subsists throughout both blocks as a thematic undercurrent. As we saw, the message that the Q people were expected to share and preach in Q 12:2–3 was the sapiential message of

---

[297] Kloppenborg 1987, 214, 217; Piper 1989, 29; Kirk 1998, 296; Johnson 2007, 51; cf. Q 12:11, 22, 25, 26, 29.

[298] Johnson 2007, 51; see Kirk 1998, 203–227; Fleddermann 2005a, 593–594, 609; cf. Allison 1997, 21.

[299] Liddell and Scott 1996, 205.

[300] Johnson 2007, 51–52; cf. Fleddermann 2005a, 610.

[301] Cf. Allison 1997, 24.

[302] Cf. Howes 2016a, 16, 18.

[303] Cf. Piper 1989, 30.

Jesus, which included most crucially the kingdom of God. The expectation to preach the kingdom message might also be reflected in Q 12:11–12. It would therefore not be entirely misguided to view the kingdom of God as another thematic link between the two blocks, even if it remains mostly unexpressed. Whereas the fourth block is about the "proclamation" (κηρύσσω) of the kingdom, the fifth block is about the "seeking" (ζητέω) of the kingdom. If the kingdom of God is a place where people live as a family and share available resources according to the principles of general reciprocity, then seeking his kingdom means contributing to the establishment of this social reality.[304] Instead of selfishly trying to secure one's own basic needs, the audience of Q is encouraged to build God's kingdom by sharing available resources, in which case they will receive what they need to survive anyway. The closing statement of Q 12:22–31 thereby links this passage directly to the theme of general reciprocity in Q 11:2–13, 33.[305] Q 12:33–34 then goes on to expose one of the main obstacles to the establishment of God's kingdom, namely greed and avarice. In this way, Q 12:33–34 harks back to Q 11:34–35.[306]

Allison finally notices a structural link between Q 11:9–13, Q 12:4–7, and Q 12:22–31.[307] These three texts use similar rhetorical structures, which include the following: (1) a λέγω ὑμῖν introductory formula (Q 11:9; 12:4; 12:22); (2) an opening imperative (Q 11:9; 12:4; 12:22); (3) a supportive statement initiated by a preposition (Q 11:10; 12:5; 12:23); (4) a practical example (Q 11:11; 12:6; 12:24); (5) another practical example (Q 11:12; 12:7a; 12:27–28); and (6) a concluding admonition against fear or anxiety (Q 11:13; 12:7b; 12:29–31). This formal linkage further reveals that all three of these texts are linked by the themes of human anxiety and divine providence.[308] Moreover, all three texts use *a minore ad maius* arguments to underline God's providential care.[309]

As in the case of the transition between blocks 2 and 3, the current transition represents not only the formative stratum, but also the Sayings Gospel Q in its final form. The only difference is that Q 12:8–10 would in all likelihood not have featured in the formative stratum, but this is inconsequential as far as the transition between blocks four and five is concerned. The same themes and catchwords remain present. In fact, the absence of Q 12:8–10 probably

---

[304] Cf. Park 2019, 47.

[305] Cf. Peters 2016, 42.

[306] See above.

[307] Allison 1997, 23–25; see also Piper 1989, 24–35, esp. 25, 35–36; cf. Kloppenborg 1987, 208.

[308] Cf. Piper 1989, 35; Allison 1997, 25.

[309] Cf. Piper 1989, 25, 26, 35; Allison 1997, 25.

strengthens the transition between the two blocks.[310] To be sure, strong catch-word, structural, rhetorical, and thematic links enable the smooth transition between blocks four and five.

10.7 The Transition from Block 5 to Block 6

Since Q 13:18–21 ends Kloppenborg's fifth block and Q 13:24 begins his sixth block, the linkage between these two blocks depends on the transition between Q 13:18–21 and Q 13:24. This transition was already discussed in chapters 6–8, when the interconnectedness and coherence of all the material in Q 13:18–21, 24–25; 14:16–21, 23 were considered. Moreover, the interconnectedness and coherence of all the material in Q 12:22–31, 33–34, 39, 42–44 have also already been discussed.[311] Between these two complexes of material stood Q 12:58–59. Scholars overwhelmingly agree that the Lukan placement of this logion represents Q.[312] If this is correct, Q 12:58–59 would have featured between Q 12:42–44 and Q 13:18–21 in the formative stratum. Hence, all that remains in order to illustrate a smooth transition between (my version of) Kloppenborg's fifth and sixth blocks is to illustrate a smooth transition between Q 12:58–59 and the material that both precedes and follows it.

Q 12:33–34 introduces the topic of "earthly treasures" (θησαυρός ἐπὶ τῆς γῆς), which finds more specific examples in the phrases "all that belongs to him" (πᾶσιν τοῖς ὑπάρχουσιν αὐτοῦ) in Q 12:39, 42–44 and "the last penny" (τὸν ἔσχατον κοδράντην) in Q 12:58–59. In other words, the two texts that immediately follow Q 12:33–34 discuss the two main types of earthly treasures that exist, namely possessions (Q 12:39, 42–44) and money (Q 12:58–59). The first way in which Q 12:58–59 links up with the material that precedes it is therefore as the second example of an earthly treasure. The second way in which Q 12:58–59 connects to the material that precedes it has to do with the kingdom of God.[313] Whereas Q 12:42–44 paints an idyllic picture of what it might look like if people implemented the kingdom of God, Q 12:58–59 provides a scary depiction of reality outside of God's kingdom.[314] The first option leads to the widespread distribution of food sources, while the second option

---

[310] Johnson 2007, 52.

[311] See esp. chapter 4 above.

[312] Piper 1989, 105; Bovon 1996, 349; see Garsky *et al.* 1997, 286–320; Howes 2018, 141–178.

[313] Cf. Fleddermann 2005a, 657; Valantasis 2005, 175, 176.

[314] Cf. Nolland 2005, 234; Rollens 2014b, 107–109.

leads to prison.[315] The first option dramatically increases one's chances of survival, while the second option dramatically increases one's chances of death.[316] Finally, the first option depicts the types of individuals who "treasure treasures in heaven" (θησαυρίζετε θησαυροὺς ἐν οὐρανῷ), while the second option depicts the types of individuals who "treasure treasures on earth" (θησαυρίζετε θησαυροὺς ἐπὶ τῆς γῆς).[317]

This stark contrast creates a thematic link between these two texts, which becomes even clearer if the conclusion of each tradition is considered. In both Q 12:42–44 and Q 12:58–59, the last sentence of the passage begins with the phrase "[Amen], I tell you" ([ἀμὴν] λέγω ὑμῖν/σοι).[318] In both cases, the conclusion that follows this phrase is hyperbolic. The difference between the two conclusions is that Q 12:44 imagines the best possible outcome, while Q 12:59 imagines the worst possible outcome. In the former, someone becomes the manager of a vast estate, which is ultimately to the economic benefit of both the slave and everyone else at the same socio-economic level. In the latter, someone gets thrown into prison, which is ultimately to the economic detriment of both the prisoner and everyone else at the same socio-economic level.[319] Despite this stark contrast between outcomes, the two traditions have the same intent, which is to endorse the kingdom of God.[320] If you promote God's kingdom by valuing "treasures in heaven," good things will follow, but if you hamper God's kingdom by valuing "treasures on earth," bad things will follow.[321] Promoting general reciprocity and making peace with one's opponents are both practical ways in which God's kingdom can be realised.[322] Implementing God's kingdom is ultimately to everyone's physical and economic benefit.[323] Hence, the two traditions are linked by the idea that implementing God's kingdom has positive economic benefits for all those involved. The traditions that follow Q 12:31 are therefore practical examples of what it means to "seek his kingdom" (ζητεῖτε τὴν βασιλείαν αὐτοῦ). These examples include: (1) not hoarding or valuing earthly treasures (Q 12:33–34); (2) sharing food with others (Q 12:39, 42–44); and (3) making peace with one's opponents, including

---

[315] Cf. Piper 1989, 106; Valantasis 2005, 175; Rollens 2014b, 107.

[316] Cf. Rollens 2014b, 107.

[317] Q 12:33; cf. Valantasis 2005, 176.

[318] Cf. Smith 2006, 105–106. The presence of ἀμήν is uncertain in both Q 12:44 and Q 12:59. In both cases, Matthew features it, whereas Luke does not. Davies and Allison (1988, 520) explain the uncertainty: "Although Matthew has sometimes added "amen" (Mt: 30–31; Mk: 13; Lk: 6) to his sources, Luke has sometimes dropped it from Mark so that we cannot be certain whether or not it was here in Q [12:59]."

[319] Jacobson 1992, 202; Bock 1996, 1200; Valantasis 2005, 175; Rollens 2014b, 107, 108.

[320] Cf. Nolland 2005, 234.

[321] Cf. Valantasis 2005, 176.

[322] Cf. Rollens 2014b, 109–113.

[323] Cf. Valantasis 2005, 176.

those responsible for economic suffering (Q 12:58–59). Finally, in addition to the phrase "[amen], I tell you," Q 12:58–59 is connected to Q 12:39, 42–44 by the catchword φυλακή ("watch" or "prison").[324]

Let us now turn to the linkage between Q 12:58–59 and Q 13:18–21. These two traditions are most visibly linked by the catchword "throw" (βάλλω).[325] Another possible catchword connection is the word "until" (ἕως) in both Q 12:59 and Q 13:21.[326] Despite these catchwords, a number of scholars have commented on how poorly Q 13:18–21 fits into its literary surroundings.[327] Yet these interpreters typically fail to appreciate not only the function of Q 12:58–59 as an exposé of economic exploitation in ancient Palestine,[328] but also the function of Q 13:18–21 to depict the kingdom as a place where people receive shelter and food.[329] Both Q 12:58–59 and Q 13:18–21 deal in some way with corporeal survival. Q 12:58–59 treats indebtedness and imprisonment, both of which enhanced poverty and hindered survival.[330] Q 13:18–21 then describes an alternative kingdom where people have sufficient accommodation and food. Whereas Q 12:58–59 describes the reality of *people*, who are often removed from their homes as a result of economic exploitation, Q 13:18–19 describes the reality of *birds*, who all seem to have a place to stay as a result of natural provision. The link between Q 12:58–59 and Q 13:18–21 is similar to the link between Q 12:58–59 and Q 12:42–44. In both cases, the kingdom of God is contrasted with the more common concurrent reality of economic exploitation depicted by Q 12:58–59. Both connections evaluate the imagined economic reality in God's kingdom favourably against the existing economic reality in the kingdom of men.[331] In chapters 7 and 8, we saw the same strategy of comparing existing reality with God's kingdom by juxtaposing Q 13:25 with Q 14:16–21, 23. In fact, this whole complex of material shifts continually between depictions of God's kingdom and depictions of lived reality: (1) God's kingdom providing food, drink, and clothing in Q 12:22–31; (2) the world

---

[324] Jacobson 1992, 203.

[325] Allison 1997, 29.

[326] Fleddermann 2005a, 657.

[327] Kirk 1998, 303; see Kloppenborg 1995, 308–311; e.g. Schürmann 1982, 161; Kloppenborg 1987, 92; Sato 1994, 173; Liebenberg 2001, 317. Kirk (1998, 303–304) finds the connection of Q 13:18–21 with its literary surroundings in the small/few-large/many contrast.

[328] See chapter 5 above.

[329] See chapter 6 above. Fleddermann (2005a, 657–658) also sees a connection between Q 12:58–59 and Q 13:18–21 based on their treatment of God's kingdom, but regards this connection as situated in the distinction between the present and future kingdoms (cf. Tuckett 1996, 158).

[330] Cf. Q 6:29–30; 11:2–4.

[331] Cf. Valantasis 2005, 175, 176; Rollens 2014b, 109.

hoarding and stealing provisions in Q 12:33–34, 39; (3) God's kingdom providing food in Q 12:42–44; (4) the world taking money, food, and shelter from people in Q 12:58–59; (5) God's kingdom providing shelter and food in Q 13:18–21; (6) the world refusing to provide shelter (and food) in Q 13:25; (7) God's kingdom providing abundant food (and shelter) in Q 14:16–21, 23. Implementing God's kingdom includes changing the existing situation by practicing "kingdom values," which include general reciprocity[332] and loving one's enemies and persecutors[333].[334] Regarding the latter, other scholars have likewise commented on the paradigmatic link between Q 12:58–59 and the command to love one's enemies in Q 6:27.[335]

The traditions that sandwich Q 12:58–59 have a lot in common. Q 12:42–44, Q 13:18–19, and Q 13:20–21 are all parables about the kingdom of God. Moreover, the kingdom of God is compared in all three parables to some form of human conduct. To be more specific, all three parables feature household tasks, namely feeding slaves in Q 12:42–44, gardening in Q 13:18–19, and cooking in Q 13:20–21. All three parables further discuss foodstuff. Q 12:42–44 features "corn/grain" (σιτομετρία), while Q 13:18–21 features "mustard" (σίναπι), "yeast" (ζύμη), and "flour" (ἄλευρον). Then as now, corn/grain was used to make flour, creating a very strong thematic link that involves chronological progression between Q 12:42–44 and Q 13:18–21. Most importantly, all three parables imagine the kingdom of God as an alternative reality where the economic needs of people are met. For these parables in particular, such economic needs include especially food and shelter. The topics of food and shelter reverberate through the entire complex of sayings that bridge the fifth and sixth blocks: (1) Q 12:39 compares a "householder" (οἰκοδεσπότης) who has shelter with a "robber" (κλέπτης) who probably lacks shelter; (2) Q 12:42–44 depicts a slave who shares "corn/grain" (σιτομετρία) with fellow slaves; (3) Q 12:58–59 depicts someone who has to substitute his home for a prison cell and is therefore unable to provide food for his family; (4) Q 13:18–19 compares the kingdom of God to a place where people always have shelter, like birds always have nests; (5) Q 13:20–21 compares the kingdom of God to enough fermented flour to feed an army; (6) Q 13:24–25 depicts someone without shelter standing outside the dwelling of a "householder" (οἰκοδεσπότης); and (7) Q 14:16–21, 23 imagines "a large dinner" (δεῖπνον μέγα) hosted by a "householder" (οἰκοδεσπότης) "so that [his] house may be filled" (ἵνα γεμισθῇ [αὐτοῦ] ὁ οἶκος).

---

[332] Q 12:42–44; cf. Q 6:30, 32, 34; 11:2–13, 33; 14:16–21, 23.

[333] Q 6:27–28, 35, 29 [incl. Matt 5:41]; cf. Q 12:58–29.

[334] Valantasis 2005, 175, 176; see Rollens 2014b, 109–113.

[335] E.g. Davies and Allison 1988, 519; Piper 1989, 107; Arnal 2001, 194; Fleddermann 2005a, 658; Luz 2007, 241; Ra 2016, 158; cf. Piper 2000, 250; Rollens 2014b, 93–113.

The sequence from Q 12:42–44 to Q 12:58–59 to Q 13:18–21 is actually very close to the final form of the Sayings Gospel. On the one hand, Q 13:18–21 probably followed Q 12:58–59 in the final form as well. On the other hand, the attribution of Q 12:49, 54–56 to the Sayings Gospel is doubtful,[336] which means that two out of the four logia that separate Q 12:58–59 from Q 12:42–46 might not have been in Q. As with Q 12:58–59 and Q 13:18–21, Q 13:24 probably followed Q 13:18–21 in the final form of the Sayings Gospel, assuming Lukan order. In other words, regarding the transition between Q 12:58–59, Q 13:18–21, and Q 13:24, the formative stratum proposed here and the final form of Q looked the same.[337] Regarding the transition from Q 12:42–44 to Q 12:58–59, the final form featured Q 12:45–46, [49], 51, 53, [54–56] in between. It is not insignificant, though, that the attribution of verses 49, 54–56 to the Sayings Gospel is uncertain and that verses 45–46 were probably added by the main redactor *ex nihilo*.

10.8 The Internal Cohesion of Block 6

In chapters 7 and 8, I argued for the continuity of Q 13:18–21, 24–25; 14:16–21, 23, of which Q 13:24–25; 14:16–21, 23 would now constitute either the end of the fifth block or the beginning of the sixth block. What remains now is to consider the internal unity and flow of the remaining material in the sixth block, since this block is not as strongly and obviously unified as the other five blocks. Instead of elaborate argumentation and carefully constructed passages, the sixth block is made up of fairly loose-standing logia. This is not the place to analyse each of these logia in detail; instead, a brief summary of the last block's unity and flow, as I see it, will suffice. The first complex of traditions to consider is Q 14:16–21, 23, 26–27; 17:33. The parable in Q 14:16–21, 23 depicts the kingdom of God as a place where everyone is welcome. Another metaphor used in the formative stratum for such inclusivity is the family of God.[338] Q 6:32 claims that you should "love" (ἀγαπάω) everyone. The parable in Q 14:16–21, 23 illustrates such inclusive love by having someone invite random strangers to his dinner party. In the formative stratum, this parable was probably followed by Q 14:26, which directs people to "hate" (μισέω) their biological family. The result is a deliberate contrast between the inclusive love of God's symbolic family and the required hate of one's biological family. This probably reflects the real-life situation of the Q people, who were forced to abandon actual family ties when joining Q's symbolic family.[339] The *Sitz im*

---

[336] See Garsky *et al.* 1997, 162–185.

[337] Cf. Hoffmann 2001, 278.

[338] Cf. esp. Q 6:32, 34, 35; 11:33; cf. Park 2019, 47.

[339] See esp. Jacobson 1995; Moxnes 2003; Howes 2015a, 144–150.

Leben of the Q movement, however, is less important here than the acknowledgement that the parable is linked to the subsequent logion by the comparison
made between God's symbolic family and people's biological families.

In both Matthew and Luke, Q 14:26 is followed by Q 14:27. This combination is therefore certain for both the formative stratum and the final form of Q.
The two logia are linked by the catchword "disciple" (μαθητής), which appears
as part of the exact same clause in both traditions, namely "cannot be my disciple" (οὐ δύναται εἶναί μου μαθητής). This clause reveals the overarching
theme of this and subsequent traditions as that of discipleship, and particularly
the hefty demands of discipleship. Whereas verse 26 points to the abandonment
of biological family as a demand of discipleship, verse 27 suggests that martyrdom and death may be real outcomes of discipleship. In fact, verse 27 is
perhaps deliberately ambiguous, denoting death and martyrdom on a literal
level, but also using the cross as a symbol for the burden of discipleship in
general. According to Matthew and the International Q Project, Q 14:27 was
followed in the Sayings Gospel by Q 17:33. The two logia are most notably
connected by similar syntax, beginning with "the one who,"[340] as well as the
logical link between "taking one's cross" (λαμβάνει τὸν σταυρὸν αὐτοῦ) and
"losing one's life" (ὁ ἀπολέσας τὴν ψυχὴν αὐτοῦ). The topic is once again
martyrdom and death as a potential cost of discipleship. However, the same
ambiguity as in Q 14:27 might be operating here, so that "losing one's life" (ὁ
ἀπολέσας τὴν ψυχὴν αὐτοῦ) might also connote some of the less ominous consequences of discipleship, like abandoning one's biological family. It might
also connote the cost of discipleship *in toto*, including all associated burdens.
One may also notice narrative progression in this material, from the abandonment of family in Q 14:26 to persecution and suffering in Q 14:27 to loss of
life in Q 17:33. The latter two items could include physical persecution and
death or social and economic persecution and "death."

According to the *Critical Edition of Q*, the saying about salt in Q 14:34–35
follows after the three logia on discipleship. At face value, the salt saying
seems out of place. Any link to the preceding discipleship logia would have to
depend on the interpretation of Q 14:34–35. Unfortunately, the salt saying is
notoriously difficult to interpret. Yet two interpretations suggest themselves
when the saying is considered in isolation. Firstly, it seems to be about evanes-
cence and caducity. According to the metaphor, nothing is permanent, not even
salt. Secondly, the saying seems to be about fulfilment of purpose. The salt's
purpose is to season food, but once it ceases fulfilling that purpose, it becomes
useless. Both of these interpretations relate specifically to the foregoing logion.
Just like salt is temporary, life is temporary, and just like the purpose of salt is
seasoning, the purpose of life is discipleship. Just like salt ceases to be salt if

---

[340] Relative pronoun ὅς with negative verbal construction οὐ λαμβάνει in Q 14:27 and
article ὁ with participle verb εὑρών in Q 17:33.

it fails to fulfil its purpose of seasoning, life ceases to be life if it fails to fulfil its purpose of discipleship. Clinging to one's life at the expense of meeting the demands of discipleship is in fact a loss of life, because one ceases then to live one's purpose. Conversely, sacrificing one's life in order to practice discipleship is in fact an acquisition of life, because one lives one's purpose. Thus interpreted, Q 14:34–35 functions as proof from the worlds of cooking and nature that losing one's life could in fact mean gaining one's life and vice versa. The link, however, depends on a certain interpretation of the salt saying, which might or might not be accurate.

The *Critical Edition of Q* features Q 16:13 next. This logion continues to discuss the demands of discipleship. In this case, the demand is to abandon any form of greed. This demand fits well with the promotion of general reciprocity in the formative stratum, particularly the instructions to give freely (Q 6:30) and refrain from hoarding (Q 12:33–34). Joining the Q movement would have had certain economic implications. On the one hand, it would have entailed sharing all available resources with other members. On the other hand, it would have entailed severing economic ties with one's family and community.[341] In the ancient world, these economic ties were crucial to survival.[342] This explains the link between Q 16:13 and the cluster of logia in Q 14:26–27; 17:33; 14:34–35. Abandoning one's family (Q 14:26) prompted not only persecution (Q 14:27) and loss of life (Q 17:33; 14:34–35), but economic suffering as well (Q 16:13). Such economic suffering is justified in Q 16:13 as a cost of discipleship. One of the consequences of implementing general reciprocity is that available resources are evenly distributed, which makes greed and hoarding impossible. Two additional connections might be relevant here. Firstly, if "mammon" (μαμωνᾶς) refers to physical coinage and not just wealth, it would relate to "salt" (ἅλας) as something that is extracted from the earth by human endeavour. In both cases, the arduous process might in itself be a metaphor for discipleship. Secondly, the catchword "hate" (μισέω) links Q 14:26 with Q 16:13. This catchword might function as a type of *inclusio* grouping together the cluster of logia in between.

In the *Critical Edition of Q*, Q 16:13 is followed by Q 16:16–18. However, the two logia in Q 16:16–17 are not attributed to the formative stratum by Kloppenborg, which means that Q 16:18 would have followed Q 16:13 in the formative stratum. It is not a far leap from the idea that one cannot serve two masters at the same time to the idea that one cannot have two marriage partners at the same time. The hypothetical "master" (κύριος) of Q 16:13, apart from representing God and/or mammon, would also have been the *paterfamilias* accord-

---

[341] See Howes 2015a, 147–148.

[342] Cf. Douglas 1995, 123; Draper 1999, 33; Horsley 1999, 52–53, 297; Jacobson 2000, 191; Destro and Pesce 2003, 212–213; Moxnes 2003, 52.

ing to ancient household structures. The professed inability to serve two masters is therefore easily translated into the inability to be married to two men at
the same time. It is true that Q 16:18 is specifically directed at men, so that the
application of Q 16:13 to women being unable to have more than one husband
creates an imperfect fit. The fit does not need to be perfect, however, in order
to be legitimate. At any rate, there is a way to make sense of this apparent
discord between the two logia. If the premises of Q 16:18 are granted (1) that
divorce and remarriage equal adultery and (2) that marrying a divorcée also
equals adultery, then the men who commit these acts place these women in the
impossible situation of serving two "masters" at the same time. The language
of Q 16:13 further strengthens the link between the two logia. Terms like "hate"
(μισέω), "love" (ἀγαπάω), "be devoted to" (ἀντέχω), and "despise"
(καταφρονέω) all relate well to the social institutions of marriage and divorce.

    Q 16:18 is followed by the saying against enticements in Q 17:1–2, accord-
ing to the *Critical Edition of Q*. These two logia are connected by the logical
correlation between seduction and adultery. The noun "enticement"
(σκάνδαλον) in Q 17:1 literally refers to a trap or a snare.[343] On a metaphoric
level, it denotes the act of causing someone to sin or stumble.[344] The verb "entice" (σκανδαλίζω), used in Q 17:2, has the same reference.[345] The most obvious example of such enticement is of course sexual seduction, here viewed in
combination with Q 16:18 as the root cause of adultery and divorce. The noun
σκάνδαλον in Q 17:1 further connotes the scandal that might result from adultery and divorce.[346] Q 17:1–2 might further link up with the previous logia in
listing another demand of discipleship, namely sexual reserve and chastity. The
Q movement must have been made up of a mixture of single and married people, including people who were still formally married to non-members. Under
such conditions, the temptation and opportunity for emotional and physical
adultery must have been great. The formative stratum attempts to counteract
such behaviour by prohibiting seduction and promiscuity. Sacrificing sexual
expression might therefore have been a consequence of joining the Q movement and is possibly listed in Q 17:1–2 as another demand of discipleship.

    Matthew and Luke differ on the sequence of the subsequent material.
Whereas Luke features Q 17:3–4 directly after Q 17:1–2, Matthew separates
these two traditions by featuring Q 15:4–5, 7 in between. The International Q
Project follows Matthew in their *Critical Edition of Q*, but I maintain that Luke
is more probable to represent Q in this case. This conclusion is supported by
two considerations: (1) whereas Matthew treats both Q 17:1–2 and Q 17:3–4
in the same literary context, Luke features Q 17:1–4 and Q 15:4–5, 7–10 in

---

[343] Liddell and Scott 1996, 1604.
[344] Louw and Nida 1993a, 775, domain 88.306.
[345] Louw and Nida 1993a, 775, domain 88.304; Liddell and Scott 1996, 1604.
[346] Liddell and Scott 1996, 1604.

different literary contexts; and (2) Q 17:3–4 follows Q 17:1–2 sequentially in both Gospels. As we saw, the word "enticement" (σκανδάλον) in Q 17:1–2 connotes sin as a possible consequence. Q 17:3–4 takes this further by teaching the forgiveness of sin. Q 17:3–4 instructs the Q people to forgive all transgressions by a fellow member, even adultery. The harsh punishment of Q 17:1–2 is here contrasted with the merciful act of forgiveness. This combination of judgment and mercy is reminiscent of Q 6:36–38.[347] It is possible that forgiveness is here listed as another demand of discipleship. According to Luke and the International Q Project, Q 17:3–4 is followed by Q 17:6. This saying is linked to Q 17:1–4 most apparently by the catchword "sea" (θάλασσα) and the imagery of someone or something being put in the sea. Q 17:6 is further connected to Q 17:3–4 by virtue of the conditional "if" (ἐάν/εἰ) and the fact that both logia are structured as conditional sentences. It is possible that "having faith" (ἔχετε πίστιν) is presented here as another demand of discipleship.

It is my view that the two parables in Q 15:4–5, 7–10 appeared next in Q, which is why Matthew treated them together with Q 17:1–4 in his Gospel. Parables are also the perfect segue in the context of Q's final form for the saying about God's kingdom in Q 17:20–21, assuming that it was present in Q. Both Q 17:6 and Q 15:4–5, 7 deal with farming. More specifically, both traditions deal with the loss of agricultural produce or livestock. There is no real need to discuss the linkage between the parable of the lost sheep (Q 15:4–5, 7) and the parable of the lost coin (Q 15:8–10) at any length, assuming that the latter featured in Q. Both are parables about God's kingdom. They deal with the topic of losing and finding something and do so with almost the exact same syntactical and narrative structures. They also feature numerous catchwords, including τίς ("who, which person"), ἔχω ("have, possess, own"), ἀπόλλυμι ("lose"), εὑρίσκω ("find"), and χαίρω ("rejoice"). In addition to the agricultural linkage between Q 15:4–5, 7 and Q 17:6, the two parables also reach back to Q 17:3–4 and the themes of forgiveness and internal cohesion. There is a reason why the stories feature a herd of sheep and a collection of coins, as opposed to a single sheep and coin. These assemblages represent the Q group, and the lost item represents the sinner in each case. According to my version of the formative stratum, Q 19:12–13, 15–24 would finally have followed in the Sayings Gospel. It is linked to the two preceding parables in Q 15:4–5, 7–10 because it is also a parable about God's kingdom. It follows particularly well after the parable of the lost coin, because it is also about ten coins. This accounts for the catchword "ten" (δέκα) and the references to numismatic denominations (δραχμή and μνᾶ) in both parables. If my interpretation of the concluding parable in chapter 9 is correct, standing up for the weak in society might be seen as another demand of discipleship.

---

[347] Cf. Howes 2015a, 247.

This accounts for the sixth block of the formative stratum: Q 13:24–25; 14:16–21, 23, 26–27; 17:33; 14:34–35; 16:13, 18; 17:1–4, 6: 15:4–5, 7–10; 19:12–13, 15–24. Although this block reads less fluently than the other blocks, each individual tradition is linked to the preceding and subsequent traditions in some way or another. And although some of these links are weaker than others, they are for the most part pretty strong. Importantly, "strong" does not here refer to complete or substantial thematic continuity, but rather to how obvious the association would have been. Superficial links are therefore legitimate if they are obvious. Traditions linked by catchword connection, for example, may be thematically incongruous, but the link is still strong because the catchword is obvious. Similarly, two traditions might be thematically contradictory, but nonetheless discuss exactly the same topic. Such a link is also strong despite the contradiction.[348]

Noteworthy is that the theme of discipleship seems to be a golden thread that runs through the entire block.[349] The cost of joining the Q movement and being a disciple of Jesus are catalogued in this block of traditions. True enough, it is not in all cases equally plausible that discipleship is in view, but if all these traditions are considered together, their cumulative weight supports the proposal that the sixth block deals in particular with the cost of discipleship as an overarching theme. The internal cohesion of the sixth block is further supported by the observation that most of the links proposed here also represent the final form of Q. This is true of the following links: Q 14:16–21, 23 to Q 14:26; Q 14:26 to Q 14:27; Q 14:27 to Q 17:33; Q 17:33 to Q 14:34–35; Q 14:34–35 to Q 16:13; Q 16:18 to Q 17:1–2; Q 17:1–2 to Q 17:3–4; Q 17:3–4 to Q 15:4–5, 7; and Q 15:4–5, 7 to Q 15:[8–10]. The only links that are not representative of Q in its final form are the following: (1) Q 13:24–25 to Q 14:16–21, 23, because of the material added in Q 13:26–35; (2) Q 16:13 to Q 16:18, because of the interpolations in Q 16:16–17; and (3) Q 15:4–5, 7–10 to Q 19:12–13, 15–24, because of the material added in Q 17:[20–21], 23–24, 26–27, 30, 34–35, 37. Moreover, many of the traditions also follow upon one another in either of the Gospels. The most obvious examples are the following: (1) Q 14:16–21, 23, 26–27 in Luke 14:16–27; (2) Q 14:26–27; 17:33 in Matthew 10:37–39; (3) Q 17:1–4, 6 in Luke 17:1–6; and (4) Q 15:4–5, 7–10 in Luke 15:4–10.

10.9 Findings

This chapter considered the overall unity and flow of Q's formative stratum. It seems justified to conclude from the foregoing analysis that the formative stratum constitutes a literary unity. Jacobson quotes secular literary critics Thrall

---

[348] Cf. Kloppenborg 1996a, 28.
[349] Cf. Kloppenborg 1987, 237.

and Hibbard to define the concept of literary unity: "The concept that a literary work shall have in it some organizing principle in relation to which all its parts are related so that, viewed in the light of this principle, the work is an organic whole."[350] As this chapter has hopefully shown, Q's formative stratum qualifies when measured against this definition. It constitutes one continuous document that flows effortlessly from beginning to end.[351] This is particularly true if my proposed additions are included in the formative stratum. The weakest linkage and flow relates to Kloppenborg's sixth block of Q^1 material. If blocks 1–5 sound like a melody or symphony from beginning to end, block 6 sounds more like staccato or jazz. This is to be expected and actually supports the idea that the formative stratum was a singular document before its elaboration by the main redactor. Other wisdom books from the ancient world likewise tend to feature their disparate logia at the end. But even with the sixth block, individual logia are unified by their thematic focus on the demands of discipleship, which is reinforced by individual links between consecutive logia.

---

[350] Thrall and Hibbard 1962, 500; Jacobson 1994, 100.

[351] One could argue against the findings of this chapter that certain individual Q traditions might not have been preserved by Matthew and Luke, but the strong connections between individual traditions and blocks in the formative stratum, as illustrated in this chapter and throughout this study, provide evidence to the contrary. Moreover, the tendency of the main redactor to retain the exact words of the formative stratum (see chapter 11 below) would suggest that the same conservatism was applied to larger traditions, so that the main redactor in all likelihood retained all of these traditions. Likewise, the redactional tendency of Matthew and Luke to retain the overwhelming majority of Markan traditions would suggest that they also retained most or all of Q in their Gospels. If traditions are missing from the formative stratum, they are probably missing from Kloppenborg's sixth block. The rest of Q^1 seems to flow too well from one tradition to the next to lack individual sayings or passages. But even with regards to the sixth block, the correlation in extent between the 30 verses of the first block and the 30 verses of the sixth block (see chapter 11 below) argues against the notion that individual traditions are lacking from the formative stratum.

Chapter 11

Concluding Remarks

This chapter will draw some conclusions. After considering Q itself, some observations will be made about the relevance of this study for the parables of Jesus and the historical Jesus.

11.1 Central Topics for Q's Formative Stratum

In addition to arguing for the unity of Q's formative stratum, this study also revealed three central themes throughout, namely discipleship, material survival, and the kingdom of God. Under the theme of material survival, general reciprocity is perhaps the most important survival strategy, enjoying independent treatment in many Q^1 passages. It is important to point out that "discipleship" does not here refer to a particularly Christian morality and lifestyle or to being a good person in general.[1] In Q's formative stratum, "discipleship" refers rather to following the wisdom instructions of Jesus, which includes above all else implementing and proclaiming his vision of God's kingdom. By the same token, the "kingdom of God" is not in Q's formative stratum a synonym for "Christians," "those who believe in Jesus," or "heaven," but is rather a term that references an alternative reality in this world, where people's daily needs are met and survival is possible for everyone. Although the term "kingdom of God" does not appear frequently,[2] the formative stratum treats this topic throughout.[3] In fact, the kingdom of God could be seen as a unifying element for Q as a whole,[4] although it does not have exactly the same meaning in the main redaction.[5] The other two themes are treated separately when considering the overarching structure of the formative stratum, but not necessarily when considering individual traditions. Let me explain. Discipleship seems to be the main topic in Kloppenborg's first and last blocks of Q^1 material. Conversely, the four blocks in between are mainly about material survival. The following overarching structure is therefore discernible:

---

[1] Cf. Horsley 1999, 228–249.
[2] Cf. Kloppenborg 1995, 287–289.
[3] Vaage 1995a, 88–89; cf. Uro 1996, 79; Park 2019, 47.
[4] Horsley 1999, 87.
[5] Cf. e.g. Uro 1996, 82–87.

- Discipleship in God's kingdom: Q 6:20–49.
- Survival in God's kingdom: Q 9:57–60; 10:2–11, 16, 21, 23–24; 11:2–13, 33–35; 12:2–7, 11–12, 22–31, 33–34, 39, 42–44, 58–59; 13:18–21, 24–25; 14:16–21, 23.
- Discipleship in God's kingdom: Q 14:26–27; 17:33; 14:34–35; 16:13, 18; 17:1–4, 6; 15:4–5, 7–10; 19:12–13, 15–24.

The first and last blocks include roughly the same amount of content, with both blocks featuring exactly 30 verses. The theme of discipleship therefore forms an *inclusio* around the theme of corporeal survival, which is developed in the middle of the overarching structure. What is more, the middle section about survival is roughly the same length as the first and last blocks taken together, with the latter adding up to 60 verses and the middle section featuring 73 verses. It follows that the formative stratum shows clear signs of deliberate structuring, presenting the material in the macro-structure as a ring composition. When the individual traditions are considered, however, the themes of discipleship and survival are not so easily disentangled. This is to be expected, since discipleship is viewed as the means through which the kingdom of God will be established on earth, while the kingdom of God is viewed as the means through which the survival of people on earth will be assured.[6] Q 9:57–60, for example, deals both with the demands of discipleship and the reality of homelessness, which makes it the perfect text to link the first block about discipleship with the middle block about survival. Another obvious example is the illustrations of how to treat one's enemies in Q 6:29–30, which are presented not only as demands for discipleship, but also as strategies for survival. The same is actually true for most or all of the material in Q's formative stratum. Survival strategies like participating in God's symbolic family, trusting in divine provenance, implementing general reciprocity, cancelling debts, standing up for those who are less fortunate, and not being litigious become the demands for discipleship that are required for the establishment of God's kingdom.[7] As such, the formative stratum as a whole discusses discipleship, survival, and God's kingdom throughout, but focuses specifically on survival in the middle block and discipleship in the first and last blocks. I should point out that I use the term "blocks" here for ease of reference, not to argue that the formative stratum can be neatly divided into separate literary blocks. Such a claim would be somewhat counterproductive in the context of my present case that Q's first redactional layer constitutes a unity that flows effortlessly from beginning to end. Part of the appeal of my analysis is that it is possible to do away with the idea of separate blocks and start viewing Q's formative layer as an inseparable unity. In fact, my analysis would seem to indicate that the formative stratum

---

[6] Cf. Häkkinen 2016, 8.
[7] Cf. Häkkinen 2016, 8–9; Park 2019, 47.

was composed from the start to function as a unified document. This goes against the criticism of some against Kloppenborg's stratigraphy that the formative stratum cannot be shown to ever have existed as a unified whole.[8] Ultimately, Q's formative stratum functions as a practical manual for establishing the kingdom of God on earth by practicing discipleship and ensuring the material survival of all God's children.

The previous sentence is very interesting when compared with Kloppenborg's statement that "it is not only the judgment and Deuteronomistic motifs that unify discrete sub-collections in Q; other subcollections are unified by their common appeal to a provident and generous God whose character serves as model of ideal human relationships."[9] Whereas judgment and deuteronomistic themes give unity to the main redaction and final form of Q, the themes of material survival (aided by "a provident and generous God") and discipleship (in imitation of Jesus and a "God whose character serves as model of ideal human relationships") give unity to the formative stratum. The focus shifted in the process of redaction from the message of Jesus about discipleship and material survival in the kingdom of God to the condemnation of outsiders for the sake of internal group identity.[10] An all-inclusive vision of how people can survive in this world was transformed into an exclusionary vision of how a sect can survive in Israel. The "kingdom of God" became more a term to distinguish insiders from outsiders in this world or the next than an expression of the radical vision of a place in this world where everyone can physically survive. This focal shift influenced the evangelists, who continued to develop not only the topics of discipleship and "helping the poor" in their Gospels, but also the topics of outsider-exclusion and apocalyptic condemnation.

11.2 Creative Redaction

The pioneer of the Old Testament Documentary Hypothesis, Julius Wellhausen, made the following statement about the composition of the Hexateuch:

Bei der Untersuchung der Komposition des Hexateuchs hat sich mir dann herausgestellt, das hier allerdings drei selbständige Erzählungsfäden fortlaufen, dass aber diese grossen Zusammenhänge *nicht bloss zugeschnitten und leicht vernäht*, sondern, vor, bei, und nacht ihrer (nicht zugleich erfolgten) Vereinigung erheblich vermehrt und überarbeitet worden sind.[11]

In investigating the composition of the Hexateuch it became apparent to me that here, to be sure, three independent narrative threads were proceeding, but these large sequences were *not simply snipped and loosely sown together*; rather, before, alongside and after being

---

[8] See chapter 10 above.

[9] Kloppenborg 2000a, 125; cf. Hoffmann 2001, 267.

[10] Cf. Kloppenborg 1987, 167–168; Uro 1996, 118; Hoffmann 2001, 268–269.

[11] Wellhausen 1871, x, emphasis added by me.

brought together (which did not occur at the same time) they had been considerably augmented and reworked.[12]

As far as Q's main redaction is concerned, a relatively simple editorial process is typically assumed. According to this understanding, the main redactor merely added (existing and/or newly created) traditions to the material of the formative stratum.[13] In addition, two interpolations were probably created *ex nihilo*: Q 6:23c functions as an interpretive gloss and Q 10:12 enables a smooth transition between Q 10:2–11 in the formative stratum and Q 10:13–15 in the main redaction.[14] If the arguments in the foregoing chapters are convincing, it would follow that the editorial process involved more creativity than this copy-and-paste style of editing. This is supported by the observation that creativity, originality, and freedom have consistently been demonstrated since the beginning of historical criticism up to the present day as features of redactional activity in ancient Judaism and Christianity.[15] This is true of textual criticism,[16] source criticism,[17] form criticism,[18] redaction criticism,[19] composition criticism,[20] and canonical criticism.[21] One only needs to consider the ways in which Matthew and Luke dealt with the traditions they inherited from Mark and Q to recognise such redactional creativity and freedom in the early church. Instead of being, in the words of Wellhausen, "simply snipped and loosely sown together," it is much more likely given these considerations that Q was formed through a fairly creative editorial process. Based on the foregoing chapters, the following examples may be listed:

- By adding Q 10:22, the sapiential message of Q 10:21, 23–24 was changed to highlight the exclusivity of Jesus as mediator of divine knowledge;
- By situating Q 11:33–35 between two extended blocks of Q^2 material, the sapiential messages of these logia were changed to now involve the judgment of outsiders;
- By adding Q 12:40 after Q 12:39, a supporting maxim was turned into a parable about the eschatological end;
- By adding Q 12:45–46 after Q 12:42–44, a parable addressing socio-economic concerns was turned into a parable about the eschatological end;

---

[12] English translation by Van Seters 2006, 236, emphasis added by me.

[13] Cf. Kloppenborg 1996a, 27–28.

[14] Cf. Kloppenborg 1996a, 19.

[15] See Perrin 1970; Den Heyer 2002, 27–51, 74–75; Van Seters 2006, 185–297; 2012, 9–22; e.g. Simon 1682; Wrede 1901.

[16] See Van Seters 2006, 298–350; e.g. Griesbach 1796, lxiv–lxxi; Epp 2012; Metso 2012; Holmes 2012; Wachtel 2012; Strutwolf 2012.

[17] E.g. Eichhorn 1803; Strauss 1860; Tyson 2012.

[18] E.g. Bultmann [1931] 1963; Gunkel [1910] 1997; McKnight 2012.

[19] E.g. Conzelmann 1960; Downing 1997a; 1997b; Keinänen 2001; Van der Meer 2004; Luz 2005, 115–142; Collins 2012.

[20] E.g. Haenchen 1968; Humphrey 2006; Ulrich 2012, 24–29.

[21] See Van Peters 2006, 351–390.

- By adding redactional material before Q 12:58–59, an admonition about avoiding courts was turned into a parable about the eschatological end;
- By adding Q 13:26–27 after Q 13:25, a maxim about the callousness of ancient masters was turned into a parable about the judgment of outsiders at the eschatological end;
- By situating Q 13:18–21 between the now-eschatological traditions of Q 12:58–59 and Q 13:24–27, the seeds were sown for changing the meaning of two parables that were originally about the divine provision of food and shelter;
- By situating Q 14:16–21, 23 after Q 13:28–29, [30], 34–35; 14:[11], a parable about sharing food was turned into an allegorical parable about boundary demarcation;
- By adding Q 17:[20–21], 23–24, 37, 26–27, 30, 34–35 before and Q 19:26; 22:28, 30 after Q 19:12–13, 15–24, a parable about standing up to an exploitative economic system was turned into a parable about eschatological judgment.

Four interesting strategies may be observed here as part of the editorial *modus operandi*. Firstly, the main redactor would at times turn logia into parables with altered messages by expanding the image. This technique was applied to Q 13:25 (expanded with the addition of Q 13:26–27). Secondly, the main redactor would at times expand parables to change their messages. This technique was applied to Q 12:42–44 (expanded with the addition of Q 12:45–46). Thirdly, the main redactor would at times adjust the message of a tradition from the formative stratum by adding a parable application and/or expository saying directly after it. This technique was applied to Q 10:21 (with Q 10:22 added), Q 12:39 (with Q 12:40 added), Q 13:25–27 (with Q 13:28–29 added), and Q 19:12–13, 15–24 (with Q 19:26 and Q 22:28, 30 added). In the case of Q 10:21–24, the addition of Q 10:22 can also be regarded as an interpolation, in which case it would be comparable to Q 6:23c and Q 10:12. Fourthly, the main redactor would often add redactional material directly before and/or after material from the formative stratum in order to change the literary context of that particular Q^1 tradition, thereby changing its message and getting it to align with the message of the main redaction. This technique was applied to Q 11:33–35 (with Q 11:16, 29–32 added before and Q 11:39, 41–52 added after), Q 12:58–59 (with Q 12:[49], 51, 53, [54–56] added before), Q 13:18–21 (with the now-eschatological Q 12:58–59 added before and the now-eschatological Q 13:24–27 added after), Q 13:24–29 (with Q 13:[30], 34–35 added after), Q 14:16–21, 23 (with Q 13:28–29, [30], 34–35 added before), and Q 19:12–13, 15–24 (with Q 17:[20–21], 23–24, 37, 26–27, 30, 34–35 added before and Q 22:28, 30 added after). In the case of some individual Q^1 traditions, these strategies were applied in combination. The best example is perhaps the maxim in Q 13:25, which was turned into a parable with the addition of Q 13:26–27, fashioned with an expository saying and/or parable application in Q 13:28–29, and placed in a redactional literary context with the addition of Q 13:[30], 34–35.

It is not always clear whether redactional additions were taken from existing traditions or created *ex nihilo*. At the very least, Q 12:45–46 and Q 13:26–27 were created anew by the main redactor. This study focused on only a few individual Q texts. Examining all the material in Q would add more examples of creative redaction and might even discover additional redactional techniques. It would seem that the main redactor worked with a fair degree of freedom when editing the document. Even so, it would seem from the evidence considered in this monograph that, for the most part, this did not include modifying the actual words and sentences of the formative stratum. Rather, the redactional strategy entailed adding existing and/or newly created material while preserving the actual verbatim content of Q^1 traditions. A measure of respect for the inherited Q^1 traditions probably lies behind this redactional strategy. The decision to keep the content of the formative stratum as close as possible to how it was received must have limited the redactional options available to the main redactor, which in turn would have required even more creativity to redirect the message of both individual Q^1 traditions and the Sayings Gospel Q as a whole. The tendency to safeguard the actual words and grammar of the formative stratum might suggest that the main redactor had the same conservatism when it came to the formative stratum as a whole, prompting her to retain as much or perhaps all of the material she inherited. From our analysis of the unity and flow of the formative stratum in chapter 10, it would certainly seem that way.

11.3 The Parables of Jesus

If my analyses are correct, it would mean that the process of adapting the parables of Jesus already started on the level of Q and in some cases perhaps even earlier, during the oral transmission of these parables. This process was taken further by the evangelists when they wrote their Gospels. Examples from this study include the parables in Q 12:42–44, Q 13:18–19, Q 13:20–21, Q 14:16–21, 23, and Q 19:12–13, 15–24. In other cases, individual logia of Jesus were turned into parables. Examples from this study include the logia in Q 12:39, Q 12:58–59, and Q 13:25. In the process, the messages of these logia and parables were typically changed to now address eschatological and polemic concerns. Very often, these logia and parables were originally about socio-economic concerns in a context where people were anxious about their daily survival. The parables in particular tend to depict the kingdom of God as an alternative reality when compared with the reigning socio-economic system(s).[22] In Q 12:42–44, a servile farm manager becomes an agent of God's kingdom and an example of discipleship in practice by feeding other slaves. In Q 13:18–21, the kingdom of God is depicted as a place where everyone has food and shelter. In Q 14:16–

---

[22] Cf. Park 2019, 47.

21, 23, an angry and wealthy householder acts as a disciple of Jesus and contributes to the establishment of God's kingdom by inviting street people to a
house party with plenty of food. In Q 19:12–13, 15–24, a city slave becomes a
model of discipleship and an ambassador for God's kingdom by standing up
against the economic exploitation of small peasants. It is interesting that these
main characters would have been unlikely candidates from the perspective of
small peasants to have established the type of reality Jesus called God's kingdom. This might suggest that Jesus imagined people from all levels of society
contributing to the establishment of God's kingdom as a new socio-economic,
politico-religious reality. The messages of these parables become particularly
potent and patent when read alongside other traditions that expose the reigning
socio-economic situation, like Q 6:29–30 (incl. Matt 5:41), Q 12:11, Q 12:58–
59, and Q 13:25.

11.4 The Historical Jesus

As explained in the introduction to this study, I maintain that Q's formative
stratum brings us very close to the historical Jesus. It might even be the closest
we can possibly hope to get to this elusive figure. I further maintain that the
formative stratum is essentially sapiential and completely lacks not only any
apocalyptic and/or futurist eschatology, but also any prophetic material.[23] In
Q's formative stratum, Jesus is portrayed as a teacher of subversive wisdom
who proclaimed the kingdom of God as a solution to the concurrent socio-economic concerns of the small peasantry and poor.[24] Given Jesus's concern for
the lower classes, Horsley's portrayal of Jesus as a social prophet is not entirely
inappropriate.[25] However, the word "prophet" in the term "social prophet" is
to my mind misleading. Notwithstanding the distinctions between different
kinds of prophets in the ancient world, the word "prophet" carries with it the
idea of predicting the future, which is not how Jesus is portrayed in Q's formative stratum. In this regard, a better designation for the historical Jesus is perhaps "social sage," giving expression to both his sapiential nature and his concern for those at the bottom of society. This does not mean that the historical
Jesus could not have used apocalyptic and/or futurist eschatology as well as
prophecy to buttress his wisdom,[26] but it is telling that such traditions are
wholly absent from the formative stratum, strongly suggesting that the historical Jesus was primarily a sage. His wisdom was all about the establishment of
God's kingdom on earth in order to address the socio-economic concerns of

---

[23] See Howes 2015a.
[24] Cf. Van Aarde 2014, 2.
[25] Horsley 2012; cf. Van Eck 2016.
[26] See Howes 2015a, 284–300.

the small peasantry and poor.[27] The followers of Jesus would succeed in realising this vision, it was believed, if they followed in the footsteps of Jesus – that is, if they practiced discipleship.

---

[27] Cf. Van Aarde 2014, 2.

Annexure A

The Extent or Scope of Q[1]

If the formative stratum is revised according to the arguments in this book, it would comprise the material featured in this annexure. I follow the reconstruction and translation of the *Critical Edition of Q*, except where I have argued for an alternative lexeme in the foregoing chapters. Regarding Q 6:37–38, I have argued for the alternative reconstruction and translation featured here in a previous publication.[1] Regarding Q 11:5–8, I feature the Greek text of Nestle-Aland 28 and the English translation of the ESV. The Greek reconstruction appears first and the English translation second. To give a sense of how the document would probably have circulated in the ancient world, I present the formative stratum as one continuous text.

A.1 Greek Reconstruction of Q's Formative Stratum

6 ²⁰<...> καὶ [[ἐπάρ]]ας το[[ὺς ὀφθαλμοὺς]] αὐτοῦ [[εἰς τοὺς]] μαθητὰ[[ς]] αὐτοῦ ...λέγ...· Μακάριοι οἱ πτωχοί, ὅτι [[ὑμετέρα]] ἐστὶν ἡ βασιλεία τοῦ θεοῦ. ²¹μακάριοι οἱ πεινῶντες, ὅτι χορτασθής[[εσθε]]. μακάριοι οἱ [[πενθ]]ο[[ῦ]]ντες, ὅτι [[παρακληθής<εσθε>]]. ²²μακάριοί ἐστε ὅταν ὀνειδίσωσιν ὑμᾶς καὶ [[διώξ]]ωσιν καὶ [[εἴπ]]ωσιν [[πᾶν]] πονηρὸν [[καθ’]] ὑμῶν ἕνεκεν τοῦ υἱοῦ τοῦ ἀνθρώπου. ²³χαίρετε καὶ [[ἀγαλλιᾶσθε]], ὅτι ὁ μισθὸς ὑμῶν πολὺς ἐν τῷ οὐρανῷ· ²⁷ἀγαπᾶτε τοὺς ἐχθροὺς ὑμῶν ²⁸[[καὶ]] προσεύχεσθε ὑπὲρ τῶν [[διωκ]]όντων ὑμᾶς, ³⁵ὅπως γένησθε υἱοὶ τοῦ πατρὸς ὑμῶν, ὅτι τὸν ἥλιον αὐτοῦ ἀνατέλλει ἐπὶ πονηροὺς καὶ [[ἀγαθοὺς καὶ βρέχει ἐπὶ δικαίους καὶ ἀδίκους]]. ²⁹[[ὅστις]] σε [[ῥαπίζει]] εἰς τὴν σιαγόνα, στρέψον [[αὐτῷ]] καὶ τὴν ἄλλην· καὶ [[τῷ θέλοντί σοι κριθῆναι καὶ]] τὸν χιτῶνά σου [[λαβεῖν, ἄφες αὐτῷ]] καὶ τὸ ἱμάτιον. ^{Matt 5:41}[[«καὶ ὅστις σε ἀγγαρεύσει μίλιον ἕν, ὕπαγε μετ’ αὐτοῦ δύο.»]] ³⁰τῷ αἰτοῦντί σε δός, καὶ [[ἀπὸ]] τ[[οῦ δανι<ζομένου> τὰ]] σ[[ὰ]] μὴ ἀπ[[αίτει]]. ³¹καὶ καθὼς θέλετε ἵνα ποιῶσιν ὑμῖν οἱ ἄνθρωποι, οὕτως ποιεῖτε αὐτοῖς. ³²... ε[[ἰ]] ... ἀγαπ[[ᾶ]]τε τοὺς ἀγαπῶντας ὑμᾶς, τίνα μισθὸν ἔχετε; οὐχὶ καὶ οἱ τελῶναι τὸ αὐτὸ ποιοῦσιν; ³⁴καὶ ἐὰν [[δανίσητε παρ’ ὧν ἐλπίζετε λαβεῖν, τί<να μισθὸν ἔχε>τε]]; οὐχὶ καὶ [[οἱ ἐθνικ]] οἳ τὸ αὐτὸ ποιοῦσιν; ³⁶[[γίν]]εσθε οἰκτίρμονες ὡς ... ὁ πατὴρ ὑμῶν οἰκτίρμων ἐστίν. ³⁷καὶ μὴ κρίνετε, ἵνα μὴ κριθῆτε· ³⁸ᾧ γὰρ

---

¹ See Howes 2015a, 221–229.

μέτρῳ μετρεῖτε μετρηθήσεται ὑμῖν. ³⁹μήτι δύναται τυφλὸς τυφλὸν ὁδηγεῖν; οὐχὶ ἀμφότεροι εἰς βόθυνον πεσοῦνται; ⁴⁰οὐκ ἔστιν μαθητὴς ὑπὲρ τὸν διδάσκαλον· ⟦ἀρκετὸν τῷ μαθητῇ ἵνα γένη⟧ται ὡς ὁ διδάσκαλος αὐτοῦ. ⁴¹τί δὲ βλέπεις τὸ κάρφος τὸ ἐν τῷ ὀφθαλμῷ τοῦ ἀδελφοῦ σου, τὴν δὲ ἐν τῷ σῷ ὀφθαλμῷ δοκὸν οὐ κατανοεῖς; ⁴²πῶς ... τῷ ἀδελφῷ σου· ἄφες ἐκβάλω τὸ κάρφος ⟦ἐκ⟧ τ⟦οῦ⟧ ὀφθαλμ⟦οῦ⟧ σου, καὶ ἰδοὺ ἡ δοκὸς ἐν τῷ ὀφθαλμῷ σοῦ; ὑποκριτά, ἔκβαλε πρῶτον ἐκ τοῦ ὀφθαλμοῦ σοῦ τὴν δοκόν, καὶ τότε διαβλέψεις ἐκβαλεῖν τὸ κάρφος ... τ... ὀφθαλμ... τοῦ ἀδελφοῦ σου. ⁴³οὐ<κ> ἔστιν δένδρον καλὸν ποιοῦν καρπὸν σαπρόν, οὐδὲ ⟦πάλιν⟧ δένδρον σαπρὸν ποιοῦν καρπὸν καλόν. ⁴⁴ἐκ γὰρ τοῦ καρποῦ τὸ δένδρον γινώσκεται. μήτι συλλέγουσιν ἐξ ἀκανθῶν σῦκα ἢ ἐκ τριβόλων σταφυλ⟦ὰς⟧; ⁴⁵ὁ ἀγαθὸς ἄνθρωπος ἐκ τοῦ ἀγαθοῦ θησαυροῦ ἐκβάλλει ἀγαθά, καὶ ὁ πονηρὸς ⟦ἄνθρωπος⟧ ἐκ τοῦ πονηροῦ ⟦θησαυροῦ⟧ ἐκβάλλει πονηρά· ἐκ γὰρ περισσεύματος καρδίας λαλεῖ τὸ στόμα ⟦αὐτοῦ⟧. ⁴⁶τί ... με καλεῖτε· κύριε κύριε, καὶ οὐ ποιεῖτε ἃ λέγω; ⁴⁷πᾶς ὁ ἀκούων μου τ... λόγ... καὶ ποιῶν αὐτούς, ⁴⁸ὅμοιός ἐστιν ἀνθρώπῳ, ὃς ᾠκοδόμησεν ⟦αὐτοῦ τὴν⟧ οἰκίαν ἐπὶ τὴν πέτραν· καὶ κατέβη ἡ βροχὴ καὶ ἦλθον οἱ ποταμοὶ ⟦καὶ ἔπνευσαν οἱ ἄνεμοι⟧ καὶ προσέπεσαν τῇ οἰκίᾳ ἐκείνῃ, καὶ οὐκ ἔπεσεν, τεθεμελίωτο γὰρ ἐπὶ τὴν πέτραν. ⁴⁹καὶ ⟦πᾶς⟧ ὁ ἀκούων ⟦μου τοὺς λόγους⟧ καὶ μὴ ποιῶν ⟦αὐτοὺς⟧ ὅμοιός ἐστιν ἀνθρώπῳ ὃς ᾠκοδόμησεν ⟦αὐτοῦ τὴν⟧ οἰκίαν ἐπὶ τὴν ἄμμον· καὶ κατέβη ἡ βροχὴ καὶ ἦλθον οἱ ποταμοὶ ⟦καὶ ἔπνευσαν οἱ ἄνεμοι⟧ καὶ προσέκοψαν τῇ οἰκίᾳ ἐκείνῃ, καὶ εὐθὺς ἔπεσεν καὶ ἦν ⟦ἡ πτῶσις⟧ αὐτῆς μεγά⟦λη⟧. 9 ⁵⁷καὶ εἶπέν τις αὐτῷ· ἀκολουθήσω σοι ὅπου ἐὰν ἀπέρχῃ. ⁵⁸καὶ εἶπεν αὐτῷ ὁ Ἰησοῦς· αἱ ἀλώπεκες φωλεοὺς ἔχουσιν καὶ τὰ πετεινὰ τοῦ οὐρανοῦ κατασκηνώσεις, ὁ δὲ υἱὸς τοῦ ἀνθρώπου οὐκ ἔχει ποῦ τὴν κεφαλὴν κλίνῃ. ⁵⁹ἕτερος δὲ εἶπεν αὐτῷ· κύριε, ἐπίτρεψόν μοι πρῶτον ἀπελθεῖν καὶ θάψαι τὸν πατέρα μου. ⁶⁰εἶπεν δὲ αὐτῷ· ἀκολούθει μοι καὶ ἄφες τοὺς νεκροὺς θάψαι τοὺς ἑαυτῶν νεκρούς. 10 ²...λεγε... τοῖς μαθηταῖς αὐτοῦ· ὁ μὲν θερισμὸς πολύς, οἱ δὲ ἐργάται ὀλίγοι· δεήθητε οὖν τοῦ κυρίου τοῦ θερισμοῦ ὅπως ἐκβάλῃ ἐργάτας εἰς τὸν θερισμὸν αὐτοῦ. ³ὑπάγετε· ἰδοὺ ἀποστέλλω ὑμᾶς ὡς πρόβατα ἐν μέσῳ λύκων. ⁴μὴ βαστάζετε ⟦βαλλάντιον⟧, μὴ πήραν, μὴ ὑποδήματα, μηδὲ ῥάβδον· καὶ μηδένα κατὰ τὴν ὁδὸν ἀσπάσησθε. ⁵εἰς ἣν δ᾿ ἂν εἰσέλθητε οἰκίαν, ⟦πρῶτον⟧ λέγετε· εἰρήνη ⟦τῷ οἴκῳ τούτῳ⟧. ⁶καὶ ἐὰν μὲν ἐκεῖ ᾖ υἱὸς εἰρήνης, ἐλθάτω ἡ εἰρήνη ὑμῶν ἐπ᾿ αὐτόν· ε⟦ἰ⟧ δὲ μή, ἡ εἰρήνη ὑμῶν ⟦ἐφ᾿⟧ ὑμᾶς ⟦ἐπιστραφήτω⟧. ⁷⟦ἐν αὐτῇ δὲ τῇ οἰκίᾳ⟧ μέν⟦ε⟧τε «ἐσθίοντες καὶ πίνοντες τὰ παρ᾿ αὐτῶν»· ἄξιος γὰρ ὁ ἐργάτης τοῦ μισθοῦ αὐτοῦ. ⟦μὴ μεταβαίνετε ἐξ οἰκίας εἰς οἰκίαν.⟧ ⁸καὶ εἰς ἣν ἂν πόλιν εἰσ⟦έρχησθε⟧ καὶ δέχωνται ὑμᾶς, ⟦«ἐσθίετε τὰ παρατιθέμενα ὑμῖν»⟧ ⁹καὶ θεραπεύετε τοὺς ἐν αὐτῇ ἀσθεν⟦οῦντας⟧ καὶ λέγετε ⟦αὐτοῖς⟧· ... ἤγγικεν ἐφ᾿ ὑμᾶς ἡ βασιλεία τοῦ θεοῦ. ¹⁰εἰς ἣν δ᾿ ἂν πόλιν εἰσέλθητε καὶ μὴ δέχωνται ὑμᾶς, ἐξερχόμενοι ἔξω τ⟦ῆς πόλεως ἐκείνης⟧ ¹¹ἐκτινάξατε τὸν κονιορτὸν τῶν ποδῶν ὑμῶν. ¹⁶ὁ δεχόμενος ὑμᾶς ἐμὲ δέχεται, ⟦καὶ⟧ ὁ ἐμὲ δεχόμενος δέχεται τὸν ἀποστείλαντά με. ²¹ἐν ... εἶπεν· ἐξομολογοῦμαί σοι, πάτερ, κύριε τοῦ οὐρανοῦ καὶ τῆς γῆς, ὅτι ἔκρυψας ταῦτα ἀπὸ σοφῶν καὶ συνετῶν καὶ ἀπεκάλυψας αὐτὰ νηπίοις· ναὶ ὁ πατήρ, ὅτι οὕτως εὐδοκία ἐγένετο ἔμπροσθέν σου. [23]μακάριοι οἱ ὀφθαλμοὶ οἱ βλέποντες ἃ βλέπετε... [24]λέγω γὰρ ὑμῖν ὅτι πολλοὶ προφῆται καὶ βασιλεῖς ...ησαν ἰδεῖν ἃ βλέπετε καὶ οὐκ εἶδαν, καὶ ἀκοῦσαι ἃ ἀκούετε καὶ οὐκ ἤκουσαν. 11 [2]⟦ὅταν⟧ προσεύχ⟦η⟧σθε ⟦λέγετε⟧· πάτερ, ἁγιασθήτω τὸ ὄνομά σου· ἐλθέτω ἡ βασιλεία σου· [3]τὸν ἄρτον ἡμῶν τὸν ἐπιούσιον δὸς ἡμῖν σήμερον· [4]καὶ ἄφες ἡμῖν τὰ ὀφειλήματα ἡμῶν, ὡς καὶ ἡμεῖς ἀφήκαμεν τοῖς ὀφειλέταις ἡμῶν· καὶ μὴ εἰσενέγκῃς ἡμᾶς εἰς πειρασμόν. [Luk 11:5]καὶ εἶπεν πρὸς αὐτούς· τίς ἐξ ὑμῶν ἕξει φίλον καὶ πορεύσεται πρὸς αὐτὸν μεσονυκτίου καὶ εἴπῃ αὐτῷ· φίλε, χρῆσόν μοι τρεῖς ἄρτους, [Luk 11:6]ἐπειδὴ φίλος μου παρεγένετο ἐξ ὁδοῦ πρός με καὶ οὐκ ἔχω ὃ παραθήσω αὐτῷ· [Luk 11:7]κἀκεῖνος ἔσωθεν ἀποκριθεὶς εἴπῃ· μή μοι κόπους πάρεχε· ἤδη ἡ θύρα κέκλεισται καὶ τὰ παιδία μου μετ᾽ ἐμοῦ εἰς τὴν κοίτην εἰσίν· οὐ δύναμαι ἀναστὰς δοῦναί σοι. [Luk 11:8]λέγω ὑμῖν, εἰ καὶ οὐ δώσει αὐτῷ ἀναστὰς διὰ τὸ εἶναι φίλον αὐτοῦ, διά γε τὴν ἀναίδειαν αὐτοῦ ἐγερθεὶς δώσει αὐτῷ ὅσων χρῄζει. [9]λέγω ὑμῖν, αἰτεῖτε καὶ δοθήσεται ὑμῖν, ζητεῖτε καὶ εὑρήσετε, κρούετε καὶ ἀνοιγήσεται ὑμῖν· [10]πᾶς γὰρ ὁ αἰτῶν λαμβάνει καὶ ὁ ζητῶν εὑρίσκει καὶ τῷ κρούοντι ἀνοιγήσεται. [11]... τίς ἐστιν ἐξ ὑμῶν ἄνθρωπος, ὃν αἰτήσει ὁ υἱὸς αὐτοῦ ἄρτον, μὴ λίθον ἐπιδώσει αὐτῷ; [12]ἢ καὶ ἰχθὺν αἰτήσει, μὴ ὄφιν ἐπιδώσει αὐτῷ; [13]εἰ οὖν ὑμεῖς πονηροὶ ὄντες οἴδατε δόματα ἀγαθὰ διδόναι τοῖς τέκνοις ὑμῶν, πόσῳ μᾶλλον ὁ πατὴρ ἐξ οὐρανοῦ δώσει ἀγαθὰ τοῖς αἰτοῦσιν αὐτόν. [33]οὐδεὶς καί<ει> λύχνον καὶ τίθησιν αὐτὸν ⟦εἰς κρύπτην⟧ ἀλλ᾽ ἐπὶ τὴν λυχνίαν, ⟦καὶ λάμπει πᾶσιν τοῖς ἐν τῇ οἰκίᾳ⟧. [34]ὁ λύχνος τοῦ σώματός ἐστιν ὁ ὀφθαλμός. ...αν ὁ ὀφθαλμός σου ἁπλοῦς ᾖ, ὅλον τὸ σῶμά σου φωτεινόν ἐστ⟦ιν⟧· ...ὰν δὲ ὁ ὀφθαλμός σου πονηρὸς ᾖ, ὅλον τὸ σῶμά σου σκοτεινὸν. [35]εἰ οὖν τὸ φῶς τὸ ἐν σοὶ σκότος ἐστίν, τὸ σκότος πόσον. 12 [2]οὐδὲν δὲ κεκαλυμμένον ἐστὶν ὃ οὐκ ἀποκαλυφθήσεται καὶ κρυπτὸν ὃ οὐ γνωσθήσεται. [3]ὃ λέγω ὑμῖν ἐν τῇ σκοτίᾳ εἴπατε ἐν τῷ φωτί, καὶ ὃ εἰς τὸ οὖς ἀκούετε κηρύξατε ἐπὶ τῶν δωμάτων. [4]καὶ μὴ φοβεῖσθε ἀπὸ τῶν ἀποκτεννόντων τὸ σῶμα, τὴν δὲ ψυχὴν μὴ δυναμένων ἀποκτεῖναι· [5]φοβεῖσθε δὲ ... τὸν δυνάμενον καὶ ψυχὴν καὶ σῶμα ἀπολέσαι ἐν τ<ῇ> γεέννῃ. [6]οὐχὶ ⟦πέντε⟧ στρουθία πωλοῦνται ἀσσαρί⟦ων δύο⟧; καὶ ἓν ἐξ αὐτῶν οὐ πεσεῖται ἐπὶ τὴν γῆν ἄνευ τοῦ ⟦πατρὸς ὑμῶν⟧. [7]ὑμῶν ⟦δὲ⟧ καὶ αἱ τρίχες τῆς κεφαλῆς πᾶσαι ἠριθμη⟦μέναι εἰσίν⟧. μὴ φοβεῖσθε· πολλῶν στρουθίων διαφέρετε ὑμεῖς. [11]ὅταν δὲ εἰσφέρωσιν ὑμᾶς ⟦<εἰς>⟧ τὰς συναγωγάς, μὴ μεριμνήσητε πῶς ἢ τί εἴπητε· [12]⟦τὸ⟧ γὰρ ⟦ἅγιον πνεῦμα διδάξει⟧ ὑμ⟦ᾶς⟧ ἐν ...ῇ τῇ ὥρᾳ τί εἴπ<ητε>. [22]διὰ τοῦτο λέγω ὑμῖν· μὴ μεριμνᾶτε τῇ ψυχῇ ὑμῶν τί φάγητε, μηδὲ τῷ σώματι ὑμῶν τί ἐνδύσησθε. [23]οὐχὶ ἡ ψυχὴ πλεῖόν ἐστιν τῆς τροφῆς καὶ τὸ σῶμα τοῦ ἐνδύματος; [24]κατανοήσατε τοὺς κόρακας ὅτι οὐ σπείρουσιν οὐδὲ θερίζουσιν οὐδὲ συνάγουσιν εἰς ἀποθήκας, καὶ ὁ θεὸς τρέφει αὐτούς· οὐχ ὑμεῖς μᾶλλον διαφέρετε τῶν πετεινῶν; [25]τίς δὲ ἐξ ὑμῶν μεριμνῶν δύναται προσθεῖναι ἐπὶ τὴν ἡλικίαν αὐτοῦ πῆχυν ...; [26]καὶ περὶ ἐνδύματος τί μεριμνᾶτε; [27]κατα⟦μάθε⟧τε τὰ κρίνα πῶς αὐξάν⟦ει⟧· οὐ κοπι⟦ᾷ⟧ οὐδὲ νήθ⟦ει⟧· λέγω δὲ ὑμῖν, οὐδὲ Σολομὼν ἐν πάσῃ τῇ δόξῃ αὐτοῦ περιεβάλετο ὡς ἓν τούτων. [28]εἰ δὲ ἐν ἀγρῷ τὸν χόρτον ὄντα σήμερον καὶ αὔριον εἰς κλίβανον βαλλόμενον ὁ θεὸς οὕτως ἀμφιέ⟦ννυσιν⟧, οὐ πολλῷ μᾶλλον ὑμᾶς, ὀλιγόπιστοι; ²⁹μὴ ⟦οὖν⟧ μεριμνήσητε λέγοντες· τί φάγωμεν; ⟦ἢ⟧· τί πίωμεν; ⟦ἢ⟧· τί περιβαλώμεθα; ³⁰πάντα γὰρ ταῦτα τὰ ἔθνη ἐπιζητοῦσιν· οἶδεν ⟦γὰρ⟧ ὁ πατὴρ ὑμῶν ὅτι χρῄζετε τούτων ⟦ἁπάντων⟧. ³¹ζητεῖτε δὲ τὴν βασιλείαν αὐτοῦ, καὶ ταῦτα ⟦πάντα⟧ προστεθήσεται ὑμῖν. ³³«μὴ θησαυρίζετε ὑμῖν θησαυροὺς ἐπὶ τῆς γῆς, ὅπου σὴς καὶ βρῶσις ἀφανίζει καὶ ὅπου κλέπται διορύσσουσιν καὶ κλέπτουσιν·» θησαυρίζετε δὲ ὑμῖν θησαυρο... ἐν οὐραν⟦ῷ⟧, ὅπου οὔτε σὴς οὔτε βρῶσις ἀφανίζει καὶ ὅπου κλέπται οὐ διορύσσουσιν οὐδὲ κλέπτουσιν· ³⁴ὅπου γάρ ἐστιν ὁ θησαυρός σου, ἐκεῖ ἔσται καὶ ἡ καρδία σου. ³⁹⟦ἐκεῖν⟧ο δὲ γινώσκετε ὅτι εἰ ᾔδει ὁ οἰκοδεσπότης ποίᾳ φυλακῇ ὁ κλέπτης ἔρχεται, οὐκ ἂν ⟦εἴας⟧εν διορυχθῆναι τὸν οἶκον αὐτοῦ. ⁴²τίς ἄρα ἐστὶν ὁ πιστὸς δοῦλος ⟦καὶ⟧ φρόνιμος ὃν κατέστησεν ὁ κύριος ἐπὶ τῆς οἰκετείας αὐτοῦ τοῦ δο⟦ῦ⟧ναι ⟦αὐτοῖς⟧ ἐν καιρῷ ⟦σιτομέτριον⟧; ⁴³μακάριος ὁ δοῦλος ἐκεῖνος, ὃν ἐλθὼν ὁ κύριος αὐτοῦ εὑρήσει οὕτως ποιοῦντα· ⁴⁴⟦ἀμὴν⟧ λέγω ὑμῖν ὅτι ἐπὶ πᾶσιν τοῖς ὑπάρχουσιν αὐτοῦ καταστήσει αὐτόν. ⁵⁸⟦ἕως ὅτου⟧ ... μετὰ τοῦ ἀντιδίκου σου ἐν τῇ ὁδῷ, δὸς ἐργασίαν ἀπηλλάχθαι ἀπ' αὐτοῦ, μήποτε σε παραδῷ ⟦ὁ ἀντίδικος⟧ τῷ κριτῇ καὶ ὁ κριτὴς τῷ ὑπηρέτῃ καὶ ⟦ὁ <ὑπηρέτης> σε⟧ β⟦α⟧λ⟦εῖ⟧ εἰς φυλακήν. ⁵⁹λέγω σοι, οὐ μὴ ἐξέλθῃς ἐκεῖθεν, ἕως τὸ⟦ν⟧ ἔσχατον ⟦κοδράντην⟧ ἀποδῷς. 13 ¹⁸τίνι ὁμοία ἐστὶν ἡ βασιλεία τοῦ θεοῦ καὶ τίνι ὁμοιώσω αὐτήν; ¹⁹ὁμοία ἐστὶν κόκκῳ σινάπεως, ὃν λαβὼν ἄνθρωπος ἔβαλεν εἰς ⟦κῆπ⟧ον αὐτοῦ· καὶ ηὔξησεν καὶ ἐγένετο εἰς δένδρον, καὶ τὰ πετεινὰ τοῦ οὐρανοῦ κατεσκήνωσεν ἐν τοῖς κλάδοις αὐτοῦ. ²⁰⟦καὶ πάλιν⟧· τίνι ὁμοιώσω τὴν βασιλείαν τοῦ θεοῦ; ²¹ὁμοία ἐστὶν ζύμῃ, ἣν λαβοῦσα γυνὴ ἐνέκρυψεν εἰς ἀλεύρου σάτα τρία ἕως οὗ ἐζυμώθη ὅλον. ²⁴εἰσέλθατε διὰ τῆς στενῆς θύρας, ὅτι πολλοί ζητήσουσιν εἰσελθεῖν καὶ ὀλίγοι ⟦εἰσὶν οἱ <εἰσερχόμενοι δι'> αὐτῆ<ς>⟧. ²⁵ἀφ' οὗ ἂν ⟦ἐγερθῇ⟧ ὁ ⟦οἰκοδεσπότης⟧ καὶ κλείσ⟦ῃ τ⟧ὴ⟦ν⟧ θύρα⟦ν καὶ ἄρξησθε ἔξω ἑστάναι καὶ κρούειν τὴν θύραν⟧ λέγοντες· κύριε, ἄνοιξον ἡμῖν, καὶ ἀποκριθεὶς ἐρεῖ ὑμῖν· οὐκ οἶδα ὑμᾶς. 14 ¹⁶ἄνθρωπός τις ἐποίει δεῖπνον ⟦μέγα, καὶ ἐκάλεσεν πολλοὺς⟧ ¹⁷καὶ ἀπέστειλεν τὸν δοῦλον αὐτοῦ ⟦τῇ ὥρᾳ τοῦ δείπνου⟧ εἰπεῖν τοῖς κεκλημένοις· ἔρχεσθε, ὅτι ἤδη ἕτοιμά ἐστιν. ¹⁸... ἀγρόν, ... ?¹⁹? ... ?²⁰? ... ²¹«καὶ < > ὁ δοῦλος < > τῷ κυρίῳ αὐτοῦ ταῦτα.» τότε ὀργισθεὶς ὁ οἰκοδεσπότης εἶπεν τῷ δούλῳ αὐτοῦ· ²³ἔξελθε εἰς τὰς ὁδοὺς καὶ ὅσους ἐὰν εὕρ<ῃς> καλέσ<ον>, ἵνα γεμισθῇ μου ὁ οἶκος. ²⁶⟦<ὃς>⟧ οὐ μισεῖ τὸν πατέρα καὶ τὴν μητέρα οὐ <δύναται εἶναί> μου <μαθητής>, καὶ ⟦<ὃς>⟧ <οὐ μισεῖ> τ<ὸ>ν υἱὸν καὶ τ<ὴν> θυγατέρα οὐ δύναται εἶναί μου μαθητής. ²⁷... ὃς οὐ λαμβάνει τὸν σταυρὸν αὐτοῦ καὶ ἀκολουθεῖ ὀπίσω μου, οὐ δύναται εἶναί μου μαθητής. 17 ³³⟦ὁ⟧ εὑρ⟦ὼν⟧ τὴν ψυχὴν αὐτοῦ ἀπολέσει αὐτήν, καὶ ⟦ὁ⟧ ἀπολές⟦ας⟧ τὴν ψυχὴν αὐτοῦ ⟦ἕνεκεν ἐμοῦ⟧ εὑρήσει αὐτήν. 14 ³⁴⟦καλὸν⟧ τὸ ἅλας· ἐὰν δὲ τὸ ἅλας μωρανθῇ, ἐν τίνι ⟦ἀρτυ⟧θήσεται; ³⁵οὔτε εἰς γῆν οὔτε εἰς κοπρίαν ⟦εὔθετόν ἐστιν⟧, ἔξω βάλλουσιν αὐτό. 16 ¹³οὐδεὶς δύναται δυσὶ κυρίοις δουλεύειν· ἢ γὰρ τὸν ἕνα μισήσει καὶ τὸν ἕτερον ἀγαπήσει, ἢ ἑνὸς ἀνθέξεται καὶ τοῦ ἑτέρου καταφρονήσει. οὐ δύνασθε θεῷ δουλεύειν καὶ μαμωνᾷ. ¹⁸πᾶς ὁ ἀπολύων τὴν γυναῖκα αὐτοῦ ⟦καὶ γαμῶν <ἄλλην>⟧ μοιχεύει, καὶ ὁ ἀπολελυμένην γαμῶν μοιχ⟦εύει⟧. 17 ¹ἀνάγκη ἐλθεῖν τὰ σκάνδαλα, πλὴν οὐαὶ δι' οὗ ἔρχεται. ²λυσιτελεῖ αὐτῷ 〚εἰ〛 λίθος μυλικὸς περίκειται περὶ τὸν τράχηλον αὐτοῦ καὶ ἔρριπται εἰς τὴν θάλασσαν ἢ ἵνα σκανδαλίσῃ τῶν μικρῶν τούτων ἕνα. ³ἐὰν ἁμαρτήσῃ 〚εἰς σὲ〛 ὁ ἀδελφός σου, ἐπιτίμησον αὐτῷ, καὶ ἐὰν 〚μετανοήσῃ〛 ἄφες αὐτῷ. ⁴καὶ ἐὰν ἑπτάκις τῆς ἡμέρας ἁμαρτήσῃ εἰς σὲ, καὶ ἑπτάκις ἀφήσεις αὐτῷ. ⁶εἰ ἔχετε πίστιν ὡς κόκκον σινάπεως, ἐλέγετε ἂν τῇ συκαμίνῳ ταύτῃ· ἐκριζώθητι καὶ φυτεύθητι ἐν τῇ θαλάσσῃ· καὶ ὑπήκουσεν ἂν ὑμῖν. 15 ⁴Τίς < > ἄνθρωπος ἐξ ὑμῶν < > ἔχ< > ἑκατὸν πρόβατα καὶ 〚ἀπολέσας〛 ἓν ἐξ αὐτῶν, οὐ〚χὶ ἀφής〛ει τὰ ἐνενήκοντα ἐννέα 〚ἐπὶ τὰ ὄρη〛 καὶ πορευ〚θεὶς ζητεῖ〛 τὸ 〚ἀπολωλὸς〛; ⁵καὶ ἐὰν γένηται εὑρεῖν αὐτό, ⁷λέγω ὑμῖν ὅτι χαίρει ἐπ' αὐτῷ μᾶλλον ἢ ἐπὶ τοῖς ἐνενήκοντα ἐννέα τοῖς μὴ πεπλανημένοις. ⁸〚«ἢ τίς γυνὴ ἔχουσα δέκα δραχμὰς ἐὰν ἀπολέσῃ δραχμὴν μίαν, οὐχὶ ἅπτει λύχνον καὶ σαροῖ τὴν οἰκίαν καὶ ζητεῖ ἕως εὕρῃ; ⁹καὶ εὑροῦσα καλεῖ τὰς φίλας καὶ γείτονας λέγουσα· χάρητέ μοι, ὅτι εὗρον τὴν δραχμὴν ἣν ἀπώλεσα. ¹⁰οὕτως, λέγω ὑμῖν, γίνεται χαρὰ <ἔμπροσθεν> τῶν ἀγγέλων ἐπὶ ἑνὶ ἁμαρτωλῷ μετανοοῦντι.»〛 19 ¹²ἄνθρωπός τις ἀποδημῶν ¹³ἐκάλεσεν δέκα δούλους ἑαυτοῦ καὶ ἔδωκεν αὐτοῖς δέκα μνᾶς 〚καὶ εἶπεν αὐτο<ῖ>ς· πραγματεύσασθε ἐν ᾧ ἔρχομαι.〛 ¹⁵... 〚μετὰ〛 ... 〚πολὺν χρόνον〛 ἔρχεται ὁ κύριος τῶν δούλων ἐκείνων καὶ συναίρει λόγον μετ' αὐτῶν. ¹⁶καὶ 〚<ἢ>λθ<εν>〛 ὁ πρῶτος λέγων· κύριε, ἡ μνᾶ σου δέκα προσηργάσατο μνᾶς. ¹⁷καὶ εἶπεν αὐτῷ· εὖ, ἀγαθὲ δοῦλε, ἐπὶ ὀλίγα ἧς πιστός, ἐπὶ πολλῶν σε καταστήσω. ¹⁸καὶ ἦλθεν ὁ 〚δεύτερος〛 λέγων· κύριε, ἡ μνᾶ σου ἐποίησεν πέντε μνᾶς. ¹⁹εἶπεν 〚αὐτ〛ῷ· 〚εὖ, ἀγαθὲ δοῦλε ἐπὶ ὀλίγα ἧς πιστός,〛 ἐπὶ πολλῶν σε καταστήσω. ²⁰καὶ ἦλθεν ὁ ἕτερος λέγων· κύριε, ²¹〚ἔγνων〛 σε ὅτι σκληρὸς εἶ ἄνθρωπος, θερίζων ὅπου οὐκ ἔσπειρας καὶ συνάγων ὅθεν οὐ διεσκόρπισας, καὶ φοβ[ηθεὶς ἀπελθὼν] ἔκρυψα 〚<τὴν μνᾶν> σου〛 ἐν 〚τῇ γῇ〛· ἴδ〚ε〛 ἔχεις τὸ σόν. ²²λέγει αὐτῷ· πονηρὲ δοῦλε, ᾔδεις ὅτι θερίζω ὅπου οὐκ ἔσπειρα καὶ συνάγω ὅθεν οὐ διεσκόρπισα; ²³〚ἔδει σε οὖν βαλεῖν〛 μου τ〚ὰ〛 ἀργύρι〚α τοῖς〛 τραπεζ〚ίταις〛, καὶ ἐλθὼν ἐγὼ ἐκομισάμην ἂν τὸ ἐμὸν σὺν τόκῳ. ²⁴ἄρατε οὖν ἀπ' αὐτοῦ τὴν μνᾶν καὶ δότε τῷ ἔχοντι τὰς δέκα μνᾶς·

A.2 English Translation of Q's Formative Stratum

6 ²⁰<...> And 〚rais〛ing his 〚eyes to〛 his disciples he said: Blessed are 〚«you»〛, poor, for God's reign is for 〚you〛. ²⁰Blessed are 〚«you»〛 who hunger, for 〚you〛 will eat 〚your〛 fill. Blessed are 〚«you»〛 who 〚mourn〛, for 〚<you> will be consoled〛. ²¹Blessed are you when they insult and 〚persecute〛 you, and 〚say every kind of〛 evil 〚against〛 you because of the son of humanity. ²³Be glad and 〚exult〛, for vast is your reward in heaven. ²⁷Love your enemies ²⁸〚and〛 pray for those 〚persecuting〛 you, ³⁵so that you may become sons of your Father, for he raises his sun on bad and 〚good and rains on the just and unjust〛. ²⁹〚The one who slaps〛 you on the cheek, offer 〚him〛 the other as well; and 〚to the person wanting to take you to court and get〛 your shirt, 〚turn over to him〛

the coat as well. $^{\text{Matt 5:41}}$ ⟦«And the one who conscripts you for one mile, go with him a second.»⟧ ^{30}To the one who asks of you, give; and ⟦from the one who borrows⟧, do not ⟦ask⟧ back ⟦«what is»⟧ yours. ^{31}And the way you want people to treat you, that is how you treat them. ^{32}... If you love those loving you, what reward do you have? Do not even tax collectors do the same? ^{34}And if you ⟦lend «to those» from whom you hope to receive, what <reward do> you <have>?⟧ Do not even ⟦the Gentiles⟧ do the same? ^{36}Be full of pity, just as your Father ... is full of pity. ^{37}And do not judge, so that you are not judged; ^{38}for that measure you measure with, it will be measured to you. ^{39}Can a blind person show the way to a blind person? Will not both fall into a pit? ^{40}A disciple is not superior to the teacher. ⟦It is enough for the disciple that he become⟧ like his teacher. ^{41}And why do you see the speck in your brother's eye, but the beam in your own eye you overlook? ^{42}How «can you» say to your brother: Let me throw out the speck ⟦from⟧ your eye, and just look at the beam in your own eye? Hypocrite, first throw out from your own eye the beam, and then you will see clearly to throw out the speck «in» your brother's eye. ... ^{43}No healthy tree bears rotten fruit, nor ⟦on the other hand⟧ does a decayed tree bear healthy fruit. ^{44}For from the fruit the tree is known. Are figs picked from thorns, or grape⟦s⟧ from thistles? ^{45}The good person from «one's» good treasure casts up good things, and the evil ⟦person⟧ from the evil ⟦treasure⟧ casts up evil things. For from exuberance of heart ⟦one's⟧ mouth speaks. ^{46}... Why do you call me: Master, Master, and do not do what I say? ^{47}Everyone hearing my words and acting on them ^{48}is like a person who built ⟦one's⟧ house on bedrock; and the rain poured down and the flash-floods came, ⟦and the winds blew⟧ and pounded that house, and it did not collapse, for it was founded on bedrock. ^{49}And ⟦everyone⟧ who hears ⟦my sayings⟧, and does not act on ⟦them⟧ is like a person who built ⟦one's⟧ house on the sand; and the rain poured down and the flash-floods came, ⟦and the winds blew⟧ and battered that house, and promptly it collapsed, and its ⟦fall⟧ was devastating. 9 ^{57}And someone said to him: I will follow you wherever you go. ^{58}And Jesus said to him: Foxes have holes, and birds of the sky have nests; but the son of humanity does not have anywhere he can lay his head. ^{59}But another said to him: Master, permit me first to go and bury my father. ^{60}But he said to him: Follow me, and leave the dead to bury their own dead. 10 ^{2}He said to his disciples: The harvest is plentiful, but the workers are few. So ask the Lord of the harvest to dispatch workers into his harvest. ^{3}Be on your way! Look, I send you like sheep in the midst of wolves. ^{4}Carry no ⟦purse⟧, nor knapsack, nor sandals, nor stick, and greet no one on the road. ^{5}Into whatever house you enter, ⟦first⟧ say: Peace ⟦to this house⟧! ^{6}And if a son of peace be there, let your peace come upon him; but if not, ⟦let⟧ your peace ⟦return upon⟧ you. ^{7}⟦And at that house⟧ remain, «eating and drinking whatever they provide», for the worker is worthy of one's reward. ⟦Do not move around from house to house.⟧ ^{8}And whatever town you enter and they take you in, eat what is set before you, ^{9}and cure the sick there, and say ⟦to them⟧: The kingdom of God has reached unto you. [10]But into whatever town you enter and they do not take you in, on going out ⟦from that town⟧, [11]shake off the dust from your feet. [16]Whoever takes you in takes me in, ⟦and⟧ whoever takes me in takes in the one who sent me. 10 [21]At «that time» he said: I thank you, Father, Lord of heaven and earth, for you hid these things from sages and the learned, and disclosed them to children. Yes, Father, for that is what it has pleased you to do. [23]Blessed are the eyes that see what you see ... [24]For I tell you: Many prophets and kings wanted to see what you see, but never saw it, and to hear what you hear, but never heard it. 11 [2]⟦When⟧ you pray, ⟦say⟧: Father – may your name be kept holy! – let your reign come: [3]Our day's bread give us today; [4]and cancel our debts for us, as we too have cancelled for those in debt to us; and do not introduce us to a trial. [Luk 11:5]And he said to them: Which of you who has a friend will go to him at midnight and say to him, Friend, lend me three loaves, [Luk 11:6]for a friend of mine has arrived on a journey, and I have nothing to set before him; [Luk 11:7]and he will answer from within, Do not bother me; the door is now shut, and my children are with me in bed. I cannot get up and give you anything? [Luk 11:8]I tell you, though he will not get up and give him anything because he is his friend, yet because of his impudence he will rise and give him whatever he needs. [9]I tell you: ask and it will be given to you, search and you will find, knock and it will be opened to you. [10]For everyone who asks receives, and the one who searches finds, and to the one who knocks will it be opened. [11]... What person of you, whose son asks for bread, will give him a stone? [12]Or again when he asks for a fish, will give him a snake? [13]So if you, though evil, know how to give good gifts to your children, by how much more will the Father from heaven give good things to those who ask him! [33]No one light<s> a lamp and puts it ⟦in a hidden place⟧, but on the lamp stand, ⟦and it gives light for everyone in the house⟧. [34]The lamp of the body is the eye. If your eye is generous, your whole body ⟦is⟧ radiant; but if your eye is jaundiced, your whole body «is» dark. [35]So if the light within you is dark, how great «must» the darkness «be»! 12 [2]Nothing is covered up that will not be exposed, and hidden that will not be known. [3]What I say to you in the dark, speak in the light; and what you hear «whispered» in the ear, proclaim on the housetops. [4]And do not be afraid of those who kill the body, but cannot kill the soul. [5]But fear ... the one who is able to destroy both the soul and body in Gehenna. [6]Are not ⟦five⟧ sparrows sold for ⟦two⟧ cents? And yet not one of them will fall to earth without ⟦your Father's⟧ «consent». [7]But even the hairs of your head all are numbered. Do not be afraid, you are worth more than many sparrows. [11]When they bring you before synagogues, do not be anxious about how or what you are to say; [12]for ⟦the holy Spirit will teach⟧ you in that ... hour what you are to say. [22]Therefore I tell you: Do not be anxious about your life, what you are to eat, nor about your body, with what you are to clothe yourself. [23]Is not life more than food, and the body than clothing? [24]Consider the ravens: They neither sow nor reap nor gather into barns, and yet God feeds them. Are you not better than the birds? ²⁵And who of you by being anxious is able to add to one's stature a ... cubit? ²⁶And why are you anxious about clothing? ²⁷⟦Observe⟧ the lilies, how they grow: They do not work nor do they spin. Yet I tell you: Not even Solomon in all his glory was arrayed like one of these. ²⁸But if in the field the grass, there today and tomorrow thrown into the oven, God clothes thus, will he not much more clothe you, persons of petty faith! ²⁹⟦So⟧ do not be anxious, saying: What are we to eat? ⟦Or:⟧ What are we to drink? ⟦Or:⟧ What are we to wear? ³⁰For all these the Gentiles seek; ⟦for⟧ your Father knows that you need them ⟦all⟧. ³¹But seek his kingdom, and ⟦all⟧ these shall be granted to you. ³³«Do not treasure for yourselves treasures on earth, where moth and gnawing deface and where robbers dig through and rob,» but treasure for yourselves treasure«s» in heaven, where neither moth nor gnawing defaces and where robbers do not dig through nor rob. ³⁴For where your treasure is, there will also be your heart. ³⁹But know this: If the householder had known in which watch the robber was coming, he would not have let his house be dug into. ⁴²Who then is the faithful ⟦and⟧ wise slave whom the master put over his household to give ⟦them⟧ ⟦a ration of grain⟧ on time? ⁴³Blessed is that slave whose master, on coming, will find so doing. ⁴⁴⟦Amen⟧, I tell you, he will appoint him over all his possessions. ⁵⁸⟦While⟧ you «go along» with your opponent on the way, make an effort to get loose from him, lest ⟦the opponent⟧ hand you over to the judge, and the judge to the assistant, and ⟦the ⟨assistant⟩⟧ throw ⟦you⟧ into prison. ⁵⁹I say to you: You will not get out of there until you pay the last ⟦penny⟧! 13 ¹⁸What is the kingdom of God like, and with what am I to compare it? ¹⁹It is like a seed of mustard which a person took and threw into his ⟦garden⟧. And it grew and developed into a tree, and the birds of the sky nested in its branches. ²⁰⟦And again⟧: With what am I to compare the kingdom of God? ²¹It is like yeast, which a woman took and hid in three measures of flour until it was fully fermented. ²⁴Enter through the narrow door, for many will seek to enter and few ⟦are those who ⟨enter through⟩ it.⟧ ²⁵When the ⟦householder has arisen⟧ and locked the door, ⟦and you begin to stand outside and knock on the door⟧, saying: Master, open for us, and he will answer you: I do not know you. 14 ¹⁶A certain person prepared a ⟦large⟧ dinner, ⟦and invited many⟧. ¹⁷And he sent his slave ⟦at the time of the dinner⟧ to say to the invited: Come, for it is now ready. ¹⁸«One declined because of his» farm. ?¹⁹?«Another declined because of his business.» ?²⁰?«A third declined because of his wedding.» ²¹«And the slave, ⟨on coming, said⟩ these things to his master.» Then the householder, enraged, said to his slave: ²³Go out on the roads, and whomever you find, invite, so that my house may be filled. ²⁶⟦⟨The one who⟩⟧ does not hate father and mother ⟨can⟩ not ⟨be⟩ my ⟨disciple⟩; and ⟦⟨the one who⟩⟧ ⟨does not hate⟩ son and daughter cannot be my disciple. ²⁷... The one who does not take one's cross and follow after me cannot be my disciple. 17 ³³... The one who does not take one's cross and follow after me cannot be my disciple. 14 ³⁴⟦The one who⟧ finds one's life will lose it, and ⟦the one who]] loses one's life [[for my sake]] will find it. ³⁴Salt [[is good]]; but if salt becomes insipid, with what will it be [[seasoned]]? ³⁵Neither for the earth nor for the dunghill [[is it fit]] – it gets thrown out. 16 ¹³No one can serve two masters; for a person will either hate the one and love the other, or be devoted to the one and despise the other. You cannot serve God and Mammon. ¹⁸Everyone who divorces his wife [[and marries another]] commits adultery, and the one who marries a divorcée commits adultery. 17 ¹It is necessary for enticements to come, but woe «to the one» through whom they come! ²It is better for him [[if]] a millstone is put around his neck and he is thrown into the sea, than that he should entice one of these little ones. ³If your brother sins [[against you]], rebuke him; and if [[he repents]], forgive him. ⁴And if seven times a day he sins against you, also seven times shall you forgive him. ⁶If you have faith like a mustard seed, you might say to this mulberry tree: Be uprooted and planted in the sea! And it would obey you. 15 ⁴Which person «is there» among you «who» has a hundred sheep, [[on losing]] one of them, [[will]] not leave the ninety-nine [[in the mountains]] and go [[hunt for]] the [[lost one]]? ⁵And if it should happen that he finds it, ⁷I say to you that he rejoices over it more than over the ninety-nine that did not go astray. ⁸[[«Or what woman who has ten coins, if she were to lose one coin, would not light a lamp and sweep the house and hunt until she finds? ⁹And on finding she calls the friends and neighbours, saying: Rejoice with me, for I found the coin which I lost. ¹⁰Just so, I tell you, there is joy before the angels over one repenting sinner.»]] ... 19 ¹²A certain person, on taking a trip, ¹³called ten of his slaves and gave them ten minas [[and said to them: Do business until I come]]. ¹⁵... [[After a long time]] the master of those slaves comes and settles accounts with them. ¹⁶And the first [[came]] saying: Master, your mina has produced ten more minas. ¹⁷And he said to him: Well done, good slave, you have been faithful over a pittance, I will set you over much. ¹⁸And the [[second]] came saying: Master, your mina has earned five minas. ¹⁹He said to [[him: Well done, good slave, you have been faithful over little,]] I will set you over much. ²⁰And the other came saying: Master, ²¹[[I knew]] you, that you are a hard person, reaping where you did not sow and gathering up from where you did not winnow; and, scared, I [[went «and»]] hid [[your <mina>]] in [[the ground]]. Here, you have what belongs to you. ²²He said to him: Wicked slave! You knew that I reap where I have not sown, and gather up from where I have not winnowed? ²³[[Then you had to invest]] my money [[with the]] money [[changers]]! And at my coming I would have received what belongs to me plus interest. ²⁴So take from him the mina and give «it» to the one who has the ten minas.

Bibliography

Aberbach, Moshe. 1994. *Labor, Crafts and Commerce in Ancient Israel.* Jerusalem: The Magnes Press.

Alexander, Loveday. 2006. "What Is a Gospel?," pp. 13–33 in Stephen C. Barton (ed.), *The Cambridge Companion to the Gospels.* Cambridge Companions to Religion. Cambridge: Cambridge University Press.

Allison, Dale C. 1997. *The Jesus Tradition in Q.* Harrisburg, PA: Trinity.

–. 2000. *The Intertextual Jesus: Scripture in Q.* Harrisburg, PA: Trinity.

–. 2001. "Q's New Exodus and the Historical Jesus," pp. 395–428 in Andreas Lindemann (ed.), *The Sayings Source Q and the Historical Jesus.* BETL 158. Leuven: Leuven University Press and Peeters.

–. 2004. *Matthew: A Shorter Commentary.* London: T&T Clark.

–. 2010. *Constructing Jesus: Memory, Imagination, and History.* Grand Rapids, MI: Baker Academic.

Amon, Josef E. 1997. "Evaluations," pp. 317–319 in Albrecht Garsky, Christoph Heil, Thomas Hieke, and Josef E. Amon (ed. Shawn Carruth), *Q 12:49–59: Children against Parents; Judging the Time; Settling out of Court.* Documenta Q. Leuven: Peeters.

Amundsen, Leiv (ed.). 1935. *Greek Ostraca in the University of Michigan Collection: Texts, Part 1.* University of Michigan Studies, Humanistic Series 34. Ann Arbor, MI: University of Michigan Press.

Andrews, Antony. 1967. *The Greeks.* The History of Human Society. London: Hutchinson.

Arnal, William E. 2001. *Jesus and the Village Scribes: Galilean Conflicts and the Setting of Q.* Augsburg, MN: Fortress.

Aubert, Jean-Jacques. 1994. *Business Managers in Ancient Rome: A Social and Economic Study of* Institores, *200 B.C. – A.D. 250.* Columbia Studies in the Classical Tradition 21. Leiden: Brill.

Bagnall, Roger S. 1993. "Slavery and Society in Late Roman Egypt," pp. 220–240 in Baruch Halpern and Deborah W. Hobson (eds.), *Law, Politics and Society in the Ancient Mediterranean World.* Sheffield: Sheffield Academic Press.

Bagnall, Roger S., and Dirk D. Obbink. 1996. *Columbia Papyri, Volume 10.* American Studies in Papyrology 34. Atlanta, GA: Scholars Press.

Bailey, Kenneth E. 2008. *Jesus through Middle Eastern Eyes: Cultural Studies in the Gospels.* Downers Grove, IL: SPCK.

Batten, Alicia J. 1994. "More Queries for Q: Women and Christian Origins," in *Biblical Theology Bulletin* 24, pp. 44–51.

–. 2014. "The Urbanization of Jesus Traditions in James," pp. 78–96 in Alicia J. Batten and John S. Kloppenborg (eds.), *James, 1 & 2 Peter, and Early Jesus Traditions.* London: Bloomsbury.

Bazzana, Giovanni B. 2015. *Kingdom of Bureaucracy: The Political Theology of Village Scribes in the Sayings Gospel Q.* BETL 274. Leuven: Peeters.

Betz, Hans D. 1995. *The Sermon on the Mount: A Commentary on the Sermon on the Mount, Including the Sermon on the Plain (Matthew 5:3–7:27 and Luke 6:20–49).* Hermeneia. English translation edited by Adela Y. Collins. Minneapolis, MN: Fortress.

Beutner, Edward F. 2007a. "A Comedy with a Tragic Turn: The Dishonest Manager," pp. 59–63 in Edward F. Beutner (ed.), *Listening to the Parables of Jesus.* Jesus Seminar Guides 2. Santa Rosa, CA: Polebridge.

–. 2007b. "A Mercy Unextended: Matthew 18:23–34," pp. 33–39 in Edward F. Beutner (ed.), *Listening to the Parables of Jesus.* Jesus Seminar Guides 2. Santa Rosa, CA: Polebridge.

–. 2007c. "Introduction: The Haunt of Parable," pp. 1–5 in Edward F. Beutner (ed.), *Listening to the Parables of Jesus.* Jesus Seminar Guides 2. Santa Rosa, CA: Polebridge.

Bilabel, Friedrich, Friedrich Preisigke, and Hans-Albert Rupprecht (eds.). 1981–1983. *Sammelbuch griechischer Urkunden aus Ägypten, Band XIV.* Wiesbaden: Otto Harrassowitz.

Blair, John F. 1896. *The Apostolic Gospel with a Critical Reconstruction of the Text.* London: Smith, Elder & Co.

Blasi, A. J. 1986. "Role Structures in the Early Hellenistic Church," in *Sociological Analysis* 47/3, pp. 226–248.

Blomberg, Craig L. 1990. *Interpreting the Parables.* Leicester: Apollos.

Bock, Darrell L. 1994. *Luke 1:1–9:50.* Baker Exegetical Commentary on the New Testament. Grand Rapids, MI: Baker.

–. 1996. *Luke 9:51–24:53.* Baker Exegetical Commentary on the New Testament. Grand Rapids, MI: Baker.

Boer, Roland, and Christina Petterson. 2017. *Time of Troubles: A New Economic Framework for Early Christianity.* Minneapolis, MN: Fortress.

Borg, Marcus J. 1984. *Conflict, Holiness, and Politics in the Teaching of Jesus.* Lewiston, NY: Edwin Mellen.

–. [1984] 1998. *Conflict, Holiness and Politics in the Teachings of Jesus.* New York, NY: Continuum.

–. 1994. *Jesus in Contemporary Scholarship.* Valley Forge, PA: Trinity.

Bork, Arne. 2014. "Moving to the Kingdom of God: The Intention of Q in Light of the Semantics of Room, Space and Characters," presented at the Society of Biblical Literature Annual Meeting, San Diego, CA: 10 pages.

Bostock, John (ed.). 1855. *The Natural History.* Medford, MA: Taylor & Francis.

Botha, Pieter J. J. 1996. "Gelykenisse in konteks: Aantekeninge oor Matteus 24:45–25:30," in *Skrif en Kerk* 17/2, pp. 271–291.

Bovon, François. 1996. *Das Evangelium nach Lukas, 2. Teilband: Lk 9,51–14,35.* Zürich: Benzinger; Neukirchen-Vluyn: Neukirchener.

–. 2001. "Tracing the Trajectory of Luke 13·22–30 back to Q: A Study in Lukan Redaction," pp. 285–294 in Andreas Lindemann (ed.), *The Sayings Source Q and the Historical Jesus.* BETL 158. Leuven: Leuven University Press and Peeters.

Bradley, Keith R. 1984. *Slaves and Masters in the Roman Empire: A Study in Social Control.* Collection Latomus 185. Brussels: Latomus.

–. 1994. *Slavery and Society at Rome.* Key Themes in Ancient History. Cambridge: Cambridge University Press.

Brenton, Lancelot C. L. 1870. *The Septuagint Version of the Old Testament: English Translation.* London: Samuel Bagster and Sons.

Broadhead, Edwin K. 2001. "The Fourth Gospel and the Synoptic Sayings Source," in Robert T. Fortna and Tom Thatcher (eds.), *Jesus in Johannine Tradition*, pp 291–301. Louisville, KY: Westminster John Knox.

Brotzman, Ellis R. 1994. *Old Testament Textual Criticism: A Practical Introduction.* Grand Rapids, MI: Baker Books.

Brown, Francis, Samuel R. Driver, and Charles A. Briggs. 1977. *Enhanced Brown-Driver-Briggs Hebrew and English Lexicon.* Oxford: Clarendon Press.

Browne, Gerald M. (ed.). 1975. *Michigan Papyri, Volume XII*. American Studies in Papyrology 14. Toronto: Adolf M. Hakkert.

Bryan, Steven M. 2002. *Jesus and Israel's Traditions of Judgement and Restoration.* SNTSMS 117. Cambridge: Cambridge University Press.

Bülow-Jacobsen, Adam (ed.). 1981. *Papyri Graecae Haunienses, Fasciculus secundus: Letters and Mummy Labels from Roman Egypt.* Bonn: R. Habelt.

Bultmann, Rudolf. [1931] 1963. *The History of the Synoptic Tradition.* New York, NY: Harper & Row.

– (trans. John Marsh). [1931] 1968. *The History of the Synoptic Tradition (Second Edition).* New York, NY: Harper & Row.

–. [1913] 1994. "What the Saying Source Reveals about the Early Church," pp. 23–34 in John S. Kloppenborg (ed.), *The Shape of Q: Signal Essays on the Sayings Gospel.* Minneapolis, MN: Fortress.

Burford, Alison. 1993. *Land and Labor in the Greek World.* Ancient Society and History. Baltimore, MD: John Hopkins University Press.

Burkett, Delbert. 2009. *Rethinking the Gospel Sources, Volume 2: The Unity and Plurality of Q.* Early Christianity and Its Literature 1. Atlanta, GA: SBL.

Carlston, Charles E. 1975. *The Parables of the Triple Tradition.* Philadelphia, PA: Fortress.

–. 1982. "Wisdom and Eschatology in Q," pp. 101–119 in Joël Delobel (ed.), *Logia: Les Paroles de Jésus; The Sayings of Jesus (Mémorial Joseph Coppens).* BETL 59. Leuven: Peeters and Leuven University Press.

Carruth, Shawn. 1995. "Strategies of Authority: A Rhetorical Study of the Character of the Speaker in Q 6:20–49," pp. 98–115 in John S. Kloppenborg (ed.), *Conflict and Invention: Literary, Rhetorical and Social Studies on the Sayings Gospel Q.* Valley Forge, PA: Trinity.

Carruth, Shawn, and Albrecht Garsky (ed.). Stanley D. Anderson. 1996. *Q 11:2b–4.* Documenta Q. Leuven: Peeters.

Casey, P. Maurice. 2009. *The Solution to the "Son of Man" Problem.* London: T&T Clark.

Castor, George D. 1912. *Matthew's Sayings of Jesus: The Non-Marcan Common Source of Matthew and Luke.* Chicago, IL: University of Chicago Press.

Catchpole, David R. 1993. *The Quest for Q.* Edinburgh: T&T Clark.

Chancey, Mark A. 2002. *The Myth of a Gentile Galilee.* SNTSMS 118. Cambridge: Cambridge University Press.

Chandezon, Christophe. 2011. "Some Aspects of Large Estate Management in the Greek World during Classical and Hellenistic Times," pp. 96–121 in Zosia H. Archibald, John K. Davies, and Vincent Gabrielsen (eds.), *The Economies of Hellenistic Societies, Third to First Centuries BC.* Oxford: Oxford University Press.

Collins, Adela Y. 2012. "Redaction Criticism in Theory and Practice," pp. 59–77 in Andrew B. McGowan and Kent H. Richards, *Method and Meaning: Essays on New Testament Interpretation in Honor of Harold W. Attridge.* SBL Resources for Biblical Study 67. Leiden: Brill.

Conzelmann, Hans. [1954] 1960. *Theology of St. Luke.* New York: Harper & Row.

Cotter, Wendy. 1995. "Prestige, Protection and Promise: A Proposal for the Apologetics of Q²," pp. 117–138 in Ronald A. Piper (ed.), *The Gospel behind the Gospels: Current Studies on Q.* NovTSup 75. Leiden: Brill.

Crenshaw, James L. 2010. *Old Testament Wisdom: An Introduction (Third Edition).* Louisville, KY: Westminster John Knox.

Crossan, John D. 1974a. "The Servant Parables of Jesus," in *Semeia* 1, pp. 17–62.

–. 1974b. "The Good Samaritan: Towards a Generic Definition of Parable," in *Semeia* 2, pp. 82–112.

–. 1974c. "Parable and Example in the Teaching of Jesus," in *Semeia* 1, pp. 63–104.

–. 1974d. "Structuralist Analysis and the Parables of Jesus: A Reply to D. O. Via, Jr., 'Parable and Example Story: A Literary-Structuralist Approach,'" in *Semeia* 1, pp. 192–221.

–. 1979. "Paradox Gives Rise to Metaphor: Paul Ricoeur's Hermeneutics and the Parables of Jesus," in *Biblical Research* 24, pp. 20–37.

–. 1983. *In Fragments: The Aphorisms of Jesus.* San Francisco, CA: Harper & Row.

–. 1985. *Four Other Gospels: Shadows on the Contours of Canon.* Minneapolis, MN: Winston.

–. 1986. *Sayings Parallels: A Workbook for the Jesus Tradition.* Philadelphia, PA: Fortress.

–. 1991. *The Historical Jesus: The Life of a Mediterranean Jewish Peasant.* San Francisco, CA: HarperCollins.

–. 1992a. "Parables," pp. 146–152 in David N. Freedman (ed.), *The Anchor Bible Dictionary, Volume 5.* New York, NY: Doubleday.

–. 1992b. *In Parables: The Challenge of the Historical Jesus.* Sonoma, CA: Polebridge.

–. 2001. "Assessing the Arguments," pp. 119–123 in Robert J. Miller (ed.), *The Apocalyptic Jesus: A Debate.* Santa Rosa, CA: Polebridge.

–. 2002. "The Parables of Jesus," in *Interpretation* 56/3, pp. 247–259.

–. 2012. *The Power of Parable: How Fiction by Jesus became Fiction about Jesus.* New York, NY: HarperOne.

Dal Lago, Enrico, and Constantina Katsari. 2008. "Ideal Models of Slave Management in the Roman World and in the Ante-Bellum American South," pp. 187–213 in Enrico Dal Lago and Constantina Katsari (eds.), *Slave Systems: Ancient and Modern.* Cambridge: Cambridge University Press.

Danby, Herbert. 1933. *The Mishnah: Translated from the Hebrew with Introduction and Brief Explanatory Notes.* Oxford: Oxford University Press.

Davies, William D. 1953. "'Knowledge' in the Dead Sea Scrolls and Matthew 11:25–30," in *HTR* 46, pp. 113–139.

Davies, William D., and Dale C. Allison. 1988. *A Critical and Exegetical Commentary on the Gospel according to Saint Matthew, Volume I: Introduction and Commentary on Matthew I–VII.* ICC. London: T&T Clark.

–. 1991. *A Critical and Exegetical Commentary on the Gospel according to Saint Matthew, Volume II: Commentary on Matthew VIII–XVIII.* ICC. London: T&T Clark.

–. 1997. *A Critical and Exegetical Commentary on the Gospel according to Saint Matthew, Volume III: Commentary on Matthew XIX–XXVIII.* ICC. London: T&T Clark.

De Vaux, Roland (trans. John McHugh). 1965. *Ancient Israel: Its Life and Institutions.* London: Darton, Longman & Todd.

De Wet, Chris L. 2018. *The Unbound God: Slavery and the Formation of Early Christian Thought.* London: Routledge.

Den Heyer, C. J. 2002. *Opnieuw: Wie is Jezus?: Balans van 150 Jaar Onderzoek naar Jezus (Vijfde Uitgebreide Druk).* Zoetermeer: Meinema.

Denaux, Adelbert. 1992. "The Q-Logion Mt 11,27 / Lk 10,22 and the Gospel of John," pp. 163–199 in Adelbert Denaux (ed.), *John and the Synoptics.* BETL. Leuven: Leiven University Press.

–. 2001. "The Parable of the Talents/Pounds (Q 19·¹2–27): A Reconstruction of the Text," pp. 429–460 in Andreas Lindemann (ed.), *The Sayings Source Q and the Historical Jesus.* BETL 158. Leuven: Leuven University Press and Peeters.

Derrett, J. Duncan M. 1970. *Law in the New Testament.* London: Darton, Longman & Todd.

Descat, Raymond. 2011. "Labour in the Hellenistic Economy: Slavery as a Test Case," pp. 207–215 in Zosia H. Archibald, John K. Davies, and Vincent Gabrielsen (eds.), *The Economies of Hellenistic Societies, Third to First Centuries BC*. Oxford: Oxford University Press.

Destro, Adriana, and Mauro Pesce. 2003. "Fathers and Householders in the Jesus Movement: The Perspective of the Gospel of Luke," in *BibInt* 11/2, pp. 211–238.

Dibelius, Martin. [1933] 1971. *From Tradition to Gospel*. New York: Charles Scribner's Sons.

Dillon, Matthew. 2002. *The Ancient Greeks: In Their Own Words*. Gloucestershire: Sutton.

Dodd, Charles H. [1935] 1958. *The Parables of the Kingdom (Revised Edition)*. Welwyn: James Nisbet.

– [1935] 1961. *The Parables of the Kingdom (Revised Edition)*. London: Fontana.

Donahue, John R. 1988. *The Gospel in Parable*. Philadelphia, PA: Fortress.

Dormeyer, Detlev. 2014. "Q 7,1.3.6b–9.?10? Der Hauptmann von Kafarnaum: Narrative Strategie mit Chrie, Wundergeschichte und Gleichnis," pp. 189–206 in Dieter T. Roth, Ruben Zimmermann, and Michael Labahn (eds.), *Metaphor, Narrative, and Parables in Q (Dedicated to Dieter Zeller on the Occasion of His 75th Birthday)*. WUNT 315. Tübingen: Mohr Siebeck.

Douglas, R. Conrad. 1995. "'Love Your Enemies': Rhetoric, Tradents, and Ethos," pp. 116–131 in John S. Kloppenborg (ed.), *Conflict and Invention: Literary, Rhetorical and Social Studies on the Sayings Gospel Q*. Valley Forge, PA: Trinity.

Downing, F. Gerald. 1997a. "Redaction Criticism: Josephus's *Antiquities* and the Synoptic Gospels (Part 1)," pp. 161–179 in Stanley E. Porter and Craig A. Evans (eds.), *New Testament Interpretation and Methods: A Sheffield Reader*. The Biblical Seminar 45. Sheffield: Sheffield Academic Press.

–. 1997b. "Redaction Criticism: Josephus's *Antiquities* and the Synoptic Gospels (Part 2)," pp. 180–199 in Stanley E. Porter and Craig A. Evans (eds.), *New Testament Interpretation and Methods: A Sheffield Reader*. The Biblical Seminar 45. Sheffield: Sheffield Academic Press.

–. 2001. "The Jewish Cynic Jesus," pp. 184–214 in Michael Labahn and Andreas Schmidt (eds.), *Jesus, Mark and Q: The Teaching of Jesus and Its Earliest Records*. London: T&T Clark.

Drake, Lyndon. 2014. "Did Jesus Oppose the *Prosbul* in the Forgiveness Petition of the Lord's Prayer?," in *NovT* 56, pp. 233–244.

Draper, Jonathan A. 1999. "Wandering Charismatics and Scholarly Circularities," pp. 29–45 in Richard A. Horsley (with Jonathan A. Draper), *Whoever Hears You Hears Me: Prophets, Performance, and Tradition in Q*. Harrisburg, PA: Trinity.

Dreyer, Yolanda. 2005. "Sexuality and Shifting Paradigms: Setting the Scene," in *HTS Theological Studies* 61/3, pp. 729–751.

Du Toit, Andrie B. 2016. "Revisiting the Sermon on the Mount: Some Major Issues," in *Neotestamentica* 50/3, pp. 59–91.

Dube, Zorodzai. 2015. "Jesus and Afro-Pentecostal Prophets: Dynamics within the Liminal Space in Galilee and in Zimbabwe," in *HTS Theological Studies* 71/1, 6 pages: http://dx.doi.org/10.4102/hts.v71i1.2748.

DuBois, Page. 2009. *Slavery: Antiquity and Its Legacy*. Oxford: Oxford University Press.

Dunn, James D. G. 2003. *Christianity in the Making, Volume 1: Jesus Remembered*. Grand Rapids, MI: William B. Eerdmans.

–. 2013. *The Oral Gospel Tradition*. Grand Rapids, MI: William B. Eerdmans.

Edgar, Campbell C. (ed.). 1925–1940. *Zenon Papyri, Catalogue général des antiquités égyptiennes du Musée du Caire*. 5 vols. Cairo: L'Institut français d'archéologie orientale.

–. 1931. *Michigan Papyri, Volume I: Zenon Papyri*. Humanistic Series 24. Ann Arbor, MI: University of Michigan Press.

Edwards, Richard A. 1969. "The Eschatological Correlative as a Gattung in the New Testament," in *ZNW* 60, pp. 9–20.

–. 1976. *A Theology of Q: Eschatology, Prophecy, and Wisdom*. Philadelphia, PA: Fortress.

Elliott, John H. 2011. "Social-Scientific Criticism: Perspective, Process and Payoff; Evil Eye Accusation at Galatia as Illustration of the Method," in *HTS Theological Studies* 67/1, 10 pages: https://hts.org.za/index.php/hts/article/view/858/1445.

Eichhorn, Johann Gottfried. 1803. *Einleitung in das Alte Testament (Erster Band)*. Leipzig: Weibmannischen Buchhandlung.

Eitrem, Sam, and Leiv Amundsen (eds.). 1931. *Papyri Osloenses, Volume II*. Oslo: J. Dybwad.

Epp, Eldon J. 2012. "Textual Criticism and New Testament Interpretation," pp. 79–105 in Andrew B. McGowan and Kent H. Richards (eds.), *Method and Meaning: Essays on New Testament Interpretation in Honor of Harold W. Attridge*. SBL Resources for Biblical Study 67. Leiden: Brill.

Etchells, Ruth. 1998. *A Reading of the Parables of Jesus*. London: Darton, Longman & Todd.

Fiensy, David A. 1991. *The Social History of Palestine in the Herodian Period: The Land Is Mine*. Studies in the Bible and Early Christianity 20. Lewiston, NY: Edwin Mellen.

–. 2010. "Ancient Economy and the New Testament," pp. 194–206 in Dietmar Neufeld and Richard E. DeMaris (eds.), *Understanding the Social World of the New Testament*. London: Routledge.

Fisher, Nick. 1998. "Rich and Poor," in Paul Cartledge (ed.), *The Cambridge Illustrated History of Ancient Greece*. Cambridge: Cambridge University Press.

Fleddermann, Harry T. 1986. "The Householder and the Servant Left in Charge," in *SBL Seminar Papers* 25, pp. 17–26.

–. 1990, "The End of Q," pp. 1–10 in David J. Lull (ed.), *SBL Seminar Papers* 29. Atlanta, GA: Scholars Press.

–. 2001. "Mark's Use of Q: The Beelzebul Controversy and the Cross Saying," pp. 17–33 in Michael Labahn and Andreas Schmidt (eds.), *Jesus, Mark and Q: The Teaching of Jesus and Its Earliest Records*. London: T&T Clark.

–. 2005a. *Q: A Reconstruction and Commentary*. Biblical Tools and Studies 1. Leuven: Peeters.

–. 2005b. "Three Friends at Midnight (Lk 11,5–8)," pp. 265–282 in Adelbert Denaux, Reimund Bieringer, Gilbert van Belle, and Joseph Verheyden (eds.), *Luke and His Readers: Festschrift A. Denaux*. BETL 182. Leuven: Leuven University Press.

–. 2014. "The Narrative of Jesus as the Narrative of God in Q," pp. 141–162 in Dieter T. Roth, Ruben Zimmermann, and Michael Labahn (eds.), *Metaphor, Narrative, and Parables in Q (Dedicated to Dieter Zeller on the Occasion of His 75th Birthday)*. WUNT 315. Tübingen: Mohr Siebeck.

Ford, Richard Q. 2016. *The Parables of Jesus and the Problems of the World: How Ancient Narratives Comprehend Modern Malaise*. Eugene, OR: Cascade.

Foster, Paul. 2014a. "The Q Parables: Their Extent and Function," pp. 255–285 in Dieter T. Roth, Ruben Zimmermann, and Michael Labahn (eds.), *Metaphor, Narrative, and Parables in Q (Dedicated to Dieter Zeller on the Occasion of His 75th Birthday)*. WUNT 315. Tübingen: Mohr Siebeck.

–. 2014b. "Q and James: A Source-Critical Conundrum," pp. 3–34 in Alicia J. Batten and John S. Kloppenborg (eds.), *James, 1 & 2 Peter, and Early Jesus Traditions.* London: Bloomsbury.

Freyne, Sean. 1988. *Galilee, Jesus and the Gospels: Literary Approaches and Historical Investigations.* Philadelphia, PA: Fortress.

–. 2000. *Galilee and Gospel: Collected Essays.* WUNT 125. Tübingen: Mohr Siebeck.

–. 2004. *Jesus, a Jewish Galilean: A New Reading of the Jesus Story.* London: T&T Clark.

Funk, Robert W. 1966. *Language, Hermeneutic, and the Word of God: The Problem of Language in the New Testament and Contemporary Theology.* New York, NY: Harper & Row.

–. 1974. "Structure in the Narrative Parables of Jesus," in *Semeia* 2, pp. 51–73.

–. 1996. *Honest to Jesus: Jesus for a New Millennium.* San Francisco, CA: HarperCollins.

– (ed. Bernard B. Scott). 2006. *Funk on Parables: Collected Essays.* Santa Rosa, CA: Polebridge.

–. 2007. "Jesus of Nazareth: A Glimpse," pp. 89–93 in Edward F. Beutner (ed.), *Listening to the Parables of Jesus.* Jesus Seminar Guides 2. Santa Rosa, CA: Polebridge.

Funk, Robert W., Bernard B. Scott, and James R. Butts (eds.). 1988. *The Parables of Jesus: Red Letter Edition; The Jesus Seminar.* The Jesus Seminar Series. Sonoma, CA: Polebridge.

Funk, Robert W., and Roy W. Hoover (eds.). 1993. *The Five Gospels: The Search for the Authentic Words of Jesus (New Translation and Commentary by Robert W. Funk, Roy W. Hoover, and the Jesus Seminar).* New York, NY: HarperOne.

Gammie, John G. 1990. "Paraenetic Literature: Toward the Morphology of a Secondary Genre," in *Semeia* 50, pp. 41–77.

Garnsey, Peter. 1970. *Social Status and Legal Privilege in the Roman Empire.* Oxford: Clarendon.

Garsky, Albrecht, Christoph Heil, Thomas Hieke, and Josef E. Amon (ed. Shawn Carruth). 1997. *Q 12:49–59: Children against Parents; Judging the Time; Settling out of Court.* Documenta Q. Leuven: Peeters.

Gathercole, Simon J. 2014. *The Gospel of Thomas: Introduction and Commentary.* Texts and Editions for New Testament Study 2. Leiden: Brill.

George, Andrew. 2003. *The Epic of Gilgamesh: The Babylonian Epic Poem and Other Texts in Akkadian and Sumerian. (Translated with an Introduction by Andrew George).* Penguin Classics. London: Penguin Books.

Glotz, Gustave. 1926. *Ancient Greece at Work: An Economic History of Greece from the Homeric Period to the Roman Conquest.* New York, NY: Barnes & Noble.

Goede, Hendrik. 2013. "Constructing Ancient Slavery as Socio-Historic Context of the New Testament," in *HTS Theological Studies* 69/1, 7 pages: http://dx.doi.org/10.4102/hts.v69i1.1297.

Gonis, Nikolaos, and Daniela Colomo (eds.), with contributions by Amin Benaissa, Livia Capponi, Walter E. H. Cockle, Janneke de Jong, Claudio Meliadò, Alberto Nodar, Angeliki Syrkou, and J. David Thomas. 2008. *The Oxyrhynchus Papyri, Volume LXXII.* Graeco-Roman Memoirs 92. London: Egypt Exploration Society.

Goodspeed, Edgar J. (ed.). 1902. *Papyri from Karanis in the Chicago Museum.* Studies in Classical Philology 3. Chicago, IL: University of Chicago Press.

Gregg, Brian H. 2006. *The Historical Jesus and the Final Judgment Sayings in Q.* WUNT 2/207. Tübingen: Mohr Siebeck.

Grenfell, Bernard P., Arthur S. Hunt, and David G. Hogarth (eds.). 1900. *Fayûm Towns and their Papyri.* Graeco-Roman Memoirs 3. London: Offices of the Egypt Exploration Fund.

Grenfell, Bernard P., Arthur S. Hunt, and Edgar J. Goodspeed (eds.). 1907. *The Tebtunis Papyri, Volume II.* University of California Publications, Graeco-Roman Archaeology 2. Reprint 1970: Egypt Exploration Society, Graeco-Roman Memoirs 52. London: Egypt Exploration Society.

Grenfell, Bernard P., Arthur S. Hunt, and J. Gilbart Smyly (eds.). 1902. *The Tebtunis Papyri, Volume I.* University of California Publications, Graeco-Roman Archaeology 1. Graeco-Roman Memoirs 4. London: Egypt Exploration Society.

Griesbach, J. J. 1796. *Novum Testamentum Græce: Textum ad Fidem, Codicum et Patrum.* London: J. Mackinlay, Cuthell & Martin. (English translation available online: http://www.bible-researcher.com/rules.html#Griesbach.)

Gronewald, Michael, and Klaus Maresch (eds.). *Kölner Papyri, Band 7.* Papyrologica Coloniensia VII, 7. Köln-Opladen: Westdeutscher Verlag.

Guelich, Robert A. 1982. *The Sermon on the Mount: A Foundation for Understanding.* Waco, TX: Word.

Guéraud, O. (ed.). 1931–1932. *ΕΝΤΕΥΞΕΙΣ: Requêtes et plaintes adressées au Roi d'Égypte au IIIe siècle avant J.-C.* Cairo: L'Institut français d'archéologie orientale.

Gunkel, H. [1910] 1997. *Genesis: Translated and Interpreted.* Macon, GA: Mercer University Press.

Haenchen, E. 1968. *Der Weg Jesu: Eine Erklärung des Markus-Evangeliums und der kanonischen Parallelen.* Berlin: Walter de Gruyter.

Hagedorn, Ursula, Dieter Hagedorn, Louise C. Youtie, and Herbert C. Youtie. 1969. Papyrologica Coloniensia IV. *Das Archiv des Petaus.* Köln-Opladen: Westdeutscher Verlag.

Hahn, F. 1969. *The Titles of Jesus in Christology.* London: Lutterworth.

Häkkinen, Sakari. 2016. "Poverty in the First-Century Galilee," in *HTS Theological Studies* 72/4, 9 pages: http://dx.doi.org/10.4102/hts.v72i4.3398.

Harding, Mark. 2003. *Early Christian Life and Thought in Social Context: A Reader.* London: T&T Clark.

Harrill, J. Albert. 2006. *Slaves in the New Testament: Literary, Social, and Moral Dimensions.* Minneapolis, MA: Fortress.

Harris, Stephen L., and Gloria Platzner. 2012. *Classical Mythology: Images & Insights (Sixth Edition).* New York: McGraw-Hill.

Hartin, Patrick J. 2000. "The Woes Against the Pharisees (Matthew 23,1–39): The Reception and Development of Q 11,39–52 within the Matthean Community," pp. 265–283 in Jon M. Asgeirsson, Kristin de Troyer, and Marvin W. Meyer (eds.), *From Quest to Q: Festschrift James M. Robinson.* Leuven: Leuven University Press and Peeters.

–. 2014. "Wholeness in James and the Q Source," pp. 35–57 in Alicia J. Batten and John S. Kloppenborg (eds.), *James, 1 & 2 Peter, and Early Jesus Traditions.* London: Bloomsbury.

–. [1991] 2015. *James and the "Q" Sayings of Jesus.* JSNTSup 47. London: Bloomsbury.

Harvey, Anthony E. 1982. *Jesus and the Constraints of History: The Bampton Lectures, 1980.* London: Duckworth.

Hays, Christopher M. 2012. "Slaughtering Stewards and Incarcerating Debtors: Coercing Charity in Luke 12:35–13:9," in *Neotestamentica* 46/1, pp. 41–60.

Hedrick, Charles W. 2004. *Many Things in Parables: Jesus and His Modern Critics.* Louisville, KY: Westminster John Knox.

–. 2014. *The Wisdom of Jesus: Between the Sages of Israel and the Apostles of the Church.* Eugene, OR: Cascade.

Heil, Christoph. 2001. "Beobachtungen zur theologischen Dimension der Gleichnisrede Jesu in Q," pp. 649–659 in Andreas Lindemann (ed.), *The Sayings Source Q and the Historical Jesus*. BETL 158. Leuven: Leuven University Press and Peeters.

Helena Visser, Jacobie M. 2017. "Following the Man on the Slippery Slide: Christ in 1 Peter," in *Neotestamentica* 51/2, pp. 337–357.

Herzog, William R. 1994. *Parables as Subversive Speech: Jesus as Pedagogue of the Oppressed*. Louisville, KY: Westminster John Knox.

Hezser, Catherine. 2005. *Jewish Slavery in Antiquity*. Oxford: Oxford University Press.

–. 2009. "Ben-Hur and Ancient Jewish Slavery," pp. 121–139 in Zuleika Rodgers, Margaret Daly-Denton, and Anne Fitzpatrick McKinley (eds.), *A Wandering Galilean: Essays in Honour of Seán Freyne*. Supplements to the Journal for the Study of Judaism 132. Leiden: Brill.

Hock, Ronald F., and Edward N. O'Neil. 1986. *The Chreia in Ancient Rhetoric: The Progymnasmata, Volume 1*. Texts and Translations 27. Graeco-Roman Religion Series 9. Atlanta, GA: Scholars Press.

Hoffmann, Paul. 1967. "Πάντες ἐργάται ἀδικίας: Redaktion und Tradition in Lc 13,22–30," in *ZNW* 58, pp. 188–214.

–. 1975. *Studien zur Theologie der Logienquelle*. Neutestamentliche Abhandlungen 8. Münster: Aschendorff.

–. 1995. "The Redaction of Q and the Son of Man," pp. 159–198 in Ronald A. Piper (ed.), *The Gospel behind the Gospels: Current Studies on Q*. NovTSup 75. Leiden: Brill.

–. 2001. "Mutmassungen über Q: Zum Problem der literarischen Genese von Q," pp. 255–288 in Andreas Lindemann (ed.), *The Sayings Source Q and the Historical Jesus*. BETL 158. Leuven: Leuven University Press and Peeters.

Hoffmann, Paul, and Christoph Heil (eds.). 2013. *Die Spruchquelle Q: Studienausgabe; Griechisch und Deutsch (4. Auflage)*. Darmstadt: Wissenschaftliche Buchgesellschaft; Leuven: Peeters.

Holladay, William L. 1971. *A Concise Hebrew and Aramaic Lexicon of the Old Testament based upon the Lexical Work of Ludwig Koehler and Walter Baumgartner*. Leiden: Brill.

Holmén, Tom. 2001. "Knowing about Q and Knowing about Jesus: Mutually Exclusive Undertakings?," pp. 497–514 in Andreas Lindemann (ed.), *The Sayings Source Q and the Historical Jesus*. BETL 158. Leuven: Leuven University Press and Peeters.

Holmes, Michael W. 2012. "What Text Is Being Edited?: The Editing of the New Testament," pp. 91–122 in John S. Kloppenborg and Judith H. Newman (eds.), *Editing the Bible: Assessing the Task Past and Present*. SBL Resources for Biblical Study 69. Atlanta, GA: SBL.

Horsley, Richard A. 1979. "Josephus and the Bandits," in *Journal for the Study of Judaism in the Persian, Hellenistic, and Roman Periods* 10, pp. 37–63.

–. 1981. "Ancient Jewish Banditry and the Revolt against Rome," in *Catholic Biblical Quarterly* 43, pp. 409–432.

–. 1991. "Logoi Prophētōn?: Reflections on the Genre of Q," pp. 195–209 in Birger A. Pearson, A. Thomas Kraabel, George W. E. Nickelsburg, and Norman R. Petersen (eds.), *The Future of Early Christianity: Essays in Honour of Helmut Koester*. Minneapolis, MN: Fortress.

–. 1992. "Q and Jesus: Assumptions, Approaches and Analyses," pp. 175–209 in John S. Kloppenborg and Leif E. Vaage (eds.), *Early Christianity, Q and Jesus*. Semeia 55. Atlanta, GA: Scholars Press.

–. 1995a. "Social Conflict in the Synoptic Sayings Source Q," pp. 37–52 in John S. Kloppenborg (ed.), *Conflict and Invention: Literary, Rhetorical and Social Studies on the Sayings Gospel Q*. Valley Forge, PA: Trinity.

–. 1995b. *Galilee: History, Politics, People*. Valley Forge, PA: Trinity.

–. 1996. *Archaeology, History and Society in Galilee: The Social Context of Jesus and the Rabbis*. Valley Forge, PA: Trinity.

– (with Jonathan A. Draper). 1999. *Whoever Hears You Hears Me: Prophets, Performance, and Tradition in Q*. Harrisburg, PA: Trinity.

–. 2003. *Jesus and Empire: The Kingdom of God and the New World Disorder*. Minneapolis, MN: Fortress.

–. 2012. *The Prophet Jesus and the Renewal of Israel: Moving Beyond a Diversionary Debate*. Grand Rapids, MI: William B. Eerdmans.

Howes, Llewellyn. 2012. *The Sayings Gospel Q within the Contexts of the Third and Renewed Quests for the Historical Jesus: Wisdom and Apocalypticism in the First Century*. Pretoria: Ph.D. Dissertation, University of Pretoria.

–. 2013a. "'Blessed are the Eyes that See': Revealing the Redaction of Q 10:21–24," in *Ekklesiastikos Pharos* 95, pp. 148–172.

–. 2013b. "'Placed in a Hidden Place': Illuminating the Displacement of Q 11:33, 34–35," in *Neotestamentica* 47/2, pp. 303–332

–. 2013c. "'To Refer, Not to Characterise': A Synchronic Look at the Son-of-Man Logia in the Sayings Gospel Q," in *HTS Theological Studies* 69/1, 12 pages: http://dx.doi.org/10.4102/hts.v69i1.1344.

–. 2014a. "The Householder, the Robber and the Son of Man: Reconsidering the Redaction of Q 12:39–40," in *Journal of Early Christian History* 4/2, pp. 54–75.

–. 2014b. Book Review of *The Story of Jesus in History and Faith: An Introduction* by Lee M. McDonald, in *Neotestamentica* 48/1, pp. 224–227.

–. 2014c. "Condemning or Liberating the Twelve Tribes of Israel?: Judging the Meaning of κρίνοντες in Q 22:28, 30," in *Verbum et Ecclesia* 35/1, 11 pages: http://dx.doi.org/10.4102/ve.v35i1.872.

–. 2015a. *Judging Q and Saving Jesus: Q's Contribution to the Wisdom-Apocalypticism Debate in Historical Jesus Studies*. Cape Town: AOSIS.

–. 2015b. "'Divided Against Itself'?: Individual Maxims and the Redaction of Q," in *Acta Theologica* 35/1, pp. 96–114.

–. 2015c. "Agricultural Slavery and the Parable of the Loyal and Wise Slave in Q 12:42–46," in *Acta Classica* 58, pp. 70–110.

–. 2015d. "'Cut in Two,' Part 1: Exposing the Seam in Q 12:42–46," in *HTS Theological Studies* 71/1 (P. G. R. de Villiers Dedication), pp. 473–477.

–. 2015e. "'Cut in Two,' Part 2: Reconsidering the Redaction of Q 12:42–46," in *HTS Theological Studies* 71/1 (P. G. R. de Villiers Dedication), pp. 478–484.

–. 2015f. "'Whomever You Find, Invite': The Parable of the Great Supper (Q 14:16–21, 23) and the Redaction of Q," in *Neotestamentica* 49/2, pp. 321–350.

–. 2016a. "'Your Father Knows that You Need All of This': Divine Fatherhood as Socio-Ethical Impetus in Q's Formative Stratum," in *Neotestamentica* 50/1, pp. 9–33.

–. 2016b. "Food for Thought: Interpreting the Parable of the Loyal and Wise Slave in Q 12:42–44," pp. 110–130 in D. Francois Tolmie (guest editor), *Acta Theologica Supplementum 23: Perspectives on the Socially Disadvantaged in Early Christianity*. Bloemfontein: SUN MeDIA.

–. 2016c. "'I Do Not Know You!': Reconsidering the Redaction of Q 13:25–27," in *Journal of Theological Studies* 67/2, pp. 479–506.

–. 2016d. "'Reaping Where You Did Not Sow': The Parable of the Entrusted Money (Q 19:12–13, 15–24, 26) and the Redaction of Q," in *Journal of Early Christian History* 6/2, pp. 18–54.

–. 2017a. "'Make an Effort to Get Loose': Reconsidering the Redaction of Q 12:58–59," in *Pharos Journal of Theology* 98, pp. 1–29

–. 2017b. "Exorcising the Kingdom Saying from the Beelzebul Story (Q 11:14–15, 17–20)," in *Journal of Early Christian History* 7/1, pp. 28–45.

–. 2018. "'You Will Not Get Out Of There!': Reconsidering the Placement of Q 12:58–59," in *Neotestamentica* 52/1, pp. 141–178.

–. 2019a. "From the Earth of Africa: Q Research in South Africa," in *HTS Theological Studies* 75/4 (HTS 75th Anniversary Maake Masango Dedication), 11 pages: https://hts.org.za/index.php/hts/article/view/5444/12663.

–. 2019b. "Q's Message to the Peasantry and Poor: Considering Three Texts in the Sayings Gospel," in *HTS Theological Studies* 75/3, 13 pages: https://hts.org.za/index.php/hts/article/view/4992/12283.

–. 2019c. "The Q Parables of the Mustard Seed and Leaven: Half-Baked and Garden-Variety Metaphors?," in *Neotestamentica* 53/2, pp. 339–374.

Huffard, Evertt W. 1978. "The Parable of the Friend at Midnight: God's Honour or Man's Persistence," in *Restoration Quarterly* 21, pp. 154–160.

Humphrey, Hugh M. 2006. *From Q to "Secret" Mark: A Composition History of the Earliest Narrative Theology.* London: T&T Clark.

Hunt, Arthur S. (ed.). 1912. *The Oxyrhynchus Papyri, Volume IX.* Graeco-Roman Memoirs 12. London: Egypt Exploration Society.

Hunt, Arthur S., and J. Gilbart Smyly, with assistance from Bernard P. Grenfell, Edgar Lobel, and Michael I. Rostovtzeff. 1933. *The Tebtunis Papyri, Volume III, Part 1.* University of California Publications, Graeco-Roman Archaeology 3. Egypt Exploration Society, Graeco-Roman Memoirs 23. London: H. Milford.

Hunt, Steven A. 2012. "And the Word Became Flesh – Again?: Jesus and Abraham in John 8:31–59," pp. 81–109 in Steven A. Hunt (ed.), *Perspectives on Our Father Abraham: Essays in Honor of Marvin R. Wilson.* Grand Rapids, MI: William B. Eerdmans.

Hunter, Archibald M. 1964. *Interpreting the Parables (Second Edition).* London: SCM.

–. 1971. *The Parables Then and Now.* London: SCM.

Husselman, Elinor M. (ed.). 1971. *Michigan Papyri, Volume IX: Papyri from Karanis, Third Series.* American Philological Association, Philological Monograph 29. Cleveland: Case Western Reserve University Press.

Jackson, Bernard S. 1972. *Theft in Early Jewish Law.* Oxford: Clarendon.

Jacobs, Theuns. 2018. "Social Conflict in Early Roman Palestine," in *Neotestamentica* 52/1, pp. 115–139.

Jacobson, Arland D. 1978. *Wisdom Christology in Q.* Claremont: Ph.D. Dissertation, Claremont Graduate School.

–. 1982. "The Literary Unity of Q: Lc 10,2–16 and Parallels as a Test Case," pp. 419–423 in Joël Delobel (ed.), *Logia: Les Paroles de Jésus; The Sayings of Jesus (Mémorial Joseph Coppens).* BETL 59. Leuven: Peeters and Leuven University Press.

–. 1992. *The First Gospel: An Introduction to Q.* Sonoma, CA: Polebridge.

–. [1982] 1994. "The Literary Unity of Q," pp. 98–115 in John S. Kloppenborg (ed.), *The Shape of Q: Signal Essays on the Sayings Gospel.* Minneapolis, MN: Fortress.

–. 1995. "Divided Families and Christian Origins," pp. 361–380 in Ronald A. Piper (ed.), *The Gospel behind the Gospels: Current Studies on Q.* NovTSup 75. Leiden: Brill.

–. 2000. "Jesus against the Family: The Dissolution of Family Ties in the Gospel Tradition," pp. 189–218 in Jon M. Asgeirsson, Kristin de Troyer, and Marvin W. Meyer (eds.), *From Quest to Q: Festschrift James M. Robinson*. BETL 146. Leuven: Leuven University Press and Peeters.

Järvinen, Arto. 2001. "Jesus as a Community Symbol in Q," pp. 515–521 in Andreas Lindemann (ed.), *The Sayings Source Q and the Historical Jesus*. BETL 158. Leuven: Leuven University Press and Peeters.

Jeremias, Joachim. [1954] 1963. *The Parables of Jesus (Revised Edition)*. London: SCM.

–. 1966. *Rediscovering the Parables*. London, UK: SCM.

– (trans. S. H. Hooke). [1952] 1972. *The Parables of Jesus (Third Revised Edition)*. London: SCM.

Johnson, Alan F. 1979. "Assurance for Man: The Fallacy of Translating *Anaideia* by 'Persistence' in Luke 11:5–8," in *Journal of the Evangelical Theological Society* 22/2, pp. 123–131.

Johnson, John de M., Victor Martin, and Arthur S. Hunt (eds.). 1915. *Catalogue of the Greek and Latin Papyri in the John Rylands Library, Manchester, Volume II: Documents of the Ptolemaic and Roman Periods*. Manchester: Manchester University Press.

Johnson, Steven R. 1997. "Evaluations," p. 319 in Albrecht Garsky, Christoph Heil, Thomas Hieke, and Josef E. Amon (ed. Shawn Carruth), *Q 12:49–59: Children against Parents; Judging the Time; Settling out of Court*. Documenta Q. Leuven: Peeters.

–. 2007. *Q 12:33–34: Storing Up Treasures in Heaven*. Documenta Q. Leuven: Peeters.

Johnson-DeBaufre, Melanie. 2005. *Jesus Among Her Children: Q, Eschatology, and the Construction of Christian Origins*. Harvard Theological Studies 55. Cambridge, MA: Harvard University Press.

Joseph, Simon J. 2012. *Jesus, Q, and the Dead Sea Scrolls: A Judaic Approach to Q*. WUNT 2/333. Tübingen: Mohr Siebeck.

–. 2014. *The Nonviolent Messiah: Jesus, Q, and the Enochic Tradition*. Minneapolis, MN: Fortress.

Joshel, Sandra R. 2010. *Slavery in the Ancient World*. Cambridge: Cambridge University Press.

Kaden, David A. 2014. "Stoicism, Social Stratification, and the Q Tradition in James: A Suggestion about James' Audience," pp. 78–96 in Alicia J. Batten and John S. Kloppenborg (eds.), *James, 1 & 2 Peter, and Early Jesus Traditions*. London: Bloomsbury.

Kase, Edmund H. (ed.). 1936. *Papyri in the Princeton University Collections, Volume II*. Princeton University Studies in Papyrology 1. Princeton: Princeton University Press.

Kee, Howard C. 1983. "Testaments of the Twelve Patriarchs (Second Century B.C.)," pp. 775–828 in James H. Charlesworth (ed.), *The Old Testament Pseudepigrapha, Volume 1: Apocalyptic Literature and Testaments*. Garden City, NY: Doubleday.

Keinänen, J. 2001. *Traditions in Collision: A Literary and Redaction-Critical Study on the Elijah Narratives 1 Kings 17–19*. The Finnish Exegetical Society 80. Göttingen: Vandenhoeck & Ruprecht.

Kingsbury, J. D. 1978. "The Verb AKOLOUTHEIN ('to follow') as an Index of Matthew's View of His Community," in *JBL* 97, pp. 56–75.

Kirk, Alan. 1998. *The Composition of the Sayings Source: Genre, Synchrony, and Wisdom Redaction in Q*. NovTSup 91. Leiden: Brill.

–. 2016. *Q in Matthew: Ancient Media, Memory, and Early Scribal Transmission of the Jesus Tradition*. LNTS 564. London: Bloomsbury.

Kloppenborg, John S. 1986. "The Formation of Q and Antique Instructional Genres," in *JBL* 105, pp. 443–462.

–. 1987. *The Formation of Q: Trajectories in Ancient Wisdom Collections*. Studies in Antiquity and Christianity. Philadelphia, PA: Fortress.

–. 1988. "Redactional Strata and Social History in the Sayings Gospel Q," presented at the Q Seminar for the SBL.

–. 1990. "'Easter Faith' and the Sayings Gospel Q," pp. 71–99 in Ron Cameron (ed.), *The Apocryphal Jesus and Christian Origins*. Semeia 49. Atlanta, GA: Scholars Press.

–. 1991. "Literary Convention, Self-Evidence and the Social History of the Q People," pp. 77–102 in John S. Kloppenborg and Leif E. Vaage (eds.), *Early Christianity, Q and Jesus*. Semeia 55. Atlanta, GA: Scholars Press.

–. [1986] 1994. "The Formation of Q and Antique Instructional Genres," pp. 138–155 in John S. Kloppenborg (ed.), *The Shape of Q: Signal Essays on the Sayings Gospel*. Minneapolis, MN: Fortress.

–. 1995. "Jesus and the Parables of Jesus in Q," pp. 275–319 in Ronald A. Piper (ed.), *The Gospel behind the Gospels: Current Studies on Q*. NovTSup 75. Leiden: Brill.

–. 1996a. "The Sayings Gospel Q: Literary and Stratigraphic Problems," pp. 1–66 in Risto Uro (ed.), *Symbols and Strata: Essays on the Sayings Gospel Q*. Göttingen: Vandenhoeck & Ruprecht.

–. 1996b. "The Sayings Gospel Q and the Quest of the Historical Jesus," in *Harvard Theological Review* 89/4, pp 307–344.

Kloppenborg (Verbin), John S. 2000a. *Excavating Q: The History and Setting of the Sayings Gospel*. Minneapolis, MN: Fortress.

–. 2000b. "A Dog among the Pigeons: The 'Cynic Hypothesis' as a Theological Problem," pp. 73–117 in Jon M. Asgeirsson, Kristin de Troyer, and Marvin W. Meyer (eds.), *From Quest to Q: Festschrift James M. Robinson*. BETL 146. Leuven: Leuven University Press and Peeters.

–. 2001. "Discursive Practices in the Sayings Gospel Q and the Quest of the Historical Jesus," pp. 149–190 in Andreas Lindemann (ed.), *The Sayings Source Q and the Historical Jesus*. BETL 158. Leuven: Leuven University Press and Peeters.

Kloppenborg, John S. 2006. *The Tenants in the Vineyard: Ideology, Economics, and Agrarian Conflict in Jewish Palestine*. WUNT 195. Tübingen: Mohr Siebeck.

–. 2007. "Evaluations," p. 53 in Steven R. Johnson (ed.), *Q 12:33–34: Storing Up Treasures in Heaven*. Documenta Q. Leuven: Peeters.

–. 2011. "Sources, Methods and Discursive Locations in the Quest of the Historical Jesus," pp. 241–290 in Tom Holmén and Stanley E. Porter (eds.), *Handbook for the Study of the Historical Jesus, Volume 1: How to Study the Historical Jesus*. Leiden: Brill.

–. 2014. "The Parable of the Burglar in Q: Insights from Papyrology," pp. 287–306 in Dieter T. Roth, Ruben Zimmermann, and Michael Labahn (eds.), *Metaphor, Narrative, and Parables in Q (Dedicated to Dieter Zeller on the Occasion of His 75th Birthday)*. WUNT 315. Tübingen: Mohr Siebeck.

Kloppenborg, John S., Marvin W. Meyer, Stephen J. Patterson, and Michael G. Steinhauser. 1990. *Q-Thomas Reader*. Sonoma, CA: Polebridge.

Klostermann, Erich. 1909. *Matthäus*. Handbuch zum Neuen Testament 2/1. Tübingen: Mohr Siebeck.

Koester, Helmut. [1968] 1971. "One Jesus and Four Primitive Gospels," pp. 158–204 in James M. Robinson and Helmut Koester (eds.), *Trajectories through Early Christianity*. Philadelphia, PA: Fortress.

–. [1968] 1994a. "The Synoptic Sayings Source and the Gospel of Thomas," pp. 35–50 in John S. Kloppenborg (ed.), *The Shape of Q: Signal Essays on the Sayings Gospel*. Minneapolis, MN: Fortress.

–. 1994b. "The Historical Jesus and the Historical Situation of the Quest: An Epilogue," pp. 535–545 in Bruce D. Chilton and Craig A. Evans (eds.), *Studying the Historical Jesus: Evaluations of the State of Current Research*. Leiden: Brill.

–. 1997. "The Sayings of Q and Their Image of Jesus," pp. 137–154 in William J. Petersen, Johan S. Vos, and Henk J. de Jonge (eds.), *Sayings of Jesus: Canonical and Non-Canonical (Essays in Honour of Tjitze Baarda)*. NovTSup 89. Leiden: Brill.

Kyrtatas, Dimitris J. 2002. "Domination and Exploitation," in Paul Cartledge, Edward E. Cohen, and Lin Foxhall (eds.), *Money, Labour and Land: Approaches to the Economies of Ancient Greece*. London: Routledge.

Lampe, Peter. 2016. "Social Welfare in the Greco-Roman World as a Background for Early Christian Practice," pp. 1–28 in D. Francois Tolmie (guest editor), *Acta Theologica Supplementum 23: Perspectives on the Socially Disadvantaged in Early Christianity*. Bloemfontein: SUN MeDIA.

Layton, Scott C. 1990. "The Steward in Ancient Israel: A Study of Hebrew ('ăšer) 'al-hab-bayit in Its Near Eastern Setting," in *JBL* 109/4, pp 633–649.

Lee, Aquila H. I. 2005. *From Messiah to Pre-Existent Son of God: Jesus' Self-consciousness and Early Christian Exegesis of Messianic Psalms*. WUNT 2/192. Tübingen: Mohr Siebeck.

Leith, David, David C. Parker, Stuart R. Pickering, Nikolaos Gonis, and Myrto Malouta (eds.), with contributions by Amin Benaissa, Daniela Colomo, Michel Cottier, Marius Gerhardt, Rosalia Hatzilambrou, Nikos Litinas, Daniela Manetti, Hiroshi Maeno, Pasquale M. Pinto, Pauline Ripat, and Manna Satama. 2009. *The Oxyrhynchus Papyri, Volume LXXIV*. Graeco-Roman Memoirs 95. London: Egypt Exploration Society.

Levine, Amy-Jill. 2014. *Short Stories by Jesus: The Enigmatic Parables of a Controversial Rabbi*. New York, NY: HarperOne.

Liddell, Henry G., and Robert Scott (revised and augmented by Henry Stuart Jones and Roderick McKenzie) 1996. *A Greek-English Lexicon (Ninth Edition)*. Oxford: Clarendon.

Liebenberg, Jacobus. 2001. *The Language of the Kingdom and Jesus: Parable, Aphorism, and Metaphor in the Sayings Material Common to the Synoptic Tradition and the Gospel of Thomas*. Berlin: Walter de Gruyter.

Louw, Johannes P., and Eugene A. Nida (eds.). 1993a. *Greek-English Lexicon of the New Testament based on Semantic Domains: Volume 1 (Domains)*. Cape Town: Bible Society of South Africa.

–. 1993b. *Greek-English Lexicon of the New Testament based on Semantic Domains: Volume 2 (Indices)*. Cape Town: Bible Society of South Africa.

Lührmann, Dieter. 1969. *Die Redaktion der Logienquelle*. Wissenschaftliche Monographien zum Alten und Neuen Testament 33. Neukirchen-Vluyn: Neukirchener.

–. [1969] 1994. "Q in the History of Early Christianity," pp. 59–73 in John S. Kloppenborg (ed.), *The Shape of Q: Signal Essays on the Sayings Gospel*. Minneapolis, MN: Fortress.

Luz, Ulrich (trans. Wilhelm C. Linss). 1989. *Matthew 1–7: A Commentary*. Augsburg: Fortress.

– (trans. James E. Crouch; ed. Helmut Koester). 2001. *Matthew 8–20: A Commentary*. Hermeneia. Minneapolis, MN: Fortress.

– (trans. James E. Crouch; ed. Helmut Koester). 2005. *Matthew 21–28: A Commentary*. Hermeneia. Minneapolis, MN: Fortress.

– (trans. James E. Crouch; ed. Helmut Koester). 2007. *Matthew 1–7: A Commentary*. Hermeneia. Minneapolis, MN: Fortress.

MacEwen, Robert K. 2015. *Matthean Posteriority: An Exploration of Matthew's Use of Mark and Luke as a Solution to the Synoptic Problem.* LNTS 501. London: Bloomsbury T&T Clark.

Mack, Burton L. 1993. *The Lost Gospel: The Book of Q and Christian Origins.* San Francisco, CA: HarperSanFrancisco.

Maehler, Herwig, Cornelia E. Römer, and Rosalia Hatzilambrou (eds.), with contributions by Matias Buchholtz, Ruey-Lin Chang, Christopher J. Fuhrmann, Marius Gerhardt, Marc de Groote, Luis A. Guichard, Andreas Hartmann, Patrick James, Ioanna Karamanou, Ruth E. Kritzer, Benoît Laudenbach, David Leith, Nikos Litinas, Katja Lubitz, Myrto Malouta, Franco Maltomini, Gianluca Del Mastro, Dominic Montserrat, T. Murgatroyd, Olga Pelcer, Carlo Pernigotti, and Angeliki Syrkou. 2010. *The Oxyrhynchus Papyri, Volume LXXV.* Graeco-Roman Memoirs 96. London: Egypt Exploration Society.

Mahaffy, John P. (ed.). 1891. *Book Title The Flinders Petrie Papyri, Volume 1.* Royal Irish Academy, Cunningham Memoirs 8. Dublin: Academy Press.

Malina, Bruce J. 1993. *The New Testament World: Insights from Cultural Anthropology (Revised Edition).* Louisville, KY: Westminster John Knox.

–. 1998. "Eyes-Heart," pp. 68–72 in John J. Pilch and Bruce J. Malina (eds.), *Handbook of Biblical Social Values.* Peabody, MA: Hendrickson.

Malina, Bruce J., and Richard L. Rohrbaugh. 2003. *Social-Scientific Commentary on the Synoptic Gospels (Second Edition).* Minneapolis, MN: Fortress.

Marriott, Horace. 1925. *The Sermon on the Mount.* London: SPCK.

Marshall, I. Howard. 1978. *The Gospel of Luke: A Commentary on the Greek Text.* NIGTC. Exeter: Paternoster.

Martinsen, Anders. 2011. "God as the Great Parasite?: Ideology and Ethics in Interpretations of the Parables," in *Journal of Early Christian History* 1/2, pp. 135–151.

Massey, Michael, and Paul Moreland. 1992. *Slavery in Ancient Rome.* Inside the Ancient World. Surrey: Thomas Nelson & Sons.

Mattila, Sharon L. 2010. Jesus and the "Middle Peasants"?: Problematizing a Social-Scientific Concept. *Catholic Biblical Quarterly* 72:291–313.

Matz, David. 2002. *Daily Life of the Ancient Romans.* Daily Life through History. Westport, CT: Greenwood.

McArthur, Harvey K. 1971. "The Parable of the Mustard Seed," in *Catholic Biblical Quarterly* 33, pp. 198–210.

McGaughy, Lane C. 2007. "Jesus' Parables and the Fiction of the Kingdom," pp. 7–13 in Edward F. Beutner (ed.), *Listening to the Parables of Jesus.* Jesus Seminar Guides 2. Santa Rosa, CA: Polebridge.

McGraw, Phillip C. 2012. *Life Code: The New Rules for Winning in the Real World.* Los Angeles, CA: Bird Street Books.

McKnight, E. V. 2012. "Form Criticism and New Testament Interpretation," pp. 21–40 in Andrew B. McGowan and Kent H. Richards (eds.), *Method and Meaning: Essays on New Testament Interpretation in Honor of Harold W. Attridge.* SBL Resources for Biblical Study 67. Leiden: Brill.

Mealand, David L. 1980. *Poverty and Expectation in the Gospels.* London: SPCK.

Meier, John P. 2011. "Basic Methodology in the Quest for the Historical Jesus," pp. 291–331 in Tom Holmén and Stanley E. Porter (eds.), *Handbook for the Study of the Historical Jesus, Volume 1: How to Study the Historical Jesus.* Leiden: Brill.

–. 2016. *A Marginal Jew: Rethinking the Historical Jesus, Volume 5: Probing the Authenticity of the Parables.* The Anchor Yale Bible Reference Library. New Haven, CT: Yale University Press.

Mendelsohn, Isaac. 1949. *Slavery in the Ancient Near East.* New York, NY: Oxford University Press.

Metso, Sarianna. 2012. "Evidence from the Qumran Scrolls for the Scribal Transmission of Leviticus," pp. 67–79 in John S. Kloppenborg and Judith H. Newman, *Editing the Bible: Assessing the Task Past and Present.* SBL Resources for Biblical Study 69. Atlanta, GA: SBL.

Meyer, Marvin W. 2000. "Did Jesus Drink from a Cup?: The Equipment of Jesus and His Followers in Q and al-Ghazzali," pp. 141–156 in Jon M. Asgeirsson, Kristin de Troyer, and Marvin W. Meyer (eds.), *From Quest to Q: Festschrift James M. Robinson.* BETL 146. Leuven: Leuven University Press and Peeters.

–. 2003. *Secret Gospels: Essays on Thomas and the Secret Gospel of Mark.* Harrisburg, PA: Trinity.

Michel, Otto (trans. Geoffrey W. Bromiley). 1967. "οἰκονόμος," pp. 149–151 in Gerhard Kittel and Gerhard Friedrich (eds.), *Theological Dictionary of the New Testament (Volume V).* Grand Rapids, MI: William B. Eerdmans.

Miller, Robert J. 2007. "The Pearl, the Treasure, the Fool, and the Cross," pp. 65–82 in Edward F. Beutner (ed.), *Listening to the Parables of Jesus.* Jesus Seminar Guides 2. Santa Rosa, CA: Polebridge.

Mouritsen, Henrik. 2011. "The Families of Roman Slaves and Freedmen," pp. 129–144 in Beryl Rawson (ed.), *A Companion to Families in the Greek and Roman Worlds.* Blackwell Companions to the Ancient World. Oxford: Wiley-Blackwell.

Moxnes, Halvor. 2003. *Putting Jesus in His Place: A Radical Vision of Household and Kingdom.* Louisville, KY: Westminster John Knox.

Murphy, Roland E. 1981. *Wisdom Literature: Job, Proverbs, Ruth, Canticles, Ecclesiates, and Esther.* Forms of the Old Testament Literature 13. Grand Rapids, MI: William B. Eerdmans.

Mussner, Franz. [1956] 1967. *Praesentia Salutis: Gesammelte Studien zu Fragen und Themen des Neuen Testamentes.* Kommentare und Beitrage zum Alten und Neuen Testament. Düsseldorf: Patmos.

Neirynck, Frans. 1982. "Recent Developments in the Study of Q," pp. 29–75 in Joël Delobel (ed.), *Logia: Les Paroles de Jésus; The Sayings of Jesus (Mémorial Joseph Coppens).* BETL 59. Leuven: Peeters and Leuven University Press.

–. 2001. "The Reconstruction of Q and IQP/CritEd Parallels," pp. 53–147 in Andreas Lindemann (ed.), *The Sayings Source Q and the Historical Jesus.* BETL 158. Leuven: Leuven University Press and Peeters.

Newman, Barcley M. 1993. *Concise Greek-English Dictionary of the New Testament.* Bible Students Series. Stuttgart: Deutsche Bibelgesellschaft.

Nielson, Bruce E., and Klaas A. Worp (eds.). 2010. *Greek Papyri in the Collection of New York University, Volume II.* Wiesbaden: Harrassowitz.

Nolland, John. 2005. *The Gospel of Matthew: A Commentary on the Greek Text.* NIGTC. Grand Rapids, MI: William B. Eerdmans.

Oakman, Douglas E. 1986. *Jesus and the Economic Questions of His Day.* Studies in Bible and Early Christianity Series 5. Lewiston, ME: Edwin Mellen.

–. 2008. *Jesus and the Peasants.* Matrix: The Bible in Mediterranean Context 4. Eugene, OR: Cascade Books.

–. 2015. *Jesus, Debt, and the Lord's Prayer: First-Century Debt and Jesus' Intentions.* Cambridge: James Clarke.

Park, InHee. 2014a. "Children and Slaves: The Metaphors of Q," pp. 73–91 in Dieter T. Roth, Ruben Zimmermann, and Michael Labahn (eds.), *Metaphor, Narrative, and Parables in Q (Dedicated to Dieter Zeller on the Occasion of His 75th Birthday)*. WUNT 315. Tübingen: Mohr Siebeck.

–. 2014b. "Oral Metonymy in Q: Mothering Images of God from the Daily Lives of Women," presented at the Society of Biblical Literature Annual Meeting, San Diego, CA: 11 pages.

–. 2019. "Women and Q: Metonymy of the *Basileia* of God," in *Journal of Feminist Studies in Religion* 35/2, pp. 41–54.

Patterson, Stephen J. 1998. *The God of Jesus: The Historical Jesus and the Search for Meaning*. Harrisburg, PA: Trinity.

Percy, E. 1953. *Die Botschaft Jesu: Eine Traditionskritische und Exegetische Untersuchung*. Lund: Gleerup.

Perkins, Pheme. 2007. *Introduction to the Synoptic Gospels*. Grand Rapids, MI: William B. Eerdmans.

Perrin, Norman. 1967. *Rediscovering the Teaching of Jesus*. New York, NY: Harper & Row; London: SCM.

Pestman, Pieter W. (ed.). 1980. *Greek and Demotic Texts from the Zenon Archive*. Papyrologica Lugduno-Batava. Leiden: Brill.

–. 1970. *What is Redaction Criticism?* London: SPCK.

Peters, Janelle 2016. "Gendered Activity and Jesus's Saying Not to Worry," in *Neotestamentica* 50/1, pp. 35–52.

Piper, Ronald A. 1989. *Wisdom in the Q-Tradition: The Aphoristic Teachings of Jesus*. SNTSMS 61. Cambridge: Cambridge University Press.

–. 1995a. "The Language of Violence and the Aphoristic Sayings in Q: A Study of Q 6:27–36," pp. 53–72 in John S. Kloppenborg (ed.), *Conflict and Invention: Literary, Rhetorical and Social Studies on the Sayings Gospel Q*. Valley Forge, PA: Trinity.

–. 2000. "Wealth, Poverty, and Subsistence in Q," pp. 219–264 in Jon M. Asgeirsson, Kristin de Troyer, and Marvin W. Meyer (eds.), *From Quest to Q: Festschrift James M. Robinson*. BETL 146. Leuven: Leuven University Press and Peeters.

–. 2001. "Jesus and the Conflict of Powers in Q: Two Q Miracle Stories," pp. 317–349 in Andreas Lindemann (ed.), *The Sayings Source Q and the Historical Jesus*. BETL 158. Leuven: Leuven University Press and Peeters.

Ra, Yoseop. 2016. *Q, the First Writing about Jesus*. Eugene, OR: Wipf & Stock.

Preisigke, Friedrich (ed.). 1997. *Sammelbuch griechischer Urkunden aus Ägypten, Band XX*. Wiesbaden: Otto Harrassowitz.

Preisigke, Friedrich, Friedrich Bilabel, and Emil Kießling (eds.). 1931. *Sammelbuch griechischer Urkunden aus Ägypten, Band 4*. Heidelberg: Verfasser.

Proctor, Mark A. 2019. "'It's probably untrue, but it wouldn't matter anyway': εἰ καί Conditions in the Greek New Testament," in *Neotestamentica* 53/3, pp. 437–458.

Rathbone, Dominic W. 2007. "Roman Egypt," in Walter Scheidel, Ian Morris, and Richard P. Saller (eds.), *The Cambridge Economic History of the Greco-Roman World*. Cambridge: Cambridge University Press.

Reed, Jonathan L. 1995. "The Social Map of Q," pp. 17–36 in John S. Kloppenborg (ed.), *Conflict and Invention: Literary, Rhetorical and Social Studies on the Sayings Gospel Q*. Valley Forge, PA: Trinity.

–. 2000. *Archeology and the Galilean Jesus: A Re-examination of the Evidence*. Harrisburg, PA: Trinity.

Reiser, Marius. 1990. *Die Gerichtspredigt Jesu: Eine Untersuchung zur eschatologischen Verkündigung Jesu und ihrem frühjüdischen Hintergrund.* Neutestamentliche Abhandlungen NF 23. Münster: Aschendorff.

Rengstorf, Karl H. 1936. *Das Evangelium nach Lukas.* Das Neue Testament Deutsch 3. Göttingen: Vandenhoeck & Ruprecht.

Robbins, Vernon K. 1996. *The Tapestry of Early Christian Discourse: Rhetoric, Society and Ideology.* London: Routledge.

Robinson, James M. 1964. "Die Hodayot-Formel in Gebet und Hymnus des Frühchristentums," pp. 194–235 in Walther Eltester and Franz H. Kettler (eds.), *Apophoreta: Festschrift Ernst Haenchen.* BZNW 30. Berlin: Alfred Töpelmann.

–. 1982. "Early Collections of Jesus' Sayings," pp. 389–394 in Joël Delobel (ed.), *Logia: Les Paroles de Jésus (The Sayings of Jesus); Mémorial Joseph Coppens.* BETL 59. Leuven: Leuven University Press and Peeters.

–. 1983. "The Sayings of Jesus: Q," in *The Drew Gateway* 54/1, pp. 26–37.

–. 1988. "Very Goddess and Very Man: Jesus' Better Self," pp. 113–127 in Karen King (ed.), *Images of the Feminine in Gnosticism.* Studies in Antiquity and Christianity. Philadelphia, PA: Fortress.

–. 1991. "The Q Trajectory: Between John and Matthew via Jesus," pp. 173–194 in Birger A. Pearson (ed.), *The Future of Early Christianity: Essays in Honour of Helmut Koester.* Minneapolis, MN: Fortress.

–. 1993. "The Jesus of the Sayings Gospel Q," presented at the Institute for Antiquity and Christianity Occasional Papers 28, Claremont, CA: 18 pages.

–. 1994a. "The Son of Man in the Sayings Gospel Q," pp. 315–335 in Christoph Elsas (ed.), *Tradition und Translation: Zum Problem der interkulturellen Übersetzbarkeit religiöser Phänomene (Festschrift für Carsten Colpe zum 65. Geburtstag).* Berlin: Walter de Gruyter.

–. 1994b. "The History-of-Religions Taxonomy of Q: The Cynic Hypothesis," pp. 247–265 in Holger Preißler and Hubert Seiwert (eds.), *Gnosisforschung und Religionsgeschichte: Festschrift für Kurt Rudolph zum 65. Geburtstag.* Marburg: Diagonal-Verlag.

–. 1995a. "The Jesus of Q as Liberation Theologian," pp. 259–274 in Ronald A. Piper (ed.), *The Gospel behind the Gospels: Current Studies on Q.* NovTSup 75. Leiden: Brill.

–. 1995b. "The *Incipit* of the Sayings Gospel Q," pp. 9–33 in *Hommage à Étienne Trocmé: Revue d'Histoire et de Philosophie Religieuses* 75.

–. 1996. "Building Blocks in the Social History of Q," pp. 87–112 in Elizabeth A. Castelli and Hal Taussig (eds.), *Reimagining Christian Origins: A Colloquium Honoring Burton L. Mack.* Valley Forge, PA: Trinity.

–. 1997a. "*Galilean Upstarts*: A Sot's Cynical Disciples?," pp. 223–249 in Willian L. Petersen, Johan S. Vos, and Henk J. de Jonge, *Sayings of Jesus, Canonical and Non-Canonical: Essays in Honour of Tjitze Baarda.* NovTSup 89. Leiden: Brill.

–. 1997b. "The Real Jesus of the Sayings 'Q' Gospel," online: http://www.religion-online.org/showarticle.asp?title=542.

–. 1998a. "The Sequence of Q: The Lament over Jerusalem," pp. 225–260 in *Von Jesus zum Christus: Christologische Studien (Festgabe für Paul Hoffmann zum 65. Geburtstag).* BZNW 93. Berlin: Walter de Gruyter.

–. 1998b. "The Matthean Trajectory from Q to Mark," pp. 122–154 in Adela Y. Collins (ed.), *Ancient and Modern Perspectives on the Bible and Culture: Essays in Honor of Hans Dieter Betz.* Scholars Press Homage Series 22. Atlanta, GA: Scholars Press.

–. 1998c. "Der Wahre Jesus: Der historische Jesus im Spruchevangelium Q," in *Zeitschrift für Neues Testament* 1, pp. 17–26.

–. 1998d. "Theological Autobiography," pp. 117–150 in Jon R. Stone (ed.), *The Craft of Religious Studies*. New York, NY: Macmillan; London: St. Martin's.

–. 1999. "From Safe House to House Church: From Q to Matthew," pp. 183–199 in Michael Becker and Wolfgang Fenske (eds.), *"Das Ende der Tage und die Gegenwart des Heils." Begegnungen mit dem Neuen Testament und seiner Umwelt: Festschrift für Heinz-Wolfgang Kuhn zum 65. Geburtstag*. Arbeiten zur Geschichte des antiken Judentums und des Urchristentums 44. Leiden: Brill.

–. 2001a. "The Image of Jesus in Q," pp. 7–25 in Marvin Meyers and Charles Hughes (eds.), *Jesus Then and Now: Images of Jesus in History and Christology*. Harrisburg, PA: Trinity.

–. 2001b. "The Critical Edition of Q and the Study of Jesus," pp. 27–52 in Andreas Lindemann (ed.), *The Sayings Source Q and the Historical Jesus*. BETL 158. Leuven: Leuven University Press and Peeters.

–. 2002. "What Jesus Had to Say," pp. 15–17 in Roy W. Hoover (ed.), *Profiles of Jesus*. Santa Rosa, CA: Polebridge.

–. 2003. "Jesus' Theology in the Sayings Gospel Q," pp. 25–43 in David H. Warren, Ann G. Brock, and David W. Pao (eds.), *Early Christian Voices: In Texts, Traditions and Symbols (Essays in Honor of François Bovon)*. BibInt 66. Leiden: Brill.

–. 2005a. "Supplement," pp. 117–118 in Christoph Heil and Joseph Verheyden (eds.), *The Sayings Gospel Q: Collected Essays by James M. Robinson*. BETL 189. Leuven: Leuven University Press and Peeters.

–. [1998] 2005b. "The Sequence of Q: Lament over Jerusalem," pp. 559–598 in Christoph Heil and Joseph Verheyden (eds.), *The Sayings Gospel Q: Collected Essays by James M. Robinson*. BETL 189. Leuven: Leuven University Press and Peeters.

–. [1994] 2005c. "The History-of-Religions Taxonomy of Q: The Cynic Hypothesis," pp. 427–448 in Christoph Heil and Joseph Verheyden (eds.), *The Sayings Gospel Q: Collected Essays by James M. Robinson*. BETL 189. Leuven: Leuven University Press and Peeters.

–. [1994] 2005d, "The Son of Man in the Sayings Gospel Q," pp. 405–426 in Christoph Heil and Joseph Verheyden (eds.), *The Sayings Gospel Q: Collected Essays by James M. Robinson*. BETL 189. Leuven: Leuven University Press and Peeters.

–. 2007. *Jesus: According to the Earliest Witness*. Minneapolis, MN: Fortress.

–. 2011. "The Gospel of the Historical Jesus," pp. 447–474 in Tom Holmén and Stanley E. Porter (eds.), *Handbook for the Study of the Historical Jesus, Volume 1: How to Study the Historical Jesus*. Leiden: Brill.

Robinson, James M., and Christoph Heil. 2001. "The Lilies of the Field: Saying 36 of the Gospel of Thomas and Secondary Accretions in Q 12.22b–31," in *New Testament Studies* 47, pp. 1–25.

Robinson, James M., Paul Hoffmann, and John S. Kloppenborg (eds.). 2000. *The Critical Edition of Q*. Hermeneia. Minneapolis, MN: Fortress.

–. 2002. *The Sayings Gospel Q in Greek and English with Parallels from the Gospels of Mark and Thomas*. Contributions to Biblical Exegesis and Theology 30. Minneapolis, MN: Fortress.

Rodriquez, A. J. 2008. *Life from on High: The Eschatology of the Gospel of John in Light of Its Vertical Dimension*. Chicago, IL: ProQuest.

Rohrbaugh, Richard L. 1993. "A Peasant Reading of the Talents/Pounds: A Text of Terror," in *Biblical Theological Bulletin* 23, pp. 32–39.

Rollens, Sarah E. 2014a. "Conceptualizing Justice in Q: Narrative and Context," pp. 93–113 in Dieter T. Roth, Ruben Zimmermann, and Michael Labahn (eds.), *Metaphor, Narrative, and Parables in Q (Dedicated to Dieter Zeller on the Occasion of His 75ᵗʰ Birthday).* WUNT 315. Tübingen: Mohr Siebeck.

–. 2014b. *Framing Social Criticism in the Jesus Movement: The Ideological Project in the Sayings Gospel Q.* WUNT 2/374. Tübingen: Mohr Siebeck.

Roth, Dieter T. 2014. "'Master' as Character in the Q Parables," pp. 371–396 in Dieter T. Roth, Ruben Zimmermann, and Michael Labahn (eds.), *Metaphor, Narrative, and Parables in Q (Dedicated to Dieter Zeller on the Occasion of His 75ᵗʰ Birthday).* WUNT 315. Tübingen: Mohr Siebeck.

–. 2018. *The Parables in Q.* LNTS 582. London: T&T Clark.

Rupprecht, Hans-Albert, and Emil Kießling (eds.). 1985–1988. *Sammelbuch griechischer Urkunden aus Ägypten, Band XVI.* Wiesbaden: Otto Harrassowitz.

Ryle, Herbert E. 1921. *The Book of Genesis in the Revised Version with Introduction and Notes.* Cambridge: Cambridge University Press.

Sabbe, M. 1982. "Can Mt 11,27 and Lk 10,22 Be Called a Johannine Logion?," in Joël Delobel (ed.), *Logia: Les Paroles de Jésus (The Sayings of Jesus). Mémorial Joseph Coppens.* BETL 59. Leuven: Leuven University Press and Peeters.

Saller, Richard. 2003. "Women, Slaves, and the Economy of the Roman Household," pp. 185–204 in David L. Balch and Carolyn Osiek (eds.), *Early Christian Families in Context: An Interdisciplinary Dialogue.* Religion, Marriage, and Family. Grand Rapids, MI: William B. Eerdmans.

Sato, Migaku. 1988. *Q und Prophetie: Studien zur Gattungs- und Traditionsgeschichte der Quelle Q.* WUNT 2/29. Tübingen: Mohr Siebeck.

–. [1988] 1994. "The Shape of the Q Source," pp. 156–179 in John S. Kloppenborg (ed.), *The Shape of Q: Signal Essays on the Sayings Gospel.* Minneapolis, MN: Fortress.

Scheidel, Walter. 2008. "The Comparative Economics of Slavery in the Greco-Roman World," in Enrico Dal Lago and Constantina Katsari (eds.), *Slave Systems: Ancient and Modern.* Cambridge: Cambridge University Press.

Schellenberg, Ryan S. 2009. "Kingdom as Contaminant?: The Role of Repertoire in the Parables of the Mustard Seed and the Leaven," in *The Catholic Biblical Quarterly* 71, pp. 527–543.

Schenk, W. 1981. *Synopse zur Redenquelle der Evangelien: Q-Synopse und Rekonstruktion in deutscher Übersetzung mit kurzen Erläuterungen.* Düsseldorf: Patmos.

Schlier, Heinrich (trans. Geoffrey W. Bromiley). 1964. "διχοτομέω," pp. 225–226 in Gerhard Kittel and Gerhard Friedrich (eds.), *Theological Dictionary of the New Testament (Volume II).* Grand Rapids, MI: William B. Eerdmans.

Schmidt, Daryl. 1977. "The LXX *Gattung* 'Prophetic Correlative,'" in *JBL* 96, pp. 517–522.

Scholtz, Jacob J. 2015. "Reading Matthew 13 as a Prophetic Discourse: The Four Parables Presented in Private," in *In die Skriflig* 49/1, 7 pages: https://indieskriflig.org.za/index.php/skriflig/article/view/1887/3023.

Schottroff, Luise. 1995. "Itinerant Prophetesses," pp. 347–360 in Ronald A. Piper (ed.), *The Gospel behind the Gospels: Current Studies on Q.* NovTSup 75. Leiden: Brill.

– (trans. Linda M. Maloney). 2006. *The Parables of Jesus.* Minneapolis, MN: Fortress.

Schröter, Jens. 2001. "The Son of Man as the Representative of God's Kingdom: On the Interpretation of Jesus in Mark and Q," pp. 34–68 in Michael Labahn and Andreas Schmidt (eds.), *Jesus, Mark and Q: The Teaching of Jesus and Its Earliest Records.* London: T&T Clark.

Schulz, Siegfried. 1972. *Q: Die Spruchquelle der Evangelisten.* Zürich: Theologischer Verlag.

Schürmann, Heinz. 1968. *Traditionsgeschichtliche Untersuchungen zu den synoptischen Evangelien.* Düsseldorf: Patmos.

–. 1969–1994. *Das Lukasevangelium.* 2 vols. Herders theologischer Kommentar zum Neuen Testament 3/1–2. Freiburg: Herder.

–. 1982. "Das Zeugnis der Redenquelle für die Basileia-Verkündigung Jesu," pp. 121–200 in Joël Delobel (ed.), *Logia: Les Paroles de Jésus; The Sayings of Jesus (Mémorial Joseph Coppens).* BETL 59. Leuven: Peeters and Leuven University Press.

–. [1975] 1994. "Observations on the Son of Man Title in the Speech Source: Its Occurrence in Closing and Introductory Expressions," pp. 74–97 in John S. Kloppenborg (ed.), *The Shape of Q: Signal Essays on the Sayings Gospel.* Minneapolis, MN: Fortress.

Schwartz, Jacques (ed.). 1963. *Griechische Papyrus der Kaiserlichen Universitäts- und Landesbibliothek zu Straßburg, Volume IV: Papyrus grecs de la Bibliothèque Nationale et Universitaire de Strasbourg.* Publications 1. Strasbourg: Bibliothèque Nationale et Universitaire de Strasbourg.

Schweizer, Eduard. 1973. *Das Evangelium nach Matthäus.* Das Neue Testament Deutsch 2. Göttingen: Vandenhoeck & Ruprecht.

Scott, Bernard B. 1981. *Jesus, Symbol-Maker for the Kingdom.* Philadelphia, PA: Fortress.

–. 1989. *Hear Then the Parable: A Commentary on the Parables of Jesus.* Minneapolis, MN: Fortress.

–. 2001. *Re-Imagine the World: An Introduction to the Parables of Jesus.* Santa Rosa, CA: Polebridge.

–. 2002. "The Reappearance of Parables," pp. 19–40 in Roy W. Hoover (ed.), *Profiles of Jesus.* Santa Rosa, CA: Polebridge.

–. 2007. "The Reappearance of Parables," pp. 95–119 in Edward F. Beutner (ed.), *Listening to the Parables of Jesus.* Jesus Seminar Guides 2. Santa Rosa, CA: Polebridge.

Shelton, John C. (ed.). 1971. *Michigan Papyri, Volume XI: Papyri from the Michigan Collection.* American Studies in Papyrology 9. Toronto: Adolf M. Hakkert.

Sijpesteijn, Pieter J. (ed.). *The Wisconsin Papyri, Volume I.* Papyrologica Lugduno-Batava XVI. Leiden: Brill.

–. 1976. *The Family of the Tiberii Iulii Theones.* Studia Amstelodamensia ad epigraphicam, ius antiquum et papyrologicam pertinentia 5. Amsterdam: Adolf M. Hakkert.

–. 1982. *Michigan Papyri, Volume XV.* Studia Amstelodamensia ad epigraphicam, ius antiquum et papyrologicam pertinentia XIX. Zutphen: Terra.

Simon, Richard. [1678] 1682. *A Critical History of the Old Testament.* London: Walter Davis.

Skeat, Theodore C. (ed.). 1974. *Greek Papyri in the British Museum, Volume VII: The Zenon Archive.* London: British Museum.

Smith, Daniel A. 2006. *The Post-Mortem Vindication of Jesus in the Sayings Gospel Q.* LNTS 338. London: T&T Clark.

–. 2014. "The Construction of a Metaphor: Reading Domestic Space in Q," pp. 33–55 in Dieter T. Roth, Ruben Zimmermann, and Michael Labahn (eds.), *Metaphor, Narrative, and Parables in Q (Dedicated to Dieter Zeller on the Occasion of His 75th Birthday).* WUNT 315. Tübingen: Mohr Siebeck.

Snodgrass, Klyne R. 1997. "*Anaideia* and the Friend at Midnight (Luke 11:8)," in *JBL* 116/3, pp. 505–513.

–. 2008. *Stories with Intent: A Comprehensive Guide to the Parables of Jesus.* Grand Rapids, MI: William B. Eerdmans.

Steck, O. H. 1967. *Israel and das gewaltsame Geschick der Propheten: Untersuchungen zur Überlieferung des deuteronomistischen Geschichtsbildes im Alten Testament,*

Spätjudentum und Urchristentum. Wissenschaftliche Monographien zum Alten und Neuen Testament 23. Neukirchen-Vluyn: Neukirchener.

Strauss, David F. (trans. and ed. Peter C. Hodgson) [1835–1836] 1972. *The Life of Jesus Critically Examined.* Philadelphia, PA: Fortress.

Strutwolf, Holger. 2012. "Scribal Practices and the Transmission of Biblical Texts: New Insights from the Coherence-Based Genealogical Method," pp. 139–160 in John S. Kloppenborg and Judith H. Newman, *Editing the Bible: Assessing the Task Past and Present.* SBL Resources for Biblical Study 69. Atlanta, GA: SBL.

Swanson, James. 2001. *Dictionary of Biblical Languages with Semantic Domains: Hebrew Old Testament (Second Edition; Electronic Version).* Oak Harbor, WA: Logos Research Systems.

Taylor, Anthony B. 1989. *The Master-Servant Type Scene in the Parables of Jesus.* New York, NY: Doctoral Dissertation, Fordham University.

Theissen, Gerd, and Annette Merz. 1998. *The Historical Jesus: A Comprehensive Guide.* London: SCM.

Thomson, William M. 1859. *The Land and the Book (Volume 1).* New York, NY: Harper.

Thrall, William F., and Addison Hibbard. 1962. *A Handbook to Literature.* New York, NY: Odyssey.

Thurén, Lauri. 2014. *Parables Unplugged: Reading the Lukan Parables in Their Rhetorical Context.* Minneapolis, MN: Fortress.

Tönsing, J. Gertrud. 2019. "Scolding the 'Wicked, Lazy' Servant; Is the Master God?: A Redaction-Critical Study of Matthew 25:14–30 and Luke 19:11–27." *Neotestamentica* 53/1, pp. 123–147.

Toutain, Jules. 1951. *The Economic Life of the Ancient World.* New York, NY: Barnes & Noble.

Tuckett, Christopher M. 1996. *Q and the History of Early Christianity: Studies on Q.* Edinburgh: T&T Clark.

–. 2001a. "The Son of Man and Daniel 7: Q and Jesus," pp. 371–394 in Andreas Lindemann (ed.), *The Sayings Source Q and the Historical Jesus.* BETL 158. Leuven: Leuven University Press and Peeters.

–. 2001b. "The Fourth Gospel and Q," pp. 281–290 in Robert T. Fortna and Tom Thatcher (eds.), *Jesus in Johannine Tradition.* Louisville, KY: Westminster John Knox.

–. 2014. "Q and Family Ties," pp. 57–71 in Dieter T. Roth, Ruben Zimmermann, and Michael Labahn (eds.), *Metaphor, Narrative, and Parables in Q (Dedicated to Dieter Zeller on the Occasion of His 75th Birthday).* WUNT 315. Tübingen: Mohr Siebeck.

Tyson, Joseph B. 2012. "Source Criticism of Acts," pp. 41–57 in Andrew B. McGowan and Kent H. Richards, *Method and Meaning: Essays on New Testament Interpretation in Honor of Harold W. Attridge.* SBL Resources for Biblical Study 67. Leiden: Brill.

Ukpong, Justin. 2012. "The Parable of the Talents (Matt 25:14–30): Commendation or Critique of Exploitation?: A Social-Historical and Theological Reading," in *Neotestamentica* 46/1, pp. 190–207.

Ulrich, E. 2012. "The Evolutionary Composition of the Hebrew Bible," pp. 23–40 in John S. Kloppenborg and Judith H. Newman, *Editing the Bible: Assessing the Task Past and Present.* SBL Resources for Biblical Study 69. Atlanta, GA: SBL.

Uro, Risto. 1996. "Apocalyptic Symbolism and Social Identity in Q," pp. 67–118 in Risto Uro (ed.), *Symbols and Strata: Essays on the Sayings Gospel Q.* Göttingen: Vandenhoeck & Ruprecht.

Vaage, Leif E. 1994. *Galilean Upstarts: Jesus' First Followers according to Q.* Valley Forge, PA: Trinity.

–. 1995a. "Composite Texts and Oral Mythology: The Case of the 'Sermon' in Q (6:20–49)," pp. 75–97 in John S. Kloppenborg (ed.), *Conflict and Invention: Literary, Rhetorical and Social Studies on the Sayings Gospel Q*. Valley Forge, PA: Trinity.

–. 2001. "Jewish Scripture, Q and the Historical Jesus: A Cynic Way with the Word?," pp. 479–495 in Andreas Lindemann (ed.), *The Sayings Source Q and the Historical Jesus*. BETL 158. Leuven: Leuven University Press and Peeters.

Valantasis, Richard. 2005. *The New Q: A Fresh Translation with Commentary*. London: T&T Clark.

Van Aarde, Andries G. 2002. "Die uitdrukking 'seun van die mens' in die Jesus-tradisie: 'n Ontwikkeling vanaf 'n landbou-omgewing na die wêreld van skrifgeleerdes," in *HTS Theological Studies* 58/4, pp. 1625–1653.

–. 2004. "Jesus and the Son of Man: A Shift from the 'Little Tradition' to the 'Great Tradition,'" in *Ephemerides Theologicae Lovanienses* 80/4, pp. 423–438.

–. 2009. "'Foxes' Holes and Birds' Nests' (Mat 8:20): A Postcolonial Reading for South Africans from the Perspective of Matthew's Anti-Social Language," in *HTS Theological Studies* 58/4, pp. 535–544.

–. 2014. "Pragmatic Dimensions in Parable Research and the Divine Economy of the *Basileia*," in *HTS Theological Studies* 70/1, 11 pages: http://dx.doi.org/10.4102/hts.v70i1.2688.

–. 2016. "The Love for the Poor Neighbour: In Memory of Her (Mt 26:6–13)," pp. 150–175 in D. Francois Tolmie (guest editor), *Acta Theologica Supplementum 23: Perspectives on the Socially Disadvantaged in Early Christianity*. Bloemfontein: SUN MeDIA.

Van der Meer, Michaël N. 2004. *Formation and Reformulation: The Redaction of the Book of Joshua in the Light of the Oldest Textual Witnesses*. Supplements to Vetus Testamentum 102. Leiden: Brill.

Van Eck, Ernest. 2011. "Do Not Question My Honour: A Social-Scientific Reading of the Parable of the Minas (Lk 19:12b–24, 27)," in *HTS Theological Studies* 67/3, 11 pages: http://www.hts.org.za/index.php/HTS/article/view/977.

–. 2013. "When Patrons Are Patrons: A Social-Scientific and Realistic Reading of the Parable of the Feast (Lk 14:16b–23)," in *HTS Theological Studies* 69/1, 14 pages: http://www.hts.org.za/index.php/HTS/article/view/1375.

–. 2015. "Die gelykenisse van Jesus: Allegorieë of simbole van sosiale transformasie?," in *HTS Theological Studies* 71/3, 10 pages: http://www.hts.org.za/index.php/HTS/article/view/3030/pdf_1.

–. 2016. *The Parables of Jesus the Galilean: Stories of a Social Prophet*. Matrix: The Bible in Mediterranean Context. Eugene, OR: Cascade Books.

Van Eck, Ernest, Wayne Renkin, and Ezekiel Ntakirutimana. 2016. "The Parable of the Feast (Lk 14:16b–23: Breaking Down Boundaries and Discerning a Theological-Spatial Justice Agenda," in *HTS Theological Studies* 72/1, 8 pages: http://dx.doi.org/10.4102/hts.v72i1.3512.

Van Seters, John. 2006. *The Edited Bible: The Curious History of the "Editor" in Biblical Criticism*. Winona Lake, IN: Eisenbrauns.

–. 2012. "The Genealogy of the Biblical Editor," pp. 9–22 in John S. Kloppenborg and Judith H. Newman, *Editing the Bible: Assessing the Task Past and Present*. SBL Resources for Biblical Study 69. Atlanta, GA: SBL.

Verheyden, Joseph. 2001. "The Conclusion of Q: Eschatology in Q 22,28–30," pp. 695–718 in Andreas Lindemann (ed.), *The Sayings Source Q and the Historical Jesus*. BETL 158. Leuven: Leuven University Press and Peeters.

–. 2007. "Evaluations," pp. 57–59 in Steven R. Johnson (ed.), *Q 12:33–34: Storing Up Treasures in Heaven*. Documenta Q. Leuven: Peeters.

Verhoeven, Paul. 2007. "The First Will Be First: The Laborers in the Vineyard," pp. 41–50 in Edward F. Beutner (ed.), *Listening to the Parables of Jesus*. Jesus Seminar Guides 2. Santa Rosa, CA: Polebridge.

Via, Dan O. 1967. *The Parables: Their Literary and Existential Dimension*. Philadelphia, PA: Fortress.

Viljoen, Francois P. 2009. "A Contextualised Reading of Matthew 6:22–23: 'Your Eye is the Lamp of Your Body,'" in *HTS Teologiese Studies* 65/1, pp. 166–170.

Von Gemünden, Petra. 1993. *Vegetationsmetaphorik im Neuen Testament und seiner Umwelt: Eine Bilduntersuchung*. Göttingen: Vandenhoeck & Ruprecht.

Wachtel, K. 2012. "The Coherence-Based Genealogical Method: A New Way to Reconstruct the Text of the Greek New Testament," pp. 123–138 in John S. Kloppenborg and Judith H. Newman, *Editing the Bible: Assessing the Task Past and Present*. SBL Resources for Biblical Study 69. Atlanta, GA: SBL.

Wanke, Joachim. 1980. "Kommentarworte: Älteste Kommentierung von Herrenworten," in *Biblische Zeitschrift* 24, pp. 208–233.

Weiß, Bernhard. 1876. *Das Matthäusevangelium und seine Lucas-Parallelen*. Halle: Waisenhaus.

Wellhausen, Julius. 1871. *Der Text der Bücher Samuelis*. Göttingen: Vandenhoeck & Ruprecht.

West, Audrey. 2009. "Preparing to Preach the Parables in Luke," in *Currents in Theology and Mission* 36/6, pp. 405–413.

Westermann, William L., and Casper J. Kraemer (eds.). 1926. *Greek Papyri in the Library of Cornell University*. New York: Columbia University Press.

Westermann, William L., and Elizabeth S. Hasenoehrl (eds.). 1934. *Zenon Papyri: Business Papers of the Third Century B.C. Dealing with Palestine and Egypt, Volume 1*. New York: Columbia University Press.

White, K. D. 1970. *Roman Farming*. Aspects of Greek and Roman Life. London: Thames & Hudson.

Wink, Walter. 2002. *The Human Being: Jesus and the Enigma of the Son of Man*. Minneapolis, MN: Fortress.

Winter, John G. (ed.), with contributions by Arthur E. R. Boak, Campbell Bonner, M. F. MacGregor, Orsamus M. Pearl, Frank E. Robbins, Henry A. Sanders, and Verne B. Schuman. 1936. *Michigan Papyri, Volume III: Miscellaneous Papyri*. Humanistic Series 40. Ann Arbor, MI: University of Michigan Press.

Wrede, William. 1901. *Das Messiasgeheimnis in den Evangelien: Zugleich ein Beitrag zum Verstandnis der Markusevangelium*. Göttingen: Vandenhoeck & Ruprecht.

Wright, Stephen I. 2015. *Jesus the Storyteller*. Louisville, KY: Westminster John Knox.

Yavetz, Zvi. 1988. *Slaves and Slavery in Ancient Rome*. New Brunswick, NJ: Transaction Books.

Yonge, Charles D. (with Philo of Alexandria). 1995. *The Works of Philo: Complete and Unabridged*. Peabody, MA: Hendrickson.

Young, Brad H. 1998. *The Parables: Jewish Tradition and Christian Interpretation*. Grand Rapids, MI: Baker Academic.

Zeller, Dieter. 1977. *Die weisheitlichen Mahnsprüche bei den Synoptikern*. Forschung zur Bibel 17. Würzburg: Echter Verlag.

–. 1982. "Redaktionsprozesse und wechselnder 'Sitz im Leben' beim Q-Material," pp. 395–409 in Joël Delobel (ed.), *Logia: Les Paroles de Jésus; The Sayings of Jesus (Mémorial Joseph Coppens)*. BETL 59. Leuven: Peeters and Leuven University Press.

–. 1984. *Kommentar zur Logienquelle.* Stuttgarter kleiner Kommentar, Neues Testament 21. Stuttgart: Katholisches Bibelwerk.

–. [1982] 1994. "Redactional Processes and Changing Settings in the Q-Material," pp. 116–130 in John S. Kloppenborg (ed.), *The Shape of Q: Signal Essays on the Sayings Gospel.* Minneapolis, MN: Fortress.

–. 2001. "Jesus, Q und die Zukunft Israels," pp. 351–369 in Andreas Lindemann (ed.), *The Sayings Source Q and the Historical Jesus*. BETL 158. Leuven: Leuven University Press and Peeters.

Zimmermann, Ruben. 2009. "How to Understand the Parables of Jesus: A Paradigm Shift in Parable Exegesis," in *Acta Theologica* 29/1, pp. 157–182.

–. 2014. "Metaphorology and Narratology in Q Exegesis: Literary Methodology as an Aid to Understanding the Q Text," pp. 3–30 in Dieter T. Roth, Ruben Zimmermann, and Michael Labahn (eds.), *Metaphor, Narrative, and Parables in Q (Dedicated to Dieter Zeller on the Occasion of His 75th Birthday)*. WUNT 315. Tübingen: Mohr Siebeck.

–. 2015. *Puzzling the Parables of Jesus: Methods and Interpretation.* Minneapolis, MN: Fortress.

Index of Ancient Sources

Hebrew Bible / Old Testament

Septuagint

Jewish Apocrypha

Jewish Pseudepigrapha

Dead Sea Scrolls

Josephus

Philo

New Testament

Early Christian Literature

Patristic Literature

Rabbinic Literature

Papyri and Ostraca

Greco-Roman Literature

Mesopotamian Literature

Index of Subjects